With Friends Like These

With Friends Like These
Entangled Nationalisms and the Canada-Quebec-France Triangle, 1944-1970

David Meren

UBCPress · Vancouver · Toronto

© UBC Press 2012

All rights reserved. No part of this publication may be reproduced, stored in a retrieval system, or transmitted, in any form or by any means, without prior written permission of the publisher, or, in Canada, in the case of photocopying or other reprographic copying, a licence from Access Copyright, www.accesscopyright.ca.

21 20 19 18 17 16 15 14 13 12   5 4 3 2 1

Printed in Canada on FSC-certified ancient-forest-free paper
(100% post-consumer recycled) that is processed chlorine- and acid-free.

Library and Archives Canada Cataloguing in Publication

Meren, David, 1972-
With friends like these : entangled nationalisms and the
Canada-Quebec-France triangle, 1944-1970 / David Meren.

Includes bibliographical references and index.
Also issued in electronic format.
ISBN 978-0-7748-2224-4 (bound); ISBN 978-0-7748-2225-1 (pbk.)

1. Canada – Foreign relations – France. 2. France – Foreign relations – Canada.
3. Québec (Province) – Relations – France. 4. France – Relations – Québec (Province).
5. Canada – English-French relations. I. Title.

FC248.Q8M47 2012   327.71044   C2011-908221-7

Canada

UBC Press gratefully acknowledges the financial support for our publishing program of the Government of Canada (through the Canada Book Fund), the Canada Council for the Arts, and the British Columbia Arts Council.

This book has been published with the help of a grant from the Canadian Federation for the Humanities and Social Sciences, through the Aid to Scholarly Publications Program, using funds provided by the Social Sciences and Humanities Research Council of Canada.

Printed and bound in Canada by Friesens
Set in Minion and Garamond Condensed by Artegraphica Design Co. Ltd.
Copy editor: Käthe Roth
Proofreader: Jenna Newman

UBC Press
The University of British Columbia
2029 West Mall
Vancouver, BC V6T 1Z2
www.ubcpress.ca

FOR MOM, DAD, AND LAURA

Contents

Acknowledgments / ix

Note on Language / xii

List of Abbreviations / xiii

Introduction: In the Shadow of the General / 1

Part 1 – Best of Times, Worst of Times: The Canada-Quebec-France Triangle, 1944-1960

1 Atlanticism in Common, Atlanticism in Question / 11

2 Stagnation amid Growth, Growth amid Stagnation / 34

3 "More necessary than ever": The Evolution of Cultural Exchanges / 58

Part 2 – The Clash of Nations: The Sources of Triangular Tensions

4 A "French" Fact: The Cultural Impetus / 85

5 *Vive le Québec libre?* The Question of Independence / 105

6 Atlanticism in Conflict: The Geopolitical Impetus / 129

Part 3 – *Le Déluge*: Triangular Relations and Triangular Tensions, 1960-1970

7 Parisian *pied-à-terre*: The Emergence of Triangular Tensions / 145

8 Crisis: From Montreal to Libreville / 164

9 Missions Impossible? Triangular Economic Relations / 182

10 Rivalry, Recrimination, and Renewal: Triangular Cultural Relations / 207

11 Is Paris Turning? Enduring Triangular Relations / 238

Conclusions / 263

Notes / 274

Bibliography / 320

Index / 337

Acknowledgments

I REACH THE COMPLETION OF this book mindful of those who helped me in the task. The only things that I am able to take full credit for are, alas, the errors that remain in the work. I am grateful to UBC Press, notably Melissa Pitts, Ann Macklem, and Käthe Roth, along with the anonymous reviewers, for their work in shepherding the book through the publication process.

This book began its life as a doctoral thesis at McGill University. My profound thanks go to Carman Miller, who supported the project from the start, and who continues to be a great source of friendship, encouragement, and intellectual exchange. I also benefited from the help of other McGill historians, notably Suzanne Morton and Brian Young, who provided comments on my thesis and aspects of this book. Special thanks are reserved for Brian Lewis, whose generosity as a fellow historian and a friend has been deeply appreciated. I write these words in his home, lent to me in these final crucial weeks of writing – the latest item to be added to the list of things for which I owe him a pint of fine ale. Perhaps two.

This book was made possible by the financial support of McGill's Faculty of Graduate and Postdoctoral Studies, the Robert and Mary Stanfield Foundation, and the Social Sciences and Humanities Research Council of Canada, and I express my gratitude to all three institutions. My two years as a SSHRC postdoctoral fellow gave me the incredible opportunity to plunge into intellectual currents in Paris and London, pursue further research trails, and forge new relationships. At the Université Paris IV-Sorbonne, I had the privilege of working with Dominique Barjot, and my thanks go as well to Georges-Henri Soutou. In London, I benefited from time spent in the London School of Economics' department of international history, for which I am indebted to Odd Arne Westad, David Stevenson, and Robert Boyce.

The staff of McGill's McLennan-Redpath Library, and the libraries at Montreal's other universities ensured that I had the needed materials, as did the staff at Library and Archives Canada, the Bibliothèque et Archives nationales du Québec, and the University of Toronto archives. In France, I owe thanks to the staff at the Bibliothèque nationale, the Archives nationales, the Archives du ministère des Affaires étrangères, and the Archives d'histoire contemporaine of the Centre d'histoire de Sciences Po. In London, I had the pleasure of a useful but too-brief sojourn at the British National Archives. Special thanks go to Jacques Monet, who granted access to the papers of Georges Vanier, and to Jean-Noël Jeanneney, for his permission to consult those of Wilfrid Baumgartner. Julie Roy was invaluable in facilitating my exploration of Marcel Cadieux's papers, and Robert Bothwell generously permitted me to consult some of his personal research files. Greg Donaghy, Mary Halloran, and Ted Kelly of the historical section in the Department of Foreign Affairs were helpful during the early phase of my research, and a special mention must go to John Hilliker for his comments on my doctoral thesis.

I benefited during the preparation of this book from the kindness, suggestions, and generosity of colleagues and friends. In Montreal, these include Elizabeth Kirkland, Nicolas Kenny, Jean-François Constant, Dan Rueck, Julie Allard, Greg Griffin, Stephanie Bolton, Anna Shea, and Matthew Kerby. Jarrett Rudy, Sebastian Normandin, and Steven Usitalo were, each in his own way, inspirational examples as they blazed their paths through their doctoral studies. Sean Mills, former flatmate but constant friend, provided me with invaluable feedback on this work at a crucial juncture. Sadly, two dear friends are not here to mark the completion of this work with me. My fellow doctoral candidate, Tom Brydon, and his partner, Laura Nagy, were taken from this world, and their absence is felt by anyone who had the privilege to count them as friends.

My friend and colleague Ryan Touhey patiently showed me the ropes at the archives in Ottawa, and, along with Andrew Burtch, has been an unwavering source of support, entertainment, and intellectual comradeship. I also relied upon the inexhaustible hospitality (and patience) of Jessica Blitt and Zane Waldman, Niall Cronin and Carolyn Konopski, and Christopher Hynes and Alison Fitzgerald. Special thanks are also reserved for Shaun and Jill Lapenskie and their family.

In Paris, I am indebted to my friends and fellow researchers at the Quai d'Orsay, Julie d'Andurain and Catherine Desos, who took this English Canadian with rather broken French under their wing. My thoughts also go to Maylis Bellocq, whose friendship and encouragement were such a source of strength during these past three years. My research trips to Paris were also made memorable and enjoyable by the friendship of Jackie Clarke, Kevin Passmore, and Orla Smyth. All of those hours filled with spirited intellectual exchange – notably around Orla's table – were brushstrokes on the canvas that is my recollection of days spent in the City of Light.

But my deepest thanks are reserved for my family. My parents, Marie and John, and my sister Laura stood beside me throughout this long journey. Without their love, patience, and support, I would not have completed it, and this book would not have seen the light of day. I dedicate it to them with love and affection.

Note on Language

WITH SO MUCH OF THIS book's content drawn from French-language sources, an issue arises regarding its presentation. After serious reflection, I have decided to translate quotations into English, except in those instances in which the meaning is readily apparent. The one exception to this rule is Charles de Gaulle's speech from the balcony of Montreal's city hall. Given the historical, cultural, and emotional significance of his remarks, I feel compelled to present them in the original French. A translation is provided in the accompanying citation.

Abbreviations

ACCT	Agence de coopération culturelle et technique
AGFC	Association générale France-Canada
AIJLF	Association internationale des journalistes de langue française
ASI	Associated States of Indochina
ASTEF	Association pour l'organisation des stages en France
AUPELF	Association des universités partiellement ou entièrement de la langue française
DEA	Department of External Affairs
EAO	External Aid Office
ECM	European Common Market
EDC	European Defence Community
ENA	École nationale d'administration
EPU	European Payments Union
ERP	European Recovery Program
GATT	General Agreement on Tariffs and Trade
MAE	Ministère des Affaires étrangères
MAIQ	Ministère des Affaires intergouvernementales du Québec
MEC	Maison des étudiants canadiens
MLF	Multilateral Force
NATO	North Atlantic Treaty Organization
NORAD	North American Air Defence Agreement
OEEC	Organisation for European Economic Co-operation
OFQJ	Office franco-québécois pour la jeunesse
PCO	Privy Council Office

PMO	Prime Minister's Office
PQ	Parti Québécois
RIN	Rassemblement pour l'indépendance nationale
SGF	Société générale de financement
SIDBEC	Sidérurgie du Québec
SNA	Société nationale des Acadiens
SOMA	Société de montage automobile
TCA	Trans-Canada Airlines
UCF	Union culturelle française
UNESCO	United Nations Economic, Social and Cultural Organization

With Friends Like These

Introduction:
In the Shadow of the General

THE WORLD HAD COME TO Montreal. Expo '67 was an overwhelming success, drawing visitors from around the globe. Taking place amid the festivities marking the centennial of Confederation, the universal exposition was also a celebration of Quebec's Quiet Revolution, the cultural, economic, and political empowerment of North America's "French fact." Situated on islands in the St. Lawrence River, the geographic feature so prominent in the history of Montreal, Quebec, and Canada, Expo's location was rich in symbolism. The riverain setting was equally a fitting metaphor for the post-war evolution of international relations, since what had been constructed in the middle of the St. Lawrence was quite literally a "global village," to coin the expression that Marshall McLuhan had popularized five years earlier.[1] With its theme *Terre des Hommes*/Man and his World, inspired by the title of a work by French author Antoine de Saint-Exupéry, Expo '67 was a tangible representation of the "merging of efforts ... uniting in the creation of a single vision: Earth, the creation of Man."[2] Indeed, the transportation and communications advances on display testified to how, in the latter half of the twentieth century, a growing portion of the global population was in closer contact, holding out the prospect of the world's national tributaries flowing into one great river of humanity.

Yet, paralleling the enthusiasm over this dizzying proposition were questions, misgivings, and hostility. McLuhan had predicted that the emergence of his global village would provoke the assertion of regional, ethnic, and religious identities. It was thus fitting, given the title *Terre des Hommes* served as Expo's leitmotif, that Saint-Exupéry should have written in this work of the need for individuals to feel that "in placing one's stone, one is contributing to building the world."[3] It was not enough for the world's diverse populations simply to contribute to the human adventure; rather, there remained an abiding need for the uniqueness of that contribution to be recognized, and for assurances that it would not be drowned under waves of homogenization.

Among those visiting Montreal was Charles de Gaulle. The French president was determined to use his trip to send an emphatic message about the enduring importance and relevance of national existence and, linked to this, the necessity of cooperation among the world's French-speaking peoples. Accompanied by Quebec's premier, Daniel Johnson, de Gaulle spent July 24 travelling up Quebec's north shore. Large crowds accorded him a rapturous welcome in the communities along his route. In Montreal, the climactic destination of a journey designed to underscore the ties of history, culture, and sentiment linking the francophone populations on either side of the Atlantic, crowds in the hundreds of thousands lined the streets to catch a glimpse of this towering historic figure. As the motorcade turned off Sherbrooke Street onto rue St-Denis and headed toward the city's old quarter, Montreal's church bells began to peal. An immense and excited throng greeted de Gaulle at the city hall overlooking Place Jacques-Cartier. He was escorted into the imposing building that stands upon what had once been the private gardens of New France's governor.[4] Very quickly, cries of "Le Général, au balcon" and "Le Québec aux Québécois" went up, joining a sea of Quebec flags, French tricolours, and placards proclaiming pro-independence slogans. Answering the calls, de Gaulle emerged onto the balcony. From this vantage point, he took in a panorama that included the teeming crowd gathered in the heat and humidity of a Montreal summer night. Within the General's view was a monument, emblematic of the historic Anglo-French struggle of which the city was so much a product, honouring British admiral Lord Horatio Nelson and his naval victories over French forces. Beyond the square lay the St. Lawrence and the Expo site. After acknowledging the crowd's acclamations, de Gaulle began to speak:

> C'est une immense émotion qui remplit mon cœur en voyant devant moi la ville de Montréal française. Au nom du vieux pays, au nom de la France, je vous salue de tout mon cœur.
>
> Je vais vous confier un secret que vous ne répéterez pas. Ce soir ici, et tout le long de ma route, je me trouvais dans une atmosphère du même genre que celle de la *Libération*.
>
> Et tout le long de ma route, outre cela, j'ai constaté quel immense effort de progrès, de développement, et par conséquent d'affranchissement vous accomplissez ici, et c'est à Montréal qu'il faut que je le dise, parce que, s'il y a au monde une ville exemplaire par ses réussites modernes, c'est la vôtre. Je dis c'est la vôtre et je me permets d'ajouter c'est *la nôtre*. Si vous saviez quelle confiance la France, réveillée après d'immenses épreuves, porte maintenant vers vous, si vous saviez quelle affection elle recommence à ressentir pour les Français du Canada,

et si vous saviez à quel point elle se sent obligée de concourir à votre marche en avant, à votre progrès!

C'est pourquoi elle a conclu avec le gouvernement du Québec, avec celui de mon ami Johnson, des accords pour que les Français de part et d'autre de l'Atlantique travaillent *ensemble* à une même œuvre *française*. Et d'ailleurs le concours que la France va, tous les jours un peu plus, prêter ici, elle sait bien que vous le lui rendrez parce que vous êtes en train de vous constituer des élites, des usines, des entreprises, des laboratoires, qui feront l'étonnement de tous et qui, un jour, j'en suis sûr, vous permettront d'aider la France.

Voilà ce que je suis venu vous dire ce soir en ajoutant que j'emporte de cette réunion *inouïe* de Montréal un souvenir *inoubliable*. La France entière sait, voit, entend, ce qui se passe ici et je puis vous dire qu'elle en vaudra mieux.

Vive Montréal! Vive le Québec! ... Vive le Québec libre!

Vive le Canada français et vive la France![5]

De Gaulle had just placed *his* stone. As if it had been thrown into a pond – a metaphor the French leader favoured – the shockwaves expanded outward in concentric circles from Place Jacques-Cartier. With the French and Quebec notables behind him still absorbing his words, the crowd erupted in a thunderous, delirious roar of approval. Farther west, in a private railcar at Montreal's Windsor Station, Canada's secretary of state for external affairs, Paul Martin, responded in panicked disbelief at what he had just seen on television. Up the river in Ottawa, the prime minister, Lester Pearson, reacted angrily to the broadcasted speech. The shockwaves reached into homes throughout Quebec, where the reaction was as varied as opinions regarding the province's political destiny; they reached a Canadian populace increasingly anxious about the country's future even as they celebrated its past; they reached across the Atlantic to France, where they provoked reactions from derision to joy; they circled the globe. De Gaulle had just dramatically drawn world attention to the debate raging over Quebec's future, laying bare Canada's unity crisis.

ALTHOUGH THE FRENCH LEADER's remarks provoked astonishment on both sides of the Atlantic, ample signs had preceded his *cri du balcon*. This was a spectacular manifestation of the complex triangular dynamic that had emerged between Paris, Quebec City, and Ottawa. The dynamic, and the tensions that erupted in the 1960s, are best understood as products of the interwoven postwar evolutions of France, Quebec, and Canada, which resulted in the confluence and clash of three nationalist reactions. To be sure, these reactions arose in, and were informed by, the unique conditions found at each point of the triangle.

But they were also shaped and exacerbated by the intersecting of local circumstances with international realities. As such, the nationalist sentiment to which de Gaulle had given voice in Montreal was symptomatic of a much larger phenomenon.

Most broadly, all three points of the triangle were contending with increasing economic interdependence and the proliferation of transnational exchanges. These trends posed challenges to the authority of the state – the fundamental unit of the international system. They also called into question the basis of ethnic, religious, and national identities, and compelled greater attention to the complexity of mediating between the local and the global, the particular and the common, and the parochial and the cosmopolitan. Here lay an apparent contradiction at the heart of twentieth-century international relations: that the proliferation of exchanges transcending state and nation should have occurred in the very moment in history when, as Benedict Anderson observes, "nation-ness [was considered] the most universally legitimate value."[6]

More specifically, all three points of the triangle had to respond to preponderant American power – military, political, economic, and cultural. Indeed, the United States bestrode the twin pillars of the North Atlantic world after 1945 like a latter-day Colossus, and it was under the gaze of the American giant that interdependence and transnationalism accelerated. Part of this trend was attributable to deliberate action by Washington, which aimed to establish and consolidate an international liberal and capitalist order. It was also the result of the expansion of American enterprise, as United States-based multinationals and cultural industries expanded their reach throughout the North Atlantic and beyond. But this trend was equally a consequence of governments – including those in Canada and France – that, even while subscribing to a liberal worldview, were seeking to contend with, influence, and constrain American power. By contributing in their own way to the growth of interdependence and transnationalism, the efforts in the triangle to carve out a space for a distinct "national" existence in the cultural, economic, and geopolitical spheres had had the ironic effect of reinforcing American predominance. The result by the 1960s, amid mounting indications of American overstretch, was growing nationalist sentiment and a desire to challenge the post-war status quo.

With these dynamics in mind, in this book I explore relations in the Canada-Quebec-France triangle in the quarter-century after the Second World War. My aim is to provide a more comprehensive and nuanced understanding of the origins and evolution of the tensions that wracked the triangle in the 1960s. Why did the "special relationship" between Paris and Quebec City suddenly emerge after nearly two centuries of minimal official contact? What did France and Quebec share that encouraged their rapprochement after 1945? What were the consequences for Franco-Canadian relations? What was Ottawa's response and what considerations informed this? The answers to these questions will shed light on domestic conditions in the three components of the triangle, but they also entail an exploration of how these conditions intersected with international developments after 1945, and how actors in the triangle responded to and were affected by global trends. It is thus crucial to place the Canada-Quebec-France triangle within the broader history of international relations.

A primary task in this regard is, as it were, to put de Gaulle in his place. To be sure, the General casts a figurative shadow over the accounts of the triangle almost as long as the one that he cast in real life.[7] This historiographical trend was encouraged by the numerous works written by participants in the events in question, upon which many of the subsequent academic accounts have been based. It was reinforced by a second generation of works sparked by the renewed debate over Quebec's political destiny in the 1990s. Inevitably, this literature has been shaped by the authors' beliefs and the political climate in which the works were produced, and it has faithfully reproduced the various linguistic, cultural, and political cleavages marking Quebec and Canada. But the preoccupation with the admittedly dramatic events of July 1967 tends to reduce actors other than de Gaulle to little more than passive observers (or perhaps bit players) and obscures the broader national and international trends at play. Taken to its logical conclusion, this "de Gaulle-centric" analysis ironically reduces the French leader's *cri du balcon* to little more than a historical footnote. However, what occurred in Montreal's Place Jacques-Cartier – and, indeed, what took place in the Canada-Quebec-France triangle – was far bigger than de Gaulle. To understand the larger significance of these events and the triangular tensions, it is essential to widen the scope of exploration. Such an approach leaves room to acknowledge the significant role played by de Gaulle, but situates his actions and the triangular dynamic in which he operated within a larger analytical framework that includes events prior to 1960, a period crucial to the origins and nature of the triangular tensions. It also involves going beyond traditional political-based narratives to engage with the cultural dimension of events.

Once again drawing upon Saint-Exupéry, what follows is my effort "to place one's stone" in the building of a greater understanding of the history of the Canada-Quebec-France triangle, its components, and its situation in international history. It is not my purpose to provide a catalogue of slights, nor do I intend to discuss only what divided Canada, Quebec, and France; rather, my objective is to demonstrate what they had in common. I thus reveal that the triangular tensions were not idiosyncratic; on the contrary, they were situated in larger international and transnational narratives. This is in keeping with the related presumption that "national" histories can be written effectively only if one pays heed to the impact of global forces upon them, and that exploring international history compels the study of developments at the state and sub-state levels.[8] Even though the devotion of so many pages to exploring four words ("Vive le Québec libre") may appear to be a classic case of academic parsing, the approach that I employ brings a new perspective to bear on the subject matter by unpacking the mythology surrounding this event – arguably the most dramatic and enduring symbol of the triangular dynamic – to reveal what it and the tensions of the period have to say about the evolution of international relations in the twentieth century and the entangled histories of Canada, Quebec, and France.

This book is divided into three parts. In the first part, I explore the Canada-Quebec-France triangle in the fifteen years from the Second World War to the advent of the Quiet Revolution. Chapter 1 delves into the geopolitical dimension of the relationship, as rising nationalist sentiment on both sides of the Atlantic to post-war challenges triggered a growing divergence between Ottawa and Paris. This division was even more apparent in the economic aspect of the bilateral relationship that is discussed in Chapter 2. With both Canada and France responding to the United States's economic strength, Ottawa saw its efforts to construct a liberalized, multilateral economic order frustrated by French protectionism and Paris's contribution to Europe's economic integration.

But the record was by no means wholly negative. Even as global trends and the linked challenge of American economic power tended to undermine the official relationship, they also encouraged a rapprochement – especially between France and Quebec. The ascendance of a new, Quebec-centric variant of French-Canadian nationalism resulted in a growing Quebec appreciation of France as an indispensable ally in preserving the province's majority francophone society in the face of the sociocultural changes accompanying urbanization and industrialization, along with intensifying interdependence and transnational flows. Informed by a discourse of "modernization," the shift in Quebec attitudes was welcomed in Paris, which sought expanded relations to ensure French Canada's cultural survival. More fundamentally, Quebec neo-nationalist preoccupations corresponded to misgivings in France over the ramifications of American economic power.

Such misgivings point to the cultural dimension of the relationship, which is explored in Chapter 3. The increasing Quebec openness toward France did not mean that contacts were free of controversy; consistent with Quebec neo-nationalist preoccupations, there were demands that France acknowledge French Canada as an equal partner and producer of francophone culture, boasting a unique contribution shaped by its North American reality. Nevertheless, there was an unmistakable trend toward increased cultural contact between France and Canada, encouraged by concerns over American cultural power. In addition to anxiety in France and Quebec over "Americanization," nationalist elements in English Canada were preoccupied with the United States's impact on Canadian life. With governments moving to support and safeguard the "national" culture at each point of the triangle, culture became more and more politicized. Paris was drawn into an increasingly rancorous intergovernmental dispute in Canada, as the collision between Canadian and Quebec nationalisms exacerbated latent tensions over the relationship between the country's two principal linguistic communities. As the 1950s drew to a close, the triangle was ripe for both cooperation and conflict.

A host of mutually reinforcing ethnocultural, political, and geopolitical motivations, combined with Canadian constitutional ambiguities, was the brew from which an increasingly fraught triangular dynamic would rise. In Part 2 of the book, I examine each of these motivations and how they shaped the triangular relationship during the 1960s. In Chapter 4, I explore how the concern with protecting and promoting North America's *fait français* – its French fact – became bound up in nationalistic projects at all three points of the triangle. Such concern fuelled notions of francophone solidarity between France and Quebec while leading to Ottawa's growing marginalization, notwithstanding a heightened English-Canadian appreciation of French Canada as a shield against Americanization. Indeed, cultural questions lay at the very core of the triangular tensions. In Chapter 5, I discuss how the acceleration of Quebec political life – and Ottawa's apparent inability to respond to this acceleration – attracted a French attention conditioned by decolonization and the primacy that Gaullism accorded to national independence. Paris, convinced that Quebec was destined to achieve a new political status, adopted an increasingly explicit position in favour of Quebec autonomy and, ultimately, independence. Ottawa faced the daunting prospect of confronting Paris and Quebec City without reinforcing their cooperation and thus harming the federal position and Canadian unity. Ottawa's response was thus confused, and this confusion was exacerbated by its having to contend with a moving target as the internal challenge of Quebec neo-nationalism and the external challenge of Gaullist nationalism progressively moved the bar. In Chapter 6, I describe how these ethnocultural and political considerations became bound up in larger geopolitical manoeuvrings, as Franco-Canadian differences spurred Gaullist France's "Quebec policy" and led to a Canadian foreign policy failure.

In Part 3, I explore how this complicated triangular relationship was manifested in the political, economic, and cultural spheres over the course of the

1960s. In Chapter 7, I discuss the early phase of the official rapprochement between Paris and Quebec City and how federal efforts to build up Franco-Canadian relations fanned the flames of rivalry between Ottawa and Quebec City, and thus spurred efforts by Paris and Quebec City to strengthen their ties. Triangular tensions were at a fever pitch and the stage was set for confrontation by the time of de Gaulle's visit, which ushered in the period of acute crisis that is the subject of Chapter 8. Following the dramatic events of that summer, Paris and Quebec City moved to strengthen relations and cooperated to achieve Quebec's distinct and autonomous participation in the Francophonie. Ottawa continued to struggle to respond to what it considered a fundamental challenge from within and without to its constitutional prerogatives and to Canadian unity.

Ultimately, the passing of the triangular crisis would owe less to the effectiveness of the immediate federal response than to other factors. In Chapter 9, I discuss the triangle's economic dimension, demonstrating the challenges and contradictions that nationalist forces encountered in altering the structure of the relationship and broader international economic conditions. In Chapter 10, I explore the cultural component that proved to be a driving force of the triangular dynamic, including the emergence and consolidation of cooperation between France and Quebec, and Ottawa's parallel efforts to assert itself as a viable interlocutor in the cultural sphere. My examination in Chapter 11 of developments in the triangle and the Francophonie after de Gaulle left the political stage, and after changes of leadership in Ottawa and Quebec City, reveals how the special relationship between France and Quebec was set to endure. All of this, along with understanding the Canada-Quebec-France triangle's broader relevance to international history, makes it essential to shine more light on this complex relationship by moving it out from under the shadow of the General.

PART 1

Best of Times, Worst of Times: The Canada-Quebec-France Triangle, 1944-1960

CHAPTER ONE

Atlanticism in Common, Atlanticism in Question

THE NORMANDY VILLAGE OF Courseulles-sur-Mer lies at the centre of what, on June 6, 1944, was Juno Beach, the Canadian sector of Operation Overlord. An imposing silver cross of Lorraine graces this stretch of shore where, days after the Allied landings, Charles de Gaulle returned to the France from which he had fled four years before. Emblematic of the change that the years of fighting had wrought on Franco-Canadian links, the Free French leader was greeted by Canadian soldiers.[1] As the war entered its final months, relations between Canada and France appeared poised to enter a new phase.

Canadian and French responses to Cold War realities, not the least of which was preponderant American power, shaped the relationship in the fifteen years after the Second World War. Bilateral contact and cooperation were greater than ever, as Ottawa and Paris viewed one another as useful and necessary allies in the realization of their respective foreign policy goals, and the two countries were bound together by a common adherence to Atlanticism. For a time, it appeared this foreign policy response, an amalgam of realist geopolitical calculations and liberal internationalist aspirations, would promote more substantive relations. However, Ottawa and Paris viewed the Cold War world through different prisms. Conditioned by diverging interpretations of the nature and organization of the international system, and the respective places that Canada and France occupied in it, the two capitals had embraced Atlanticism with unique expectations. To be sure, both recognized that circumstances had pushed them into the United States's geopolitical orbit, and both viewed Atlanticism as a means to influence and even constrain Washington. From the outset, however, there were fundamental differences between Ottawa and Paris over how close one could come to the American sun without getting burned. This divergence was increasingly apparent as it became clear that rather than controlling the American giant, the Atlantic framework was in many respects facilitating its predominant position in the West.

By the mid-1950s, the discrepancy between the Canadian and French understandings of Atlanticism was making it a source of discord. Paris, wrestling with reduced international stature and with decolonization, chafed under the constraints of Atlanticism and resented the realities of an alliance increasingly perceived as a thorn in the side of French interests. Such frustration fuelled a progressively more nationalist foreign policy and culminated in the Fourth Republic's collapse and de Gaulle's return to power. The shifting French position presented Ottawa with a dilemma. Nationalist concern over Canada's thickening web of links with the United States grew throughout the post-war period, in parallel with the declining importance of relations with Britain and the Commonwealth. As the 1950s progressed, Ottawa continued to consider Atlanticism an essential tool for managing Canada's asymmetrical relationship with Washington and maximizing an international influence that was in decline as Europe recovered. Boasting a foreign policy establishment oriented culturally toward the Anglo-American world and inclined ideologically to engage in the Cold War, Ottawa strove to act as a linchpin and reconcile France with its allies, in the hope of preserving the transatlantic framework at the heart of Canadian foreign policy. The result was a growing Franco-Canadian divergence on an array of global issues and a deterioration of the bilateral relationship in the geopolitical sphere that was crucial to the origins and evolution of the triangular tensions of the 1960s.

IN THE NEARLY TWO CENTURIES from Britain's conquest of New France to the German occupation of France in 1940, official links between France and Canada were tenuous. Formal contact between British North America and France was established only in the 1850s, and Confederation had little immediate impact on the relationship – the fledgling Dominion remained a colony in international affairs, so that relations were conducted chiefly through London. However, in the decades after Confederation, contacts with France proved instrumental to Canada's gradual emergence as an autonomous international actor – notwithstanding occasional fears in Paris about provoking British annoyance. The Quebec and Dominion governments, in turn, opened offices in Paris. Quebec premiers Adolphe Chapleau and Honoré Mercier were fêted in the French capital, as was prime minister Sir Wilfrid Laurier. The First World War saw tens of thousands of Canadians spill their blood at the Somme, Vimy Ridge, and beyond. These losses on French territory ultimately spurred Canadian bids for international autonomy. After the Balfour Declaration (1926) recognized Canada's right to conduct its own foreign relations, Ottawa and Paris established equivalent diplomatic representation. France – after Britain and the

United States – was the third country in which Canada operated a diplomatic mission. Even after this, however, relations remained anemic.²

Franco-Canadian links took on unprecedented importance following France's collapse before the German blitzkrieg in 1940. Ottawa suddenly confronted the dilemma of which rival French authority to recognize: the Vichy regime headed by Marshall Philippe Pétain, or de Gaulle and his Free France movement. The question quickly became bound up in Canadian domestic affairs as the conflict between the rival Frances was transposed onto Quebec's ideological and political debates. The prime minister, Mackenzie King, responded to the situation with characteristic caution, guided by his overarching goal of avoiding a recurrence of the national disunity that had rocked Canada during the First World War. Ottawa pursued its "Vichy gamble," maintaining relations with the increasingly collaborationist regime until late 1942. Beyond domestic considerations, the decision was motivated by the urgings of London, which wanted to keep open a line of communication with Vichy, and by Washington's maintaining relations with Pétain's government. Canada's wartime links with France were thus influenced heavily by the Anglo-Americans' complicated and shifting relations with Vichy and the Free French. This was apparent in the Saint-Pierre-et-Miquelon affair at the end of 1941, when, to American consternation, Free French forces acting on de Gaulle's orders seized these French islands off the Newfoundland coast. The dynamic was similarly evident in Canadian efforts, with Ottawa shifting toward a pro-Free French stance, to have Washington and London recognize de Gaulle's Gouvernement provisoire de la République française as France's legitimate government.³

Ottawa and Paris emerged from the war believing that they could expand and employ their strengthened links to mutual benefit. The symbolic elevation of their diplomatic legations to full embassies after Canada, in tandem with the other allies, recognized France's provisional government in October 1944 signalled the importance that both capitals assigned to the relationship. Ottawa's enhanced appreciation of France stemmed from recognition of that country's centrality to the post-war settlement, not least its role in a restored European counterweight to the United States. Paris's support of Canadian claims to "middle power" status were appreciated in Ottawa, where it was envisaged that the country's alleged vocation as a linchpin between Britain and the United States could be expanded to an intermediary role between those two countries and France. French diplomats noted their country's increased stature in the Canadian capital, evident when the secretary of state for external affairs, Louis St. Laurent, described France as an "indispensable element" of Canada's international life during his 1947 Gray Lecture at the

University of Toronto, remembered as the most comprehensive declaration of Canadian post-war foreign policy.[4]

Paris certainly recognized Canada's enhanced international position. When de Gaulle visited for the first time, in July 1944, his briefing notes described Canada as an interpreter between Europe and North America by virtue of geography, and between the Anglo-Saxon and Latin worlds owing to its ethnic origins. During a second trip, in 1945, de Gaulle used a press conference in Ottawa to refer to Canada's rise in the global ranks as justification for taking the bilateral relationship to a new level, and he asserted that Canada and France could only benefit from close cooperation. A report prepared by the Ministère des Affaires Étrangères (MAE) in 1949, perhaps the most comprehensive account of Paris's post-war attitudes regarding Canada, emphasized the country's increased importance and argued that this could only grow with immigration and the development of its natural resources. The report even suggested that Canada could displace Britain as the Commonwealth's centre of gravity and predicted that, with an increasing population, it would not be long before Canada was one of the world's most powerful countries.[5]

Paris was especially impressed by Ottawa's growing international assertiveness. The MAE saw Ottawa's positive disposition toward France as stemming partly from a Canadian concern with counterbalancing American influence, and French attention was drawn to Mackenzie King's declaration that Canada would act more and more independently of the Commonwealth in pursuing its national interests.[6] Such claims to independence resonated in Gaullist ears. Paris recognized that this increasingly powerful, autonomous Canada could be a very useful ally. France's ambassador to Ottawa, Francisque Gay, described Canada as exerting a certain French influence in the Commonwealth that London had to acknowledge. French interest similarly arose from Ottawa's links with the United States, reinforced by King's claims that Canada could serve as an intermediary between Paris and Washington. Gay suggested that by virtue of France's close relations with Canada, Paris could call upon Ottawa to intercede with the Americans when necessary.[7]

Ottawa's perceived influence with the British and Americans meant that Paris considered Canada well placed to advance French interests in international forums. On the eve of King's March 1945 visits to Washington and London, Paris sought to use his influence with Franklin Roosevelt and Winston Churchill to advance the French position regarding the emerging United Nations organization. France's ambassador emphasized to King the similarity of French and Canadian policy, as well as the fact that Paris's proposals would enhance the influence of middle powers such as Canada. Although they differed somewhat over the question of the veto for the permanent members of the Security Council, the Canadian and French delegations generally supported one another at the subsequent San Francisco conference.[8] This cooperation endured at the United Nations. Francisque Gay claimed that there was no other country with which France found itself "more commonly, more completely, and more amicably in agreement." He also remarked upon the Canadian efforts to serve as intermediary between the French and Anglo-American delegations.[9]

The Cold War provided additional incentive for cooperation: faced with the deteriorating international situation, Ottawa and Paris embraced Atlanticism, reflected in their participation in the founding of the North Atlantic Treaty Organization (NATO). Atlanticism was meant to bind North America and Western Europe together against the perceived Soviet threat. As such, it was a manifestation of realist calculations about the global balance of power. At the same time, however, Atlanticism was grounded in liberal internationalism – the belief that peace and stability were best promoted by states ceding a portion of their sovereignty to act collectively to confront common challenges. The tension between Atlanticism's realist and liberal internationalist dimensions was apparent in the complicated role that the United States played in the alliance and in the relationship between it and other members. As the apotheosis of the liberal project undergirding Atlanticism, the United States was considered a crucial source of protection and support; however, alliance members were also preoccupied with influencing and curbing American power. Reflecting the reality that, "as with all faiths, the tenets [of Atlanticism] were understood differently by its adherents," Ottawa and Paris adopted this foreign policy with differing motivations and expectations.[10]

In the immediate post-war period, Paris had hoped to regain international influence by serving as an intermediary between the Soviets and Anglo-Americans, its foremost concern being to block any German revival. Such aims were soon overtaken by events. French efforts to cultivate the Russians were revealed to be a failure by the testy Franco-Soviet exchanges during the Moscow Conference of Foreign Ministers in 1947. This was quickly followed by the Soviet-backed coup in Czechoslovakia and the Berlin blockade. In France, meanwhile, de Gaulle had resigned in early 1946, fed up with the machinations of France's political parties. Anxiety over the communists' political strength and mounting labour strife throughout 1947 resulted in the expulsion of the Parti communiste française from the government, and the emergence of the Third Force coalition of socialists, liberals, and Christian democrats arrayed against the communist and Gaullist extremes of French political life. Evidence of Paris's shift from a quasi-neutralism into the Western camp was its concluding the Brussels Treaty, a mutual defence pact – and, more broadly, an appeal for North American assistance – with Britain and the Benelux countries.

As the talks leading to the North Atlantic treaty got underway in mid-1948, the foremost French concern, beyond securing American aid, protecting against a Soviet invasion, and resisting Anglo-American pressures for German rearmament, was to use the nascent alliance to regain Great Power status and establish itself as the pre-eminent continental power. For Paris, such status required having a voice in the strategic direction of the West equal to that of London and Washington, along with arrangements to help France retain its overseas possessions, especially in North Africa. The realist hue to French Atlanticism was evident in Paris's irritation at not being included in secret preliminary talks between American, British, and Canadian officials in March 1948. The exclusion, a result of American security concerns, rankled all the more since Paris had been pushing for joint strategic planning and some form of alliance with Washington.[11]

This early dispute pointed to a fundamental tension at the core of French Atlanticism. If Atlanticism appeared to be the best means available to promote France's geopolitical interests, concealing French weakness under the cloak of North Atlantic solidarity, France's past as a Great Power ill prepared it to accept second-tier status in the alliance.[12] Yet the shift in the global balance of power ruled out French predominance, as did the fact that Atlanticism was grounded in the ties of history and culture linking the United States, Britain, and Canada. Indeed, the core personalities involved in NATO's founding were overwhelmingly "Anglo-Saxon," making the new alliance "an Anglo-American concept, an Anglo-American creation."[13] All of this rendered problematic Paris's bid for a privileged partnership with the new American hegemon and parity with Britain. It was hardly surprising, therefore, that shortly after the North Atlantic treaty was concluded complaints could be heard that France had become the "tail to a kite flown in Washington."[14] Although France boasted staunch Atlanticists such as Robert Schuman, Jean Monnet, and Raymond Aron, ambivalence marked French attitudes about the new transatlantic order; the nationalistic aspects of French Atlanticism overlapped with the neutralist sentiment popular among France's intellectual left, along with enduring desires for a Europeanist "third way" between the two superpowers.

In contrast to France's ambivalent embrace of Atlanticism, Canada's experience as the junior member of the "North Atlantic triangle," along with the Anglo-American cultural orientation of its diplomatic corps, conditioned Ottawa to seize what the Department of External Affairs (DEA) under-secretary, Norman Robertson, described as the "providential solution" of Atlanticism – a reasonable compromise of sovereignty in exchange for an autonomous, nominally equal voice in the West's councils of power.[15] Moreover, following the wartime acrimony between English and French Canada, Atlanticism stood as the best prospect for a consensus on the country's international life.

A ribbon of liberal internationalism ran prominently through Canadian Atlanticism. The debate over article 2 of the North Atlantic treaty, intended to facilitate economic, cultural, and political cooperation, reflected Canadian desires that NATO be more than a military alliance – that it serve as a rejoinder to the Soviet worldview and promote an integration culminating in the emergence of an "Atlantic community." Not too far behind such lofty ambitions, however, lurked more prosaic geopolitical calculations. Certain members of Canada's foreign policy establishment – notably Ottawa's ambassador to Washington, Hume Wrong – gave short shrift to Atlanticism's idealistic dimension and were more concerned with responding to the more immediate challenge of the post-war balance of power.[16] The exponential growth of American power and Britain's concomitant decline had upset the delicate balance that Ottawa sought to maintain between Washington and London. Matters were not helped by Canada's failure to secure a tangible "middle power" status at the United Nations, considered the surest vehicle for autonomous Canadian international action. Combined with Ottawa's concern over the Soviet threat and what this portended for relations with Washington, Atlanticism appeared an attractive option indeed. It offered Ottawa the ability to influence the Americans while safeguarding Canada's autonomy: NATO would expand the traditional European counterweight from a weakened Britain to include France and Western Europe. Canadian nationalism thus "marched hand in hand with internationalism."[17]

Even as Paris and Ottawa embraced Atlanticism, their differences over what this entailed were evident. In addition to French indifference and lip service to article 2, the St. Laurent government was discomfited by Paris's insistence that the NATO treaty should cover North Africa, fearing that it would make the alliance a vehicle for the perpetuation of colonialism. Ottawa overcame its reticence only when faced with Paris's *sine qua non* that Algeria be included in the treaty. Amid French hesitation about the emerging alliance, Lester Pearson, recently appointed secretary of state for external affairs, instructed Georges Vanier, Canada's ambassador to Paris, to "talk some sense into his French friends, who, of all people, should be the most enthusiastic."[18] Although the NATO shield provided an arena for greater Franco-Canadian contact, it was apparent early on that it was also a multilateral sword that could cut both ways.

The peak in Franco-Canadian cooperation during this Atlanticist moment occurred during the Korean War. Although Paris and Ottawa backed the United Nations resolution condemning North Korea's invasion of South Korea, both capitals were concerned about the United States-led action on the peninsula and feared a larger conflict. By the end of 1950, Ottawa and Paris had recognized their common concerns over Korea, and used their influence to counter "the more impetuous aspects" of American policy.[19]

The strength of the relationship was evident throughout 1951. Against the backdrop of Canada sending an army brigade and air division to Europe as part of NATO's integrated force, France's prime minister, René Pleven, travelled to Ottawa, where he commented to Canadian officials "upon the remarkable extent to which French and Canadian views coincided on the most important world problems."[20] Pleven's visit had been preceded by Louis St. Laurent's first trip to France as prime minister. French officials interpreted the sojourn as a signal that Ottawa viewed relations with Paris as equal in importance to those with London and Washington, and as a means to emphasize Canadian autonomy from the British and Americans. The MAE took advantage of St. Laurent's presence to demonstrate Paris's desire for a strong collaboration, especially regarding relations with the Americans, since it considered Canada better placed than any other country to present views not easily accepted in Washington. During their talks, Pleven complained to St. Laurent about what he decried as American and British attempts to establish an "Anglo-Saxon leadership" of NATO.[21]

In April 1951, France's president, Vincent Auriol, became that country's first head of state to visit Canada. The trip took place amid heightened anxiety over Korea, following American General Douglas MacArthur's threats to expand the war to China if Beijing did not negotiate with the UN. During the visit, Pearson reiterated to his French counterpart, Robert Schuman, that Ottawa and Paris had similar misgivings about the trend of American policy. Referring more than once to Canada's "courageous policy," Auriol and Schuman affirmed that Ottawa could criticize Washington much more emphatically than Paris dared given France's reliance on American military and economic aid.[22]

Pearson's subsequent speech to Toronto's Canadian Club, in which he declared over the era of "easy and automatic relations" between Canada and the United States, was welcomed in French official circles as an expression of concern over the bellicose climate in Washington and the prospect of the Korean War escalating into a global conflagration. France's embassy characterized Pearson's remarks as a bid to maintain Atlantic solidarity, sending the Americans a message that likely would have been ignored had it come from another ally. The ambassador, Hubert Guérin, even claimed that Pearson deserved some credit for American president Harry Truman's subsequent firing of MacArthur, and remarked upon the community of interests and intentions between Canada and France.[23] Guérin cited Canadian public opinion's support of France's "peace offensive" at the 1951 UN General Assembly, and the fact that Auriol's opening remarks on this occasion were better received in Ottawa than in Washington as proof of a greater Canadian understanding of Western European positions on the Cold War.[24]

Yet storm clouds were already gathering over this common ground. Although France and Canada shared an Atlanticist response to Cold War realities, this masked and even exacerbated their differences. There was French disappointment over Ottawa's decision in 1949 not to recognize the Associated States of Indochina (ASI), owing to Canadian doubts about the viability and independence of the Paris-backed regime. Despite repeated French requests and fears that Ottawa was signalling non-confidence in French policy and a lack of sympathy for Paris's domestic challenges, Canada withheld recognition until 1952. News of the Viet Minh's growing strength prompted Ottawa to grant recognition as a way to encourage Franco-Vietnamese forces and support France to show Atlantic solidarity.[25]

The episode demonstrated that a shared Atlanticism by no means guaranteed harmony; to the contrary, it had sown discord. Paris was preoccupied with re-establishing France as a Great Power, which entailed regaining control of its overseas possessions, and it expected support from its Canadian ally. Such expectations clashed, however, with Canadian liberal internationalism and Ottawa's quest for middle power status, one based partly on its Commonwealth ties. Indeed, the withholding of Canadian recognition had been informed by the fact that India, with which Ottawa sought a "special relationship," questioned the ASI's legitimacy. To Ottawa's subsequent surprise, New Delhi was influential in arranging to have Canada serve on the International Commission for Supervision and Control established in 1954 to oversee the Geneva settlement of the conflict in Indochina. As Canadian diplomats prepared to take up the task, Lester Pearson warned them to be cautious in their dealings with the French.[26]

Differences over Indochina were the harbinger of a growing divergence between Ottawa and Paris over foreign policy approaches and objectives. To be sure, by the early 1950s, the idealistic dimension of Canadian Atlanticism had declined in relative importance, as reflected in Ottawa's failure to propose concrete measures regarding article 2. Yet Canada's foreign policy establishment continued to view Atlanticism as the best available way to respond to the Cold War and contend with American power, even though such an approach was reinforcing American predominance.[27] Across the Atlantic meanwhile, with the acute phase of French vulnerability past, Paris assumed an increasingly nationalist stance. French Atlanticism was predicated on Paris having an equal voice in Western decision-making, yet this appeared increasingly unattainable given the "growing hegemonic impulse" in Washington being fed by pessimistic appraisals of Western European military capabilities.[28] French nationalist disenchantment encouraged Ottawa to pursue a "helpful fixer" role to mitigate transatlantic dissension. When Auriol told Vanier of the growth of "a violent anti-American sentiment" in France, the Canadian ambassador was moved to warn Ottawa that the president's thinly veiled criticism of the United States in an October 1952 speech revealed a "growing [French] impatience in foreign policy matters." This made it urgent, Vanier argued, for Ottawa to act as a linchpin between Paris and Washington; an active Canadian presence in NATO would reinforce French faith in the alliance and strengthen the hand of Atlanticist politicians in Paris.[29]

Canadian concern with maintaining Atlantic solidarity was evident during the acrimonious debate over the European Defence Community (EDC). The deepening Cold War and the fighting in Korea had increased the sense of urgency regarding Western European defence. Responding to European calls for an integrated NATO force in Europe that included a North American troop commitment and an American commander, Washington began pushing for West German rearmament within NATO under a single, unified command. These developments jeopardized France's entire post-war strategy. Beyond posing a security risk, German rearmament would upset the European balance of economic, political, and military power and raised the spectre of an eventual Anglo-American withdrawal from the continent. Paris responded with the Pleven Plan, the EDC's progenitor; German rearmament was to be realized under the supranational cloak of European integration, although in practice the EDC would come under NATO control. The scheme was fatally weakened, however, by its ambitiousness and British non-participation. Paris's objectives throughout the ensuing protracted debate were consistent: ensuring French parity with the Anglo-Americans and integrating West Germany into the Western camp on terms favourable to France. Despite the EDC's French origins, fears grew that the scheme threatened French interests. De Gaulle and his Rassemblement du peuple français condemned the plan as an excessive concession of sovereignty that relegated France to second-tier status relative to Britain and the United States. The project was depicted as a plot to ensure that the Anglo-Americans would become the sole possessors of independent armed forces, with the continental European powers falling under their control.[30] The EDC soon became a foundling, adopted by a Washington that also wanted to be midwife to the birth of a united Europe.

The Atlantic ideal guided Ottawa's response, informing its attempts to reconcile Paris and Washington and see the EDC realized. Although Paris was aware of Canadian desires for a prompt ratification of the treaty, it also appreciated Ottawa's linchpin efforts as proof of understanding and moderation. Pearson's sympathetic remarks at the December 1953 meeting of the North Atlantic

Council that saw the United States's secretary of state, John Foster Dulles, threaten an "agonizing reappraisal" of American policy if the EDC collapsed, earned Pearson his French counterpart's deep gratitude. Georges Bidault, France's foreign minister, found it "moving that a Canadian of British origin should express the French position with such clarity, understanding and goodwill."[31] Bidault was perhaps drawn more to the sympathetic elements of Pearson's remarks than to the deeper Atlanticist message that he repeated in acknowledging Bidault's thanks:

> Because of our history, our traditions and our origins we are ... able to understand somewhat more clearly than our American neighbours the feelings of our friends in France, especially when questions of Franco-German relationships are under consideration. It would be surprising if it were not so.
>
> At the same time, because we are North Americans, we also appreciate and share the anxiety of ... Washington that European arrangements should soon be completed which will make it easier for us on this continent to cooperate to the full within the North Atlantic coalition by associating Germany in some form.[32]

The EDC, however, was doomed. After France's new prime minister, Pierre Mendès-France, failed in the face of American opposition to remove the treaty's supranational components, he refused to engage his government's future over it. This prompted the National Assembly to block ratification, effectively killing the project. Ottawa welcomed the subsequent compromise arrangement of the Western European Union;[33] however, it was anxious that this should not undermine the Atlanticist framework by encouraging a "Europeanist" solution.[34] Notwithstanding such concerns, there was official optimism in Ottawa about Mendès-France, who was perceived as more capable than his predecessors in responding to France's challenges. For his part, Mendès-France regarded Pearson as a useful ally who could explain French actions to the Americans. Paris had appreciated Pearson's sympathetic reaction to the EDC's failure, and Guérin was instructed to ask him to use his influence in Washington to help with the difficult situation. Pearson did so, lobbying Dulles in advance of Mendès-France's November 1954 visit to the American capital. Stopping in Ottawa en route, Mendès-France acknowledged, in talks with St. Laurent, the reality of American leadership of the West, but he emphasized Western Europe's need to lessen its dependence on the United States as a prerequisite to a more flexible foreign policy. St. Laurent offered his empathy in reply, explaining that Canada, possibly more than any other country, was aware of and had to contend with American public opinion.[35]

With the EDC debate resolved after providing opportunities for cooperation between Ottawa and Paris, it was not surprising that Canada's ambassador, Jean Désy, should have claimed that the relationship had "never been more active or useful."³⁶ The transatlantic bonhomie, however, hid the broader trend: rather than sympathy for the French position, Ottawa had been motivated by its concern to preserve the Atlanticist framework. For France, meanwhile, the debate had constituted a national reawakening that included a growing antipathy for Atlanticism. Notwithstanding the EDC's French parentage, Washington's intense pressure for ratification had made it appear to be an American *diktat*. Rejecting it constituted an assertion of independence from Washington, a refusal to accept what had come to be seen as an excessive concession of sovereignty in pursuit of the Atlantic ideal, and a rejection of a two-tiered NATO that would see France treated differently.³⁷ Although Ottawa and Paris continued to operate within the Atlanticist framework, they were increasingly working at cross-purposes.

THE DIVERGENCE BETWEEN Canada and France was increasingly apparent as events in North Africa spilled into the North Atlantic. Part of the French calculus for NATO had been to shift part of the rearmament burden onto Washington, freeing up resources that Paris could use to shore up control of its overseas territories. This was all the more important given that the war had enhanced the importance of empire in French minds as a guarantor of Great Power status and pre-eminence in Europe. North Africa loomed large in this regard, but France's collapse and the arrival of Anglo-American forces in 1942 had disrupted French authority, encouraged local nationalist movements, and attracted international attention to the region's future. The Fourth Republic's attempts at reform were no match for the rising anti-colonial tide in Morocco, Tunisia, and Algeria. Nationalist calls for "internal independence" were quickly overtaken by demands for full sovereignty, and a vicious cycle of popular unrest, repression, and nationalist appeals to international opinion further eroded France's position.³⁸

Canada's support for decolonization in the abstract was conditioned in practice by the priority that it attached to Atlantic solidarity and broader Cold War considerations. Initially, Ottawa was indulgent toward Paris and its actions in North Africa; however, as French difficulties began to have a deleterious effect on Western interests and NATO unity, Ottawa attempted to reconcile France to the broader priorities of its allies, particularly Washington. The dynamic was evident during the Pinay affair of autumn 1952, when the American delegation to the UN abstained on a vote regarding inscription of the Tunisian situation on the General Assembly's agenda. Paris considered the abstention a betrayal that, combined with Washington's reduction of offshore procurement aid to France, provoked the French prime minister, Antoine Pinay, to decry American interference in his country's affairs. In contrast, the Canadian delegation's votes against resolutions urging France to recognize Tunisian and Moroccan independence earned Pinay's gratitude. French diplomats ascribed Ottawa's sympathetic reaction to its own challenges with Washington.[39]

In fact, the more immediate reason for Canada's stance was Ottawa's fear that criticizing France could provoke Paris to reject the EDC or withdraw from Indochina, or that it could even bring an anti-NATO government to power. The Atlanticist preoccupation informing Canadian policy was apparent in the fact that during the same period, Ottawa supported inscription of the Tunisian and Moroccan issues on the General Assembly agenda, in the hope that such a discussion would mollify Arab and Asian members and thereby safeguard Western interests in North Africa and beyond.[40]

If Ottawa drew satisfaction from Paris's subsequent adoption of liberal policies that led to Moroccan and Tunisian independence, it was increasingly alarmed as France grappled with its most vexing colonial challenge: Algeria. The idea of France's *mission civilisatrice* in Algeria was long in dying; the bloody French reaction to the 1945 Sétif uprising, combined with events in Morocco and Tunisia, stoked an Algerian nationalism that erupted in a full-blown anti-colonial insurgency in November 1954. For Paris, accommodation was a non-starter. France had been humiliated in 1940 and in Indochina, its position had become untenable in the rest of North Africa, and the EDC's collapse had announced a heightened nationalistic sensitivity. France's military and a vast swath of the political class were adamant that Algeria would not – could not – be another defeat.[41]

Ottawa had been loath to extend the provisions of the North Atlantic treaty to Algeria, but even if it harboured a certain sympathy for the Algerian desire for self-determination, its preoccupation with Atlantic unity and belief that NATO interests were best served by French control of the Mediterranean littoral prompted it to support the attempt by Paris to crush the insurgency. This support included indirect funding of the French war effort, as Canada sent military equipment to France under the auspices of NATO's Mutual Aid program. However, mounting evidence throughout 1955 of French difficulties, along with the Bandung Declaration on self-determination that fuelled Canadian fears of a rift between the West and the Third World, provoked second thoughts in Ottawa. When Paris weakened the NATO deterrent by transferring an army division from West Germany to Algeria, Pearson became convinced that French actions were undermining the Atlanticist cause.[42] France's ambassador to Canada, Francis Lacoste, was soon reporting on the deepening anxiety in Ottawa over Algeria and the Canadian predisposition toward the anti-colonial position.[43]

As the French government of Guy Mollet adopted an all-out war effort in 1956, Canada's Paris embassy warned that a French defeat would unleash extremism and bitterness transcending anything witnessed since the end of the Second World War. Canadian hopes of satisfying Algerian aspirations without harming French (and, by implication, NATO) interests were stymied by Paris's adamance that fighting in Algeria – by law an integral part of France – was a domestic affair. When Ottawa attempted to use the 1956 North Atlantic Council meeting to push Paris to embrace a liberal solution similar to that in Morocco and Tunisia, it was pre-empted by France's request for the NATO allies to foreswear interference and declare unqualified support of French efforts.[44]

France's deteriorating position in Algeria precipitated the Suez Crisis. It is fitting, given the growing divergence between Ottawa and Paris over Atlanticism, that what is remembered as a Canadian diplomatic triumph – Lester Pearson's contribution to defusing the crisis – should have occurred in conjunction with what was arguably the foreign policy nadir of the Fourth Republic. Paris's response to Egypt's nationalization of the Suez Canal in July 1956 was motivated partly by a concern with safeguarding French investments. There was also a general aversion to Egypt's president, Gamal Abdel Nasser, particularly his anti-Israeli position and pan-Arabism; democratic Europe's failure to confront the totalitarian challenge in the 1930s could not be repeated with what was viewed as a quasi-fascist regime. The foremost French aim, however, was to use the crisis to halt Cairo's material aid to the Algerian insurgency. Increasingly exasperated over what it considered a temporizing American approach, Paris was determined to remove Nasser and halt Egyptian arms shipments to the insurgents, and it began acting as an intermediary between the British and Israelis in organizing a military riposte.[45]

The Canadian response recalled that of the EDC debate – the objective being to defuse the crisis and preserve Atlantic solidarity. Ottawa was all too aware of the growing strains within NATO; the previous year, Pearson had reiterated Canada's desire to enhance the alliance's civilian dimension and achieve greater consultation between its members. Even as the Suez Crisis unfolded, Pearson was promoting these objectives as a member of NATO's "Three Wise Men" committee that had been established to find ways to strengthen non-military cooperation and reinvigorate the Atlanticist cause.[46] Aware that the French blamed Egypt for the fighting in Algeria, Ottawa viewed Paris's and London's actions as a dangerously flawed bid to destroy Nasser. The French and British veto of the American resolution in the Security Council condemning Israel for its prearranged attack on Egypt at the end of October, followed by the Anglo-French military intervention, was the nightmare scenario for Canadian Atlanticism: an open split in NATO between its foremost allies. Ottawa used the General Assembly to facilitate a solution that would extricate the British and French while minimizing damage to Atlantic solidarity and the Commonwealth. Initially, therefore, there was no Canadian public condemnation of Paris or London for violating the UN Charter; rather, Pearson built support for a peacekeeping force to defuse the explosive situation. His efforts bore fruit when the Security Council mandated the secretary-general, Dag Hammarskjöld, to assemble an emergency military force to act as a buffer between Egyptian and Israeli forces. The crisis deepened, however, following the landings of Anglo-French paratroopers, an action that led Moscow to threaten an atomic attack on Paris and London. Before Anglo-French military objectives could be realized, intense American financial pressure forced Britain's prime minister, Anthony Eden, to inform his French counterpart, Guy Mollet, that he was compelled to accept a ceasefire and the deployment of a peacekeeping force without British or French participation.[47]

Atlantic solidarity was shaken to its core. The debacle meant that Paris sank further into the Algerian quagmire, having enhanced Nasser's prestige in the Arab world at a corresponding cost to French influence. Mollet believed that he had been betrayed by Eden and abandoned by Washington. Indeed, the American economic coercion and refusal to respond to Soviet sabre-rattling confirmed French suspicions that the alliance was a fig leaf concealing a naked American bid for hegemony. Referring to the "undercurrent of satisfaction that Nasser ha[d] been shown up ... and that France had reacted vigorously" and independently of Washington, Canada's Paris embassy warned against underestimating French nationalist sentiment; although NATO was still considered indispensable to France's security, this was paralleled by a growing determination to safeguard French independence within the alliance.[48]

News from London was even more alarming. Canada's high commission cited a Foreign Office source in reporting that senior French Cabinet members, including Mollet and foreign minister Christian Pineau, had seriously considered the "emasculation, if not the actual break-up, of NATO" to free France from the American embrace.[49] Such reports heightened Canadian anxiety over French intentions; DEA officials feared the ramifications of Paris's increased assertiveness for European integration in the wake of Suez. St. Laurent was reminded that it was "axiomatic" for Canada that "Western Europe should develop and integrate as part of the Atlantic community ... in every major field of policy."[50]

Suez and its aftermath were thus a dramatic illustration of the Franco-Canadian dynamic, already apparent during the EDC debate, arising from the divergence over Atlanticism. In both situations, Ottawa had sought to minimize the damage to Atlantic solidarity in response to an increasingly pronounced French nationalism. But there was a crucial difference between the two episodes:

whereas Canadian efforts had earned French gratitude regarding the EDC, these were less appreciated in Paris two years later, as their aim was to preserve the solidarity of a transatlantic alliance that a growing portion of French decision makers criticized as unresponsive, even hostile, to French interests. Indeed, Suez was crucial to France's subsequent relations with "les Anglo-Saxons," fuelling nationalist frustration over preponderant American power, concern over decolonization, and a belief that French interests were ill served by the structures of Western strategic decision-making.[51] Although French bitterness toward Ottawa was not as intense as it was toward London and Washington, Paris's ambassador did relay St. Laurent's reproach of France and Britain for their unilateralism, notably his assertion that the era when the "supermen of Europe" ruled the world was over. Lacoste ascribed the remarks to St. Laurent's Irish blood, combined with the vehement anti-colonialism, egocentrism, and isolationism linked to his French-Canadian heritage.[52]

With Suez having undermined France's position in Algeria, the Franco-Canadian divergence over Atlanticism was exacerbated. Although Ottawa continued to respond to Paris's growing alienation, it was frustrated over what it viewed as French intransigence and the consequences of this for NATO. The DEA did not disguise its annoyance over Paris's "stubbornness ... [to] not ... face certain basic facts," and the under-secretary of state for external affairs, Jules Léger, warned that it was "becoming very difficult" for Ottawa to support French actions in Algeria.[53]

The Fourth Republic collapsed amid this growing transatlantic exasperation. The Eisenhower administration's attitude toward Paris was considerably less indulgent after Suez, as Washington continued to bring its economic power to bear to hasten a resolution of the Algerian conflict. French outrage over an Anglo-American arms shipment to Tunisia, due to fear the weapons would fall into Algerian hands, was followed in early 1958 by French forces bombing the Tunisian village of Sakiet-Sidi-Youssef to strike at Algerian insurgents in the border community. Washington made clear to France's ambassador its deep anger over the attack that had resulted in considerable civilian deaths, and ratcheted up the pressure for a settlement by establishing an Anglo-American "Good Offices" mission to address Franco-Tunisian tensions.[54] In Ottawa, Léger suggested to Lacoste that Paris should take advantage of the mission to resolve not only the immediate crisis but the broader Algerian issue. The ambassador reluctantly agreed to relay the message after Léger emphasized Ottawa's worry that Tunisia would use the Sakiet affair to bring the Algerian question before the Security Council, in which case Ottawa would be forced to consider its response jointly with the other allies.[55] The exchange revealed a growing official Canadian impatience: Ottawa was siding with London and Washington and bringing its own pressure to bear on Paris, hoping to avoid another public transatlantic rupture, less than two years after Suez, that would result from a Security Council debate.

French opinion interpreted American president Dwight Eisenhower's April 1958 letter to French prime minister Félix Gaillard as supportive of Algerian independence; combined with Washington's ongoing economic pressure that threatened a French balance-of-payments crisis, the Gaillard government's subsequent acceptance of the Good Offices mission was viewed as a sell-out. The result was explosive: a protracted ministerial crisis culminating in de Gaulle's return and the demise of the Fourth Republic. The dramatic events were in many respects an "anti-American revolt" – a nationalist rejection of the United States-dominated Atlanticist framework.[56] Canada's embassy reported on the prevalence of anti-American and anti-NATO sentiment, reminding Ottawa that the nationalist reaction was not "just the isolated rantings of right-wing extremists," but present "in a wide segment of French public opinion."[57] The assessment of the embassy's Henry Davis was that "there are many in France and many more in Algeria who want to show that France still has courage and determination ... that France is still vigorous and master of its own destinies."[58]

Despite misgivings about de Gaulle's attitude about Atlanticism, Ottawa considered the General the best hope for French political stability and a solution in Algeria. Ottawa therefore continued to support France at the UN and refrained from applying pressure privately; however, Canadian concern over the French leader's ability and willingness to settle the Algerian issue continued until his September 1959 announcement that Algerian Muslims would be called upon to exercise their right to self-determination in a referendum. Although the announcement by no means resolved the matter, it ended the period during which North African decolonization affected Franco-Canadian relations most directly. Lacoste reported on Canadian satisfaction over de Gaulle's decision and the DEA's eagerness to assist France at the UN. Paris had generally recognized in the months preceding the announcement that Ottawa was torn between its position on decolonization and a desire not to add to French difficulties; however, tensions had not been avoided. The Diefenbaker government had refused to employ Canada's Commonwealth links to prevent African and Asian members from recognizing the Cairo-based Gouvernement provisoire de la République algérienne. And the news in the summer of 1958 that Jules Léger was to meet with representatives of the Conference of Independent African States lobbying on behalf of Algerian nationalists provoked a strong French reaction. A senior French bureaucrat even warned against undue Canadian interest in Algeria by suggesting that this was tantamount to Paris involving itself in the political destiny of part of Canada.[59]

De Gaulle's return to power also meant that even as the conflict in Algeria lurched toward a conclusion, Ottawa had to contend with a determined French effort to provoke fundamental change in the transatlantic framework. The issue of nuclear proliferation provided an example, early in the life of the Fifth Republic, of the implications of the Franco-Canadian divergence over Atlanticism. The potential for atomic issues to split Ottawa and Paris had been illustrated in 1955, when French officials expressed interest in Canadian uranium for France's nuclear energy research program. Complicating the proposed sale was the question of command and control. Guided by its liberal internationalism and proliferation fears, Ottawa favoured international controls as a condition of the sale. The position was equally informed by a concern to avoid the disruption to NATO that it was felt France's atomic military capability would provoke. The Canadian stance was at odds with a French nationalism quickly approaching critical mass; reflecting a growing resentment over its second-tier status in NATO, Paris rejected any external controls, and no deal was concluded.[60]

Franco-Canadian differences over nuclear proliferation were exacerbated by Paris's decision after Suez to pursue a nuclear weapons program. This was meant to obtain for France the influence that it desired in NATO, thwarting the apparent Anglo-American condominium over the Alliance. Washington's lacklustre response to Soviet threats during the crisis had also confirmed French fears over the reliability of the American atomic deterrent. Returned to office, de Gaulle ordered the weapons program accelerated and made it clear that France would have an independent nuclear capability. This Gaullist position clashed with an increasingly avowed Canadian disarmament stance.[61]

A confrontation came in 1959, when the Afro-Asian bloc at the UN protested France's first atomic explosion in the Algerian desert. Lacoste invoked Atlantic solidarity in urging Ottawa to vote against any resolution linked to French testing, but the appeal was ineffective. Paris regarded it as a betrayal when Canada's delegation supported calls for France to refrain from nuclear tests in the Sahara. Charles Lucet, the MAE's second-ranking official, raised the issue with Canada's ambassador, Pierre Dupuy, asking why, after years of large American, British, and even Soviet tests, Canada had chosen the occasion of a "little French explosion" to censure France.[62] Dupuy warned Ottawa of the potential consequences of the dispute, after the head of the MAE's European division told him that de Gaulle would see Canada's vote as further proof of the hollowness of Atlantic solidarity. The disarmament issue resurfaced during de Gaulle's visit to Canada a few months later. When the prime minister, John Diefenbaker, reiterated Ottawa's opposition to atomic testing, de Gaulle was unrepentant, stating that France could stop testing only if all nations destroyed their warheads.[63]

Beyond heralding a French nuclear capability, the mushroom cloud that rose over the Sahara was an ominous testament to a more explicitly nationalist French foreign policy. Despite repeated French efforts since NATO's inception, the alliance was not a partnership of equals entailing global solidarity. What had been adopted in a bid to overcome a French sense of inferiority had ultimately reinforced this; the effective exclusion of Paris from the Anglo-American inner circle of strategic cooperation fuelled a sense that France's "association with NATO ha[d] required her to make concessions, even sacrifices, without being compensated by comparable advantages."[64] Although the Three Wise Men committee on which Pearson served had taken into account French concern about the operation of the alliance and the need for members to discuss matters outside the NATO area, this concern was watered down in its final report, which contained a thinly veiled rebuke of the French and British for their actions regarding Suez.[65]

Strikingly evident in the dying days of the Fourth Republic, French dissatisfaction with the Atlantic status quo only increased amid the birth of the Fifth. In 1944, de Gaulle had groused that the United States was "'already trying to rule the world.'"[66] The Yalta Myth, positing France's exclusion from the superpowers' divvying up of the globe, with a compliant Britain as junior partner to the Americans, figured prominently in Gaullist thought. The rapidity with which Washington and London had apparently healed their rift over Suez only reinforced this belief. De Gaulle scorned the Fourth Republic's Atlanticism as an effort to please others, claiming that it had used Atlantic solidarity to camouflage France's "self-effacement," subjecting France "to the hegemony of the Anglo-Saxons."[67]

Gaullist thought held that French independence required the prevention of any de facto collusion among the superpowers that would enable them to maintain hegemony in their spheres of influence. In practical terms, this led to de Gaulle's challenge of the Cold War order as he strove to end what he considered an unhealthy subservience to Washington. This included building on the Fourth Republic's efforts to achieve reconciliation and a partnership with West Germany, meant to facilitate France's leadership of a Western Europe that would be an equal partner of the United States. De Gaulle's return to power did not change so much the substance of French international action as the worldview underpinning it: a realist approach according the nation-state the highest political value supplanted Atlanticism's liberal internationalism. France would continue to confront the Soviet threat alongside the United States and the NATO allies, but a foremost Gaullist aim was to ensure that, in so doing, France would recover its rightful geopolitical rank in the West and increase its influence with and autonomy from Washington.[68]

As the Gaullist storm broke, Ottawa lashed itself to the mast of Atlanticism and its self-appointed linchpin role. Notwithstanding NATO's apparent shortcomings, a persuasive combination of culture, ideology, and geopolitical circumstance encouraged Canada's foreign policy establishment to keep faith with the Atlantic ideal. The DEA believed that "careful diplomacy and delicacy" were the order of the day, and that Ottawa should help calm the waters between France and its allies. There was even discussion about reappointing Georges Vanier to Paris given his wartime friendship with de Gaulle. Canada's embassy warned of the "fissiparous tendencies" that a failure to consult Paris would provoke; Ottawa was therefore urged to "take every opportunity to consult the French" and to encourage London and Washington to do likewise.[69]

Such anxieties were borne out by de Gaulle's annoyance over not being consulted prior to the July 1958 Anglo-American military interventions in Lebanon and Jordan, and by Washington's handling of the Second Formosa Straits crisis that erupted the following month. Both events had the potential to escalate into a larger conflict involving the NATO allies, and the Lebanese operation had involved American forces based in France. Consistent with Paris's efforts since NATO's creation to possess an equal voice in allied strategic planning, de Gaulle responded by proposing a US-UK-France "directorate" through which France would transform the structure of transatlantic relations and achieve the political equality with the British and Americans that it had sought since the 1940s.[70]

The response in Ottawa to de Gaulle's proposal was cool – coming, as it did, as Canada was itself experiencing a nationalist reaction to Cold War realities, notably its deepening relations with the United States. If anti-American sentiment in Canada was less pronounced after the Second World War than it had been in earlier periods, by the mid-1950s nationalist rumblings were increasingly audible. It was all too apparent that, notwithstanding the rhetoric that had surrounded NATO since its creation, the actions and inaction of its members – Canada included – had ensured that it was "an alliance of the old kind."[71] Although Atlanticism had offered Ottawa opportunities to influence Washington, it had also contributed to American predominance in the West and institutionalized Canada's asymmetrical relationship with the United States. Ottawa's failure to support London during the Suez Crisis had provoked a considerable section of anglophone Canadian opinion, which condemned the St. Laurent government's response as indicative of its continentalist predilections. Many suggested that Canada had become the "chore boy" to Washington, a better friend to Nasser than to London and Paris. The nationalist charge that Liberal governments since the 1930s had led Canada into the American embrace was reinforced by the release of the Gordon Commission's preliminary report outlining the scope of the American economic presence in Canada.⁷² It was in this charged atmosphere that the Norman affair erupted. Commentators blamed the suicide of Canadian diplomat Herbert Norman on American communist witch-hunts. The controversy, described by Pearson at the time as the most severe instance of anti-Americanism that he had ever experienced, galvanized nationalist anxieties and led to the emergence of modern Canadian anti-Americanism as a potent political force.⁷³

John Diefenbaker and his Progressive Conservatives reaped the electoral benefit, incorporating the nationalist angst into a larger narrative about a Liberal government that had overstayed its welcome and lost touch with Canadians. However, despite Tory accusations that the Liberals had undermined Canada's independence by tacking too closely to Washington, there was a foreign policy continuity between the Diefenbaker government elected in 1957 and that of its predecessor. The core preoccupation continued to be finding a counterweight to the United States, as demonstrated by the new government's concern with reviving links with Britain and the Commonwealth. Ottawa therefore continued to adhere to Atlanticism. Indeed, this policy took on even greater importance after the Diefenbaker government approved the North American Air Defence Agreement (NORAD), which provided for a joint military command between Canada and the United States in air defence.⁷⁴

Diefenbaker reacted "very strongly" to de Gaulle's proposed directorate, dismissing it as "a totally unrealistic assessment of France's power and influence in NATO."⁷⁵ The sense in the DEA was that even if the General had correctly identified the challenge of preponderant American influence in NATO, his "remedy could well kill the patient."⁷⁶ Ottawa feared that a directorate would lead to a formalized, two-tiered NATO at odds with the rationale for Canadian Atlanticism: a US-UK-France strategic partnership would reduce Ottawa's ability to use the alliance to influence the Great Powers; the decline of Canada's international stature since 1945 would be institutionalized; and Ottawa would effectively be denied its European counterweight, leaving Canada more vulnerable in its relations with the United States.⁷⁷ The scope of the divergence over Atlanticism was laid bare: what to Gaullist eyes was a means to ensure French independence and international influence was, refracted through Ottawa's Atlanticist prism, a threat to Canada's autonomy and ability to act internationally.

Meeting de Gaulle for the first time in Paris in 1958, Diefenbaker expressed Canada's opposition forcefully. The French leader responded by declaring it unacceptable that Washington alone should make decisions affecting NATO allies and that the organization's strategic planning be carried out by the American and British high commands. When Diefenbaker claimed that Ottawa wanted greater consultation in NATO, but not at the price of a two-tiered alliance, de Gaulle rejoined that Canada already accepted this in practical terms, citing Ottawa's acquiescence to the Great Powers' decisions regarding the Middle East, Asia, and disarmament. Diefenbaker did not address this charge but intimated that if the directorate were established and NATO's geographic scope extended to reflect French extra-European interests, Ottawa would have to reconsider its NATO commitments.[78] The exchange was emblematic of the evolution of the bilateral relationship since 1945. The cooperation stemming from the two countries' shared Atlanticism had faded; Paris now felt that its interests were better served by challenging the Atlantic framework, whereas Ottawa continued to believe that this framework was the best means to safeguard and promote Canadian interests.

The dispute contributed to a growing concern in Ottawa over the state of a relationship that, despite being "regularly described as close and sympathetic due to ... ties of culture and history," had been subject to "recurring difficulties and frictions."[79] A DEA report to Diefenbaker warned that Ottawa and Paris tended to take their bilateral links for granted; it expressed concern that Canada's complex relations with Washington and London were poorly understood in France and that Ottawa had failed "to convince [Paris] of our independent involvement in international affairs."[80]

The DEA analysis skirted the core issue. A fundamental – and growing – difference existed between the cultures of the two countries' foreign policy establishments over exactly *what* constituted the best means to achieve "independent involvement in international affairs," a point that Canada's ambassador to France, Pierre Dupuy, emphasized:

Many Frenchmen, even in government circles, tend to think that Canada, in the Washington-Ottawa-London triangle, is more often than not the recipient of advice, which we usually act on ... Only by emphasizing Canada's independent course in international political and economic affairs, and her initiatives, could one hope to gain that measure of influence likely to enable us to "sell" our policies to [Paris].[81]

Paris was certainly aware of the growth of Canadian nationalist sentiment and the concern with not appearing to be an American satellite. Indeed, the Progressive Conservatives' election had been interpreted in French circles as a symptom of this nationalist reaction. As the Diefenbaker government continued in office, however, French officials were struck by the disparity between its nationalist rhetoric and continentalist reality. Francis Lacoste argued that after eighteen months, "Conservative" Canada had scarcely reduced, and certainly not eliminated, the American influence for which the Liberals had been reproached. To the contrary, the ambassador considered the new government to have markedly *increased* Canadian dependence on Washington through its hasty acceptance of NORAD and a joint ministerial defence committee.[82] Such developments, given the Diefenbaker government's stated intentions, fuelled a French belief that Canada was locked into the United States's orbit.

The extent to which Franco-Canadian relations had deteriorated was reflected in the doubts in both capitals when de Gaulle visited Canada in 1960. Beyond a concern that the trip would be cancelled as a result of Canada's vote at the UN regarding France's atomic testing, the DEA wondered if Ottawa was being sent a signal when, despite prior French knowledge, the visit was scheduled for dates that conflicted with Diefenbaker's planned trip to Mexico. Conversely, the apparent lack of warmth and enthusiasm in Ottawa during the visit drew comments from a French delegation perplexed at the public indifference and an absence of pomp that contrasted poorly with extraordinary receptions in Britain and the United States. Lacoste gamely attributed the difference to a Canadian temperament shaped by its ethnic origins, history, and even the northern climate, and claimed that even the most popular royal visitors did not attract the crowds that France's president had drawn.[83]

THE AMBASSADOR'S VALIANT, if questionable, effort to assuage the presidential ego aside, the reality was that the hopes at the end of the Second World War for a more substantive relationship between Canada and France had been buffeted by rough Atlantic seas. Although membership in NATO had facilitated increased contact and cooperation between the two countries, their differing post-war experiences meant that Atlanticism had evolved into a source of divergence. As it became apparent that this foreign policy response was reifying rather than restraining American hegemony in the West, Franco-Canadian relations were gradually hollowed out. Notwithstanding growing doubts and anti-American sentiment, Ottawa remained wedded to Atlanticism. Indeed, for members of Canada's foreign policy establishment, the evolution of the Cold War international order and Canada's place in it seemed to leave Ottawa little alternative. In France, by contrast, the Gaullist government accepted the necessity of transatlantic cooperation, but demanded that it be a true partnership among equals that did not impinge on French sovereignty. Combined with developments in the economic and cultural spheres of Franco-Canadian relations, this nationalist-inspired divergence over Atlanticism – and, more broadly, relations with the United States – would loom large in the ensuing triangular tensions.

CHAPTER TWO

Stagnation amid Growth, Growth amid Stagnation

IN 1855, THE FRENCH CORVETTE *La Capricieuse* sailed majestically up the St. Lawrence, charged with re-establishing official contacts between France and its former colony. In a context of increasingly liberalized international trade, Paris's aims were primarily economic; it viewed British North America as a source of cheap commodities and a vast market for France's expanding manufacturing sector. A parallel goal, as Napoleon III's France preoccupied itself with economic development amid the rise of the United States, was to protect the colonies from excessive American influence. Indeed, this goal appeared all the more pressing given the reciprocity agreement that colonial authorities had recently concluded with Washington following the dismantling of Britain's mercantile system. Beyond commerce, cultural considerations were on Captain Paul Henri de Belvèze's mind: he argued that increased economic links would inoculate the *Canadiens* against assimilation into American civilization, preserving them as a French partner after the United States emerged as a major economic power. However, despite a triumphal visit, a glowing report on the colonies' development, and the subsequent establishment of a French consulate, exchanges remained limited. International conditions, private sector indifference, and the failure of either side to accord the relationship priority proved to be insurmountable obstacles.[1]

Ninety years later, there were renewed hopes for expanded Franco-Canadian economic relations. France's post-war recovery needs corresponded to Ottawa's desire to see exchanges grow as part of its liberal internationalist trade policy and its quest for secure markets for Canada's war-enhanced industrial sector. A parallel Canadian aim was to restore the European economic counterweight to the United States that Britain's decline had removed. But, as had occurred in the wake of *La Capriceuse*, ambitions for a more substantive relationship were frustrated. Consistent with their divergence over Atlanticism, Ottawa and Paris differed in their responses to domestic and international economic conditions, not least American predominance. Paris's preoccupation with recovery, including a nationalist-inspired concern to reduce its dependence on the United States and secure a leadership position on the continent, led it to employ a protectionist commercial policy oriented increasingly toward Europe. Canadian liberal internationalism was stymied; Europe's economic integration encouraged that of North America, as the United States offered Canada the surest markets and sources of capital.

Yet Franco-Canadian economic relations were more complex than a cursory reading of statistics would suggest. Notwithstanding the divergence of the two countries' policies that contributed to the *relative* stagnation of the relationship, the global trend of increasing economic interdependence and transnationalism produced an *absolute* growth of exchanges between France and Canada. This fuelled hopes for a more substantive partnership – hopes informed by nationalist anxieties on both side of the Atlantic about the consequences of the United States's economic strength and, more broadly, the "American way of life."

A discourse of "modernization," one in which the United States loomed large as both promoter and example, framed post-war efforts in Canada and France to emulate the dynamism and standard of living associated with the American socio-economic model. Paralleling such efforts, however, were preoccupations over the economic and sociocultural impact of modernization, which was closely linked to the question of "Americanization," since the United States was considered the apotheosis of liberal capitalist modernity. At each point of the triangle, the aim was to modernize on one's own terms, to reconcile liberal capitalism with local specificity and thereby promote a distinct national existence. Although the Keynesian variant of liberalism, with its provision for moderate state involvement in the economy, provided opportunities in this regard, the broader reality was that the generalized acceptance of liberal capitalism in the triangle helped to reinforce an international economic order in which the United States was predominant and in which the acceleration of interdependence and transnationalism challenged the ability of governments to shape "national" economic life. Heightened nationalist sentiment flowed from this dynamic.

Nationalist preoccupations in Canada were especially acute given that Ottawa and Quebec City's proclivity for a liberal economic policy, combined with the shortcomings of Canadian commercial strategy, meant that the American presence in the economy was that much more pronounced. By the mid-1950s, increasingly pointed questions were arising about the implications for Canada's development, identity, and independence, including in Quebec, where the rise of French-Canadian neo-nationalism was accompanied by a growing interest in economic links with France. To neo-nationalists contending with Quebec's deepening integration into the North American economy, a France experiencing the *trente glorieuses* – the post-war years of economic boom and transformation – was a vital partner that could help Quebec respond to the twin challenges of economic transformation and cultural survival by offering an alternative to "Anglo-Saxon" capital for industrial development and a means to realize francophone economic empowerment.

Paris shared these desires for cooperation, especially with Quebec. French motivations recalled the ambitions of Captain Belvèze a century before, as they were informed by a preoccupation with American economic and cultural power. Even as France pursued its modernization drive as part of its reconstruction efforts, there were concerns about the sociocultural implications of this, as well as about what was alleged to be France's Americanization. The dynamic encouraged a projecting of French concerns onto an increasingly urbanized and industrialized Quebec. Paris was well aware of the opportunities throughout Canada; however, amid Europe's recovery and on the eve of the Quiet Revolution, such awareness was being eclipsed by a growing sense of francophone solidarity, as two French-speaking populations moved to ensure their success in the liberal capitalist system and safeguard their cultural specificity in the face of preponderant American economic power.

THE FOREMOST CHARACTERISTIC of the post-1945 international economic order was American predominance. Convinced that a sustainable peace depended on a prosperity that was realizable only through multilateral, liberalized trade, Washington built on its pre-war efforts and strove in this "liberal moment" to establish a framework beneficial to Western liberal capitalism. This framework was to be achieved through the institutions that emerged from the 1944 Bretton Woods conference: the International Monetary Fund, the International Bank for Reconstruction and Development, and the ill-fated International Trade Organization, all under the watchful gaze of the international economy's new American hegemonic manager.[2]

Canada participated actively in these efforts. It had emerged from the war in a strengthened economic position both relatively and absolutely as a result of its extensive wartime diversification and industrialization. Ottawa contributed to the construction of the post-war order as a convinced disciple of multilateral, liberalized trade as the prerequisite for peace. Yet, as in the geopolitical sphere, there was a nationalist dimension to Canadian liberal internationalism: the aim was secure export markets to ensure Canada's post-war reconstruction and prosperity, a complicated task given the post-war conjuncture. The years of fighting had encouraged North American interdependence; Britain's dire situation meant that Ottawa had effectively lost its European counterweight to the United States, and hence had an interest in an international regime that could help diversify Canada's economic relations and thereby dilute the American presence in the economy.³

The delicacy of Canada's situation was demonstrated by the 1947 balance of payments crisis provoked by Canadians' voracious appetite for American consumer goods. Combined with Britain's halting of the pound's convertibility and the fact that European purchases of Canada's exports were financed largely by loans extended by Ottawa, the result was the rapid depletion of Canada's foreign reserves. The response to the crisis reinforced the trend toward North American interdependence; Washington permitted European countries to use Marshall Plan aid to purchase Canadian goods, thereby assuring Ottawa a vital source of American currency. There were also efforts to increase American purchases of Canadian products, not least strategic materials. Notwithstanding Prime Minister Mackenzie King's refusal to sanction a free trade deal between the two countries, Canada was in fact increasingly locked into the United States's economic orbit.⁴ King's Liberal government was reluctant to impede the flow of American capital; mindful of prosperity's electoral rewards, it was all too aware that the size of Canada's debt limited its capacity to spend on economic development and that Western European sources of capital were exhausted. Ottawa therefore courted American investment in the industrial sector, believing that beyond the initial investment, the corresponding reduction in imports would permit Canada to hold on to its American dollars.⁵

Canada's challenge in adjusting to preponderant American economic power after the war was dwarfed by that of France, which faced "a fragmented market, a shattered industry, [and an] exhausted work force."⁶ The Blum-Byrnes Agreement of 1946 underscored France's dependence. It effectively extinguished France's wartime debt and provided crucial financial aid, but Paris had to agree to Washington's international trade proposals in advance of the talks to establish the International Trade Organization and undertake measures to liberalize French commercial policy. France's deteriorating economic situation and the accompanying labour unrest in 1947 reinforced American concern about the political consequences of Western Europe's economic situation and thus contributed to the announcement of the Marshall Plan. The ensuing European Recovery Program (ERP) meant that French security and prosperity depended more than ever on the United States; between 1948 and 1952 France received US$2.63 billion, or 20 percent of Marshall Plan aid. Some French deputies decried what they viewed as a "colonizing" intent in the provisions of the 1948

Franco-American ERP agreement, and only 38 percent of French adults surveyed in mid-1948 believed that the Marshall Plan did not pose a serious threat to France's independence.[7] The foremost goal of French economic policy during this period was thus recovery. The Monnet Plan outlined a reconstruction program comprising newly nationalized and non-nationalized sectors of the economy that envisaged France as the dominant continental economic power, in partnership with the British and Americans.[8]

With reconstruction such a priority, there was hope on both sides of the Atlantic to see more substantive Franco-Canadian economic relations, which had historically been anemic. It was indicative of the value that Quebec was accorded in the French Atlantic world that it had been ceded to the British in the Treaty of Paris (1763), Guadeloupe and Martinique being more highly prized on account of the slave and sugar trade.[9] The Conquest and global events conspired to disrupt economic links well into the nineteenth century. Despite an Anglo-French maritime treaty in 1826 opening British North American ports to French vessels, Canadian participation in the universal exposition in Paris in the same year that *La Capricieuse* visited, and the opening of a French consulate in Quebec City, progress remained limited. The global downturn of the 1870s saw both countries shift toward economic nationalism, so that it was not until the 1890s that there was any significant growth in trade between them. Even then, the two clashing protectionisms – as Paris safeguarded France's agricultural sector and Ottawa shielded Canada's nascent manufacturing base – meant that the expansion of commercial ties remained weak in relative terms. The dearth of trade was matched by a paucity of investment. French financial houses were more interested in the opportunities in Eastern Europe, Latin America, and the expanding French Empire.[10]

The collapse of the international commercial system accompanying the First World War took with it this limited economic relationship. To be sure, there were opportunities for Canadian business as France was forced to import, given the occupation of a large swath of its industrial heartland, but this also meant that France lost its position in the Canadian market. The result was a trade balance increasingly in Canada's favour, so that relations remained unsettled through the 1920s, a situation aggravated by the fact the war had transformed France into a debtor nation. The Great Depression upset this already delicate situation; in 1931, the Bennett government denounced a trade accord that Paris and Ottawa had signed less than a decade earlier. Two years passed before the two countries were able to reach a new agreement, and the return of war interrupted efforts to build on this progress. The Franco-German armistice brought trade to a standstill; any exchanges that occurred were almost entirely unidirectional, in the form of Canadian aid to the Free French.[11]

As the guns fell silent, Paris was aware that Canada had emerged as one of the world's foremost industrial powers.[12] Canadian shipyards helped to rebuild the French merchant marine, Charles de Gaulle's 1944 and 1945 visits were dominated by his efforts to secure assistance, and Ottawa aided France in purchasing Canadian foodstuffs and other essential supplies.[13] Following official overtures, talks resulted in Ottawa granting France a thirty-year loan of $242.5 million to facilitate the purchase of Canadian goods. The loan was a case of enlightened self-interest; beyond concern over the geostrategic implications of French political instability, it was motivated by Ottawa's search for secure export markets.[14] Such calculations were highlighted when Ottawa responded with a sympathetic no to French inquiries about a second loan even as the ink was drying on the formal agreement regarding the first. The first loan had caused some hesitation in the department of trade and commerce, in which there was scepticism over the potential trade benefits; a second loan was considered even less commercially justified, a potential risk to Canada's economic health, and liable to be unpopular. The negative response was apparently well received by French officials; Paris withdrew its request, and it was agreed that there would be no public reference to the episode.[15]

Although Canadian post-war aid was motivated partly by a desire for French markets, this assistance was part of a broader strategy to realize a multilateral, liberalized economic order to reduce Canada's dependence on the United States.[16] The failure of the International Trade Organization threatened this goal, as did European reluctance to reduce non-tariff trade barriers as part of the subsequent provisional solution of the General Agreement on Tariffs and Trade (GATT). These developments informed Canadian Atlanticism's economic dimension. Believing that Western military cooperation would be strengthened by stronger economic links, and mindful of Canada's need for some of the American aid dollars that Europeans were spending, Ottawa championed article 2 of the North Atlantic treaty. The goal was an economically interdependent North Atlantic that would promote multilateral liberalized trade and restore Canada's European economic counterweight. Canadian hopes for this aspect of the alliance, however, went unrealized, not least owing to Ottawa's failure to follow through with concrete proposals. More broadly, the disappointing outcome was consistent with the stagnation of Canada's economic relations with Western Europe, which tended to use Marshall Plan aid to purchase American goods and concentrate on intra-European trade.[17]

This dynamic was evident as the divergence between Ottawa and Paris over commercial policy frustrated ambitions for a more substantive relationship. The immediate concern following the post-war normalization of economic relations was a trade imbalance overwhelmingly in Canada's favour: Canadian exports to France in 1944 approached $15.9 million, whereas a meagre $9,000 of French exports reached Canada. The imbalance was even greater the following year, and Paris's concern led the foreign minister, Robert Schuman, to propose a bilateral committee of officials that could meet regularly to discuss economic issues.[18] There was, however, significant bureaucratic opposition in Ottawa; the view in the DEA was that although informal consultations were possible, there was little need for a permanent committee, a point that the department of finance echoed in expressing worry that Paris's proposal would encourage French requests for bilateral payments agreements and further loans. Reflecting its multilateral and Atlanticist inclinations, Ottawa suggested that the two countries cooperate to realize the potential of article 2.[19]

But Paris was anxious to see the committee established, and its diplomats lobbied Canadian officials persistently. These efforts, Ottawa's interest in expanding trade, and a concern that Paris could take umbrage given the existence of a Canada–United Kingdom committee led to a view in Ottawa that at least one exploratory meeting was required.[20] This was arranged, but the secretary of state for external affairs, Lester Pearson, warned Canada's ambassador, Georges Vanier, that the meeting should *not* be considered the first of a formal, permanent economic committee: although Ottawa wished to promote exchanges with France and hold discussions when appropriate, it also wanted to avoid "unprofitable meetings and unnecessary trans-Atlantic journeys."[21] The talks resulted in Paris obtaining the bilateral committee, but it was agreed that there would not be regularly scheduled meetings.[22]

The episode was emblematic of the Franco-Canadian divergence in the economic sphere. Paris viewed a bilateral approach as the most effective way to advance its interests and develop relations; the push for regular meetings of a formal committee that would oversee the expansion of exchanges was consistent with its *dirigiste* reconstruction and development strategy, as was the French suggestion during the talks that Ottawa could intervene to help France secure a larger share of Canadian markets. Ottawa was of a different view. Its tepid response to the French overtures had been shaped by its liberal predilections, a point underscored during the subsequent meeting when its delegation advocated a more ad hoc approach that assigned primacy to private sector initiative.[23]

The differing policies were consistent with the radically dissimilar economic situations in which Canada and France found themselves in the immediate post-war period. Ottawa was well placed to embrace multilateralism; indeed, Canada's support of liberal capitalism, combined with the economic strength of its southern neighbour, compelled Ottawa to employ the country's economic strength to fashion an international order favouring a liberalized, multilateral trade regime. Conversely, although France subscribed to liberal capitalism, its sense of vulnerability during the years of recovery, along with the prominence of economic nationalism in French history and the support for *dirigisme* in the aftermath of the interwar upheavals, prompted Paris to favour a more bilateral, protectionist approach.[24]

The Cold War's economic impact and the conflicts in Indochina, Korea, and North Africa made France's road to recovery a bumpy one. In the early 1950s, France experienced a spike in inflation that put a brake on manufacturing and exports; this exacerbated its trade and current accounts deficits, depleted its dollar and gold reserves, and produced a ballooning budget deficit. The deteriorating situation delayed France's economic liberalization within the Organisation for European Economic Co-operation, making France one of its most protectionist members. French officials played for time regarding the convertibility of the franc in order to give Paris a chance to bring its external and internal finances into line and develop responses to the commercial implications of convertibility. Among these implications was the anticipated loss of much of the protection that France's industry enjoyed in its overseas territories, which, in the mid-1950s, absorbed more than a third of French exports.[25]

A consequence of France's fitful recovery was Paris's turn – after some initial reluctance – toward Europe. French reticence regarding the American-backed European Payments Union (EPU), established to facilitate monetary relations among the countries of Western Europe and thereby encourage trade between them, had been overcome by the realization of Paris's proposed European Coal and Steel Community. The creation of this entity had established French leadership of a European integration movement that offered the attractive prospect of liberalization within a larger protected environment. As an EPU member, France had little incentive to move on currency convertibility and liberalize its trade; beyond a feared inability to compete with the United States, Paris claimed that France's dollar shortage and the imperatives of reconstruction made such discrimination necessary. French exports to EPU countries increased by 42 percent – a rate far exceeding that of its exports to dollar countries – between 1952 and 1954.[26]

France's protectionism and the growing orientation of its commercial policy toward Europe contributed to the relative stagnation of the Franco-Canadian relationship. Paris's ambassador to Canada, Hubert Guérin, complained that it was difficult to recruit French firms to participate in an exposition that Paris organized in Montreal in 1954.[27] In a similar vein, Canadian exports to France declined sharply after Paris reimposed the customs duties on a number of raw materials that it had suspended in order to spur reconstruction. Pearson subsequently expressed concern to Guérin about the two countries' "noticeable divergence" over commercial policy and urged "the speediest possible development of multilateral trade."[28]

Ottawa was unenthusiastic when Paris suggested that it purchase French military equipment to help address French balance-of-payment difficulties; during a 1953 visit to Canada, France's prime minister, René Mayer, was told that the problems plaguing the economic relationship could not be solved in a narrow bilateral framework and that Paris should follow the Canadian multilateralist example.[29] Nor was Ottawa impressed when Paris decided to accord favourable treatment to synthetic rubber imports from two American firms in exchange for their assistance in establishing a French factory. The move put at risk one-fifth of total Canadian exports to France. Ottawa lobbied against the action and threatened retaliatory measures, arguing that the deal contravened the GATT. With Ottawa and Paris at an impasse, Canada's ambassador, Pierre Dupuy, castigated Ottawa for not following through on its threat, claiming that this would encourage French protectionism.[30]

Although worry over the low volume of French exports to Canada prompted Ottawa to temporarily exempt these from dumping duties in response to the rebate that French industry received for social security charges, the issue quickly became yet another irritant.[31] During discussions about renewal of the measure, the consensus among senior Canadian officials was that Paris was not displaying "sufficient awareness of the importance of more liberal commercial policies" and was "less conscious than [it] should be of the Canadian point of view."[32] A senior department of finance official complained it was "difficult to see why we should deliberately ... favour ... a country which so resolutely maintains its rights to discriminate against us."[33] Despite Ottawa's belief that the exemption ran contrary to liberal principles and worries that Canada could be compelled to extend similar treatment to American goods, the renewal was granted, owing largely to the feared impact of increased prices on the already meagre level of French exports.[34] Yet the dispute endured, even becoming bound up in France's purchases of Canadian wheat as Paris sought to induce Ottawa to grant a long-term exemption. The irritant was removed only when Paris ceased reimbursing French exporters for social security charges.[35]

The emergence of the European Common Market (ECM) underscored the Franco-Canadian divergence over foreign economic policy. It was indicative of French economic nationalism that Paris was initially reluctant to establish a common market among the six European Coal and Steel Community members, as it feared West German domination. French reticence gave way to enthusiasm, however, as it became clear that German concessions offered Paris a continental economic arrangement in which it would enjoy preponderant influence. The economic pressure that Washington imposed during and after the Suez Crisis was a bitter reminder of the need for France to reduce its dependence on the United States and confirmed Paris's conversion to the cause.[36] Although Canadian decision makers favoured European economic integration in the abstract, their support was predicated on integration occurring in an Atlanticist framework, so that a recovered, united Europe would counterbalance the United States in Canada's economic relations. The record of intra-European organizations such as the EPU, however, suggested what could be expected from the proposed scheme. Consequently, Ottawa's relative neutrality at the outset was quickly superseded by disquiet; Canadian officials suspected a French hand in the ECM's protectionist elements.[37]

The Treaty of Rome provided for the establishment of a common market among France, West Germany, Italy and the Benelux countries; however, the emergence of this European trade bloc, as ECM members moved toward internal free trade and a common external tariff, marked the failure of Ottawa's efforts to achieve a multilateral liberal trading order that would dilute the American presence in the Canadian economy. Indeed, the economic integration of Western Europe was spurring North America's: faced with nationalist policies, such as those of France, and the need for secure export markets to ensure Canadian prosperity, the web of links between Canada and the United States only thickened. In 1957, nearly 60 percent of Canadian exports went south of the border, from where Canada obtained more than 70 percent of its imports. By comparison, between 1958 and 1963, ECM countries never absorbed more than approximately 8 percent of Canadian exports, and they were the source of only 5 percent of Canada's imports.[38]

More immediately, the treaty institutionalized the post-war dynamic of Franco-Canadian economic relations. Canadian liberal internationalism was trumped by French protectionism – or, more precisely, a bounded liberalism operating within a supranational framework. To Ottawa's chagrin, the trade liberalization that Paris embraced was to be realized within the relative protection of the Common Market. Despite the post-war hopes for a more substantive relationship, Canada and France were oriented increasingly toward their respective continental markets.[39]

The relative stagnation of Franco-Canadian economic relations was all too apparent. In 1958, France ranked eleventh as the destination for Canadian products, taking only $45.2 million worth of goods, in stark contrast to the $2.83 billion that Canada shipped to the United States. Similarly, the poor showing of French exports to Canada was consistent with a broader lack of West European interest (notwithstanding superior British, West German, and Belgian export performances) in the Canadian market.[40] The dynamic was the same regarding direct investments. The value of French investments in Canada had declined considerably in the immediate post-war period as Paris sought the currency required to finance reconstruction, and the 1950s saw anemic growth. French investment in Canada was a modest $40 million, amounting to only 3 percent of foreign direct investment in the country in 1957. Belgium outstripped France in 1959, and the rate of West German investment in Canada was twice the French rate.[41] In Hubert Guérin's estimation, despite boasting a wealth of opportunities, Canada was a secondary concern for French business.[42] The feeling was mutual, as France was of marginal interest to Canada's entrepreneurs. By the early 1960s, Canadian direct investment in France amounted to an equally modest $130 million. Only thirteen Canadian firms had direct investment establishments in France, and five of these – Polymer, Massey-Ferguson, Alcan, the Royal Bank of Canada, and the Banque canadienne nationale – accounted for the lion's share.[43]

Having emerged from the war years in radically different economic situations, Canada and France had responded in diverging ways to post-war economic conditions. The common challenge of preponderant American economic power had not translated into a more substantive relationship; instead, relations stagnated in relative terms as each country pursued different foreign economic policies and priorities. Yet this divergence should not be exaggerated; the gap between Ottawa and Paris was one of method more than ideology; both capitals subscribed to the logic of Keynesian liberalism and, as constituents of the "liberal core," contributed actively to the development of the post-war capitalist international system, one in which the United States occupied the "fulcrum" position, notwithstanding French and Canadian ambivalence and efforts to mitigate the impact of this.[44] Neither country had realized the primary objective of its commercial policy; rather, both had been forced by events beyond their control into a continental partnership that was a second choice. There was, however, a crucial difference; whereas Paris remained able to employ the emerging ECM to pursue an economic nationalist agenda, this option was not available to Ottawa in its continental context. Canadian officials continued to hope for a larger Atlantic economic community that would dilute the American presence in Canada's economy, but the regionalization of international trade and Ottawa's adherence to a liberal commercial policy rendered such ambitions increasingly derisory.

YET THIS TALE OF DIVERGING integrations in the North Atlantic is only half the story, for there was growth amid this stagnation. Advances in communications and transportation, combined with efforts to forge a liberalized international economic order, facilitated an economic interdependence that has been characterized as quantifiably and qualitatively unprecedented.[45] Although the Cold War encouraged a bipolar international system, it also contributed to this integration as it "enmesh[ed] the entire world in the struggle between two politico-economic systems, [each] claiming universal applicability."[46] From 1948 to 1958, the global economy grew on average by 5.1 percent per year; trade increased at an annual rate of 6.2 percent, outpacing production for the first time since 1914 and intensifying the transnational movement of capital, goods, and people. Europe and Japan's post-war recovery only reinforced the trend, so that by 1964 world exports of manufactured goods were 228 percent higher than their 1953 levels. Accompanying this trend was a sharp acceleration of foreign direct investment as the number and significance of non-state actors, notably transnational corporations, increased.[47] The dynamic contributed to a blurring of the line between domestic and foreign policy, raising questions about the ideal of state sovereignty upon which the post-1945 order was based and presenting a challenge for governments preoccupied with achieving and maintaining the economic conditions necessary to keep their populations content.[48]

The growth, in *absolute* terms, of Franco-Canadian trade and economic links was consistent with this global trend. This included a number of foreign direct investments by major French companies. Air Liquide expanded its longstanding operations to twelve installations across Canada. Shortly after the war, Les Grands Travaux de Marseille took over Alban Janin et Compagnie, a public works firm. Groupe Schneider was a major participant in West Canadian Oil and Gas, which was involved in Alberta's post-war petroleum boom. Rhône-Poulenc established a pharmaceutical factory in Montreal in 1956. The public works firm Fougerolle, after establishing a Canadian subsidiary that partnered with Quebec-based Key Construction Company, was involved in a number of high-profile projects, including the construction of Montreal's Champlain Bridge and a portion of the St. Lawrence Seaway, as well as the expansion of Dorval Airport.[49] Les Ciments Lafarge established operations in Montreal in 1948; eight years later, it founded another subsidiary in British Columbia.[50] An array of other French banks and Air Liquide, in collaboration with Quebec's Banque Beaubien, created the Confederation Development Corporation to promote further French investment.[51]

The establishment of direct air service between France and Canada encouraged increased economic links. Air France inaugurated a weekly service in 1950, and the following year a pair of beavers, gifts to the Paris zoo, were the star passengers that helped Trans-Canada Airlines launch its twice-weekly service.[52] Regular air travel facilitated the growing number of trade missions and expositions.[53] Montreal was witness to the most significant exposition of the period, spearheaded by France's embassy in 1954. Ambassador Guérin had urged Paris against any half-measures and he was not disappointed as the MAE seized the opportunity to boost France's profile in Quebec. Montreal authorities responded with equal enthusiasm, and the city's press was full of praise. Prime minister Louis St. Laurent, minister of trade and commerce C.D. Howe, Quebec provincial secretary Omer Côté, and Cardinal Paul-Émile Léger attended, and 14,000 visitors flocked to the exposition on its first full day. The embassy revelled in the success: according to Guérin, French Canadians had never seen so many French products gathered together or had such an opportunity to appreciate the vitality of modern French industry.[54]

A reciprocal opportunity to raise Canada's economic profile in France arose in conjunction with the centenary of the visit of *La Capricieuse*. The MAE extended invitations to Ottawa, Quebec City, and Toronto to send representatives to festivities in the French port city of La Rochelle. Canada's ambassador, Jean Désy, argued for a strong presence, as it was "an excellent occasion" to build economic contacts. Much to the regret of Désy and France's embassy, however, there was little official interest: only the federal minister of labour accompanied Désy.[55] There was greater interest three years later, however, in an exposition on Canada's provinces at the Grands Magasins du Louvre in Paris. Désy approached the provincial governments to urge their participation, and Quebec and Ontario answered the call. More than a hundred thousand visitors passed through the exposition during its first week. Quebec had pride of place, with the Duplessis government determined to show off the province's development and increase awareness of its economic opportunities.[56]

The proliferation of organizations promoting Franco-Canadian economic relations offered additional opportunities. When the Canada-France Economic Committee met in October 1950, the French delegation proposed expanding the Comité franc-dollar, established to promote Franco-American business ties, to include Canada. Ottawa agreed, but, consistent with its more liberal approach, on the understanding that initiative would be left primarily to the private sector.[57] In 1953, the Chambre de commerce française de Montréal, in existence since the 1880s, established the Comité France-technique. Headed by the French embassy's commercial counsellor, the organization promoted French technical and scientific methods.[58] Two years later, Désy helped French business figures establish the Institut France-Canada, citing growing French private sector interest in Canada and the absence of a service independent of the Canadian embassy to promote exchanges. The Institut's economic committee was rechristened the Chambre de Commerce France-Canada in 1957. Cooperating with the embassy and local chambers of commerce, it brought France's business community into contact with Canadian personalities and organized expositions throughout France vaunting Canada, including the one held at the Grands Magasins du Louvre.[59]

Although the results of such efforts ultimately remained limited in the face of a generally unresponsive private sector, they were nonetheless significant in that they pointed to another dimension of the evolution of Franco-Canadian economic relations after 1945. To be sure, the absolute growth of trade between the two countries was consistent with the acceleration of interdependence and transnational exchanges. However, nationalist elements concerned about this international phenomenon – and, more specifically, the American economic power at once promoting and resulting from it – paradoxically seized upon the absolute growth in the relationship as proof that a more substantive relationship was not only possible, but essential.

This nationalist-inspired economic interest was informed at all points of the Canada-Quebec-France triangle by a preoccupation with modernization and linked to this, questions of Americanization. Flowing from longstanding discussions about the "modern,"[60] the discourse and theory of modernization was predicated upon a linear understanding of history positing the economic and political development of the European world as a normative model that the rest of the planet should – and eventually would – follow.[61] The diverse articulations of modernization theory posited a dichotomous relationship between the traditional and the modern, with the latter ultimately sweeping the former away.[62] Moreover, it was claimed that the rise of technical and industrial civilization was promoting the erosion of differences between national societies. Some relished the prospect, but voices at both ends of the ideological spectrum decried the materialism and alienating aspects of a society alleged to accord higher value to social and economic efficiency than to the human individual and community.[63]

Although the European colonial powers and the Soviet Union propounded their respective versions of modernization, the United States's rise to global predominance meant that modernization discourse was bound up in notions of Americanization, that is, "the adoption ... of [American] patterns of production, consumer behaviour and ways of life."[64] By the interwar period, the American example had become a point of reference; the United States's economic power had given it the ability to assert itself as *the* socio-economic model. Doubts during the Great Depression about such claims were soon dispelled by the outcome of the Second World War. The United States's preponderant economic and military power, in combination with the Cold War, encouraged a conflation between the concepts of modernization and Americanization. Washington's public diplomacy accompanying the Marshall Plan contributed to the defining of the "modern," and the global competition with the Soviet alternative spurred American social scientists to articulate a modernization theory that, notwithstanding its pluralistic and transnational origins, was "a sustained projection of American identity."[65]

Although modernization theory was developed in the context of and concerned primarily with the "developing" world, its precepts also informed a discourse in the West marked by a preoccupation – positive and negative – with the American socio-economic model. The United States occupied pride of place in Walt Rostow's *The Stages of Economic Growth*, a foremost statement of modernization theory. Even as Rostow, who would hold prominent roles in the Kennedy and Johnson administrations, discussed the modernizing of the Third World, his "non-communist manifesto" explored why continental Europe had trailed the United States in achieving a mass-consumption economy. Canada also appeared in the work, with Rostow citing a "still-lagging" Quebec as an example of a "traditional society."[66] The tendency to conflate "modern" with "American" – either implicitly or explicitly – raised serious questions. Was it possible to be modern without being American? Did Americanization go hand in hand with modernization? Such questions were of growing relevance amid the expansion of a "culture of consumption [that was] facilitating a consumption of [American] culture."[67]

The debates swirling around modernization and the attendant issue of Americanization were apparent on the Canadian side of the Atlantic, where in the post-war period "aspects of tradition and modernity" were in "constant negotiation and tension."[68] A discourse of modernization was evident in the "reconstruction" discussions of the latter war years. Leonard Kuffert has observed how the priority assigned to post-war "planning" reflected "an implicit belief that existing flaws in the Canadian economic and social order could be designed away."[69] Ottawa's plans for peacetime emphasized the need for the "modernization" of Canada's industrial and agricultural sectors, the importance of "a higher degree of productive efficiency" to boost employment and income levels, and the necessity of expanded scientific research to raise "the whole technical level of Canadian industry."[70]

Paralleling such enthusiasm, however, was a pronounced concern among a group of conservative English-Canadian intellectuals about the rise and consequences of technological civilization associated with modernization.[71] Amid the post-war consumer-driven economic boom, these critics despaired that although Canada was prospering materially, it was suffering from a spiritual impoverishment. As North America's interdependence deepened, such opposition translated quickly into anxiety over the scope of the American presence in Canada's economy. By 1948, historian Harold Innis was bemoaning the fact that Canada had "moved from colony to nation to colony."[72] His colleague Donald Creighton decried Canadians' acceptance of "the American credo of 'continual economic growth,'" which prompted them "'to sacrifice their independence ... and endure all the hideous evils of modern industrialization and urbanization,' [and internalize the] 'imperial religion,'" that is, the cult of technological progress.[73] Influenced significantly by the writings of his French counterpart Jacques Ellul about the concept of *technique,* philosopher George Grant railed that Canada was "being challenged to defend itself against a barbaric Empire that puts its faith in salvation by the machine."[74]

These nationalistic attitudes were increasingly apparent in Canadian public life. Hubert Guérin cited the extensive press coverage that the October 1953 meeting of the Canada-France Economic Committee received as evidence of growing Canadian worries over North America's integration. St. Laurent subsequently expressed to the French diplomat his preoccupation over Canada's dependence on the United States, and from this his desire for increased trade with France.[75] The prime minister's remarks came as Ottawa established the Royal Commission on Canada's Economic Prospects, chaired by Walter Gordon. Although a Gallup poll at the beginning of 1956 indicated that nearly seven-tenths of Canadians viewed American investment positively, this opinion had changed by the end of a year that saw a rancorous parliamentary debate over American involvement in construction of the trans-Canada natural-gas pipeline and the release of the Gordon Commission's preliminary report that sounded the alarm over the United States's dominance in the growth of foreign direct investment in Canada. The Progressive Conservative opposition, led by John Diefenbaker, seized upon nationalist fears to lambaste the Liberals and win the 1957 election. Diefenbaker's ensuing proposal to divert 15 percent of Canada's import trade from the United States to Britain was interpreted in French circles as evidence of the new government's desire for greater economic independence.[76]

Paralleling the broader Canadian nationalist response to American economic influence was Quebec's emerging neo-nationalist reaction that was shaped by similar preoccupations about modernization and Americanization. If there were growing misgivings in Canada as a whole about the continentalist trend, anxiety was that much more pronounced among the rising generation of Quebec nationalists. The Depression had drawn attention to French Canada's economic marginalization and encouraged nationalist attempts to reconcile the liberal capitalist economic system and the accompanying challenges of urbanization and industrialization with traditional French-Canadian society – that is, to "modernize" on French-Canadian terms.[77] Ultimately, however, the interwar socio-economic crisis had fuelled a belief, particularly among the younger generation, that traditional nationalism, with its attachment to the past, respect for order and authority, emphasis on a more conservative Catholicism, ambivalence about liberalism, and hostility toward left-wing ideas, was unable to cope with modern challenges, and thus no longer an effective guarantor of Quebec's majority francophone society. The result was the ascendance of a more explicitly Quebec-centric *neo*-nationalism, one more open to an activist state in the service of the province's francophone majority.[78] Even more conservative and traditionalist elements, among which there existed serious differences over the exact measures to be taken, expressed a growing openness to seeing the Quebec state assume its regulatory function and intervene in the province's social, economic, and cultural life – albeit in a manner consistent with the social doctrine of the Catholic Church.[79]

Such sentiments, however, confronted the obstacle of Quebec premier Maurice Duplessis. His Union Nationale government preached the language of traditional nationalism to maintain itself in power, but practised a classical liberalism that simultaneously drove Quebec's socio-economic transformation and left little room for government to respond to the accompanying challenges. Quebec's renewed industrialization during and after the Second World War increased the pressure on traditional French-Canadian society, as well as the sense of urgency about coming to terms with the modern.[80] Hence, the Asbestos strike prompted Pierre Trudeau to denounce those French-Canadian institutions that he accused of standing in the way of Quebec's modernization, while at the other end of Quebec's ideological spectrum, the Tremblay Report, which has been described as the most succinct response of traditional French-Canadian nationalism, sought to reconcile economic and political modernization with the traditionalist worldview.[81] The post-war perpetuation of Duplessisme, abetted – if ambivalently – by the traditional nationalist elites fuelled neo-nationalist frustration over what was condemned as a lackadaisical and insufficient response to a set of challenges alleged to pose a threat to French Canada surpassing that of the Conquest.[82]

In a dynamic similar to that in English Canada, the preoccupation of Quebec francophones with modernization was framed by nationalist misgivings over the growing American economic presence accompanying the province's development, notably in the resource sector. This flowed into the broader resentment over anglophone domination of Quebec economic life.[83] The Tremblay Report warned of the dangers of "centres of influence ... clearly foreign to the population's cultural tradition" arising from Quebec's economic evolution.[84] Similar notions informed the Société Saint-Jean Baptiste de Montréal's complaint in the mid-1950s about what it decried as a meek French-Canadian entrepreneurism, and its calls for the development of large-scale enterprises that could compete with non-francophone-owned rivals, as well as the creation of a government department to manage the development of Quebec resources.[85]

Building on longstanding traditionalist calls for francophone economic empowerment, neo-nationalist historians Michel Brunet, Maurice Séguin, and Guy Frégault blamed Quebec's economic inferiority on the Conquest and its consequences, including traditional nationalism's preoccupation with non-economic priorities, which they claimed had facilitated anglophone economic predominance. Other neo-nationalist figures, such as journalist André Laurendeau and Gérard Filion, publisher of *Le Devoir*, denounced American and Anglo-Canadian economic dominance of Quebec, charging the Duplessis government with selling off Quebec's natural resources to foreign interests.[86] In a similar vein, journalist Jean-Marc Léger's encounter with French economist François Perroux, who was preoccupied with the question of safeguarding national independence in an age of increasing interdependence, informed his subsequent claim that French Canada's economic liberation could not take place without political liberation.[87] Léger's stance typified how neo-nationalist economic concerns fuelled demands for a more activist, dynamic, francophone-oriented state to realize development and protect Quebec's francophone majority amid the acceleration of transnational exchanges. Challenging traditional nationalist hostility to anything approaching *dirigisme* or socialism, neo-nationalists feared that in the absence of such action, the homogenizing effects of industrialization and urbanization would end in French Canada's assimilation.[88]

The neo-nationalists' concern regarding Quebec's industrial development and the need to gain control of the economic levers of power stimulated their interest in greater cooperation with France. To be sure, there was some interest in Duplessis's Quebec City in economic links with the Hexagon. Cabinet ministers such as Antoine Rivard and Paul Beaulieu visited Paris in an effort to attract French investment to Quebec, and Beaulieu, the minister of trade and commerce, was viewed in French circles as a prominent champion of more substantive relations. In his encounters with French diplomats, Beaulieu spoke constantly of Quebec's need for French capital and technical expertise. Not willing to accept economic difficulties as an excuse, he bemoaned France's insufficient and ineffective economic profile in Quebec.[89]

Both Beaulieu and Paris had to contend, however, with Quebec's premier. Duplessis certainly paid lip service to the value of French investment, bragging of the opportunities in "Nouvelle France" that could only benefit from French contributions and expertise. His appeals were often made in the context of his expressing the desire to dilute anglophone, notably British and English-Canadian, economic influence; he alluded to possible favourable treatment for French firms, and even cited Britain's growing profile in Quebec in a bid to shame French officials into acting. In practice, however, Duplessis's words were trumped by an antipathy for France informed by traditional French-Canadian nationalism, and by his government's laissez-faire economic policy that precluded active government efforts to develop links. Indeed, major French businesses in Quebec complained that they often received less favourable treatment than did other foreign firms – even when they contributed to Union Nationale coffers.[90]

Quebec neo-nationalism was predisposed not only to discard the traditional nationalists' ambivalence for *France moderne* – considered a stalking horse for secular liberal materialism – but to embrace a more activist role for government in pursuing economic collaboration with Paris. Growing Quebec interest in France as a potential economic partner in the face of American power was evident amid the Coca-Cola controversy in that country at the end of the 1940s. The efforts by the company, a potent symbol of Americanization, to establish itself in France became a lightning rod for anti-American sentiment: the communist daily *L'Humanité* warned of France's "coca-colonisation," and French wine-growers condemned the soft drink as a threat. An intense legal battle erupted when Paris denied Coca-Cola the right to import the ingredients that it needed, and the French embassy in Ottawa was impressed by the sympathy that Quebec's francophone press expressed for the French position.[91] Similarly indicative of the turn to France was *La Presse*'s welcoming the Chambre de commerce de la province du Québec's announcement in 1959 that it would be organizing a mission to France to encourage investment in the province. The paper argued that it was essential to develop links with Europe – and France in particular – to reduce American economic influence.[92]

The growth of nationalist anxiety in Canada was mirrored across the Atlantic. The Coca-Cola controversy pointed to French worries about American economic power and its impact. Beyond misgivings about the political ramifications of France's economic dependence, the United States was perceived as at once "a model and a menace," prompting a debate over whether American-style prosperity and consumerism could be achieved while safeguarding France's cultural specificity. Even the United States's greatest proponents in France harboured doubts about the economic and sociocultural costs of the "American way of life."[93] As Alfred Grosser has argued, the simultaneity of France's Americanization and the post-war wave of anti-Americanism was not at all paradoxical; the former was a scapegoat for everything perceived as a negative consequence of France's post-war economic development, giving rise to the latter as the spread of ideas associated with modernization were denounced as symptomatic of foreign (that is, American) rule.[94]

Indeed, French anxiety over American economic power was subsumed within the broader discourse and debate surrounding modernization. A leader of the "second industrial revolution" of the late nineteenth and early twentieth centuries, France had been hit hard by the interwar economic crisis and the Second World War: much of the industrial and agricultural equipment that had survived was outdated compared to that of Britain and the United States. A pre-war concern that France's economy was structurally and technologically *retardé* informed recovery discussions. Calls for modernization came from across the French political spectrum. Reports depicted France as a quasi-developing country, the result of a business community accused of being Malthusian in outlook and hostile to innovation.[95] Even as France sought to impart its own model of modernity in its overseas territories, a current of opinion in the metropole argued that safeguarding France's future demanded decisive action to correct its underdevelopment by adopting lessons learned from the American model.

The demands of reconstruction gave French "modernizers" the opportunity to act on the ambitions that they had been nurturing since before the war. The Conseil National de la Résistance had drawn up a *dirigiste* recovery strategy that subordinated free enterprise to state planning in a bid to overcome what was condemned as the structural sclerosis of the French economy.[96] Harnessing the modernization discourse, the famed diplomat and technocrat Jean Monnet, appointed Commissaire au Plan, sold his vision of France's post-war reconstruction to de Gaulle in 1945 as a massive modernization effort crucial to realizing French *grandeur*. Aided by a series of modernization commissions, Monnet developed and executed an economic plan involving major industrial restructuring that took part of its inspiration from the American model. Paris sent numerous research missions to the United States, and approximately five hundred more toured American factories, farms, stores and offices under Marshall Plan auspices.[97]

As was the case on the Canadian side of the Atlantic, notions of modernization and the related issue of Americanization had their French opponents. Indeed, there were tensions at the very heart of France's modernization drive; even though it took part of its inspiration from the American example and was facilitated by American aid, it was informed by an ambivalence regarding the United States. The eruption of the Poujadiste movement and its surprise electoral success in 1956 was symptomatic of a certain hostility toward modernization and Americanization. This right-wing movement, which began as a tax revolt born of a sense of powerlessness and nostalgia, engaged in Vichy-style rhetoric against the Fourth Republic's *dirigisme* and the socio-economic changes of the period.[98] At the opposite end of France's political landscape, Simone de Beauvoir similarly condemned France's modernization efforts as leading to Americanization and the Hexagon's economic and cultural colonization.[99] And somewhere in between, writer and intellectual François Mauriac, commenting on American economic and cultural influences, bemoaned the cult of technology and the mania for speed that he felt were fundamentally at odds with French *génie* and civilization.[100]

Notions of modernization and the accompanying nationalist apprehensions over Americanization informed official views of France's economic relations with Canada. Shortly after the war, an MAE report argued that Paris should seize the opportunity for stronger cooperation offered by the complementarity of French reconstruction requirements with Canada's conversion to a peacetime economy and Ottawa's desire to escape the Anglo-American embrace.[101] Concern that France should be perceived as modern was evident in Paris's representatives calling for a more effective promotion in Canada of France's scientific and technical achievements as the prerequisite to strengthening its economic presence. Posted to Ottawa in the mid-1950s, the French ambassador, Francis Lacoste, strove to correct what he alleged was a strongly rooted view among both francophone and anglophone Canadians that France was unproductive and not scientifically advanced, and that its population was resistant to the sacrifices required for modernization.[102]

As at the time of the voyage of *La Capricieuse,* cultural considerations were prominent in French economic interest in Canada. Paris continued to view Quebec as a gateway to the Canadian and North American markets, with an MAE report recommending that Paris take advantage of cultural affinities to increase France's economic profile. In the immediate aftermath of the war, France's ambassador in Ottawa, Jean de Hauteclocque, called on Paris to favour French-Canadian involvement in France's reconstruction efforts over any other foreign industrial interest, in order to help French-Canadian-owned industry resist absorption into larger North American enterprises.[103] De Hauteclocque's suggestion revealed a view of French Canada as a collectivity requiring economic assistance to ensure its survival, and demonstrated the converging interests between French and Quebec nationalism as two francophone populations worked to realize economic development while safeguarding their cultural specificity. Perhaps most significant for the subsequent triangular tensions, MAE reports shortly after the war claimed that France was well positioned to assist French Canada realize its technical and economic potential, so that its population would achieve socio-economic equality with English Canada.[104]

Quebec's ongoing transformation amplified the cultural dimension of French economic interest. Hubert Guérin, one of de Hauteclocque's successors as ambassador, affirmed in 1954 that earlier French depictions of Quebec as a francophone, Catholic, artisan enclave no longer applied, and France's consulate general in Montreal subsequently remarked upon what it viewed as an increasing francophone economic assertiveness.[105] Consistent with broader French worries about Americanization, Paris's awareness of the changes afoot in Quebec provoked misgivings over the growing American influence in the province. Before the close of the 1940s, the consulate in Quebec City was linking the rapid developments in French-Canadian life to the expanding American presence, observing that after two centuries of resisting the Anglo-Saxon influence represented by Britain, Quebec appeared to be rapidly embracing that of the United States. French representatives also warned of the threat to francophone culture represented by the importation of American technical terminology that corrupted the language spoken in Quebec's industrial centres.[106]

French fears were stoked by the Duplessis government's industrialization policy that explicitly favoured American capital, owing partly to the premier's determination to avoid being beholden to Quebec's anglophone financial and industrial elites. Minds were not set at ease when, in early 1958, Duplessis refused publicly to open a Quebec commercial office in Paris, arguing that it would be a waste of money as "Europe is the past." The pronouncement prompted Francis Lacoste to observe the irony that "Canada ... britannique," in condemning the premier's remarks and in valuing Europe as a counterweight to the United States, demonstrated that it understood far better the significance of Europe and France to the resistance to American influence.[107]

Despite the ambassador's analysis, the intersecting of French and Quebec nationalist anxiety contributed to a trend in the triangular relationship that favoured the France-Quebec axis. Part of the explanation, of course, was a question of history. In addition to longstanding links between France and Quebec, Canada's economic capital well into the twentieth century was Montreal. Paris opened a commercial office in Toronto only in 1949.[108] Another important factor was the question of cultural affinity. Guérin, for example, had remarked upon English Canada's underwhelming participation in, press coverage of, and attendance at the 1954 French exposition in Montreal, and he suggested that such relative indifference demonstrated that Quebec should be the primary target of French efforts.[109] Moreover, although the expanding American economic presence in Canada encouraged an official French interest in increasing cooperation with Quebec, such a consideration did not carry the same weight outside the province, even though francophone minority communities existed across the country.

Added to questions of history and culture, however, were positive French assessments of Quebec's economic potential. An internal MAE report in 1957 judged Quebec to be the Canadian province destined to have the most brilliant economic future. France's prime minister, Guy Mollet, and foreign minister, Christian Pineau, were highly impressed with Quebec's development when they visited that same year.[110] Duplessis's death only further roused French interest; Lacoste reported that notwithstanding traditional French-Canadian ambivalence for France, Paris needed to respond to the growing desire for expanded economic links, since Quebec boasted the greatest opportunities in Canada.[111]

To be sure, French officials acknowledged that more should be done to develop their country's presence outside Quebec; the embassy considered France's participation in Toronto's annual Canadian International Trade Fair as tangible proof of Paris's determination to develop its economic profile throughout Canada, and the development of Alberta's petroleum industry prompted Paris to appoint a consul general to Edmonton.[112] Lacoste deplored the lack of a substantial French presence in Ontario, noting that provincial authorities were contacted by more German industrialists in a month than by representatives of French firms in more than a year.[113]

Official French attention, however, was focused increasingly on Quebec, a dynamic that was apparent when de Gaulle visited in 1960. The French leader's briefing notes remarked on the clear preference that Quebec's government was displaying for French industry over that of the British or Americans.[114] During the trip, de Gaulle noted the "Anglo-Saxon" economic domination of Montreal and the lament of its mayor, Sarto Fournier, over the paucity of French investment in the metropolis.[115] De Gaulle publicly alluded to French interest in Quebec's industrialization, and, diplomatically ignoring anglophone economic dominance, praised it as "a great French success" that, had it not been realized, would have meant the diminution of the international French fact.[116] The remarks suggested that as Quebec grappled with the challenge of reconciling economic development with the preservation of its cultural specificity, it was to Gaullist eyes becoming a proxy for a France confronting similar challenges.

The growing convergence of Gaullist and Quebec nationalist preoccupations in the economic sphere assumed tangible form following the Quebec government's decision to reopen a commercial office in Paris that it had closed in 1912. Plans in the late 1930s by the premier, Adélard Godbout, to appoint a trade commissioner to Paris had been overtaken by wartime events, but the idea had not disappeared. With the return of peace, Paul Beaulieu told a senior French embassy official of his desire for a Quebec commercial representative in Paris, since neither Canada's embassy nor its francophone personnel were staunch defenders of Quebec interests.[117] *La Tribune de Sherbrooke* took up the cause after France's consul general in Quebec City publicly raised the idea during a Comité France-Amérique luncheon in 1958. Despite Duplessis's flirtation with the idea, it was not until after his death that any substantive progress was made. In March 1960, the premier, Antonio Barrette, indicated that Quebec would open offices in Paris and London.[118] The Union Nationale's subsequent defeat, however, meant that the task would fall to the Lesage government.

Economic relations between Canada and France in the fifteen years following the Second World War therefore present a mixed record. Although at a governmental level and in relative terms they were stagnant and even diverging, economic contacts between the two countries grew in absolute terms. This growth was certainly evident in a monetary sense, but, even more significantly, it was also reflected in a thickening web of interpersonal contacts that were contributing to an emerging sense on both sides of the Atlantic that a more substantive relationship would be beneficial to both sides – and not in strictly economic terms. Indeed, cultural questions were emerging as central to the unfolding triangular dynamic. Assessments of the value of strengthened economic relations were encouraged by the modernization discourse and anxieties arising from American economic influence and its consequences. International economic conditions had intersected with and exacerbated Quebec, French, and Canadian nationalist sentiment, a crucial precursor to the triangular tensions. However, as these interacting nationalisms spurred increased cooperation and conflict in the economic sphere, an important question remained to be answered: how effective would the combined nationalist-inspired efforts be in the face of the international trends and structural realities to which they were responding?

CHAPTER THREE

"More necessary than ever": The Evolution of Cultural Exchanges

A FURORE ERUPTED IN 1946 over two private French-sponsored colleges in Montreal, as traditional French-Canadian nationalists denounced what they claimed was a corrupting influence on Quebec's education system. From its editorial pages, *Le Devoir* urged French Canada to defend itself against a fifth column of foreign secularism and Masonic elements, and called for Action catholique and Quebec ecclesiastical authorities to move swiftly against the "present danger."[1] A senior French embassy official described it as difficult to grasp the scope of the emotion that had been unleashed.[2] Two decades after what was dubbed the Abadie affair, however, *Le Devoir*'s attitude toward French cultural influence had shifted considerably; it reported approvingly on the visit to Paris of Quebec's minister of education, Paul Gérin-Lajoie, to sign an agreement with his French counterpart establishing a cooperation program touching on every facet of the province's education system.[3]

The contrast between these two reactions highlights Quebec's sociocultural transformation and the accompanying evolution of attitudes toward France. Indeed, although the geopolitical and economic components of official Franco-Canadian relations were anemic, and even deteriorated, in the fifteen years after the Second World War, the same cannot be said of the cultural sphere, in which contacts multiplied. The growth and evolution of exchanges between France and francophone Quebec was especially significant. Reflecting broader developments in the province, links of a more religious and conservative hue declined in importance relative to those of a more secular and progressive nature.

As the controversy over the colleges demonstrated, the change was not without tension. Quebec's cultural development meant that rather than a dependent consumer and agent of French culture, French Canada saw itself increasingly as a cultural producer. The expansion of Franco-Canadian cultural contacts also testified to the post-war proliferation of transnational exchanges. This trend contributed, paradoxically, to a more defensive impetus to develop links; growing anxiety that socio-economic changes in Quebec were promoting

"Anglo-Saxon" – notably American – cultural influences that threatened French Canada's survival encouraged an increased openness in Quebec toward *France moderne*. This was symptomatic of the broader ideological, generational, and class conflict in nationalist ranks and beyond over the preservation of Quebec's majority francophone society. Interest in links with France was especially pronounced among, but certainly not limited to, the rising generation of Quebec neo-nationalists. Leading figures of this community were living testimonials to the evolving cultural exchanges between Quebec and France, as they drew upon French thought and their experiences in the Hexagon to criticize conditions in Quebec. For this group, the cultivation of links with France by an activist Quebec state represented an inoculation against Americanization.

The shifting Quebec nationalist interest in France coincided with a French preoccupation with the United States's cultural strength. An anti-Americanism that crossed France's deep political divides was evident well before the Second World War; after 1945, protecting and promoting French culture at home and abroad was a priority for France's political class and intelligentsia. This preoccupation extended to Canada, and it included a growing concern over the state of French culture in Quebec. Paralleling such nationalist sentiment in France and Quebec was English-Canadian apprehension over American cultural influence. Already apparent in the interwar period, this nationalist reaction rooted in traditional English-Canadian hostility toward the United States intensified after the Second World War.

A consequence of the heightened nationalist sensitivities was pressure at all points of the triangle for greater state activism regarding culture. This growing politicization of cultural affairs sowed the seeds for conflict. Even as France reinforced its cultural diplomacy, Ottawa and Quebec City were increasingly at odds over culture in the 1950s. Their jurisdictional wrangling foreshadowed the tensions of the following decade, as three nationalist reactions – Canadian, Québécois, and French – contended with preponderant American cultural power, and more broadly, the acceleration of transnational cultural flows.

CULTURAL CONTACT BETWEEN France and French Canada was never completely severed after the Conquest and reflected an array of political and ideological positions. Quebec's traditional nationalist elite, however, distinguished between *France éternelle* and *France moderne,* favouring the former, pre-1789 incarnation as an ally in maintaining French Canada's religious and linguistic specificity. *France moderne* was condemned as a Trojan horse for secular and materialist influences that would bring about the ruin of French-Canadian civilization.[4] Paris was aware of this ambivalence. To win over public opinion and counter pro-Vichy sympathies in the Quebec church, there were efforts to arrange visits of French clergy with pro-Resistance sympathies.[5] The MAE described relations with Quebec ecclesiastical authorities as one of the most important and delicate questions for France's representatives; indeed, Francisque Gay was appointed ambassador to Ottawa partly because of his Catholic activism and leadership role in France's Christian Democratic movement.[6] A heated debate in Quebec's francophone press over French Catholicism in the early 1950s prompted Gay's successor, Hubert Guérin, to claim that the one attitude not to expect from French Canadians was indifference, given their tendency to invoke France in their internal quarrels, as either a target or an ally.[7]

The references to France in Quebec's post-war debates were consistent with what has been described as the "prelude" to the Quiet Revolution, and they highlighted the evolving cultural exchanges between Canada and France.[8] France's wartime collapse had facilitated francophone Quebec's exposure to French intellectual currents – notably via New York's French exile community – that traditional nationalist elites had previously filtered out. Another factor was Ottawa's permitting Canadian publishers to breech copyright and reprint French works that the fortunes of war had rendered inaccessible. Combined with the opportunity to publish the works of French writers in exile, Quebec publishing received an intellectual infusion.[9] The industry grew rapidly and dramatically, enabling it to support local talent, so that France's wartime effacement facilitated Quebec's cultural *épanouissement*. As the task of helping to maintain and propagate French culture fell to Quebec, there was growing awareness in the province of the universality of "French" culture; France was not its sole agent and French Canada could be a major contributor to the international francophone community. This cultural assertiveness was reflected in remarks that Adrien Pouliot, dean of Université Laval's mathematics faculty, made to a French audience in 1948 in his capacity as a representative of the Comité permanent de la survivance française. Pouliot explained that beyond promoting francophone rights in North America, his organization sought to convince France that French Canada was no longer a subordinate population, but a sister nation desiring to work on a basis of equality to promote French culture.[10]

In the years after the Second World War, contacts of a more secular and progressive nature multiplied between France and French Canada. An immediate reason for the changing dynamic was the predicament in which France's Catholic right found itself as a result of its dalliance with Vichy and collaboration. This is not to suggest, however, that religion ceased being a major vehicle for exchanges. To the contrary, the spiritual sphere was at the centre of Quebec's intellectual and ideological upheaval, and had been since the interwar period.

The influence of the body of French Catholic thought dubbed personalism was felt increasingly in Quebec from the 1930s onward.[11] Personalism was the effort of an array of Catholic intellectuals to come to terms with the industrial age and achieve the social and political institutions that would permit individuals to realize their full spiritual and material potential. The ideas of Emmanuel Mounier and his magazine *Esprit*, which advocated a left-wing Catholicism combining Christian belief with Marxism and existentialist philosophy, were especially influential in Quebec after 1945. Personalism inspired the rival neo-nationalist and liberal *Citélibriste* challenges to Quebec's established order, including comprehensive critiques of the Catholic Church and traditional French-Canadian nationalism, and damning indictments of Duplessisme.[12]

A barometer of the growing influence of personalism was the hostility that it and its proponents provoked in Quebec's traditional nationalist circles. An issue of *Esprit* devoted to French Canada produced a strong response to its criticism of Quebec cultural life, notably the contributors' condemnation of a domineering clerical influence.[13] Assigning the French Catholic left the lion's share of blame for Quebec's contemporary problems, expatriate French historian Robert Rumilly condemned the neo-nationalists and *Citélibristes* for entering into an unholy alliance with French communists. He accused them of having been seduced by left-wing and anti-clerical ideas and of hastening French-Canadian assimilation by their efforts to denationalize Quebec youth at the service of English Canada.[14]

Rumilly's accusations notwithstanding, personalism, as an effort to rejuvenate the Catholic faith in an urban and industrial milieu, was not only a vehicle for contestation but served as a crucial intergenerational bridge between the traditional French-Canadian order and its neo-nationalist and *Citélibriste* challengers. The latter groups found their intellectual inspiration in France as they sought to rethink and reform Quebec society in a manner that kept faith with its Catholic heritage.[15] In this sense, personalism was a means by which a Quebec trying to reconcile aspects of tradition and modernity could come to terms with a similarly bifurcated France.

It was the temporal domain, however, that saw the most significant proliferation of contacts. The return of peace meant a normalization of and increase in educational exchanges between France and Canada. More than a thousand Canadian students visited France on some form of government scholarship in the decade after 1945, and many others, far surpassing the number awarded funding, spent time in France at their own expense.[16] After its wartime closure, the Maison des étudiants canadiens at the Cité universitaire in Paris reopened. This student residence, in addition to offering the chance to encounter major

French intellectual and cultural figures, was a key meeting place for expatriate Canadians, the majority of them from Quebec and some of whom would play prominent roles in the triangular tensions of the 1960s.[17]

The flow of students was accompanied by a flow of teachers. Numerous French professors and intellectuals visited Canada to renew ties that the war had interrupted. By the late 1940s, Paris's diplomats were remarking on the large number of French professors that Canada's francophone universities were requesting, the numerous applicants for scholarships to study in France, and the fact that it was in Canada, and Quebec especially, that touring French speakers drew the largest audiences.[18] The embassy boasted in 1953 that France's contribution to Canadian university life had never been so significant, with French professors occupying permanent posts at Dalhousie University, Université Laval, Université de Montréal, McGill University, Queen's University, and the University of Toronto.[19]

Growing intellectual contacts and increased interest in *France moderne* did not mean the disappearance of French-Canadian ambivalence toward France. Indeed, this ambivalence was glaringly apparent in the differences between the history departments of Université Laval and Université de Montréal. The former maintained close connections with French historians, notably those with links to the Annales school, and actively recruited French historians who ended up as crucial conduits for students pursuing graduate studies in France. The Université de Montréal, by contrast, boasted in its ranks the neo-nationalist historians Guy Frégault and Michel Brunet, who took France to task for its post-Conquest abandonment of its North American outpost, and often evinced a veritable Francophobia. The French ambassador, Francis Lacoste, reported on such antipathy, including an instance when Brunet made remarks considered so hostile that the university rector invited Lacoste to deliver a speech as a way to make amends.[20]

The expansion and evolution of Franco-Canadian cultural contacts was even more apparent in the artistic sphere. A year after the war, France's embassy reported on the younger Quebec generation's keen interest in new French literary works, contemporary art shows, and visits by French theatre companies.[21] Jean-Paul Sartre's *Huis clos* played at the Jesuit-run Théâtre Gesù, a surprising venue explained by the fact that the existentialist philosopher and the implications of his work remained relatively unknown in Quebec at the time.[22] Conversely, French Canada's blossoming theatre sector enjoyed success in France, as evidenced by the warm critical welcome that the Théâtre du Nouveau Monde received in 1955. Paris was interested in the growth of Canada's French-language theatre, particularly when the company's director claimed that a significant Quebec audience had been created as a result of televised French-language productions and touring French troupes. Among the latter was the Comédie française, which performed to acclaim in Montreal, Quebec City, Ottawa, and Toronto during its first North American tour.[23]

Once again, however, French Canada's complex relationship with France and its heightened cultural self-awareness meant that increased contacts led to complications. The growth of Quebec's publishing industry that had resulted from its wartime reprinting of French works was one source of conflict. Quebec publishers hoped to continue their lucrative activity, but this ambition clashed with Paris's determination, as part of its reconstruction efforts, to re-establish the monopoly that France's publishers had previously enjoyed. Quebec's publishing industry plunged into crisis as a number of houses collapsed; the consequent hampering of the emergence of an autonomous literature over the short term meant that the dispute reinforced the French-Canadian desire for an independent literary evolution.[24]

The Charbonneau affair similarly exposed the differences generated by evolving Quebec attitudes regarding French Canada's cultural relationship with France. The controversy arose when France's Comité national d'écrivains condemned Quebec publishers Variétés and Éditions de l'Arbre for publishing authors deemed collaborators and blacklisted in France. Robert Charbonneau, co-founder of Éditions de l'Arbre and president of the Association des Éditeurs canadiens, defended the decision to publish the authors. An avowed anti-fascist, Charbonneau asserted the importance of the free dissemination of ideas; a Francophile, he nonetheless resisted what he viewed as interference in Quebec's literary life, denouncing French cultural colonialism and urging French Canadians to abandon the idea that they were merely North American interpreters of French thought. Yvan Lamonde and Gérard Bouchard have referred to the clash as consistent with Quebec's embracing its *américanité* – that is, a New World society that has broken with the ideologies, references, and cultural models of its metropole.[25]

These publishing disputes, at once commercial and cultural, underscored the shifting dynamic of Franco-Canadian cultural relations, since the crux of both lay in French Canada's role as a cultural producer. France's embassy, for example, tended to dismiss Charbonneau's protests as commercially motivated.[26] Such tensions were exacerbated by the ambitions of French publishers. To be sure, the Centre du livre français established in 1950 became an important feature in Montreal's cultural landscape, offering its clientele previously unknown access to French intellectual currents and ideas emerging from Quebec's cultural ferment.[27] It was also, however, along with other initiatives, part of a concerted

French effort to win a greater share of the Canadian market, and hence a threat to Quebec publishers.[28] Matters were scarcely better in France, where Quebec publishers complained that they were at a serious disadvantage due to the quasi-monopoly enjoyed by the major French organizations. Moreover, French publishers and booksellers tended to marginalize French-Canadian authors by denying them adequate marketing support and favouring only those writers who had already succeeded in Quebec.[29]

Notwithstanding occasionally strained relations, however, the unmistakable trend was toward increased literary contact. French officials were pleased as, fuelled by the growing consumer culture, the amount, by weight, of French books sold in Quebec rocketed from 480 to 2,700 tonnes between 1955 and 1966.[30] And for all of the transatlantic recrimination that they generated, disputes such as the Charbonneau affair had the salutary effect of attracting the French intelligentsia's attention to the existence of French-Canadian literature and helping to legitimize it as a distinct, autonomous form. This was reflected in the growing critical acclaim for French-Canadian authors in France and the fact that by the late 1950s, French publishers were demonstrating a readiness to take a chance on first editions of new Quebec writers.[31]

Beyond academic and artistic contacts, the expansion of transnational exchanges was reflected in the proliferation of groups promoting cultural links between France and Canada. With the return of peace, French intellectual personalities such as André Siegfried and Georges Duhamel visited to help revive the Alliance française, the private French organization devoted to promoting French culture. New Alliance branches were established in Rimouski, Rivière-du-Loup, Sherbrooke, and Saint-Hyacinthe, adding to a longstanding network of clubs that included Montreal, Ottawa, Toronto, and Halifax. Jean-Paul Sartre, Jean-Albert Sorel, François de La Noë, Vercors, and Maurice Bedel were just a few of the French intellectual figures who visited under Alliance auspices.[32]

New organizations were also established. The Fédération Normandie-Canada, founded clandestinely in 1942 to commemorate Canadian sacrifices in Normandy, set as its post-war mission the cultivation of exchanges, especially with French Canada.[33] More significant was the Accueil Franco-Canadien, organized to welcome Canadians visiting France.[34] In 1951, the two were subsumed within a new umbrella organization, the Association générale France-Canada (AGFC), established to introduce greater coordination of the proliferating friendship groups' efforts. During its first six years of existence, the AGFC assisted nearly three thousand Canadians at its Paris reception centre and organized hundreds of cultural events. By the end of the decade, it had eight thousand members and had established the annual Prix France-Canada to honour a French-Canadian literary work.[35] For all of the association's efforts, however, the Canadian embassy tended to dismiss it as inconsequential. Ambassador Jean Désy's doubts about the organization prompted him to help found the Institut France-Canada, hoping to correct what he claimed was the inefficiency of existing groups that were relevant only to the intellectual community.[36]

Across the Atlantic, Accueil Franco-Canadien (which bore no relation to its Gallic predecessor) was established in 1951. Inspired by the motto "Même sang oblige," the organization boasted a membership in the hundreds by the end of its first year, and held numerous cultural and social events. It also opened an office to provide recent French immigrants with loans and with legal, medical, and employment services. Earning the praise of France's president, Vincent Auriol, and Canada's prime minister, Louis St. Laurent, Accueil opened branches in Quebec City and Ottawa and cultivated links with France-based organizations such as the AGFC.[37]

Although the vast majority of the populations in Canada and France were unaffected by and unaware of such groups, there were other avenues through which cultural contacts increased, not least the growth of tourism facilitated by post-war prosperity, advances in transportation, and the city twinning movement. The number of tourist visas issued by French offices in Canada nearly doubled from 1948 to 1949, and the effective waiving of visa requirements and establishment of transatlantic air service encouraged tourism over the following decade.[38] A hundred thousand Canadians visited France in 1963, representing an annual growth rate since 1950 of 12 percent. Half of this number came from Quebec – many of them French Canadians tracing their ancestral roots – and their average stay was nearly five times longer than those coming from other provinces.[39]

But it was the growing mass media that offered the greatest scope for expanded cultural contact. Agence France-Presse opened a Montreal bureau in 1946, the same year as *Le Monde français* and *Carrefour* began publishing Canadian editions.[40] In 1947, the CBC and Radiodiffusion Française concluded a program-exchange agreement. This was the precursor to Radio-Canada joining the Communauté radiophonique des programmes de langue française, founded in 1955. Two years later, Radio-Canada posted permanent correspondents to Paris.[41]

The flow of French films to Canada also resumed after the wartime interruption. Paris's diplomats cited the cinema as a valuable tool for combating Anglicization and contributing to French-Canadian cultural life.[42] That this latter aspect could generate controversy was demonstrated in 1947 when

Quebec's censor banned the French film *Les Enfants du paradis*. This decision drew a protest from Francisque Gay, who used the French embassy's extraterritorial rights to screen the film. Consistent with the enduring traditional nationalist hostility toward *France moderne*, the ambassador's actions provoked protests in the Quebec press.[43] Notwithstanding the controversy, by 1954, nearly a quarter of new feature films screened in Canada were French – the bulk playing in Quebec cinemas. France's embassy cited the considerable success of the first Semaine du Film Français, held in Montreal in 1958, as evidence of the Canadian market's potential – in Quebec and beyond. Conversely, actor Gratien Gélinas visited Paris in 1953 to premiere the Quebec film *'Tit-coq*, and by the close of the 1950s, Claude Jutra, the future dean of Quebec's feature film industry, had arrived in France, where he immersed himself in New Wave cinema, established friendships with famed directors such as François Truffaut and Jean Rouch, and drew inspiration from Jean-Luc Godard to produce his critically acclaimed *À tout prendre*.[44]

Links were also forged between French and Canadian television. By the late 1950s, Montreal was the world's largest French-language production centre. With nearly nine-tenths of households owning a TV set by the end of the decade, the new medium was at the forefront of Quebec's sociocultural and even political life, a dynamic underscored by the nationalistic fervour surrounding Radio-Canada's strike in 1959.[45] The dynamic was not lost on France's embassy, which emphasized television's importance to its cultural diplomacy, noting that French visitors were regularly invited to appear on Radio-Canada.[46]

Notwithstanding this evolution of Franco-Canadian cultural contacts, there existed some continuity between the pre- and post-1945 periods. Whereas spiritual links were declining in relative importance, the same could not be said of the other primary vehicle of cultural relations: language. *Indépendantiste* André d'Allemagne, for example, claimed that for all of the Société Saint-Jean Baptiste's efforts, its "refrancisation" campaigns did not hold a candle to the impact of the post-war influx of French-language detective novels, magazines, and even the *Tintin* albums that arrived from Belgium.[47] French Canadians were prominent in the founding of non-governmental organizations employing the transnational bond of the French language. One was the Association internationale des journalistes de langue française (AIJLF), which held its congress in Montreal in 1955.[48] Another group was the Union culturelle française (UCF), founded the previous year to defend the French language and culture internationally and to connect all groups and territories in which French was the principal or secondary language; by the end of 1954, thirty associations and organizations were members of the Canadian section. The UCF was an important forerunner of the Francophonie, reflected in the fact that at its first congress in Versailles in 1955, Léopold Sédar Senghor, who went on to serve as Senegal's first president and become a driving force in the Francophonie, invoked the "new universalism of the French language."[49] In a similar vein was the Université de Montréal's effort to establish an international association of French-language universities. The founding meeting of the Association des universités partiellement ou entièrement de langue française (AUPELF) was held in 1961 in Montreal, which became the organization's headquarters.[50]

The proliferation of these linguistic-inspired organizations pointed to a heightened concern about the status and quality of the French language spoken in Quebec, one that the province's socio-economic transformation encouraged. Urbanization meant that the language of the working class – which had traditionally been denigrated as a corruption of the purer French spoken by rural Quebecers – was becoming the language of the francophone majority, and hence an object of concern.[51] By the 1950s, with a growing proportion of Quebec's francophones living in Montreal, an array of private groups was protesting that city's English visage. Similarly telling was the Congrès de la Refrancisation in 1957; France's ambassador, Francis Lacoste, suggested that the congress highlighted the broader evolution of Quebec attitudes, given that at the height of the traditional nationalist order, French Canadians had frequently asserted that the quality of French spoken in Quebec was purer than its Parisian equivalent. Lacoste suggested that, among Quebec's intelligentsia at least, a concern with preserving the French language was inspiring demands for a cultural rapprochement with France.[52] As Chantal Bouchard has observed, this interest reinforced Quebec concerns about the French spoken on the shores of the St. Lawrence: if it differed too radically from the French spoken on the banks of the Seine, communication – and the desired rapprochement – would be hampered.[53] Such sentiments were reflected in the scathing denunciations of Quebec's education system in Jean-Paul Desbiens's *Les insolences du Frère Untel,* in which the linguistic situation was compared to someone sleeping while their house burned.[54]

The broadening array and increasing number of cultural contacts resulted in the emergence of a group of individuals in Quebec, many of whom had spent time in France, who were interested in building stronger contacts with *France moderne*. Paul-Émile Borduas, who fled post-war Quebec for Paris, described the attraction and significance of France as a place of intellectual awakening for French Canadians. In *Refus global,* the manifesto that condemned Quebec's traditional order and anticipated the upheavals of the 1960s, he explained how time in Paris forever changed "the frontiers of our dreams."[55] Among the rising Quebec generation who had spent time in France was André Laurendeau. Oriented initially toward *France éternelle,* upon arriving in Paris in 1935 he strolled along intellectual avenues that encouraged him to develop his acute critique of Quebec's traditional nationalism. Paul Beaulieu – who was to serve at Canada's embassy in Paris – and Robert Charbonneau also spent time in France before presenting French personalist ideas to Quebec through their magazine *La Relève*.[56]

After the Second World War, Paris was at the centre of European intellectual life, as "the tenor of French political arguments epitomized the ideological rent in the world at large."[57] Expatriate Quebecers found themselves in a city in which existentialists, red Catholics, doctrinaire Marxists, and anarchists were all discussing the need for societal transformation.[58] Gérard Pelletier has emphasized the importance of Paris to members of his generation and described it as their intellectual point of reference.[59] As these Quebecers immersed themselves in the intellectual tumult in Paris before and after the war, the lines became blurred between traditionalists and progressives, and between the intellectual left and the Catholic left. The dynamic was encouraged by concerns on both sides of the Atlantic over the cultural implications of urban, industrial, and technological civilization, and the related issue of Americanization. This intellectual cross-fertilization was a crucial precursor to the rapprochement – official and otherwise – between France and Quebec.

Jean-Marc Léger was perhaps the foremost example of the increased openness in Quebec toward *France moderne* and the larger international francophone community. An avowed Francophile and tireless advocate of cultural exchanges, Léger had been influenced significantly by an encounter with Georges Duhamel when the French writer visited Montreal in 1945, as well as by talks that other visiting French figures gave at Montreal's Alliance française. Léger stayed at the Maison des étudiants canadiens (MEC) and studied at the Institut des sciences politiques in Paris. It was during this sojourn that his efforts and those of his classmate d'Iberville Fortier led to their editing of the issue of *Esprit* on French Canada. Léger has recalled how he found it "absurd" when he realized that his fellow students from the French Empire were "legally French" whereas he, "issue of French ancestors and with French as a mother tongue," was a foreigner. He returned to Montreal preoccupied with the question of Quebec's political future, the state of the French language in Canada, and the need for an international organization for francophone peoples that would permit French Canada, and Quebec especially, to act internationally. Indeed, it was Léger who founded the Montreal-based Accueil Franco-Canadien and was a driving force behind the UCF, AIJLF, and AUPELF; he was appointed secretary-general of the last organization in 1961.[60]

Another neo-nationalist figure interested in cultivating cultural relations with France was André Patry. Fascinated by the larger international francophone community, Patry was the subject of a French consulate general report after he gave a public address in which he declared that the world was witnessing the end of French imperialism in Africa.[61] Serving in turn in Université Laval's newly established positions of external relations secretary and director of cultural relations, Patry was responsible for promoting the university's international contacts. In 1954, he travelled to France, where he met with cultural relations officials at the MAE and members of various groups involved in building links between France and Canada. Dissatisfied at Laval, Patry left to work for NATO in Paris, where he promoted cultural exchanges within the alliance.[62]

THE INCREASING QUEBEC interest in *France moderne* points to another dimension of Franco-Canadian cultural relations after 1945. The proliferation of cultural contacts was consistent with the acceleration of transnational exchanges. Accompanying this global trend was a defensive response that, paradoxically, provided an additional spur to those interested in strengthening the bonds between the French and Canadian populations. The advances in transportation and communications promoting cultural interpenetration also fuelled nationalist concern for local culture and a determination to preserve it in an era of profound and rapid change. Apprehension over what appeared to be a trend toward cultural homogeneity became linked to discussions surrounding Americanization.[63] In the cultural context, Americanization may be understood as the advent of a consumer society in the image of the United States, entailing the influx of American cultural products from jazz to rock music, from comic books to Hollywood films. The phenomenon was especially pronounced among the younger generations and popular classes, making its corollary – anti-Americanism – the purview predominantly of socio-economic and cultural elites. The United States, because it constituted the foremost cultural power by virtue of its enhanced geopolitical and economic strength, its role as the centre of mass media-driven popular culture, and its cultural diplomacy, was the object of particular anxiety. Nationalist hostility to Americanization, already apparent in the interwar period, intensified after 1945.[64]

This defensive impetus informed a growing state involvement in cultural affairs and the rise of cultural diplomacy. The late nineteenth century had witnessed the emergence of "cultural internationalism," predicated on a belief that such exchanges would promote international peace and prosperity. Private philanthropic organizations such as the Carnegie Foundation strove to realize this vision. Although the First World War stood as a horrific rejoinder to such idealism, the enhanced prominence of cultural diplomacy in the wake of the carnage was evident in the establishment of the International Committee on Intellectual Cooperation as part of the League of Nations. The interwar period saw the establishment of a number of non- and quasi-governmental organizations such as the Deutsche Akademie and the British Council. The crises of these years and the Second World War accelerated states' appropriation of cultural activities so that cultural diplomacy took on even greater importance, culminating in the founding of the United Nations Educational, Scientific and Cultural Organization (UNESCO) in 1945.[65]

The French state's involvement in cultural life dated back at least to the sixteenth century, but it was Louis XIV who put the diffusion of France's cultural influence at the centre of his policy, and it was increasingly taken for granted that France had a mission as the guardian of Europe's cultural heritage.[66] Little surprise, then, that France was a pioneer of cultural diplomacy. Quasi-private efforts following the debacle of the Franco-Prussian War, such as the Alliance française and the Comité France-Amérique, anticipated the gradual incorporation of culture into French foreign policy in the interwar period. France's diminished stature after 1945 meant that Paris attached even greater importance to cultural diplomacy as a way to make France's voice heard in a world in which the superpowers dominated the conversation. The priority was to preserve what was claimed as France's role as a cultural leader and model, and it was reflected in the establishment of a distinct cultural relations division in the MAE.[67]

The increased importance of culture in French foreign policy was also reflected in Paris's innovation of appointing cultural councillors to fourteen of its diplomatic posts, including its Ottawa embassy.[68] Quebec was accorded a high priority, with the French ambassador to Canada, Jean de Hauteclocque, asserting that the survival of a hardy, prolific, faithful, and influential "élément français" in the Americas was invaluable to France.[69] The view at the Quai d'Orsay was that Quebec and France should cooperate for the promotion of French culture in North America by virtue of their common language and their shared religious and intellectual heritage. The MAE, mindful of Canada's linguistic and cultural cleavages and aware of English-Canadian desires to see French influence foster a more progressive, liberal spirit in Quebec, argued that Paris could be pleased if its cultural action produced the integration and "fusion morale" of the "deux Canadas." Such aspirations were tempered, however, by awareness that the success of France's cultural activities depended on these actvities never appearing to be in service to English Canada.[70]

French efforts were by no means limited to Quebec, but boasted a distinctly pan-Canadian hue. The MAE acknowledged the value of targeting francophones outside Quebec, notably the Acadian community, and efforts were made to cultivate cultural links with the population.[71] English Canada was considered especially promising, not least because it did not share French Canada's complex feelings for France. In 1950, Paris's ambassador, Hubert Guérin, claimed that interest in French artistic and intellectual activities was as pronounced among English Canadians as it was among their francophone fellow citizens. He welcomed the subsequent release of the Massey Report on Canada's cultural life as an opportunity to adapt French efforts to Canadian objectives and enhance links.[72] Guérin's reaction reflected Paris's desire for a Canadian interlocutor with which it could realize expanded cultural exchanges and a readiness to engage with Ottawa in this regard.

The MAE employed the linguistic ties between France and Canada as a primary vehicle for its cultural diplomacy, reflective of the primacy that its cultural relations division assigned to the international diffusion of the French language after the Second World War as a means for France to regain its international influence.[73] The MAE accordingly facilitated study visits to France for Canadian French-language professors, and, after a wartime interruption, Paris resumed providing a modest subsidy to the Comité permanent de la survivance française, which was at the forefront of French-language advocacy. Similarly indicative was the high-level French delegation that attended the Congrès de la langue française in Quebec City and Montreal in 1952 that discussed the condition of North America's francophone communities.[74]

The French government also contributed significantly to post-war intellectual contacts. This was accomplished partly through the support and expansion of groups such as the Alliance française, and, to a greater extent, through educational links. Despite the controversy that had been associated with the French-sponsored Collège Stanislas as a result of the Abadie affair, the MAE considered it one of the foremost vehicles for France's intellectual penetration of Quebec – a means to improve the quality of education and promote greater openness toward *France moderne*. Luc Roussel has noted the effectiveness of the institution and its female counterpart, Collège Marie de France, as cultural agents; beyond the significant growth of the two schools' populations, the students tended to be members of Montreal's privileged class, magnifying the impact.[75] Paris also strove to increase the number of Canadians studying in France; even before the Second World War ended, the MAE announced an annual program of forty scholarships for Canadian students, a number equal to the scholarships accorded to American and British students. Divided approximately evenly between students from Quebec and the rest of Canada, eight hundred Canadians had benefited from the program by 1956.[76] Indeed, the MEC owed much of its post-war success to the French government's initiative.

But French cultural diplomacy faced a number of official obstacles across the Atlantic. Whereas Paris was a leader in cultural diplomacy, Ottawa was much slower to act. Part of the explanation was constitutional: Canadian cultural diplomacy was complicated by the fact that many aspects of cultural affairs fell under exclusive provincial or shared jurisdiction. This was especially problematic because a court ruling had effectively restricted Ottawa's ability to implement treaties unilaterally to matters under exclusive federal jurisdiction.[77]

Added to these constitutional considerations was an institutional bias. In the case of Franco-Canadian relations at least, the bias arose partly from federal awareness of Quebec's complex relationship with France – and the complications this could present Ottawa. During the Abadie affair, DEA under-secretary Norman Robertson spoke to France's ambassador about Ottawa's misgivings over a foreign power operating educational institutions (even indirectly) on Canadian soil, and noted that Ottawa had discouraged a similar plan by the British Council. Taking Jean de Hauteclocque aback with his claim that the colleges had an incontestably "colonial face," Robertson urged that Paris instead expand its program of scholarships and exchanges of professors. The DEA official added that he and a large number of his colleagues owed their education to British scholarships that had allowed them to keep their "purely Canadian mentality" while acquiring respect and affection for Britain.[78]

Alongside such domestic considerations was a pronounced inferiority complex – a fear that what was viewed as Canada's cultural underdevelopment would render its cultural diplomacy ineffectual, if not embarrassing.[79] However, the most significant reason for the limited Canadian cultural diplomacy was that it was generally under-appreciated in Ottawa. When the DEA's information division was established in 1944, it was denied a mandate to promote cultural relations.[80] The institutional obstacle was also evident in the federal response to claims that Oscar Drouin, Quebec's minister of trade and commerce, made about his province's desire to promote cultural and commercial relations with Latin America. Lester Pearson, then serving at Canada's legation in Washington, conceded that Drouin's remarks revealed Quebec's dissatisfaction with the content of Canadian foreign policy, but claimed that it was premature to set up a cultural relations division in the DEA. Robertson was even doubtful about Pearson's modest alternative of appointing an official to coordinate cultural activities with the United States, Britain, and Latin America. His assessment was that it would be difficult to convince Parliament of the value of cultural diplomacy.[81]

Although Ottawa appointed a cultural and press attaché to its Paris embassy after the war, this had more to do with questions of reciprocity given the equivalent French appointment than with any significant policy shift.[82] In 1946, Paul Beaulieu, second secretary at the embassy, voiced frustration that he had neither the time nor the resources to develop cultural exchanges with France, even though the DEA had told him that this would be his main task. Beaulieu decried the paucity of Ottawa's effort and warned that Canada's unprecedented popularity in France resulting from the war was fleeting and would be difficult to regain.[83]

Matters improved somewhat during the 1950s. Using the monies that France repaid it for Canada's wartime material assistance, in 1952 Ottawa established the Canadian Government Overseas Awards, which facilitated year-long sojourns in France for Canadian students and artists. To avoid constitutional complications, the program was administered by the Royal Society of Canada.[84] Canada's embassy took advantage of the MEC to pursue its cultural action in Paris, and René Garneau, the embassy official responsible for cultural and press affairs, was active and enjoyed considerable prestige in Paris intellectual circles.[85] Although cultural diplomacy remained a secondary consideration in the Massey Report, its authors nonetheless claimed that "the promotion abroad of a knowledge of Canada is not a luxury but an obligation."[86] By acting on the recommendation to establish the Canada Council for the Arts, Letters, Humanities and Social Sciences, Ottawa acquired a vehicle to pursue cultural diplomacy indirectly: beyond the organization's domestic mandate, it was also tasked with promoting Canadian culture abroad. In addition to funding Canadian students in France, the Canada Council awarded fellowships enabling French students and academics to study in Canada and Canadian universities to host foreign professors.[87]

The broader reality, however, was that Ottawa still accorded little priority to cultural diplomacy. Louis St. Laurent had revealed his ideological leanings at the outset of the Massey Commission, when he declared that the federal government should not be "subsidizing ballet dancing." Although the prime minister's attitude evolved, his foremost concern remained avoiding another dispute from which Maurice Duplessis could benefit. He also had to contend with a distinct absence of support for the measure in the Cabinet, with C.D. Howe particularly opposed.[88] The six years that elapsed between the Massey Report and the creation of the Canada Council, along with the fact that its initial endowment came from a onetime windfall of succession duties arising from the death of two millionaires, underscored the institutional reticence that continued to exist in Ottawa regarding governmental involvement in cultural affairs. The DEA's relative indifference was reflected in the fact that Jean Désy, who served as Canada's ambassador to France in the 1950s and had a reputation as a relentless self-promoter with an undisputed interest in cultural diplomacy, appears to have acted largely on his own initiative in expanding cultural links between France and French Canada, and did so with limited budgetary resources.[89] The embassy complained to Ottawa about the funds it had to cultivate exchanges, emphasizing the political significance of culture in "this country which was once very rightly described as 'La République des Professeurs.'"[90] By the early 1960s, $71 million of France's foreign affairs budget – 39 percent – was directed to cultural and technical cooperation,[91] whereas the DEA budget's cultural element was a meagre $8,000, the majority of this in the form of book presentations.[92]

In addition to Ottawa's relative disinterest, Paris had to contend with an official ambivalence in Quebec City toward state involvement in cultural affairs, not least when it came to exchanges with France. To be sure, there was a history of Quebec governmental cultural action, notably the interwar efforts of the provincial secretary, Athanase David.[93] Examples of the Duplessis government's efforts to cultivate links with France, by contrast, were conspicuous for their rarity. These included a contribution to the post-war reconstruction of the university in Caen. The resumption, after a wartime interruption, of an annual $5,000 subsidy to the MEC occurred more out of a sense of tradition than any real interest in educational links.[94] And it was only with the well-placed effort of Jean Bruchési, under-secretary of the province, that Jean-Marc Léger's UCF obtained the one-time subsidy that permitted it to launch its activities.[95]

Much more typical was the failure of the Association canadienne-française pour l'avancement des sciences to convince Quebec City to establish a scholarship program to enable French students to pursue doctoral studies in Quebec. Although the Duplessis government resumed the pre-war practice of granting bursaries to Quebec students interested in pursuing their studies in Europe, minimal sums were allocated and the program stagnated. Further complicating matters was the intense politicization of the system by which funds were awarded, a principal criteria being friendliness to the Union Nationale and ideological suitability. Such bias resulted in a decreasing proportion of the bursaries awarded being used for studies in France.[96]

Notwithstanding such official obstacles and Ottawa and Quebec City's trailing Paris in cultural diplomacy, the broader trend was a shift of Franco-Canadian cultural relations from the private to the public sphere. The dynamic was encouraged by growing nationalist anxiety over American cultural power. French concern about the rising United States had been evident in the latter decades of the nineteenth century and transcended France's political and ideological divides. The country's weakened position relative to the United States after the First World War exacerbated the situation, so that French cultural nationalism took on an increasingly defensive hue as questions multiplied about the implications of Americanization for France's culture and identity.[97] French personalism, by virtue of its antipathy toward capitalism, liberalism, and materialism – and a United States that was regarded as the apotheosis of these – was a crucial conduit for the transmission of anti-American discourse between France and

French Canada. Indeed, this was a crucial aspect of the role of personalism in fostering a rapprochement between the two francophone populations. There was an "unsurpassed crest," an efflorescence of French works on the United States in the late 1920s and early 1930s that was crucial to the vulgate of French anti-Americanism.[98] It was in these turbulent intellectual waters that expatriate French Canadians such as André Laurendeau immersed themselves in Paris, and the waves that these literary works generated were still rolling by the time a new group of French Canadians plunged into the French milieu after the Second World War.

French nationalist objections to American cultural influences only grew after 1945. As the 1950s progressed and France's Americanization was increasingly apparent, a debate about its sociocultural impact suffused the country's intellectual and political life. With the French Right in eclipse as a result of the war, the Left took up the anti-American torch; however, the question across the political spectrum was whether France's national identity – or, more precisely, a certain conceptualization of this identity – could survive the cultural onslaught. As Philippe Roger explains, what was at stake was "Frenchness" – a "quintessentialized" France that, with its "unparalleled joie de vivre," its idealized depiction of family, neighbourhood, and village life, and its "culinary rituals and religious or electoral rites," stood in stark contrast and radical opposition to the "American Way of Life."[99] Works such as Cyrille Arnavon's *L'américanisme et nous* sounded the alarm against the colonizing aspects of American culture, and Albert Camus warned that the faster airplanes flew, the less important countries such as France, Spain, and Italy would be; alluding to French culture's folklorization, he asserted that what once had been nations had become provinces and soon would be villages.[100] As Roger claims, those aspects of American culture that were embraced enthusiastically in France, such as jazz, rock 'n' roll, westerns – even Jerry Lewis – were simultaneously manifestations, paradoxically, of the anxiety over Americanization, as they appeared either to be dissident or subversive within American culture – that is, un-American.[101]

Paris's disquiet over American cultural influence in Canada and its interest in the opportunities that this situation presented for developing Franco-Canadian relations was evident shortly after the war, and was by no means restricted to French Canada. The French embassy in Ottawa reported on growing English-Canadian interest in Western Europe as a response to Americanization. France's diplomats similarly remarked that with the traditional nationalist antipathy for France being eclipsed in Quebec, a desire for stronger cooperation was increasingly apparent among the elites of both of Canada's linguistic communities, fuelled in large measure by their shared concern over American influences.[102]

Quebec quickly became the North American theatre of the Franco-American cultural war. In the late 1940s, French diplomats expressed concern as Quebec audiences flocked to American films. Similarly troubling was the impact of the United States's influence on Quebec university life, notably the prolific flow of American books into the province and the wartime legacy that saw a growing proportion of Quebec graduate students heading south of the border. The embassy subsequently warned that in many respects, the general French-Canadian population was even more susceptible to American influences than was its anglophone counterpart, as it did not possess the British and Irish heritage through which English-Canadians refracted American culture.[103]

The French preoccupation with American influence in Quebec helps to explain the reaction of France's consul general in Quebec City, François de Vial, to a speech that Lionel Groulx gave at the 1953 annual meeting of the Conseil de la Vie française. De Vial was struck by the traditional nationalist's "dénonciation fanatique" of Ottawa, as well as his complete lack of openness to cooperation with English Canada, and what de Vial described as a lamentable failure to display greater concern about French Canada's rapid Americanization. Indeed, the French diplomat considered this a far more immediate threat, and in this regard could not understand Groulx's refusal to turn to France as a bulwark for French-Canadian culture.[104]

Other figures in Quebec demonstrated a greater willingness to turn toward France. Writer François Hertel, from his self-imposed exile in Paris, where he sought escape from the growing American presence and what he considered a stifling atmosphere in Quebec, used the pages of *Cité libre* to plead for renewed ties with France as an antidote to Americanization. Arguing that English- and French-Canadian cultural survival was to be found in links with Britain and France, he declared it the duty of the elites of both linguistic communities to embrace these two countries.[105] Antoine Rivard, solicitor-general of Quebec, told sailors of the French ship *Aventure,* marking the centenary of the *La Capricieuse* visit, that Quebec's struggles were comparable to those of the French Resistance. He warned that French culture in the province was at risk due to French-Canadian "promiscuité" with the United States, so that contacts with France were "more necessary than ever." The French diplomat attending the event found Rivard's remarks particularly significant, as they were a rare public affirmation by a senior Duplessis government figure of the need to maintain relations with France to counter American influence.[106]

By the mid-1950s, the French embassy's cultural service was remarking upon French Canada's "rapide évolution de la mentalité," as earlier debates in Quebec over the desirability of links with France had been overtaken by an almost total acceptance of French intellectual influence and a belief that cultural contacts were invaluable. Paris was told that the foremost debate in Quebec cultural life arose from the efforts among French Canada's elites to reconcile traditional and modern Quebec, with the intellectual elites displaying a marked preference for French culture over Americanization.[107]

The embassy analysis underscores a significant class dimension to nationalism in Quebec with important implications for attitudes toward France. The acceleration of Quebec's Americanization during and after the war widened a cleavage, the origins of which were visible by the late eighteenth century, between a bourgeois nationalist elite oriented more toward France and the popular classes more interested in the United States and their immediate North American environment.[108] Perhaps mindful of an analogous dynamic in France, Paris's diplomats emphasized that whereas Quebec's expanding cultural avant-garde wished to purify French-Canadian culture through more intense contact with French civilization, it was increasingly alienated from a general population that embraced Americanization.[109] As Quebec grappled with its *américanité*, anxiety over the accompanying threat that Americanization was alleged to pose cut across the multiple currents of nationalism, so that Lionel Groulx's claim in 1941 that one day history would recognize French Canada's accomplishment in resisting "le continentalisme américaine" found its post-war echoes in André Laurendeau's warning of the "danger mortel" of the United States's "influence uniformisante" and, in the 1960s, the leftist radicalism of *Parti pris*.[110] Just as anti-Americanism was a point of convergence between France's sociopolitical extremes, so too did it serve as a meeting place for nationalists across French Canada's ideological spectrum.

Where differences arose was over the exact nature of the American peril, and the related question of which incarnation of France could best help preserve French Canada's cultural specificity in the face of the American threat. Traditional nationalists such as Lionel Groulx evinced a deep suspicion of *France moderne*, seeing in its materialistic, liberal secularism a menace to French Canada's survival as great as that of English Canada and the United States. The younger generations, however, were more inclined to see *France moderne* as a useful and necessary ally as Quebec came to terms with its urban and industrial reality. For the growing ranks of neo-nationalists, the francophone urban proletariat was to be protected from Americanization – and assimilation – by a greater communion between *Québec moderne* and its French counterpart. The neo-nationalist embrace of *France moderne* recalled that of the traditional nationalist turn to *France éternelle*: both entailed a nationalist elite pursuing its self-appointed mission of preserving Quebec's majority francophone culture. Where traditional nationalists had accorded the spiritual dimension a higher priority and thus looked askance at *France moderne,* neo-nationalists attached greater importance to the temporal realm, and were consequently eager to engage with France's post-revolutionary incarnation.

The neo-nationalists' desires for expanded cultural links with France were consistent with their calls for a more activist Quebec state that would preserve and promote French-Canadian culture. Though more pronounced from neo-nationalists, there were demands across the political spectrum for Quebec City to abandon its laissez-faire approach to culture. The Tremblay Report argued that French Canada's survival required a Quebec state with the ability and willingness to intervene to safeguard the national culture. Léopold Richer, founder of the weekly newspaper *Notre Temps*, called in 1953 for a government agency that would promote the use of French in Quebec, as did former politician Paul Gouin and writer Jean-Paul Desbiens.[111]

Indicative of the mounting nationalist pressure on the Duplessis government was the growing clamour for a Quebec office in Paris. Amid a public debate over low levels of francophone immigration to Canada in the early 1950s, *Le Devoir* and the Fédération des Sociétés Saint-Jean Baptiste du Québec urged the establishment of an office that, among other tasks, would promote French immigration to Quebec.[112] Gouin prevailed on Quebec City to take responsibility for promoting French-Canadian culture overseas by appointing an agent to the French capital, explaining that the French Canadians responsible for culture at Canada's Paris embassy were "fédéralistes" whose work constituted an attack on Quebec autonomy.[113] There were also repeated calls for such an office in the legislature, not least from the leader of the Opposition, Georges-Émile Lapalme. A former federal member of Parliament with a marked affinity for French culture, Lapalme emphasized the need for increased links with France to safeguard Quebec's majority francophone culture.[114]

The growth of nationalist sentiment favouring a more activist Quebec state that would forge cooperation with France as part of its broader vocation to promote francophone culture in North America helped to set the stage for conflict with Ottawa. The seeds of the explosive jurisdictional dispute lay in the nebulous treatment of culture in the *British North America Act*. Responsibility for "culture" as such was not assigned to any one level of government, although the provinces had (at least in theory) exclusive control over education. In a dynamic mirroring that in Quebec and France, however, Canadian nationalist worries over Americanization pushed Ottawa to increase its cultural activity. The trend had been visible in the first half of the twentieth century in response to the influx of American periodicals, radio, and movies, and prompted Ottawa to establish the CBC. After the war, the English-Canadian nationalism and cultural anti-Americanism apparent in the Massey Report shared with its

French-Canadian and French counterparts the view that maintaining cultural independence from the United States would allow for the construction of a more civilized society.[115] And, as occurred in France and Quebec, there was a convergence of English-Canadian nationalist opinion regarding the American challenge. Aspects of the more conservative nationalism that figures such as George Grant espoused served as part of the foundation upon which were built the more liberal and left-wing critiques that emerged in the 1950s and later decrying American "cultural imperialism."

To be sure, English-Canadian cultural nationalism shared a positive dimension with its Quebec neo-nationalist counterpart. With Canada having evolved "from colony to nation" constitutionally, diplomatically, and militarily, the cultural sphere seemed a logical extension of this project of national rule; if Canada was to tread the boards of the world stage, it had to offer products that reflected its national life.[116] Yet, it was a measure of the preoccupation with American cultural influence that Britain and France continued to figure prominently in the nationalist calculus. English-Canadian activists drew inspiration from the British cultural metropole, but the French example also loomed large in their lobbying for an enhanced cultural infrastructure, one modelled along European rather than American lines. There were striking parallels between the "cultural democratization" movement in Canada and similar efforts in France, as there were ambitions in both countries to expose the masses to high culture as an inoculation against the challenges of modern life, mass culture, and ultimately, Americanization.[117]

Also encouraging the nationalist push for Ottawa's involvement in cultural affairs was an evolving English-Canadian appreciation of French Canada as a shield against Americanization. Poet, public intellectual, and constitutional expert Frank Scott described Quebec as a rampart against American influences and ambitions.[118] In a similar vein, the Anglophilic Vincent Massey, chair of the royal commission that bore his name, described Canada's bicultural dimension as a strength that protected both linguistic communities from American cultural power.[119] Such sentiment informed a belief in the necessity of active federal promotion of Canada's two founding cultures, since a dynamic biculturalism offered the best defence against the United States, the greatest prospect for a distinctly Canadian cultural life inspired by the cultural heritage of France and Britain, and, more generally, a means to promote national unity. Massey's de facto co-chair, Georges-Henri Lévesque, dean of Université Laval's faculty of social sciences, shared and advocated this pan-Canadian approach, arguing that because Quebec and French Canada were not synonymous, it was incumbent upon Ottawa to cultivate Canada's bicultural reality.[120]

But federal cultural activism remained hotly contested in Quebec. When Ottawa acted on the Massey Report's recommendation that it use the constitution's residual powers clause to justify its action, which included funding post-secondary educational institutions and the establishment of the Canada Council, André Laurendeau warned against an Ottawa-directed, pan-Canadian culture that posed a clear threat to French Canada. If a federal presence was tolerated in some quarters, notably Quebec's cash-starved universities, in the main Quebec nationalists of all stripes considered Ottawa's cultural activism and the justification offered for it to be illegitimate, in Canada and abroad. This was grounded in a belief that the spirit, if not the text, of the constitution made culture an exclusive provincial jurisdiction. Quebec neo-nationalists rejected Lévesque's argument for federal activism on behalf of biculturalism as naïve; although ready to acknowledge that Americanization presented a serious challenge to French Canada's cultural specificity, they argued that it by no means justified ceding any of Quebec autonomy. To the contrary, notwithstanding the growing English-Canadian appreciation for Canada's "French fact," it was unthinkable that Quebec should turn over even the smallest measure of its cultural development to federal institutions controlled by the anglophone majority; French Canadians had no choice but to entrust the maintenance, defence, and expansion of their culture to their national government – in Quebec City, not Ottawa.[121]

Accordingly, Quebec nationalist appeals for the Duplessis government to take a more activist role in cultural affairs were inspired significantly by a concern with asserting Quebec's autonomy in the face of federal encroachments and thereby safeguarding the province's francophone majority. As Michael Behiels has observed, at the crux of the conflict was a dispute over which level of government could best ensure the survival and well-being of French and English Canada in the face of the American challenge.[122] Canada's two nationalist reactions to Americanization, and the two levels of government under pressure to combat the phenomenon, were on a collision course.

The competing Quebec and Canadian nationalist responses, and the increasingly rancorous intergovernmental rivalry that they fuelled, had serious implications as they intersected with the French nationalist response to Americanization. In 1959, an official of Canada's embassy in Lima encountered France's new minister of culture, the famed intellectual André Malraux, at a dinner in the Peruvian capital. The new ministry for which Malraux had been given responsibility was the latest chapter in the story of French governmental involvement in cultural affairs. Malraux spoke to the official of France's deep interest in Canada and desire to expand cultural relations; the official came away with the impression that France was undertaking a "vast cultural offensive" of which Canada would be a significant part.[123] The following year, during his

1960 visit to Canada, de Gaulle praised French Canada's survival and success as a cultural entity. He emphasized the significance that he attached to French Canadians' will to survive, claiming that what they were was very important not just for Canada, but for France and indeed, the world, since it was crucial that a thriving "French entity" exist on the American continent to help ensure that the world was not reduced to a sort of "uniformity."[124]

THESE SENIOR FRENCH FIGURES' remarks were consistent with Paris's abiding and growing interest in Canada, especially French Canada. But the interest was also symptomatic of broader French preoccupations about American cultural strength; although increased transnational exchanges had led to an increase and evolution of Franco-Canadian cultural contacts, the global trend was also sparking nationalist concern for the strength of French culture at home and abroad. Yet the expansion of cultural exchanges was a trend to which French governmental action was not only reacting, but contributing. Two years before de Gaulle's return to power, the MAE had been reorganized to give greater prominence and resources to France's cultural diplomacy; in the final days of the Fourth Republic, a committee of senior French civil servants had developed a comprehensive program of cultural action.[125] These developments occurred as Paris found itself faced with two interested (and increasingly competing) interlocutors, one in Ottawa and the other in Quebec City. Although this situation held out the prospect of expanded exchanges, French diplomacy had to determine how it was to conduct its activity in Canada. The heightened nationalist sensitivity surrounding cultural affairs and encouraging a more substantive role for governments meant that such exchanges were poised to become a major source of conflict. Combined with the hollowing out of the official bilateral relationship in the geopolitical and economic spheres, as well as the emerging rapprochement between France and Quebec in the economic domain, the stage was set for a new dynamic – and tensions – in the Canada-Quebec-France triangle.

PART 2

The Clash of Nations:
The Sources of Triangular Tensions

CHAPTER FOUR

A "French" Fact: The Cultural Impetus

IN 1944, DURING THE MONTHS of delay preceding Allied recognition of the Gouvernement provisoire de la République française as France's legitimate government, one of Ottawa's diplomats, Tommy Stone, warned that Canada's future was "bound up" in the debate. Predicting a post-war rapprochement between France and what he described as an increasingly liberalized Quebec, Stone expressed his fear that French nationalism, spurred by France's bitter wartime experience, would "make a big play for the sympathy and moral support of its American outpost." Although rather Francophilic, he admitted to anxiety about the potential threat to Canada's unity and wondered if there was nothing Ottawa could do "to divert the Flood."[1]

Such warnings appeared remarkably prescient on the eve of Charles de Gaulle's 1967 visit. Quebec neo-nationalism, aiming to equip the Quebec government to serve as French Canada's "national" state and the promoter of North America's *fait français* – French fact – had found an enthusiastic partner in Paris. Gaullist France was preoccupied with countering American cultural power, and this extended to concern for Quebec, where debate was raging over what it meant to be "Québécois," and the political consequences that flowed from this. If French concerns about French Canada's survival were not new, the manner in which they were manifested was transformed following the coming to power of Gaullist nationalism. The primacy of "nation" in the Gaullist worldview, which emphasized the importance of a historically enduring national consciousness, the centrality of the nation-state in the international system, and the importance of a political regime capable of promoting the national interest, predisposed Paris to embrace the "two nations" constitutional thesis about Canada. Increasingly prominent after 1945, this thesis posited Canada's duality as a compact between an anglophone nation with its capital in Ottawa, and a francophone nation with its capital in Quebec City. More and more, Paris favoured Quebec City, viewing it as the seat of the only viable national entity with the ability – aided by France – to resist the American embrace.

The resulting special relationship between Paris and Quebec City was paralleled by Ottawa's marginalization, a dynamic that aggravated federal unease about Canada's unity. Such sensitivities were all the more acute because, similar to the Quebec and French anxiety over Americanization, English Canada was experiencing a nationalist reaction to the United States's influence. This English-Canadian reaction was part of a broader debate over the nature and future of Canada as links to Britain and the Commonwealth declined in importance. Especially after the Pearson government's election, Ottawa was preoccupied with employing Canada's *fait français* as a source of differentiation from the United States and as a vehicle for cultivating relations with France to ensure a viable European counterweight. More fundamentally, it was determined to embrace biculturalism and bilingualism as part of a reimagining of the Canadian community and a reforming of the federation in a manner that it was hoped would foster unity. The intersecting of these three nationalist reactions, all of which were preoccupied in one way or another with the future of French Canada and responding to American cultural strength, proved to be a critical mass for the emergence of triangular tensions.

As Stone's wartime analysis reflected and foreshadowed, a degree of cultural essentialism characterized the triangular dynamic of the 1960s. It was presumed and feared in equal measure that ethnocultural affinities between France and Quebec made them natural allies. But while there existed a great deal of complementarity between Gaullism and Quebec neo-nationalism, this by no means dictated perfect harmony or identical interests, especially given the history of ambivalence between France and French Canada, as well as Quebec's complexity. Even amid the multiplying references to cultural solidarity, there was a certain disconnect between these two nationalist reactions that were ultimately using one another to advance their respective political agendas.

IN HIS EXPLORATION OF THE origins of French nationalism, David A. Bell observes how its eighteenth-century architects sought, in a period of "vertigo-inducing change," a "new form of civic harmony ... [that lay] in giving a large and disparate community ... a shared culture – common language, customs, beliefs, [and] traditions."[2] In the mid-twentieth century, amid the eclipse of the spiritual by the secular, the upsetting of the geopolitical order, and the dramatic changes provoked by technological civilization, such efforts appeared all the more relevant to nationalists on both sides of the Atlantic. To be sure, nationalisms are never static; they are constantly contested and reflect larger political objectives. But that is just the point: the heightened nationalist sentiment at all points of the Canada-Quebec-France triangle was a response to the destabilizing impact of intersecting domestic and international conditions. These conditions provoked a rethinking of preconceived notions of the nation even as they posed troubling questions about its integrity and future. The fact that the acceleration of interdependence and transnational exchanges was occurring under the auspices of preponderant American power meant the United States often served as a foil against which the nation could be defined. Anti-Americanism acted as a life preserver to which the various nationalisms could cling in another period of vertigo-inducing change.

The dynamic was evident in the respective evolution of English- and French-Canadian nationalism. The development of these nationalisms did not occur in a vacuum; rather, it built upon a lengthy history of symbiosis.[3] With both nationalisms in a state of profound flux after the Second World War, Canada's two principal linguistic communities had something in common that ultimately ended up dividing them.

The ascendance of Quebec neo-nationalism was symptomatic of what has been called the "break-up" of French Canada.[4] A growing number of Quebec nationalists dismissed as outdated the French-Canadian nationalism that figures such as Henri Bourassa had espoused – one advocating a non-territorial biculturalism and entailing solidarity between Canada's francophones that transcended provincial boundaries and fought for equality of rights and opportunities across the country. This pan-Canadian approach, one conceiving of the French-Canadian nation in a minority position, was increasingly challenged by its Québécois rival, which envisioned North America's French fact in a majority position within the boundaries of Quebec. Fuelled by the evolution of Canada's political life and the often-strained relations between French and English Canada, the struggle between these two different strands of French-Canadian nationalism became more and more pronounced throughout the twentieth century. By the early 1960s, the conflict raging in French Canada was evident in writer Hubert Aquin's warning that as Quebec struggled to achieve independence, English Canada was not the main obstacle; rather, it was "the French Canadians we have to fight."[5]

The rise of Quebec neo-nationalism intersected with and influenced similar nationalist soul-searching in English Canada. Post-war demographic changes to Canada's population and the declining importance of links with Britain relative to those with the United States contributed to an undermining of the ethnocultural component of the English-Canadian identity and the strand of Canadian nationalism that emphasized Canada's "Britishness." The process was not an easy one. Expressions of regret in the press that Canada was somehow "incomplete" and complaints about the slow growth of a distinctive national identity were the legacy of an ethnic-based understanding of Canada – that is, a desire for one English-speaking and "British" pan-Canadian nation.[6] Although conservative nationalist George Grant willingly described French Canada as the keystone of the Canadian nation and condemned John Diefenbaker's "One Canada" concept for disregarding French-Canadian communal rights, in the main this British-oriented conceptualization of Canada tended to view the country's dualism as a handicap – an obstacle to be overcome to achieve national maturity.[7]

Yet, by the early 1960s this conservative, more ethnic-based nationalism was increasingly eclipsed by a more liberal and civic-based variant that claimed that Canada's identity and unity would best be assured in the adoption of distinctive symbols, some form of greater recognition of the country's "two nations," and federal activism to promote the country's cultural duality. This would culminate in what José Igartua has characterized as Canada's "other quiet revolution," as the British definition of Canada was discarded over the course of the decade.[8] Encouraged by the rise of the internal challenge of Quebec neo-nationalism and the external challenge of preponderant American power, this vision of Canada posited the country's biculturalism as a strength, considering the country's "French fact" a guarantor of a national life distinct from the United States. Sharing the pan-Canadianism of its French-Canadian counterpart, the rise of this version of Canadian nationalism meant that the federal government took on enhanced importance as Ottawa was accorded responsibility for fostering Canada's dualism.

The trend could be seen in 1961, when the *Toronto Star* declared that Canada was a product of the cooperation between two linguistic and cultural communities and praised Quebec nationalism's quest for "a better life for its own people," arguing that this could "only benefit our nation of two peoples and two cultures."[9] Lester Pearson reflected this evolution when he invoked the importance of biculturalism in a speech to the Association des hebdomadaires de langue française du Canada. The new prime minister warned the congress of French-language publications that neither an independent Quebec nor a truncated Canada would be able to resist the embrace of the United States, and he appealed for English and French Canadians to unite against what he characterized as an American cultural and economic invasion.[10] Pearson's nationalist call came amid his government's efforts to increase French-Canadian influence in Confederation, and Ottawa especially, reflected in its establishing the Royal Commission on Bilingualism and Biculturalism. By the end of the decade, constitutional squabbles, increasingly pointed questions about Canada's future, and the Trudeau government's election meant Ottawa was promoting a nationalism positing Canada as a bilingual country, in which the federal government had the task of promoting equality between the country's two principal linguistic groups. However, although it shared the pan-Canadianism of its predecessors, this vision of Canada was grounded in the language of individual rather than communal rights; the "two nations" thesis was rejected, along with the notion of any special status for Quebec. Ottawa was to have primary responsibility for preserving and promoting the country's *fait français*, which simultaneously would be safeguarded within and reinforce the Canadian project of national rule.[11]

With the rival Québécois and Canadian nationalisms, each in its own way, preoccupied with the future of North America's *fait français* and mindful of its centrality to their duelling political projects, it did not take long for each to turn to France. A year into office, Quebec premier Jean Lesage told a Université de Montréal audience that French Canada could not escape international realities: no more protective barriers stood between it and the outside world, and history showed that the peoples that survived were those that were best able to adapt to change.[12] Lesage's remarks highlighted a question that the traditional nationalist order's passing was only making more relevant: how to ensure French Canada's cultural survival amid Quebec's sociocultural transformation, and, more broadly, the acceleration of economic interdependence and transnational exchanges. Consistent with the more positive neo-nationalist disposition toward *France moderne*, an important part of the answer was for Quebec City to cultivate relations with France and the international francophone community.

The priority assigned to this task underscores the tremendous symbolic importance of Lesage's visit to Paris in 1961. Beyond opening the new Maison du Québec, the trip was intended as a dramatic announcement that at an official level Quebec desired closer links with France and that the Quiet Revolution was not to be confined to the province's borders. This dimension of the trip was apparent during the preparations, when Quebec's deputy premier and minister of cultural affairs, Georges-Émile Lapalme, emphasized to France's ambassador that the reception should be as impressive as possible, to reflect the extraordinary importance that the Lesage government attached to developing relations.[13]

The visit *was* spectacular. A delegation of some three hundred Quebecers – including half the Cabinet – descended on Paris in an atmosphere "reminiscent ... of relatives returning home after a long absence," and a motorcade of twenty-six limousines whisked them to their lodgings at the luxurious Hôtel Crillon.[14] De Gaulle took a personal interest in the arrangements; although protocol considerations prevented his attending the Maison's inauguration, he sent André Malraux to represent him, and hosted a sumptuous dinner at the Élysée during which he hailed the fact that after having separated them for so long, history was conspiring to bring Quebec and France back together in common purpose. For his part, Lesage announced that in the face of modern realities, ensuring French Canada's survival made it crucial for Quebec to affirm its presence abroad and multiply contacts with other countries, with France at the forefront. Overwhelmed by the welcome, he subsequently paraphrased Louis XIV's celebrated quip regarding the Pyrenees, declaring, "The Atlantic no longer exists!"[15]

Yet even as Quebec sought a greater communion with France to buttress its cultural specificity, Lesage's trip highlighted the province's determination to participate as a distinct and equal member of the international francophone community. In this sense, the visit pointed to tensions at the heart of the Quiet Revolution, and indeed, to Quebec's broader complexities. To be sure, a defensive impetus drove the Quiet Revolution. Nationalist concern about Americanization and preserving Quebec's majority francophone society compelled a turn to France as a means to reinforce its French cultural heritage and to help realize the neo-nationalist vision of Quebec as the political expression of the French-Canadian nation. But interwoven with this defensive aspect was a more positive dimension: the Quiet Revolution was equally a moment of national affirmation, an effort to come to terms with Quebec's *américanité,* its self-recognition as a cultural entity distinct from France, a New World francophone society shaped by its North American situation.[16]

Although Lesage frequently invoked the idea of cultural solidarity between France and French Canada, he reminded his Parisian hosts that French Canada's duty was to be itself, not merely an "appendice nordique de la France," and that the international francophone community's strength was to be found in its diversity. When Malraux visited Canada two years later, Lesage repeated this message, declaring that French Canada's French heritage did not render it any less Canadian.[17] Lesage's successor, Daniel Johnson, similarly emphasized French Canada's distinctiveness. Amid the soaring rhetoric of cultural solidarity during de Gaulle's 1967 visit, Johnson made a point of referring to Quebec's North American dimension, claiming that even before the Conquest the *Canadien* population of New France had acquired certain traits differentiating them from "their French cousins."[18]

Those advocating more dramatic action than Lesage and Johnson also made sure to highlight Quebec's distinctiveness – even as they appealed for French support. During his 1963 visit to Paris, the vice-president of the Rassemblement pour l'indépendance nationale (RIN), André d'Allemagne declared that it was only natural that the Quebec independence movement's first appeals for support should be to "a brother people" and claimed that there existed a nation in Quebec – the oldest in North America and, by virtue of its population, the largest French-speaking nation in the world after France.[19] The RIN candidate in Gaspé wrote to de Gaulle to express his dream to see a "France-Québec" republic established to serve as an "Israël francophone" in which North America's French-speaking diaspora could find their Pernod in the corner café, even if this took the form of apple cider.[20] The avowedly Francophilic journalist Jean-Marc Léger also made a point of asserting Quebec's distinctiveness. Léger argued that although the world's francophone peoples recognized France as a spiritual homeland and head of the French-speaking community, they were no longer willing to defer culturally to France, and expected to be treated as partners in promoting the international *fait français*.[21]

The debate over language in Quebec was a barometer of efforts to reconcile Quebec's French heritage and its North American reality – a debate made all the more intense as language was eclipsing religion as the primary component in the construction of the francophone Quebec identity associated with neo-nationalism.[22] Chantal Bouchard has observed how the dynamic provoked both a wave of "'parisienisme'" among Quebec's more educated population, and, conversely, a reaction against Francophilism. For cultural figures such as Jacques Renaud and Jacques Godbout, as well as members of the Parti pris movement, working in *joual* – the name given to the language spoken by Montreal's popular classes – was a means to empowerment, a way to denounce feelings of domination and alienation.[23] The rise to prominence of the term *joual* in 1960 set off a heated debate in Quebec over what it meant to be a francophone in North America and, specifically, the relative weight assigned to the French and North American components in the production and promotion of francophone Quebec's identity. What to some was a means to assert French Canada's distinctiveness was for others a betrayal of Quebec's French heritage; writer Jean-Paul Desbiens, for example, condemned it as a vector of Americanization. *Joual* became a lightning rod for all of the preoccupations about French Canada's socio-economic and political marginalization, and the destiny of North America's *fait français*.[24]

It was symptomatic of the debate over identity that the French spoken in Quebec was increasingly compared to "international French," rather than to that of Paris. This situation was encouraged by the growing awareness of French Canada's membership and participation in a transnational linguistic community and a preoccupation with ensuring that the French spoken in Quebec reflected local conditions and realities, thus serving as a vehicle for independent cultural development. The dynamic was evident in the second Biennale de la langue française, held in Quebec City in September 1967. The meeting resulted in the launch of the Conseil international de la langue française, which offered Quebec nationalists the best of both worlds: ongoing engagement with the international francophone community and a universal French culture, but in a manner that decentred France and acknowledged Quebec's unique contribution.[25]

The assertions of Quebec's distinctiveness and accompanying invocations of francophone cultural solidarity underscore how the neo-nationalist efforts to cultivate relations with France were inseparable from notions of Quebec's historical vocation. One such notion posited Quebec as Canada's bulwark against American cultural power: Jean Lesage argued that the best way for French Canada to be faithful to its French origins was to remain in Confederation and inoculate Canada's two founding cultures against Americanization. In Paris, he described it a "delicious paradox" that the most enlightened elements of English Canada, the beneficiary of the Conquest, wished for the survival of French culture in Canada as ardently as did French Canadians, to protect against the American invasion.[26]

The scope of Quebec's mission grew in parallel to that of nationalist assertiveness. Daniel Johnson argued that Quebec was destined to serve as the link between Europe and North America, given that it was the product of French civilization as well as a full and integral participant in North American civilization.[27] Jean-Marc Léger and Gaston Cholette, assistant commissioner-general for cooperation in Quebec's ministry of intergovernmental affairs, went even further, claiming that by virtue of being simultaneously a First World country and "colonisé," Quebec had the potential to serve as a bridge between the West and the Third World.[28] Léger argued that Quebec had a special role in building the Francophonie, since it had no imperialist past or political ambitions and could achieve agreements with newly independent states that France might not be able to secure.[29]

As such remarks make clear, the Union Nationale's return to office in 1966 did not herald a return of the Duplessiste antipathy for *France moderne*; to the contrary, references to cultural solidarity between the French and French-Canadian nations multiplied. Just before visiting Paris in 1967, Johnson told the French ambassador to Ottawa, François Leduc, that his goal was to confirm at the highest levels of France's government that Quebec City could count on support in ensuring the French-Canadian nation's survival, and assistance in responding to modern cultural and economic realities.[30]

Amid the unfolding official rapprochement between France and Quebec, there was an increased appreciation in Ottawa of the French-speaking world. To be sure, part of this federal interest was related to broader foreign policy concerns; DEA elements believed that Canada's francophone dimension offered an opportunity to develop relations with France so that Ottawa could mitigate the growing estrangement between Paris and other NATO capitals. It was also claimed that a greater orientation of Canadian foreign policy toward the French-speaking world could only benefit Canada as a whole by reinforcing its identity in the face of American strength. There was also, however, a more immediate domestic issue: by 1963, concerns were growing over where the Quiet Revolution was headed, and the newly elected Pearson government hoped that cultivating relations with France would demonstrate its commitment to biculturalism and thereby help to contain Quebec nationalism. The new secretary of state for external affairs, Paul Martin, summed up the array of federal motivations when he urged that French Canada's cultural affinities with France be "exploited in the best sense of the word" to strengthen the bilateral relationship and national unity.[31] Accordingly, when Pearson visited Paris in a bid to build up Franco-Canadian relations, he made sure to highlight the importance that his government attached to promoting the French fact, explaining to the prime minister, Georges Pompidou, that Canada's best hope in maintaining a distinctive national life lay in its bilingual and bicultural reality.[32]

THE INTEREST ON THE CANADIAN side of the Atlantic in strengthening links with France to protect against American influences found a ready audience. The power of the United States appeared all the more problematic to a France still healing the deep wounds that the Second World War inflicted, and seeking, through its cultural life, a restored sense of identity and renewed sense of purpose.[33] French sensitivities were reflected in the release of Étiemble's polemic *Parlez-vous franglais?* in which he railed against American cultural strength and condemned the increasing anglicization of the French language. An issue of *Esprit* in 1962 surveyed the state of French around the world, announced that the fate of the language was at stake, and urged cooperation among the world's francophone peoples to protect and promote it.[34] As what would become known as the Francophonie rose from the ruins of France's collapsed imperial edifice, Jean de Broglie, French secretary of state for foreign affairs, predicted that the era of battles for political and economic supremacy was coming to a close and it was necessary to prepare for future struggles centred on questions of cultural independence.[35] Situating anti-Americanism in a global context, journalist Claude Julien claimed that student demonstrations in Latin America had been directed not simply against corrupt and ineffective dictatorships, or even against neo-imperialist exploitation; rather, they were a revolt against American "colonisation culturelle."[36] France's cultural anti-Americanism would culminate in the upheaval of May 1968, inspired in part by a rebelling against the conformism, consumerism, and alienation identified with Americanization.[37]

French nationalist anxieties were projected across the Atlantic. If French notions of nationhood – including those predating the Revolution of 1789 – have been predominantly *political* in orientation, they have also been marked by efforts to achieve *cultural* unity.[38] Moreover, the ethnocultural dimension has at times overshadowed the civic and political attributes. In the nineteenth century, for example, heightened nationalist sentiment in Europe, France's defeat by Prussia, and a growing conflation of ethnocultural considerations with national movements led to the emergence of a more ethnic conceptualization of the *nation*, one all too apparent during the Dreyfus Affair and that would resurface under Vichy.[39] Indeed, Gary Wilder has argued that the post-1789 history of the French nation-state may be understood as a series of crises linked to questions of membership in a claimed universalism. Wilder emphasizes that the Third Republic's "very logic and instruments of republican universalism – a rational(izing) administration, social scientific knowledge, and assimilating techniques – worked to particularize segments of the population."[40] His analysis highlights the fact that, notwithstanding claims to political-civic notions of nationalism and identity, the very efforts to achieve these carry ethnocultural content within them; efforts to achieve the universal draw attention to, distinguish, and ultimately oppose the particular. Hence, the value placed on any a priori understanding of "Frenchness" (or, for that matter, "Canadianness" or "Québecité") has the potential to lend itself to a chauvinistic nationalism. After 1945, as France's multi-ethnic empire dissolved and concerns about Americanization grew, the ethnocultural dimension of French identity took on greater salience, making it logical that there should have been increased openness to and appreciation of *French* Canada.

Thus, despite numerous assertions by Quebec figures about French Canada's distinctiveness, de Gaulle tended to view it as a branch of the French nation and to project onto Quebec France's efforts to distance itself from the "Anglo-Saxons." During a French Cabinet meeting in which Quebec was discussed, de Gaulle insisted that the terms "Français" and "Anglais" be used rather than "francophone" and "anglophone."[41] It was similarly telling that when Ottawa's ambassador to Paris, Jules Léger, presented his credentials in 1964, de Gaulle declared provocatively that France was present in Canada by virtue of the fact that numerous Canadians were of French blood, language, culture, and thought, and were "essentially French" in all areas except that of sovereignty.[42] In the months before the General's 1967 visit, the Élysée's diplomatic counsellor explained to a senior Canadian diplomat that French Canadians were "of course" Canadians, but they were also "former Frenchmen," making them a "very special case" to which "normal rules do not apply."[43]

There certainly were French acknowledgments of Quebec's "American" dimension; an internal MAE report explained that amid the budding special relationship, Paris had to remain mindful of Quebec's Canadian and North American character and recognize that France and Quebec had followed separate historical paths since the Conquest.[44] André Malraux even came away from a 1963 visit prepared to argue that neither those seeking greater autonomy for Quebec nor the general population were anti-American or opposed to the American lifestyle; rather, they were anti-English-Canadian, desirous to see Montreal's skyscrapers owned by francophones.[45]

Yet even as Malraux made his observation, the United States was occupying an increasingly central position in Quebec nationalist critiques.[46] The French minister's analysis was also noteworthy for running counter to the Gaullist tendency to conflate the world's various English-speaking populations into the category of "les Anglo-Saxons." Nevertheless, his remarks were significant in that they underscored the urgency of the situation: such awareness of Quebec's North American reality fuelled French fears that the growing American influence in the province threatened its francophone majority and French cultural heritage.[47] The Académie française's hosting Jean Lesage for one of its sessions during his 1961 visit underscored the French concern with maintaining Quebec's *francité* – its Frenchness – as did its subsequent awarding the premier a medal in recognition of his government's efforts on behalf of the French language. Members of the French National Assembly's foreign affairs committee who visited Canada declared it France's national interest and duty as a "sister nation" to intensify economic and cultural links with Canada, especially Quebec, to protect it from falling irretrievably into the American orbit.[48]

If the French Left tended in general to approach the Quebec nationalist cause with some reticence, events in the province were regarded in certain French intellectual circles as having an important relevance to France. Jean-Marie Domenach, editor of *Esprit,* described Quebec as a testament to American civilization's shocking assimilatory capacity and to the tremendous challenge of maintaining a distinct political and socio-economic system while embracing the American way of life.[49] He claimed that what was at stake went beyond Quebec and Canada to encompass the world – that is, whether the United States was going to dominate the Americas and in so doing reduce other cultures to insignificance and folklore.[50] French sociologist Joffre Dumazedier, who spent time teaching at Université de Montréal, declared that the very future of France's culture, society, and economy was at play in Quebec's "feverish revolt" against the Anglo-Americans. Dumazedier hoped that Quebec could invent "a second America, an America of French culture, in which the values of justice, liberty, truth, and beauty would be better incarnated in communal and individual daily life."[51]

Most significant to the emergence of the triangular tensions were the efforts of the "Quebec lobby," a group of French politicians, civil servants, and other personalities interested in developing links with Quebec. Although members of this informal lobby differed in ideological and political affiliations, and even disagreed to an extent over the ideal political status for Quebec, they shared a nationalist-inspired concern for the international influence of French culture and were thus inclined to sympathize with Quebec neo-nationalism and the promotion of North America's *fait français*.[52] Indeed, for them the survival of the French-speaking population in the New World stood as an inspiration as France contended with American cultural power. Even though the majority of lobby members had never visited Canada or had done so only briefly, they displayed a predilection encouraged by a "francolâtre" – an excessive love of France – to imagine Quebec as part of a transatlantic French community, rather than to acknowledge its Canadian and North American dimensions.[53]

Part of this predilection stemmed from the fact that many Quebec lobby members had been born and come of age at a time when the discourse of "Greater France" – an imaginary in which France's colonies were conceptualized as "integral, if legally ambiguous, parts of the French nation" – remained prominent in France's political life.[54] Inspired by a nationalism grounded in an anti-American discourse dating to the nineteenth century that posited a global struggle between "Anglo-Saxons" and "Latins," certain figures prominent in the triangular tensions began to take an interest in Quebec in the late 1950s.[55] Among these was French diplomat Bernard Dorin, who, while posted to Ottawa, encountered the prominent neo-nationalists Jean-Marc Léger, journalist Yves Michaud, historian Denis Vaugeois, and international law professor Jacques-Yvan Morin.[56] Dorin was a colleague of fellow French national Philippe Rossillon. Interested in Quebec and French Canadians as a result of his travels in Canada, Rossillon was a central figure in an organization dubbed Patrie et progrès, founded at the dawn of the Fifth Republic and committed to a "socialisme patriotique" and France's imperial mission in Africa.[57] There was a pronounced strain of ethnocultural nationalism in the group's manifesto, and members urged that, to avoid being trapped in a Europe organized by the United States and West Germany, France should strengthen its links with "countries of French ethnicity or language."[58] Rossillon was subsequently appointed rapporteur-general of the Haut comité pour la défense et l'expansion de la langue française, established in 1966 under the authority of France's prime minister and charged with promoting the purity, unity, and diffusion of French.[59] Dorin and Rossillon would soon be joined by other Quebec sympathizers in France.

AMPLIFIED FRENCH INTEREST in Quebec's *francité* encouraged Paris and its representatives to shift from a pan-Canadian approach to an increasingly explicit "two-nation" policy regarding Quebec and Canada. The shift was consistent with neo-nationalist ambitions. The neo-nationalist argument, grounded in frustration over Canada's evolution since 1867 and a rejection of its French-Canadian rival's pan-Canadianism, was that Confederation was a compact between two nations – anglophone and francophone – with the latter being the responsibility of the Quebec government, which accordingly should possess all of the powers and resources needed for it to serve as the guardian of francophone culture in North America. This vision underpinned the growing chorus of demands for special constitutional status, greater autonomy for Quebec within a Canada refashioned into a true confederation, and, ultimately, calls for independence.[60]

Paris's evolution toward a two-nation approach was also a logical consequence of French history. A legacy of the Revolution of 1789 was that "the nation" was the source of all authority, with French republicanism informed by a belief that political boundaries should correspond to cultural ones. The prominence in French political culture of the notions of the united nation and the "one and indivisible" republic influenced a search for perfect unity and an antipathy for federalism, which was associated with division. The result was a French predisposition to favour those political entities allegedly best placed to assure unity and indivisibility – and hence a readiness to embrace the two-nation thesis.[61]

More specifically, the two-nation approach was consistent with the Gaullist worldview, which accorded primacy to the nation and its relationship with the state, the primary task of the latter being at all times to defend and promote what were posited as the enduring interests of the former.[62] Gaullism, with its early-nineteenth-century conceptualization of nation, considered Canada, with its marginalized francophone population, an anachronism – a holdover from a dynastic era brought to a close by the French Revolution and rise of national self-determination.[63]

De Gaulle himself possessed a strong predisposition toward the two-nation thesis. He had come of age at the turn of the twentieth century, a period marked by a surge of French anti-Americanism following the Spanish-American War, and amid the growing popularity of notions of ethnography that assigned "races" specific, intangible characteristics. In de Gaulle's view, the only tangible reality on the world stage was the nation-state, a product of history and founded upon a national conscience.[64] As early as his 1960 visit, he explicitly equated Quebec and French Canada, and it was telling that upon meeting a group of Canadians studying at the École nationale d'administration in Paris in 1965, he raised his arms and exclaimed "Ah, the real Canada!" when informed that the majority were from Quebec.[65]

Paris's attention was thus drawn to Lesage's describing Quebec as the "mère patrie" – homeland – of North America's francophones, his appeals for co-operation with France to facilitate Quebec's cultural mission, and his government's establishing a cultural affairs ministry that included an Office de la langue française.[66] The trend of French thinking was apparent in the weight that Paris accorded the notion of French Canada as a bulwark against Americanization. During Lesage's 1961 visit, de Gaulle declared that a strengthened French fact in North America could only benefit French Canada, Canada as a whole, and the larger international community.[67] When Pearson visited three years later, de Gaulle told him that Paris's interest in Quebec's newfound dynamism derived partly from the fact that it would assist Canada as a whole to differentiate itself from the United States.[68] Even as harsh a critic of de Gaulle as French journalist Claude Julien urged English Canadians to embrace bilingualism and biculturalism, and to unite in common cause with a French Canada reacting against its Americanization.[69]

André Malraux's visit in 1963 reflected the significance that Paris attached to relations with Quebec. In improvised remarks in Montreal, the French culture minister lauded the affinities between France and French Canada and, inviting French Canadians to face the future in cooperation with France, exclaimed that nowhere in the world was French energy on display as much as it was in Quebec. Malraux cast a jaundiced eye over what he viewed as the science- and technology-dominated civilizations developing in the United States and Soviet Union, and this informed his rousing declaration to his Quebec hosts that "we will build the next civilization together!"[70]

Malraux's call to arms was an example of the multiplying references to cultural solidarity between the francophone populations on either side of the Atlantic. The French ambassador, Raymond Bousquet, described how Canada's francophone elite viewed the visit as a spectacular recognition of the Quiet Revolution and a promise of fraternal support from a revitalized France. Bousquet was also enthusiastic about a *Le Devoir* column in which academic and writer Jean-Éthier Blais urged French Canadians to get over their traditional ambivalence and forge links with France. The diplomat described the article as dramatic proof that French Canada keenly experienced France's grandeur and weaknesses, citing Blais's contention that Quebecers would not have dared assert themselves since 1960 had France, under de Gaulle's skilled leadership, not regained its confidence, international prestige, and authority.[71] Paris was undaunted by the Lesage government's defeat at the hands of the Union Nationale in 1966; Robert Picard, the French consul general in Quebec City, claimed never to have heard the will for collaboration between France and Quebec expressed so strongly or clearly as in Cabinet minister Marcel Masse's public remarks on the necessity of linguistic cooperation with Paris. Picard predicted a deepening special relationship that would ensure that Quebec's language and culture could only become "more authentically French."[72]

The corollary of France according Quebec City higher priority was Ottawa's marginalization. During the initial stages of the official rapprochement, Paris sought to conduct relations with Quebec City in a manner that did not offend Ottawa.[73] There were signs, however, of French scepticism regarding Ottawa's willingness and ability to promote the *fait français*. De Gaulle made his preference clear as early as 1963, when he declared that Paris could not allow its direct cooperation with Quebec to be drowned under federal efforts to expand bilateral links on a pan-Canadian basis.[74]

The emerging special relationship between France and Quebec only reinforced Gallic doubts about Ottawa's overtures, notably the drive for bilingualism. De Gaulle told Ambassador Léger that although Paris would do nothing to hamper the Pearson government's bilingualism policy, he felt it was in all likelihood impossible to achieve.[75] Rossillon, from the vantage point of the Haut comité pour la défense et l'expansion de la langue française, condemned Ottawa's bilingualization efforts as a trap – an attempted assimilation by stealth.[76]

The marginalization of Ottawa extended to the short shrift that Paris gave French Canadians active at the federal level. De Gaulle privately described prime ministers Laurier and St. Laurent as "marionette[s]" whose strings English Canada had controlled.[77] When Jean Marchand, the federal minister of manpower and immigration (and Pearson's preferred heir), was denied an audience with de Gaulle after the Élysée had received a number of Quebec figures, Jules Léger expressed frustration that the welcome reserved for Canadian ministers depended on the level of government they represented.[78] The Gaullist preference for Quebec would become even more pronounced after July 1967. When Gérard Pelletier, the federal secretary of state, visited Paris in 1969, the Élysée chastised France's foreign minister, Michel Debré, for not obtaining prior authorization before approving the visit and reminded him of de Gaulle's antipathy toward federal personalities who he felt were betraying their French origins.[79] Indeed, de Gaulle described Pierre Trudeau as "the enemy of the French fact in Canada."[80]

The most dramatic manifestation of the notion of ethnocultural solidarity between France and Quebec was, of course, de Gaulle's 1967 visit. On the eve of the General's arrival, Daniel Johnson predicted that it would signal to the world that "we exist," making Quebecers more conscious of their unique existence and demonstrating their participation in a universal francophone culture.

René Lévesque, at the time a member of the Liberal opposition, declared that Quebecers should not be afraid to acknowledge their need for France, and urged them to put on a spectacular welcome.[81]

For his part, de Gaulle was determined to use the occasion to highlight the cultural links uniting France and Quebec; English Canada and, by extension, Ottawa were distant secondary considerations. Conscious of the weight of history, de Gaulle had recalled how he had felt himself "an instrument of fate" at the time of the Liberation; so too did he now see himself as history's agent, repaying the debt of Louis XV – the idea that France had abandoned the colonists of New France after the Conquest. Upon embarking at Brest in July 1967, de Gaulle confided to his son-in-law that it was the "last chance to rectify the cowardice of France."[82] It was telling of the General's preoccupation with his place in history that in the wake of the dramatic events that unfolded, he claimed that had he not acted he "would no longer have been de Gaulle."[83]

Gaullism has been described as being at least as much an emotion as an ideology, and so it was fitting that de Gaulle's triumphal tour was bathed in historical and cultural symbolism.[84] The French president had played a significant personal role in its planning. The MAE had originally suggested that instead of travelling down the Chemin du roy, he would sail up the St. Lawrence at night with bonfires of greeting along the shore. Such an arrangement, however, meant that de Gaulle would be denied the direct contact he desired with the population. Reading the proposal, he became enraged, crumpling the document and exclaiming "bureaucratic asswipe!" Matters were quickly put right. The arrival of France's head of state recalled the route taken by French explorers and colonists of past centuries and the visit of *La Capricieuse*. He arrived in Quebec City on the naval cruiser *Colbert,* named for the French minister who had played a pivotal role in the development of New France. Triumphal arches and flags abounded along Quebec's north shore, as did the blue *fleur de lys* painted at two-metre intervals on the pavement. Villages along the route were designated to represent the various regions of the Hexagon, the Johnson government declared a public holiday, and buses were arranged to transport the population to the spectacle, bringing them into communion with the famed French leader.[85]

De Gaulle's remarks during his stay, not least the speech from the city hall of "la ville Montréal française," were replete with references to cultural solidarity between France and Quebec, going so far as to intimate that French Canadians were members of a transatlantic French nation acting to counter American cultural power and promote the French fact in North America and around the world. On the last day of his visit, after acknowledging their differing circumstances, de Gaulle affirmed that the tasks before the "Français de Canada" and the "Français de France" were bound inextricably together and derived from a common inspiration.[86]

In the days following the visit, de Gaulle wrote Johnson to urge a redoubling of cooperation efforts for "our French community."[87] The letter followed an account of the visit sent to all of Paris's diplomatic posts that cited the rapturous welcome accorded to the French leader. Ottawa's negative reaction, meanwhile, was ascribed to federal authorities acting under pressure from "Canadiens britanniques." The account concluded by emphasizing the importance of assisting the Johnson government as it strove to ensure the progress of North America's "nation française."[88]

De Gaulle's remarks during his visit, the explanations for them, and subsequent French actions were consistent with the Gaullist predisposition to conflate the interests of French and Quebec nationalism. Edgar Faure, France's agriculture minister, confirmed to Ambassador Léger that his president's actions had been inspired by a belief that the French population had to be made aware of the Quebec example. Similarly, Georges Gorse, the French minister of information, emphasized that challenging American hegemony was a primary motivation for de Gaulle, who believed it essential to strengthen and facilitate the development of Quebec and its francophone personality, and to help it resist Americanization.[89] In his November 1967 press conference in which he prophesied Quebec's independence, de Gaulle quoted French literary figure Paul Valéry in declaring that "the fact there exists a French Canada is a comfort to us, an inappreciable element of hope. This French Canada affirms our presence on the American continent, demonstrating our vitality, our endurance, and the worth of our effort."[90]

To be sure, de Gaulle's visit and its aftermath had been an occasion for the vaunting and celebration of cultural solidarity between France and Quebec. The *indépendantiste* Pierre Bourgault was pleasantly astonished at what he described as Quebecers' enthusiastic demonstration of their *francité* during the visit, recalling that "despite their history, despite the English, despite the notables, and alas, despite us, the Québécois had stayed French. I could not get over it. This people had no need to be told to assert their French pride to the entire world."[91] Quebec writer Claude Jasmin was similarly moved to lay claim to his French heritage. Observing that "we had forgotten that we were sons of France, and grandsons of Navarre, Normandy, Britanny or Berri," he asserted that "I have a right to Corneille and Lafontaine, Renan is a relative of mine, Pasteur is part of my family, Lumière is French and I am French too," and finally commanded, "stand up, Frenchmen of the New World!"[92]

Yet in de Gaulle's enthusiastic support of Quebec nationalism, his tendency to see French Canada as a branch of the French nation, and his preoccupation with countering American power, de Gaulle tended to ignore the aspects of Quebec – not least its Canadian component – that distinguished it from France. Some Quebec nationalists rejected the implications of de Gaulle's message; Quebec writer Hubert Aquin, an avowed advocate of independence, was sarcastic and scathing in dismissing the suggestion that the Québécois were part of a transatlantic French nation.[93] And even though prominent conservative nationalist François-Albert Angers was adamant that Quebec needed to be united in support of de Gaulle's intervention and should seize the opportunity to advance the cause of independence, he also warned that "we must stay Québécois vis-à-vis France, just as we asked Canadians to [stay Canadian] vis-à-vis England."[94]

It was Jean Drapeau, Montreal's Francophile mayor, who perhaps best captured the complexities of the debate surrounding francophone Quebec's identity. In remarks at a luncheon that he hosted the day after de Gaulle's *cri du balcon*, Drapeau acknowledged the affinities of history and culture between France and Quebec but asserted that French Canada's roots were planted deep in Canadian soil. He explained that although French Canadians were grateful for de Gaulle's interest, they nevertheless harboured a certain ambivalence for the country that he led, arising from the struggle for survival that they had waged alone for two centuries. Declaring that "we are attached to this immense country," Drapeau ventured the hope that with France's assistance, French Canada would be able to contribute to the betterment of Canada as a whole. In the weeks that followed, a poll showed that it was the mayor's response to de Gaulle's actions that received the greatest level of support from Quebecers.[95]

If Quebec nationalism had found a useful ally in its Gaullist counterpart, it was increasingly apparent that this was not without complications. The Gaullist embrace was occasionally a bit too tight for elements in Quebec City, where the French president's multiplying references to the "Français du Canada" caused discomfort. When Jean Chapdelaine, who had left the DEA to take up the post of Quebec representative in Paris, suggested gently that Quebec City preferred the term "Canadiens français," the effort yielded only a smile from his interlocutors, who warned him that there was little hope of changing the language used by de Gaulle.[96]

Quebec's nationalist reaction had become intertwined with that of France, making it difficult at times to distinguish between the two. De Gaulle's New Year's message for 1968 referred to "la nation française au Canada" as part of the larger French nation comprising France and its overseas territories. When Daniel Johnson died that September, de Gaulle sent a message of condolence describing the premier's passing as a great loss "for all Frenchmen, those of France and those of Canada." Prefects throughout France were instructed to lower the French flag to half-staff on public buildings on the day of the funeral.[97]

IN 1946, FRANCE'S AMBASSADOR, Jean de Hauteclocque, had come away from a discussion at the DEA regarding France's cultural diplomacy shaking his head. He claimed that remarks made by the department's under-secretary, Norman Robertson, revealed a mentality common among English Canadians – that North America's "'French stain'" was to be slowly but surely removed in the interest of Canadian nationalism. De Hauteclocque declared that such an attitude underscored the importance of France's cultural action.[98] Such concern for the future of North America's French-speaking population – notably Quebec's majority francophone society – was apparent two decades later. And as de Hauteclocque's comments had presaged, the question was bound up in discussions surrounding "the nation" and nationalism at each point of the Canada-Quebec-France triangle.

De Gaulle may have been the personality who took the most advanced position and actions regarding the special relationship between France and Quebec, but by no means was he alone in advocating the idea of a cultural solidarity between "the French living on both sides of the Atlantic."[99] Indeed, he may be viewed as the personification of broader French nationalist preoccupations over Americanization. Such preoccupations and the Gaullist worldview combined to encourage Paris to favour the two-nation thesis of Confederation, to treat with Quebec directly in a bid to reinforce its *francité*, and to marginalize Ottawa. This cultural calculus would loom large in the French response to the debate over Quebec's political future. It would also become linked to Gaullist geopolitical manoeuvrings to counter the hegemony of "les Anglo-Saxons."

De Gaulle was thus a compelling figure for Quebec nationalists of all stripes, and not just because of his avowed support. He stood for a *France moderne* that had emerged from its post-war upheavals as a confident and assertive power, a sister francophone society equally determined to preserve its cultural specificity in a period of profound change. As such, Gaullist France was an inspiration to and partner for a Quebec experiencing the simultaneous crises and opportunities of the Quiet Revolution. Quebec nationalists certainly took issue with the idea of a transatlantic French nation, but they were nonetheless quite prepared to invoke notions of cultural solidarity. This stemmed not simply out of a sense of euphoria over the official rapprochement, but out of a more calculated recognition that the Gaullist worldview corresponded to Quebec neo-nationalist ambitions to preserve the province's majority francophone society and secure for

Quebec City – seat of the Québécois nation – the powers and responsibility to preserve and promote North America's *fait français*.

Despite the very real differences between Gaullism and Quebec neo-nationalism, the broader community of interest between these two nationalist reactions brought them into an increasingly rancorous conflict with a third – a Canadian one centred in but by no means exclusive to English Canada. Quebec was not alone in its crisis of identity and attempts to come to terms with its *américanité*. Post-war international and domestic realities, notably the growth of American influence in Canada and the Quiet Revolution, were conspiring to provoke a rethinking of Canadian national existence. Amid the adoption of new national symbols such as the maple leaf flag and the heightened appreciation of Canada's francophone population as a point of differentiation from the United States, federal sensitivity grew over the proclivity of Paris and Quebec City to treat directly with each other. The internal logic of Gaullism and Quebec neo-nationalism, and their cooperation, stoked a Canadian nationalism grounded in a pan-Canadianism and a federal activism at odds with the political projects being espoused in Quebec City and Paris. It was from this clash of nationalisms that the triangular tensions arose.

CHAPTER FIVE

Vive le Québec libre?
The Question of Independence

IN THE MID-1960S, AMID RISING triangular tensions, federal officials casting about for ways to build up Franco-Canadian relations struck upon the idea of having the governor-general, Georges Vanier, and his wife, Pauline Vanier, undertake a state visit to France. Charles de Gaulle had met the couple in London in the darkest days of 1940. The Vaniers had been stalwart supporters ever since, and they saw such a visit as the natural culmination of their public careers. The proposal, however, became bound up in Gaullist opposition to Canada's constitutional status quo. De Gaulle offered to receive the governor-general only as a close personal friend, not as Canada's head of state, since this was Elizabeth II. Despite federal protests that the Queen could not fulfil this role internationally, given that when she travelled outside the Commonwealth she did so as Britain's head of state, the visit was not realized, angering and disappointing Ottawa and the Vaniers. Months later, as Quebec premier Daniel Johnson was welcomed in Paris almost as a head of state, de Gaulle confided to him that although he was grateful for Vanier's longstanding and dogged support of France, he disagreed with his avowedly federalist and anglophilic inclinations.[1]

The dispute symbolized how the debate over Quebec's political destiny was contributing to the triangular tensions. Although aware of changes in Quebec after 1945, Paris had maintained a discreet attitude supportive of Canada's federal reality. In the early 1960s, however, French attitudes began shifting. Paris came to view Quebec's development as necessitating fundamental change to the Canadian political order. The neo-nationalist push for greater autonomy met with an enthusiastic response in French circles, arising not least from the Gaullist preoccupation with national independence. France's encounters with anticolonial nationalism reinforced the trend, as did its history of constitution-making. Consistent with the belief that a new political status for Quebec was a historical inevitability, the French leader's visit in 1967 was meant as a *coup de pouce* – a boost – to the cause of Quebec self-determination.

There was apprehension in Ottawa over the constitutional and political implications of the growing solidarity between Gaullism and Quebec neo-nationalism. Both clashed with a Canadian nationalism fanned by a preoccupation with maintaining the country's independence from the United States. The greater value being assigned to Canada's bicultural dimension meant that there was increased sensitivity over anything perceived as encouraging Quebec nationalism. The federal margin of manoeuvre was limited; Ottawa had to respond to French actions in a manner that avoided fuelling separatist sentiment; this was all the more difficult given the acceleration of Quebec's political life and the increasing boldness of Gaullist interventions. But Ottawa was not alone in its difficulties in keeping up with developments. In Quebec too, there were misgivings. Although independence advocates hailed the *cri du balcon*, the Union Nationale government was anxious that French assistance be limited to increasing Quebec's autonomy within Canada and not precipitate secession. Conversely, de Gaulle's expectations of Quebec's rapid accession to independence were dashed as they encountered the hesitation of the province's political class and general population. The French leader's miscalculation reflected the fact that Gaullism and Quebec nationalism, each with their unique interests and agendas, were increasingly talking past one another. More broadly, the misreading was a manifestation of different political cultures. The result was disappointment and confusion in Paris, which found itself asking the same question as English Canada: "What does Quebec want?"

CANADIAN INTERGOVERNMENTAL dynamics after 1945 were marked by an enduring clash that was a legacy of the Depression years, the Second World War, and a heightened English-Canadian nationalism arising from the slackening of ties to Britain and concomitant growth of American influence. Ottawa preached a centralizing "new federalism" that faced off against the autonomist position of Quebec's Union Nationale government. As the scope of federal involvement in Canadian life increased in parallel to Quebec's socio-economic development, the neo-nationalist critique of both the federal and Duplessiste positions became increasingly pronounced. Neo-nationalists bemoaned Ottawa's interference and, at the same time, what they alleged was Maurice Duplessis's ineffectual, passive approach to autonomy and French-Canadian marginalization. Quebec nationalists of all stripes, however, clamoured for fundamental constitutional reform to alter the federation's balance of power, preserve provincial autonomy against federal encroachments, and confirm Quebec as the *foyer* of French Canada.[2]

Whereas the Duplessis government resisted such demands, the same could not be said of Quebec's Liberal Party. It seized upon the report of the Tremblay

Commission that Duplessis had appointed to examine the province's relationship with Canada as a rejoinder to the centralizing trend. The report's recommendations were transformed by the Liberals into a political platform calling for an expanded, activist, and more autonomous Quebec state. In so doing, they attracted a wave of neo-nationalist support that carried them to victory in 1960.[3]

France's representatives were conscious of this quiet evolution. As early as 1952 the ambassador, Hubert Guérin, explained how certain Quebec political and intellectual circles were espousing ideas radically opposed to traditional nationalism, and that although the province's political life had not undergone a similar change, it was aligning itself socially and economically with the rest of Canada and becoming increasingly integrated with North America. Consistent with the pan-Canadian approach marking French policy, Guérin evinced the hope that even as it retained "a certain nationalism" to maintain its language, French Canada would become more aware of its membership in the larger Canadian entity and discover a sense of solidarity with English Canada.[4]

French awareness of currents in Quebec meant that Duplessis's antipathy for France was reciprocated. Guérin expressed concern about France's foreign minister, Robert Schuman, attending Université Laval's centennial celebrations, as he feared that it would benefit a government that Paris had "no reason" to support.[5] The death of Duplessis – who Guérin once described as "autocratic ... crafty, prickly and egocentric" – was welcomed as ushering in a long-overdue period of reform.[6] Visiting in 1960, de Gaulle met with Jean Lesage, who was girding for the upcoming provincial election by advocating fundamental change. As was the case among many English-Canadian observers at the time, the Lesage government's election was hailed in French circles as the definitive end of Duplessisiste conservatism and proof of a growing public appetite for Quebec to take a more assertive role in Canada and beyond.[7]

The Quiet Revolution provoked an evolution of French attitudes. There was an exponential increase in references to Quebec in the French press, to the extent that the Canadian embassy became concerned and complained about the apparent lack of balance in the coverage.[8] The growing assertiveness of Quebec nationalism impressed French diplomats, who noted the calls for the Lesage government to accelerate the pace of reform. From the outset, the new premier was under pressure to embrace the neo-nationalist vision that combined a desire for linguistic equality with a commitment to modernizing every aspect of Quebec, not least relations with the rest of Canada. The French assessment was that the trend of public opinion could only encourage Lesage to adopt a tougher approach with Ottawa. Amid multiplying references to the "État du Québec" and "principes de souveraineté,"[9] France's consul general in Montreal, Raymond de Boyer de Sainte-Suzanne, believed that developments made it necessary for Paris to adopt a "'state of availability'" regarding Quebec requests.[10]

The eruption of the independence movement on Quebec's political landscape influenced French analyses. Writing amid the stir provoked by Marcel Chaput's *Pourquoi je suis séparatiste,* Guérin's successor as ambassador, Francis Lacoste, confessed amazement over the speed with which separatist ideas had gained so much interest and support, notably among young people.[11] Lacoste's own successor was equally impressed; in early 1963, Raymond Bousquet described the existence of an "irreversible trend" that would lead to either total equality between Canada's linguistic groups or Quebec independence.[12]

Quebec's accelerating metamorphosis shaped French attitudes regarding Canada and its constitutional regime. During the Duplessis era, mutual official antipathy between Quebec City and Paris had reinforced a very correct French approach; an internal MAE report in 1949 emphasized the importance of not interfering in federal-provincial relations, especially between Ottawa and Quebec City. Guérin nonetheless characterized Canada as a typical federation in that, notwithstanding any legal guarantees, the central government tended to dominate the sub-national governments. France's history of centralizing political authority from the Ancien Régime through the Revolutionary era and beyond conditioned a French predisposition to look askance on this centralizing tendency, given that the same trend was linked in French political culture with state efforts to enforce a cultural homogeneity associated with creating and maintaining the "French" nation.[13] Indeed, the ambassador attributed Canada's internal tensions to the *British North America Act,* arguing that the constitutional document had set a francophone minority preoccupied with autonomy against the centralizing tendency of the anglophone majority. All too aware of the power disparity between English and French Canadians, Guérin bemoaned the fact that although an increasing number of French Canadians held senior positions in Ottawa, the price of success appeared to be repudiation of their French traditions, so that English was more dominant than ever. In this regard, he emphasized the need for figures such as Louis St. Laurent to champion the federalist cause, as they would ensure that Ottawa's actions did not provoke a true French-Canadian resistance. The implication was that senior Quebec figures in Ottawa were hostages to English Canada, their main role being to ensure federal (that is, anglophone) ascendancy.

But French perceptions of Quebec and its relationship with the rest of Canada were also significantly affected by the global phenomenon of decolonization. In an ironic twist, the very anti-colonial movements that had emerged in opposition to French imperialism served, in the Quebec context, to encourage a France-Quebec rapprochement. The decolonization phenomenon influenced

Quebec's intellectual life profoundly. The work of the neo-nationalist "Montreal School" of Quebec history was crucial to providing fertile ground upon which the ideas of decolonization fell, positing the notion of French Canadians as victims of a transfer from one colonial authority (France) to another (Anglo-Canadian and American). Quebecers were also exposed to the anti-colonial struggles through the mass media and the accounts of missionaries – religious and a growing number of the lay variety – returning from working in the Third World.[14] Equally significant was the growing number of Quebecers serving as aid workers under the auspices of non-governmental organizations such as the Canadian University Service Overseas.[15]

Quebec had been swept up in the global tide of urbanization, the dislocation and growth accompanying the population movement from countryside to city that was the basis for the "landscape of discontent" upon which decolonization played out. Indeed, Montreal's "two solitudes" evoked the racial discrimination of imperialism that saw most colonial cities organized in a manner that kept the privileged and marginalized populations separate and unequal.[16] Although decolonization had an impact across Quebec's ideological spectrum, its most far-reaching impact was on the Quebec left; intellectuals drew on the anti-colonial literature, such as Aimé Césaire's *Discours sur le colonialisme*, Albert Memmi's *Portrait du colonisé*, and Frantz Fanon's *Les damnés de la terre*, to reimagine Quebec as a colony, situating it and French Canadians within a global movement of anti-colonial resistance and revolution.[17]

The ideas and implications of decolonization quickly spilled into Quebec politics. The right-wing separatist movement Alliance laurentienne advocated Quebec decolonization, as did the left-wing Rassemblement pour l'indépendance nationale (RIN). The discourse of anti-colonial resistance also had an impact much closer to the centre of Quebec's political mainstream. The arrival in power of Quebec neo-nationalism was accompanied by its drawing upon Third World anti-colonial nationalism, considered more legitimate than its discredited European counterpart, to help justify and portray itself as a progressive force. Indeed, the very terms linked to the Lesage government's reforms – "Quiet Revolution," "Maîtres chez nous" – evoked decolonization, and Quebec officials did not shy from employing the phenomenon to explain their actions. René Lévesque, then Quebec's minister of natural resources, responded to doubts about the nationalization of Quebec's hydroelectric sector by pointing out that despite condescending scepticism, the Egyptians had proven that they could operate the Suez Canal when Cairo took it over.[18]

France's post-war experience meant there was receptiveness to the decolonization discourse emanating from Quebec. To be sure, this receptiveness was encouraged by a projecting of France's relationship with the United States onto the province; French misgivings about American imperialism had been evident since the latter decades of the nineteenth century, anticipating the popularity of the "France as colony" metaphor after 1945.[19] A more immediate reason, however, was the tendency in French circles to refract developments in Quebec through the prism of Third World independence. Todd Shepard has described the "invention of decolonization" that accompanied the end of France's rule in Algeria, whereby after years of fighting, there emerged across the French political spectrum the certainty that "decolonization" was a stage in the forward march of history, part of a progress narrative that had begun in France with the Revolution of 1789.[20] Just as nineteenth-century France had embraced an imperialism justified by a *mission civilisatrice* to compensate for its reduced international power, Gaullist France now embraced a *mission libératrice*, presenting itself as a champion of self-determination, decolonization, and the developing world.[21]

Whereas observers such as Jean-Marie Domenach and *Le Monde* cautioned against drawing too direct a comparison between Algeria and Quebec, Jacques Berque, a Collège de France professor and decolonization scholar who taught at the Université de Montréal in 1962, did not hesitate; he affirmed in *France-Observateur* that Canada's French-speaking population was colonized. The Tunisian-born Albert Memmi, whose *Portrait du colonisé* was so influential in inculcating the idea of Quebec as colony, overcame his initial hesitation and demonstrated a certain openness to the idea.[22] The decolonization discourse also carried resonance for the Quebec lobby; many of its members had spent time in or had responsibilities connected to France's African colonies during the empire's twilight years and had thus witnessed anti-colonial nationalism on the march.[23]

Amid the culmination of the Algerian Revolution, Bousquet issued steady reports on what appeared to be a similar *prise de conscience* in Quebec. The numerous references to Quebec's "émancipation" and "libération" in Bousquet's reports were no accident: he cited the decolonization phenomenon as the most significant factor contributing to developments in the province and argued that Quebec and French Canada's subordinate status was increasingly untenable at a time when colonies in Africa and Asia were achieving independence.[24] Visiting Quebec in 1963, André Malraux was struck by the copious references to decolonization; he described the anger of French Canadians as having grown so great that they now had the will to be something other than "angry men." That same year, de Gaulle remarked to Alain Peyrefitte, the minister responsible for resettling French Algerians, that just as France had granted Algeria self-determination, Canada should have to do the same for the French of Canada.[25]

In some French minds, then, francophone Quebecers had taken on the role of Algeria's Muslim majority, with Canada cast in the role of France and anglophone Quebec that of the *pied-noir* population. Yet, in a complicated mixing of analogies, Quebec's francophones also served as a metaphor for the French themselves as they faced down the United States's bid for imperial hegemony; English Canada in this case served as the proxy for the American overlord. The convergence of these analogies – Quebec as Algeria, Quebec as France – was not surprising given the conflation of France and Algeria in the French nationalist imaginary, and they added up to a compelling rationale for intervention.

Indeed, beyond serving as an inspirational example for Quebec *indépendantistes,* Algeria and the other anti-colonial movements had significant implications in the Canadian context. According to Matthew Connelly, events in Algeria and throughout the decolonizing world constituted a "diplomatic revolution" that encouraged a breaking down of the barrier between the ostensibly separate domestic and international spheres. The dynamic, notably the ascendancy of self-determination as an international norm, promoted foreign interest and involvement in what international law had, to that point, deemed strictly internal affairs.[26]

If Quebec to French eyes was Algeria, then Canada was the Fourth Republic: an inherently flawed regime best discarded in favour of a new entity able to respond to political realities. The decolonization analogy pointed to an important difference between the political cultures of France and Canada – Quebec included. Tony Judt has emphasized the centrality in French political culture of the memory of not just the 1789 Revolution, but any revolution (even a "quiet" one). "Revolution," in this sense, is "the only possible route from the past to the future."[27] Since 1791, France had produced sixteen constitutions, contributing to and revelatory of a political culture welcoming efforts to remake, rebuild, and refound in the name of *liberté* and *égalité*.[28] This Cartesian approach to regime change, rooted in France's revolutionary past, contrasted with Canada's more pragmatic and incrementalist constitutional tradition, one in which Quebec was a participant.[29]

Preoccupations in Paris that the budding special relationship with Quebec City should not come at the expense of Franco-Canadian relations were increasingly overshadowed by the consensus emerging in French circles that developments in Quebec necessitated fundamental and comprehensive changes to Canada's constitutional order.[30] The 1962 federal election results confirmed a French sense of Canadian *immobilisme* recalling the worst days of political gridlock under the Fourth Republic. Bousquet described the Progressive Conservatives' minority win as leaving Canada politically weaker, with a government in Ottawa that had lost the confidence of Canadians at a moment that demanded imaginative and dynamic leadership. Reporting on his sense of being witness to the "end of a reign," Bousquet welcomed the prospect as being in the interest of Canadians, who faced a choice between achieving a productive coexistence or the independence of the "colonie anglo-saxonne" that was Quebec.[31]

French hopes shifted to Opposition leader Lester Pearson and his Liberals to accomplish the fundamental changes required. Pearson's calls in Parliament in December 1962 for a "national cultural, economic and political co-sovereignty" between English and French Canadians fuelled expectations that he was the man for the moment.[32] The subsequent Liberal victory was welcomed in French circles, with the MAE considering that the strong Quebec contingent on the government benches – including a record number of francophones in the Cabinet, was the best-case scenario for achieving francophone equality.[33]

Notwithstanding the high French hopes, the Pearson government had to contend with increasing neo-nationalist assertiveness and, accompanying this, a deepening French belief that Quebec was destined to achieve a new (if as yet unclear) political status. Malraux told the French Cabinet that the enthusiasm with which he had been received in 1963 was not entirely natural and that pro-autonomy sentiment was much stronger than Paris had thought, suffusing Quebec's political life and widespread among the general population.[34] René Lévesque's condemnation of the constitutional status quo and raising the possibility of separation drew French attention, as did a conversation that Bousquet had with Montreal mayor Jean Drapeau, who derided Pearson's "cooperative federalism" and claimed that the real choice was between independence and, as Drapeau claimed to prefer, a binational confederation.[35]

Although Pearson offered assurances during his 1964 visit to Paris that Canada would remain united in a manner reflecting the country's bicultural reality, he left France's leadership with the impression he was not fully conscious of the implications of the Quiet Revolution, thus contributing to an erosion of faith.[36] French hopes for the Pearson government's prospects declined amid the deepening tension between Ottawa and Quebec City over the federal spending power and national social programs, and as a series of scandals linked to the federal Liberal Quebec caucus undermined government fortunes in the province. The pitched battles in Quebec City streets at the time of the Queen's 1964 visit and the bitter debate over Canada's new flag reinforced French doubts about Ottawa's capacity to respond. Paris believed that Pearson had reached the limits of the concessions that he could offer at the very moment when Quebec realities made it impossible for the Lesage government to curtail its demands.[37]

The release in February 1965 of the first volume of the report of the Royal Commission on Bilingualism and Biculturalism, which warned that Canada was traversing "the worst crisis in its history," confirmed the French view that a fundamental change to the Canadian political order was on the horizon.[38] Pearson subsequently told France's new ambassador to Ottawa, François Leduc, that he wanted an "Austro-Hungarian solution" for Canada – though he qualified this as being short of two independent states.[39] The failure of the proposed Fulton-Favreau constitutional amending formula, meant to facilitate the patriation of Canada's constitution, and the subsequent Liberal failure to win a majority in the 1965 federal election was interpreted in French circles as a repudiation of Pearson's attempts at conciliation, prompting de Gaulle to observe to Canada's ambassador, Jules Léger, "You are at a difficult moment ... You are two entities, perhaps two states, one French-speaking, and the other English-speaking."[40]

De Gaulle's comment demonstrates how the belief in the logic and necessity of a new political status for Quebec reached the highest levels of the French administration. Despite declaring publicly to Pearson in Paris that France had "no intention" of involving itself in Canadian affairs, de Gaulle had, during preparations for this visit, predicted, "French Canada will inevitably become a state, and it is in this perspective that we must act."[41] He suggested to Lesage later that year that he saw Quebec as ultimately achieving some form of independence, and he subsequently repeated this opinion to Quebec ministers Paul Gérin-Lajoie and Pierre Laporte. Indeed, de Gaulle's son Philippe has recalled his father being greatly affected after reading Daniel Johnson's *Égalité ou indépendance* and asking himself what assistance he could provide to Quebec.[42]

Jean Lesage was a casualty of the evolving French attitudes. The Quebec premier was increasingly viewed in French circles as *dépassé*, especially after he assured de Gaulle that there was "no question" of Quebec independence, explaining that separation would harm the population's standard of living and that the province's best option was to develop within a diverse Canada.[43] Leduc came away from his first visit to Quebec City as ambassador commenting that a number of Lesage's collaborators appeared freer of the past and better able to envision the future through the prism of Quebec than of Canada.[44]

Following the Lesage government's defeat in 1966, Leduc quickly reassured Paris that the Union Nationale's return would not be accompanied by that of Duplessiste passivity, citing as proof the remarks made by the new premier, Daniel Johnson, to the Société Richelieu, in which he asserted Quebec's need to exercise its right to self-determination to ensure French-Canadian freedom. Leduc declared that the task of affirming Quebec would continue, even if the new government were less dynamic. He also predicted that the Johnson government's profound mistrust of federal authorities made inevitable a further deterioration of relations between Quebec City and Ottawa.[45]

Paris's interest in Quebec was thus correlated to the Johnson government's assertiveness. De Gaulle told Johnson that the growing France-Quebec cooperation was only a beginning given the "brilliant future unfolding in Quebec."[46] He told Jean Chapdelaine, Quebec's representative in Paris, that France could be counted on to do everything it could to assist, but that assistance would be much easier to accomplish once Quebec achieved a new constitutional arrangement with Canada.[47] Johnson visited Paris a few months after this exchange. A conservative, pragmatic nationalist who had embraced the Quiet Revolution's key aims, he considered French assistance invaluable to maximizing Quebec's autonomy within Canada. Explaining to de Gaulle the importance that he attached to de Gaulle's Quebec visit as his government sought a new constitutional settlement with Ottawa, the premier allegedly implored, "General, Quebec needs you. It's now or never."[48]

Johnson's appeal coincided with a similar plea for French assistance in Gérard Bergeron's *Le Canada-Français après deux siècles de patience*. This work, which de Gaulle is alleged to have read en route to Quebec, predicted that independence could be expected within fifteen years.[49] Jean-Daniel Jurgensen, a confirmed Gaullist and a senior Quebec lobby member in his capacity as head of the MAE's Amérique division, claimed that French Canada was at a turning point in its history, a view that Leduc echoed in late June 1967, when he declared that a certain moment of truth was at hand, since the only viable political option left was Johnson's demand for a comprehensive negotiation of a new constitution – to be conducted bilaterally between Quebec City and Ottawa.[50] Emphasizing that the increasingly rancorous debate over Quebec's destiny was a source of conflict as much among Quebecers as between the province and the rest of Canada, Leduc characterized it as consistent with broader international trends: the shrinking of the globe and acceleration of ideas had provoked concerns about French Canada's survival, leading its elite to strive for recognition of their nation's right to organize itself and be treated as an equal.[51]

THIS WAS THE BACKGROUND against which de Gaulle's 1967 visit to Canada – or, more accurately, to Quebec – must be understood. The trip was conceived in French circles as providing a boost to the cause of Quebec self-determination. More than a year before the visit took place, Jurgensen characterized it as absolutely crucial for French Canada's future.[52] As planning began, de Gaulle was adamant that the trip be limited to Quebec. Although Ottawa was subsequently included on the itinerary, an Élysée document confirms that the French leader understood his visit as being to "Canada français," responding to the invitation of its leader, Daniel Johnson; the Ottawa portion was to have only a "symbolic character."[53] Far from improvised, the trip was planned meticulously. Bernard

Dorin, a Quebec lobby member involved in the preparations, has recalled the awareness and understanding in Paris that it was meant to assist Quebec nationalism.[54] Dorin's claim is substantiated by the warning that Canada's ambassador to Washington, A.E. Ritchie, received from the American secretary of state, Dean Rusk, on the eve of the French president's arrival. Rusk's sources in Paris claimed that "nothing de Gaulle is likely to do or say in Canada will bother Washington, but it may worry Ottawa."[55]

Indeed, the corollary of Paris's emphasis on Quebec was an implicit – and increasingly explicit – rejection of the Canadian status quo. When Ottawa requested a congratulatory message from de Gaulle that could be broadcast at the outset of Canada's centennial year, the MAE's Amérique division recommended that the content be carefully weighted to ensure that it maintained a strict neutrality regarding the *British North America Act*. But even this was too much for de Gaulle, who retorted that France had no reason to celebrate the incorporation of "a part of the French people" into a British political entity that sprang from a French defeat and had become very "precarious."[56] It was only through Jules Léger's persistence that the MAE agreed to a reference to Confederation's anniversary in the official announcement of the visit; even at this, the reference was made in connection with the organization of Expo '67, rather than being cited as a reason for the French leader's trip.[57] Material prepared for de Gaulle in advance of his visit explained that Quebec rejected, in principle, Canada's constitution because it did not accord the province special status and had not created the conditions that Canada's French-speaking population required; virtually the entire federal organization was in the hands of the "Britanniques," and French Canadians were second-class citizens in fact if not in law. He was also told of the "dilatory manner" in which Ottawa was approaching the question of constitutional reform, in contrast to the more assertive approach of Quebec City, which was actively seeking a confrontation.[58]

By the mid-1960s, federal authorities were increasingly concerned about French interest in Quebec's political status and what this portended for Canadian unity. The remarks of Quebec lobby member Xavier Deniau in support of Quebec independence gave pause, especially given his position as rapporteur of the French National Assembly's foreign affairs committee and his apparent links to the Élysée.[59] Marcel Cadieux, the under-secretary of state for external affairs, was especially concerned over the dynamic between France and Quebec. He harboured an abiding mistrust of France, notably its Gaullist incarnation. Although he had never served abroad in an ambassadorial post, instead spending much of his career rising through the DEA's administrative ranks, he had witnessed the patronizing way that Paris treated the Walloons in Belgium after the war, and he came away from serving on the International Commission on

Supervision and Control in Indochina predisposed to view French actions with suspicion.[60] Cadieux was all the more sensitive to French interventions given his avowed opposition to Quebec nationalism. The son of a postman, born and raised in the northern Montreal suburb of Ahuntsic, Cadieux was an avowed advocate of the federal cause, a member of a generation of French Canadians that had opted for a career in Ottawa and made inroads in the anglophone-dominated capital. An expert in international law known for his firmness, frankness, and explosive temper, Cadieux had a heavy personal stake in the tensions; amid the challenge to the pan-Canadian vision of French Canada that he championed, he was well aware that as one of the most senior and influential French Canadians in Ottawa, he was unlikely to be welcome in an independent Quebec.[61]

Cadieux was particularly disturbed over an RCMP report suggesting that a well-known terrorist had visited Canada, and that in addition to linking up with Quebec extremists this person had met numerous times with Bousquet and his assistants.[62] The under-secretary was also very concerned by the account of a conversation that the Vaniers had had with France's minister of finance, Michel Debré, who visited Canada at the beginning of 1967. Georges Vanier spoke "frankly" to Debré, but the minister offered no response, except when Pauline Vanier emphasized the necessity of not forgetting the Canada existing outside of Quebec, to which Debré replied ominously that Paris was "aware of many things."[63] Indicative of the anxiety taking hold by early 1967 was the recommendation that the secretary of state for external affairs, Paul Martin, made a couple of weeks later regarding the need to be watchful of the "clandestine activities" of certain French nationals supportive of separatism. Pearson agreed to regular information exchanges with Brussels and Bern, which harboured similar concerns about French intentions regarding their own francophone communities.[64]

Amid the mounting tensions, Ottawa and its embassy in Paris were generally agreed that a non-confrontational, quiet diplomatic response was preferable, given the need to avoid public controversies that would have negative repercussions in Quebec and undermine Canadian unity. The approach was informed by a federal fixation on de Gaulle. Jules Léger argued that Ottawa should wait out France's ageing leader; in the interim, it should maintain a bland, positive approach at the senior governmental level while defending the federal cause at lower official levels. Léger was another member of the wartime generation of French Canadians who had taken the road less travelled to Ottawa. Throughout a brilliant diplomatic career, he had strived to correct what he described as the "blind spot" that Pearson and other senior DEA officials had regarding French Canada.[65] His more pragmatic, nonconfrontational approach was consistent with this background, and was informed by his ambassadorial role, the challenges of his mission, and the many years that he had spent in Paris, first as a doctoral student at the Sorbonne and later as Canada's ambassador to NATO. It was an approach to the triangular dynamic markedly less hard-line than that advocated by his colleague, rival, and friend, Marcel Cadieux.

In keeping with this de Gaulle-centric analysis, in early 1967, Paul Martin, whose prime ministerial ambitions encouraged him to court Quebec opinion and thus favour Léger's approach, ventured that if France's leader was not satisfied with the "pre-1960 vintage" of the Canadian federation, he probably did not *consciously* intend to weaken Canada. Martin confessed to worrying, however, that de Gaulle's attitude could be "misunderstood" in Quebec and exploited in France.[66] Indeed, Ottawa maintained the wishful belief that de Gaulle's actions were best explained by ignorance; Martin even suggested that Pearson write the French president because he did not "fully comprehend the Canadian situation."[67] Cadieux echoed this sentiment, expressing frustration over Ottawa's apparent inability to make de Gaulle understand the potential consequences of his actions, and he asked Léger if he could think of any French personality with sufficient influence to make the General see the error of his ways.[68]

Another factor contributing to Ottawa's quiet diplomacy was the confidence placed in Paul Martin's working relationship with his French counterpart, Maurice Couve de Murville. Léger claimed that France's foreign minister could be counted upon "rather completely," in that he behaved very correctly and liked Martin.[69] Cadieux, however, was sceptical of the value of Couve de Murville's friendship. And according to Jean Chapdelaine, whose belief that Martin and Cadieux were stifling his career progress had prompted him to leave the DEA, reports on the nature of the dialogue between the two foreign ministers were greatly exaggerated: his Quai d'Orsay contacts claimed that it consisted mainly of Martin "keeping his mouth open, as if swallowing flies, in reverential admiration as Monsieur Couve de Murville does the talking."[70] To be sure, Couve de Murville was, by virtue of his professional diplomatic sensibilities and his cautious nature, reluctant to endorse the most provocative aspects of Paris's Quebec policy, and thus worked to round off its sharper edges. However, his ability to influence events was somewhat circumscribed by the Élysée's primacy in foreign affairs and de Gaulle's personal interest in Quebec. More significantly, such an approach tended to underestimate the (growing) support that Quebec enjoyed at the Quai d'Orsay and in the broader French administration.[71]

Ottawa's last, best chance to affirm its position was Martin's June 1967 visit to Paris; however, this was lost when Martin opted for a cautious approach during his audience with de Gaulle. He explained subsequently that although he could have raised Ottawa's desire that the French leader's visit not be permitted to undermine Canadian unity, he had decided not to, given the cordiality of the meeting and the fact that the discussion focused mainly on international questions. The dynamic, according to Martin, was the same during talks with Couve de Murville. This outcome fuelled a general sense of resignation in the DEA that although de Gaulle might make inopportune remarks during his time in Canada, there was "nothing we can effectively do at this point to avoid it."[72] It also contributed to Marcel Cadieux's deepening contempt for Martin. Cadieux's strongly held views on the proper conduct of a diplomat and the running of the DEA collided with his minister's ambition. Their differing personalities and priorities made for a rocky relationship. As early as May 1964, Cadieux had criticized Martin for using the DEA as a vehicle for self-promotion; an increasingly scathing Cadieux used his private diary as an outlet for his intense irritation over what he viewed as his minister placing his leadership aspirations ahead of his duty to confront the Gaullist and Quebec nationalist challenges.[73]

De Gaulle's visit began propitiously enough, with the French leader declaring, upon his arrival in Quebec City, that there could never be anything but high esteem between France and Canada "as a whole."[74] Hard on the heels of the warm words, however, were hints of the dramatic events to follow. During a banquet hosted by Daniel Johnson, de Gaulle referred to Quebec's right to self-determination, claiming that it was only natural that its population should "become their own masters" and, with other Canadians, pursue efforts to forge a new political arrangement.[75]

The twin themes of self-determination and the need for fundamental change to the Canadian political order dominated de Gaulle's remarks the following day as he travelled to Montreal. Reflecting the differences in political culture between Canada and France and influenced by his country's constitutional history, to which he had added the latest chapter, de Gaulle told Johnson that Quebec participation in an upcoming constitutional reform conference would be a waste of time, since a deficient political regime could never be reformed from within. Throughout the day, Canada was not included in the list of *vivats* punctuating the end of his speeches, and his calls for Quebec self-determination grew more and more pronounced. This culminated in his *cri du balcon*, which, with its references to France's wartime liberation and lauding of the Quiet Revolution, was intended as a dramatic declaration of support for the Quebec cause.[76] In the ensuing controversy, de Gaulle affirmed his belief in the justness and necessity of his intervention. At the luncheon hosted by Jean Drapeau, he claimed that he had gotten to the "heart of things" regarding French Canada's realities, and expressed the hope that his visit had contributed to Quebec's élan.

On his way back to Paris, an enraptured de Gaulle declared, "I have saved them ten years!"[77]

Notwithstanding the thunderous cheer that greeted "Vive le Québec libre!" the reaction in Quebec to the French leader's actions was complicated, reflecting the fact that if there was a complementarity between Gaullist and Quebec nationalism, there were also differences. Gallic Cartesianism was faced with what Jocelyn Létourneau has described as the centrality of ambivalence in the francophone Quebec historical experience, a legacy of the "forced interdependence" that is Canada – one in which, for all of the challenges that its francophone population encountered, Quebec had participated and helped build.[78] The complexity of Quebecers' reactions was apparent: a poll taken shortly after de Gaulle's intervention revealed that 60 percent of respondents opposed it. Yet, just a few weeks later, another poll revealed that a majority now approved of the visit and de Gaulle's remarks in Montreal; however, these were interpreted not as a call to separate but as an invitation to "enhance the measure of freedom that Quebec already possesse[d] within Canada."[79]

The political class mirrored this complexity of opinion. Whereas *indépendantistes* such as Pierre Bourgault and Gilles Grégoire were jubilant over the boost to their cause, Jean Lesage, speaking on behalf of a divided Liberal caucus, rejected de Gaulle's intervention and blamed the Johnson government for the controversy. Daniel Johnson, for his part, had privately expressed misgivings even before the French leader's motorcade reached Montreal. De Gaulle, noting that the premier looked worried after the *cri du balcon*, asked him if he had embarrassed him in any way; Johnson replied bluntly, "Yes, you have just used a slogan which was exploited to good effect against me ... in the recent Quebec political campaign."[80] Following the General's departure, Johnson confided to friends that what had transpired was regrettable. Forced to manage a government divided increasingly between its moderate and nationalist wings, he sought to minimize the controversy while profiting from it. In an official statement, he condemned press attacks on de Gaulle, characterizing his remarks as courageous and lucid, and claimed that in calling for Quebec emancipation and self-determination France's leader had echoed the Quebec government position.[81]

News of the events in Montreal provoked a mixture of incredulity, bemusement, and opposition in France. The public and the press generally disapproved of de Gaulle's action.[82] There was support from the Gaullist left; a group of French politicians, the Groupe de 29, lauded the French leader's actions and claimed that it was only just that Quebec should obtain what Algeria and the other African states had obtained from the Fifth Republic.[83] The non-Gaullist Left, however, expressed disapproval. Leading socialists Gaston Deferre, François

Mitterrand, and Guy Mollet, each in his turn, condemned the interference in Canadian affairs.[84] De Gaulle also took hits from the non-Gaullist right; Valéry Giscard d'Estaing, for instance, condemned "the solitary exercise of power."[85] Doubts existed even among de Gaulle's colleagues, including members of the Cabinet. Ministers summoned to Orly airport to greet their returning president groused openly as they waited, and Edgar Faure, the minister of agriculture, marked his disapproval by refusing to go.[86]

There certainly were misgivings at the Quai d'Orsay. Couve de Murville confided to Alain Peyrefitte that de Gaulle's actions in Montreal had been wrong and that he needed to realize that the Quebec independence that he was trying to provoke would end in disaster. But the foreign minister's disapproval was not absolute; in discussing the visit with an unnamed Cabinet colleague, he excused de Gaulle, saying, "If you had been swept up as I was in that wave of enthusiasm, you would understand better. It was unimaginable, that Chemin du roy, unimaginable."[87]

A notable dissenter was France's ambassador, François Leduc, who was in the impossible position of trying to keep Ottawa content while carrying out Paris's instructions. Although Leduc believed that a reordering of the Canadian state was essential in order to enhance Quebec's political status, he disagreed with de Gaulle's intervention. As a result of questioning the logic of supporting independence and his calls for improved relations with Ottawa, the embattled ambassador fell into disfavour with the Élysée. His end-of-mission report praised de Gaulle for drawing attention to Quebec and the new special relationship but bemoaned the damage done to Franco-Canadian relations.[88] The assessment reflected a view that was widespread among France's political class outside the core of de Gaulle's supporters and the Quebec lobby: even if de Gaulle's actions in Montreal were opposed as an unwarranted, ill-advised provocation, there was general agreement on not just the need but the inevitability of change to Canada's political order to accommodate Quebec's demands.[89]

As for the federal reaction, de Gaulle was provoking concern in Ottawa even before he arrived in Montreal. Although Paul Martin politely rose and applauded at the Quebec City banquet, he was alarmed over the French leader's comments that effectively endorsed the Johnson government's constitutional position. Consistent with the quiet diplomatic approach that he and Ottawa had been pursuing, however, Martin recommended against creating a public issue and making de Gaulle a martyr to the Quebec nationalist cause; instead, the French leader's remarks could be discussed in private when he reached Ottawa. Martin rationalized that de Gaulle had not specifically pronounced on *what* the result of Quebec self-determination should be, and he had even referred to Quebecers finding a solution with other Canadians.[90]

The loud roar of approval that rose from Montreal's Place Jacques-Cartier following the *cri du balcon* served as a dramatic announcement that Ottawa's quiet diplomacy had failed. Silence was no longer a viable option, especially given the backlash that could be expected from English Canada. Initially in a hope-induced state of denial, Martin quickly contacted Lester Pearson, who was particularly offended over de Gaulle's comparing the atmosphere in Quebec to France's Liberation. Léger, in keeping with the federal fixation on de Gaulle, mindful of his diplomatic mission, and consistent with his more indulgent approach to the triangular dynamic, counselled a prudent response that took into account the broader Franco-Canadian relationship, a position that Martin shared in advocating as conciliatory a reply as possible. By contrast, Cadieux and Gordon Robertson, clerk of the Privy Council, believed that it was no longer possible for de Gaulle to visit Ottawa and should be told to leave.[91] This more hard-line stance was echoed during an emergency Cabinet meeting, notably by Pierre Trudeau and Jean Chrétien, who prevailed on Pearson to make clear that the French leader's behaviour was "unacceptable." After a lengthy debate, it was agreed to include this term in the official government response, along with a categorical rejection of the Liberation metaphor.[92]

The French response to Pearson's public statement was swift: de Gaulle cut short his trip and returned home, notwithstanding a last-ditch federal bid to see the Ottawa portion of the visit realized. Paris released an official communiqué that included Quebec in the French revolutionary tradition, claiming that the "Canadian French" held a unanimous conviction that Canada's constitution had failed to assure them liberty, equality, and fraternity in their own country. De Gaulle, it was explained, had sensed their will for self-determination, prompting him to offer assurances that they could count on France's support. The General explained his actions further in a televised address three weeks later, declaring that it was France's vocation to support the right to self-determination of all peoples as the basis for international harmony.[93]

Subsequent French actions were guided by a conviction that Quebec was on the threshold of some form of independence, reflected in de Gaulle's claim to Johnson that with Quebec having been brought to world attention so dramatically, it was clear that "solutions" were necessary that would lead to Quebec's self-determination "in every respect."[94] The French leader used his November press conference to condemn Canada's federal system as a threat to French Canada's survival. Arguing that it was essential to resolve the question of Quebec's future, he predicted that this would entail independence in an associative partnership with a truncated Canada.[95] In a subsequent conversation between Jules Léger and André Bettencourt, the French secretary of state responsible for cooperation with Quebec, constantly employed the "Quebec as colony" analogy. Bettencourt argued that if France, with all the means at its disposal, had been unable to maintain its grip on an Algeria whose population demanded independence, it was only logical to conclude Ottawa would be unable to stop Quebec.[96]

Gaullist analyses of the situation initially appeared to be confirmed by Paris's Quebec interlocutors. Chapdelaine emphasized to de Gaulle the impact of his visit, claiming that public opinion now generally accepted that Quebec should, at a minimum, be accorded special constitutional status. Quebec's minister of cultural affairs, Jean-Noël Tremblay, told Jean-Daniel Jurgensen that he and other senior Quebec personalities believed that complete independence, followed by the establishment of a common market with Canada, was inevitable in a few years.[97]

But the broader reality was a growing disconnect between Paris and Quebec City. There was discomfort in the Quebec capital over the accelerating pace of events and the French interventions. When Alain Peyrefitte visited in September 1967 as de Gaulle's envoy, Johnson revealed a sense of being overwhelmed. He warned Peyrefitte that things were going too fast and that disaster would result if Quebec moved as quickly and forcefully as France's president desired. The premier made clear that what he wanted was a strong Quebec in a united Canada, with increased autonomy as a means to *avoid* independence.[98] Worried that matters were escaping his control and threatening his goal of fundamental constitutional reform, Johnson temporized, a response that warnings from Quebec's business community encouraged. As early as October 1967, the MAE noted that he was moderating his public remarks. When word of de Gaulle's November press conference arrived during the Confederation for Tomorrow constitutional talks in Toronto, Johnson's close adviser Marcel Faribault characterized it a deliberate attempt to torpedo the negotiations and urged him to disavow the French leader. However, facing threats of ministerial resignations if he did so, Johnson kept silent.[99]

From Paris, Chapdelaine grumbled that although the MAE was making an effort to avoid further confrontations, de Gaulle considered Quebec sovereignty inevitable and was thus unfazed by adverse federal reactions. Chapdelaine urged Johnson to raise the issue personally, as, notwithstanding de Gaulle's stature, it was unhealthy to have an external authority pronounce repeatedly on Quebec's future.[100] Claude Morin, the enigmatic Quebec deputy minister of intergovernmental affairs, echoed such concern, telling Chapdelaine that although he was certain that French assistance would be "extremely useful" in pursuing Quebec's interests over the long term, he was worried about the potential short-term consequences.[101]

Reticence in Quebec City about French actions was paralleled by consternation and frustration in Ottawa over its apparent ineffectiveness in responding to the Gaullist and Quebec nationalist challenges. Federal options in the months after de Gaulle's visit remained circumscribed by the same factors that had determined its reaction prior to July 1967: Ottawa had to strike a careful balance between responding to French interventions and avoiding bringing de Gaulle's prophecies to fruition. This challenge was all the greater following the *cri du balcon,* as federal authorities were seeking the time necessary to permit the emergence of a pragmatic, evolutionary solution to Canada's unity problems. Such an approach, however, was unacceptable to the increasingly impatient de Gaulle.

Allan Gotlieb, head of the DEA's legal division, acknowledged the scope of Ottawa's vulnerability and warned that it would have little recourse if Paris moved to recognize Quebec as an independent state. A report that he wrote even alluded to discreetly sounding out Washington over the possible applicability of the Monroe Doctrine, the nineteenth-century statement of American foreign policy warning against European interference in the Western hemisphere.[102] Marcel Cadieux recognized that there was little hope of Ottawa influencing the Élysée, but, reflecting his desire for a more assertive response, hoped to bring pressure to bear on Paris. He ruminated about opening a consulate in Strasbourg with a view to exploiting what he believed was growing Alsatian nationalism, and he wished to pursue the same strategy through new missions in Guadeloupe and Martinique. Cadieux was able to secure Pearson's approval to request access to American intelligence as a means to combat French initiatives, and the prime minister even expressed a willingness to explore electronic eavesdropping on France's embassy.[103]

It was no surprise, given events, that Ottawa remained fixated on the figure of de Gaulle. A DEA analysis concluded that the French leader was "solely responsible" for the tenor of his visit. Jules Léger confirmed this view – and reiterated his preference for a more dovish policy – in subsequently reporting that French ministers and officials were simply carrying out Élysée orders. Such analysis informed the continuation of the pragmatic, quiet diplomatic approach; Ottawa believed that a "business as usual" policy was the only reasonable short-term response. It was recognized, however, that such a policy was practicable only so long as Ottawa could count on the discreet good will of French figures, not least Couve de Murville.[104] In late September, Martin had his first opportunity to discuss recent events with his French equivalent, and he conveyed federal concern and dissatisfaction in a "good, frank talk." To Martin's relief, Couve de Murville expressed a desire "to remain friends." He also gave assurances that

Ottawa had nothing to worry about, characterizing "Québec libre" as a call for cultural autonomy rather than political separation. Martin challenged this interpretation given subsequent French declarations, not least the Couve de Murville's own claim that "the Canadian problem is a French national question."[105]

De Gaulle's prediction of Quebec independence during his press conference two months later underscored Ottawa's difficulties. Whereas Pearson believed that the French leader's comments dispelled any lingering doubts about his attitude, the Paris embassy urged a response guided by an understanding that Canadian interests were best served through maintaining relations with Paris, which made it crucial to distinguish between the Élysée and France.[106] The view in the DEA was similar. Although Cadieux railed that de Gaulle was "not content to prophesy" and was trying to "speed up the process of Canada's disintegration," he emphasized that the critical front was in Quebec, not France. He warned against giving in to the temptation of a violent reaction that would force Johnson to indulge more radical elements.[107] A Cabinet debate resulted in the position that de Gaulle was acting on his own with little domestic support, and Pearson made a firm statement in Parliament in which he disputed de Gaulle's analysis of Canada's history and political situation. He described this latest intervention as an "intolerable" attempt to undermine Canada's unity, and, declaring that Canadians would decide their country's future, appealed to them to be restrained in their reactions to avoid playing into the hands of those seeking to divide them.[108]

In the wake of the latest controversy, Martin acknowledged the desire to react forcefully, but, consistent with his desire for appeasement (and with an eye on the imminent Liberal leadership campaign), he counselled maintaining the "business as usual" policy. He argued that to contain de Gaulle and buy the constitutional reform process crucial time, Ottawa should make every effort to engage moderate Quebec opinion, including reaching an understanding, even on an interim basis, that would involve a federal shift toward the Quebec constitutional position. Martin's rationale was that even if Johnson did not cooperate, Ottawa would at least have a greater awareness of his intentions and could plan more serious measures. Pearson generally agreed with Martin's assessment, but insisted on the need to take diplomatic notice of de Gaulle's latest pronouncement and voiced doubts about the viability of the business-as-usual approach. Giving vent to his frustration, Pearson complained that Johnson would "try to ignore and avoid the necessity for *any* choice" between Ottawa and Paris.[109]

Growing Canadian fears over Quebec separation and French actions fanned Canadian nationalist flames and helped to pave Pierre Trudeau's road to power. A few months after succeeding Pearson, Trudeau had occasion to question

French policy when Couve de Murville, by this time prime minister, visited Quebec City to attend the funeral of Daniel Johnson. Trudeau challenged the logic of Paris's actions, characterizing them as interference in Canada's affairs that, taken to their logical conclusion, entailed French support for Quebec separatism. Couve de Murville disputed the suggestion and claimed that independence would lead ultimately to the assimilation of Quebec francophones. Reflecting afterward on the exchange, Trudeau expressed doubt about his French counterpart's truthfulness and ruminated that Paris seemed unable – or unwilling – to acknowledge the contradictions and consequences of its policy.[110]

Indeed, notwithstanding federal protests, Couve de Murville's assurances, and the reticence in certain Quebec circles, Paris continued to believe that it was only a matter of time before the province achieved sovereignty. French officials accordingly tailored their behaviour to serve this end, favouring those elements in Quebec that could bring it to fruition. As the Gaullist worldview collided with Quebec realities, de Gaulle was increasingly disillusioned with Daniel Johnson. In the weeks following his Quebec visit, the French leader expressed profound disappointment over Johnson's failure to seize the opportunity to make history that his intervention had created. According to Peyrefitte, de Gaulle's November press conference remarks were designed partly to push the premier to follow the course of action that he believed was inevitable. De Gaulle was eventually moved to regret that Johnson was apparently a politician lacking courage, rather than a true statesman.[111]

Paris and its representatives cast an even more doubtful eye over Johnson's successor, Jean-Jacques Bertrand, whom they saw as too conciliatory to Ottawa. The French embassy predicted, however, that Bertrand's timidity would propel more nationalist elements in the Union Nationale or the Opposition to power, thereby returning Quebec to the path to sovereignty. When Bertrand cancelled a visit to France in late 1968, MAE officials breathed a sigh of relief, believing that Paris had no interest in increasing his stature. News that the premier was instead sending Jean-Guy Cardinal, the minister of education and an avowed nationalist, was welcomed at the Quai d'Orsay as a serendipitous opportunity to cultivate relations with a more determined champion of Quebec.[112]

Paris's faith in the inevitability of Quebec independence was reinforced by changes on the province's political landscape. The founding of the Mouvement Souveraineté-Association and its successor, the Parti Québécois (PQ), was interpreted in French circles as indicative of future developments. Jean-Marie Domenach was moved to endorse Quebec independence in the pages of *Esprit*,[113] and French diplomats considered the PQ's emergence to be consistent with the acceleration of Quebec political life. Paris's representatives noted that voters now possessed a choice between federalism and independence and that the latter was growing in popularity; indeed, unnamed Union Nationale and Liberal sources confided that the political situation in Quebec was evolving toward independence. France's new consul general in Quebec City, Pierre de Menthon, speculating that the PQ could hold the balance of power after the upcoming Quebec election, predicted that a moment of decision was at hand: the growing desire for autonomy was irreversible and suggestive of the path that Quebecers would take.[114]

De Menthon's appraisal of the PQ's electoral chances proved overly optimistic, as it only won seven seats in the 1970 election; however, the party did attract nearly a quarter of the popular vote. Leduc's successor as French ambassador to Canada, Pierre Siraud, opined that in spite of the Quebec Liberals' victory under their new leader, Robert Bourassa, Quebecers still faced the ultimate question of whether their future was to be found in Canada or in some form of independence, and that the need to resolve the question was increasingly apparent to a growing number of them. In a similar vein, back in Paris, Jean-Daniel Jurgensen, promoted to assistant director of political affairs at the MAE, warned a Canadian embassy official against entertaining any illusion that the election results had solved Canada's difficulties.[115]

To the contrary, Jurgensen, a leading Quebec lobby member, appeared determined to ensure this was not the case. After the election, he made an unsolicited offer to the PQ's treasurer, telling him that France was prepared to provide the party with substantial financial assistance. Here was another example of the disconnect between Gaullism and Quebec nationalism, for the offer provoked a strongly negative reaction from PQ leader René Lévesque. Mindful of how it would appear if news of it leaked out, Lévesque keenly resented the compromising position in which his party had been placed, especially as it had just established itself as a viable political force. It was made crystal clear to Jurgensen that his offer could not be accepted.[116]

Jurgensen's suggestion notwithstanding, Paris was in fact evolving toward a more wait-and-see position. By early 1969, although de Gaulle remained persuaded that Quebec's accession to sovereignty would occur eventually, he no longer believed that it would be as rapid as he had hoped or intended.[117] At the end of the year that saw the General leave office, France's foreign minister, Maurice Schumann, argued that Paris was well advised to adopt a lower profile amid Canada's deepening unity crisis; such an approach would ensure that no one could blame France for the difficulties arising from the constitutional negotiations underway, including provincial complaints that the Trudeau government's intransigence was stoking Quebec separatism. The Élysée's new occupant,

Georges Pompidou, agreed with Schumann's analysis and characterized a French embassy report on the constitutional talks as proof of the need for Paris to stand firm in maintaining its Quebec policy.[118] The assessment was consistent with the French lack of faith in the pragmatic, evolutionary response to Canada's constitutional conundrum.

The wisdom of this shift in approach appeared to be confirmed when unnamed officials in Quebec's ministry of intergovernmental affairs informed Paris in the early autumn of 1970 that Ottawa was rapidly exhausting the Bourassa government's goodwill and, with this, federalism's last best chance. An MAE analysis reflected French bewilderment over developments by citing the fact that although at least a third of Quebec francophones were pro-independence and fervent PQ supporters, Quebec's hesitation made the future difficult to predict. In counselling circumspection, the report also reflected MAE misgivings over the more provocative aspects of the Quebec policy that Paris had been pursuing.[119]

Indeed, the evolution of events after July 1967 had revealed that de Gaulle had erred in his reading of Quebec. To be sure, he had done much to embroider himself into the tapestry of the nationalist narrative – that is, that Quebec's "natural" destiny was some form of independence – and so was a hero to those subscribing to this narrative. But he could never bring himself to accept the ambivalence of the Quebec condition. To the contrary, he saw this as flying in the face of the logic of history. The answer that Gaullism gave to Quebec's *question nationale* was one that Quebec was not – at least not yet – prepared to accept. Moreover, although the *cri du balcon* boosted the cause of Quebec self-determination and those favouring independence, viewed from another angle, de Gaulle's interventions – with their implicit rejection of the gradualist dimension of Quebec political culture – may reasonably be construed as a setback for Quebec. In provoking a crisis in the triangle, de Gaulle fanned Canadian nationalist flames, thereby contributing to Pierre Trudeau's election and bringing an end to the more conciliatory approach of the Pearson era that had been leading to growing Quebec autonomy.[120]

Yet, de Gaulle's actions had had an impact on French policy, reflecting the broader shift of French perceptions of Quebec and Canada and their linked political future. Much more than a sentimental gesture thought up on the spur of the moment, de Gaulle's intervention was also informed by ethnocultural considerations and, as we shall see, Gaullist geopolitical calculations. The result was a dualistic, two-nation approach predicated on the belief that it was a question of not *if* but *when* Quebec would achieve a new political status. The most provocative aspects of Paris's Quebec policy faded as it became apparent that they were not going to produce the desired result as rapidly as had been hoped. By the start of the 1970s, they were giving way to an approach more consistent with the MAE's preference for caution, but one that ensured that as Quebec debated its destiny, it could continue to count on Paris's support. In the words of one MAE official, France had provided Quebec with a number of unanticipated political trump cards; it was now up to Quebecers to play them.[121]

CHAPTER SIX

Atlanticism in Conflict: The Geopolitical Impetus

As Canada's centennial year dawned, Lester Pearson was finding his celebrated diplomatic skills taxed severely. At home, the growing ranks of *indépendantistes* in Quebec testified to the difficulty that he was having in maintaining national unity. Abroad, Paris's withdrawal from NATO's integrated military command had been a "major setback" for Canadian diplomacy.[1] The situation was all the more vexing since what at first blush appeared to be two disparate challenges – one domestic, the other international – were in fact mutually reinforcing. If Atlanticism had been an effective means to realize Canadian domestic and international priorities in the post-1945 world, this appeared no longer to be the case by the 1960s. Indeed, the triangular tensions are impossible to understand without situating them in their geopolitical context. With heightened nationalist sensitivity on both sides of the Atlantic, notions of ethnocultural solidarity and the debate over Quebec's future intersected with global events, so that the complex triangular dynamic became bound up in the acrimony between Paris and Washington. The Franco-Canadian divergence over Atlanticism, already apparent by the late 1950s, had a corrosive effect on the bilateral relationship at the very moment that Ottawa was most anxious to strengthen links with Paris.

The Gaullist challenge to Atlanticism was predicated on a belief that NATO had evolved from a necessary deterrent against Moscow into a vehicle for American hegemony in the West. Ottawa's view was that the alliance, although flawed, remained the most effective means available to counterbalance the United States and influence Washington; Paris's efforts to establish a strategic partnership between the United States and a French-led Western Europe sparked Canadian fears that the resulting "two pillar" alliance – one pillar North American and the other European – was fundamentally at odds with Canadian Atlanticism, in that it would force Canada even further into the American orbit. Confronted with this prospect, Ottawa fell back on its self-appointed linchpin role, striving to reconcile Paris and Washington and preserve the Atlantic framework.

But whereas Ottawa's past efforts on behalf of Atlanticism had contributed positively to Franco-Canadian relations, the contradictions and shortcomings inherent in Canada's response to the Gaullist challenge fatally undermined such action in the 1960s. The general aim of Canadian diplomacy to strengthen relations with France was based on an erroneous presumption that bilateral links could be employed to minimize disruption of the Atlantic framework; conversely, it was believed that assisting Paris in the multilateral sphere would yield benefits in the bilateral domain. Equally problematic for the denizens of the DEA was the fundamental tension between the international and domestic motivations underpinning Canadian efforts to expand relations with Paris. At the same time as Ottawa was moved to mitigate the Gaullist challenge to Atlanticism, it was striving to respond to Quebec nationalist charges that Canada's foreign policy inadequately addressed the province's needs for relations with the francophone world. This domestic motivation was increasingly pronounced as the decade unfolded, and informed Ottawa's concern to ensure French neutrality in Canada's increasingly rancorous internal affairs.

Whatever the relative weight of external and domestic considerations, the Pearson government's efforts to develop relations with France and act as transatlantic linchpin were suspect to Gaullist eyes. The more that Paris challenged the Atlantic framework and was implicated in Canada's unity debate, the more Ottawa strove to forge links. Yet this only confirmed a French conviction that Canada had become the servant of American geopolitical interests and a satellite of the United States. As such, Ottawa's efforts on behalf of Atlanticism contributed to the deterioration of Franco-Canadian relations and encouraged Paris to pursue direct relations with Quebec. Indeed, the Gaullist intervention arose partly from a desire to hasten the emergence of a sovereign Quebec partnered with the rest of Canada in a new entity better able to resist American pressures and serve as a useful ally of France. Although one could argue (and it was argued) that this approach failed to recognize that a collapse of the Canadian federation would enhance the United States's geopolitical strength, to de Gaulle's eyes the status quo was already producing this result, and action was therefore justified.

BY THE EARLY 1960S, FOLLOWING the Anglo-American spurning of de Gaulle's directorate proposal, Paris and Washington were at loggerheads over the organization of the strategic leadership of the West. The lack of progress on the longstanding French aim of a meaningful tripartite arrangement with the United States and Britain had prompted France to withdraw its Mediterranean fleet from NATO command and refuse to integrate its domestic air defence squadrons with the alliance. Nor was de Gaulle satisfied with Washington's handling of the Berlin crisis, as he believed that the new president, John F. Kennedy, had been insufficiently forceful in assuring the security of Western Europe. The question of command and control of American nuclear weapons in France further poisoned relations; the Kennedy administration's "flexible response" strategy raised the spectre of nuclear weapons not being used in the event of a Soviet attack on Western Europe. All of this confirmed de Gaulle's belief that the Atlanticist status quo threatened French interests.[2]

The Franco-American discord was reflected in the rival "Grand Designs" for the transatlantic relationship. The Kennedy White House took up the Eisenhower administration's idea of "Atlantic Community"; disarray in the Western camp in the aftermath of Suez was to be ended by promoting European integration within a framework that safeguarded the United States's preponderant influence and avoided the emergence of an autonomous (and potentially rival) West European bloc. The clearest expression of American aims was Kennedy's "Declaration of Interdependence" speech in July 1962. Kennedy's geopolitical vision collided with Gaullist sensibilities. Viewed from Paris, the "Declaration of Interdependence" was simply another – if eloquent – extolling of the benefits of American hegemony. Gaullist antipathy was subsequently reinforced by the outcome of the Cuban missile crisis, which, combined with the Sino-Soviet split, convinced de Gaulle of the United States's strategic superiority and the passing of any genuine Soviet threat. France was thus able and encouraged to take a more assertive, autonomous position.[3]

The debate in NATO over the command and control of nuclear arms only reinforced the Gaullist challenge. The December 1962 Nassau agreement that gave Britain access to American Polaris missiles to modernize its nuclear force confirmed Paris's belief that the alliance was a vehicle for Anglo-American hegemony. Indeed, the agreement also included Washington's rejoinder to France's recently acquired *force de frappe:* the Multilateral Force (MLF), an integrated European nuclear force that was to come under the NATO umbrella, making it effectively American-controlled. Paris rejected this nuclearized version of the ill-starred European Defence Community, considering it a bid to reaffirm Anglo-Saxon unity and maintain American nuclear supremacy.[4]

Having publicly condemned the Atlantic Community as an unacceptable subordination to Washington, de Gaulle responded with his Europeanist Grand Design. Freed from the distraction of decolonization following Algerian independence, the Gaullist view was that the only rational response to the new geopolitical conjuncture was an independent, French-led Western Europe in strategic partnership with (and acting as a counterweight to) the United States. This was to be part of an ambitious re-organizing of the international order along multipolar lines; the Soviet Union would be similarly reduced to size as it was shorn of its Eastern European satellites, and China would join the ranks of the great powers. Gaullist ambitions were reflected in de Gaulle's cultivation of a Franco-German partnership – with Bonn in a decidedly junior position – that culminated in the Élysée friendship treaty of 1963, de Gaulle's riposte to Kennedy's "Declaration of Interdependence." The French leader also condemned London for betraying Europe by signing the Nassau agreement, and cited this as a primary reason for his vetoing British membership in the European Common Market (ECM).[5]

Washington moved swiftly to counter the Gaullist challenge. It succeeded in having Bonn include a preamble to the Élysée treaty that reaffirmed West German friendship with the United States, effectively stripping the treaty of its Europeanist raison d'être. Thwarted in the realization of his Grand Design but determined to challenge preponderant American power, de Gaulle looked elsewhere: Paris recognized the People's Republic of China, over Washington's objections, and moved to counter American influence in the Third World.

Gaullist eyes also turned to Canada, where nationalist reactions were increasingly pronounced. Amid the duelling Grand Designs, France's ambassador, Raymond Bousquet, reported that Canadians, torn between their European history and American geography, were posing difficult questions about Canada's identity and place in the transatlantic order.[6] The appearance of works such as James Minifie's *Peacemaker or Powder-Monkey*, a best-selling excoriation of the country's defence relationship with the United States and a panegyric to neutrality, reflected the heightened sensitivities. John Diefenbaker, conscious of the nationalist tide on which his government had sailed into office and conditioned by a series of cross-border disputes, was especially sensitive to the curdling public mood. Canadian foreign policy accordingly took on a more nationalist hue, a trend that the sour personal relationship between Diefenbaker and Kennedy encouraged. Britain's bid to join the ECM only added to Canadian frustration over what was an increasingly scalene North Atlantic triangle; the Macmillan government's decision threatened the Commonwealth link that Diefenbaker and his party considered vital to countering American influence. The result was strains upon Ottawa's otherwise slackening ties with London.[7]

There thus existed some common ground between Diefenbaker and de Gaulle. Although they differed over Atlanticism, both were seeking greater autonomy from the United States and opposed British membership in the ECM. There was even a certain Gaullist tinge to Diefenbaker's dismissal of Pearsonian "quiet diplomacy," with its pragmatic incrementalism and concern with keeping disputes out of the public eye, and his assertion that Canada's defence cooperation with the Americans should never entail subservience.[8] But although French officials noted Canada's deteriorating relationship with the United States in the early 1960s, Paris was most impressed by what it considered the inefficacy of the Canadian nationalist response as represented by the Diefenbaker government. A 1961 MAE report affirmed that Canada and the United States were more tightly linked than ever; two years later, French parliamentarians returned from a study mission warning that geography and Cold War dynamics were putting Canada in peril of being absorbed by its southern neighbour.[9]

Canada's tempestuous debate over American nuclear warheads was emblematic of the Franco-Canadian divergence over Atlanticism. The origins of the controversial episode lay in the Soviet acquisition of the hydrogen bomb and the launch of Sputnik, which forced a reassessment of NATO strategic doctrine, the stockpiling of tactical nuclear warheads for alliance forces, and the installation of medium-range missiles in Western Europe. As was the case in other NATO capitals, a primary concern in Ottawa was how to reconcile the stationing of American warheads with the preservation of national sovereignty. In the late 1950s, the Diefenbaker government sent signals suggesting that it would accept the warheads under some form of joint control system, including the announcement that Ottawa would acquire the American, nuclear-capable Bomarc missiles.[10]

Diefenbaker and de Gaulle discussed the issue during the latter's 1960 visit. The latter was unequivocal: even if there was a willingness to associate the United States in some manner with their control, France-based warheads and the circumstances of their use had to be under Paris's authority. De Gaulle's stance stood in stark contrast to the Diefenbaker government's apparent acceptance of the "double-key" system and illustrated the two capitals' perceptions of their respective geopolitical positions.[11] Canadian acceptance was founded on the belief that the proposed arrangement would prevent the United States from launching Canada-based weapons without (in theory) Ottawa's agreement. Under the circumstances, this seemed to Canada's foreign policy establishment to be a reasonable arrangement consistent with Canadian Atlanticism and aspirations to middle-power status. For Paris, however, the proposal was an unacceptable compromise of sovereignty that could lead to a situation in which Washington could effectively veto the use of its warheads in France.

The warhead issue became caught up in the heightened nationalist sentiment in Canada and an increasingly vocal disarmament movement that counted among its converts Howard Green, the secretary of state for external affairs, and his deputy, Norman Robertson. The Diefenbaker government vacillated and prevaricated on the question for four years, even as the Cuban missile crisis provided a terrifying demonstration of the need to resolve the growing irritant in its relations with Washington. Diefenbaker's subsequent failure to act on what appeared to have been a Canadian commitment to acquire warheads for the

Bomarcs provoked a cross-border crisis that culminated in the fall of his government in February 1963.[12]

The ensuing election campaign was a bitter contest fought largely over questions of Canada's relations with the United States. Tellingly for French doubts about the viability of Canadian nationalism and independence, it was the first vote in the country's history in which the side championing the anti-American position did not carry the day. Although troubled over the prospect of acquiring nuclear warheads, Pearson had effectively reversed the Liberal party's stance in the weeks preceding the campaign; he argued that the Diefenbaker government had undertaken a commitment to acquire the weapons and that a Liberal administration would honour this as a precursor to negotiating a "more effective and realistic [i.e., non-nuclear] role" for Canada.[13]

Canada's quasi-Gaullist reaction, embodied (if ineffectively) by Diefenbaker, appeared to be stillborn. In its place, the personality most closely identified with Canadian Atlanticism returned to power leading a government committed to improving relations with Washington and London. Although occasionally frustrated with the Americans and not immune to the growing nationalist and anti-nuclear sentiment, Pearson remained convinced that the foremost priority of Canadian foreign policy had to be managing relations with the United States.[14]

To this end, the transatlantic framework to which Pearson had devoted so much of his working life remained, in his view, the best available way for Canada to reconcile its national and international priorities. Admittedly, the grand post-war dream of an Atlantic community had gone unrealized; moreover, as time wore on doubts about the alliance would grow within the ranks of the Pearson government and even in the mind of the prime minister. This second-guessing also pointed to a broader ambivalence over links with a United States stuck in Vietnam and subject to increasing levels of international opprobrium, not least from Canada's nationalist communities. Notwithstanding such considerations, the culture of Canada's foreign policy establishment predisposed it to remain wedded to Atlanticism. Ottawa feared that the Gaullist challenge threatened not only the Western deterrent, but what remained of Canada's European counterweight and the means to make the Canadian voice heard on the world stage. Although the Pearson government would demonstrate considerable openness to reforming NATO, this did not extend to abandoning the liberal internationalist core of its Atlanticist foreign policy.[15]

The Pearson government was thus compelled to respond to the Gaullist challenge to Atlanticism. The fixation on Canada's alleged linchpin role was evident amid the establishing of a DEA taskforce and an interdepartmental committee, both mandated to examine and recommend measures to develop relations with France. Similarly, the secretary of state for external affairs, Paul Martin, declared it crucial to develop the relationship following a conversation with the American secretary of state Dean Rusk, who told him of the absence of substantive dialogue between Washington and Paris. Martin suggested to Rusk that Ottawa could assist, invoking what he claimed was Canada's special links to France. Following this encounter, Martin told Bousquet that Ottawa was considering how it could help reactivate the Franco-American dialogue and claimed repeatedly in conversations with other NATO foreign ministers that, by virtue of its bicultural heritage and historic ties to France, Canada was well positioned to improve the climate between France and the NATO allies.[16]

Ottawa's concern with developing relations with France so that it could act as a transatlantic linchpin was on display when Pearson visited Paris in 1964. De Gaulle explained to him that Washington had become used to a leadership role that was no longer appropriate given Europe's recovery, and that it would have to accept a true partnership more reflective of the transatlantic balance of power. Pearson responded by stressing the importance of the Atlanticist framework, and he urged French understanding of American global responsibilities. He also acknowledged the closeness of Canada's relations with Washington, citing this as the reason that Ottawa assigned such a high priority to strong transatlantic links; tensions between Europe and the United States forced Ottawa into the impossible position of having to choose between the two. A concern to prevent this was at the heart of Canada's support for an Atlantic community.[17]

Pearson's visit fuelled hope in Ottawa for a healthier bilateral relationship that would enable Canada to realize its international vocation and mitigate tensions in the alliance.[18] But this was wishful thinking. Ultimately, the circle could not be squared between the Canadian aim to help resolve the divisions plaguing NATO and Paris's determination to provoke fundamental change. What one nationalist reaction demanded, the other could not concede without renouncing itself. Thus, Ottawa attempted to use the December 1964 NATO ministerial meeting to launch a re-examination of the role and structures of the alliance. But both the initiative and a subsequent Canadian discussion paper on reform that was circulated met with little immediate success, owing to a lack of cooperation from alliance members – not least France.[19]

Even those points on which Ottawa and Paris could agree demonstrated their divergence over Atlanticism, as was the case regarding their common opposition to the American-backed MLF. Indeed, Martin provoked Washington's ire by supporting the French position, but whereas Paris opposed the concept because of its integrationist dimension, Ottawa had no difficulties with this so long as Canada had a say in nuclear decision making; rather, Canadian opposition stemmed from a belief that the proposal was unworkable and thus disruptive to an alliance already under serious strain. Additionally, the MLF ran counter to Ottawa's stance on nuclear proliferation, something not figuring into Gaullist calculations.[20]

In November 1964, senior DEA officials had a "free-wheeling exchange" about NATO with Bousquet. The French ambassador blamed American policy for wrecking the alliance and insisted that the British and Germans, in supporting the proposed MLF, were "placing themselves in the position of American satellites," something that Paris was unwilling to do. This drew a strong response from the Canadian diplomats, who argued that Ottawa "did not want to be in bed alone with the Americans" and pointed out that "in a large bed occupied by countries on both sides of the Atlantic no one country need dominate the others." Bousquet acknowledged that Paris preferred "an old fashioned '19th century' military alliance with North America, ready in case of war, but not involving any integration of foreign ... or defence policy ... still less an Atlantic Community." The Canadian diplomats expressed alarm over the implication that Canada was to be denied its European counterweight and left to its own devices with the United States. This, they warned, was at odds not only with Canadian Atlanticism, but with "the basic lines of Canadian policy for the past two centuries."[21]

In addition to the incompatibility of Canadian and Gaullist aims, Ottawa's bid to strengthen links with Paris was being undermined by the tensions between its international and domestic motivations. At the same time as the Pearson government was spurred to build up Franco-Canadian relations to realize its goals in the multilateral arena, domestic concerns were also pushing it to act. Ottawa's actions were encouraged by a concern – increasingly pronounced – to demonstrate to French Canada its commitment to a bicultural foreign policy. The Pearson government was also aware, amid the intensifying unity debate, of the need for French benevolence. If Ottawa's objectives regarding relations with France were thus far more complex than simply a bid to contain Quebec nationalism, the outline of a looming foreign policy failure was already discernible as the Pearson government took office; Ottawa's desire for stronger links with Paris – the product of a complicated calculus of international and domestic considerations – was occurring at the very moment when the two capitals' differences in the multilateral arena were driving them apart. As Canada's complicated wartime relationship with France had foreshadowed, Ottawa's difficulties would arise in large measure at the point at which these domestic and international considerations intersected.

The DEA's under-secretary, Norman Robertson, alluded to the tension inherent in the Canadian approach at the outset of Ottawa's review of Franco-Canadian relations in 1963. Mindful of the national unity implications, he expressed concern over the negative effect that could result from the view –

already widespread among the diplomatic corps in Ottawa – that Canada's primary motivation in strengthening links with France was to reconcile Paris and Washington. In his estimation, Ottawa would be better positioned for this task the less it was discussed. Accordingly, when he met with Couve de Murville in October 1963, Martin, reflecting the growing importance that Ottawa attached to relations with Paris for their own sake, emphasized the bilateral rather than multilateral dimension of the relationship. During their talks, Martin abjured a "helpful fixer" role for Canada, claiming that it was "not [Ottawa's] intention at all" to "play ... intermediary between France and the United States."[22] Such assurances, however, rang rather hollow coming from someone who in the preceding months had emphasized repeatedly that this *was* Canada's objective. Indeed, by the end of 1963 French officials were interpreting the Pearson government's overtures for expanded bilateral relations as being motivated by Atlanticist calculations.[23]

The French perception that Ottawa's interest in developing links stemmed primarily from a concern with maintaining the Atlantic framework was informed by Paris's sense of Canada's satellization. The success of Ottawa's efforts to strengthen the relationship depended upon its ability to convince Paris of its independence from the United States and Britain and its desire to alter fundamentally the Atlantic status quo. Yet this was at odds with Ottawa's overarching goal of preserving the transatlantic framework as the most realistic guarantor of Canadian independence. The Canadian position was summed up in a DEA memorandum arguing that as Ottawa sought strengthened relations with France, it "must not weaken" its ties with Washington and London.[24]

The French assessment of Canada's geopolitical situation surfaced during Pearson's Paris trip. France's prime minister, Georges Pompidou, told Pearson that rather than questions of unity, Canada's real challenge was maintaining its independence and distinctiveness from the United States. The Canadian embassy sensed a French "assumption" that Ottawa's policies were shaped primarily by its relations with Washington. Indeed, Pierre Trottier, the embassy's cultural counsellor, claimed subsequently that de Gaulle tested Pearson in Paris by dangling the prospect of French cooperation in exchange for undertaking to move Canada out of the American geopolitical orbit. When Pearson did not rise to the bait, he confirmed Gaullist analyses.[25]

In the years after Pearson's visit, amid multiplying indications of a dramatic French move regarding NATO, the Franco-Canadian divergence over Atlanticism was all too apparent to Canada's ambassador in Paris, Jules Léger, who questioned the wisdom of Ottawa's attempts to reconcile Paris to Atlanticism. He argued that there was scant prospect of Canada (or any other NATO ally) persuading France to adopt a less nationalist position. Emphasizing that de

Gaulle had dismissed the idea of a Canadian linchpin role, he ventured that it was more realistic for Canada to place less priority on Atlantic integration and seek a pragmatic solution to the divisions in NATO. He even proposed that Ottawa facilitate a modified version of de Gaulle's directorate proposal, noting that although this meant conceding on a core principle, it would serve the larger Canadian interest of salvaging what remained of the transatlantic alliance.[26] More fundamentally, Léger dared to question Canada's enduring Atlanticism, describing it as symptomatic of the DEA's tendency to situate Canada's development in the anglophone and North American world, something that put Ottawa immediately at odds with Gaullist priorities. The ambassador warned that so long as de Gaulle maintained an anti-American policy, Ottawa's efforts to foster a rapprochement with Paris would be frustrated.[27]

Léger's misgivings cast a stark light onto how the Franco-Canadian divergence over Atlanticism was rotting the bilateral relationship. Ottawa's approach was fundamentally flawed as it presumed, erroneously, that the French viewed (or wished) Canada as a linchpin. Moreover, Gaullist preoccupations conditioned Paris to view anything short of a challenge to the transatlantic framework as proof of satellization, making it all too ready to dismiss Ottawa's claims that Atlanticism constituted the most realistic response to Canada's geopolitical situation.

Ottawa's efforts to reconcile France to Atlanticism came to naught in March 1966, when de Gaulle announced that France was withdrawing from NATO's integrated military command and that allied forces would be asked to leave the Hexagon. Pearson was left in "despair and angry frustration" that France could be "so stupid and so shortsighted." The fact that France remained in the alliance was of cold comfort, since, in Pearson's view, NATO derived its value from the principle of collective organization.[28] Allowing his irritation to overcome his usual diplomatic demeanour, Pearson asked a senior French embassy official whether the Canadian forces moving to West Germany should take with them the hundred thousand dead Canadians that lay in French fields.[29]

Yet de Gaulle's announcement was the logical culmination of the divergence between the Canadian and French versions of Atlanticism since the founding of NATO and, more immediately, the differences between Gaullist and Pearsonian diplomacy. Canada, as a purported middle power, given its geopolitical realities and the historical experience conditioning the culture of its foreign policy establishment, continued to see the alliance, even with its admitted imperfections, as something to be preserved and reformed from within. Ottawa's prescription for curing the alliance's ills was a more profound integration. This was anathema to Gaullist France. A belief that national defence was the state's foremost raison d'être, the dogged pursuit of *grandeur* and national independence, and opposition to the Cold War order informed Paris's position that the Atlantic status quo and any form of military integration were unacceptable concessions of sovereignty that had to be challenged.

For want of any viable alternative, and mindful of the need for French benevolence amid Canada's deepening unity crisis, Ottawa's impulse for conciliation endured. Pearson wrote to de Gaulle explaining his determination to expand bilateral relations regardless of the two countries' differences over international issues. Paris's attention was also drawn to Pearson's remarks in the United States in June 1966, in which, although reaffirming the need to preserve the Atlanticist framework, he acknowledged Gaullist concerns and the need to recognize Europe's post-war recovery. Indeed, in the wake of the announced French withdrawal from NATO's integrated command, Pearson and Martin each expressed support for what amounted to a two-pillar approach to NATO; both men were willing to forsake a core principle of Canadian Atlanticism in a desperate bid to somehow preserve it.[30] Martin argued well into 1967 that Ottawa should be "helpful to the French government" in multilateral forums to convince Paris of the benefits that accrued from strong Franco-Canadian relations. Just ten days before de Gaulle's arrival in Canada, Martin was ruminating about Ottawa facilitating a meeting between the French president and his American counterpart.[31] But he had matters upside-down; instead of strengthening the Canadian position, Ottawa's efforts to reconcile France with the NATO allies only reinforced the Gaullist belief of Canada's satellization.

The reality was that Ottawa's position had become untenable: the contradictions between the bilateral and multilateral dimensions of its relations with France were apparent, its ability to serve as a transatlantic linchpin was clearly exhausted, and the Atlanticist moment that it had shared with Paris early in the Cold War was well and truly past. This situation had been emerging since the mid-1950s, but, conditioned by its Atlanticist policy, preoccupied with its evolving relationship with the United States and Britain, and blinded by the ties of sentiment and the memory of wartime and early Cold War cooperation, Ottawa had failed to comprehend the scope and ramifications of the divergence between Canadian and French foreign policy. The result was that Canada had shifted from being the North Atlantic's self-appointed linchpin to being caught in the vise-grip of the geopolitical struggle between Paris and Washington.

The consequences of this foreign policy failure were by no means limited to the international arena. The differences between Ottawa and Paris over the transatlantic order had a significant impact on Canada's domestic situation as they contributed significantly to the triangular tensions. Confronted with a

Canada that it believed to be firmly ensconced in the Anglo-Saxon world and an American satellite by virtue of its persistent Atlanticist efforts, Gaullist France was encouraged to establish direct, privileged relations with Quebec. Attributing Canada's geopolitical orientation to an anglophone-dominated federal state, de Gaulle sought to provoke a fundamental change to the Canadian political order. Brought about with French assistance, a sovereign Quebec partnered with the rest of Canada would ensure the independence of the "Canadas" from American power, enabling them to realize their historic vocation of counterbalancing the United States on the North American continent.[32]

The evolution of French policy toward this position could be seen in the years preceding de Gaulle's *cri du balcon*. French diplomats described French Canada as a driving force behind Canada's autonomy from Britain and the United States. In his memoirs, de Gaulle claimed that he took a particular interest in Quebec during his 1960 visit, seeing in it a countervailing influence to American hegemony in the Western hemisphere. Although this may conceivably have been a post hoc justification of subsequent events, his comment to Pearson in 1964 that a renewed French Canada was the best guarantor of Canadian independence is not so easily dismissed.[33] Nor was his analysis idiosyncratic: his remarks echoed a report prepared by members of the French National Assembly who visited Canada in 1963. Even a prominent French critic of de Gaulle and his Quebec policy, Claude Julien, appreciated Canada's geopolitical significance. Decrying European ignorance of Canada's importance, the acclaimed *Le Monde* journalist argued that European independence was at stake in Canadian efforts to resist the American embrace. In Julien's view, the key issue was whether Canada could be strengthened to act as a counterweight to the United States and thereby enable Europe to engage in a true dialogue with Washington.[34]

Ottawa also demonstrated an awareness of Quebec's geopolitical significance and its importance to the bilateral relationship; however, consistent with the broader Canadian foreign policy failure, the analysis was refracted through an Atlanticist prism. Notwithstanding the all-too-apparent failure of Ottawa's linchpin efforts, Gordon Robertson, clerk of the Privy Council, affirmed that France's main interest in Canada stemmed from "our influence internationally and our influence with the United States specifically." He claimed that Paris had to be made to understand that a Canada without Quebec could not "be counted on as being understanding of, or sympathetic to[,] the French position." To the contrary, what could be expected would be a revulsion as "unreasonably 'Anglo-Saxon' as the attitude of a bitter Northern Ireland."[35] Robertson's analysis reflected the mistaken belief in Ottawa – notably Martin's – that de Gaulle was using Quebec to gain leverage over Canada in international forums. It was further flawed in its suggestion that Canadian linchpin efforts over the preceding decade had been conditioned primarily by Quebec, rather than by the Atlanticism at the core of Canadian foreign policy.

To be sure, there were misgivings in French official circles about de Gaulle's geopolitical manoeuvrings. Georges Gorse, France's minister of information, told Léger that the General was ignoring the danger that too great an independence for Quebec would push the rest of Canada into the arms of the United States.[36] This view was shared by many French figures who questioned the logic of Paris's Quebec policy, not least ambassador François Leduc, who warned Paris that all Canadian observers estimated that Quebec's separation would be followed by the United States absorbing what remained of Canada, thereby significantly increasing American power and material advantages over Europe. Leduc also emphasized that the American component of French Canada's identity and its concern with maintaining a high living standard meant that if Quebec achieved independence, it would orient itself toward the United States.[37] Such critiques of Gaullist policy, however, failed to take into account the pro-Quebec elements in Paris, de Gaulle foremost among them, who believed that the Canadian status quo was already producing the feared enhancement of American geopolitical strength. This view had been reinforced by the Pearson government's linchpin efforts that, ironically, sought to safeguard Canadian autonomy. De Gaulle simply dismissed Ottawa's approach as wrong-headed and symptomatic of Canada's inability – in its current incarnation – to extricate itself from the American orbit.

Geopolitical considerations thus figured prominently in de Gaulle's visit in July 1967. His biographer, Jean Lacouture, argues that his speech at the Quebec City banquet was in a sense more provocative than were his Montreal remarks in that he called not only for Quebec self-determination, but for Canada as a whole to free itself from American tutelage. Not only was Quebec to be sovereign, but in saving itself, it would save the rest of Canada.[38] Indeed, the account of the visit that the Quai d'Orsay sent to all French diplomatic posts explained that de Gaulle's actions had been intended to underline that the ferment in Quebec would produce a new political order ensuring a better "general equilibrium" in North America.[39] One Gaullist baron, the French finance minister Michel Debré, echoed this idea in describing the *cri du balcon* as "a warning against U.S. hegemony over Quebec, the rest of Canada, and indeed much of the rest of the globe."[40] A few days after returning to Paris, de Gaulle told one of his closest advisers that French Canada would one day become a "great power," making it crucial that France have "a foothold over there," since Paris's help today would yield future benefits.[41]

By 1967, RELATIONS BETWEEN Canada and France had fallen dramatically from the heights of the early post-war period. Yet, there was a thematic consistency between these two moments. Paris's interest in Canada in the 1940s and early Cold War period derived from a view that it was a useful ally in pursuing French goals and an effective intermediary with the British and Americans. Similarly, Ottawa had emerged from the war viewing relations with France as central to restoring Canada's traditional European counterweight to the United States, something considered all the more essential given the exponential growth of American strength. With the return to power of de Gaulle and Pearson – the respective champions of Gaullism and Atlanticism – the stage was set for conflict. As the Gaullist challenge proceeded, Ottawa continued, and even redoubled, its efforts to minimize disruption to NATO. Rather than being viewed as a useful ally and counterweight to Britain and the United States, however, Paris now considered Canada an American satellite. This outcome was especially problematic because Ottawa was increasingly motivated to cultivate relations with France out of a more domestic concern: the need to respond to the more immediate challenge of Quebec nationalism. Ottawa's Atlanticist priorities interfered with its attempts to cultivate the bilateral relationship, since Gaullist eyes viewed such efforts as being on behalf of a transatlantic framework and a Canadian status quo at odds with French geopolitical designs. Atlanticism had evolved from a source of strength in Franco-Canadian relations to one of conflict, serving as a crucial part of the geopolitical justification for the Gaullist intervention.

PART 3

Le Déluge:
Triangular Relations and Triangular Tensions,
1960-1970

CHAPTER SEVEN

Parisian *pied-à-terre*: The Emergence of Triangular Tensions

WHEN THE QUEBEC GOVERNMENT OPENED an office in New York in 1943, Marcel Cadieux, then a junior DEA officer, warned that although it was perfectly constitutional for the province to operate agencies abroad, these could become vehicles for a nationalist agenda if Quebec City decided that it could promote the province's overseas interests more effectively than Ottawa. Cadieux worried that if the DEA confined itself to matters under federal jurisdiction, the provinces would eventually seek to project their personalities beyond Canada's shores, presenting Ottawa with a fundamental challenge regarding the conduct of foreign affairs and the very essence of Canadian federalism.[1] Two decades later, as under-secretary of state for external affairs, Cadieux had the dubious satisfaction of seeing his prophecy fulfilled. Against the backdrop of overlapping ethnocultural, political, and geopolitical factors giving rise to the triangular tensions, the Quiet Revolution was marked by neo-nationalist efforts to have Quebec act as French Canada's voice on the world stage. Although an initial neo-nationalist motivation was to protect against federal encroachments on provincial jurisdiction, many nationalists envisaged establishing a separate international personality for Quebec as a step on the path toward independence, drawing inspiration from the example of Canada's constitutional evolution and achievement of independence from Britain.

At first welcomed in federal circles, the emerging special relationship between Paris and Quebec City quickly became a source of tension and rivalry regarding the constitutional responsibility for Canada's foreign affairs. As the 1960s progressed, Quebec City demonstrated a growing determination to act autonomously on the world stage and serve as the international voice of French Canada, and relations with France were central to such efforts. With Ottawa striving to contain the Quebec nationalist challenge by pursuing a more bicultural foreign policy, Paris was increasingly implicated in the intergovernmental dispute, provoking federal annoyance as France's government appeared to favour Quebec. In responding to the situation, Ottawa had to balance defence of the federal position in foreign affairs against the need to maintain cordial relations with Paris and avoid fuelling Quebec nationalism. The evolving dynamic also caused discord in Paris between the Élysée, which was determined to achieve direct relations with Quebec City, and more cautious elements among the professional diplomats at the Quai d'Orsay, which strove to act on Élysée orders and respond to Quebec requests while hoping to avoid confrontations with Ottawa. By the time that preparations for de Gaulle's 1967 visit were underway, the stage was set for confrontation.

IT IS IMPOSSIBLE TO UNDERSTAND the events in the triangle during the 1960s without taking account of the ambiguous treatment of foreign affairs in Canada's constitution. Conceived as a measure to facilitate internal self-government, the *British North America Act* did not contain an explicit assignment of responsibility for foreign affairs except for a provision enabling the Dominion government to implement treaties that the British Empire (that is, London) had concluded. Ottawa subsequently argued that the spirit of this provision, in combination with the constitution's residual powers clause, meant that it possessed exclusive responsibility for foreign affairs. Following Canada's accession to international sovereignty with the *Statute of Westminster* (1931), the provinces used the courts to challenge Ottawa's claims, notably regarding the treaty power, out of fear that an exclusive federal responsibility would inevitably encourage Ottawa to encroach on provincial jurisdiction. Such concerns appeared to be borne out in 1932 by the *Radio Reference*, which, although distinguishing between the treaty-*making* and treaty-*implementing* power, argued that the former fell under federal purview. The implication was that Ottawa could acquire authority over provincial matters if legislation was required to carry out a treaty that the federal government had signed. But Ottawa's apparent victory was short-lived: five years later, the *Labour Conventions* case resulted in the Judicial Committee of the Privy Council limiting Ottawa's ability to implement treaties to subjects under federal jurisdiction; if Ottawa entered into a treaty affecting provincial authority, the provincial legislatures had to pass the enabling legislation. Moreover, the decision remained silent on the question of which level of government possessed the treaty-making power.[2]

The DEA's legal division subsequently described this constitutional ambiguity as "the most important single obstacle limiting and confining the scope of Canadian foreign policy."[3] Although acknowledging the provinces' right to operate overseas agencies in areas of their jurisdiction, Ottawa opposed any provincial *jus tractatuum*: only the federal government had the right to treat with foreign powers – even in matters of provincial jurisdiction.[4] Prior to

Confederation, the British North American colonies had possessed offices to promote trade and immigration abroad, and after 1867 the provinces continued to project their interests beyond Canadian shores; the Quebec government operated an agency in Paris from 1882 to 1912. The Duplessis government abolished all of Quebec's foreign posts in 1936; although the Godbout Liberals reversed the measure, wartime circumstances dictated that only the New York office was opened.[5]

Provincial offices took on enhanced importance after 1945; Ottawa's preoccupation with asserting its control over foreign affairs grew as, consistent with the acceleration of transnational exchanges and economic interdependence, the content of international relations shifted increasingly from its more formal aspects to technical matters that had been previously considered to be of domestic concern. Such subjects were less likely in federal systems to be the responsibility of the central government, thus encouraging sub-national governments to project themselves abroad.[6] The proliferation of overseas offices operated by Canada's provinces testified to this global trend. So, too, did a joint request that provincial representatives in London made in 1948 for privileges that would have made them equal to other foreign representatives. Although it rejected this request initially, four years later the British government (with Ottawa's approval) granted the provincial agents-general privileges equivalent to consular representatives. Federal preoccupations were reflected in the DEA's estimation that the sizeable staff of Canada's Paris embassy was essential, as it conducted "a lot of work for the Province of Quebec." A.D.P. Heeney, the undersecretary of state for external affairs, argued that the alternative was a Quebec office that could become a "source of embarrassment."[7]

As Marcel Cadieux had emphasized in the 1940s, the question of responsibility for foreign affairs was linked to a broader issue of the place of francophones in Canada's foreign policy establishment. No French Canadians were on the DEA's original staff when it was established in 1909, and little thought was given to the idea that the new department should reflect Canada's duality. Attempts to increase the francophone presence in the decades that followed were haphazard and problematic; the few French-Canadian officers tended to encounter discrimination in a work environment that, like the rest of the civil service, was English-speaking. Only in 1934 did a French Canadian join senior management. The war years, which saw the closure of Canada's Paris and Brussels legations, only reinforced the DEA's anglophone character. A report that Cadieux prepared on Canada's Paris embassy after the war was telling: certain anglophone officers had made no effort to learn French or to expose themselves to French culture and politics; instead, they relied on francophone staffers to translate despatches and preferred to entertain their anglophone diplomatic counterparts. The embassy's effectiveness also suffered from the sour relations between the ambassador, Georges Vanier, and his officers, notably those from Quebec.[8] When Lester Pearson, then secretary of state for external affairs, offered the position of under-secretary to the department's two senior francophones, Jean Désy and Pierre Dupuy, neither accepted; this supports John Hilliker's claim that French-Canadian officers tended to prefer being posted abroad as this offered greater opportunity to work in their mother tongue than existed in Ottawa.[9]

It was not until 1954 that the DEA was headed by a francophone. Beyond a strong record as a foreign service officer and secondments to the prime minister's office, Jules Léger owed his appointment over more senior officers to the fact that Pearson and St. Laurent believed that a French Canadian should be named to the post.[10] Léger's efforts to encourage the use of French as a workplace language produced mixed results: although the DEA undertook to make French lessons available to its employees, it was on a voluntary basis – the Treasury Board refused to cover tuition costs on the grounds that French was not a foreign language. Léger also worked to stimulate recruitment in Quebec and strengthen French-Canadian influence in Canada's foreign policy establishment.[11]

Léger was aided in this task by Marcel Cadieux. Indeed, consistent with his dedication to the federal cause and his hostility to Quebec nationalism, Cadieux emerged as a sort of godfather to the DEA's francophone contingent. His time as head of the personnel division placed him in a position to oversee the careers of French-Canadian officers and ensure that they toed the federal line. This position was not without complications; owing partly to his awareness of the second-tier status of French Canadians in Ottawa, Cadieux was a hard taskmaster, and his high expectations and rather unyielding manner often produced resentment among his francophone charges.[12]

Nonetheless, the efforts of individuals such as Léger and Cadieux helped somewhat to correct the DEA's anglophone orientation; of the 368 officials who joined the department between 1946 and 1964, eighty were francophone, and nearly 22 percent of foreign service officers were francophone on the eve of the Quiet Revolution. This said, French Canadians remained woefully underrepresented in the upper administrative ranks.[13] In a review of *Le Diplomate canadien*, a book that Cadieux wrote to recruit francophones, André Patry acknowledged the DEA's increasing awareness of the contribution that French Canadians could make, but he emphasized how Cadieux's account drew attention to the department's anglophone-dominated work environment.[14]

The evolving attitudes in Quebec toward France accompanying the rise of neo-nationalism made the relative marginalization of francophones and the French-speaking world in the DEA an even greater source of resentment. As early as 1951, the MAE described Louis St. Laurent's visit to France as motivated partly by a concern with responding to French-Canadian complaints that Canada's foreign policy was tied too closely to Britain and the United States.[15] French president Vincent Auriol was received warmly during his visit that year; the mayor of Montreal, Camillien Houde, assured him that French Canada no longer feared *France moderne,* and both Auriol and the French foreign minister, Robert Schuman, were moved to comment on the enthusiastic welcome.[16] The reception was even warmer in 1954 for Pierre Mendès-France; the French prime minister was greeted enthusiastically in Montreal and Quebec City by crowds demonstrating a spontaneity that drew the attention of the French journalists who accompanied him.[17] There was discernible sympathy in Quebec's francophone press as France grappled with its international challenges. The French ambassador to Ottawa, Hubert Guérin, ascribed this interest to Quebecers wishing to see France maintain its status and influence as a Great Power, a situation he compared to English Canada's attachment to Britain.[18] The evolving Quebec interest was discernible even in the actions of premier Maurice Duplessis; although he repeatedly turned down invitations to visit Paris, by the time France's prime minister, Guy Mollet, and foreign minister, Christian Pineau, visited in 1957, he was moved to personally greet them at the airport, host a luncheon and dinner, and insist on accompanying the visitors back to the airport, earning the praise of Cadieux, who remarked upon the Quebec government's cooperativeness.[19]

The constitutional and cultural complexities of Canada's relations with France were apparent when Vanier retired as ambassador in 1953. The French embassy described choosing his replacement as a delicate task, given the pressure on Ottawa to find someone who could reconcile federal and Quebec views as much as possible. The consul-general in Quebec City reported on the impatient anticipation of Vanier's departure among a large segment of French Canadians, notably Duplessis's entourage and the cultural and intellectual communities, who considered him "Ottawa's man." Vanier's successor, Jean Désy, was considered to have a much better reputation since French Canadians considered him to be "truly of their language and blood."[20]

Indeed, it was a measure of the intercultural dynamic in the DEA, and more generally of the latent tensions between Quebec and pan-Canadian nationalism, that as Désy prepared to step down as ambassador in 1957, he lobbied Duplessis to be appointed, even unofficially, Quebec's representative in Paris. Désy explained that it would permit him to end his career "devoting [himself] to the cause of our people, without having to fight against the contrary and often hostile influences of our so-called anglophone brothers."[21] Such nationalist resentment was also evident in the Conseil de la Vie française decrying the inadequate level of bilingualism in the DEA and among Canada's diplomats. In a similar vein, Montreal's Jeune Chambre de Commerce and *Le Devoir* mounted a campaign condemning the discrepancy between Canada's aid to the African members of the Commonwealth and that accorded to francophone Africa.[22]

The clearest indication of the evolving Quebec attitude regarding France and the need to act internationally, however, was the Maison du Québec that opened in Paris in 1961. There were plans afoot for such an office in the final days of the Union Nationale regime, but it was the Lesage Liberals who brought them to fruition, even though their electoral platform had not mentioned international relations. The deputy premier and former Liberal leader, Georges-Émile Lapalme, was the driving force. Visiting Europe a few months after the Quebec election, Lapalme met with France's minister of culture, André Malraux, who told him of de Gaulle's interest since his 1960 visit in developing links with French Canada, and encouraged him to proceed with the project.[23] Charles Lussier, named Quebec's representative in Paris by Lapalme, was given no written instructions or mandate regarding his dealings with French authorities. He was simply told that it was up to him to establish the office. The improvised nature of the project was underscored during preparations for premier Jean Lesage's visit to inaugurate the Maison du Québec, when Lussier was forced to recruit Quebec students in Paris to pass themselves off as provincial officials for meetings at the Quai d'Orsay.[24] Reflecting the initiative's neo-nationalist underpinnings, the title "delegate-general" was selected for Lussier to signal a qualitative departure from the province's prior overseas representation; the traditional appellation of agent-general was done away with as an awkward translation from English.[25]

Federal reactions were mixed. In the late 1950s, during the earliest discussions about the Maison du Québec, Duplessis had been told that Canada's ambassador to Paris, Pierre Dupuy, favoured the initiative. The DEA bridled at the suggestion, however, that the embassy was an ineffective spokesperson for Quebec, arguing that the mission always emphasized affinities between France and Quebec outside official political circles, and that Quebec enjoyed greater prominence in Paris than did any other province. Although the DEA was convinced that the proposed office would "raise certain problems," there was a willingness to adapt, albeit with the proviso that any new arrangements would have to respect federal authority in foreign affairs. Dupuy did not foresee any difficulties, and the DEA recommended that the embassy facilitate the project to preserve relations with Quebec and maintain its pre-eminent position in Paris.[26]

Federal authorities were reassured in this early phase of the official rapprochement between France and Quebec by the clear desire in the MAE that it should not cause problems in relations with Ottawa. The MAE's Amérique division shared the view of the French ambassador, Francis Lacoste, that Paris should take no action regarding the proposed office without Ottawa's prior approval and that the responsibilities of the Canadian embassy and the Quebec agency would have to be carefully delineated. Similarly, the DEA believed that Lussier would not cause any difficulties; indeed, he publicly disavowed the idea of a separate Quebec diplomatic power.[27]

The desire for harmony continued during Lesage's visit to Paris. The premier remained circumspect, emphasizing repeatedly that the Quebec initiative was consistent with Canadian constitutional realities and that, rather than an attempt to usurp Ottawa, the Maison du Québec was part of a collaborative Canadian effort. Despite Canadian press chatter about the lavishness of the reception, the DEA's assessment was supportive, arguing that although the premier had been received "almost like a head of state," Paris had stressed the Quebec office's provincial character, and de Gaulle had emphasized that French cooperation with Quebec was perfectly compatible with Franco-Canadian relations. Although Dupuy allowed that the fine French wines had caused Lesage to engage in some rhetorical flourishes, he felt that the premier had generally been "very cautious" in his statements and that the visit had clarified the Maison's mandate in French minds. The ambassador's only concern was whether those appointed to the new office would follow Lesage's discretion.[28]

Dupuy's misgivings pointed to the potential pitfalls of the evolving triangular dynamic. In the short term, the most vexing issue was the status of Quebec's new representation. Reflecting the initiative's nationalist dimension, Quebec City expressed a desire that Lussier and his staff have a status as close as possible to that enjoyed by diplomats; Lesage confided to Lacoste that he did not wish to appear too submissive to Ottawa, and so the less Quebec had to pass through Canada's embassy the better.[29]

Mindful to ensure that any new arrangement respected federal prerogatives, Ottawa proposed that Lussier be accorded the privileges – but not the rank – of a consul or vice-consul, an arrangement analogous to that for provincial representatives in London. No such provision existed under French law, however, for sub-state actors. The MAE felt that the easiest solution was for Ottawa to put Lussier on the Canadian embassy's diplomatic list, but the DEA opposed this as unconstitutional since it amounted to a province appointing members of Canada's overseas representation.[30] Faced with appeals from Lesage and Lapalme for federal help to secure formal status for the Maison du Québec and its three senior officials, the DEA's under-secretary, Norman Robertson, recommended that the request be acted on quickly and effectively to avoid "the danger of disputes and rivalries."[31] Attempting to come to terms with the Quiet Revolution's international dimension in a manner respecting federal authority, Ottawa prevailed on Paris to consider an ad hoc arrangement, or even a change in French law, to facilitate Quebec's request for an official status. The lack of progress, however, persuaded Lussier that the DEA was hostile to Quebec's presence in Paris.[32] Although Dupuy continued to press the "British solution," the issue remained unsettled when Lesage visited Paris a second time in 1963. Increasingly impatient with French bureaucracy, the premier toyed briefly with enacting unspecified reprisals to push Paris to act, before opting to prevail upon the newly elected Pearson government.[33]

Although the federal Liberals came to office committed to a more open approach to Quebec, they were equally anxious to safeguard Ottawa's primacy in foreign affairs. To reconcile these two somewhat contradictory goals, bilingualization of the foreign policy establishment and efforts to develop a bicultural Canadian foreign policy became a priority. France's ambassador, Raymond Bousquet, characterized a speech on Franco-Canadian relations that Paul Martin delivered in Quebec City as an appeal to French Canada and an attempt to demonstrate the importance that Ottawa attached to the relationship, in a bid to ensure that events evolved in a manner consistent with federal interests.[34]

Indeed, there had been mounting Quebec nationalist criticism over the paucity of Canadian representation in francophone Africa, and in July 1963 Jean-Marc Léger wrote a series of articles in *Le Devoir* arguing the necessity of Quebec having stronger links with France and the newly independent francophone states. Acknowledging that past French-Canadian indifference had contributed to the federal neglect, Léger applauded Lesage for opening the Maison du Québec, since only Quebec City could ensure contacts between French Canada and the francophone world. Léger also argued that such contacts were a crucial precondition to French Canada's emancipation.[35]

Robertson warned Martin that what Léger was proposing would have "very grave" national and international repercussions. To "reduce the pressure for separate Quebec external policies and representation," he recommended that steps be taken to accelerate bilingualism in the DEA, expand Canada's diplomatic presence in francophone Africa, increase cultural relations with the francophone world, and, above all, strengthen relations with France.[36] Martin agreed to Robertson's suggestion to set up a DEA task force to examine Franco-Canadian relations, and a larger interdepartmental committee was charged with developing a government-wide response. Members of the former were told that their "primary objective" was of a domestic nature, part of the Pearson government's broader effort to increase French-Canadian participation in federal activities. The instructions reflected Ottawa's predisposition to view the evolving triangular dynamic primarily through a domestic lens and its preoccupation with responding to the Quebec nationalist challenge.[37]

It was in this context of growing federal concern over the Quiet Revolution's international implications and, more broadly, Canadian unity, that prime minister Lester Pearson visited Paris. To assert Ottawa's primacy in foreign affairs, the DEA insisted that he be greeted with at least the same level of pomp that Lesage had been accorded three years earlier. Pearson told Bousquet in advance of the visit that he wanted it to focus largely on bilateral questions, so that he could return claiming that Franco-Canadian relations had entered a new, more substantive phase.[38] Pearson and Martin used their time in the French capital to strengthen ties and increase Ottawa's credibility at home and abroad as an interlocutor with the francophone world. With Canada's embassy pronouncing the trip an "undoubted success," Pearson returned reassured that relations with France rested on a firmer foundation and cooperation between France and Quebec would be conducted in a manner respecting the constitution. Such was Pearson's relief that he described the visit to Maurice Lamontagne, the federal secretary of state, as the most significant of his career.[39]

The status of Quebec's representation in Paris, however, remained a thorn in the side of the triangular dynamic. Expectations in Quebec that the Pearson government would facilitate a rapid solution were soon dashed, provoking frustration and suspicions of federal intransigence.[40] In fact, Ottawa continued to hope and work for an informal agreement with Paris over the question of privileges. The DEA was thus annoyed when Jean-Marc Léger publicly lambasted Ottawa for the impasse and accused federal officials of working to prevent Quebec's office from obtaining the facilities and privileges that it required. The view in the DEA was that the primary obstacle was French law.[41]

Lapalme met with Malraux in May 1964 to complain that the Maison du Québec's nebulous status was hampering the development of Quebec's links with France. Indicative of the emerging special relationship, Malraux reportedly raised the issue with de Gaulle, who sent word to the MAE to resolve the impasse.[42] In Ottawa, meanwhile, the federal Cabinet, facing an increasingly impatient Quebec, was anxious to resolve the question, reflected in Pearson's prevailing upon Georges Pompidou to intervene in the matter.[43] On the eve of Lesage's November 1964 visit to France, and partly in gratitude for his contribution to the success of recent federal-provincial negotiations, Pearson agreed to Paris extending the rank and privileges of consul general to Quebec's delegate-general, although his name would not appear on the diplomatic list. Whereas federal officials considered the status similar to that of provincial representatives in Britain, Quebec's representative and the Maison du Québec (henceforth called the delegation-general) in fact enjoyed a higher position in France's diplomatic hierarchy, analogous to that of an embassy.[44]

The protracted dispute had demonstrated the complications arising from the unfolding triangular dynamic. If the Quebec state was the political expression of French Canada, neo-nationalist logic dictated that the post-war evolution of international relations meant this principle should extend beyond Quebec's borders and Canadian shores.[45] Nationalists such as Jacques Brossard, a former Canadian diplomat, Jacques-Yvan Morin, an international law professor at the Université de Montréal, and Louis Bernard, a senior legal officer in Quebec's new department of federal-provincial affairs, argued that French officials should be persuaded to sign an intergovernmental agreement, thereby establishing a precedent that would lend support to a Quebec treaty-making power and the externalization of the province's constitutional jurisdiction.

Claude Morin was equally determined see Quebec negotiate international agreements in its areas of jurisdiction independently of Ottawa, and interpreted the federal efforts to expand relations with France as a counter-offensive aimed at containing Quebec.[46] Remembered by a senior federal official as a "most astute schemer" and "a master" at creating no-win situations for his opponent, Morin had been hired to write speeches for Lesage before being named deputy minister of federal-provincial affairs, emerging as a key player in the Quiet Revolution. Before entering active political life and formulating the Parti Québécois's *étapiste* (step-by-step) strategy for achieving independence, Morin worked tirelessly in the 1960s to maximize Quebec's autonomy within Canada's federal system, and he saw the constitutional ambiguity surrounding foreign affairs as a crucial aspect of this task.[47]

The efforts of Morin and his colleagues testify to the fact that more than just intergovernmental jockeying for power was at stake; the deepening rivalry over foreign affairs was a manifestation of French Canada's "break-up," as the pan-Canadian ideal of a transcontinental biculturalism was being eclipsed by a territorially bounded Québécois vision. Jean Chapdelaine's arrival in Paris testified eloquently to the dynamic. He had started his career in the DEA, but frustration over the second-tier status of francophones in Ottawa and his professional and personal differences with Martin and Cadieux had led him to jump at the chance to serve as delegate-general. Despite the best efforts of Cadieux and Jules Léger, the embittered Chapdelaine could not be dissuaded, prompting Léger to characterize the episode as "a very sad tale" for the three colleagues.⁴⁸ With Chapdelaine declaring that Cadieux simply could not understand Quebec's need for international action, the division among the DEA's senior francophone members reflected the broader cleavages in Quebec society. Indeed, whereas in 1962 André Patry had been full of praise for Cadieux and his considerable service on behalf of French-Canadians, he and Claude Morin would subsequently describe him and other DEA francophone officers as self-loathing French Canadians and handmaidens to the anglophone establishment.⁴⁹

The opportunities for discord only grew as Quebec's challenge to federal control of foreign affairs intensified. The neo-nationalist colours were nailed to the mast in a speech that Paul Gérin-Lajoie, minister of education and deputy premier, made to the consular corps in Montreal in April 1965. He declared that Quebec possessed an international personality by virtue of its sovereignty in its areas of jurisdiction. A constitutional expert and prominent neo-nationalist, Gérin-Lajoie contended that in light of the *Labour Conventions* case, which had circumscribed Ottawa's treaty-implementing power to matters under exclusive federal jurisdiction, it was reasonable to posit that the provinces' authority in their areas of jurisdiction included a competence to negotiate and sign international agreements. He considered this all the more important because matters under provincial jurisdiction were increasingly in play internationally. Although Gérin-Lajoie subsequently denied that he was calling the federal foreign policy prerogative into question, he reflected neo-nationalist thinking when he argued that Ottawa represented an entity more anglophone than francophone, making it essential for Quebec, boasting the continent's only majority francophone government, to have responsibility for French Canada's contacts with the francophone world.⁵⁰

Morin confessed to Lesage that he was unsure whether the "Gérin-Lajoie doctrine" could be proven legally, but he argued that this was beside the point: a political solution was required, given that the status quo was unacceptable. Characterizing the issue as a matter of "national pride," Morin claimed that regardless of legal obstacles or federal opposition, and without provoking Canada's dissolution, Quebec had to obtain the ability to negotiate, sign, and implement international agreements in its areas of jurisdiction.⁵¹ Although Gérin-Lajoie had spoken without the authorization of the Quebec Cabinet or Lesage, the fact that he was able to repeat and expand upon his remarks ten days later revealed that he had at least the premier's tacit support. Indeed, although he wanted to avoid provoking Ottawa, Lesage publicly endorsed the idea of Quebec concluding "agreements" (which he distinguished from treaties) in its fields of jurisdiction. His acceptance of the Gérin-Lajoie doctrine, along with the more prosaic concern with controlling the increasingly assertive nationalist elements in his Cabinet, led to the creation of an interministerial committee that Morin chaired, with André Patry serving as technical adviser. The committee was mandated to coordinate departmental activities to facilitate a coherent Quebec foreign policy.[52]

The pronouncement of the Gérin-Lajoie doctrine stoked federal anxiety. Canada's Paris embassy had earlier warned of the need to convince French Canada that Ottawa could serve its interests in relations with France just as well as Quebec City could; if the idea of exclusive relations between France and Quebec were encouraged, it would sow disunity and eventually draw France "willy-nilly" into Canadian affairs.[53] Under criticism from the *Globe and Mail* and John Diefenbaker in the aftermath of Gérin-Lajoie's speech, Paul Martin publicly reaffirmed exclusive federal control over foreign affairs. He declared an independent provincial treaty-making power unconstitutional and emphasized Ottawa's efforts to ensure that Canada's foreign policy reflected the country's bicultural reality.[54]

When Morin visited Ottawa soon after, he encountered an irate Marcel Cadieux, who accused Quebec of bad faith and offered sarcastic congratulations on its declaration of independence. Cadieux, who had succeeded the ailing Norman Robertson as under-secretary, made clear federal unwillingness to countenance even a limited international capacity for any province. He warned that Ottawa could alert all countries that it would consider any direct contact with Quebec City to be interference in Canadian affairs. Morin dismissed the suggestion as an empty threat, claiming that Ottawa would sign its death warrant by thus provoking Quebec and revealing Canada's profound divisions to the world.[55]

Days after the stormy exchange, Pearson met with Lesage and Gérin-Lajoie to discuss the controversy. Pearson was advised in advance that "there should be no weakening, or appearance of weakening, in the paramountcy of the Federal position," although it was acknowledged that active Quebec cooperation was necessary and that the present arrangements "could stand improvement."[56] Although the conciliatory Pearson was willing to concede powers to Quebec in this regard, an agreement in principle reached during this meeting remained a dead letter. Cadieux warned Pearson that his concessions went against existing policy, were unconstitutional, and called into question Canada's international unity. Consistent with the clash between the pan-Canadian and Quebec nationalist visions framing the intergovernmental dispute, Cadieux was ready to channel Quebec's international activity into a broader, bicultural Canadian foreign policy. He adamantly refused, however, to countenance anything suggesting that Quebec City had a "national" role to play on the world stage or was to be responsible for Canada's relations with the francophone world.[57]

Similarly indicative of the internecine conflict in French Canada was the extent to which Quebec's representatives in Paris were subject to criticism. Although Lussier had been Lapalme's personal choice as delegate-general, he failed to live up to his minister's expectations. Lapalme went so far as to question Lussier's commitment to Quebec and its population.[58] Federal assessments were hardly better; Cadieux described Lussier as "weak and incompetent," possessing a "poor character and mediocre intelligence," and Jules Léger interceded with his colleague to advise against appointing Lussier head of the DEA's new cultural relations division.[59]

Criticism of Lussier's successor was equally harsh. Jean Chapdelaine and Jules Léger had agreed to work together and keep one another informed while respecting their individual prerogatives. Léger's readiness to cooperate even extended to using his diplomatic privileges to circumvent French customs authorities and keep the delegation-general supplied with alcohol and cigarettes until its status was resolved.[60] Guy Frégault, who had been lured from the delights of academe to serve as the province's deputy minister of cultural affairs, was concerned about the dynamic, fearing that Chapdelaine was passing too much information to Ottawa. Senior officials in the delegation-general echoed these worries, criticizing Chapdelaine as arrogant and subservient to the embassy. The complaints of Quebec lobby members such as Jean-Daniel Jurgensen and Xavier Deniau, who accused Chapdelaine of destroying everything achieved between France and Quebec in recent years, reinforced such doubts.[61]

The campaign to assert Quebec's international personality only intensified following the Union Nationale's return to power. Shortly after the election, Daniel Johnson told Morin that he favoured Quebec's international activity and described himself as a pragmatist who wished to avoid "explosive scandals" – firm on core principles but flexible on details.[62] The new premier followed Chapdelaine's advice and wrote de Gaulle assuring him of Quebec's interest in relations with France. He also sent two of his closest aides to Paris with the message that not only did his government support the federally sanctioned cooperation agreements that Paris and Quebec City had recently concluded, but he wanted to improve, enlarge, and surpass them. Quebec Cabinet ministers Jean-Noël Tremblay and Marcel Masse, both avowed nationalists, told France's ambassador, François Leduc, of their determination to wrest from Ottawa the responsibility for Quebec's contacts with the francophone world. This reinforced Leduc's belief that cooperation between France and Quebec could only grow.[63]

By this point, Paris was increasingly implicated in the clash between Ottawa and Quebec City over foreign affairs. From the outset of the official rapprochement between France and Quebec, some MAE elements, not least the foreign minister, Maurice Couve de Murville, had demonstrated a more cautious, nuanced approach to the triangular dynamic. Visiting Ottawa a few months after the Pearson government's election, Couve de Murville had acknowledged that federal involvement in the exchanges between Paris and Quebec City was indispensable. Two years later, Leduc cautioned that in cultivating links with Quebec City, Paris should move in a methodical and orderly way to "balance the impetuosity of our Quebec friends."[64] He subsequently welcomed the Johnson government's establishing Quebec's Ministère des Affaires intergouvernementales (MAIQ) as a means of facilitating cooperation with France across all government departments in a manner that would help minimize triangular tensions by permitting the expansion of relations without new agreements. There certainly was strong support at the Quai d'Orsay for increasingly direct links with Quebec, but this was tempered by a concern among France's professional diplomats to avoid conflicts with Ottawa as much as possible, in contrast to the Élysée's relative indifference.[65]

Yet by the mid-1960s French diplomats were coming away from discussions with Quebec officials convinced that Quebec City would soon have "mains libres" – free hands – regarding its international activities.[66] The Lesage government's interministerial committee on foreign relations was interpreted in French circles as an official sanction of the Gérin-Lajoie doctrine and proof of Quebec's determination to project itself abroad. Patry was even more explicit, telling Malraux that the committee marked another step on Quebec's path toward "émancipation politique."[67] Quebec's growing boldness prompted Paris to reassess the conduct of its relations with Canada and Quebec. The shift in approach was consistent with the evolving French estimation of Quebec's destiny and resulted in Paris increasingly subscribing to the Gérin-Lajoie doctrine. De Gaulle had certainly made up his mind: in December 1964, when Leduc was posted as ambassador, he described him to his Cabinet as Paris's de facto ambassador to Quebec in anticipation of the day when France and Quebec formally exchanged representatives. Perhaps mindful of the French diplomatic corps's professional sensibilities, de Gaulle emphasized that Leduc would have to adapt to the new reality that Quebec's evolution was dictating.[68]

Daniel Johnson's visit to France in May 1967 reflected the shifting French attitude. De Gaulle had invited the premier after Johnson first wrote to him. The lavishness of the reception, including the French leader's intervention to ensure that only Quebec flags flew at the airport and that Johnson was received twice at the Élysée, surpassed that accorded to Lesage six years prior and signalled that Paris considered Quebec City a viable interlocutor.[69] It also reflected the fact that growing presidential interest in the Quebec file was trumping what desires existed in the MAE for a more nuanced approach. Indeed, the Quai d'Orsay was finding it an increasingly impossible challenge to keep satisfied an emboldened Élysée, an assertive Quebec City, and a sensitive Ottawa.

Paris's emerging special relationship with Quebec was apparent in Ottawa's progressive marginalization. As early as the period when the Maison du Québec was first under discussion, de Gaulle acknowledged Canada's federal reality but told his advisers that Paris could not be dissuaded from establishing special links with Quebec just because Ottawa might find them "disagreeable."[70] Jules Léger subsequently bemoaned the fact that the expansion of Franco-Canadian relations following Pearson's visit was almost entirely a result of Ottawa's initiative, and that Paris did not appear to be reciprocating the federal effort.[71]

Léger was himself subject to this marginalization, the trajectory of his diplomatic ostracization serving as a useful gauge of French attitudes. Three months into his ambassadorial mission, he was cautiously optimistic, believing that de Gaulle had sent word that he was to be assisted in his efforts to develop links. Léger compared the situation to his boyhood village's church organ, which had periodically needed a good cleaning given the organist's penchant for throwing her chewing gum into the pipes; he was confident that the combined efforts of Ottawa and its embassy would "clean out the pipes" of the bilateral relationship. Confirmed as the DEA's under-secretary a few months before, Cadieux believed his colleague's posting was off to a "good start."[72]

Yet, a couple of months later Léger was complaining to a departmental colleague that "this devil of a man in this devil of a country is creating a devil of a situation."[73] His standing in the French capital had suffered as a result of de Gaulle having taken exception to remarks he made during his letters of credence ceremony. Léger had suggested that Canada's development could proceed without France in a bid, ironically, to encourage greater French involvement. Reporting on the ceremony, he emphasized the terseness and provocativeness of de Gaulle's response.[74] Months later, when Léger was not invited to an Élysée luncheon for Lesage, it was interpreted in federal circles as proof that Léger had given offence. Martin was advised to use a meeting with Couve de Murville to reaffirm Ottawa's confidence in its ambassador. Notwithstanding this intervention, and Léger's prediction that the embassy's relations with the French administration would improve given the resolution of the delegation-general's status and the signing of a number of cooperation agreements, he was on the outs in Paris for the rest of his ill-starred posting.[75] The letters of credence incident was significant, but the ambassador's diminished standing ultimately had more to do with his representing the federal authority and the increasingly overt Gaullist preference to deal directly with Quebec.

As Ottawa struggled to respond to French actions, it also had to contend with the rapidly evolving situation in Quebec. The DEA welcomed the Lesage government's interministerial committee on external relations as proof that the premier wanted to maintain control and that, notwithstanding Gérin-Lajoie's pronouncements, a majority of the Quebec Cabinet still favoured working with Ottawa. Favouring a collaborative approach that would discourage independent initiatives from more radical quarters, Cadieux recommended that federal authorities work with those elements – among whom he still counted Claude Morin – that envisaged Quebec's international activity within a federal framework.[76]

Ottawa's approach to Couve de Murville's September 1966 visit highlighted the federal dilemma. Quebec officials were determined that Daniel Johnson should meet privately with the French minister. Beyond a concern with emphasizing the special relationship with France and contesting a federal *droit de regard* – supervisory right – Quebec officials were contemplating a general cooperation agreement to facilitate future exchanges in areas not covered by existing ententes between France and Quebec and, even more significantly, to institutionalize the relationship irrespective of future political and constitutional developments.[77] Paul Martin was initially quite firm that he should be present during any meeting between Couve de Murville and Johnson, and he even threatened to cancel the Quebec City portion of the visit. In the face of Quebec's resolve, however, and over the dismayed protests of Cadieux, who opposed the precedent regarding private meetings between Quebec and French authorities, Lester Pearson conceded the point in order to avoid a public controversy. It was arranged that Martin would absent himself on the pretext of an "emergency" Cabinet session, in exchange for Quebec officials agreeing to generate a minimum of publicity regarding the meeting and promising that there would be no spectacular declarations. John Halstead, head of the DEA's European division, was the federal standard bearer in Quebec City; while Johnson and Couve de Murville met privately, he escorted their wives to a museum.[78]

The DEA considered the visit a success. Halstead claimed that nothing was said or done that could embarrass Ottawa or complicate its relations with Quebec City, relaying assurances from Leduc and Chapdelaine that Johnson had been "absolutely correct" in respecting provincial jurisdiction. Despite such reports and the claim by Couve de Murville's chief of staff that the discussion had been of "no real importance," the wisdom of Ottawa's approach was questionable. In addition to the matter of Quebec's participation in the emerging Francophonie,

Johnson and Couve de Murville had discussed the proposed general cooperation agreement. Both issues entailed the assertion of a Quebec international personality and constituted a direct challenge to the federal stance regarding foreign affairs.[79]

The episode underscored the escalating competition between Ottawa and Quebec City over foreign affairs in the months after the Johnson government's election. The scope of federal anxiety was apparent when Johnson announced the establishment of the intergovernmental affairs ministry in February 1967. The stern federal reaction was informed by awareness in Ottawa of the historical parallels to the creation of the DEA and its contribution to Canada's distinct international personality and independence from Britain. Pearson declared publicly that Ottawa would resolutely oppose any Quebec effort to use the MAIQ as the basis for signing international agreements independently. A hardening of federal attitudes was also evident in the establishment of a DEA task force, chaired by Allan Gotlieb, head of the department's legal division, to work closely with the Prime Minister's Office and the Privy Council Office to monitor Quebec's international activity and expand links with the international francophone community.[80]

Reflecting the intergovernmental conflict and the broader clash between Canadian and Quebec nationalism, federal authorities tended to assign Quebec the larger share of blame for the triangular tensions. Ottawa's view was that although Quebec nationalist actions were meeting a ready French response, Paris was simply responding to Quebec government initiatives. Martin maintained that the road to an improved triangular dynamic went through Quebec City, which made "close cooperation and mutual confidence" between the two levels of government essential.[81]

Yet, the federal preoccupation with containing Quebec blinded Ottawa to the scope of the French challenge. There was certainly awareness by mid-1964 that the emerging special relationship between France and Quebec was having a deleterious effect on Ottawa's dealings with Paris. Cadieux expressed concern to Bousquet about the difficulties arising from the tendency of French authorities to contact Quebec City prior to raising matters with Ottawa.[82] With the DEA questioning the "somewhat unusual courtesies" being extended to Quebec personalities in Paris, Pearson was advised to raise federal unease with Bousquet and explain that nationalist elements were exploiting French gestures, provoking reactions in the rest of Canada that hampered Ottawa's ability to expand relations with France.[83] By the end of 1965, Cadieux was complaining to Jules Léger that Quebec's "one-upmanship" was encouraging Paris to behave inappropriately.[84] Federal apprehension only grew over news that prior to his defeat, Lesage had maintained a monthly correspondence with de Gaulle. The suggestion that the two leaders might have discussed many of the Lesage government's initiatives cast recent events in a more ominous light and, in Cadieux's view, implied a "very worrying" degree of French involvement in Canadian affairs.[85]

The federal tendency to blame Quebec for the deteriorating situation, however, combined with Ottawa's hope for French benevolence and its preoccupation with building up Franco-Canadian relations, meant that concern about French actions was accompanied by a desire to extend Paris the benefit of the doubt. This was not entirely unwarranted, given the initial MAE efforts to reconcile special relations with Quebec and the broader Franco-Canadian relationship. At the end of 1965, Cadieux opined that the French "surely" would hesitate to encourage Quebec City so long as they were better informed and viewed Ottawa as a useful and profitable partner.[86] Martin argued that the source of the tensions was an ignorance of Canada's constitutional complexities in certain French circles that Quebec elements were exploiting. He ascribed differences between Ottawa and Paris less to ill will than to an ongoing adjustment of the bilateral relationship to accommodate political developments, and in February 1967 he declared cheerfully that "honest misunderstandings" were declining thanks to a federal policy of "alertness, firmness, and friendliness."[87]

To the extent that Ottawa did assign France blame, this was laid at the feet of de Gaulle. Jules Léger claimed that the relative importance that the French leader attached to relations with Quebec City and Ottawa was dependent on his estimation of Quebec's political future and that he would accept whichever interlocutor came to him. Reflecting his more conciliatory attitude, the ambassador argued that a good deal of Ottawa's difficulties would be resolved soon enough; de Gaulle's Quebec policy was a passing phenomenon that, like de Gaulle himself, was nearing its natural end, since no successor would be able to revive it.[88]

As nature took its unforgiving course, however, Ottawa was increasingly disturbed by what it viewed as de Gaulle-inspired actions. Federal suspicions were reinforced when the French leader received Chapdelaine in February 1967. The meeting was characterized as the latest example of Paris bypassing Ottawa and meddling in Canadian affairs.[89] In the weeks prior to Johnson's May 1967 visit to Paris, Martin blamed de Gaulle for the fact that arrangements were being handled directly between the delegation-general and the Élysée, marginalizing Canada's embassy. Pearson was reduced to approaching the Quebec premier to ask him to intercede so that Canada's ambassador would be "included, where possible" during the visit; indeed, it was only Johnson's intervention that ensured that the hapless Léger was invited to attend the luncheon hosted by de Gaulle.[90]

THE INCREASINGLY PRONOUNCED triangular diplomatic relationship meant that tensions were rife on the eve of de Gaulle's 1967 visit. Global conditions, notably the acceleration of economic interdependence and transnational exchanges, had intersected with Canada's constitutional peculiarities, encouraging a Quebec nationalism determined to protect against federal encroachments, assert Quebec City as the French-Canadian nation's international spokesperson, and, in its most advanced form, use foreign affairs as a means to obtain independence. Neo-nationalist efforts – and the ensuing triangular tensions – were a logical consequence of Canadian domestic realities, notably the ambiguity of the foreign policy power and a diplomatic establishment that in form and content had tended to neglect Canada's francophones. Although such neglect could be explained to the extent of traditional French-Canadian ambivalence for *France moderne,* Ottawa had failed to keep pace with the changing attitudes in Quebec accompanying its sociocultural transformation. This was symptomatic of a foreign policy culture – and a broader system of power – in which Canada's francophone population had been systematically marginalized. Federal authorities were thus left scrambling to respond, with diminishing success, to the expanding special relationship between France and Quebec. Cadieux's wartime prediction had come true: Quebec believed it could more effectively promote its interests internationally than could Ottawa.

Motivated by a sense that Quebec was evolving toward a new political status, notions of ethnocultural solidarity, and its broader geopolitical concerns, Paris was compelled to favour Quebec's bid for a distinct international personality. Encouraged by members of the Quebec lobby, the Élysée took the lead in this regard. But even within the MAE, where there was scepticism about the more provocative aspects of the Quebec policy and elements favouring a more orthodox, nuanced, and non-confrontational approach, Quebec's advocates ensured that the trend was toward direct relations. Paris's strengthening links with Quebec City, accompanied by a deterioration of its relationship with Ottawa, were a barometer of the broader interaction of the nationalist reactions in play, and a crucial precursor to the triangular crisis that would erupt in July 1967.

CHAPTER EIGHT

Crisis: From Montreal to Libreville

Two months before the dramatic events of July 1967, an exasperated François Leduc confessed his frustration to Claude Morin. Never in his life, the French ambassador complained, had he experienced so many difficulties as he was encountering in organizing his president's visit. Leduc grumbled that whatever de Gaulle ended up doing, someone in Canada would be upset.[1] Indeed, de Gaulle's visit was the occasion for the most dramatic episode of the triangular tensions that had emerged over the preceding decade, and it ushered in a period of crisis as Canadian, Québécois, and Gaullist nationalisms collided.

As Quebec City intensified its efforts to act as the international voice of French Canada, Paris demonstrated a proclivity to deal directly with Quebec. This became a significant aspect of Gaullist strategy: Quebec would obtain independence by achieving a distinct international personality. The dynamic was evident in the preparations for de Gaulle's visit, measures to institutionalize direct relations between Paris and Quebec City after the *cri du balcon*, and efforts to achieve Quebec's autonomous participation in the Francophonie. Ottawa faced the same dilemma as it had throughout the 1960s: how could it counter Gaullist interference and Quebec nationalism without exacerbating the unbalanced triangular dynamic and undermining Canadian unity abroad and at home? In the months after de Gaulle's visit, the federal camp was increasingly divided over the appropriate response, torn between the continuation of a pragmatic, quiet diplomacy and the alternative of a harder line. The sense of crisis in Ottawa only grew as it became apparent that neither approach was particularly effective in countering the Gaullist and Quebec nationalist challenges.

During the Quebec election campaign that brought the Johnson government to power, Canada's ambassador, Jules Léger, sounded out Paris about de Gaulle visiting Canada during Expo '67. Ottawa, fearing the reaction in Quebec if word of the informal inquiries leaked out during the campaign, had Léger ask the French officials to keep the matter strictly confidential.[2] Following the

Union Nationale victory and Daniel Johnson informing Ottawa that he would ask de Gaulle personally, the French leader received two invitations. The first was from the governor-general, Georges Vanier, who formally invited France's president to celebrate Canada's centennial and attend the universal exposition in Montreal. A week later, Quebec's delegate-general, Jean Chapdelaine, delivered the second personal invitation from Johnson. Consistent with Paris's evolving two-nation approach, de Gaulle responded separately to the messages. His sympathies were reflected in his answers. In a warmer tone and at greater length, he welcomed the Quebec premier's message. He confessed that he was unable to give an answer but offered assurances that France recognized Expo's significance to Quebec. The response to Vanier was more restrained; de Gaulle explained that unspecified conditions raised equally unspecified questions about the proposed visit that it was necessary to examine "at leisure."[3]

The episode was a harbinger of the triangular dynamic that suffused every aspect of de Gaulle's visit. By the first weeks of 1967, Ottawa had lost effective control of the itinerary as Paris, and the Élysée especially, embraced Quebec City as its interlocutor. Telling Chapdelaine in mid-February that he would visit barring any surprise in France's legislative elections, de Gaulle instructed that the matter be kept secret and that he would inform Ottawa later. He outlined an itinerary to the delegate-general, subject to Johnson's approval, that would see him arrive by boat in Quebec City before heading to Montreal, followed by a perfunctory stop in Ottawa.[4]

Chapdelaine's audience at the Élysée spelled trouble for Ottawa. Federal officials planning the visit in anticipation of a positive French response were anxious to ensure that the Quebec portion of the visit did not dominate, in order to deny new ammunition to those advocating a separate international personality for Quebec. When an official in the Prime Minister's Office (PMO) noted that federal plans meant that de Gaulle would stay twice as long in Ottawa as other heads of state, Marcel Cadieux rejoined that "the longer we keep the General in Ottawa, the better."[5] There was consternation in DEA corridors when the *Ottawa Journal* broke the news that de Gaulle planned to arrive in Quebec City by boat; such an arrangement precluded the visit beginning in Ottawa to emphasize that France's leader was visiting Canada and thus avoid the appearance of the federal government being relegated to second-tier status. The PMO swiftly took over responsibility for the visit from Lionel Chevrier, the federal commissioner in charge of official visits to Expo. With Ottawa still not having an answer to Vanier's invitation, Léger asked the MAE if de Gaulle had decided to visit.[6]

The *Ottawa Journal* article added to the deepening reservoir of mistrust and ill feeling between Paris and Ottawa. This was all too evident at the time of

Georges Vanier's death. Still smarting over de Gaulle's failure to sanction her husband's state visit, Pauline Vanier considered it an insult that Claude Hettier de la Boislambert, chancellor of France's Ordre de la Libération, represented the French government at the funeral. For his part, de la Boislambert felt that he was treated shabbily and resented the disparaging remarks that the governor-general's widow made to him about de Gaulle. As her last official act before leaving Rideau Hall, Vanier called in Leduc and asked him to convey to the Élysée the terse message "1940," recalling the vice-regal couple's longstanding support for France and its president.[7]

Another incident, this one surrounding ceremonies commemorating the fiftieth anniversary of the battle of Vimy Ridge, stoked further resentment. De Gaulle took exception to Ottawa organizing the event without consulting Paris, especially given the fact that he was invited to attend the commemoration after Prince Phillip, who was to represent Canada's monarch. The MAE made clear the Élysée desire that the affair be a strictly Franco-Canadian event, meaning that French representation would be affected if the British prince attended. Both capitals rested on their positions, with Ottawa fearing that to concede would be a sign of weakness and invite more radical French commentaries on Canadian constitutional realities. Consequently, the ceremony went ahead with Prince Phillip in attendance, and without a high-level French presence or guard of honour.[8]

Visiting Paris for discussions, Leduc confided to Léger that "things were not going well in Ottawa" and that various incidents were affecting French attitudes negatively. In addition to the Vanier and Vimy irritants were conversations that John Halstead had with the Élysée's diplomatic counsellor, René de Saint-Légier de la Saussaye, and senior MAE officials. The DEA official's warnings about the constitutional implications of France appearing to favour Quebec City as interlocutor had found their way to "high places," where the implicit criticism had been ill received. Canada's diplomats confessed that they had noticed an increased chill on the banks of the Seine.[9]

The banks of the Rideau were scarcely warmer. Pearson declared that if the rumours that de Gaulle might not stop in Ottawa proved true, the trip could not go ahead. Paul Martin told Maurice Couve de Murville that although the federal government was "not ... setting any condition," federal authorities wanted de Gaulle to begin his visit in Ottawa, "the heart of the nation." Martin explained that France's special relationship with Quebec made this even more important and emphasized that if de Gaulle had Canada's unity and interests at heart he would land in the federal capital.[10]

Martin's entreaties notwithstanding, Ottawa had in fact already effectively conceded the point. Although federal authorities had reached an agreement with André Patry, Quebec's recently appointed Chef du protocole, that all official visits to Canada for Expo would begin in Ottawa, the federal decision to permit the Austrian, Ethiopian, and West German heads of state to begin their visits elsewhere was seized upon in Quebec City as grounds for de Gaulle to begin his visit there. When Johnson and Pearson met in May, the premier made clear his expectations in this regard, following which the PMO decided that Ottawa would not contest the issue if de Gaulle insisted on arriving in the Quebec capital. Although not pleased, Cadieux rationalized that having the visit conclude in Ottawa would permit the federal government to "have the last word and ... correct any undesirable impressions the General's visit to Quebec City might create."[11]

Ottawa's preoccupation with safeguarding its constitutional position was paralleled by Quebec City's efforts to promote a distinct international personality. Upon learning of a proposed compromise that would have seen de Gaulle arrive in Montreal, Morin made the Johnson government's disappointment clear to Leduc and accused Paris of caving in to federal pressure. Morin pressed for even a brief stop in Quebec City before Montreal, but the ambassador responded that the proposed arrangement appeared to be the only possible solution given de Gaulle's determination to begin his visit in Quebec and the opposing federal desire to see him arrive in Ottawa. Leduc argued that Morin was asking Paris to choose openly between Canada and Quebec, whereas de Gaulle could indicate his choice implicitly by arriving in Montreal (that is, on Quebec territory) and visiting Quebec City immediately after. Visiting Paris days later, Johnson raised the question with de Gaulle, citing his earlier meeting with Pearson as he claimed that the prime minister was "indifferent" about the question and accepted the idea of a Quebec City arrival since the governor-general would greet France's leader wherever he arrived. A convinced de Gaulle informed Jules Léger of the changed itinerary.[12]

Although Johnson overstated Pearson's indifference over the question, he was correct on the core issue: the prime minister had agreed to accept the change from Montreal to Quebec City. This concession, however, was predicated partly on Ottawa's being responsible for the official greeting, leading to a dispute over the scope of the federal profile in the Quebec capital. The squabble was over whether the French leader was to be escorted to the Citadelle by the governor-general or Quebec's premier, or both, and was resolved only when Johnson proposed a compromise: the governor-general would receive de Gaulle and then proceed alone to the Citadelle, where he would greet him again after Johnson escorted him through Quebec City's streets.[13] Cadieux bemoaned the fact that Pearson had conceded everything regarding de Gaulle's itinerary, as he feared that this would confirm in French minds that Quebec City, with

Paris's backing, would win every time – a conclusion that would only "further complicate our relations" with France.[14]

Such protocol debates might have been arcane and verged on the farcical, but they pointed to the larger rivalry between Ottawa and Quebec City over foreign affairs. They formed one strand – a highly visible one – in the rope that the two levels of government were struggling over in their jurisdictional tug-of-war. In this struggle, the federal side was at a growing disadvantage owing to the French anchor assisting Quebec. The extent of Ottawa's marginalization was evident in the federal exclusion from planning sessions between Quebec officials and France's protocol officers and the fact that many of the visit's details were worked out in Paris between Quebec's representatives and senior Quebec lobby members. The intergovernmental conflict was vividly illustrated on the eve of de Gaulle's arrival as federal and Quebec authorities held separate, concurrent press briefings.[15]

Ottawa's last chance to assert its position with Paris regarding the constitutional responsibility for foreign affairs came when Paul Martin visited the French capital in June 1967. The DEA had recommended an intermediate approach, rejecting the opposing alternatives of an aggressive stance and remaining silent as ineffective and liable to encourage further French interventions. Martin was urged to explain that although Ottawa welcomed France developing links with Quebec within a federally sanctioned framework and would be rather flexible regarding demonstrations of friendship between France and Quebec, it could not countenance direct relations. Martin's decision not to convey any message, however, meant that Canada's quiet diplomacy was rendered completely silent.[16]

Shortly after de Gaulle's arrival in Quebec City, the DEA warned Pearson that France's leader was "adopting explicitly and in public the attitude which has been implicit for some time in his treatment of relations between France and Canada on one hand and France and Quebec on the other ... [stressing] ... the priority he gives to France-Quebec relations."[17] Throughout the following day, de Gaulle's remarks emphasized that Paris regarded Quebec City as a viable interlocutor. At every stop along the Chemin du roy, de Gaulle made clear the importance he attached to the special relationship, highlighting the growth of the official rapprochement and praising the cooperation between France and Quebec.[18]

Following the visit, Paris and Quebec City moved quickly to consolidate direct, privileged relations. Declaring that the two capitals were passing from words to action, Johnson sent Morin to Paris to discuss a more systematic organization and expansion of links.[19] A report on relations with Quebec prepared at the behest of the Élysée and Couve de Murville reflected the high-level interest in Paris, as did de Gaulle's convening the Cabinet to decide upon the next phase of cooperation between France and Quebec City. Senior French governmental figures also attended discussions in this regard at the delegation-general.[20]

De Gaulle sent France's minister of education, Alain Peyrefitte, to Quebec in September to meet with Johnson and his ministers to establish a comprehensive program of political, economic, and cultural cooperation. Peyrefitte was a confidant of de Gaulle's, having served as minister of information and overseen the settlement in France of the *pied-noir* population. He had been converted to the Quebec cause by his diplomatic counsellor, Bernard Dorin. De Gaulle urged Peyrefitte to convince Johnson of the need for an intergovernmental organization to institutionalize and manage the special relationship. The French leader envisaged the initiative as a means to hasten Quebec's independence by helping to establish its separate international personality; he explained that what Paris was proposing was an ever-increasing bilateral cooperation that would end up in France treating Quebec as a de facto sovereign state.[21]

Although not prepared to go either as far or as fast as de Gaulle, Johnson nevertheless expressed to Peyrefitte his strong desire for strengthened interministerial structures to increase the scope and efficiency of cooperation. Leduc ascribed the Quebec preoccupation with political and administrative structures to a mix of electoral considerations, the desire for prestige and efficacy, and a concern to avoid anything suggesting submission to a French imperium. Indeed, Johnson insisted that in the communiqué announcing the vastly expanded co-operation between France and Quebec, a passage be included referring to how this was occurring on an "equal to equal" basis. Among the items in the Johnson-Peyrefitte agreement were the creation of a permanent secretariat, periodic consultations between the French and Quebec ministers of education and economic affairs, and provision for regular meetings at the "highest level."[22]

The extent of French support for direct relations with Quebec was underscored when Chapdelaine was subsequently summoned to the Élysée. De Gaulle pushed for Johnson and his principal ministers to visit France that autumn to act upon, and even accelerate, the initiatives that had been established.[23] Similarly, when Leduc warned that no thaw in Franco-Canadian relations would occur without some triangular compromise, the MAE noted that this was of scant concern to the Élysée. With 1967 drawing to a close, Leduc told Morin that notwithstanding federal objections, Paris stood ready to act on any Quebec request in terms of formal relations, including further agreements.[24]

Another barometer of Paris's intentions was the reorganization of France's diplomatic representation. A new consul general, Pierre de Menthon, was appointed to Quebec City. He was told that his mission would differ qualitatively from that of his predecessors; the consulate general was to be expanded considerably and given responsibility for relations with Quebec, while the embassy would oversee relations with the rest of Canada. Barring exceptional circumstances, de Menthon was to communicate directly with Paris rather than through the embassy. Consistent with its two-nation approach and sympathy for Quebec's constitutional position, Paris was effectively operating two embassies in Canada. Indeed, the growth of the consulate general's personnel after 1967 meant France's combined representation in the province soon exceeded that in Ottawa.[25]

BY THE SPRING OF 1968, LÉGER was bemoaning the obvious second-tier status of Franco-Canadian relations relative to Paris's rapidly expanding links with Quebec City, noting that scarcely a week passed without Quebec ministers, senior officials, or experts visiting France.[26] Mindful that a robust alliance between France and Quebec would eviscerate any retaliatory measures, the DEA's first instinct in responding to these strengthening ties had been to maintain its pragmatic, quiet diplomatic response. This reaction was informed by the federal fixation on de Gaulle; the hope in Ottawa was that given the negative French public reaction to his Montreal pronouncements, Gaullist leaders would restrain him from attempting to establish a state-to-state relationship.[27]

The flaws in the federal response, however, were laid bare in September 1967 when Peyrefitte only visited Quebec, with Ottawa not formally consulted or even informed in advance. The agreement between Peyrefitte and Johnson was viewed in federal circles as a deliberate escalation, notably the references to the new intergovernmental organization and regular ministerial meetings. Martin advised Pearson that these amounted to French recognition of "a measure of [international] sovereignty" for Quebec, given the lack of prior notification of, consultation with, or authorization from Ottawa, the glaring absence of any reference to the federal government, and the suggestion that the intergovernmental organization would be organized on a basis of equality. A memorandum prepared for the then minister of justice, Pierre Trudeau, argued that the agreement constituted a grave threat to Canadian unity and that a failure to challenge it raised the risk of being seen as an acceptance of a de facto independent Quebec international personality.[28] Federal anxiety would have been even more pronounced had Ottawa found the briefcase that Peyrefitte forgot in front of his Montreal hotel. Inside were a number of highly sensitive documents, not least a duplicate of the letter from de Gaulle that he had just delivered to Johnson in which France's leader lauded the cause of Quebec self-determination. The briefcase was not missed until the French delegation reached the airport.

Panicked that it could fall into RCMP hands, Dorin raced back downtown; however, to his astonishment and relief, it was still sitting on the sidewalk.[29]

Ottawa continued to keep its powder dry. The federal response to the Johnson-Peyrefitte agreement was relatively restrained, limited to asking Paris for more information and inquiring how it could be reconciled with international law and the existing framework for Franco-Canadian relations. The measured reaction was meant as a positive signal to moderates in Paris in the hope of reducing tensions. However, Martin's subsequent talks with Couve de Murville and Leduc, combined with the embassy's exchanges with the MAE led him to admit that direct relations between France and Quebec would continue, increasingly undermining Ottawa's claim to control over foreign affairs.[30]

The result of the ongoing crisis was growing division in federal circles between those advocating the pragmatic "business as usual" approach and those favouring a more assertive, legalistic response. The dispute was all the more intense because it overlapped with the conflict raging in French Canada between the Quebec-centric and pan-Canadian worldviews. The federal rift was most apparent between Jules Léger and Marcel Cadieux. The two men were, by virtue of their differing experiences, roles, and geographic locations, virtually destined to be driven apart over the best response to the interlaced challenges of Quebec nationalism and Gaullism. The divergence between the DEA's two senior francophones had been foreshadowed in early 1967, when Léger expressed concern over what he viewed as Ottawa's hardening attitude, whereas Cadieux claimed that the impact of French actions on federal prerogatives and Canadian unity trumped the importance of maintaining good relations with Paris. Cadieux was subsequently instrumental in blocking publication of an article that Léger had written that called for a depoliticization of the questions surrounding Quebec's international activities, including its participation in the Francophonie, in order to achieve an intergovernmental compromise.[31]

The crisis atmosphere that reigned after de Gaulle's visit exacerbated the differences between the two men. Léger, favouring a pragmatic and conciliatory approach, believed it essential to avoid further incidents until the situation stabilized; he recommended that Ottawa avoid the Élysée as much as possible, support initiatives in Paris in which federal and Quebec interests coincided, and steer clear of activities in areas in which there were differences. He also voiced misgivings over instructions that he received following Peyrefitte's visit. Indicative of the frustration that he must have been feeling over his difficulties in Paris, he complained that lodging a protest would accomplish nothing except annoy de Gaulle and complicate things further for the embassy. The embattled diplomat suggested that he could instead meet with French Cabinet members and urge them to visit Ottawa during any travels to Quebec, letting the DEA pursue the Peyrefitte trip with Leduc. He also urged federal authorities to be more flexible regarding French ministerial visits and accept that certain ministers would go to Quebec without stopping in Ottawa.[32]

Léger's suggestions did not sit well with Cadieux, arguably the voice in the DEA calling for the toughest response. The Peyrefitte visit had severely eroded his support for the "business as usual" strategy, leading him to push a more aggressive defence of federal interests. The DEA under-secretary believed that it was crucial to make Paris aware of Ottawa's opposition and willingness to react. He complained that given the constitutional and legal issues at stake Léger's approach was unacceptable, expressing annoyance that it appeared to rule out a protest even for the record. Cadieux also questioned Léger's logic, arguing the Élysée would be just as likely to find out and be equally annoyed if Ottawa registered its protest about the Peyrefitte visit through the French embassy instead of in Paris.[33]

The scope of the dispute between the two men was apparent when Léger cited the growth of links between France and Quebec in suggesting that despite recent events, it was a mistake to claim that Franco-Canadian relations had deteriorated. Acknowledging the tempestuous triangular dynamic of the preceding years, he argued that it was only natural that progress had been confined to Quebec; this at least offered the prospect of an expansion to other provinces. Léger also warned against an "overly legalistic" approach that would benefit only Quebec City. This was too much for Cadieux, who thundered that Léger would "never see the constitutional and political implications" of France-Quebec relations. He dismissed Léger's intimation that France's cooperation with Quebec was benign, arguing that in addition to the province being treated as a distinct international entity, it was undermining federal biculturalism efforts.[34] The two men had what Cadieux described as a "difficult" and "heated" discussion in Paris. A thoroughly exasperated Cadieux was determined to make Léger understand that Ottawa could not remain indifferent to the fact Paris was treating Quebec as an independent state. Cadieux left the French capital believing that he had persuaded his colleague that Ottawa's approach was not entirely negative and that, rather than preventing the development of Quebec's relations with France, it sought to place these in a framework that respected Canadian sovereignty.[35]

To be sure, although there were clear differences between Cadieux and Léger, there is a risk in overstating their dispute. In the immediate wake of de Gaulle's visit, for example, Cadieux was inclined to take solace from Léger's reports from Paris, citing them as he expressed his cautious belief that the crisis could be contained and that Ottawa would be able to stabilize the domestic situation as a precursor to normalization. Cadieux extended an olive branch to his colleague after their Paris confrontation, declaring that their differences were only natural and obliged them to develop a response better suited to the situation. And the two men did have a mitigating effect on each other: beyond Cadieux's effort to convince Léger of the wisdom of a more assertive approach, he was subsequently at pains to demonstrate to his colleague Ottawa's efforts to maintain communication with Quebec City and reach a compromise over foreign affairs.[36] Ultimately, both men agreed on the common goal, what they differed over was how to achieve it. Their differences were attributable as much to the crisis atmosphere, their responses to Quebec nationalism, and their differing responsibilities in the foreign policy establishment as to any tactical disagreement. In this sense, their dispute reflected the broader turmoil in French Canada and Canada at the time, and how, as Léger noted, relations with France had a unique capacity to magnify the country's internal divisions.[37]

Ottawa's difficulties in responding to the institutionalization of the Franco-Québécois special relationship did not escape Jean Chapdelaine's attention. The delegate-general explained how, with Paris's support, Quebec City was able to present Ottawa with faits accomplis and leave it to the lawyers to work out the details.[38] His assessment underscores how Ottawa had to be mindful of domestic repercussions in responding to French actions. Indeed, Martin's favouring of Léger's approach stemmed significantly from his holding Quebec City chiefly responsible for the tensions. Arguing that Quebec officials were "play[ing] into" de Gaulle's hands, Martin contended throughout the autumn of 1967 that the triangular challenge was ultimately internal, as it was unrealistic to expect Paris to accept the federal position without Quebec's agreement. Convinced that the situation demanded "imaginative action" and struck by the need for greater consultation with the provinces on foreign affairs, he told Pearson that Ottawa should "not be in a position of letting France have better and more extensive contacts with Quebec than Quebec has with us."[39]

This informal axis between Martin and Léger annoyed Cadieux, who decried Martin's handling of the triangular crisis. Cadieux's growing disdain for Martin was increasingly personal; in addition to disagreeing on issues ranging from relations with France to Canadian policy regarding Vietnam and NATO, he had little patience for what he saw as Martin's obsession with succeeding Pearson. The result was an increasingly toxic relationship. On the eve of de Gaulle's visit, Cadieux railed that his minister refused to believe that the French leader had malevolent intentions. If Cadieux found any consolation in the *cri du balcon*, it was that Martin had been made to grasp the scope of the Gaullist danger. Cadieux was furious, however, when Martin manipulated him into allowing Jules Léger to lobby de Gaulle to not cut his visit short, as this ran counter to Pearson's expressed view.[40]

His contempt for Martin notwithstanding, Cadieux could agree that improving relations with Paris depended on engaging Quebec. Toward the end of 1967, he believed that although Quebec City was unprepared to renounce its international activities, it was not deliberately trying to achieve independence through precedents in the international sphere, so that the more satisfaction Quebec City could be given in foreign affairs within the existing constitutional framework, the less tempted it would be to draw on Parisian favours. He deemed it crucial to avoid placing Daniel Johnson in a position in which he was forced to treat with de Gaulle and cater to pro-independence elements, especially given the premier's plans to visit Paris and the outstanding question of Quebec's place in the Francophonie. Cadieux remained cautiously optimistic, however, that Johnson wished to compromise.[41]

EVENTS IN AFRICA QUICKLY put paid to Cadieux's cautious optimism. The notion of *francophonie* – cooperation among the world's French-speaking populations – had been discussed since the late nineteenth century; in the ensuing decades, a number of private initiatives had sought to foster such cooperation. With France's colonies achieving independence, calls came from the leadership of some of these new states for an enduring relationship with France. Notwithstanding a concern in Paris to avoid measures that could lead to accusations of neo-imperialism – or the opposite worry, an undermining of its bilateral links with its recent possessions – France considered cultural affinities a means to maintain its influence with its former colonies and retain its international stature. Indeed, there was a pronounced neo-imperialist hue to the emerging Francophonie, inseparable from France's broader relationship with francophone Africa.[42]

Federal officials initially welcomed the prospect of an international francophone organization, believing that it would reinforce Ottawa's claims to serve as the international voice of French Canada and offer an opportunity to demonstrate the federal commitment to a bicultural foreign policy. There was also awareness, however, that failure to take the initiative would encourage domestic and foreign elements seeking a distinct international personality for Quebec. The DEA's legal experts argued that although it was constitutional for the provinces to participate in an association of francophone states under federal auspices, an independent Quebec membership would constitute endorsement of the Gérin-Lajoie doctrine and recognition of Quebec as a state under international law.[43]

The growing federal interest in the Francophonie paralleled Quebec City's. Paul Gérin-Lajoie had called for an association of francophone countries in a speech in Montpellier in 1961, and he subsequently discussed the matter with de Gaulle and Couve de Murville.[44] The Johnson government took a keen interest in the file, concerned with avoiding federal involvement in any potential organization. Throughout the latter half of 1966, there was talk of Quebec hosting an international meeting of francophone education ministers. In discussing the question with Jean Basdevant, head of the MAE's cultural relations division, Quebec's junior education minister, Marcel Masse, acknowledged that it would provoke Ottawa; he nevertheless affirmed Quebec's determination to prevail. Indeed, the Quebec Cabinet mandated AUPELF and its secretary-general, Jean-Marc Léger, to organize the proposed meeting. In a bid to outflank Ottawa, Léger was given his instructions informally so that it could be reasonably claimed that the proposed meeting was a non-governmental affair.[45]

Paul Martin, worried by Johnson's public remarks about the Francophonie and French intentions, used Couve de Murville's September 1966 visit to express federal concerns regarding the modalities of Quebec participation in international meetings of francophone education ministers. When Johnson announced that Quebec intended to host a francophone ministerial conference, Martin declared that it was Ottawa that would sponsor any intergovernmental conference in Canada.[46] Federal preoccupations were also apparent following the Élysée's arranging for Quebec's minister of justice to be invited to a meeting of the Institut international de Droit d'Expression et Inspiration française, a private association of francophone legal experts. Ottawa took steps to secure an invitation, and Pearson's parliamentary secretary, Pierre Trudeau, was dispatched to the meeting in Lomé and afterward toured francophone African capitals to promote the federal cause. Back in Canada, Cadieux called in Leduc to remind him that "there was only one address ... for correspondence relating to [the] Francophonie and that was Ottawa."[47]

In an attempt to pre-empt any dispute with Paris and avoid an evolution of the Francophonie inimical to federal interests, Martin used a speech to the Jeune Chambre de Commerce de Montréal to present Ottawa's proposal for a private umbrella organization that national governments would mandate to coordinate the activities of non-governmental organizations dedicated to promoting French language and culture. Taken by surprise, the MAE was annoyed, a reaction that Canada's embassy interpreted as pique at the Quai d'Orsay being caught out at its own game.[48] In fact, the Canadian proposal had come hard on the heels of the founding in Paris of the Association de solidarité francophone. Although it was ostensibly private, the organization boasted significant official involvement, including that of France's secretary of state for foreign affairs, Jean de Broglie, several Quebec lobby members, and Quebec's delegate-general. Raymond Bousquet, the former ambassador to Ottawa, had spearheaded the effort.[49]

The issue of Quebec's participation in the Francophonie took on greater urgency following de Gaulle's *cri du balcon*. The DEA now feared the nascent organization as "a barely-disguised mechanism for ... intrusion in our internal affairs."[50] Ottawa saw itself and francophone minorities outside Quebec bypassed as Quebec lobbyist Philippe Rossillon succeeded in rebuffing repeated federal overtures and facilitating exclusive Quebec participation in the newly created Conseil international de la langue française – another quasi-private organization receiving French governmental largesse.[51] Anxiety levels only increased when Georges-Henri Lévesque, rector of the Université Nationale du Rwanda, returned from the founding of the Association des universités africaines in Morocco sounding the alarm about Jean-Marc Léger, who he claimed had used the meeting to lobby for Quebec's direct participation in the Francophonie. Lévesque urged Ottawa to appoint a prominent diplomat to neutralize Léger's efforts, lest he achieve his "Austerlitz" before being presented with a "Trafalgar."[52]

The battle, as it turned out, came in the Gabonese capital of Libreville, in the context of a meeting of francophone ministers of education hosted by the Organisation commune africaine et malgache, established to facilitate cooperation among the newly independent francophone African states. The Quebec lobby was instrumental in the "Gabon affair." Bernard Dorin has recalled ensuring Quebec's separate participation at the conference as the most beautiful "coup" that he and fellow lobbyist Rossillon achieved. There was no difficulty in getting de Gaulle's approval; he was "enchanté" by the "bonne farce" sprung on federal authorities. The French leader made it clear that although Quebec should participate in the Libreville meeting, he had no desire to see Ottawa attend, a position consistent with his strategy of establishing a separate Quebec international personality.[53] Added to such motivations was the consideration that Quebec participation in the Francophonie, by widening membership beyond the France-Africa binary, provided useful cover against charges of neo-imperialism.

As for Daniel Johnson, he was convinced Quebec should be invited directly to Libreville as an observer, seeing it as a means to strengthen the province's claims to international action. Although he had no objection to Ottawa being informed, he refused to countenance any direct federal involvement given that the conference dealt with education. Claude Morin informed Ambassador Leduc of the premier's firm position at the end of December 1967 and assured him that Quebec City would handle any difficulties with Ottawa. Leduc came away from the exchange believing Quebec's interest in Libreville was purely political, motivated by the question over which Ottawa was most sensitive – the foreign policy power. As such, Leduc believed that Quebec City was deceiving itself by underestimating the scope of the inevitable federal reaction.[54]

Meanwhile, Chapdelaine pressed the matter in Paris. Reflecting its more nuanced approach, the MAE hoped to realize Quebec's participation in Libreville without exacerbating the Franco-Canadian crisis. Jean-Daniel Jurgensen referred to a federally proposed compromise that would have seen Ottawa appoint Quebec's minister of education, Jean-Guy Cardinal, head of a federally sponsored Canadian delegation. Chapdelaine responded unequivocally: Quebec had no interest in attending if it was not invited directly, and it rejected any arrangement meant to placate Ottawa. He later told Morin that Jurgensen's reaction to his determined stance was as good as could be desired given the MAE's efforts to "please everyone and his father."[55]

As discussions were taking place between Quebec City and Paris, anxiety grew in Ottawa as word arrived from its ambassador in Niger that Quebec would be invited to Libreville. The DEA's European division urged a provisional arrangement with Quebec City regarding international francophone meetings – even one falling short of federal principles – to prevent Quebec from using the help of France or other francophone states to achieve arrangements harmful to Canada's international unity. Pearson accordingly wrote Johnson at the beginning of December to emphasize Ottawa's willingness to include Quebec representatives in Canadian delegations to international conferences and cooperate regarding Quebec's participation in the Francophonie.[56]

The federal efforts and the hope that Paris would not frustrate them, however, appeared increasingly unrealistic. Pearson's letter to Johnson ominously went unanswered, as did a request for Paris to help Ottawa secure an invitation to send observers to Gabon. When Marcel Cadieux met with Johnson in early 1968, the latter carefully avoided committing himself to anything when the Libreville meeting was discussed. Recounting the conversation to Jules Léger, Cadieux conceded that he did not know what Quebec City would decide but hoped that it would opt for compromise, since in his estimation, the jurisdictional battle over foreign affairs would then be resolved and Paris, faced with the agreement, would stop its meddling.[57]

Cadieux was to be disappointed. A couple of days before, Gabon's president, Omar Bongo, had met Maurice Couve de Murville in Paris. The French foreign minister had initially not been enthusiastic about Libreville inviting Quebec directly to the conference; he preferred to procrastinate in the hope that Ottawa and Quebec City would reach a compromise. It was now arranged, however, that the Gabonese education minister would invite Cardinal to attend the meeting. Jacques Foccart, de Gaulle's shadowy and strongly influential adviser on African affairs, provided Bongo with a draft of the invitation that Paris wished sent. Foccart also supplied a series of rebuttals to potential criticism, including the claim that a direct invitation to Quebec was "the only possible procedure" since education was an exclusively provincial jurisdiction. Whereas the French draft provided for Cardinal attending as an observer, this qualification was dropped in the final version, in which the Quebec minister was asked to participate as the representative of French Canada.[58]

Scarcely a week after Bongo visited Paris, Johnson announced triumphantly that Quebec had been invited to the Libreville conference. Consistent with the federal fixation on de Gaulle, Martin emphasized to Pearson the MAE's efforts to avoid another confrontation. Federal resentment was reserved especially for Quebec's premier, who had been "much less helpful" in his public remarks than what he had led Pearson to believe when the two men had discussed the matter the previous day. Indeed, Johnson made no attempt to minimize the legal and constitutional implications of Quebec receiving the invitation; rather, he declared it a "happy precedent" that demonstrated the necessity of not having "too rigid" an approach to foreign affairs. Cadieux, shaken, described the decision as "disastrous."[59]

Sent to Libreville with Johnson's instructions to take a "strong line," Cardinal headed a delegation that was treated as if it were representing an independent, sovereign state. Quebec flags flew throughout the Gabonese capital and Cardinal was lodged at the presidential mansion. The only other guest at the mansion was France's education minister, Alain Peyrefitte, who used his public remarks to draw attention to Quebec's participation in the conference not as an observer but as a member of the Francophonie. All such measures were meant to emphasize Quebec's arrival on the international stage.[60] Peyrefitte also emphasized that the Francophonie was being established on a basis of equality among its members, citing Quebec's presence as proof that France did not consider Africa its private sphere of influence.[61]

The Gabon affair fuelled dissension in the federal camp over the appropriate course of action. After its last-ditch efforts to secure an invitation failed, Ottawa suspended relations with Gabon and lodged an oral protest with the MAE. The response was far milder than what Cadieux wished; however, he had been overruled by Martin, who argued that Ottawa did not have the "luxury of 'gestures of annoyance,'" since no protest would prompt de Gaulle to modify his policy and that, to the contrary, such a response could give him grounds to suspend relations with Ottawa.[62] Cadieux found the latest crisis all the more perilous since Pearson's authority was waning and Martin was preoccupied with the Liberal leadership contest at the very moment when Canada needed strong and forceful leadership. He was dismayed when Martin betrayed Cabinet solidarity, undermined the federal position, and infuriated Pearson by claiming publicly that Ottawa would soon re-establish relations with Libreville and that there was no question of Canada breaking ties with France. Cadieux viewed this as blatant pandering to Quebec in a bid by Martin to outflank his harder-line leadership rival, Pierre Trudeau. He was disgusted when he subsequently caught Martin lying to the House of Commons about a fictional Gabonese representative whom he was to meet with, in another bid to differentiate himself from Trudeau on the eve of the leadership convention. Cadieux's contempt only grew when he learned that Martin had repeated the lie to his Cabinet colleagues; he condemned his minister for having "no scruples" as he indulged his ambition.[63]

The renewed sense of crisis also exacerbated Cadieux's differences with Jules Léger, who contacted him in a personal capacity to express his fear that the situation was at risk of spinning out of control. Holding out little hope for a change in de Gaulle's behaviour, Léger argued that only through an agreement with Quebec City would Ottawa be able to emerge from this latest triangular controversy. Cadieux, along with Pearson, shared Léger's fear and expectation that Canada was headed toward a suspension of its relations with France. Yet, in Cadieux's view, Léger's prescription was too simplistic: so long as Quebec could count on French support, Johnson would remain master of the situation and have no incentive to compromise. Cadieux agreed on the need for an agreement with Quebec City, but he pointed out that it was not responding to Ottawa's letters "ninety-nine percent" of the time and was taking actions directly opposed to federal interests. Recognizing that if Ottawa took no action it would quickly face a "catastrophe," he despaired that Ottawa had run out of room for manoeuvre; he was forced to conclude that the only option available was to play for time, riding out the Gaullist storm until de Gaulle departed and the constitutional reform process that the Pearson government had initiated produced results.[64]

Concern, however, was not limited to Ottawa. Quebec authorities were caught by surprise at the intensity of the federal reaction to Libreville's invitation, notably Ottawa's suspending relations with Gabon. Although Johnson decried the move as an overreaction, his bluster reflected awareness that while Quebec had achieved a tactical victory, the Gabon affair had left it vulnerable in its bid for autonomous international action and the larger objective of a new constitutional settlement. Indeed, the Quebec Cabinet expressed concern over the affair's impact on the upcoming constitutional reform conference.[65] Such concerns appeared to be borne out when, during this meeting in Ottawa, Cadieux rebuffed Morin when he proposed negotiations to settle the foreign affairs rivalry.[66]

The constitutional struggle was all the more relevant because the close of the Libreville conference was the end of only the first phase of the crisis, as Ottawa suspected that Paris intended to invite Quebec to participate in the follow-up meeting in the French capital. In one of his last acts as prime minister, a plaintive Pearson wrote to Johnson on the eve of the April meeting to suggest that

Quebec's minister of education should chair Canadian delegations to future francophone education ministers' conferences. He urged a solution to the intergovernmental rivalry over foreign affairs that respected the internal competences of the provinces while preserving Canada's international unity.[67]

Contrary to Pearson's hopes, and consistent with the Gérin-Lajoie doctrine, the view in the premier's office was that Quebec should agree to participate in a Canadian delegation to Paris only if a full-blown crisis erupted. Moreover, to safeguard the principle of provincial autonomy, André Patry would countenance only a delegation composed of provincial representatives that received instructions from and spoke on behalf of their respective capitals. He argued that such a position was necessary to check Ottawa's persistent efforts to decide unilaterally which aspects of foreign affairs it controlled. Patry acknowledged that negotiation was the only solution, but claimed that this made it crucial to accumulate precedents favouring the Gérin-Lajoie doctrine. Johnson therefore responded to Pearson's repeated overtures only just before the Paris meeting, and, in so doing, invoked the Gérin-Lajoie doctrine to assert Quebec's right to attend.[68]

The Gabon affair, however, had left its mark on Quebec City. Mindful of the earlier federal reaction, Morin told the French consul general, Pierre de Menthon, that although Quebec was determined to participate in the Paris follow-up meeting, no official invitation was necessary or, in the current climate, even preferable. To be sure, a good deal of Quebec's caution was related to the unfolding federal Liberal leadership contest. Paris learned from its Ottawa embassy that although Quebec City wished to avoid another controversy as Pearson's successor was chosen, the atmosphere in the Quebec capital was profoundly intransigent.[69]

In an attempt to outflank Paris and Quebec City, Ottawa enlisted the Ontario and New Brunswick governments to emphasize to Johnson the illegitimacy of Quebec's claim to speak on behalf of the francophone minorities in their provinces, and to intercede with Paris to call for a pan-Canadian delegation under federal auspices. Ottawa also released two policy papers spelling out its position regarding Quebec's international activities and the case for exclusive federal responsibility for foreign affairs. For good measure, Leduc was summoned to the DEA and warned of "serious repercussions" if Paris did not respect the federal stance.[70] Having won the Liberal leadership and been sworn in as prime minister just days before the conference, Pierre Trudeau used a subsequent speech to the Chambre de commerce de Montréal to underscore federal opposition and criticize Paris and Quebec City.[71]

To Johnson's expressed satisfaction, Paris did not issue a formal invitation to Quebec; instead, the MAE argued that the meeting was simply a continuation of the Libreville conference. This facilitated Quebec participation while stealing the federal thunder by shifting the blame from Paris to all of the conference participants, thereby avoiding a full-blown crisis. Quebec made it clear that it wanted its delegation to be accorded a low-level reception and wished to avoid any spectacular protocol measures. Nevertheless, the Quebec attendees were accorded the same level of recognition and participation as the other delegations, without Ottawa ever being informed officially of their status. Moreover, de Gaulle had given specific instructions that if a federally sponsored delegation tried to crash the meeting, it was to be barred from attending.[72]

Although Jules Léger presented a note of protest to the MAE, federal complaints proved to be of limited utility. Meeting with Léger on Couve de Murville's behalf, Louis Joxe, France's minister of justice, abjured any French desire to interfere in Canadian affairs. He then immediately contradicted himself, however, by explaining that Paris would accept any agreement that Ottawa reached with Quebec City, the implication being that French actions were governed foremost by Quebec desires. Joxe also questioned the federal position that Canada's constitution did not permit Paris to host a Quebec delegation for an international conference.[73] The new secretary of state for external affairs, Mitchell Sharp, could only reiterate Ottawa's opposition to Leduc, who denied French interference in Canadian affairs and ultimately pronounced Sharp's concern a trivial legalism.[74] The fruitless exchange encapsulated the triangular dynamic of the preceding years: Ottawa's efforts to safeguard the federal prerogative in foreign affairs, and more broadly, Canadian unity, had been frustrated by Paris's sympathy for the Gérin-Lajoie doctrine and its encouragement of a distinct international personality for Quebec.

Leduc's meeting with Sharp was the last before he left Ottawa after what could only be described as a tumultuous ambassadorial posting. Indeed, Pearson was so furious with Leduc that he refused to receive him or even be in the same room.[75] Similarly, Jules Léger was soon to leave Paris, exhausted from weathering the diplomatic storm unleashed by the three intersecting nationalist reactions. Even more significant, however, were the political changes afoot. In Ottawa, Pierre Trudeau had taken over from Pearson as prime minister. Dramatic events in Paris and Quebec City were also to lead to changes at the other two points of the triangle. What remained to be seen after the months of crisis was what these changes portended. Ultimately, changes in political leadership would be only part of the reason for the passing of the period in which tensions were most acute. Developments in the economic and cultural spheres were crucial in this regard, and so it is these aspects of the triangular dynamic that must first be examined.

CHAPTER NINE

Missions Impossible?
Triangular Economic Relations

IN THE CHORUS OF CELEBRATION accompanying Confederation, Paris's representatives in the fledgling Dominion had sounded a sour note. They feared that the union of British North America's principal colonies was a first step toward Canada's absorption by its southern neighbour, and thus potentially at odds with French interests. As the young federation grappled with difficult economic conditions in its first decades, one French diplomat urged that Quebec's premier be convinced to seek French economic assistance to help guarantee Canadian independence from the wakening American giant.[1]

Similar considerations were present a century later as each point of the Canada-Quebec-France triangle contended with American economic power and more broadly, the challenge of achieving success in a global liberal capitalist order while safeguarding cultural specificity. The economic dimension of the Quiet Revolution, as Quebec's neo-nationalists sought francophone empowerment as a means to preserving the province's majority francophone identity and achieving greater autonomy amid deepening North American interdependence, coincided with Gaullist priorities. Paris was determined to challenge the economic predominance of the United States and resist Americanization; however, it was equally resolved to ensure that France was equipped with a modern economy permitting it to achieve success on the world stage.

The complementarity of the Quebec neo-nationalist and Gaullist agendas was reflected in the proliferation of official initiatives meant to increase economic cooperation. These were not without contradictions. Quebec was often portrayed and perceived as requiring "émancipation" from anglophone economic influence; consistent with broader French views, a discourse of decolonization often surrounded cooperation discussions. At the same time, however, Quebec was presented as a partner, a francophone society boasting a modern, industrial economy. France and Quebec were to serve as gateways to one another's continental market; together, the two francophone populations would challenge

Anglo-American predominance and realize a thriving, modern industrial economy *en français*.

Whereas nationalist anxiety over American economic strength and the concern to reconcile modernization with the maintaining of cultural distinctiveness encouraged France and Quebec to cooperate, it tended to drive Ottawa and Paris apart. English Canadians were similarly preoccupied with ensuring that their country possessed a modern industrial economy; as the decade unfolded, concerns grew that the American economic presence was ultimately at odds with this goal and, more broadly, a Canadian national existence. Although federal authorities held out hope for more substantive relations with France as part of a strengthened European economic counterweight, Ottawa's ambitions were frustrated as the Franco-Canadian economic divergence widened. A series of disputes contributed to Paris's view of Canada's satellization, which, to federal chagrin, reinforced the impetus for cooperation between France and Quebec. Ottawa was increasingly marginalized, even as it sought to cultivate economic links with France to respond to Quebec nationalism.

DEBATE OVER AMERICAN ECONOMIC power only intensified in the 1960s. Samuel P. Huntington described the "transnational organizational revolution" stemming from the diffusion of technologies developed largely in the United States, which gave rise to an American empire marked by the *penetration* (rather than *acquisition*) of new territories.[2] Until the late 1950s, American investment in France was relatively restrained, a condition encouraged by the country's political and economic situation and by what was considered an onerous regulatory regime. By the close of the decade, however, American dollars were flowing in, spurred by the growing liberalization of the French economy, the emergence of the ECM, the rise of European consumer spending, and the strong American dollar. American direct investment in Western Europe as a whole grew more than fourfold, rising from US$2.1 billion to US$8.9 billion in constant dollars, outpacing the growth of European investments in the United States.[3]

To foster a liberal capitalist international order in which it retained leadership, Washington worked to strengthen the Atlantic framework's economic component amid Europe's post-war recovery and integration. It initiated the Dillon Round of GATT negotiations aiming to lower the ECM's external tariff. It spearheaded the establishment of the Organisation for Economic Co-operation and Development, successor to the OEEC and counting Canada and the United States among its members, in a bid to ensure that matters evolved in a manner consistent with American economic interests. In a similar vein, the Kennedy administration supported British membership in the ECM and enacted the

Trade Expansion Act (1962) launching the GATT's Kennedy Round. These measures were the economic dimension of Kennedy's Grand Design.[4]

It was against this backdrop that the Maison du Québec opened in Paris. For premier Jean Lesage, economic motivations were the foremost consideration.[5] His stance was consistent with the neo-nationalist wish to see strengthened links with France dilute "Anglo-Saxon" influence in Quebec's economy, promote francophone economic empowerment, and facilitate greater autonomy. Although French Canadians were present in Quebec corporate life by the mid-twentieth century, francophone empowerment appeared all the more important by the early 1960s as Quebec was increasingly integrated into the North American liberal capitalist system.[6] Speaking at the Maison's inauguration, Lesage cited his province's need to increase its profile in Europe, telling his hosts that only through partnering with France could Quebec achieve the development that it required while preserving its majority francophone identity. Indeed, senior officials at Université Laval subsequently ascribed the official rapprochement to Quebec's yearning to offset two centuries of virtually exclusive Anglo-Saxon investment that had dispossessed French Canada of its industry and finance and made Montreal a centre of anglophone commerce.[7]

Neo-nationalist preoccupations were evident in the shift to a more *dirigiste* economic policy inspired partly by the French example, and the determination to see the Quebec state take a more activist role to correct French Canada's economic marginalization. In pursuing his policy of "grandeur" – a deliberate invocation of the Gaullist shibboleth – Lesage hoped to see French capital and engineers involved in establishing a Quebec steelworks christened SIDBEC.[8] In addition to being consistent with the centrality of industrialization in notions of modernization so popular at the time, the initiative stemmed from longstanding neo-nationalist resentment over the Duplessis-era Ungava deal. In 1949, the Quebec government had granted the Iron Ore Company of Canada – a consortium boasting a strong American presence – cheap access to Quebec's iron ore, and the company shipped it out of province for processing. Neo-nationalists condemned the deal as disastrous, arguing that it could be offset only by establishing a government-owned corporation; beyond breaking Quebec's dependence on the steel mills of the Great Lakes region, this would encourage development of tertiary industry in the province.[9] There had been talk of French involvement in a Quebec steel plant in the late 1950s; now, Quebec ministers crossed the Atlantic urging participation, part of a broader appeal for French assistance as Quebec pursued its modernization and economic independence "in a French orbit."[10]

Neo-nationalist interest in economic cooperation with France was inseparable from the broader concern with safeguarding Quebec's majority francophone society. Senior Quebec figures invoked cultural solidarity in their calls for collaboration. According to Gérard-D. Lévesque, the minister of industry and commerce, French investments would help francophone culture thrive in North America.[11] Meeting with Charles de Gaulle in July 1965, Quebec's delegate-general, Jean Chapdelaine, argued that French participation in the Quebec economy was crucial to ensuring that French became the workplace language and claimed that francophone economic empowerment was a precondition to expanding cultural relations.[12] Beyond being employed in defensive terms, ethnocultural ties were cited to induce French investment. Lesage invoked such considerations in lobbying de Gaulle to intercede to ensure that French automobile manufacturers Renault and Peugeot would establish their Canadian assembly plant in Quebec, claiming that start-up problems would be resolved more easily between partners sharing the same language and whose common ethnic roots would encourage mutual understanding.[13]

Cultural affinities underpinned another argument in favour of French investment: the portrayal of Quebec as a bridgehead, a gateway to the United States market, and a strategic observation post from which to monitor American innovation. Turning nationalist concerns about American power on their head, it was argued that France and Quebec should cooperate to conquer North American markets. Chapdelaine told de Gaulle that beyond political motivations, France should increase its economic presence in Quebec because it was a natural springboard and would ensure that North America never would or could become entirely "Anglo-Saxon." It was no accident that plans drawn up at the time of Expo '67 for the ultimately unrealized Paris-Montreal tower envisaged a structure soaring to 1,066 feet – a nod to the Norman victory at Hastings.[14]

Quebec's overtures were well received in a France experiencing a "révolution invisible," the social transformation accompanying the country's economic development, notably the eclipse of the agricultural sector amid the rise of urbanization and consumer society.[15] The post-war growth of economic interdependence and transnational exchanges blurred the line between the foreign and domestic spheres and constituted a challenge to the core Gaullist principle that the state's primary duty was to achieve the utmost level of independence by organizing all internal resources to this end. Although Gaullism was preoccupied with independence, France enjoyed tremendous economic success in the 1960s amid its integration into the increasingly globalized economy.[16] This apparent contradiction is explained by the fact that economic development was central to and symptomatic of Gaullist efforts to harness and exploit international realities to national benefit. Beyond the financial stabilization of the late 1950s, the Fifth Republic oversaw industrial mergers to create "national champions," notably in the high-technology sector, part of a general effort to develop and project French economic might. Industrialization was an absolute imperative, a crucial means for France to maintain and increase its international stature.[17]

When he returned to power, de Gaulle accepted the ECM, sharing his predecessors' view that it would permit France to modernize and build its economic strength within a broader protected environment. He was determined to take advantage of Europe's political opportunities, employing it as the foundation for France's global influence and the Gaullist challenge to the Atlantic status quo. The continent's post-war recovery provided Paris with an additional incentive to achieve a more symmetrical economic relationship with the Americans. Determined to block any semblance of transatlantic free trade, Paris kept Britain, and the European Free Trade Association that it backed, at a distance. It championed the enactment of the ECM's common external tariff two years earlier than planned, thereby consolidating European integration in a manner that favoured France. The move foreshadowed de Gaulle's veto of British membership in the ECM in 1963. Intent on realizing interdependence on French terms, the Gaullist republic also strove to limit the ECM's supranational tendencies; rather than being one voice in a European chorus, France strove to maximize its autonomy while leading the rest of Europe.[18]

As Paris moved to make the ECM a vehicle for Gallic economic nationalism, trade liberalization measures adopted early in the life of the Fifth Republic were superseded by an increasingly selective policy. After a number of high-profile corporate takeovers in 1964, Paris announced a series of initiatives to discourage foreign (that is, American) investment in France and urged its ECM partners to do likewise.[19] France also launched a "gold offensive," hoping to precipitate a devaluation of the American dollar and thereby challenge its preponderant role in the international monetary system.[20] Gaullist determination to safeguard French sovereignty converged with an array of opinion, including the left's hostility to alleged American imperialism, and traditional protectionist elements, to make common cause against the United States's economic power. The best-selling book published in France in the 1960s was Jean-Jacques Servan-Schreiber's *Le défi américain*, which captured the nationalist anxiety over American economic influence and advocated a supranational approach to European integration along with a selective Americanization to prevent Europe's eclipse and France's satellization at the hands of United States-based multinationals.[21]

Little wonder, then, that French officials viewed the Quiet Revolution as a tremendous opportunity. France's ambassador, Francis Lacoste, enthused that France would be well placed to reap the benefits if it seized the opportunity to make a significant contribution to Quebec's development.[22] The heightened French interest in Quebec was reflected in the economic mission that Wilfrid

Baumgartner led to Canada in 1962. Baumgartner, a former French minister of finance and one-time governor of the Bank of France, subsequently described Quebec as "a chosen land for European foreign direct investment."[23] There was a major French trade exposition in Montreal the following year; nearly three hundred thousand visitors toured the show, which boasted a significant French economic delegation, numerous peripheral demonstrations, and events highlighting France's industrial achievements.[24] When the Lesage government established the Société générale de financement (SGF), a public-private joint venture to develop the francophone small- and medium-sized business sector, a consortium of mostly private French banks purchased 4 percent of the SGF's initial share offering. Five years later, a group that included France's public-controlled Caisse des Dépôts et Consignations and a dozen other financial institutions purchased nearly half the shares of the SGF's second offering, leading to an administrative post being allocated to a French representative.[25]

Consistent with their broader view of events in Quebec, and encouraged by France's imperial legacy and the popularity of "coopération" following decolonization, French officials interpreted Quebec interest in strengthened links as a bid for economic liberation. They tended to perceive Quebec as an industrializing, even developing, society requiring assistance to escape Anglo-Saxon tutelage. Indeed, posing the rhetorical question of whether it was desirable for France to cultivate economic links with Quebec's English-Canadian and American communities when the expressed goal was to liberate Quebec as much as possible from their presence, Lacoste's successor as ambassador, Raymond Bousquet, responded that French efforts should be conducted with discretion until the day when the result would speak for itself.[26] It is similarly telling that in his memoirs, Maurice Couve de Murville groups Quebec into a discussion of development and cooperation in Algeria and francophone Africa.[27] Little surprise then, that the idea of economic liberation was prominent during de Gaulle's visit in 1967: having told the French Cabinet four years prior of how he was struck by French Canada's economic colonization, the French leader now rejoiced that Quebec, no longer willing to submit to preponderant foreign influences or accept an auxiliary role in its development, was equipping itself with its own elites, universities, and research centres.[28]

Underpinnning Paris's tendency to situate economic cooperation with Quebec in a liberation framework was a cultural calculation informed by the Gaullist determination to overcome the technological imbalance with the United States, equip France with a dynamic and high-tech economy, and position it on the world stage as a modern, industrial power.[29] Even before the advent of the Fifth Republic, scientific and technical education had been assigned the highest priority in plans to expand French cultural diplomacy, on the understanding that the cultural influence of nations was dependent upon the prestige of their scientific and technical achievements.[30]

Indeed, notwithstanding the decolonization analogy, Quebec was also perceived and portrayed as a sister francophone society striving to achieve economic modernization while maintaining its cultural specificity in the face of preponderant American power. France and Quebec's situations were conflated as a commercial counsellor in France's Ottawa embassy called publicly for an "alliance franco-québécoise." He explained that beyond wanting to assist Quebec, Paris wished to avoid France and Europe becoming an exclusively consumer society for the benefit of American enterprise.[31] Efforts to portray Quebec as a North American bridgehead drew French attention; Georges Pompidou referred to Quebec as a springboard to the conquest of American markets, since Quebec lived at the pace and level of the United States. François Leduc insisted that economic cooperation be on equitable terms, not just out of consideration for Québécois psychology, but because France had much to learn from Quebec.[32]

Perhaps the most tangible example of this facet of the economic relationship was Montreal's Métro system, which opened in 1966. There had been longstanding talk of French participation in a subway, but ultimately, it was Jean Drapeau's efforts that proved paramount in overcoming pressures for American involvement. In an announcement made with fanfare in 1960, Montrealers were promised a state-of-the-art system with stations – some boasting stained-glass windows, others ceramic art – that were "cathedrals to modern transportation."[33] Montreal's representatives worked closely with two French engineers, and the city's Vickers plant constructed the cars under licence. The priority accorded to the project's cultural dimension was underscored when France's minister for public works, Louis Joxe, attended the system's inauguration.[34]

De Gaulle especially was attached to the idea of Quebec as an example of francophone economic achievement. When he visited Montreal and Expo '67 – a celebration of all that was modern, not least the majority francophone society hosting it – he praised the city as the "exemplary city" of modernization and rejoiced that, far from having lost its "French soul," Montreal had emerged as an economic metropolis whose population, in refusing to sacrifice what was human as they took the path of modernization, stood as an example for France.[35] At the Université de Montréal, de Gaulle referred more explicitly to economic cooperation between France and Quebec in resisting Americanization, reminding his audience that Quebec lived in the shadow of a "colossal power" that threatened its very existence. He declared that together, France and Quebec would live and modernize on their own terms.[36] References to francophone economic solidarity only increased after the visit. De Gaulle returned repeatedly to the theme, and his abiding concern with seeing francophone Quebec students trained as engineers resulted in a significant increase in the value and number of French technical cooperation bursaries. In de Gaulle's view, Quebec and France were engaged in the same fight on two continents – that of holding onto their cultural specificity while pursuing modernization.[37]

THE ARRAY OF NATIONALIST concerns inspiring the efforts to increase the economic links between France and Quebec was mirrored by those encouraging Ottawa to turn to France. Notwithstanding Canadian frustration over French protectionism and the Diefenbaker government's Commonwealth emphasis, federal authorities remained interested in the Hexagon as a way to diversify Canadian economic relations. France's improved situation and liberalization measures at the close of the 1950s stoked such interest. Canadian exports to France doubled over 1959-60, and the more equitable trade balance with Canada that Paris had sought since the war's end was finally achieved. The cut to the EEC's common external tariff in 1959, extended to all GATT members, gave Ottawa reason to think that there might still be a European solution to its American challenge. Federal optimism was reinforced by the Baumgartner economic mission, members of which met with John Diefenbaker and other senior government figures. Subsequent missions that French companies carried out similarly fuelled Ottawa's tentative hope that the relative stagnation of Franco-Canadian economic relations was at an end. Although Canada's diplomats cautioned against expectations of any "dramatic [trade] breakthroughs," they believed that direct investments could facilitate closer relations, especially since French businesses were looking for a "new hinterland now that their future in Africa and Asia appears limited."[38]

These developments had greater resonance in the atmosphere accompanying the release of the Gordon Report, "a watershed in Canadian economic, political, and intellectual life" that legitimized and provoked nationalist anxiety over the extent and impact of American influence in the Canadian economy.[39] The report warned of the distortive effect on Canada's development of American-owned subsidiaries that relied on the research and decision making of their parent companies, and of the logic of political union that flowed from an ever-deepening economic integration. Britain's bid for ECM membership only exacerbated the nationalist angst, as it meant that Canada faced a further reduction of its European counterweight. North America's accelerating interdependence and an increase in Canada's unemployment rate in the early 1960s tapped into longstanding fears that Canadians were fated to be "hewers of wood and drawers of water" for Uncle Sam, as their country's "silent surrender" to American multinationals promoted its deindustrialization and reliance on a resource-based economy. As the 1960s unfolded, the protests against the continentalist trend by conservative nationalists such as George Grant were joined and gradually overshadowed by a left-wing critique arguing that Canada's liberal, multilateral commercial policy was placing it in a neo-colonial relationship with the United States.[40]

A concern with diversifying Canada's foreign economic relations was thus prominent when Ottawa reviewed Franco-Canadian links in 1963. The primary mandate of the interdepartmental committee created for the purpose was to examine the economic and financial aspects of the relationship, it being hoped that stronger ties with France could be used over the longer term to influence European economic and trade policy.[41] Canadian ambitions were apparent as Lester Pearson arrived in Paris. While conceding to his hosts that American investment and markets were crucial to Canada, Pearson emphasized Ottawa's hope to dilute the United States's economic presence. Returning home, the prime minister promised Bousquet that the upcoming federal budget would provide incentives to French manufacturers.[42]

But if Ottawa's desire to cultivate economic links with France arose partly from longstanding nationalist concerns about American influence, the Quiet Revolution and the accompanying need to respond to Quebec nationalism provided an additional spur. Indeed, preoccupations with Canada's unity and federal control of foreign affairs were prominent in Ottawa's review of the economic relationship. Responding to officials who, in keeping with the orientation of post-war Canadian commercial policy, expressed reservations about encouraging bilateral trade relations with Paris, Norman Robertson emphasized that domestic considerations made supplementary bilateral contacts essential. In Paris a few months later, Pearson admitted to de Gaulle that Ottawa's interest in enlarged economic relations with France was, to a significant extent, inspired by Quebec's increased role and influence in Canadian political life.[43]

FOR ALL OF THE NATIONALIST-INSPIRED desire at each point of the triangle to see the economic dynamic change, serious obstacles remained. The challenge was especially pronounced along the Paris-Ottawa axis owing to the two capitals' divergence over commercial policy stemming from their broader political agendas. Irrespective of the motivations driving Ottawa to develop links, it had to contend with the Gaullist challenge's economic dimension. This was certainly the case regarding European integration. Ottawa's concern about the emergence of a "Fortress Europe" that would force Canada further into the American orbit meant that the ECM was a source of discord. Whereas the Diefenbaker government had looked askance on British membership in Europe, its successor was of another view. Pearson may have been concerned about the implications of too heavy a reliance on American markets and capital, but he was ultimately more an Atlanticist than an economic nationalist, believing that the solution to Canada's dilemma lay in a broader transatlantic framework that would facilitate diversification of its foreign economic relations. When Pearson raised the British membership issue in Paris, he emphasized the importance that Canada attached to this membership as part of its broader desire to expand trade with Europe. De Gaulle's response, however, was that Europe would stay united economically to protect itself from being drowned under the American tide.[44] A similar dynamic shaped Ottawa's and Paris's policies regarding the Kennedy Round. Ottawa's ambition to see the ECM lower its common external tariff and thereby ensure that Canadian exports, from wheat to manufactured goods, would enjoy access to Europe had to contend with French protectionism, notably in the agricultural sector.[45] Although there was thus "no lack of trade and economic questions" to discuss, Canadian officials were at a loss to cite those that could lend themselves to mutually beneficial talks, given France's "more rigid national patterns and conceptions of national interest." A DEA report warned that such discussions would be counter-productive if they produced only "sterile confrontation."[46]

Ottawa's effort to strengthen economic relations was also hampered by non-economic factors. In late 1962, Paris expressed interest in signing a ten-year contract for annual purchases of five hundred tons of uranium for use in its nuclear energy program. Paris considered that Pearson, during his 1964 visit, had committed himself to seeing the deal realized. This fact, combined with the depressed state of the global uranium market, Canada's surplus product, and the fact France could obtain South African uranium without controls, led French officials to believe that the purchase could proceed without Ottawa attaching the supervisory conditions that had blocked a deal in the 1950s. French estimations were incorrect. The proposed purchase languished for two years as Ottawa and Paris sparred over the control issue.[47] At one point, Alain Peyrefitte, the French minister responsible for nuclear affairs, approached Jean Chapdelaine to express France's disappointment over the Canadian stance, suggesting that Quebec could not be indifferent to Ottawa treating the French differently from the Anglo-Americans. Chapdelaine interpreted the encounter as Paris's attempt to employ its budding special relationship with Quebec to bring pressure to bear on Ottawa. Meanwhile, Canada's ambassador urged Ottawa to reconsider its stance in light of France's having joined the nuclear club. Jules Léger characterized the uranium issue as by far the most significant and troubling since he had taken up his post the previous year. The purchase, however, went unrealized, foundering on the rocks of Gaullist determination not to be constrained in nuclear affairs and Ottawa's equally unyielding commitment to its non-proliferation policy.[48]

The disappointing outcome had political repercussions, as nuclear research "epitomized the link between French radiance and technological prowess" and was a foremost symbol of France's modernization drive.[49] De Gaulle had monitored the affair closely as the dispute became entangled in Washington's efforts to deny Paris access to uranium sources owing to American opposition to the *force de frappe*. With Ottawa's stance interpreted in French circles as being conditioned by its relations with the United States, the failed deal seemed to confirm Canada's satellization.[50]

Indeed, by the early 1960s, Paris's representatives were remarking that the Diefenbaker government's economic nationalism was more storm than substance, and that many in the business community were claiming in hushed tones that the future was a North American customs union. Lacoste predicted that with regionalization of international trade, Ottawa would eventually be compelled to adopt an economic policy associated with, if not identical to, Washington. Days after the 1963 federal election, Bousquet observed that the victorious Liberals had drawn their support from those regions where economic integration with the United States was most advanced and profitable, an outcome obliging the Pearson government to adopt a more favourable attitude to the Americans.[51]

Such analysis appeared vindicated amid the debacle of the subsequent Gordon budget that proposed a number of nationalist-inspired *dirigiste* measures to dilute the American profile in the Canadian economy, which were then withdrawn following "violent and ... bitterly hostile" protests from the business community on both sides of the border.[52] Paris was well aware as, despite a professed intention to reduce Canada's economic dependence on the United States, the Pearson government oversaw "a dramatic and significant increase in North American economic integration."[53] This trend included the 1965 auto pact, the origins of which, ironically, lay in a nationalistic bid to use the automotive sector to develop Canada's secondary industry and reduce its dependence on American capital. Similarly telling were the cooperation between Canada and the United States during the Kennedy Round, and the 1965 Merchant-Heeney Report that, notwithstanding the nationalist uproar it provoked, endorsed deepening continental economic integration.[54]

Leduc argued that North American interdependence was less the product of a deliberate policy for which the risks had been properly assessed than the result of two equally liberal governments ceding the initiative to the private sector. The ambassadorial verdict as Canada entered its centennial year was damning: having chosen a high standard of living and a civilization of comfort, Canadians were simply incapable of the material sacrifice required to recover their economic independence. In a similar vein, French journalist Claude Julien, although a critic of Paris' Quebec policy, suggested that the loss of Canada's economic potential to the United States would be a defeat for Europe far more serious than that which France had experienced on the Plains of Abraham.[55]

GALLIC ASSESSMENTS OF CANADA'S economic satellization were a crucial part of Paris's justification for forging links with Quebec; however, notwithstanding the soaring rhetoric accompanying the official rapprochement, here, too, the immediate results were disappointing. Successes such as the road construction company Routière Colas, which began operating in Quebec in 1962, and Compagnie Générale d'Électricité, established the following year and heavily involved in the James Bay hydroelectric project, were conspicuous by their rarity. Undaunted, Jean Lesage responded effusively when de Gaulle asked about the results of his economic discussions during his 1964 trip to Paris.[56]

The Quebec premier's optimism belied the fact that although Gaullist and Quebec nationalist objectives coincided, tangible progress remained limited, owing largely to private sector reluctance. Part of this reticence stemmed from international economic realities, notably the ongoing regionalization of international trade. France's private sector preferred the greater opportunities available in the ECM. Europe's integration and the Kennedy Round acted as further disincentives to French industry's establishing new overseas operations; instead, the priority was to reinforce, consolidate, and regain industrial interests in France. Washington's July 1963 decision to tax outgoing capital in response to its balance-of-payments deficit reinforced the trend while simultaneously reducing Quebec's value as a North American bridgehead.[57]

French private sector hesitation was also linked to concerns related to the Canadian, and specifically Quebec, market. The Duplessiste laissez-faire legacy endured as numerous French business figures were driven away by the belief that Quebec opposed economic planning. An even greater concern, however, was the French view of business in Canada as an Anglo-American preserve – an attitude encouraged, according to Quebec's delegate-general, Charles Lussier, by anglophone dominance of Canada's diplomatic corps. Lussier expressed frustration over what he cited as a major factor behind the French private sector's apparent reluctance to participate in the Montreal trade exposition that Paris organized in 1963 and the veritable "state of panic" provoked any time he raised the idea of French firms competing in the Quebec market.[58]

Notwithstanding the rhetoric of ethnocultural solidarity, tension existed between Quebec's New World reality and the Quebec and Gaullist nationalist efforts to cultivate links. Accustomed to North American business methods and oriented toward North American markets, many Quebec businesspersons felt more at ease with their anglophone partners, to the extent that they subscribed to North American stereotypes of French business as inefficient and excessively cautious. Indeed, only months after his triumphal visit to Paris in 1961, Lesage courted New York's financial community, and the commercial section of Quebec's office in that city was expanded. Three years later, amid complaints about the meagre French investment in the Quiet Revolution, Montreal's business weekly *Les Affaires* opined that whereas French business was hesitating to contribute to Quebec's industrial development, the Americans were not, so that it made sense to seek the latter's assistance.[59]

Beyond considerations of geography and the international economic conjuncture, Quebec's political situation, specifically the growth of the *indépendantiste* movement, dampened French private sector enthusiasm. Amid the reverberations of the Front de Libération du Québec's first bombs in the spring of 1963, Charles Lussier reported how all of the French financial figures he encountered expressed stunned disbelief over the rise of separatism, unable to fathom what Quebecers could hope to gain. The delegate-general warned of his contacts' reluctance to establish operations in a part of Canada that could become "a new Katanga," referring to the bloody secession of the resource-rich Congolese province.[60] Canada's embassy initially dismissed suggestions that talk of separatism or acts of terrorism were driving away French investors; by the beginning of 1965, however, Jules Léger confessed to having misread the situation. He cited conversations with senior economic figures who confirmed a growing French private sector concern and corresponding reduced interest in Quebec.[61]

Private sector hesitation reinforced a belief on both sides of the Atlantic that a political push was needed to alter the prevailing economic dynamic. Lussier argued that if major French firms, particularly those over which Paris had a degree of influence, could be persuaded to locate in Quebec, others would follow.[62] This approach was evident in the establishment of the Société de montage automobile (SOMA), an automotive assembly plant opened by Peugeot and the state-owned Renault under the aegis of Quebec's SGF. Jean Deschamps, Quebec's deputy minister of industry and commerce at the time, has recalled the initiative as strictly political and possessing no economic logic, a result of Lesage's and de Gaulle's interventions.[63]

A similar dynamic surrounded SIDBEC. Viewing the proposed steelworks as a unique opportunity to demonstrate a commitment to Quebec's economic independence, Leduc argued strongly for French participation, notwithstanding the French steel industry's financial difficulties. In Leduc's estimation, Quebec was seeking a tangible and reciprocal sign of French confidence in its economic efforts. Couve de Murville echoed this assessment when he described SIDBEC as part of a broader effort to diminish the relative strength of American capital in Quebec's economy, and he recommended investment in the project as tangible proof of French interest in the province's development.[64]

The complications arising from the political push for expanded economic relations were foreshadowed by the quasi-official agreement between France and Quebec on engineering exchanges and technical cooperation, a prominent part of the joint effort to promote francophone economic empowerment. Paris and Ottawa had concluded an internship agreement in the 1950s, but the results were disappointing, with no French nationals trained in Quebec. Notwithstanding a modest system of bursaries operated by the Comité France-technique, there was concern by the early 1960s that it was easier for French-Canadian engineers to pursue post-graduate studies in the United States than in France.[65] Bousquet consequently received enthusiastic responses in Quebec political and academic circles when he proposed an intergovernmental technical cooperation program to help train Quebec engineers, a scheme that he sold to Paris as a way to stimulate future French investment.[66] When Lesage visited Paris in 1963, he discussed technical cooperation with de Gaulle, and by the end of the month officials had drafted an agreement between Quebec City and France's quasi-official Association pour l'organisation des stages en France (ASTEF). The accord provided for an array of internships, mixed professional training centres, technical documentation in French, an engineering association to maintain links forged by the exchanges, and a bilateral committee to coordinate the various programs. Consistent with Quebec's international ambitions, Paul Gérin-Lajoie's letter to the head of ASTEF during the negotiations made no reference to Canada or Canadians, and revealed an ambition to see a system of exchanges that extended far beyond engineering, to include everything that could facilitate Quebec's modernization.[67]

The DEA expressed little concern when it learned of the discussions between France and Quebec. Nonetheless, the agreement that Gérin-Lajoie was to sign was with a private association receiving support from France's government and subject to its policy direction. To safeguard federal prerogatives, Paul Martin therefore expressed publicly in writing Ottawa's approval. Federal officials were also put at ease by a parallel agreement between ASTEF and the University of Toronto: mindful of the complications arising from Canadian constitutional realities, and in a bid to pre-empt any anglophone recrimination, Bousquet had suggested that the Quebec agreement be supplemented by one with a private, Ontario-based organization.[68]

More problematic for Ottawa was the Caravelle affair. In March 1963, France's state-owned Sud-Aviation began lobbying Trans-Canada Airlines (TCA) to purchase its Caravelle airliner. The Caravelle had special economic and cultural significance given that this "prodigal child of French aviation" was the symbol of France regaining the leadership position in aviation that it had enjoyed earlier in the century.[69] The Sud-Aviation bid had an advantage over those of its British and American competitors, given that Montreal's Canadair was to assemble the airliner. The employment opportunities and the project's value as a symbol of the modern, high-tech economy prompted Jean Lesage to pledge total support to the lobbying effort in Ottawa. The federal minister of transport, Léon Balcer, was similarly supportive, telling Bousquet that Sud-Aviation was best placed to win the contract, given the Diefenbaker government's insistence that the winning bid should offer the maximum direct benefit to Canada's economy. Rising French expectations were reinforced by the Pearson Liberals' election, especially since the strong Quebec contingent on the government benches would increase the pressure to favour the Caravelle for the government-owned TCA.[70]

Difficulties, however, quickly surfaced. The chair of the Air Transport Board argued that there was "no North American market" for the French airliner, as it had reached the limits of its technical development. The British and American alternatives were considered more appropriate to TCA needs, and Ottawa concluded that it would be of greater economic benefit to have Toronto-based De Havilland produce components for the American Douglas DC-9, given its greater sales potential.[71] Bousquet expressed concern to Martin about the "strong opposition" to the Caravelle, reminding him that the sale was also a question of prestige and making clear that economic issues had implications for Ottawa's desire to strengthen Franco-Canadian relations. Martin encouraged the ambassador to continue lobbying and promised to tell Pearson of his own personal support for Sud-Aviation's bid.[72]

Although it appears that Martin fell short of doing so, he did characterize the Caravelle purchase as an opportunity to establish "a community of interest" with Paris. He reminded Pearson of the overlapping domestic and international reasons to give serious consideration to the French airliner; all else being equal, the potential impact on employment in Montreal and on Canada's ability to act as a transatlantic linchpin meant that Sud-Aviation's bid merited serious consideration. Pearson's response was that the Caravelle was at a considerable disadvantage to its British and American competitors, but he remained circumspect with Bousquet a few days later, telling him that although TCA's independent recommendation would be essential to the final decision, the Cabinet could take political contingencies into account if it was judged that technical factors among the competitors were roughly equal.[73]

By this point, Bousquet's lobbying of Quebec figures had become a source of annoyance in Ottawa, where his efforts were viewed as an unsubtle attempt to bring pressure to bear. This strategy bore fruit, however, when many Quebec members of Parliament asked the minister of transport to confirm press reports that TCA had selected the Douglas DC-9, and the federal Liberal Quebec caucus issued a press release supporting the Caravelle. Meanwhile, in Quebec, a Cabinet discussion resulted in a public statement emphasizing the Lesage government's support of the Sud-Aviation bid.[74]

Matters degenerated quickly after the official announcement of the winning Douglas bid, when Gordon MacGregor, president of TCA, made disparaging comments about the Caravelle before the House of Commons Transport Committee. Bousquet compared the ensuing controversy to the preceding year's Gordon affair,[75] reporting that MacGregor had been subjected to intense questioning from the committee's francophone members and that protesters had marched on TCA's Montreal office. MacGregor's remarks were interpreted in nationalist circles as an insult against not simply Sud-Aviation, but Quebec. Coming as they did amid francophone frustration and disappointment over the failed deal, the comments went to the heart of sensitivities over French Canada's economic marginalization and neo-nationalist determination to develop Quebec's technical capacity and industrial base.[76]

Federal authorities were even more alarmed over discussions between Quebec City and Paris regarding a French loan to Quebec. Two years into his posting as ambassador, Bousquet observed that only the United States's banking system was able to assure Quebec the means needed for its investment and nationalization policy; unless European market conditions changed, any new francophone state would face the same reliance on American capital markets as did Canada. Shortly after Bousquet made this report, word arrived from Lussier in Paris that an unnamed French minister had confided to him that France's government was studying a possible financial agreement with Quebec equal to that recently initiated with Mexico, suggesting Quebec could expect to obtain approximately $150 million.[77]

Progress proved slow and difficult. Nothing had transpired by the time the Union Nationale returned to power, at which time Daniel Johnson was told that the matter was dividing the French administration: one camp favoured a loan to help Quebec establish SIDBEC, whereas another preferred a direct loan to the Quebec government. Even more frustrating was the news that no one within the French government had truly taken up the issue. Paris's early reimbursement of its post-war debt to the United States that autumn led Quebec officials to anticipate a similar repayment of the $67 million outstanding from Canada's loan to France in 1946. Seizing the opportunity, Quebec officials developed a daring proposal: France should pay the debt back early, but with a stipulation that these monies should go to Quebec City. Johnson's economic adviser, Jacques Parizeau, and the deputy minister of finance, Marcel Cazavan, outlined an arrangement whereby a consortium of banks in Quebec would hold the funds temporarily and lend them to the Quebec government, which would then pay Ottawa back according to the original repayment schedule.[78]

The Élysée recommended in favour of the Quebec proposal – with the proviso that it receive Couve de Murville's agreement. Consistent with the MAE's more nuanced and orthodox approach to the triangular relationship, however, the scheme got a cool reception at the Quai d'Orsay. The secretary-general, Hervé Alphand, told Chapdelaine about the MAE's reservations, especially its belief that Ottawa would not accept a situation in which its position as debt holder was effectively usurped. With Couve de Murville apparently opposing the plan for fear of the federal reaction, Chapdelaine could only decry Ottawa's intransigence.[79]

Indeed, news of the Quebec proposal had reached Ottawa. The federal Cabinet was strongly opposed, fearing that it would be perceived as interference in Canadian affairs and as French aid to Quebec that Ottawa was unable or unwilling to extend. Marcel Cadieux suggested an alternative: Ottawa could agree on condition that the monies were made available to all provinces. Another option was for Paris to make the funds available to a private consortium in France for relending to Quebec, in order to obviate any suggestion of a government-to-government arrangement. Jules Léger took a more indulgent view, observing that the unusual arrangement was an acceptable price for the benefits of strengthened Franco-Canadian relations.[80]

Federal objections, however, meant that Paris's answer to Quebec's proposal was no. Undaunted, Chapdelaine continued his lobbying, even raising the matter with de Gaulle. He explained that Ottawa could be persuaded to support the measure but that this was beside the point, since what was proposed would not affect Ottawa being reimbursed according to the original loan schedule. De Gaulle promised to re-examine the matter when Chapdelaine emphasized the loan's symbolic benefit, citing the fact that Jean Drapeau had wished to see Montreal's Métro built with French capital but had been forced to opt for American funding. Ultimately, the unusual financial deal was not realized; Paris was willing only to facilitate a new loan on French financial markets.[81]

Taking place amid these loan discussions, the visits that de Gaulle and Johnson undertook in 1967 were designed partly to boost economic relations between France and Quebec. The premier sought assistance for Quebec's financial and technical needs when he travelled to Paris. He also lobbied successfully for the creation of a joint committee of senior public and private sector figures to recommend measures to strengthen relations – the Comité franco-québécois sur les investissements. De Gaulle lauded the economic cooperation between France and Quebec during his own visit, and Paris reinforced its efforts afterward: the monies allocated for technical cooperation for 1968 jumped nearly ten-fold.[82] Although Johnson never made his second trip to France, during his final press conference he insisted that the primary objective of his planned visit was to increase French investment in Quebec and strengthen economic relations. It was telling of French official attitudes that senior figures believed that the premier should leave Paris with something to show for it: when the head of French petroleum giant Société nationale des pétroles d'Aquitaine, a subsidiary of the state-owned Entreprise de recherches et d'activités pétrolières, expressed reluctance over participating in a proposed Quebec oil refinery project, Michel Debré, recently appointed as foreign minister, made clear to him that the refinery project had a political dimension, and was thus a foregone conclusion.[83]

Paris and Quebec City's efforts to overcome structural economic realities created a growing dilemma for Ottawa as it engaged in its own political push to promote exchanges between France and the whole of Canada. Federal officials saw their initiatives hampered as relations with Paris deteriorated in the economic sphere and beyond. Ottawa tried to revive the Canada-France Economic Committee, moribund since 1953. Memories of the committee's limited effectiveness were softened somewhat by initial federal optimism that Paris appeared to be trying to boost French investments in Canada. But the circumstances under which the committee had been established had long since changed; Ottawa was now the *demandeur* and it was Paris's turn to be lukewarm. The MAE was noncommittal when Pearson proposed that the committee be revived and raised to a ministerial level to make it equivalent to Canada's arrangements with the British and Americans. Pearson also raised the matter with de Gaulle, who replied that to justify such high-level meetings, any committee had to possess sufficiently important subject matter, and in his view France and Canada simply did not have enough in common. Couve de Murville echoed this assessment (and Ottawa's response of thirteen years prior) when he claimed that although Paris greatly desired to develop relations and hold talks as the need arose, a formal ministerial committee with regular meetings posed challenges in terms of workload and timing.[84]

Undaunted by Paris's tepid reaction, federal officials worked to revive the committee at an official level, and Paris gave in to Ottawa's lobbying at the end of 1964.[85] The divergence between the two countries' commercial policies, however, remained an obstacle. There was frustration in the DEA over French reluctance to discuss multilateral issues such as the ECM or GATT. When the revived committee finally met in November 1965, François Leduc denigrated Ottawa's interest by suggesting that it stemmed from a concern with having a federal, institutional counterweight to Quebec's economic links with France. While acknowledging the utility of talks and federal officials' hope to dilute

American economic influence, he nonetheless emphasized the meeting's rather meagre results.[86]

Leduc's assessment of federal motivations, if somewhat uncharitable, was generally correct. Growing cooperation between France and Quebec reinforced Ottawa's determination to cultivate economic relations; in 1960, Canadian investments in France had stood at only $24 million, approximately 1 percent of Canadian overseas holdings, while French investments in 1959 were similarly estimated at constituting only 1 percent of foreign direct investment in Canada. As for the trade relationship, notwithstanding the progress seen in 1959-60, the ongoing relative stagnation cried out for action, as did the fact that Canada's principal exports to France tended to be wheat and semi-fabricated iron, steel, and non-ferrous metals, while the principle French goods that Canada purchased were steel-making products, alcoholic beverages, and textiles. Of particular concern was the considerable decline in sales, after some initial success, of French automobiles.[87] Federal concern about the triangular dynamic's economic component was apparent when the DEA instructed Léger to take advantage of an encounter with Lesage to enquire how Ottawa could participate in SOMA and SIDBEC to give them a "more solid Canadian character."[88] Anxious to ensure SOMA's success, federal officials moved swiftly to resolve tariff issues and secure an exemption from Canadian content regulations. When the automotive assembly plant later encountered financial difficulties, a federal sales tax break was arranged to dissuade Renault and Peugeot from abandoning the operation. Indeed, Ottawa harboured hopes of seeing another French assembly plant established, this one located outside Quebec – and preferably in Martin's Windsor riding.[89]

Ottawa organized a trade mission to France to reciprocate for the Baumgartner mission. Canada's industry minister, Charles Drury, led the federally sponsored delegation to France, which included the deputy minister of commerce, a deputy governor of the Bank of Canada, the director of Quebec's SGF, and members of Canada's business community, including senior Quebec figures. In addition to the Drury mission, the department of trade and commerce doubled Canadian participation in French trade fairs, boosted the number of economic officers in the Paris embassy, and intensified its publicity work. Ottawa was even able to take solace from an agreement that it reached with Paris in September 1968 providing for the sale of Canadian plutonium for use in France's nuclear reactors.[90]

Yet the unavoidable reality was that the broader record was less than satisfying for Ottawa. Two years after visiting Paris, Pearson expressed disappointment to de Gaulle over the limited progress and urged a greater effort. Although the absolute value of trade between the two countries had grown, exports to France had actually *diminished* as a percentage of Canada's export trade, and France's exports were flowing increasingly to its ECM partners. De Gaulle conceded the importance of developing exchanges but asserted that the private sector had to take the lead, even as he invoked the French protectionist tradition to explain that it would take time for France to adjust to international competition. The French leader's ungenerous response stood in stark contrast to the active political engagement marking his attitude toward economic links with Quebec.[91]

In the aftermath of de Gaulle's *cri du balcon,* federal frustration over the difficulties in cultivating the economic relationship was superseded by concern that Paris and Quebec City were pursuing their cooperation in a manner that threatened federal prerogatives and Canadian unity. The provisions in the Johnson-Peyrefitte agreement for regular economic meetings between French and Quebec ministers prompted the DEA to warn Leduc of the potential encroachment on federal jurisdiction, arguing that the meetings could not be carried out under the auspices of a France-Quebec intergovernmental organization.[92] As part of the broader federal response to the triangular crisis, Ottawa decided to renegotiate its 1933 commercial agreement with France. Cadieux recognized that de Gaulle was not influenced by such material considerations and that the disguised denunciation of the treaty was not likely to provoke "riots in French cities," but he welcomed it as a tangible and symbolic signal to Paris that there were consequences for its actions.[93] Whatever satisfaction might have been gained from the gesture was matched by annoyance when, following the January 1969 report of the Comité franco-québécois sur les investissements established during Johnson's Paris visit, Quebec's minister of education, Jean-Guy Cardinal, and Michel Debré exchanged letters establishing a permanent committee charged with developing economic links. Ottawa was informed only at the last moment.[94]

Yet, Ottawa's marginalization is insufficient as an explanation of its apparent inability to realize more fruitful relations with France. De Gaulle's response to Pearson's entreaties for greater trade pointed to a factor crucial not just in Franco-Canadian economic relations, but in the efforts of Paris and Quebec City to boost exchanges. Although de Gaulle possessed "no particular affinity for capitalism or capitalists" and rejected American economic leadership, Gaullism proved in many respects to be a sheep in nationalist wolf's clothing: moderate economic nationalism and use of the state as an agent of modernization were the order of the day even as France's economy was increasingly integrated into the liberal capitalist international system. Indeed, the Fifth Republic's economic policy was meant to ensure French success in this system, as was apparent in Paris's lowering of tariffs in 1959, and the subsequent IVth Plan that sought to reduce the level of government intervention in favour of market forces.[95] Although Gaullist nationalism was dedicated to challenging American predominance, it was not at odds with – and, indeed, actively participated in – the liberal capitalist order, so that the conflict was between "two different economic organizations within the same philosophical framework" rather than "two opposing ideologies."[96]

The dynamic points to the central role that broader economic structural realities, flowing from the ideological predispositions on both sides of the Atlantic, occupied in the triangular relationship. Although not without some qualification, the participation of Ottawa, Quebec City, and Paris in the liberal capitalist system meant their incorporation into a network of relations in which the economic freedom of market actors was expanded whereas the power of government to place restrictions on that freedom was circumscribed.[97] During the colonial era, French authorities had warned of the effective rivalry between the economies of New France and its metropole; for all that had changed since that time, the French and Canadian economies remained more competitors than complementary, and both were oriented toward their respective continental markets. Canadian investments in France had more than doubled to $58 million by 1967, but still accounted for only about 1 percent of Canadian overseas holdings. While the value of Canada's exports to France grew by 53 percent in absolute terms in 1969, only 13 percent of these exports were manufactured goods. Similarly, although the value of French direct investment in Canada as a whole had tripled between 1955 and 1967, it remained negligible relative to total foreign investment in the country.[98]

These structural factors were similarly decisive in the outcome of Paris and Quebec City's efforts to develop economic links. As his posting to Paris came to an end in 1970, Patrick Hyndman, the delegation-general's economic counsellor, praised the growth of French investment in Canada over the preceding years and noted that Quebec had attracted the majority of secondary industry investment. Hyndman was forced to admit, however, that the level of French industrial investment remained far below the province's needs. Trade statistics were similarly disappointing: in 1968, France was ranked ninth among countries purchasing Quebec goods, well behind the United States, Britain, West Germany, and Japan. French products fared little better, placing sixth on the list of Quebec imports. It would not be until the 1980s that any significant relative change would occur in this aspect of the relationship, and even then the results would remain limited. Notwithstanding the political effort of the preceding decade, the expansion of economic relations between France and Quebec had encountered a number of obstacles.[99]

Most dramatic among these obstacles were the economic repercussions of the events of May 1968. France's political earthquake set off a cycle of production disruptions and a deteriorating commercial position that provoked a major currency crisis and France's largest balance-of-payment deficit since the Second World War. The Fifth Republic's economic success and French *grandeur* were threatened. The crisis obliged France to review its foreign policy, rejoin the international gold pool, and make massive spending cuts that affected core Gaullist priorities. Paris was also forced to seek American support to avoid a devaluation of the franc, pushing France toward a greater dependence on Washington than it had experienced in recent years and signalling the effective end of the Gaullist challenge to American economic leadership.[100] If Gaullist economic nationalism had correctly identified the challenges arising from preponderant American economic power, it was not able to escape its internal contradictions and was bested by the interdependence and transnational exchanges to which it was reacting – and contributing. Paris's capacity to foster economic cooperation with Quebec was thus undermined. The priority instead, at least in the immediate term, was domestic economic recovery.[101]

But even before the economic crisis of 1968, Paris was having to come to terms with the shortcomings of the Gaullist economic challenge. Paris had been outflanked in its effort to discourage American foreign direct investment, as this had flowed toward other ECM members, notably West Germany. Fears that such a trend could result in France falling behind its European partners, especially in the high-technology sector, compelled Paris to revert to a more liberal policy in 1966. Paris's offensive against the American dollar was also in tatters. France found itself isolated among its European partners in the face of the crisis that struck the American dollar over the winter of 1967-68, as they opted to support the beleaguered American currency and existing international monetary system. It would fall to Georges Pompidou to oversee the devaluation of the franc that de Gaulle had resisted so tenaciously.[102]

These outcomes point to the final major obstacle to the realization of a more substantive relationship between France and Quebec: private sector attitudes. The bitter, yet unavoidable, truth was that for all of the political prodding, the French and Quebec private sectors remained rather unenthusiastic about the special relationship and oriented toward their respective continental markets. A significant part of the explanation for private sector reticence was its misgivings over the rise of Quebec separatism; the concern over where political events could lead discouraged it from rising to the nationalist bait. In this sense, there was a contradiction in the logic of those who were moving to expand economic relations between France and Quebec as a means to realizing greater Quebec autonomy. Yet there was a surprising lack of sensitivity in the French corridors of power to the ramifications of the independence debate and, more broadly, the province's economic health. De Gaulle, for example, dismissed the notion that the question would scare off American investors. When André Bettencourt, the secretary of state for foreign affairs, told Chapdelaine that Quebec was destined for sovereignty given its popularity among the younger generations, the exasperated diplomat had to keep from retorting that the province's development nevertheless depended upon the older generations who controlled the levers of economic power and were less inclined to embark on political adventures. In an analysis fundamentally at odds with the notions of liberation underpinning efforts to develop cooperation between France and Quebec, and with the very logic of the Quiet Revolution, Bettencourt and the Élysée's diplomatic counsellor, René de Saint-Légier de la Saussaye, admitted that the United States would remain Quebec's main source of foreign direct investment, but opined that American dollars would continue to flow regardless of events so long as Quebec had natural resources.[103]

Even the transatlantic links that were forged did not necessarily follow the political lead of Paris and Quebec City. French tire manufacturer Michelin announced that its new North American plant would be in Nova Scotia, a decision motivated by Halifax's ice-free port and by what François Michelin described as his company's need for "English immersion."[104] A similar scenario played out when French aluminum giant Péchiney decided against locating its North American plant in Quebec. High-level political interventions by Paris and Quebec City could not overcome the fact that Péchiney found Hydro-Québec's power rates too high and Quebec's alleged value as a bridgehead trumped by the savings on customs duties and transportation gained by locating in the United States.[105]

Emblematic of the decidedly mixed record of political efforts to expand economic relations was SOMA, which was bedevilled by difficulties from the moment it opened. The doubling of sales figures in 1968 fuelled cautious optimism about the assembly plant, as well as claims about what a committed political will could accomplish in the economic sector. The reality, however, was that the operation was not profitable. As federal minister Jean Marchand had noted sarcastically, even the most nationalist Quebecer could not be convinced to prefer a Peugeot or Renault over an American vehicle. Despite interventions by the highest levels of the French and Quebec governments, the problem-plagued plant fell silent at the end of 1972.[106]

Such developments had negative repercussions, given the Quebec public's demand for French investment as proof of the tangible benefits of the special relationship. Leduc had observed that whereas the nationalist elite was preoccupied with using economic links with France to advance its political project, the general population was interested in the more prosaic concerns of employment opportunities and an improved standard of living. The Michelin decision provoked an especially strong reaction: the new Quebec Liberal leader, Robert Bourassa, exploited the situation by criticizing the Union Nationale for its "Parisian splendours" and accusing France of not matching its rhetoric with action.[107]

IN 1965, FRENCH INTELLECTUAL Jean-Marie Domenach had offered a pessimistic prediction that the margins of manoeuvre and the potential for success of *dirigisme* were heavily circumscribed in a liberal capitalist international order. Five years later, his analysis was being borne out.[108] Despite political efforts on both sides of the Atlantic, and despite the progress that had occurred in absolute terms, the combined efforts of Gaullism and Quebec neo-nationalism had been unable to overcome the international economic realities spurring their collaboration and the broader official rapprochement. Although the political will existed, there did not appear a way around transnational exchanges, interdependence, and the regionalization of international trade. For all of the ambivalence about liberal capitalism and its implications that had informed the evolution of Quebec nationalism and Gaullism, as well as their cooperation, these two nationalist reactions ultimately subscribed to the logic of this economic model, and the private sector simply was not willing to dance to the tune that Paris and Quebec City were calling.

In this sense, the disappointing results of Paris and Quebec City's efforts can be viewed as the counterpart to the Diefenbaker government's unsuccessful bid to restore and strengthen the British economic counterweight to the United States. In both cases, the attraction of the putative partners' respective continental markets proved stronger and thus precluded the realization of more substantive economic relations. The parallel between these two examples is a useful reminder that attempts by the Pearson government, with its mild economic nationalism, to alter the dynamic of relations in the triangle were found similarly wanting. The relative value of Canadian exports to France was actually *lower* in 1970 than it had been a decade earlier. The trend was equally disappointing regarding French goods, the relative value of which had grown only slightly. As the 1960s drew to a close, the post-war economic dynamic in the triangle remained: the efforts of the three capitals had contributed to the absolute growth of trade between Canada and France, an outcome consistent with global trends; however, the relationship remained stagnant in relative terms.

Yet there was a profound irony to this outcome. The Gaullist republic's failed challenge to the United States's economic leadership – and, more broadly, its inability to harness the accompanying international economic trends to nationalist ends – provoked a period of profound political and economic turmoil in France. Among the consequences of this upheaval was Paris's reduced ability to pursue its Quebec policy, mitigating the most immediate threat to Canadian sovereignty represented by the Gaullist interventions. Thus, the preponderant American economic power and international economic trends over which Canadian nationalist angst had only grown in the 1960s ultimately proved a crucial – if inadvertent – Canadian ally in the face of the Gaullist and Quebec neo-nationalist challenges.

CHAPTER TEN

Rivalry, Recrimination, and Renewal: Triangular Cultural Relations

MARCEL CADIEUX WAS FURIOUS. As 1965 drew to a close, Quebec's relations with France were reaching new heights while Ottawa was increasingly at a disadvantage. The DEA under-secretary had just learned from newspaper reports of the lavish welcome that Paris had accorded Quebec's minister of education, Paul Gérin-Lajoie, and minister of cultural affairs, Pierre Laporte. In addition to meeting more French Cabinet ministers in one week than federal ministers had encountered in an entire year, the two Quebecers had been granted an audience with de Gaulle, who had hosted a luncheon from which Canada's ambassador, Jules Léger, had been pointedly excluded. The scope of the reception appeared to be an endorsement of the doctrine to which Gérin-Lajoie had lent his name. Refusing to see the federal government left out in the cold, Cadieux confided to Léger that his initial inclination was to find a retaliatory measure to demonstrate that Ottawa was not naïve about the special relationship between France and Quebec, and that its patience had limits. Despite his anger, however, Cadieux acknowledged the need to proceed cautiously, as any reprisals ran the risk of Paris forging stronger links with Quebec City.[1]

The episode demonstrates the centrality of cultural affairs in the triangular relationship. Culture was a driving force of the tensions, for what was at stake was nothing less than which level of government was to be French Canada's international voice and have responsibility for preserving and promoting North America's *fait français*. This jurisdictional struggle only grew in salience as the state became increasingly involved in the cultural sphere. Education issues loomed especially large. In an immediate sense, education was the epicentre of the triangular dynamic, the point where Canadian intergovernmental rivalries and the Gaullist and Quebec nationalist reactions converged. The importance of education to the Quiet Revolution, combined with neo-nationalist determination to see Quebec serve as French Canada's national state, prompted Quebec to project its jurisdiction in cultural affairs abroad, seeking out cooperation with France and challenging federal activism. Quebec's cultural diplomacy was received enthusiastically in Paris. Gaullist interest in challenging all facets of American power, the growing belief that Quebec was destined to achieve a new political status, and a preoccupation with promoting French culture in North America made for a potent nationalist cocktail.

It was Ottawa, however, that suffered the hangover. Federal officials welcomed increased cultural exchanges between France and Quebec in the abstract, but misgivings grew as Paris and Quebec City concluded a series of cultural agreements of expanding scope and an increasingly official nature. With cultural diplomacy combining the jurisdictional rivalry over culture and foreign affairs, the fear in Ottawa was that Quebec City – with French connivance – was undermining the federal constitutional position and, along with this, the Pearson government's biculturalism efforts and national unity. Determined to protect its prerogative in foreign affairs and assert its capacity to serve as an interlocutor with the francophone world, Ottawa sought its own agreement with Paris. As federal actions collided with those of an equally determined Quebec City, the intergovernmental struggle was internationalized and France was drawn into Canadian affairs.

This race for agreements was a barometer of the intensifying rivalry and, more broadly, the intersecting nationalist reactions spurring the triangular dynamic. As cultural cooperation deepened between France and Quebec, Ottawa was increasingly left out. Indeed, Paris and Quebec City employed the agreements that they concluded in 1965 not simply to cultivate exchanges, but to justify increasingly direct relations and, by implication, assert Quebec's international capacity. Ottawa was ill placed to respond effectively, and its eclipse appeared to be confirmed as Paris bypassed it in dealings not only with Quebec but with francophone communities outside the province. Long marginalized within Canada, members of these communities – notably the Acadians – seized the opportunity for assistance, becoming participants and pawns in the triangular tensions. To safeguard its increasingly undermined authority, Ottawa fought a rearguard action that involved ramping up Canadian cultural diplomacy in France, boosting aid to francophone minority communities, and protesting what it condemned as abuses of the cultural cooperation agreements that it had sanctioned. When these agreements came up for renewal in 1970, Ottawa faced an unpalatable choice between continuing the difficulties of the preceding years and rejecting renewal, thereby exacerbating the triangular crisis.

ALTHOUGH CULTURAL COOPERATION with France was not Quebec premier Jean Lesage's foremost priority when the Maison du Québec opened, it was certainly a much higher concern for other members of his Cabinet, notably Georges-

Émile Lapalme and Paul Gérin-Lajoie. The Francophilic Lapalme had been in Paris in 1958, when André Malraux was handed responsibility for France's newly created ministry of culture, and it inspired him to recommend such a ministry for Quebec. He viewed Quebec's new Paris office primarily in cultural terms, as reflected in his selection of Charles Lussier as delegate-general; the former director of the Maison des étudiants canadiens, Lussier had been involved in Quebec's education links with France.[2] Despite its initially vague mandate, the Maison du Québec set about strengthening French Canada's cultural presence, including participation in a number of art exhibitions, hosting colloquia, sponsoring book launches, and promoting Quebec literature. By the end of 1962, a year that saw a cultural counsellor added to the Maison, Lussier declared that its mere existence was contributing to a heightened profile for French Canada.[3]

Quebec City's interest corresponded to that of Paris. After his 1960 visit, de Gaulle was determined to see increased cultural relations with French Canada. The MAE accordingly reorganized France's cultural representation in Canada in a manner that foreshadowed Paris's two-nation approach; the cultural attaché in Ottawa was transferred to a new cultural office in Montreal and a second attaché was appointed to Quebec City. The French ambassador, Francis Lacoste, opposed the measure, warning that it could signal that Paris's cultural activity was becoming Quebec-centric and be interpreted in federal circles as an encouragement of French-Canadian "particularism" and even a threat to Ottawa's authority in foreign affairs. The MAE's Amérique division shared Lacoste's concern and echoed, in vain, his call for the second attaché to be appointed to Toronto instead of Quebec City to demonstrate France's neutrality and desire to conduct pan-Canadian activities.[4]

Lacoste's misgivings proved astute. The under-secretary of state for external affairs, Norman Robertson, considered the reorganization provocative.[5] Lacoste was called to the DEA, where he was told that "extremist groups" in Quebec "anxious to involve French representation in their schemes" could exploit Paris's decision. Ottawa also requested that Paris not proceed with, or at least delay, appointing the Quebec City attaché. Jean Basdevant, head of the MAE's cultural relations division, assured Canada's ambassador, Pierre Dupuy, that the appointments would be made with "maximum discretion," intimating that an attaché would be appointed to Toronto in the future. On the basis of this exchange, Cadieux, at the time assistant under-secretary, concluded that Ottawa could realistically take no further action except urge Paris to proceed as quickly as possible on the Toronto appointment.[6]

The attaché episode, combined with the new Quebec office in Paris and the founding of the Association des universités partiellement ou entièrement de la langue française (AUPELF) fuelled DEA interest in expanding Canada's cultural relations. Cadieux, exceptional in the department for the value that he attached to cultural diplomacy, expressed hope that AUPELF would serve as a vehicle for federal participation in scholarship exchanges with francophone countries. He also wanted a special inter-agency committee created to review Canada's cultural links with France, believing it essential, given the new Maison du Québec, that the embassy be able to count on the support of all federal organs involved in cultural affairs.[7]

Consistent with its troubled relationship with French Canada, however, the Diefenbaker government's response to cultural relations with the francophone world remained lacklustre. Whereas Ottawa had allocated $3.5 million annually since 1959 to African members of the Commonwealth for education purposes, the newly independent francophone states in Africa were initially given only small, one-time gifts of scholarships. Cadieux's efforts secured a $600,000 annual education aid fund to send Canadian teachers to francophone Africa, but the secretary of state for external affairs, Howard Green, halved the amount, and only with Robertson's and Cadieux's sustained lobbying did the funds remain dedicated to francophone Africa.[8]

The Pearson government arrived in office with a greater sense of urgency to develop cultural relations with France, spurred by the multiplying questions in Quebec regarding the federal will and ability to cultivate links with the francophone world. The DEA accelerated study of a proposal, supported enthusiastically by Paul Martin, that Ottawa should spearhead the creation of a multilateral cultural cooperation program among francophone countries that would build on the education aid program for francophone Africa. It was hoped that the program would also promote greater cooperation between Ottawa and Quebec City and thereby strengthen national unity. In outlining the federal initiative and the broader cultural strategy to Martin, Cadieux suggested avoiding constitutional difficulties by having the Canada Council administer it under DEA supervision. Mindful of the Pearson government's goal of cooperative federalism, Cadieux recommended consultations with Quebec City prior to any announcement, and he even raised the possibility of Quebec making a financial contribution to the program.[9]

The federal proposal was stillborn, however, as Paris preferred to keep cultural relations with its former colonies on a bilateral basis, and it thus opposed the initiative.[10] Faced with this setback, the DEA created a $250,000 budget for cultural exchanges with francophone Europe. But the apparent significance of the move was belied by the fact that it simply consolidated funds that Ottawa was already distributing, formalizing and focusing their dispersal in order to fly the federal flag more prominently. By late 1963, such considerations were increasingly important, as a DEA report described Quebec's expanding cultural links with France as "a classic example" of Quebec City taking Ottawa's place as a result of federal difficulties in operating in the domain.[11]

Yet even as the DEA bemoaned Ottawa's apparent usurpation, elements in Quebec City were anxious about the impact on Quebec's francophone majority of the clash between Canadian and Quebec nationalism and, more specifically, the jurisdictional dispute between the federal and Quebec governments over culture. Although education was an exclusive provincial jurisdiction, the acrimonious post-war debate over federal funding of post-secondary institutions had exposed the difference between theory and practice. In an internal Quebec government report, Université de Montréal law professor Jacques-Yvan Morin ascribed increasing federal cultural activism to the growth and evolution of English-Canadian nationalism. He feared that, having engaged on this path, Ottawa would be sorely tempted to assume responsibility for the protection and promotion of francophone culture, which would threaten the neo-nationalist shibboleth that Quebec City should possess exclusive responsibility for the *fait français*. Morin declared that it was crucial for Quebec to assert its cultural leadership by accumulating precedents and establishing the administrative capacity to counter federal encroachments, thereby ensuring that Quebec City would serve as the interlocutor between France and North America's francophones.[12]

Quebec accordingly challenged Ottawa's proposed cultural exchange program. The deputy minister for cultural affairs, Guy Frégault, derided it as a public relations stunt in anticipation of Pearson's 1964 visit to Paris, a brazen attempt to steal Quebec's thunder. In addition to expressing concern that Quebec participation in the initiative would simply encourage federal incursions, he cited the parsimonious budget as proof that the principle aim was publicity. After the Quebec Cabinet discussed the dispute, Claude Morin, the deputy minister of federal-provincial affairs, was dispatched to Ottawa. In a difficult meeting with Cadieux, Morin emphasized that Quebec City could entertain only a token federal role in cultural relations, since too high a profile would encourage Paris to take a pan-Canadian approach to exchanges and divert resources better concentrated in Quebec.[13]

The dispute was but one example of an evolving triangular dynamic that Malraux's visit to Canada in 1963 underscored. Meeting with Martin in Ottawa, the French minister offered assurances that Paris had no hidden objectives in its relations with Canada; rather, it hoped that expanding cultural and technical exchange programs would contribute to "the evolving country that is Canada."[14] The cryptic remark was consistent with Paris's progressive shift toward an overtly two-nation approach, as Quebec was the priority. Both the Quebec and French governments had only recently equipped themselves with cultural affairs ministries – the ranks of the latter swelled by an influx of returning bureaucrats as a result of decolonization – making a cooperation program attractive as each ministry established itself on its respective governmental landscape.[15] During the Quebec portion of the visit, Malraux and Lesage agreed that after some initial smaller projects, a more formal cooperation program would be developed. Lesage welcomed the prospect, but his foremost priorities remained economic, whereas the much more enthusiastic Lapalme recalled Malraux's visit as the "grand départ" of Quebec's cultural cooperation with France.[16]

From Paris's perspective, the trip was a great success, even if diplomats in the MAE were taken aback by some of Malraux's improvised remarks. Bousquet dismissed rumours that Pearson was trying to hamper cultural cooperation between France and Quebec and argued that, to the contrary, federal authorities wished to encourage such cooperation but in a manner allowing for their input.[17] Indeed, Ottawa was generally pleased with the visit, since it served as the occasion to sign a cinematography agreement to facilitate co-productions between Canada's National Film Board and the Centre nationale de la cinématographie française. Although the tenor of some of Malraux's remarks prompted some concern – they could lend themselves to a nationalist interpretation if taken out of context – a DEA analysis ascribed them to the French minister's literary background; calls for French Canadians to "take France's hand" were explained as an attempt to emphasize that French Canadians (and, through them, all Canadians) were participants in the cultural values of France and Western Europe. Ottawa was also reassured by the fact that Malraux had emphasized that his improvised remarks were to be understood within a strictly cultural context; there was no question of encouraging Quebec to become a French political satellite.[18]

Ottawa's foremost concern was Quebec City. Although federal officials felt that Lesage had kept a proper measure in expressing Quebec sympathy for France, they were annoyed with Lapalme. His failure to associate federal representatives with Quebec-sponsored events during the visit was resented as a flagrant attempt to marginalize Ottawa. René Garneau, the Canadian embassy's cultural counsellor, derived comfort from the surprise that visiting French officials had expressed over the deputy premier's attitude, citing this as proof that Paris had not lost "the correct sense of things." Garneau reassured his colleagues that although Quebec would likely continue to make a minimal effort to inform federal authorities of its cultural activities with France, the embassy's contacts would ensure that Ottawa was kept informed.[19] The diplomat did not address the question, however, of what would happen if French attitudes shifted.

THE TRIANGULAR DYNAMIC GREW more pronounced following Malraux's visit, with cultural affairs a source of thickening tension as Ottawa and Quebec City competed to be Paris's primary interlocutor and the French capital increasingly favoured the latter. An early example came in the form of an agreement facilitating the studies of Canadian bureaucrats at France's École nationale d'administration (ENA). The origins of the agreement lay in contacts between ENA and Quebec university figures, notably Monsignor Irénée Lussier, the rector of the Université de Montréal, who had been at the forefront of establishing AUPELF and was the brother of Quebec's delegate-general. After enthusiastic responses from Quebec City and Ottawa, an exchange of letters during Pearson's visit to Paris established the program.

The project reflected growing French interest in Quebec, as the Élysée had intervened (allegedly at the behest of Quebec lobby members Philippe Rossillon and Bernard Dorin) to ensure that there were funds for the exchanges. The agreement also provided an occasion for differences between Ottawa and Quebec City. The latter considered the exchange of letters a federal encroachment on Quebec's education jurisdiction, made all the more bitter by two of the dozen posts going to federal bureaucrats instead of all being reserved for Quebec's civil servants. Constitutional sensitivities had also been aggravated by Bousquet's failing to inform Ottawa that the Quebec government had already reached an agreement in principle with the ENA, so that the subsequent federal participation appeared to Quebec officials to be a blatant attempt to outflank the province.[20]

The dispute not only previewed subsequent tensions but testified to how education questions drove them. Eric Hobsbawm has written of the global "education revolution" that saw the rapid expansion of educational and university systems. Beyond the demographic impetus of the baby boom, education was of heightened importance as it was considered an essential vehicle for modernization and economic success in the latter half of the twentieth century, the only means through which countries could avoid the unwelcome fate of being left behind.[21] Interwar concern in Quebec that the education system was inadequate and contributing to French Canada's socio-economic marginalization only grew after 1945. Education reform was prominent on the public agenda by the mid-1950s, with activists and critics viewing it as essential to contend with the challenges of modernization and preserve the province's *francité* and Catholic values.[22] Changes to the education system, notably an enhanced role for the Quebec state, were meant to reaffirm a sense of national cohesion and integrity in a society experiencing rapid socio-economic change. Education was thus a centrepiece of the Quiet Revolution. Linking it explicitly to francophone economic empowerment, Lesage declared that the revenge of the cradle no longer guaranteed French Canada's future, which was henceforth to be assured through "the re-conquest of the mind."[23] As the Quebec state expanded its control over education, it assumed the heady responsibility for preserving and promoting the province's francophone majority. Quebec City was determined to live up to this mission at home and abroad, and thus was unwilling to brook federal interference. Such neo-nationalist aims clashed, however, with Ottawa's equally strong determination to maintain its prerogative in foreign affairs, as well as to fund the post-secondary education and research deemed crucial for Canada's development.[24]

The importance of education to cultural triangular relations and the trend toward increasingly formal relations between Paris and Quebec City was apparent soon after Quebec's ministry of education was created in 1964. Gaston Cholette, head of Quebec's Service de la coopération avec l'extérieur, had previously approached Bousquet to propose an education cooperation agreement. Visiting Quebec that spring, Xavier Deniau, a deputy in France's National Assembly prominent in the Quebec lobby, discussed the idea with Bousquet, Lesage, and Gérin-Lajoie. After the French embassy informed the DEA of the exploratory talks the following month, Martin explained that Ottawa welcomed expanded education links between Paris and Quebec City, but that to respect the federal prerogative in foreign affairs, any agreement would require Ottawa's explicit consent. Given the time constraints involved and the concern in the DEA with avoiding the accusation that it was interfering in provincial jurisdiction, it was agreed that the ASTEF agreement would serve as a model: negotiations would be mainly between Paris and Quebec City, with Ottawa joining at the final stage to signal its consent through an exchange of letters with French authorities. Ottawa also made clear, however, that it considered any agreement provisional, to be superseded by an eventual France-Canada cultural accord.[25]

With Ottawa having signalled its consent, discussions between Paris and Quebec City intensified. The negotiations offered a window into neo-nationalist thinking. In seeking de Gaulle's support, Lesage described the initiative as a crucial tool to help Quebec build the structures indispensable to its future. He claimed that it was necessary in order to realize the Quiet Revolution's full potential, and as a means to solidify Quebec's links with France and the larger international francophone community. As such, the agreement was intended to help Quebec achieve its modernization while retaining its cultural specificity.[26] Indeed, nationalist preoccupations with Quebec's *francité* and protecting the general population from Americanization loomed large in the project. During his February 1965 visit to Paris, Gérin-Lajoie confided to Alain Peyrefitte, at the time France's minister of information, that he viewed the agreement as a tool that would help him fight *joualistes* such as playwright Michel Tremblay and singer Robert Charlebois and purify the French spoken in Quebec.[27] The remarks underscored that notwithstanding the eclipse of traditional nationalist hostility for *France moderne*, profound divisions remained among Quebec nationalists, and notably between the bourgeois elite and popular classes, over the "French" and "American" components of francophone Quebec's identity.

Beyond revealing neo-nationalist aspirations, the education agreement negotiations were a measure of growing Quebec assertiveness. It was initially envisaged that Gérin-Lajoie would sign a series of agreements with a quasi-public organization to be established in Paris and overseen by a joint France-Quebec committee. Gérin-Lajoie and Lesage subsequently pronounced this insufficient, however, and proposed a more ambitious scheme that also provided for direct government financing instead of leaving the responsibility for funding to the universities. Gérin-Lajoie explained that this would enable Quebec's fledgling education ministry to gain greater control over the province's post-secondary institutions and ensure that they served Quebec's national interests.[28]

Federal nervousness about the negotiations grew over the autumn of 1964. A letter from Lesage to de Gaulle referring to Quebec as a "pays" and using the term "accord" – significant in international law – in referring to the proposed agreement gave Ottawa pause. Anxious over developments and their impact on Canadian unity, the DEA instructed Léger, in presenting Lesage's letter to the Élysée, to convey Ottawa's "reservation" that Quebec's interpretation of the proposed agreement went beyond that envisaged by federal authorities, who considered that it would be replaced with a formal Franco-Canadian accord.[29] The ambassador carried out the *démarche* reluctantly, fearing that it would signal federal reticence and that the Élysée would be annoyed to be dragged into Canadian constitutional quarrels, which could only harm the federal position. Cadieux conceded the point in the abstract, but, mindful of the broader context, cited the need to take English-Canadian opinion into account, reminding his colleague that this opinion was not as prepared to extend the benefit of the doubt to France and that, if provoked, it would undermine Ottawa's biculturalism efforts. Léger believed that his misgivings were vindicated, however, when he was not invited to attend the subsequent Élysée luncheon for Lesage.[30]

Further proof that the triangular dynamic was becoming complicated came during discussions over the letters that Ottawa and Paris were to exchange; Cadieux was unable to secure a reference in them to the effect that the proposed agreement was to be provisional. When Basdevant argued that Quebec authorities would object to the term "interim," Cadieux agreed to have the exchanged letters simply take note of the arrangements between France and Quebec and refer to the cultural accord that Ottawa and Paris were to negotiate.[31] Conversely, Cadieux opposed Claude Morin's suggestion that the agreement be styled a "joint declaration"; he argued that this would give it a more formal tone and lead press and public opinion to think that Quebec was seeking a separate international personality. The dispute was resolved only after the two officials agreed on the term "entente" for the agreement that, in its final form, provided for exchanges of university professors, researchers, and students; teacher training; the improvement of technical instruction; increased harmonization of the educational systems in France and Quebec; and the creation of the Commission permanente de coopération franco-québécoise to facilitate collaboration.[32]

Although federal prerogatives were ostensibly safeguarded by letters that Martin exchanged with the French embassy on the day the France-Quebec Education Entente was signed with great pomp in Paris in February 1965, Cadieux feared that Quebec nationalists were exploiting the cultural agreement to advance their broader political agenda.[33] Indeed, members of the Quebec delegation that Gérin-Lajoie led to Paris did not disguise their belief that Quebec was signing its first international agreement. Gérin-Lajoie minimized Ottawa's role, describing it as a "consenting observer" and declaring that Quebec had acted completely independently. The federal mood soured further owing to the welcome that the Quebec minister of education received, including a hastily arranged private audience at the Élysée, and the fact that his French counterpart, Christian Fouchet, referred to the entente as an "accord" and a "treaty" at its signing.[34]

Even as Quebec City congratulated itself on strengthening its claim to the internationalization of its education jurisdiction, Ottawa was moving swiftly to reinforce its cultural links with Paris through an *accord cadre* – umbrella agreement – that would provide a clearly defined framework for future ententes between France and Quebec (or other provinces) and thereby safeguard federal authority. All too aware that Canada's international sovereignty had been achieved in large measure through the gradual accumulation of precedents, DEA officials had insisted early in the negotiations of the education entente that it could not serve as a basis for future agreements. Ottawa was thus compelled to develop a long-term policy to facilitate cultural links between provinces and foreign states in a manner that balanced respect for provincial jurisdiction with the federal interpretation of the foreign policy power.[35] The *accord cadre* was meant to achieve this by acting as an a priori ratification and providing for a coordinating mechanism between Ottawa, Paris, and the provinces. What the DEA wished to avoid above all was an unconditional and unfettered provincial competence to negotiate independently with France; rather, it sought a *droit de regard* – a supervisory role. To federal thinking, this meant that Paris would be obliged to consult Ottawa, inform it of its intentions to negotiate with any province, and communicate any proposed agreement in advance. This would allow federal authorities to determine whether it fell within the *accord cadre*'s purview, was consistent with Canadian foreign policy, and had Ottawa's "explicit consent." Equally important, Ottawa viewed the *accord cadre* as a means to encourage French cultural diplomacy along pan-Canadian lines. Consistent with the Pearson government's biculturalism drive, the concern was to ensure that francophone minorities outside Quebec and English Canadians were not neglected.[36]

Quebec City was deeply suspicious of the federal initiative. Briefed on the *accord cadre* during his visit to Ottawa following the pronouncement of the Gérin-Lajoie doctrine, Morin was told that Ottawa, aware of Quebec sensitivity over anything that could be construed as reducing the education entente's significance, was now prepared to include a provision permitting provinces to follow the procedure followed for the France-Quebec entente – a concession contradicting the original federal motivation for the *accord cadre*. Morin questioned Ottawa's good faith in this prior consultation, however, after the minister of forestry and rural development, Maurice Sauvé, confided to him that the draft proposal he had been given was at that very moment before the Cabinet, which hoped to approve it in advance of Paul Martin's imminent visit to Paris. Morin convinced Sauvé to ensure that any decision was delayed until after Lesage and Gérin-Lajoie had the chance to discuss the matter with Pearson a week later.[37]

Paris was confronted with – and increasingly implicated in – this intergovernmental rivalry. France's ambassador, François Leduc, informed Paris of Quebec's reservations about the *accord cadre*, including Gérin-Lajoie's pledge that Quebec would not avail itself of the federally sponsored framework but would, instead, use the procedure employed for the education entente. Although the federal initiative was perceived at the Quai d'Orsay as an obvious rejoinder to the France-Quebec entente, the feeling was that Paris should seize the occasion to expand its cultural contacts at the federal level, profiting from the rivalry to increase French cultural activities throughout Canada, albeit with the primary focus remaining on Quebec.[38] Throughout the *accord cadre* negotiations, the MAE strove to respond to federal overtures in a manner that respected Quebec objections and objectives. Despite Ottawa's expectations and earlier apparent French assurances, when Cadieux proposed placing the education entente formally in the *accord cadre*, Leduc opposed this on the grounds that it would raise difficulties with Quebec City. Jean-Daniel Jurgensen, the new head of the MAE's Amérique division, argued that to avoid having Paris being forced to act as a de facto federal agent in Canada's jurisdictional squabbles, it should be up to Quebec to inform Ottawa of any new agreement, with France's responsibility limited to an exchange of letters with federal authorities.[39]

The triangular dynamic was evident in the back-channel contacts between French representatives and Quebec City during the negotiations between Ottawa and Paris. Consistent with the Gérin-Lajoie doctrine, Lesage told Leduc that Quebec could not accept without public protest the idea of consultations between Ottawa and Paris on the subject matter of Quebec's cultural agreements with France. The premier also expressed a desire to see any reference to the need for Ottawa's "explicit consent" dropped.[40] The impact of these parallel talks was quickly apparent as Basdevant obtained appropriate changes to the text. Indeed, although the MAE official was willing to indulge federal desires to see an agreement concluded as rapidly as possible, his cooperation had its limits: Jean Chapdelaine crowed that Basdevant had ensured that the *accord cadre* would not contravene the core principles of the Gérin-Lajoie doctrine, thereby defusing the "bomb" Ottawa had intended it to be.[41] Such actions revealed growing pro-Quebec sympathies at the Quai d'Orsay: consistent with Jurgensen's earlier recommendation, Paris's responsibility to keep Ottawa apprised of negotiations with Quebec was limited to a basic notification, with the onus on Quebec City to keep federal authorities informed. Nor was there any reference to Ottawa's constitutional stance regarding foreign affairs; this was relegated to an accompanying exchange of letters consisting of a federal declaration of which Paris simply took note.[42]

The resulting France-Canada Cultural Agreement provided for the development of educational, cultural, scientific, technical, and artistic exchanges between the two countries. Ottawa obtained its framework agreement, but it fell short of the original federal aims: Paris had only to "inform" Ottawa, the reference to education exchanges was watered down to respect Quebec jurisdictional concerns, and there was no acknowledgment in the text that France recognized federal claims to exclusive control of foreign affairs. Moreover, André Patry, serving as counsellor to the Quebec government, had lobbied his French contacts, helping to ensure that the *accord cadre* was signed by Leduc instead of the foreign minister, Maurice Couve de Murville, thereby reducing its symbolic importance. The agreement's raison d'être had been undermined further by the federal concession that future ententes between France and provincial governments could refer either to the *accord cadre* or simply follow the exchange of letters procedure used for the education entente. All told, in the estimation of Jean Chapdelaine, Quebec's capacity for autonomous international action remained secure.[43] Thanks in no small measure to French assistance, Quebec City appeared to be gaining the advantage over Ottawa not only in the cultural sphere, but the conduct of foreign affairs.

Why did Ottawa accept an agreement that fell short of its original motivations? The answer to this question lay to a significant extent in the fact that in parallel to the *accord cadre* negotiations, Paris and Quebec City were reaching a second, more expansive cultural cooperation entente. The initiative came from Quebec's new minister of cultural affairs, Pierre Laporte. Frégault, his deputy, saw the second agreement as advancing Quebec's claims to international action in the face of Ottawa's proposed *accord cadre*. Indicative of the intensifying centrifugal forces in the Lesage government, the initiative was also designed to match Gérin-Lajoie's success regarding the education entente and to avoid having cultural cooperation with France fall under the education ministry's control. Indeed, Laporte announced publicly that he would go to Paris to negotiate the agreement, notwithstanding Lesage's explicit instructions against declarations regarding Quebec's international activities.[44]

Basdevant agreed to Laporte's proposal. Mindful of federal sensitivities, the MAE official suggested initially that the agreement could be finalized once the *accord cadre* was concluded. Leduc disagreed. The ambassador argued that Quebec's concerns over the emerging France-Canada agreement, or any federal effort to thwart the province's international activity, argued in favour of Paris and Quebec City moving rapidly to draft, negotiate, and sign the second entente before the *accord cadre* negotiations were too far advanced. Quebec could also count on support at a much higher level: de Gaulle expressed personal interest in what Chapdelaine described to him as the first-ever agreement engaging two French-speaking populations to cooperate to promote the respect, purity, and propagation of the French language.[45]

Although the possibility of Quebec City pursuing another agreement with Paris had been referred to vaguely when Lesage and Gérin-Lajoie met with Pearson in early May 1965, eyebrows went up in Ottawa when news of the proposed entente broke a few days later, a reaction exacerbated by the fact that Quebec officials informed the DEA only after Laporte left for Paris. When Laporte announced an agreement in principle after meeting with Malraux, Canada's embassy made it clear to the MAE that Ottawa desired to facilitate Quebec's international activity but expected to be consulted in advance of any formal talks. In the interim, federal authorities took solace from the *accord cadre* negotiations that were underway.[46]

The DEA was consequently alarmed when Canada's embassy reported at the end of August that negotiations on the second agreement were well advanced. Cadieux was annoyed and frustrated, considering the fait accompli a betrayal by the French. He was particularly exercised over the fact that the French government's proposed text that Morin had provided to him appeared to release Paris from any obligation to inform Ottawa when it entered into future agreements with Quebec, thereby providing for direct relations between France and Quebec in violation of the stated federal position regarding foreign affairs. An incensed Cadieux was determined to make French officials understand that international law and diplomatic courtesy dictated that no country could treat with a part of another without informing its central government. Far from exporting Canada's constitutional debate, Cadieux believed that the time had come to defend against foreign interference.[47]

Ottawa's consternation was matched by Quebec City's quiet satisfaction. Morin believed that Quebec had been wise to express its international ambitions through the pronouncement of the Gérin-Lajoie doctrine. He argued, however, for a more discreet attitude as negotiations of the second entente reached a conclusion, and in anticipation of similar agreements with other countries. He reasoned that the new entente could only strengthen Quebec's bid for an international personality, making it essential to avoid scuttling the opportunity through too cavalier an attitude. Lesage accordingly instructed the Cabinet to avoid any public or private comments that Ottawa could seize upon to block the initiative.[48]

Morin and Cadieux remained in contact amid the mounting tensions. Cadieux even secured a number of revisions that made the proposed text more acceptable to Ottawa. But such revisions came at a price. Federal authorities accepted that there would be no reference to the *accord cadre* in this second entente, reflective of neo-nationalist preoccupations with asserting the Gérin-Lajoie doctrine and Quebec's autonomy in cultural affairs. In any event, Morin felt that the Quebec position was secure enough that he could be conciliatory. He boasted to Chapdelaine that his "goodwill" move of providing Cadieux with the proposed drafts had been motivated by the fact that, since Paris would inform the DEA anyway, it was better to offer a "courtesy gesture" that could actually redound to Quebec's advantage.[49]

Cadieux was not the only person in touch with Morin: French officials were concerned when Ottawa insisted on a reference in the accompanying exchange of letters to the effect that it had been involved in the negotiations. Paris's and Quebec City's actions, however, had meant that this was patently not true; federal authorities had been informed only after the agreement was reached. Leduc accordingly paid a secret visit to Morin, urging him to ask the DEA about the proposed letters to ensure that Quebec had no objections. When Morin did so, federal officials confirmed the reference to Ottawa's involvement, telling him it was designed to protect against any repetition of the claims of independent Quebec action that had accompanied the education entente. Despite Paris's bid to eliminate any reference to trilateral negotiations, Quebec officials conceded the point, given the gains that Morin had secured from Cadieux, not the least being references in the entente to it being between the "Government of Quebec" and the "Government of the French Republic."[50]

The only disappointment for Quebec was related to the signing of the entente: although Quebec lobbied heavily to have Malraux sign, the French culture minister declined the honour with the excuse that he felt ill placed to do so since the agreement dealt with a great deal of subject matter not under his purview.[51] Faced with the news, Leduc suggested that Paris grant Laporte and Gérin-Lajoie a particularly lavish welcome during their upcoming stay in Paris. It was also hastily arranged that the entente would be signed in a manner identical to that for the *accord cadre* with Ottawa, thereby allowing Quebec to present the procedure as emphasizing Quebec's international capacity. Leduc and Laporte accordingly signed the entente with great pomp in Quebec's legislative council chamber, and in the presence of Lesage and the Cabinet.[52]

Although news of Laporte and Gérin-Lajoie's visit to Paris would quickly change his opinion, Cadieux initially expressed relative satisfaction with the outcome of the latest episode; even if the cultural cooperation entente was more detailed than its predecessor had been, no doubt had been left about Ottawa being kept informed of its negotiation and about federal prerogatives. This second agreement, however, was more formal in tone and much broader in scope; it was to facilitate the panoply of cultural links and expanded the mandate of the Commission permanente de coopération franco-québécoise. As such, it was justly interpreted as a further step toward the recognition of a Quebec right to negotiate and conclude agreements with other countries independently in its areas of jurisdiction.[53]

A final example of the triangular dynamic in this race for agreements arose over the question of timing. Morin was initially adamant that Quebec City should sign its cultural agreement before the *accord cadre* to pre-empt Ottawa's claim that it fell within the new federally sanctioned framework, as this would render the Gérin-Lajoie doctrine a dead letter. For the same reason, Ottawa was just as determined to see the *accord cadre* concluded first. Well aware of the federal stance, French officials conceded the point during talks with Cadieux. The federal success, however, was more apparent than real. It occurred only after Paris was assured that Lesage and Morin were satisfied that the *accord cadre* had been watered down to the point that it would not restrict Quebec's international activities and were therefore willing to compromise over timing. Moreover, Cadieux had had to agree that the *accord cadre* would be signed by France's ambassador rather than Couve de Murville. Ottawa had won the race for agreements, but the federal concessions extracted throughout suggested a pyrrhic victory.[54]

As THEY RUSHED TO CONCLUDE their agreements with Paris, Ottawa and Quebec City engaged in a parallel competition abroad, with each government striving to establish itself as the primary voice of French Canada in France. This rivalry only intensified after the pronouncement of the Gérin-Lajoie doctrine, since the Quebec minister's speech made it "more necessary than ever for the Federal Government to assert its powers in the cultural field."[55] The embassy warned in mid-1965 that Quebec was fast supplanting Canada's image in France and urged a long-term effort to cultivate the French media and facilitate visits of Canadian cultural and intellectual figures to the Hexagon. Reflecting the increased importance that Ottawa was assigning cultural diplomacy, the cultural relations program with francophone Europe that it had created the previous year saw its budget quadrupled to $1 million, to be administered by the DEA's new cultural affairs division. More ambitious still were the plans for a Canadian cultural centre in Paris. Léger and the embassy's cultural counsellor, Pierre Trottier, lobbied heavily for such a facility in order to increase Canada's profile in the French capital, demonstrate Ottawa's desire for a special relationship, and consolidate and expand federal cultural initiatives. Approval to purchase a building to house the centre was granted in June 1967.[56]

Quebec nationalist circles viewed the increasing federal cultural activity with a jaundiced eye. A white paper on cultural affairs that ultimately went unpublished justified the Quebec state's cultural activism in explicitly biologic terms: it would permit the population to "breathe more easily" and form a moral person possessing the "organs" necessary to live and grow. Extending the metaphor, the Quebec state was to serve as an immune system that would protect the body politic from cultural contagion – notably "anglo-américanisation."[57]

The cultural ententes had both revealed and stoked French interest in Quebec, and the delegation-general had certainly increased its cultural activity, but this was of limited comfort to Jean-Marc Léger, who returned from a fact-finding visit to Paris complaining that Canada's ambassador and embassy had become very "présent," acting as feverish apostles of Franco-Canadian cultural relations, such that the Quebec mission was being eclipsed.[58] Morin expressed mixed feelings over the situation. Although resentful that Ottawa had greater financial means to pursue the intergovernmental rivalry, he ventured that the federal effort would not damage French-Canadian culture. He even suggested that once Quebec's international personality was achieved, there would be room enough for both levels of governments in France. Chapdelaine was less sanguine; declaring that Quebec's position in Paris was under threat, he maintained that Quebec City, notwithstanding its inferior resources, had to act to counter the federal menace to its jurisdiction over education and culture.[59]

Given what was at stake, it is not surprising that cultural questions ranked high on the agenda when premier Daniel Johnson visited Paris in 1967. The Quebec delegation was determined to build on the momentum of the preceding agreements to increase Quebec's profile in France.⁶⁰ Cultural cooperation took on even greater importance during the visit because in the weeks preceding it, the intergovernmental rivalry had been aggravated when Ottawa moved to conclude an *accord cadre* with Belgium and present Quebec with a fait accompli. Quebec officials, in contact with their Belgian counterparts since the mid-1960s regarding increased exchanges, were furious when formally informed of the agreement only five days before Prince Albert of Liège was to sign it in Ottawa. No federal action could have been more provocative to a Quebec City jealously guarding what it considered its jurisdiction and equally determined to be recognized as the international voice of French Canada. The Johnson government quickly dissociated itself from the agreement on the grounds that Ottawa had flagrantly violated provincial jurisdiction.⁶¹

Faced with the intensifying Canadian intergovernmental rivalry, Paris attempted to respond to federal overtures in a manner that did not impinge on the developing special relationship with Quebec City. It was increasingly apparent that for French authorities, Quebec was not only the priority but, more and more, their primary interlocutor in cultural relations. The trend could be seen in the discussion of youth exchanges. Federal officials contacted France's embassy to express Ottawa's interest in funding a program, and the minister of manpower and immigration, Jean Marchand, reiterated Canadian desires during his December 1966 visit to Paris. The French reaction was shaped by Quebec City's: worried at being outflanked by Ottawa after Marchand's visit, Quebec officials lobbied for an exclusive France-Quebec program. Leduc expressed bemusement over the intergovernmental one-upmanship but argued that, regardless of the origins of Quebec's proposal, Paris would have to act. The federal initiative thus went ignored while the Commission permanente de coopération franco-québécoise studied youth exchanges.⁶²

The dynamic was similar regarding immigration. The Pearson government was interested in increasing immigration from France as part of its biculturalism policy; indeed, this had been the primary motivation for the new consulates general that Ottawa opened in Bordeaux and Marseille.⁶³ The immigration issue was of special concern to Jules Léger, who considered it the most important long-term issue in the bilateral relationship given the federal commitment to Canada's cultural duality.⁶⁴ Again, however, interest was not limited to Ottawa. Under pressure from nationalist groups and the Opposition, the Lesage government had established an immigration service attached to the ministry of cultural affairs in 1965. A report in early 1967 called for Quebec City to take an active role in immigration in order to maintain the province's francophone majority, a recommendation that led to the creation of an immigration ministry in late 1968.⁶⁵

Paris again favoured the Quebec initiative over Ottawa's. In advance of Marchand's visit to the French capital, Leduc advised the MAE that any talks regarding immigration should be noncommittal and play for time, given the overture anticipated from Quebec officials, who considered the federal minister a potential obstacle to establishing a Quebec immigration service. From his vantage point at the Quai d'Orsay, Jurgensen argued that French interests would be best served through favouring Quebec City, since French immigrants would have the most beneficial impact in Quebec and be at risk of assimilation in the rest of Canada. There was also a broader political calculation: French concern about non-francophone immigration to Quebec, notably the tendency of new arrivals to assimilate into the anglophone cultural milieu, which, it was feared, would strengthen the federalist position in the debate over Quebec's future. De Gaulle's diplomatic counsellor, René de Saint-Légier de la Saussaye, raised the spectre of French Canada's "demographic asphyxiation."[66] Léger was deeply disappointed over what could only be characterized as a lukewarm response, viewing it as a blow to the Pearson government's biculturalism drive and efforts to strengthen Franco-Canadian relations, as well as further evidence, if such was necessary, of Ottawa's marginalization.[67]

EFFORTS TO REINFORCE cooperation between Paris and Quebec City in the wake of de Gaulle's visit only fanned the flames of the Canadian intergovernmental rivalry. French cultural aid to Quebec increased across the board. The number of teachers Paris sent to Quebec was raised from three hundred to a thousand, and the number of Quebec bursary students was increased nearly sevenfold. Reflecting the Gaullist preoccupation with countering American influence, Paris boosted the value of the bursaries to make them competitive with those of universities in the United States. These measures and others were discussed during Peyrefitte's September 1967 visit to Quebec. All were designed to safeguard Quebec's *francité* and help its government realize its cultural vocation.[68]

Johnson subsequently told Cadieux that he believed deeply that French Canada's survival required substantial cultural assistance from France, and that Quebec City could not tolerate federal interference in this regard. Conceding that direct financial assistance would not be substantial, Johnson argued that it was essential for Quebec to draw upon French technology, know-how, and cultural resources.[69] Indeed, a few months later, Basdevant was able to boast that in many areas cooperation was surpassing the objectives agreed to during Peyrefitte's visit, and that a fruitful cultural, technical, and scientific "osmosis" was taking place.[70] By the close of the decade, Paris and Quebec City were spending a total of $8.8 million on exchanges related to the 1965 cultural ententes.[71]

Consistent with France's increasingly explicit recognition of Quebec as a viable interlocutor, diplomatic personnel on both sides of the Atlantic were reorganized to facilitate the enhanced cooperation. The Quebec portion of the French embassy's cultural section was transferred to the consulate general in Quebec City. These officers now worked under the authority of the new consul general, Pierre de Menthon, rather than the ambassador. De Menthon had been selected partly because of his extensive experience in the MAE's cultural relations division, and he received instructions directly from de Gaulle regarding the importance of increased exchanges. Paris's moves were matched by Quebec City's appointing two new cultural attachés to the delegation-general.[72]

Facing this strengthening France-Quebec axis, Ottawa did its best to assert itself as an interlocutor. From Paris, Jules Léger sounded the alarm: years of institutional reticence regarding cultural diplomacy had come home to roost. Canada's embassy was in a permanent state of inferiority to France's information services and the delegation-general's resources, which included a full-time press liaison.[73] The embassy, stressing the need for a more coordinated effort to lend credibility to Ottawa's claims to being a viable interlocutor, established a committee that brought together members of all federal agencies involved in cultural affairs in France. This was part of a long-overdue strengthening of the mission's cultural and information resources that included the addition of a full-time press officer. Two years later, in April 1970, a guest list of nearly eight hundred that included leading French and Canadian cultural personalities helped to inaugurate the Canadian Cultural Centre.[74]

Ultimately, the 1965 cultural agreements proved to be the greatest source of rivalry and recrimination, especially after de Gaulle's *cri du balcon*. It was soon all too apparent to federal officials that they had erred in their expectation that Ottawa's primacy in foreign affairs had been safeguarded. To the contrary, Paris and Quebec City employed the ententes and the *accord cadre* to pursue direct relations, marginalizing Ottawa and challenging its constitutional position. Morin has recalled that even before the ink had dried on the *accord cadre*, Jean Lesage was interpreting it far more "libéralement" than Ottawa had intended.[75] Although this agreement led to increased exchanges, federal authorities were concerned over Paris's apparent lack of interest in the Commission mixte franco-canadienne that had been established, prompting Cadieux to warn Leduc of the "invidious comparisons" to its France-Quebec counterpart that might arise.[76]

It was not just the *accord cadre* that became a source of dispute. Only a few months after the education entente was signed, the MAE was examining how it could be stretched to cover questions related to cultural, linguistic, and artistic cooperation.[77] Press reports of the April 1967 meeting of the Commission permanente de coopération franco-québécoise prompted the DEA to send Léger to the Quai d'Orsay to assert Ottawa's claim to a *droit de regard* regarding the 1965 ententes and its opposition to any new project that did not have prior federal knowledge and consent. Unbeknownst to Ottawa, the MAE's legal division had recommended that, since federal sensitivities constituted a serious obstacle, Paris should act where it could claim that there was implicit federal agreement to direct relations with Quebec City, citing the cultural entente as an example.[78]

Federal frustration over the application of the agreements grew commensurately with the expanding cooperation between Paris and Quebec City. Ottawa particularly resented what it considered an abuse of the *accord cadre* in which so much federal hope had been invested. After Peyrefitte's visit, Cadieux and Pearson in turn expressed Ottawa's annoyance to Leduc; both explained that although France's growing cultural exchanges with Quebec were to be applauded, they wanted France to pursue relations with Canada as a whole. Cadieux, who complained that the French were behaving like "pigs" regarding exclusive ministerial visits to Quebec, conceded that it appeared that the matters Peyrefitte had discussed followed the letter of the 1965 agreements, but he nonetheless warned Leduc that Ottawa could not tolerate learning of such visits through press reports.[79]

The subsequent visit to Quebec by François Missoffe, France's youth minister, and word of a planned intergovernmental organization to facilitate youth exchanges between France and Quebec, provided the occasion for a more heated exchange between Cadieux and Leduc. When Leduc asked what Ottawa expected Paris to do when it received invitations from Quebec, an exasperated Cadieux retorted, "What international law prescribes and all other countries do, you come to us."[80] Beyond serving as a vehicle for direct relations between Paris and Quebec City, the proposed Office franco-québécois pour la jeunesse (OFQJ) was meant to act as a crucial component in the promotion of a rapprochement between the two francophone populations and, by explicitly targeting youth, the reinforcement of Quebec's *francité*.[81] Léger carried Ottawa's objections to the Quai d'Orsay, citing the initiative as the perfect example of the proclivity of Paris and Quebec City to conduct negotiations in areas beyond which they had explicit federal consent. This, he argued, violated the spirit and letter of the 1965 agreements, as it amounted to France's endorsing the Gérin-Lajoie doctrine and, thus, interfering in Canadian affairs.[82]

Despite the federal protests, Paris and Quebec City proceeded on the OFQJ in a manner that virtually bypassed Ottawa. Leduc had recommended that Paris take Quebec City's cue in the formal establishment of the organization.[83] Concerned with avoiding undermining its bargaining position during the February

1968 constitutional reform conference, Quebec City preferred that the protocol establishing the OFQJ be announced afterward. Accordingly, the MAE telephoned the Canadian embassy the day that the conference ended – twenty-four hours before the protocol was signed – and sent it a copy of the protocol that Paris maintained was authorized under the terms of the education entente.[84]

Coming as it did on the heels of the constitutional conference and amid the Gabon affair, the fait accompli provoked federal anger. DEA officials argued that even though the subject matter appeared to fall within the scope of the education entente, the last-minute notice had stripped Ottawa of its right to prior consultation and consent, and was thus tantamount to Paris reserving for itself and Quebec City the right to decide whether the protocol conformed to the entente and, more broadly, Canada's constitution. Federal dismay over French actions and the outcome of what had originally been Ottawa's initiative was aggravated by the fact that even though the DEA had not been properly consulted, it was obliged to go through the farce of approving the protocol to safeguard what was an increasingly illusory federal prerogative in foreign affairs. Altogether, the DEA considered the episode a dangerous precedent that made it essential to adopt measures to prevent a recurrence in another area.[85]

But the wish was parent to the thought; despite Ottawa's efforts, the dynamic was repeated regarding satellite cooperation. This was part of a larger dispute between Ottawa and Quebec City over communications and, indeed, cultural affairs. The *Radio Reference* had resulted in the courts endorsing a federal responsibility for communications. As early as the Massey Commission, the Ligue d'Action nationale and other organizations were urging Ottawa to reduce its involvement in the sector, fearing that the authority it had won would lead to its interfering in education. Calls for a Quebec broadcasting capacity and an overhaul of the constitutional responsibilities for broadcasting soon followed.[86]

As Ottawa and Quebec City struggled over communications, what was at stake was far more profound than governmental jurisdictions: it was the future of the communities for which they were asserting rival claims of responsibility. Johnson considered satellite cooperation with France essential, given the anticipated impact of American satellite programming and the consequent need for a French-language equivalent to ensure French Canada's well-being in an age of ever-growing mass communications. The matter was discussed during Johnson's visit to Paris, with the premier declaring that "the heavens should speak French" and Quebec officials expressing enthusiasm about helping to finance a satellite with a broadcast range that would cover Quebec.[87] Jules Léger, meanwhile, considered satellite technology a promising arena for Franco-Canadian relations. He was encouraged in this regard by what appeared to be French interest; Jurgensen had told him of being impressed by a French physicist's claim that no language would survive in the space age without its own satellites; noting that Canada would be bombarded by American television shows, the MAE official referred to a possible joint effort to maintain a "linguistic equilibrium" in satellite communication. The embassy urged Ottawa to act rapidly to ensure that any progress was not overtaken by Quebec initiatives.[88]

Even as the embassy issued this warning, however, Quebec officials believed that they had secured French assistance for independent Quebec action in satellite communications.[89] Indeed, Jurgensen instructed the head of France's Centre nationale d'études spatiales to avoid any commitments with Ottawa because Paris attached greater importance to working with Quebec. Acknowledging that telecommunications was a federal jurisdiction, Jurgensen nonetheless reminded his MAE colleagues of the Johnson government's efforts to achieve greater autonomy in the domain, so that Paris should engage – prudently – in discussions with Quebec.[90]

Federal anxieties were aroused by the news that Morin had discussed satellite cooperation during his trip to Paris after de Gaulle's visit. These anxieties only grew when the French space agency's head of foreign relations travelled to Quebec on a fact-finding mission, but claimed that his busy schedule prevented him from visiting Ottawa. Rubbing salt into the wound, federal authorities were informed of the visit only three days before it took place. An enraged Cadieux condemned as "shameful" and "disgusting" the French actions that marginalized Ottawa and implied that Quebec possessed a competence in satellite communications.[91]

A flurry of federal protests ensued, but Paris held fast to its dualistic approach. It accepted that satellite cooperation with Ottawa could exist in parallel to that with Quebec City; however, it was decided that to forestall any federal interference, a declaration with Quebec on satellite cooperation should occur prior to any links with Ottawa. Meeting with Quebec's education minister, Jean-Guy Cardinal, France's foreign minister, Michel Debré, declared that Paris had made its choice: Quebec was to be accorded priority over Ottawa in satellite cooperation.[92]

Aware of the possibility of an agreement in principle between France and Quebec, Ottawa viewed the situation as akin to the OFQJ episode. It made clear to Paris that it expected to be consulted in advance and asserted its jurisdiction over telecommunications. A fatalistic Mitchell Sharp, however, warned that Ottawa would have to be realistic: if Quebec City wanted federal authorities excluded, Paris would act accordingly.[93] Fears of another fait accompli were borne out when, in addition to agreements on French assistance in establishing the Université du Québec and the forming of the permanent committee on economic cooperation, Cardinal and Debré exchanged letters that provided for Quebec's participation in the Franco-German Symphonie satellite, as well as planning for a France-Quebec satellite to be called *Memini* – Latin for "I remember" – echoing Quebec's unofficial motto, "Je me souviens."[94]

Once again, Canada's embassy was informed at the last moment. The DEA considered the proposed scheme unconstitutional as it exceeded the scope of the 1965 agreements. French authorities dismissed the charge of interference, with the Élysée rationalizing that there was no conflict with federal jurisdiction (and therefore no need for prior consultation) because the letters exchanged referred only to a joint study, not to any practical consequences.[95] Ultimately, it was only Quebec's hesitation that prevented a further escalation. By the time the Bourassa government arrived in power in 1970, budgetary constraints and technical setbacks had convinced Quebec officials to quietly shelve the planned cooperation.[96]

In addition to these multiplying cases of relations between France and Quebec, Ottawa was highly sensitive to Paris treating directly with francophone communities outside Quebec. France had certainly cultivated contacts with private francophone organizations before 1960, but in the wake of the *cri du balcon* these intensified and appeared more ominous in that they deliberately bypassed the *accord cadre* meant to facilitate such exchanges, thus reinforcing Ottawa's marginalization in cultural relations. This went to the core of the struggle between the pan-Canadian and two-nation visions of Canada, posing a direct challenge to federal biculturalism efforts and drawing the francophone communities into the triangular crisis. Earlier in the decade, leaders of these communities had called for federal cultural assistance, and, in a dynamic recalling that of the Massey Report, Ottawa seized upon the recommendations of the Royal Commission on Bilingualism and Biculturalism to justify its asserting its responsibility for official-language minority groups and to expand its cultural action.[97] Yet the legacy of decades of Canada's marginalizing its francophone population was apparent; there was scepticism over the depth of the federal commitment to bilingualism and biculturalism, and hence a willingness among members of the francophone communities to embrace the French cultural assistance being offered. This, combined with Paris's dismissal of Ottawa's claims to responsibility for promoting the country's *fait français*, sowed the seeds of conflict.

The first instance involved the Acadian community. During Peyrefitte's visit, Quebec lobby members Bernard Dorin and Philippe Rossillon interrupted him in the middle of shaving to introduce senior figures of the Société nationale des Acadiens (SNA). Peyrefitte and Rossillon were instrumental in cultivating the

Acadians, putting them in touch with the Élysée and facilitating their January 1968 visit to Paris, where they were received as guests of the French government, were welcomed warmly by de Gaulle, and met with senior officials to establish a cultural exchange program. This included new French cultural centres in Moncton and Bathurst, funding amounting to 10 percent of the money earmarked for exchanges between France and Quebec, and a significant subsidy to the Acadian newspaper *L'Évangéline* and the SNA.[98]

Paul Martin rejected French claims that the Acadians' visit was a private affair. He decried it as an overtly political act with serious consequences, especially for the Pearson government's biculturalism efforts. He expressed frustration that France's cultural activities in Canada were being channelled through Quebec "as the 'Government of French Canadians,' and ... francophone groups elsewhere, without reference to Ottawa or ... provincial governments."[99] Cadieux agreed, estimating that de Gaulle was intervening in Canadian affairs in the most inconvenient, untimely, and dangerous fashion. Convinced that Paris was carrying out similar activities in Manitoba, he complained that Ottawa could soon find itself completely outflanked by Paris in terms of French Canada. Cadieux could not keep from privately regretting, however, that the reason Paris had succeeded in this latest intervention was that Canada had not found the means, a century after Confederation, to be fair to its francophone population. He found it "extremely moving and sad" to see how the leadership of these communities had abandoned hope of obtaining justice from Ottawa and the provinces, and were looking abroad for support.[100]

Indeed, notwithstanding questions regarding their legitimacy as spokespersons for all Acadians, the SNA representatives strove to ensure direct, privileged relations with Paris in a manner bypassing a federal authority that had for too long been unresponsive to French-Canadian needs. They lobbied Paris – unsuccessfully – for an Acadian delegation-general and a Commission mixte franco-acadienne similar to the one that had been established with Quebec.[101] When Basdevant and Jurgensen visited New Brunswick in March 1968 to discuss the expanding cooperation, the Acadian representatives rebuffed federal efforts to attend; during the talks, Léon Richard, head of the SNA, expressed the desire that Franco-Acadian cooperation be realized without provincial or federal authorities acting as intermediaries. Over the ensuing months, as the Trudeau government boosted financial aid to francophone minorities, the SNA prevailed repeatedly on Paris to help it maintain financial independence from Ottawa.[102] Nor was Ottawa alone in being marginalized. French officials gave short shrift to New Brunswick's first Acadian premier, Louis Robichaud, viewing his effort to channel French cultural action through his government and the DEA as

Ottawa's thinly veiled attempt to block the establishment of direct links with the Acadian community.[103]

After the MAE officials' visit, Cadieux and Leduc had a stormy meeting. Cadieux argued that French cooperation with the Acadians fell under the *accord cadre* and should therefore involve both federal and New Brunswick authorities. Leduc replied that cultural affairs were not a federal jurisdiction, and then parried Cadieux's strong objection by claiming that it was standard practice for French cultural attachés to pursue activities with private groups and characterizing Ottawa's reaction and demands as "unreasonable and suspicious." A thoroughly exasperated Cadieux could only protest that the reaction was perfectly reasonable given the multiplying examples of Gaullist interference.[104]

Leduc's protests notwithstanding, Paris's relations with the Acadians were consistent with the two-nation approach underpinning Gaullist Quebec policy. Paris was soon conducting its cooperation with the Acadian community through structures and institutions meant to facilitate Franco-Québécois exchanges. The French interdepartmental committee established to oversee relations between Paris and Quebec City, for example, was accorded responsibility for cooperation with the Acadians and Canada's other francophone communities.[105]

But the upheaval wracking French Canada meant that France quickly confronted complications arising from its two-nation approach. The Acadian visit to Paris raised Quebec eyebrows; Jean-Noël Tremblay, the cultural affairs minister, looked askance on the development and went so far as to suggest a triangular arrangement with Quebec City and Paris in a bid to ensure that Quebec retained its lead role in exchanges with France.[106] Leduc subsequently claimed that Quebec authorities would "probably" not object to the Acadians benefiting from arrangements made for them, so long as this did not negatively affect the funds that Quebec had been accorded. He even suggested that Quebec would see it as advantageous to be considered as possessing "a sort of jurisdiction" regarding Canada's francophone minorities. He emphasized, however, the need to keep the Acadian community ignorant of the fact that commitments that Paris had made in its regard were being realized with monies established for cooperation with Quebec. Leduc noted that the question of administering cooperation with the Acadians pointed to a larger issue: conducting relations with francophone minorities that refused to recognize Quebec's primacy.[107]

The heightened interest in Canada's francophone minorities at all points of the triangle set the stage for another confrontation. In September 1968, months after the Trudeau government's election, Philippe Rossillon undertook what was billed as a private visit to Manitoba at the behest of the Association culturelle de la Vallée de la Rivière Rouge. In discussions with numerous Franco-Manitoban representatives, he raised the prospect of Paris appointing a cultural attaché to Winnipeg, and he urged them to follow the Acadian example and prepare a list of requests as a precursor to sending a delegation to Paris. When Rossillon's hosts informed federal authorities of the visit, Ottawa alerted the RCMP and sent an official to sit in on the discussions. The Manitoba government, apprised of the situation by Ottawa, made clear to Rossillon that it expected any agreements to be realized through the *accord cadre*.[108]

Notwithstanding the French embassy's claim that it had no prior knowledge of the visit, Cadieux estimated that the Acadian episode had demonstrated all too clearly that political consequences followed in Rossillon's footsteps.[109] Indeed, the visit underscored Ottawa's vulnerability – and the willingness of francophone communities to exploit the triangular tensions. During the ensuing controversy, a spokesperson for the Association d'éducation des Canadiens Français du Manitoba declared that the question of whether the Franco-Manitoban community would pursue further relations with France would be determined by "whether Mr. Trudeau translates into facts his theories on national unity," and he noted that assistance from the federal and provincial governments had to that point been "extremely minimal."[110]

Coming as it did on the heels of the Acadian visit and after more than a year of acute tensions, Rossillon's unannounced visit was viewed in Ottawa as a deliberate, provocative, and malevolent French action that demanded a response.[111] Such considerations informed the forceful public reaction of Pierre Trudeau, who was intent on embarrassing Paris to prevent any recurrence. Severely reprimanding the French official and Paris, Trudeau was quoted in the *Globe and Mail* as saying, "If French Canadians are more or less going to plot with secret agents of France in Canada, this can harm ... French-Canadian interests," and adding that "Nothing could be more harmful to the acceptance of the bilingual character of Canada in the [majority anglophone] provinces."[112] Although debate remains over whether Trudeau was misquoted in characterizing Rossillon as a secret agent, the result was a media storm and further strain on Franco-Canadian relations.[113] The Trudeau government was castigated on both sides of the Atlantic for manufacturing the crisis and overreacting. French authorities rejected the accusation, and journalist Georges Broussine accused Trudeau of carrying out an anti-French, anti-de Gaulle campaign. France's new ambassador, Pierre Siraud, considered Ottawa's aggressiveness retaliation for de Gaulle's having, a few days before, compared Canada's political difficulties to Nigeria's civil war and criticizing its federal system as an example of neo-colonialism akin to Rhodesia, Malaysia, and Cyprus. For his part, de Gaulle told his advisers that Trudeau's "francophobe" attitude was jeopardizing Franco-Canadian relations.[114]

More than a year after the *cri du balcon*, it appeared that things might spiral out of control. Called to the Quai d'Orsay to hear MAE secretary-general Hervé Alphand's half-hearted defence of Rossillon and gentle pleading for Ottawa to drop the matter, Léger reminded Alphand that such incidents could be easily avoided if Paris respected the *accord cadre*. Cadieux seethed privately over Ottawa's difficult position, notably the fact that it could not reveal its intelligence about Rossillon, so that the media did not share Ottawa's sense of outrage and Paris was able to play the part of a wronged party. He dearly wished to announce that, according to Ottawa's sources, Rossillon was a member of France's intelligence services working for the Élysée's Jacques Foccart.[115]

Rossillon was a slippery figure, but it does not appear that he was a French spy as Cadieux believed and has been implied elsewhere, notably in J.F. Bosher's account of the "Gaullist attack" on Canada.[116] Rather, he is best described as a *franc-tireur* – an individual who acted on his own initiative and used his position to promote francophone culture around the world. Siraud subsequently remembered him as a "passionate," but ultimately minor, figure. Nor did he and his activities meet with universal approval in Paris. Frédéric Bastien has alleged that French intelligence had kept Rossillon under surveillance, as he was suspected of trafficking in gold and arms. And an MAE assessment of the Haut Comité pour la défense et l'expansion de la langue française described how, under Rossillon's influence, its activities had often exceeded its mandate and caused difficulties for French cultural diplomacy.[117]

Reflecting on the controversy at the time, Jurgensen considered it curious that Trudeau faulted Rossillon for encouraging Franco-Manitobans to defend their language, since the community could scarcely do otherwise, and the absence of any question of separatism meant that Rossillon's activities in Manitoba posed no political problem.[118] What Jurgensen was unable – or unwilling – to recognize was that Ottawa had responded forcefully because it viewed Rossillon's actions as symptomatic of the broader trend of Paris's cultural action in Canada. Since the beginning of the 1960s, Paris had increasingly treated Quebec City as French Canada's spokesperson and marginalized Ottawa and its claims to represent French Canadians in and outside of Quebec. The Trudeau government's determination to arrest this trend as part of its broader effort to promote a bilingual and bicultural Canada was at the heart of the tempest.

THIS WAS THE TENSE AND UNHAPPY experience informing the federal deliberations over the fate of the *accord cadre*, which was set to expire in 1970. The DEA favoured a qualified renewal, with a revised exchange of letters to make crystal clear the federal expectations regarding prior consultation and consent. Officials were encouraged in this regard by their hope that, with de Gaulle having abruptly left office in April 1969, a gradual normalization of relations was achievable. The DEA rejected a wholesale renegotiation, fearing that this would provoke Gaullist ire and an aggressive Quebec response that would scuttle what potential there existed for a rapprochement.[119]

Canadian diplomats in Paris shared this assessment. Eldon Black, the embassy's second-in-command, argued that aside from some changes to address Ottawa's concerns, maintaining the (admittedly imperfect) arrangement that had emerged since 1965 better served the federal interest than the uncertainty and intensified conflicts that would inevitably accompany a major confrontation over renegotiation or permitting the *accord cadre* to lapse. Black was also encouraged by the fact that in the aftermath of the Rossillon affair, a conciliatory MAE had agreed to the Commission mixte franco-canadienne discussing France's assistance to francophone minorities outside Quebec. The positive results of this meeting encouraged Ottawa to believe in the potential for meaningful change, especially when Paris moved to implement a broader pan-Canadian program of cultural exchanges.[120] Rather than simply the manifestation of a desire for a rapprochement, however, the French shift was also likely a consequence of the MAE recognizing the difficulties arising from its two-nation approach to cultural cooperation with francophone communities outside Quebec.

The view in the PMO over the *accord cadre* was more ambivalent. In his first meeting with Pierre Siraud, Trudeau had made clear that although he saw great advantages in stronger cultural links between Quebec and France, the record of Paris's actions regarding the umbrella agreement rendered hollow the claim that France bore no ill will toward Canada. During a January 1970 conversation with Black, Trudeau appeared unworried when the diplomat referred to the potential risks and the consequences of failure if Ottawa insisted on a full renegotiation. Responding to Black's appeal for a more cautious, pragmatic approach, Trudeau simply observed that given Paris's behaviour there did not seem much point in "going out of our way to co-operate."[121]

Four months later, however, Trudeau was in agreement that given the impossibility of a renegotiation, qualified renewal was the best alternative. The shift in attitude was owed partly to Mitchell Sharp's relatively successful visit to Paris to inaugurate the Canadian Cultural Centre. The reception that he was given suggested that the new Pompidou government was taking tentative steps to normalize relations. The decision for qualified renewal was also made more palatable by the Bourassa Liberals' election win, which brought to power what was considered a more pro-federalist government. A convinced Francophile, Robert Bourassa assured federal authorities that he intended to take a "low-key" approach regarding cultural triangular relations: so long as the core of Quebec

City's cooperation with Paris was intact, he had no desire to waste time over problems of form.[122]

As these deliberations took place on the Canadian side of the Atlantic, there was not a great deal of worry in Paris over the fate of the *accord cadre*. French confidence derived from a belief that Ottawa was unlikely to scuttle the agreement. Albert Féquant, the new head of the MAE's Amérique division, boasted to a Canadian embassy official that even if it expired, Paris and Quebec City had, by virtue of the education entente's indefinite nature, the means to continue their cultural cooperation. When the unnamed official asked why Paris insisted on regarding cooperation with Quebec City and Ottawa as mutually exclusive, making a choice that Quebecers themselves had not made, Féquant explained that it arose from Paris's assessment of Canadian realities, notably what it viewed as a hard-line Trudeau government and doomed federal bilingualization efforts.[123]

In informing Siraud that Ottawa was proceeding with a qualified renewal of the *accord cadre,* Sharp emphasized that federal authorities considered its stipulations equally applicable to the 1965 France-Quebec education and cultural ententes. The secretary of state for external affairs also underlined that in addition to being given prior notice of French ministerial and official visits, Ottawa expected to be informed of any intentions that Paris had to negotiate with any province, to have a *droit de regard* regarding discussions in progress, and to be provided with the content of any agreement well in advance of its conclusion. Finally, Sharp outlined Ottawa's desire for joint discussions in the event of future difficulties regarding the *accord cadre*.[124]

The first instinct of France's foreign minister, Maurice Schumann, was to protect the French position. Georges Pompidou had earlier made clear his view that the 1965 agreements did not provide the federal government with a supervisory role, and so Schumann accordingly instructed that there be no written response to Sharp's message. Anticipating a discussion of the issue with his Canadian counterpart during their upcoming meeting in Rome, Schumann instructed the consulate general in Quebec City to sound out Bourassa to ensure a coordinated approach. Indeed, despite Bourassa's conciliatory attitude, Quebec officials, not least Claude Morin, were determined to safeguard the province's privileged, direct relations with France. It emerged from discussions between Morin, Bourassa, and the minister for intergovernmental affairs, Gérard-D. Lévesque, that as far as Quebec City was concerned the *accord cadre* should be renewed as a whole and without alteration; anything suggesting systematic federal control over the content of cultural cooperation between France and Quebec would contravene the agreement's raison d'être. The only concession that Quebec was prepared to make was regarding Ottawa's concern that Paris provide prior notification of French ministerial and official visits to Quebec.[125]

Ottawa's latest effort to assert itself as a viable interlocutor in cultural relations and as the international voice of French Canada had thus to contend with Quebec City's determination to act internationally in the cultural domain and the enduring France-Quebec solidarity that flowed from this position. Indeed, according to Pompidou, it was necessary to hold fast, declaring "we have agreements, we will use them."[126] The presidential decree, combined with the Bourassa government's stance, informed the approach that Schumann took when he met Sharp in Rome. He offered his Canadian counterpart assurances that Paris had no desire to weaken Canada and would make a greater effort to harmonize its relations with Quebec to those with the rest of the country. Schumann asserted, however, that the 1965 ententes would be applied in the manner that Quebec believed conformed to Canada's constitution, and that Paris opposed any systematic consultation with Ottawa regarding their implementation. Sharp responded to the promise of continued triangular tensions by reiterating Ottawa's position: it was not up to Quebec City to interpret Canada's constitution to France, nor was it for Paris to do this on Quebec's behalf; France had to deal with the federal government, as only this jurisdiction possessed an international personality.[127]

THE EXCHANGE BETWEEN THE two foreign ministers was symptomatic of what was proving to be a painfully slow normalization of triangular relations. Even the Bourassa government, more pro-federalist than its predecessor, recognized the importance of cultural cooperation with France. By the early 1970s, the Bourassa government would be calling for Quebec's "cultural sovereignty," as Canada's intergovernmental rivalry over culture continued. Consistent with the dynamic that had accompanied the race for agreements and their implementation, French policy remained guided foremost by its links with Quebec City, and aimed to maintain the core of the special relationship.

Faced with the enduring cooperation between the Gaullist and Quebec neo-nationalist positions, Ottawa had opted for – or, more accurately, been compelled to adopt – a pragmatic approach regarding the renewal of the 1965 agreements. Federal authorities, all too aware of the difficulties that had been encountered, believed nonetheless that the negative consequences of provoking a collapse of the framework for cultural cooperation were ultimately a greater menace than those accompanying a qualified renewal.

To be sure, after boosting its cultural activism abroad and at home and striving to demonstrate its commitment to bilingualism, Ottawa was gaining increased recognition of its interlocutor role in the cultural realm. And notwithstanding its motivation, Paris appeared open to using the *accord cadre* to conduct more pan-Canadian activities. Yet as Ottawa proceeded with a qualified renewal, it had effectively signalled tacit acceptance of the reality that direct relations between Paris and Quebec City would endure. Indeed, the conditions it attached to renewal in order to safeguard federal primacy in foreign affairs offered a guarantee that was effectively no greater than that in the cultural agreements that had spawned so many disputes. The triangular dynamic thus appeared set to endure, a point that was being underscored by the consequences flowing from political changes at all three points of the triangle, and by the evolution of the Francophonie.

CHAPTER ELEVEN

Is Paris Turning?
Enduring Triangular Relations

CHAMPAGNE AND RELIEF FLOWED freely at Canada's embassy when Charles de Gaulle announced his resignation on April 28, 1969, after his proposed reforms of France's Senate and regional administration were defeated in a referendum.[1] Beyond satisfaction at seeing the departure of someone who had caused Ottawa such difficulty, the bursting corks and euphoria reflected de Gaulle's prominence in federal analyses and the expectation that his exit would usher in normalized relations in the triangle. This appeared all the more likely as the dramatic developments in France had followed those on the other side of the Atlantic. The death of Quebec's premier, Daniel Johnson, the previous autumn had brought to power the less assertive and more federalist-minded Jean-Jacques Bertrand. Meanwhile, Trudeaumania had produced the first majority government in Ottawa since 1962, and the new prime minister was determined to stare down Quebec nationalism and France's involvement in Canadian affairs.

If changes at the top contributed to the passing of the acute phase of the triangular crisis, it was soon clear that Ottawa had erred in its de Gaulle-centric analysis. The ethnocultural, geopolitical, and political bases of the nationalist reactions driving events remained present. Tensions continued as Ottawa strove to reassert its exclusive control of foreign affairs, Paris maintained its two-nation approach, and the question of Quebec's participation in the Francophonie came to a head. Indeed, francophone Africa became a battleground as each point of the triangle sought to gain influence there in order to advance its respective political agenda. Nor were the tensions limited to Ottawa's relations with Paris and Quebec City; even as Quebec navigated the fluid situation in pursuit of a distinct international capacity, it had to contend with pressures from Paris, which, given the larger French interests at stake, was increasingly frustrated with Quebec's temporizing. Although the outlines of a fragile *modus vivendi* began to appear by 1970 amid the institutionalization of the Francophonie, it was also apparent that the complicated diplomatic triad was set to endure.

PIERRE TRUDEAU ARRIVED IN THE Prime Minister's Office (PMO) after having worked closely with the DEA team charged with developing responses to the French and Quebec challenges to federal control of foreign affairs. He had personally offended France's ambassador and mused publicly in the days following de Gaulle's visit about what the reaction would be if a visitor to France were to shout "Bretagne aux Bretons!" In Cabinet, Trudeau had excoriated the Pearson government's response to the unity crisis as "pragmatic and incoherent," lacking an overall strategy and leadership.[2] In the 1968 election campaign, Trudeau had made clear that he would consider a victory a mandate to challenge Quebec's extraterritorial ambitions. A foreign policy review announced shortly after the Liberal majority victory was intended partly as a riposte to the "extraordinary external threat" of Gaullist France.[3]

The under-secretary of state for external affairs, Marcel Cadieux, welcomed the change, characterizing the transition from Pearson to Trudeau as a shift from a doomed passivity to a clear and constructive alternative. He admitted that history might record that Pearson had bought the federalist cause necessary time, but he remained convinced that the outgoing leader had ultimately made things worse by being so conciliatory.[4] For his part, Jules Léger was apprehensive about Trudeau's apparent desire to visit the French capital to have a "frank confrontation" with de Gaulle, as he knew that such an encounter could not go well.[5]

Trudeau nonetheless used his first press conference after winning the Liberal leadership to extend an olive branch; he stated that, tensions aside, as a French Canadian he welcomed expanded relations with France. Asserting Canada's willingness and ability to promote francophone culture, Trudeau even suggested that he was open to meeting with de Gaulle. Sworn in as prime minister in the wake of the Gabon affair, Trudeau told the federal Cabinet that he desired a calmer climate with Paris and Libreville.[6] France's ambassador, François Leduc, remained unconvinced. He predicted that the new leader would be "a significant but difficult partner," especially because his idea of federalism did not allow any concessions regarding Quebec's international personality. This said, amid the heightened tensions surrounding the Paris follow-up meeting to the Libreville conference, Leduc suggested that France should take advantage of the change of leadership to reopen a dialogue.[7] But de Gaulle would have none of it; no invitation to Paris was forthcoming, as he declared, "We are not to offer any concession or even any kindness to Mr. Trudeau."[8]

The new government's commitment to a more assertive approach, part of its broader effort to confront the Quebec nationalist challenge, was underscored by the PMO taking over responsibility for the France and Francophonie files from the DEA.[9] Ottawa's handling of the Rossillon affair was similarly indicative of the new approach. In the wake of the media controversy and Paris's strong reaction, however, Trudeau made a conciliatory statement on Franco-Canadian relations. He subsequently told Mitchell Sharp, secretary of state for external affairs, that, having made its point publicly, Ottawa could now return to quiet diplomacy to avoid future incidents. Indeed, days later Pierre Siraud, who had succeeded Leduc, came away from his first encounter with Trudeau with a sense that he was trying to create a more serene atmosphere.[10] The apparent return to a more Pearsonian approach demonstrated that Ottawa still faced the dilemma of navigating between the Scylla of Gaullist interference and the Charybdis of Quebec nationalism. Ultimately, neither the aggressiveness nor the effectiveness of the federal response led to the passing of the acute crisis phase of the tensions; this had more to do with factors in Quebec City and Paris.

One of these factors was Quebec's hesitation. Daniel Johnson was certainly determined that his province should have an international capacity, and he recognized the leverage that its French-assisted activity could provide in the broader constitutional struggle with Ottawa. In the wake of de Gaulle's visit, however, he was increasingly concerned that French actions were pushing Quebec down a path further and more quickly than was desirable. When French minister Alain Peyrefitte visited, Johnson expressed profound misgivings about the formal intergovernmental organization that Paris was proposing, notably the provision for reciprocal head of government visits every six months. It was only with Peyrefitte's gentle and persistent persuasion that this provision was included in the resulting communiqué. Even at this, Johnson stipulated that the visits be at the prime ministerial level; moreover, to limit the legal implications of the Johnson-Peyrefitte agreement, there was no formal signature.[11] Repeated postponements of Johnson's second visit to Paris compelled Quebec officials to assure their French counterparts that there was no question of diplomatic illness. It was not just Paris left speculating: Cadieux was ecstatic over word that Johnson had delayed his trip, mistaking the premier's deteriorating health for a political message. Johnson never saw Paris again, as he succumbed to a heart attack just days before the rescheduled visit.[12]

It appeared initially that Jean-Jacques Bertrand's accession to power would change little in the triangular relationship. Claude Morin, deputy minister of intergovernmental affairs, told Pierre de Menthon, France's consul general in Quebec City, that the new premier wished to travel to Paris as soon as possible.[13] The reality, however, was that although Bertrand was not prepared (or able) to countenance a return to the *status quo ante*, relations with France and affirming Quebec's international personality were lower priorities for him. With the special relationship established, and facing divisions within his government and party over the value and wisdom of Quebec's international forays, Bertrand was amenable to normalized relations between Paris and Ottawa.[14] Gallic eyebrows went up when, after suffering a heart attack of his own, Bertrand cancelled his trip to Paris. A red-faced Morin explained to de Menthon that the premier was obsessed with the notion that he would suffer the same fate as his predecessor and die either before or during the visit to France. Although Bertrand waxed enthusiastic over the subsequent visit undertaken by the deputy premier, Jean-Guy Cardinal, and the minister of industry, Jean-Paul Beaudry, MAE officials remained sceptical of his commitment.[15]

French reservations about Quebec City's willingness to assert a separate international personality and pursue the special relationship had been preceded by questions on the Canadian side of the Atlantic about the direction of French policy. May 1968 shook the Fifth Republic to its foundations. Jean Marchand, federal minister of manpower and immigration, rejoiced over the collapse of de Gaulle's policy of *grandeur*, reflecting Ottawa's hope that the political earthquake would force Paris to reorder its priorities and result in reduced triangular tensions. However, Cadieux was disappointed when it became clear that the "old bandit" had retained power. Federal authorities quickly recognized that the Élysée was unlikely to change its attitude substantially, especially given the strong Gaullist victory in subsequent legislative elections and the fact the new foreign minister, Michel Debré, was an avowed Gaullist.[16] Indeed, Debré assured Quebec's delegate-general, Jean Chapdelaine, of his interest in the Quebec file and promised to monitor it personally and directly. He reiterated this commitment publicly, confirming a quiet Quebec confidence that little had changed: de Gaulle remained in power; Maurice Couve de Murville, appointed prime minister, was intimately familiar with the Quebec question; Debré was the most "ultra" of the anti-Ottawa senior ministers; and the existence of the Quebec lobby meant that the province had friends in high places.[17]

Although the events of May 1968 and their economic consequences diminished Paris's capacity to take as advanced a position, France could still help Quebec achieve a separate international personality, notably in the context of the emerging Francophonie. The policy was consistent with the two-nation approach underpinning Gaullist policy: there was no place for Ottawa, capital of an anglophone political entity, in the Francophonie; rather, it was Quebec City, capital of the French-Canadian nation, that had the rightful claim to a seat at the table. Also informing such considerations was the value to France that Quebec's participation represented as a defence against charges of neo-imperialism. The ironic flip side of such logic was Paris's determination to combat what it considered a Canadian bid to undermine France's influence in Africa. It opposed federal efforts to establish a multilateral dynamic involving Canada along with Belgium and Switzerland; the increasingly pronounced view in senior French circles was that the Trudeau government was trying to establish a "solid Canadian presence" in Africa, so that what was at stake for Paris went far beyond Canadian constitutional jousting to include France's "essential interests."[18]

Notwithstanding Bertrand's more conciliatory attitude, he appointed Marcel Masse, an avowed advocate of Quebec's autonomous international action, as intergovernmental affairs minister. Moreover, key figures involved in the official rapprochement with France remained in place and determined to see Quebec retain what it had achieved during the Gabon affair. Morin insisted that a separate Quebec delegation to the January 1969 francophone education ministers conference in Kinshasa was essential, since participation in a federal delegation would contravene the Gérin-Lajoie doctrine and imply acceptance of a de facto federal international responsibility for education that Ottawa would eventually use to interfere in Quebec affairs.[19] Quebec aims regarding Kinshasa applied equally to the meeting in Niger's capital, Niamey, meant to discuss the establishment of a permanent intergovernmental organization to facilitate cultural and technical cooperation.

Ottawa's immediate concern, by contrast, was to assert and safeguard the federal position regarding foreign affairs. Cadieux had pushed to have the French-speaking African states bring pressure to bear on the Élysée in advance of the Paris follow-up meeting to the Libreville conference, but Pearson had overruled him.[20] The change of leadership in Ottawa, however, accelerated the exporting of the triangular tensions to Africa, as Ottawa pressed its case with the francophone African states. Paul Martin, now a senator, was sent on a tour of francophone African capitals in November 1968 to plead the federal cause as part of a larger effort to heighten Canada's profile.

The most substantive aspect of the federal effort came in the form of development assistance, through which Ottawa hoped to gain influence with and obtain the help of francophone Africa. The Gabon affair had coincided with a Canadian aid mission to the region. Led by former federal minister Lionel Chevrier, the mission has been described as the Pearson government's "outright and deliberate attempt" to outflank Quebec. More immediately, the aim was to resolve difficulties plaguing the delivery of Canadian aid to French-speaking Africa, some of which were the result of the Anglocentrism that had marked the External Aid Office (EAO) since its creation in 1960, whereas others were attributable to logistical challenges on the ground.[21] The controversy over the Libreville conference prompted federal authorities to cancel the mission's stop in the Gabonese capital; along with the suspension of Canada's minimal aid, this was meant as a warning to other African capitals against siding with Quebec. The reprisals were not without effect: Libreville was soon in touch with Paris asking it to facilitate a normalization of its relations with Canada so that it could obtain some of the Chevrier mission's aid.[22] Cadieux subsequently expressed the hope that Canadian aid could be used to win two or three French-speaking African states over to the federal side and thereby force Paris to revise its plans. He took particular comfort from the fact that May 1968 had forced France to scale back its aid program, meaning that its leverage over its African satellites was diminishing at the very moment when Canadian aid to them was skyrocketing.[23]

Ottawa's neo-imperialistic use of foreign aid highlights how the question had become entangled in the triangular tensions. Consistent with their broader rivalry, the federal and Quebec governments had been at loggerheads throughout much of the 1960s over Canadian development assistance. As part of its broader commitment to biculturalism, the Pearson government oversaw an exponential increase in the amount of aid to francophone Africa, which jumped from $300,000 to $4 million in 1964 and to $7.5 million the following year. Quebec City sought an agreement between its Service de la coopération avec l'extérieur and the EAO to facilitate Quebec participation in the administration of Canadian aid. The expressed long-term goal was for Quebec City to assume almost total responsibility for assistance to the francophone world.[24] Although Ottawa was open to senior Quebec officials working with the EAO, negotiations ended in failure owing to federal fears that the agreement would be viewed as another step toward a separate Quebec international personality, and Quebec City's balking at the concessions that Ottawa demanded to prevent its marginalization. The dispute was further aggravated by federal efforts to block repeated Quebec attempts to reach an aid agreement with francophone African countries, notably Tunisia.[25]

The debate over development assistance, already a thorn in the side of relations between the Pearson and Lesage governments, only grew after the Johnson government's election. Federal sensitivities were that much more acute given that the hopes surrounding an aid cooperation agreement that Pearson had concluded in Paris had gone unrealized. French officials were not enthusiastic over the idea of Canadian aid – from whichever level of government – to francophone Africa, as they saw it as intruding into France's sphere of influence.[26] The reality, however, was that as Paris pursued a neo-imperialistic drive to shore up its influence in Africa, it was increasingly having to take into account an Ottawa and Quebec City all too willing to employ foreign aid to exert their own measure of control as they pursued their respective constitutional ambitions.

Indeed, in Mitchell Sharp's estimation, Ottawa had to ensure a presence in Africa wherever Quebec City was engaged in development activities in order to prevent it from accruing any constitutional advantage. Federal ambitions were apparent as francophone Africa was receiving more Canadian aid than was Commonwealth Africa by 1970.[27] Conversely, hopes in Quebec City that the Gabon affair would give it the leverage to gain control of Canadian aid to francophone countries were matched by a fear that Ottawa's greater resources would win francophone Africa over to the federal cause. Quebec officials prevailed on Paris for help regarding the Chevrier mission, emphasizing that they had not been consulted about it. Accordingly, the Quai d'Orsay received the Canadian delegation but instructed French diplomatic posts in Africa to give it no advice or support beyond general information.[28]

The foreign aid rivalry continued in advance of the Kinshasa and Niamey conferences. Although they were in an increasingly awkward position, the African capitals seized the opportunities that the triangular dynamic afforded. With Ottawa multiplying its aid offers to Congo, Paris suggested that Quebec could assure itself of a separate invitation to Kinshasa with an aid offer of its own. Chapdelaine felt that the proposed $500,000 for construction of a school or another project was a rather exorbitant price for a separate invitation; however, he recognized the utility of foreign aid and that Quebec consequently faced a dilemma regarding its participation in the Kinshasa meeting, and more broadly, the Francophonie. The delegate-general took comfort, however, from the fact that federal leverage in Africa was somewhat ephemeral: Ottawa could not withdraw its development assistance from one country without risking the collapse of its support in other African capitals, where the crass attempt at manipulation would be resented.[29]

Quebec nonetheless attempted to influence francophone Africa with aid promises. When Ottawa suspended its aid to Gabon, Quebec offered to provide technical assistance to Libreville. Similarly, Pierre de Menthon told Paris that Quebec City was making every effort to obtain an invitation to Kinshasa by proposing a major education cooperation program to Congolese authorities. Meeting with Jean-Daniel Jurgensen in advance of the Niamey conference, Morin asked what development assistance Quebec could provide to certain African countries and noted that the immediate priority was Niamey, given that it was hosting the conference.[30]

Quebec was also able to count on French help. When Niger's president, Hamani Diori, expressed reticence over issuing Quebec a separate invitation to the Niamey conference for fear that Ottawa would withdraw its financial contribution for the talks, Paris pledged to cover any losses that Niger incurred.[31] Added to such carrots were French sticks: Paris warned Niamey of its profound displeasure when Ottawa provided Niger with a gift of 20,000 tonnes of wheat. France's ambassadors also reminded the various francophone African capitals of the obligations that flowed from Paris's aid.[32]

The foreign aid competition was but one aspect of the triangular tensions surrounding the Francophonie conferences. Morin and other Quebec figures were in touch with France's consulate general to convey Quebec City's determination to participate in the Kinshasa meeting, and Bertrand wrote to Congo's president, Joseph-Désiré Mobutu, seeking an invitation.[33] In a bid to outflank Ottawa and undermine its ability to pressure Kinshasa or other African capitals for an invitation, Paris arranged to have the conference secretariat in Dakar summon the participants – Quebec included.[34]

Ottawa, however, was able to achieve a measure of success in advance of the meeting. Whereas Gabon was a former French colony, Congo's colonial master had been Belgium, with which Canada enjoyed good relations by virtue of a mutual concern over French actions. France's reduced leverage, combined with the influence of Canadian aid offers, resulted in what appeared initially to be a federal victory: Mobutu sent Ottawa an invitation. French diplomats were soon describing how federal authorities were exploiting the opportunity to force Quebec to participate in a unitary Canadian delegation. At a loss as to how to contend with Ottawa's success, Morin and Chapdelaine contemplated a boycott to protest and undermine its ability to form a credible delegation.[35]

Paris's intervention, however, made this unnecessary. Indeed, in the months preceding the Kinshasa conference, French authorities demonstrated a determination to see the Libreville precedent respected and, even more importantly, to prevent the Bertrand government from "dangerous and disappointing" backsliding. De Menthon made clear to Morin that Paris would find it very "regrettable" if Quebec retreated from its position regarding the Libreville and Paris meetings and opted to participate in a Canadian delegation.[36] The MAE bristled when Morin subsequently ventured that the most Quebec could hope for was a compromise with Ottawa permitting Quebec to participate in a delegation of Canadian provinces. Pressuring Quebec City to hold fast, Paris sent word that it would view what Morin had outlined as a retreat, strongly prejudicial to "the Francophonie, Franco-Québécois relations, and Quebec itself."[37] Meanwhile, the French ambassador to Kinshasa made clear that although France could tolerate a federal Canadian delegation attending the conference, it would boycott the meeting if Quebec was not invited to attend in its own right. The threat prompted Congolese authorities to acquiesce in order to avoid having the meeting collapse; the conference secretariat accordingly issued the appropriate invitation to Quebec.[38]

From Quebec City, de Menthon gloated that the "bataille de Kinshasa" appeared to be won: although the Libreville precedent had not been strictly followed, Quebec had obtained a separate invitation, thwarting an outright federal victory and preventing any substantive loss of what had been achieved in Gabon.[39] But this apparent win was effectively undone when Mobutu effectively disinvited Quebec by making clear his expectation that its delegation would be part of the Canadian contingent. However, just as Mobutu's disinvitation arrived, Ottawa and Quebec City reached a compromise permitting Quebec's delegation to be identified as such and to express itself in its areas of jurisdiction. Although Quebec City and Paris were forced to accept a federal presence in Kinshasa and Quebec's participation in a Canadian delegation, the compromise represented an achievement vis-à-vis the federal power and Quebec's ability to speak on the world stage. Quebec's junior education minister, Jean-Marie Morin, co-chaired the contingent alongside New Brunswick's premier, Louis Robichaud, who had been selected to demonstrate that French Canada was not synonymous with Quebec. The outcome was too much for de Gaulle, however, who castigated the Bertrand government as spineless for compromising.[40]

Although Ottawa and Quebec City had come to an arrangement for Kinshasa, and federal officials could be pleased that a federally sponsored delegation attended a Francophonie conference for the first time, tensions were pronounced during the meeting. Instead of the united, co-chaired delegation envisaged, what arose were two quasi-independent contingents. Indeed, participants at the Kinshasa conference considered Quebec to be a full member, whereas Ottawa was relegated to observer status. Canadian embassy officials complained to the Élysée afterward about the French delegation members who "had felt unable to indulge in [even] the most elementary courtesy" toward Robichaud.[41]

A similar dynamic marked the Niamey conference in February 1969. Tensions were all the more pronounced given the institutionalization of the Francophonie under discussion, which raised the thorny question of Quebec's membership and thus went to the core of the triangular tensions. Ottawa was determined to see its prerogative regarding foreign affairs protected – the federal government would represent Canada (including Quebec) in the proposed international organization. In Claude Morin's view, meanwhile, everything that Quebec City had gained throughout the preceding decade was at stake and would be reduced to a historical footnote if Ottawa blocked a separate Quebec membership and participation in the new cultural and technical cooperation agency. Morin's anxiety was heightened by what he saw as Quebec's vulnerability arising from its reliance on French assistance in its constitutional gamesmanship. He considered Quebec to be in a heavily dependent position, a political object rather than a subject – a situation that could not last for long without Quebec losing control over its affairs.[42]

It was Ottawa, however, that was at the immediate disadvantage. Paris's expressed aim was to see Quebec participate in the meeting in its own right, not as part of a Canadian delegation.[43] Quebec lobby members Philippe Rossillon and Bernard Dorin were responsible for most of the ideas and documentation regarding the conference, which they had prepared on the presumption that Quebec would be sending an autonomous delegation. Their influence was apparent in the proposed statutes for the new organization, which were drafted in a way that marginalized Ottawa's involvement and provided a prominent position for Quebec, referred to throughout as an "État" or "pays." The federal government was mentioned only once in the thirty-page text, whereas "Québec" or "Québécois" appeared on virtually every page.[44]

Diori, who had initially accepted Ottawa's position regarding the question of Quebec participation in the meeting, came under strong French pressure to invite Quebec separately in respect of the Libreville precedent. Paris's ambassador to Niamey conveyed Debré's message that although Paris could accept the presence of two governments at the meeting, what had to be avoided "at all costs" was the inclusion of Quebec representatives in a united Canadian delegation.[45] Faced with the conflicting demands of Paris and Ottawa, in mid-November 1968 Diori sent federal authorities an invitation suggesting that Quebec's minister of education could be part of the Canadian delegation. He sent Bertrand a similar letter, and Niger's minister of education sent his Quebec counterpart, Jean-Guy Cardinal, a personal invitation. Diori's "unpleasant surprise" was ascribed in DEA circles to French pressure. By contrast, Claude Morin was thrilled, as he considered Diori's letter consistent with the Gérin-Lajoie doctrine and thus liable to strengthen Quebec's position regarding foreign affairs in advance of constitutional talks taking place the following month.[46]

It was not just Diori, however, who was the target of French pressure. Notwithstanding Morin's enthusiasm, Paris's representatives were soon warning the MAE that the Bertrand government was divided over Quebec's participation in the Niamey conference. Pierre de Menthon claimed that the trend was toward compromise with Ottawa, since the premier and senior Quebec officials saw a single Canadian delegation as unavoidable, and that there was little appetite for taking an action that many would consider a bid for independence. Indeed, just days after claiming that Diori's invitation exceeded the Libreville precedent in importance given that it was liable to facilitate an enduring settlement with Ottawa regarding foreign affairs, Morin was trying to justify to French officials Quebec's participation in a federally sponsored Canadian delegation to Niamey.[47]

Back in Paris, there was impatience and frustration. An annoyed Jurgensen characterized Quebec's approach as "highly unsatisfactory and full of risks" and declared that if Quebec could not attend alone, the only acceptable alternative was for Ottawa and Quebec City to send delegations that remained "absolutely distinct." Anything less would be a "very serious" reversal. Although he conceded that it was up to Quebecers to decide their fate, Jurgensen argued that Quebec had to be made to understand that its actions would affect those of France, which had done its utmost to assist Quebec in affirming its international personality under very challenging circumstances.[48]

Jurgensen's protests notwithstanding, Ottawa and Quebec City came to another compromise, a result of Bertrand's appetite for appeasement, the arrangements made for the Kinshasa meeting, and the fact that the subject matter under discussion in Niamey strengthened federal claims to participate. For the first time, a federal minister, Gérard Pelletier, led a Canadian delegation to a Francophonie conference, strengthening Ottawa's claim to be the international voice of French Canada. As at Kinshasa, Quebec's delegation was part of the Canadian contingent, with Ottawa agreeing reluctantly that Canada would abstain from voting[49] in the event of any internal disagreement during the conference.[50]

Although not marred by scandal, the Niamey conference was rife with tension. Beyond a dispute over the flags flying over the conference site, the Quebec lobby was active in the corridors promoting separate Quebec participation in the proposed Agence de coopération culturelle et technique (ACCT). Objecting strongly to the "bastard compromise" that had been concluded, Masse declared that the Quebec delegation that he led was completely autonomous and subject only to instructions from Quebec City. He dismissed the existence of a Canadian delegation as such; in Quebec's view, there was only a Canadian "representation," as much of the ACCT's activity would fall under provincial jurisdiction, meaning that Ottawa was not able to delegate anyone to speak in its name – only Quebec had this capacity. Matters were not helped when Pauline Julien cried "Vive le Québec libre!" during Pelletier's remarks, to which the Canadian minister deftly responded that the Quebec chanteuse sang better than she shouted.[51]

The conference resulted in a provisional secretariat being established to write the ACCT's charter and an agreement among participants to meet again in Niamey to finalize it and formally establish the organization. Conference participants assigned Diori the task of overseeing the work and the organization of the second conference. The provisional executive secretary appointed to assist him was none other than the indefatigable Jean-Marc Léger. Federal officials were not enthusiastic, but Léger, an avowed champion of the Francophonie and

Quebec's international activity, received Ottawa's backing after he assured Pelletier, a long-time colleague, that he would not use the post to promote independence.[52]

Reflecting on what Quebec had achieved on the road from Libreville to Niamey, and amid increasing federal involvement in the Francophonie, Morin and Chapdelaine were agreed that a moment of truth had arrived: Quebec should use the advantages of precedent and French assistance to obtain from Ottawa, at a minimum, distinct and autonomous participation for Quebec delegations under Canadian auspices at all international conferences touching on provincial jurisdiction. Both were of the view that it had to be made crystal clear to federal authorities that, if they refused to adapt to the new reality that had been brought about in large measure by the special relationship with Paris, they would force Quebec down a path that would be worse for all concerned.[53]

THE FLUID SITUATION IN THE triangle was underscored a few weeks after Niamey when de Gaulle resigned. May 1968 had reinforced a preoccupation in both Ottawa and Quebec City with preparing for the post-de Gaulle era, and each capital sought links with the non-Gaullist right- and left-wing personalities such as François Mitterrand.[54] The reaction in Quebec circles to the General's departure was confidence that the special relationship would continue. Morin and Chapdelaine both believed that Paris's Quebec policy would survive the loss of its champion; de Gaulle would retain influence out of office, senior French bureaucrats generally favoured the Quebec position, and the change of government meant that certain Quebec lobby members were now even better placed to render assistance. Chapdelaine considered it unlikely that the new administration could turn its back on Quebec without being accused of betraying Gaullism. Allowing that French actions would likely be less provocative, the two officials reflected the mixed feelings in Quebec City over preceding events when they suggested that the new conjuncture would be healthier as Quebec would be taking the lead, rather than reacting to French initiatives.[55]

Quebec nevertheless moved to safeguard its position. Following the presidential election that sent Georges Pompidou to the Élysée, Morin visited Paris to emphasize Quebec City's determination to maintain direct links. The official met with Pompidou's foreign affairs advisers, Jean-Bernard Raimond and Martial de la Fournière – the latter a Quebec lobby member. Morin was pleased that he had arrived while the new government was still determining its priorities and before federal representatives had made their contacts. He also derived comfort from what he described as a rather weak Canadian diplomatic presence; to his eyes, the embassy was hard-pressed to counter France's pro-Quebec position. Morin's assessment was shared by federal officials: Jules Léger's departure in October 1968 had left a vacuum. The effectiveness of his successor, Paul Beaulieu, was undermined by health troubles, personal problems, and his being overwhelmed by his task.[56]

Morin returned believing that the Pompidou government was just as sympathetic to Quebec as its predecessor had been, and that despite differences in nuance and form, direct relations would endure. He described the new foreign minister, Maurice Schumann, as "entirely acquired"; if the Gaullist baron wished to avoid pointless troubles with Ottawa, he was definitely not a federal supporter. Indeed, Morin's interlocutors told him to not publicize Schumann's pro-Quebec sentiment so that federal officials would retain the impression he was favourable to them. Finally, Schumann was surrounded by prominent Quebec lobby members, not least his friend Jean-Daniel Jurgensen.[57]

But confidence also reigned in federal circles. Cadieux rejoiced over de Gaulle's departure.[58] The embassy's immediate reaction was that regardless of the outcome of the ensuing presidential contest, and with the proviso that any dialogue would have to be initiated carefully and constructively, Ottawa would be able to engage the victor and his government; moreover, the MAE would now be able to establish a more independent position. The embassy accordingly recommended a prudent attitude during the election to avoid squandering any opportunity for rapprochement.[59]

Officials in Ottawa, however, thought differently. When Pierre Laurent, an avowed Gaullist and the new head of the MAE's cultural relations division, declined an invitation to come to Ottawa during his upcoming visit to Quebec City for a meeting of the Commission permanente de coopération franco-québécoise, an emboldened DEA decided that it was the "the ideal moment" to deal once and for all with Paris's two-nation approach to visits.[60] The embassy begged the DEA to reconsider, arguing that the result would be a pyrrhic victory at best; Beaulieu warned that by giving the impression that it was trying to bring pressure to bear at a moment during the election when Pompidou's opponent, Alain Poher, appeared a credible threat, Ottawa would have difficulty improving relations if Pompidou won.[61]

Beaulieu's warnings proved correct; when the embassy delivered the DEA's admonition for Laurent to travel to Ottawa, he cancelled his visit to Quebec. After Pompidou's victory, the ambassador was called in to the MAE and told of the bad impression that the federal message had made. In Paris a few weeks later, Morin was told repeatedly of the incident, with French officials characterizing Ottawa's action as "extremely crass behaviour."[62] As he left the Quai d'Orsay to take up his new post as defence minister, a furious Debré declared that

Quebec's supporters in Paris would have their revenge. Consistent with the centrality of de Gaulle in federal analyses, his resignation had led Ottawa to misread the situation and overextend itself.[63]

This episode notwithstanding, Ottawa remained cautiously optimistic, interpreting an apparently friendlier attitude in Paris, including a Dominion Day message from Schumann, as signs of a thaw.[64] The Laurent affair, however, was a harbinger of continuing tensions. To be sure, Pompidou had characterized the *cri du balcon* – about which he maintained that he had no warning – as a "folie," reflecting a far less personal engagement. Quebec lobby members feared that this fact, combined with Pompidou's limited exposure to Canada and Quebec, meant that Paris was set to abandon its Quebec policy.[65] The Gaullist jeremiad, however, proved unfounded; although he desired improved relations with Ottawa, the new president was unwilling to countenance any fundamental change.

Domestic political considerations were an immediate reason for this steadfastness: attempting to consolidate and expand his presidential coalition, Pompidou could not risk alienating the General's loyalists. There had been a growing rivalry between de Gaulle and his successor, especially after May 1968. The fact that Pompidou had not participated in the Resistance did not help his credibility with the Gaullist core, and certain barons resented him for what they alleged was his pushing de Gaulle toward an early retirement. With a number of groups sprouting up to watch over the General's legacy, Pompidou was effectively on probation.[66]

More broadly, however, the conditions that had given birth to the triangular tensions remained in place, and Pompidou, despite a different political style, remained a firm adherent to the Gaullist heritage. To be sure, Franco-American relations were improving; a shift had been apparent even before de Gaulle left office, and Pompidou built on this to make a number of friendly overtures. The changing dynamic between Paris and Washington, however, reinforced the value of the Quebec policy as political cover and a relatively costless way for Pompidou to flaunt his Gaullist geopolitical credentials. Questions of ethnocultural solidarity remained as salient as ever, especially amid the institutionalization of the Francophonie and given Pompidou's preoccupation with the international influence of the French language; moreover, the new president harboured the same doubts as his predecessor regarding Ottawa's bilingualization efforts. Finally, the conventional wisdom in Paris remained that Quebec would achieve – if more slowly than expected – a new political status, and that France had a stake in this.[67]

In short, Pompidou hoped for good relations with Ottawa but wanted excellent relations with Quebec. In practical terms, this entailed maintaining the two-nation approach, meaning that tensions were set to endure. The contradictions inherent in the Pompidolien policy were apparent when Morin visited Paris. Senior officials told him that France had no wish to intervene directly in Canadian affairs, but was ready to assist Quebec in its efforts to achieve greater autonomy; Ottawa would have to get used to a special relationship meant to enable Quebec to assert itself in North America and the Francophonie. Morin also encountered a desire to make a few symbolic concessions and correct the excesses of the de Gaulle era, if only to minimize federal complaints. When asked if Quebec City would object to Paris respecting protocol norms a bit more, he signalled his tentative approval, rationalizing there was nothing to lose by giving Ottawa the impression that Paris was observing diplomatic form, especially when it could be made clear to federal officials that any apparent improvement in Franco-Canadian relations was not the result of federal efforts, but because Quebec City had deigned to allow it.[68]

The new government's attitude was revealed in Pompidou's response to a question from a Canadian reporter about French designs on Quebec. Playfully observing that Jacques Cartier and Montcalm were dead, he ridiculed the suggestion that Paris intended to annex Quebec; however, he made clear that strong and friendly relations with the "Français du Québec" were only natural given ties of history, ethnicity, and culture. Ottawa and Quebec City interpreted the statement similarly: the onus was on federal authorities to ensure that the special relationship did not prejudice Franco-Canadian relations.[69] By the end of July 1969, the initial burst of federal optimism was dissipating. The DEA recommended that Ottawa continue its longstanding policy of engaging Paris while defending its constitutional position and doing everything to avoid unnecessary confrontations, in the hope that normalized relations would take hold.[70]

The flaws in Ottawa's de Gaulle-centric analysis and hopes for a rapid rapprochement were revealed over the ensuing months. The most significant incident occurred in October 1969 over the visit of France's secretary of state for foreign affairs, Jean de Lipkowski, an ardent Gaullist and Quebec supporter. Federal officials considered the visit a litmus test of the Pompidou government's intentions and deemed it essential that he stop in Ottawa.[71] Although Morin and France's representatives endorsed de Lipkowski visiting the Canadian capital to placate federal authorities, Schumann opposed the move, arguing that because France's minister of justice, René Pleven, had recently visited Ottawa for a conference, federal officials might conclude erroneously that Paris was abandoning its Quebec policy.[72] With Pompidou forbidding any measure that could suggest that Paris was modifying its position, de Lipkowski declined Ottawa's invitation with the unconvincing explanation his visit to Quebec was only "touristic."[73]

Mitchell Sharp expressed Ottawa's concerns to Schumann in what proved to be a tempestuous first encounter, insisting that France should conduct its relations with Quebec in a manner respecting Canada's constitution. Schumann downplayed federal objections to Paris's apparent continued support for a separate Quebec international personality, and he rejected the claim that only if de Lipkowski visited Ottawa could Paris avoid another triangular crisis and prove its goodwill.[74]

Informed of the federal objections, Pompidou complained to a Canadian reporter that "they are absurd in Ottawa," which the embassy interpreted as a deliberate signal of extreme presidential annoyance over the firm federal stance.[75] Indeed, Pompidou felt it necessary to hold fast and not "give in to blackmail"; Paris would maintain its position that French officials could visit Quebec without having to cross the Ottawa River. Pompidou consequently forbade de Lipkowski from visiting the federal capital, a move encouraged by the fact orthodox Gaullists were mounting a challenge to his leadership, making the maintenance of the Quebec policy a crucial credibility test. Pompidou therefore rejected Schumann's suggestion – as did federal officials – that de Lipkowski could go to Ottawa the following month when he visited New York, thereby maintaining the appearance of a separate visit to Quebec.[76]

With Trudeau annoyed and Ottawa warning that the French secretary of state risked having his visit being interpreted as a deliberate challenge, the stage was set for confrontation. De Lipkowski visited Quebec, and federal anger only grew when he commented publicly on the constitution, including an apparent endorsement of the Gérin-Lajoie doctrine and references to Quebec independence. Trudeau now entered the fray, instructing Sharp to prepare a strong response for Cabinet discussion. This pleased Marcel Cadieux, who believed that "a brutal and immediate reaction" was "indispensable."[77] For the first time since de Gaulle's November 1967 news conference, the triangular tensions were debated in Cabinet. Although Ottawa decided to play down the incident at home, the Cabinet agreed to seize the opportunity to privately press its demands with Paris regarding the circumstances of French visits. A DEA task force began studying possible punitive measures in the event that talks with Paris floundered. For his part, Trudeau publicly denounced de Lipkowski's "insolence," dismissing him haughtily as a minor French minister.[78]

The reaction in Paris was one of resolve. With Schumann abroad, Paul Beaulieu had the awkward and unwelcome task of discussing the de Lipkowski affair with the man who had lent his name to the controversy. De Lipkowski, by contrast, had the pleasure of conveying Schumann's annoyance over Trudeau's personal attacks after a number of goodwill gestures from Paris. For his part, Pompidou considered the prime minister's remarks "inadmissible" and decreed that Canadian protests were to go unanswered. When Beaulieu subsequently met with Schumann, there was "absolutely no meeting of minds," with the French minister observing that relations were "worse than ever."[79]

There was irritation and disappointment in the DEA over the latest tempest, a reaction informed by what had been an overly optimistic expectation that the Pompidou government would break rapidly with its predecessor. Ottawa considered the de Lipkowski affair a setback, proof that the new French administration was unwilling – or unable – to dissociate itself from Gaullist policy.[80] But hope remained in federal circles; Canada's embassy believed that despite the suspicion and hostility engendered, the controversy had demonstrated the limits of the Trudeau government's patience, so that even if Paris was not changing the core of its Quebec policy, an important bridge had been crossed and Ottawa was favourably placed to pursue more positive action and dialogue. Cadieux shared this qualified optimism, venturing that friendly French gestures since Pompidou's takeover suggested that better relations between Ottawa and Quebec City would lead to reduced differences with Paris, and that Quebec was no longer able to count on France to the same degree. Characterizing the recent controversy a "bump in the road," Cadieux claimed that the question was not *if* but *when* French policy would change, and that Ottawa could expect a certain French neutrality, even an inactivity and disengagement toward Quebec.[81]

DEVELOPMENTS IN THE FRANCOPHONIE once again revealed Cadieux's assessment as premature. The under-secretary had shared a belief widespread in Ottawa that de Gaulle's resignation meant that the international francophone community would shift from being an arena of conflict with Paris to one of cooperation. The embassy was delighted with Jacques Foccart's departure from the Élysée and boldly predicted that the Francophonie would be less politicized under Pompidou, arguing that the compromises that Ottawa and Quebec City had reached for the Kinshasa and Niamey conferences would limit Paris's room for manoeuvre.[82] Yet Morin returned from his July 1969 visit to France reassured that the new government was prepared to facilitate Quebec's participation. Michel Jobert, the Élysée's new secretary-general, was a convinced partisan of the Francophonie and Quebec, and Pompidou was a staunch advocate of the emerging organization, having claimed to support it even more strongly than de Gaulle.[83]

The first indication of enduring triangular tensions regarding the Francophonie came in connection with the Paris follow-up meeting to the Kinshasa conference. Fearing that Ottawa would be bypassed and only Quebec would be asked to attend, federal officials tried to turn the previous year's Gabon affair to their advantage by arguing that Ottawa was automatically invited because it had sent a delegation to Kinshasa.[84] As far as the MAE was concerned, however, only Quebec should be invited; although it recognized that Quebec was likely to want to make some concessions to Ottawa, it felt that Quebec officials needed to be encouraged to hold fast in the face of federal pressure.[85]

Morin made clear to French representatives that the Quebec government wished a direct invitation to the meeting; this would signal that Paris was maintaining its Quebec policy and thereby strengthen the province's constitutional bargaining position. However, Bertrand's more conciliatory attitude and, according to Morin, the desire to avoid a full-blown crisis that could jeopardize Quebec's gains in the Francophonie, resulted in Morin expressing the government's desire to receive a low-key invitation and have Ottawa informed of it and of the meeting. Paris dutifully extended Quebec a direct invitation. Ottawa was told of it and the conference, along with the fact that France had no objections to other provinces attending.[86]

This procedure, combined with the fact that the exact nature of Canada's representation at the meeting was not resolved by the time of the de Lipkowski affair, meant that things quickly became acrimonious when Sharp and Schumann discussed the question in New York. Each foreign minister blamed the other's capital for undermining the compromise that Ottawa and Quebec City had reached regarding Kinshasa.[87] "Dismayed" over the encounter, especially since Paris believed that Trudeau and Cadieux had given their verbal consent regarding the meeting, Schumann sent Siraud to 24 Sussex Drive. Trudeau extended an olive branch; he suggested that compromise was possible if Quebec refrained from claiming that it alone had been invited, the Kinshasa compromise were maintained, and there were no efforts to undermine any agreement that Ottawa and Quebec City reached. Siraud was at pains to plead Paris's desire to avoid the difficulties of the past, and he warned Ottawa against expecting too much, too soon, alluding to the new government's limited margin of manoeuvre.[88] The ambassador's protestations, however, were overstated: angered over the de Lipkowski affair, Pompidou had instructed the MAE not to cede to Ottawa. Ultimately, another controversy was avoided only because Ottawa and Quebec City reached a compromise that saw Quebec's junior education minister, Jean-Marie Morin, lead a Canadian delegation that included representatives of other provinces and federal advisers.[89]

The de Lipkowski affair certainly fuelled federal anxiety over French intentions in advance of Niamey II, but the general view in Ottawa in the early autumn of 1969 was that efforts to cultivate the various African capitals meant that the federal position was rather favourable. This view appeared to be borne out by the fact that the draft ACCT statutes provided only for the participation of "pays" (sovereign states), and thus federal responsibility for Canada's membership. The federal cause appeared strengthened as well when the government of Mauritania invited Ottawa – not Quebec City – to the February 1970 francophone education ministers' conference in Nouakchott.[90] Spurred by Claude Morin's repeated requests, Paris's efforts to secure a separate invitation for Quebec fell short, as the Mauritanian president, Moktar Ould Daddah, was unwilling to move on the question. Ultimately, the compromise reached for the Paris follow-up meeting was renewed for the Nouakchott conference.[91]

Yet Ottawa's guarded optimism and the federal position were eroded under France and Quebec's combined efforts in advance of Niamey II. Paris's actions revealed the tensions at the heart of the Pompidolien approach to the triangular dynamic. An internal MAE report claimed that a wholly separate membership for Quebec in an international organization dealing with matters beyond Quebec's jurisdiction was not "realistic" as it constituted a direct attack on Ottawa. At the same time, however, it also dismissed exclusive federal participation as unacceptable. Rather than encouraging a "sterile rivalry" between Quebec City and Ottawa, the Quai d'Orsay aimed to facilitate an enduring compromise between them. As such, Paris was to avoid anything preventing Quebec's distinct participation at Niamey II and in the ACCT, since this was tantamount to endorsing the federal position, something that would have serious consequences within Canada and in terms of the special relationship.[92]

For his part, Pompidou considered it "indispensable" that Diori send Quebec a direct invitation to the conference. Responding to numerous Quebec requests for help, Paris prevailed repeatedly on Diori to invite Quebec directly, rationalizing that inviting both Ottawa and Quebec City would force the two governments to reach a "pragmatic arrangement."[93] It was a barometer of the shifting federal fortunes that Pompidou reappointed Foccart to his former post. Having returned after a brief absence, the powerful official brought his own pressure to bear on Niger's leadership. French efforts extended to mobilizing Diori's African counterparts against him. The president of Côte d'Ivoire, Félix Houphouet-Boigny, advised Diori against adopting a stance that ran counter to the French position, since the aid available from Canada was simply not comparable to that of France. Houphouet-Boigny emphasized that he did not wish to find himself in a situation in which he was obliged, out of a sense of African solidarity, to defend a "poor cause."[94]

Diori was extremely discomfited to see his country drawn into a quarrel that did not concern it. He was tempted to delay Niamey II to give Ottawa and Quebec City time to reach a compromise, and he even raised the prospect of cancellation given the apparent impasse between the French and Canadian positions. However, notwithstanding the pressure from Paris and his fellow African leaders, Diori opted to write to Bertrand and only *inform* him of the upcoming conference, doing so in a manner that underscored the federal constitutional position regarding foreign affairs.[95] The MAE was unimpressed and attributed Diori's decision to the "very strong and constant pressure" to which the Canadian government had subjected him. A portion of blame was also reserved for Quebec City; the MAE groused that it had not made much of an effort in Niamey, even as Paris acted on its behalf. The reaction in Quebec City was hardly better. Morin considered Diori's letter particularly disappointing and unhelpful as negotiations with Ottawa over the conference reached their climax.[96]

Paris and Quebec City ultimately had greater success regarding the revision of the ACCT's proposed statutes that marginalized Quebec and thus imperilled its bid for a distinct international personality. Acting on a request from Quebec City, where there was consternation over the draft charter, de Lipkowski interceded with Diori to make clear that Quebec, not Canada, should be a member of the ACCT. This early intervention was soon followed by others, since Paris wished to see references to "pays" or "États" replaced with a term that would facilitate Quebec's distinct participation in a manner that Ottawa would be obliged to tolerate. De Lipkowski subsequently told Diori's personal envoy that Canada could not be permitted to impose its views on the Francophonie and that, in the final analysis, French and Quebec aid should be the decisive factor.[97]

But just as Quebec's participation in the Francophonie was meant to serve broader French interests, Paris's concern about the draft statutes went far beyond the question of Quebec's membership. Although Paris wished to see the project realized, it also wanted the new agency to act as a vehicle for France to maintain influence with its former colonies and keep a watchful eye over cooperation among them. At the same time as the ACCT was to provide France with a multilateral cloak to shelter it from accusations of neo-imperialism, it was also meant to stand as proof – not least to Paris's European partners – of France's enduring geopolitical, cultural, and technical influence. However, the proposed statutes threatened French influence by virtue of the ambitious multilateral organization that Jean-Marc Léger and his collaborators envisaged and Ottawa wanted.[98]

By early February 1970, Ottawa was forced to recognize that its position was under attack.[99] Federal worries only grew when word arrived of de Lipkowski's approaching the various African capitals to emphasize that Quebec would not participate in Niamey II without a direct invitation and to explain that it would be a "shame" if an "anglophone country" succeeded in imposing its will on the

Francophonie. Any solace that Ottawa took from its belief that de Lipkowski had acted on his own initiative was tempered by worries that he was backed by Gaullist protectors, which at best made Pompidou hostage to pro-Quebec advisers. In fact, Pompidou had sent de Lipkowski to Africa, fearing that failure of a direct Élysée initiative to secure Quebec an invitation would harm his international credibility.[100]

Ottawa did its best to bring its own pressure to bear. Jean-Marc Léger told Paris that he felt he had no room to manoeuvre regarding the statutes given Ottawa's demands.[101] The numerous federal warnings to Diori against inviting Quebec, combined with Ottawa's pledge to finance the construction of Niger's national highway, proved effective: Diori's letter informing Quebec of Niamey II was written under the close supervision of the cultural counsellor at Canada's Dakar embassy.[102] As for the French side of the equation, Trudeau sent word to Pompidou that Canada would oppose any initiative at Niamey II that was at odds with the principle of state sovereignty, and warned of serious differences that could threaten the ACCT and the normalization of Franco-Canadian relations.[103]

Pompidou's reaction was that Trudeau's approach was "a bit much," so that when the Canadian embassy sought the Élysée's reaction, Jean-Bernard Raimond, the foreign policy adviser, would say only that there would be no difficulties so long as Ottawa and Quebec City came to an agreement regarding Quebec's participation in the meeting.[104] Raimond was much more forthcoming with the Élysée's secretary-general, Michel Jobert, to whom he expressed doubt over whether creating the ACCT was worth the threat to France's position in Africa. He also recommended that Paris seek a postponement of Niamey II, since, beyond specific French interests, Diori's actions meant that it appeared that Quebec would be unable to participate in its own right, and therefore Paris risked having to contend with a Canadian delegation "à vocation anglophone" along with representatives of African states under Ottawa's "considerable influence."[105]

Decisions in Paris, however, were ultimately determined by the broader calculus of France's African interests and by scepticism over Quebec's reliability. This had been foreshadowed when Morin first sounded out French authorities on their potential reaction to a Quebec boycott. Hervé Alphand, head of the MAE, skirted the issue by declaring that on such a fundamental question, it was up to Quebec alone to decide its course of action.[106] Pompidou's initial view was that because Paris was building the Francophonie "for Quebec," it would be "completely ridiculous" to proceed without it.[107] At the same time, however, he wished to avoid Quebec City's using France's support to strike at Ottawa, since Paris would suffer the consequences. Consistent with Gallic bewilderment over developments in Quebec, Pompidou had derided it as "a very sluggish partner" beset by internal division; this made it necessary for Paris to avoid finding itself in an exposed position. Foccart agreed, and persuaded Pompidou that the conference should take place even if Quebec boycotted, to prevent a diplomatic setback for France and a loss of influence in African capitals that would be disappointed to see the ACCT collapse.[108] De Menthon was told to convey the news to his Quebec interlocutors and reassure them that France was going to Niamey II with the "very firm" intention of ensuring that Quebec would be able to join the ACCT at a later date.[109]

The debate in the French capital reveals how tensions between Ottawa and Paris over Niamey II were inseparable from the parallel differences between Quebec City and Ottawa. With the federal hand strengthened as a result of Diori's non-invitation to Quebec, and concerned over French intentions, Trudeau wrote Bertrand to reiterate Ottawa's opposition to Quebec's bid for separate ACCT membership. He alluded to a withdrawal of federal support from the proposed organization if France or any other country acting on Quebec's behalf undermined federal authority, and he predicted that Quebec City, by virtue of its obstinacy, would be blamed if the multilateral initiative failed.[110]

Facing the firm federal stance and what he decried as a "French reversal" as Paris strove for a solution that could rally the African delegations while ensuring future Quebec participation in the Francophonie, Claude Morin was pessimistic in the days preceding Niamey II about Quebec's ability to influence events. In his view, the only trump card that Quebec City held was the threat of boycott. Bertrand alluded to this in a press conference and, responding to Trudeau's earlier warnings, referred obliquely to a boycott in asserting there was a point beyond which Quebec City could not make any concessions. He declared it crucial that Quebec's presence and activities in the Francophonie be adequately identified; he also insisted that Quebec be able to speak in its own name in the ACCT and make engagements in its areas of jurisdiction.[111]

Unprepared for the threat of a boycott given its confidence that Quebec's interest in attending Niamey II would ultimately outweigh its objections to federal conditions, Ottawa now agreed to most of Quebec City's demands for distinctive identification of its delegates and conceded that the head of Quebec's delegation could speak in the province's name in matters under provincial jurisdiction, as well as serve as vice-chair of Canada's delegation. The question of Quebec's participation in Niamey II was thus resolved, but there remained no guarantee against Ottawa using the finalizing of the ACCT charter to reverse Quebec's international gains and block its separate membership in the Francophonie.[112]

Any federal hope that the compromise with Quebec City would encourage French cooperation was quickly dashed. Pompidou wrote to Trudeau, explaining that Paris respected the principle of state sovereignty but believed that ACCT membership should be available to universities, private associations, and non-sovereign governments (such as Quebec). Further evidence of French intentions came when Gérard Pelletier, head of Canada's delegation, stopped in Paris en route to Niamey. He was given a copy of France's proposed revisions to the ACCT statues that provided for a distinct Quebec membership. In his meeting with members of the French Cabinet and senior Quai officials, Pelletier was warned that Paris would not abandon Quebec and would move to establish an organization excluding Canada if Niamey II ended in failure.[113]

The extent to which the federal position had eroded was apparent as discussions got underway in Niamey. Jurgensen and Rossillon were in attendance as advisers to France's contingent. With Bertrand having just called an election, Quebec's delegation was led by Julien Chouinard, secretary to the Quebec Cabinet. As expected, France's representatives proposed that "participating governments" with constitutional competence for matters under the ACCT's purview be permitted to sign the charter. Reticence from some African delegations prompted the French to add the qualification that such governments should have the approval of the sovereign state of which they were a part. Paris had outflanked Ottawa in its efforts to prevent a distinct Quebec participation in the ACCT; Trudeau initially refused to countenance the French proposal, but an awkward federal effort to block it proved fruitless.[114] The dearth of support for its desperate rearguard action and the prospect of being blamed for the collapse of the conference and the ACCT forced Ottawa to accept the change.[115]

Understandably, Quebec City was pleased. With Chouinard signing the ACCT charter on its behalf, Quebec effectively became a member of an international organization, and the core of the Gérin-Lajoie doctrine – that Quebec was entitled to act internationally in its areas of jurisdiction – appeared confirmed and institutionalized. While the victory was qualified in that it had been dependent on federal consent and the modalities of Quebec's participation were still to be negotiated, Ottawa had fallen short in its attempt to assert exclusive control of foreign affairs and been forced to accept Quebec as a participating government in the Francophonie. Chapdelaine opined that federal authorities had failed to understand that they had overreached in trying to put Quebec in its place, and as a result had instead been put in their place. Echoing Chapdelaine's appraisal and using a poker analogy, Morin claimed that Quebec had beat a flush with a pair of twos, thanks in large measure to French help in the face of the stronger federal position.[116]

Paris was satisfied with the outcome of its efforts. France's post-colonial interests in Africa were preserved, as a large number of African states signed on to the ACCT charter and the new organization was headquartered in Paris, giving France the means to exercise a satisfactory measure of control over it. Jurgensen hailed the "clear diplomatic success" for France and Quebec, while Pierre Billecocq, secretary of state for national education and co-chair of France's delegation, reported to an equally satisfied Pompidou on the provision for distinct Quebec participation that had received Ottawa's reluctant blessing.[117]

Indeed, the assessment of Niamey II in federal circles was much more ambivalent. A member of the Canadian delegation confessed disappointment to Jean-Marc Léger, observing that Ottawa had believed that it "had more friends in Africa."[118] Although Trudeau declared the Francophonie the only winner, the DEA view was that any satisfaction over the ACCT's creation and Canada's membership had to be balanced against the circumstances of its birth and the fact that, contrary to federal expectations informed by a de Gaulle-centric analysis, the MAE appeared to be maintaining the Quebec policy. From Paris, Eldon Black complained that Ottawa appeared weaker for having been forced to accept the French-inspired compromise, and expressed fear that Quebec's sympathizers would be emboldened, making it more difficult to convince Paris to abandon its dualistic approach.[119] A subsequent DEA report acknowledged that although France had rounded off some of the sharp edges of its Quebec policy, Paris had not modified its core position from 1967. Even worse, according to the analysis, the Quai d'Orsay appeared to have adopted de Gaulle's policy as its own, and neither Pompidou nor Schumann appeared willing to engage his authority to change the situation.[120]

Faced with the reality that its de Gaulle-centric analysis had proved flawed and that the Pompidou government was maintaining privileged relations with Quebec City, Ottawa had to content itself with incremental steps toward normalized relations. Among these were the welcome that Sharp received during his April 1970 visit to Paris. Schumann assured him that Pompidou desired normalized relations more than ever and responded with obvious discomfort when Sharp criticized recent French actions in Africa. The French government spokesman, Léo Hamon, told a DEA official that Ottawa could expect an "inflexion" – a shift – of French policy. Although Sharp interpreted the welcome as proof of a desire for a rapprochement, the veterans at Canada's embassy were unconvinced. Indeed, in advance of Sharp's arrival Pompidou had instructed officials to be sure to maintain Paris's policy regarding Quebec's distinct participation in the Francophonie and its dualistic approach to French ministerial visits.[121]

Paris could, in any event, afford to be friendlier toward Ottawa. Quebec's apparent hesitation regarding its political future made it difficult for France to pursue a more aggressive policy – this had been recognized even before de Gaulle's departure. In the interim, the renewal of the cultural cooperation agreements meant that the core of the special relationship between France and Quebec was secured. Combined with the outcome of Niamey II, the neo-nationalist objectives for Quebec's international activity had largely been achieved: although Ottawa had established itself as a viable interlocutor with the international francophone community and was continuing to claim a right to involvement in the special relationship, Quebec City remained able to maintain what amounted to direct, privileged links with Paris and the Francophonie in a manner consistent with the Gérin-Lajoie doctrine.

The road to normalization thus promised to be slow and not without detours. Notwithstanding the founding of the ACCT, the question of responsibility for Canada's foreign affairs remained unresolved, as was quickly demonstrated by renewed conflict between Ottawa and Quebec City over the province's accession to the organization preceding the ACCT conference in the two capitals in 1971.[122] This continued rivalry could only endure amid the debates over constitutional reform and Quebec's future. Moreover, Quebec's new premier, Robert Bourassa, was resolute that the core of the province's cooperation with France should be maintained and was supported in this regard by officials dedicated to Quebec's international action. Most broadly, despite political changes at all three points of the triangle, the complex relations were poised to continue by virtue of the continued resonance of nationalist sentiment on both sides of the Atlantic. Quebec City still had to contend with its *question nationale*. The Trudeau government, of course, had its own answer to this question: a reformed federalism, but one in which Quebec enjoyed no special status – not least in foreign affairs. Indeed, maintaining Canada's unity abroad and at home appeared more important than ever as Ottawa managed the country's relations with the United States. Finally, France had to come to terms with the Gaullist legacy. For all of de Gaulle's efforts on behalf of "a certain idea of France," the shortcomings of the nationalist reaction to preponderant American power that he had embodied were evident even before he had left the stage. Combined with the ongoing acceleration of interdependence and transnational exchanges, the nationalist reactions in the triangle were fated to clash in the years to come.

Conclusions

CHARLES DE GAULLE'S *CRI DU BALCON* was an electric moment of high political theatre, an occasion for catharsis as he gave succour to Quebec nationalist aspirations, vaunted the ties binding France and Quebec, and urged solidarity between their two populations. Far from marking the beginning of the triangular tensions, much less giving rise to the debate over Quebec's *question nationale* and Canada's unity crisis, the significance of the French leader's remarks derived from their being the dramatic climax to the entangled post-war evolution of the triangle's components. De Gaulle's actions may have been in the avant-garde, but he was by no means alone in the sentiments he expressed. Indeed, he may be viewed as the embodiment of the nationalist reactions that had arisen on both sides of the Atlantic in response to the interaction between local circumstances and global realities. Montreal's Place Jacques-Cartier was the location on 24 July 1967 for the dramatic convergence of these nationalist reactions.

This exploration of the Canada-Quebec-France triangle has been shaped by two overlapping paradoxes at its core. The first is that the conditions that encouraged a rapprochement in the triangle, notably between France and Quebec, were the same ones that helped to spawn the tensions of the 1960s. The second is that, even as nationalist concerns in the triangle's three components motivated them to respond to preponderant American power and the acceleration of interdependence and transnational exchanges accompanying this, their replies contributed to the very international conditions that had fuelled the nationalist pressure for a response in the first place.

As such, the triangular tensions are significant as a historical episode not just in and of themselves, but for the insight that they provide into the respective yet interwoven development of Canada, Quebec, and France, and for the light that they shed on the history of international relations after 1945. Indeed, the Canada-Quebec-France triangle was at the centre of debates marking the international relations of the period: most broadly, developments in the triangle were driven to a great extent by the concerns arising from the acceleration of what is referred to today as globalization – a deepening integration and interconnection resulting in the expansion and intensification of social relations that cut across traditional political, economic, cultural, and geographical boundaries.[1] Indeed, the word "globalization" seems to have first appeared just five years before the *cri du balcon*, and apparently took its inspiration from the French word *mondialisation*, coined almost a decade earlier.[2] Each component of the triangle contributed to promoting the liberal capitalist variant of this phenomenon, with its implications for sovereignty, identities, and the efficacy – as well as relevance – of "the nation" and nationalism. Notwithstanding ongoing debates over the nature of globalization's impact on state sovereignty, the *perception* in the period that this book has examined was that the power and authority of national governments were being eroded under the rising tide of interdependence and transnationalism. This perception was all the more significant since it coexisted in the same historical moment with the ideal of an international order based upon sovereign nation-states and a Keynesian liberalism according an important role to national governments. More immediately, each point of the triangle was preoccupied with the preponderant power of the United States and strove in its own way to respond to the American challenge. These two debates were bound tightly together, especially during the quarter-century after the Second World War. As has been observed, "The twentieth century was neither the end of history nor the beginning of globalization. But it was conspicuously American."[3]

The emergence and rise to power of Quebec neo-nationalism and the Gaullist variant of French nationalism were the crucial precursors to a rapprochement between France and Quebec that was first visible in the private sphere, but manifested increasingly in the public sphere. The ascendance of and growing allegiance between these two nationalisms presented a dilemma for a Canadian nationalism that was in profound flux after the Second World War, and was reacting to the same international conditions as its French and Quebec counterparts. Quebec neo-nationalism called into question the conceptualization and even the unity of Canada as a project of national rule. In combination with Gaullism, it challenged fundamental assumptions and objectives of Canadian nationalism. The dynamic was equally true in reverse, and the result was an increasingly complex triangular dynamic in which cooperation proliferated alongside suspicion, tension, and confrontation.

The conditions for this convergence and clash of nationalisms ripened throughout the post-1945 period. Bilateral contact and cooperation between Canada and France was greater than ever in the decade after the Second World War. In contending with American geopolitical strength and the Cold War,

Ottawa and Paris viewed each other as useful and necessary allies, reflected in their cooperation in multilateral forums and their adoption of Atlanticism. Yet this liberal internationalist approach, which sought to secure the protection of the United States while simultaneously constraining its influence, ultimately ended up reifying American predominance in the West, thereby contributing to the American phase of globalization. Having embraced this foreign policy response with different expectations conditioned by their unique pasts and diplomatic cultures, Atlanticism soon evolved into a source of discord. French foreign policy took on an increasingly nationalist hue, chafing over a transatlantic order that a growing segment of opinion viewed as an ill-disguised American hegemony. Canadian nationalist concern over the United States also grew during the period, but Ottawa adhered to Atlanticism, viewing it as the most effective means available to maximize Canada's autonomy and international action. Ottawa accordingly worked to mitigate dissension in the North Atlantic, but by the latter half of the 1950s, this Franco-Canadian divergence over Atlanticism contributed to a hollowing out of the bilateral relationship.

Nationalist-inspired differences were even more pronounced in the economic sphere. Although emerging from the war in radically different situations, Canada and France each had to contend with the United States's economic strength and their dependence on it for prosperity. Paris responded with a more protectionist approach, notably in the form of a bounded liberal economic policy axed increasingly on Europe. This was at odds with Canada's liberal internationalism, which aimed to dilute the American presence in the Canadian economy through a multilateral and liberalized commercial order. Differences between French and Canadian foreign economic policy, and the regionalization of world trade flowing from this, led to the relative stagnation of the economic relationship.

Yet there was another dimension to the economic relationship in the fifteen years after the Second World War. Consistent with the global trend toward increased economic interdependence and transnationalism, exchanges between Canada and France grew in absolute terms, not just monetarily but also in terms of interpersonal contact. The three points of the triangle contributed to this international phenomenon since, for all the differences between them over the appropriate level of government involvement in the economy, each ultimately subscribed to the logic of liberal capitalism. Even as they contributed to the construction of an international order based on this, one in which the United States occupied the central position, Paris, Quebec City, and Ottawa sought to reconcile this order with understandings of their respective national interests. The dynamic fuelled interest in a more substantive relationship as an end in itself, but also out of a more defensive calculus arising from concern about the broader consequences of American economic power. Consistent with a larger Canadian anxiety over the United States's growing economic profile in Canada, the rise of neo-nationalism in Quebec was marked by increasing interest in France as a source of support as the province adapted to new socio-economic realities, strove to preserve its francophone majority, and sought francophone economic empowerment. The dynamic was encouraged by the preoccupation throughout the triangle with "modernization," which overlapped with debates surrounding Americanization and efforts to reconcile the modern with local conditions – that is, to modernize on one's own terms. Such nationalist concern found a receptive audience in France, where there was concern about the effect of the American way of life on a certain idea of Frenchness.

Preoccupations over Americanization also helped shape cultural relations in the triangle, which were marked by substantial growth and change. The trend was especially pronounced between France and French Canada, and it highlighted Quebec's sociocultural transformation as the traditional nationalist order was eclipsed by elements favouring exchanges of a more secular and progressive nature. Not only did these exchanges reflect Quebec's evolution in the decades preceding the Quiet Revolution, they were a vital contribution to it. This included a shift in francophone Quebec's self-perception as a cultural producer with a unique contribution to international francophone culture that merited recognition.

As was the case in the economic sphere, there was a more defensive impetus accompanying the expanding cultural contacts. The growth was consistent with the global proliferation of transnational cultural exchanges, notably the expansion of American cultural influence that Peter J. Taylor claims was inseparable from the political and economic components of the United States's hegemonic cycle.[4] Consistent with the longstanding French-Canadian nationalist mission to perpetuate North America's *fait français,* elements of the neo-nationalist elites turned to France as a source of protection against Anglo-Saxon – especially American – cultural influences, considered all the more a threat since Quebec's urbanization and industrialization, combined with communications and transportation advances, were allegedly promoting the general population's Americanization. Neo-nationalist interest in France was part of a larger drive to see a more activist Quebec state act as the guardian of North America's francophones. This ambition was framed by a constitutional rivalry with Ottawa over culture and the broader question of French Canada's place in Canada's federal system. For it was not just Quebec francophones coming to terms with their "American" reality. Already evident in the interwar period, English-Canadian nationalism and anti-Americanism pushed Ottawa to increase its cultural activism. Federal efforts clashed with Quebec nationalist sensibilities that, informed by history, held that French Canada's survival required Quebec to jealously guard its autonomy in cultural affairs.

The increasing politicization of cultural affairs in Canada was part of the global trend toward greater state involvement in culture. Indeed, an array of constitutional, institutional, and ideological factors meant that Ottawa and Quebec City lagged behind as culture occupied an increasingly important place in international relations. Paris was much further advanced, employing culture to compensate for its diminished geopolitical and economic power. The postwar strength of the United States's cultural industries and the Americanization phenomenon – not to mention Washington's own cultural diplomacy – provided the French state with a further impetus for involvement in cultural affairs: despite its geographic location, France, like Canada and Quebec, had to contend with the American challenge.

By the end of the 1950s, amid word that Quebec would open an office in Paris to promote economic and cultural cooperation, the complex combination of estrangement and rapprochement that the post-war years had produced in the triangle meant the stage was set for cooperation and confrontation. An array of mutually reinforcing ethnocultural, political, and geopolitical motivations gave rise to the triangular relations and tensions. Gaullism, preoccupied with "the nation" and the realization of French *grandeur,* was attracted to Quebec neo-nationalism's bid to have Quebec serve as French Canada's nation-state. Interest in Quebec was especially pronounced in Gaullist circles and among members of the Quebec lobby in Paris. However, the community of interest that had arisen from the growth of cultural exchanges, and French anxiety over American cultural strength, fuelled a broader French interest in Quebec founded upon notions of ethnocultural solidarity in the face of "les Anglo-Saxons."

The rapprochement between France and Quebec was strengthened further by the acceleration of Quebec's political life. Into the 1960s, Paris maintained a discreet attitude regarding Canada's federal system. The advent of the Quiet Revolution, however, led to a growing consensus among the French political class about the necessity of fundamental change to Canada's constitutional and political order. Paris accordingly shifted toward an approach in its relations with Canada – or, more accurately, "the Canadas," consistent with the two-nation thesis of Confederation. In its most advanced form, this Quebec policy entailed not only support for but active encouragement of Quebec independence.

The shift in French policy was consistent with the ethnocultural motivations driving the triangular dynamic, France's turbulent political history, and the priority that the Gaullist worldview accorded national independence. It was also the product of the decolonization phenomenon and France's experience of this. Decolonization was in many respects a function of the acceleration of globalization. The relative rapidity with which it took place owed much to the liberal victory in the Second World War, the ascendancy of liberal notions of national self-determination flowing from this, and the rapid transnational flow of ideas and images that reached a planetary audience, including francophone Quebecers.[5] Yet at the same time, as Robert Latham has observed, decolonization posed a fundamental challenge to liberal doctrine and a liberal international order founded upon sovereign states and non-intervention, notably in terms of how these could be reconciled with questions of self-determination.[6] As Paris found out to its chagrin in North Africa, the result was multiplying examples of the apparent permeability of what was posited as a barrier between the domestic and international spheres. In the aftermath of Algeria, France would add to these examples by its interventions on behalf of Quebec self-determination.

Initially supportive of Quebec City's efforts to cultivate relations with France so long as they respected federal authority, Ottawa's ensuing marginalization provoked a growing federal unease that intersected with Canadian nationalist anxiety over the nature of the country's identity, its unity, and American influence. The future of North America's *fait français* took on heightened importance, as it was central to the political projects accompanying the various nationalist reactions in the triangle. Ottawa moved to cultivate relations with France and the francophone world, consistent with its concern to promote a pan-Canadian biculturalism and bilingualism that would contain the Quebec nationalist challenge, safeguard unity, and ensure the development of French and English Canada as cultural entities distinct from and independent of the United States.

Herein lay a fundamental source of the tensions, as the Gaullist and Quebec neo-nationalist position was that Ottawa was incapable of conducting relations with France in a manner consistent with French Canada's interests. In any case, it was unwelcome; rather, Quebec City believed, given the constitutional ambiguity surrounding culture and foreign affairs, that logic, provincial rights, and French-Canadian survival dictated that Quebec's jurisdiction did not stop at Canadian shores. Longstanding debates over the nature of Canada and its federal system were internationalized amid the pronouncement of the Gérin-Lajoie doctrine. Ottawa opposed this resolutely, arguing that the unity of Canada's international personality, and by implication the country itself, demanded federal primacy in foreign affairs irrespective of the subject matter. Paris increasingly favoured the Quebec position. Although the Élysée was at the forefront of encouraging direct relations with Quebec City, the influence of Quebec's supporters at the Quai d'Orsay meant that the MAE also cultivated links, even while displaying concern to minimize federal objections and diplomatic incidents.

Beyond ethnocultural considerations and questions of Quebec's political destiny, Ottawa found itself further marginalized owing to its widening divergence with Paris over Atlanticism. The more Paris challenged the transatlantic order and the more Franco-Canadian relations deteriorated, the more Ottawa strove to forge links with Paris, hoping to earn French amity and preserve the Atlanticist framework that remained a central component of Canadian foreign policy. The perverse result, however, was confirmation of Gaullist suspicions that Canada was an American satellite, which provided Paris with the geopolitical rationale for its Quebec policy.

This was the context in which the triangular relations unfolded. It was apparent in the economic sphere, as Quebec neo-nationalists sought francophone economic empowerment as a means to achieving greater autonomy and ensuring the industrial and technological development of Quebec in a manner that reinforced its majority francophone society. Such objectives meshed nicely with the Gaullist challenge to American economic leadership and Paris's efforts to facilitate French success in the global economy. The corollary of this growing francophone economic solidarity was the frustration of federal efforts to cultivate links with France, a condition aggravated by disputes between Ottawa and Paris arising from their ongoing differences over foreign economic policy. Such disputes also confirmed the Gaullist view of Canada's satellization, and thus encouraged Paris's drive for cooperation with Quebec City.

It was in the cultural domain that the triangular dynamic was most visible, as the post-war rivalry between Ottawa and Quebec City over culture intersected with that over foreign affairs. Quebec was increasingly assertive in pursuing cooperation with France to realize its neo-nationalist-inspired cultural vocation as the national government of French Canada. Paris responded enthusiastically, and the result was a series of cooperation agreements that sparked concern in Ottawa over the apparent threat to the federal constitutional position, even as the Pearson government sought to ramp up its cultural relations with the francophone world as part of its biculturalism drive.

The increasingly direct relations between France and Quebec were symptomatic of Paris's favouring the province's claims to an international capacity, and became enmeshed in the efforts of Quebec's French advocates to help it achieve a new political status. De Gaulle's visit in 1967 was the most dramatic illustration of this policy, ushering in an acute crisis that saw the French leader pronounce explicitly in favour of Quebec independence, and Paris's efforts to ensure a distinct Quebec participation in the Francophonie. Ottawa faced the challenge of responding to Gaullist and Quebec nationalist initiatives in a manner that did not reinforce the lopsided triangular dynamic and threaten Canadian unity. If the Trudeau government's arrival in power was marked by Ottawa adopting a more assertive position, this was more a question of degree than of fundamental change, since federal authorities still confronted their principal dilemma in responding to the triangular dynamic.

In an immediate sense, changes of political leadership at the three points of the triangle hastened the passing of the acute phase of the triangular crisis. However, this development had much to do with more profound domestic and international factors. In the economic sphere, for example, the complementarity of Quebec neo-nationalism and Gaullism led to increased contacts and exchanges. Yet, despite the concerted political efforts of Quebec City and Paris, these exchanges never attained the scope that advocates of such cooperation desired. Even with Ottawa's efforts to cultivate economic relations (admittedly motivated by a different set of considerations), the three components of the triangle were unable to overcome interrelated domestic and international conditions and change the structure of economic relations in the triangle. With each of the triangle's components operating within a liberal capitalist logic, the reality was that the French and Quebec (and, for that matter, Canadian) private sectors were oriented toward their respective continental markets, so that the relative stagnation of the economic relationship continued. Moreover, the inescapable irony was that for Quebec to realize the francophone economic empowerment that it sought, the required capital was only available in the United States.

The shortcomings of economic cooperation between France and Quebec were all the more evident in the aftermath of the events of May 1968, which undermined Paris's ability to assist Quebec. Canadian nationalist George Grant had predicted three years before that Gaullism was destined to fail in the face of liberalism; as Paris found itself increasingly isolated in its bid to challenge American economic leadership and compelled by the dictates of interdependence to moderate its foreign policy positions, Grant's lament for the French nation appeared prescient indeed. The dynamic was underscored by the mounting private sector reticence to follow the political lead of Paris and Quebec City, arising from a concern over instability. Such an outcome demonstrates the broader significance of the Canada-Quebec-France triangle to the history of international relations, as it suggests the limited efficacy of nationalist responses to the liberal capitalist variant of globalization.

The outcome of cultural triangular relations was more nuanced. Here again, the nationalist reactions at each point of the triangle contributed to the post-war trends to which they were responding. Cultural cooperation between Paris and

Quebec City grew in the second half of the 1960s, founded upon a belief that only Quebec was able and willing to ensure French Canada's survival in an era of proliferating transnational exchanges, and that it required the assistance of a Paris preoccupied with promoting the international reach of French culture in the face of American cultural power. The period was also marked by Paris's proclivity, consistent with its two-nation approach, to treat directly with francophone minority groups outside Quebec. The trend fuelled federal fears, not just in terms of what Ottawa asserted was an encroachment on its prerogative in foreign affairs, but about the impact on federal efforts to foster pan-Canadian biculturalism and bilingualism to reinforce Canada's unity and promote an identity distinct from that of the United States. Throughout the latter half of the 1960s, Ottawa struggled to safeguard its position. It increased its cultural activities in France and asserted its role as a viable interlocutor to facilitate contacts between France and French Canada – including Quebec. Exploration of the dynamic reveals how events in the international sphere factored into the adoption of the *Official Languages Act* and the extension of federal aid to Canada's francophone minority communities.

The record of cultural triangular relations also has implications for understandings of Canadian federalism. With the cooperation agreements that it reached with France, Quebec demonstrated a willingness and ability to bend the federal system to its needs. For all of the disputes of the 1960s over the circumstances under which cultural exchanges were to be carried out, and notwithstanding the fact that neither Ottawa nor Quebec City achieved complete satisfaction in this regard, Canadian federalism proved an adaptable beast. Despite its expressed reservations, Ottawa tacitly accepted that the core of privileged cultural cooperation between France and Quebec would endure. This decision was encouraged by Paris's apparent willingness to engage with Ottawa regarding Canada's francophone minority communities – a development that resulted partly from the challenges French Canada's divisions posed to the two-nation approach underpinning France's Quebec policy.

The nature of Canada's federal system, and Quebec's place in or outside of it, was of course at the core of the political triangular relationship. Quebec was able, with increasingly overt French assistance, to exploit the constitutional ambiguities over the competence for foreign affairs, project itself abroad, and achieve a distinct (if circumscribed) international personality, notably in terms of its participation in the Francophonie. This was not without complications; consistent with the fact Gaullism and Quebec neo-nationalism were using one another to promote their unique political agendas, frustration arose occasionally between Paris and Quebec City over what each viewed as the other's failure to understand its fundamental interests. Nevertheless, Quebec's growing international activity was a significant achievement for neo-nationalism, something that it deemed essential to safeguard and promote. More broadly, the achievement was exemplary of the international phenomena of the transformative impact of "low politics" after 1945, which saw the multiplying efforts of sub-state entities to act internationally, thereby posing a challenge to the notions of state sovereignty upon which the international order was based.

This trend was especially relevant to Canada by virtue of the debate over responsibility for foreign affairs, the country's cleavages, and the enduring discussion over constitutional and political arrangements. The complementarity between the Gaullist and neo-nationalist positions was reflected in the Lesage and Johnson governments using French interest in and support for Quebec as leverage against Ottawa to obtain greater autonomy. There were limits, however, to this complementarity; even as federal authorities awoke to the scope of the challenge of the allied Gaullist and Quebec neo-nationalist reactions, there was a growing disconnect between them. In the main, Quebec's political class and population appreciated French support (and, to a significant extent, the *cri du balcon*) as a validation of Quebec's national existence. To the confusion of Paris and the disappointed expectations of de Gaulle, however, Quebec was not prepared to act so rapidly or definitively on the French leader's proposed answer to the *question nationale*. Instead, consistent with a pragmatism conditioned by Quebec, Canadian, and North American realities, the advocates of the Quebec neo-nationalist and Canadian nationalist responses continued to engage each other within the existing federal framework. Yet, the genie that de Gaulle had released could not be put back in the bottle. In addition to having had a strong impact on the political life of Quebec and Canada, the French president's actions tied Paris to the sovereignty debate so that in the decades since the General's visit, France and its attitudes regarding Quebec's political future and Canadian unity have remained under scrutiny.

Triangular tensions were thus set to continue into the 1970s. The nationalist reactions that had arisen on both sides of the Atlantic were continuing to play out and interact, and the domestic and international conditions that had fuelled them remained salient. As globalization accelerated, France had to come to terms with the Gaullist legacy, and the new Pompidou government, pushed by Quebec lobby members, was determined to pursue privileged relations with Quebec to ensure the development of the *fait français*. Although the trend was toward a less interventionist policy, the expectation in Paris remained that Quebec was destined to accede to a new political status. In Canada, beyond concern over the scope of American influence, the dispute over responsibility for foreign affairs remained unresolved, part of the much wider constitutional debate, and there was a determination to recover the federal position as Ottawa moved to stare down Quebec nationalism. Even with the Bourassa government's election and the appearance of the outlines of a fragile compromise, the question of Quebec's political future remained to be answered, a point that the growing strength of the Parti Québécois underscored. For all of these reasons, then, it was more accurate to describe the Canada-Quebec-France triangle as having entered a period of truce rather than rapprochement, as the echoes from de Gaulle's *cri du balcon* and the clash of nationalist reactions to which it had given voice continued to be heard on both sides of the Atlantic.

Notes

Introduction: In the Shadow of the General

1 McLuhan, *Gutenberg Galaxy*, 31.
2 Roy, "The Theme Unfolded by Gabrielle Roy," 28-30.
3 Saint-Exupéry, *Terre des hommes*, 55.
4 McKenna and Pucell, *Drapeau*, 135.
5 Lescop, *Le pari québécois*, 165-166 (emphasis added).

> My heart is filled with profound emotion as I see before me the *French* city of Montreal. In the name of the old country, in the name of France, I salute you with all my heart.
>
> I am going to tell you a secret that you will not repeat. Here tonight, and all along my route, I have found myself in an atmosphere similar to that of the *Liberation*.
>
> Beyond this, all along my route I have noted what an immense effort of progress, development, and, consequently, of emancipation you are accomplishing here, and it is in Montreal I must say it, because, if there is a city in the world whose modern successes stand out, it is *yours*. I say it is yours, and I permit myself to add that it is *ours*.
>
> If you knew what confidence France, awakened after immense struggles, has in you, if you knew what affection it is beginning to feel again for the French of Canada, and if you knew to what extent it feels the need to contribute to your march forward, to your progress!
>
> This is why it has concluded with the Government of Quebec, with that of my friend Johnson, agreements enabling the French of both sides of the Atlantic to work *together* in a common *French* undertaking. And, moreover, France knows that the increasing assistance it will provide here will be returned, since you are in the midst of establishing for yourself the elites, factories, businesses, laboratories that will impress everyone and that one day, I am sure of it, will enable you to help France.
>
> That is what I have come to tell you this evening in adding that I will take away an *unforgettable* memory from this *extraordinary* Montreal reunion. All of France knows, sees, hears what is happening here, and I can tell you, it is the better for it.
>
> Long live Montreal! Long live Quebec! Long live a *free* Quebec! Long live French Canada and long live France!

6 Anderson, *Imagined Communities*, 3.
7 For a review of the literature, see Meren, "Strange Allies," 6-16.
8 Mazlish, "Comparing Global History," 385-391; Mazlish and Iriye, "Introduction," 3.

Chapter 1: Atlanticism in Common, Atlanticism in Question

1 DEA/5692/1-A(s)/4 – Office of the Representative of Canada to the French Committee of National Liberation, Algiers to DEA, 27 June 1944.
2 Penisson, "Commissariat canadien à Paris," 357-376; Hilliker, *Canada's Department*, 17-18, 26, 112.
3 Amyot, *Québec entre Pétain et de Gaulle*; Couture, "The Politics of Diplomacy"; Hilliker, "Canadian Government," 87-108; Langer, *Our Vichy Gamble*.
4 DEA/5724/7-CS(s) – Supplementary Note on Yalta Commentary, 11 May 1945; DEA/5693/1-E(s) – Robertson to King, 9 June 1944; MAE/34 – de Hauteclocque to MAE, Amérique, 17 January 1947.
5 ANF/3AG1/259/1 – Aide Mémoire pour le Voyage du Général de Gaulle; MAE/43 – Service d'Information Français, Conférence de Presse du Général de Gaulle, 29 August 1945; MAE/Schuman/105 – L'importance internationale du Canada, 10 September 1949.
6 MAE/43 – Entretien du Général de Gaulle avec M. Mackenzie King, 29 August 1945; MAE/43 – L'intérêt que présente le développement des relations franco-canadiens, undated [circa 1946].
7 MAE/Schuman/105 – L'importance internationale du Canada, 10 September 1949; MAE/43 – Note pour le Secrétaire Général, 20 September 1944.
8 MAE/37 – Dejean, MAE, Amérique, to French Embassy, Ottawa, 6 March 1945; MAE/37 – Fouques-Duparc, San Francisco, to MAE, Amérique, 19 May 1945; MAE/43 – L'intérêt que présente le développement des relations franco-canadiens, undated [circa 1946]; Chapnick, *The Middle Power Project*, 135-138.
9 DEA/3284/6956-40/1 – European Division to the Under-Secretary, 3 November 1949.
10 English, *Worldly Years*, 112. For a discussion of the linkages between liberalism and the post-war geostrategic situation, see Latham, *Liberal Moment*.
11 Brogi, *Question of Self-Esteem*, 89-90; Cogan, *Forced to Choose*, 3-74; Soutou, "Sécurité de la France."
12 Harrison, *Reluctant Ally*, 27; Soutou, "Sécurité de la France," 35, 45-46.
13 Reid, "Birth of the North Atlantic Alliance," 433. See also Cogan, *Forced to Choose*, 41; Reid, *Time of Fear*, 67; Roger, *American Enemy*, 325-328.
14 DEA/3775/7839-40/1 – Canadian Embassy, Paris to SSEA, 19 February 1950.
15 Reid, *Time of Fear*, 108-109, 132, 139; Champion, "Mike Pearson at Oxford."
16 Reid, *Time of Fear*, 133-142.
17 Granatstein, *Man of Influence*, 137. See also Chapnick, *Middle Power Project*; Simpson, "Principles of Liberal Internationalism."
18 Pearson, *Mike: The Memoirs ... volume 2*, 50. See also Milloy, *North Atlantic Treaty Organization*, 30; Reid, *Time of Fear*, 60, 213-218.
19 MAE/39 – MAE, Amérique, to Director, Affaires Politiques, 7 December 1950; DEA/2492/10463-P-40 – Annual Review for 1950, 16 January 1951. See also Kitchen, "From the Korean War to Suez," 220-240; Stairs, *Diplomacy of Constraint*; Stueck, *Korean War*.
20 DEA/3284/6956-40/1 – Memorandum, 6 February 1951; Bothwell, *Alliance and Illusion*, 96.
21 MAE/44 – Guérin to MAE, 25 December 1950; MAE/44 – Note pour le ministre, 11 January 1951; DEA/3775/7839-40/1 – Note to File, 14 February 1951.
22 DEA/8300/9908-AD-2-40/3.2 – Pearson to Under-Secretary, 7 April 1951.
23 MAE/41 – de Laboulaye to Schuman, MAE, Amérique, 27 April 1951; MAE/45 – Guérin to Schuman, MAE, Amérique, 11 April 1951; MAE/44 – Guérin to MAE, 19 April 1951.
24 MAE/39 – Guérin to Schuman, 12 December 1951.

25 DEA/4620/50052-40/4 – Memorandum to the Cabinet, Draft, 17 February 1950; DEA/4620/50052-40/4 – Ritchie to Under-Secretary, 21 February 1950; DEA/4620/50052-40/5 – Canadian Ambassador, Paris to SSEA, 3 March 1950; MAE/36 – Guérin to MAE, Amérique, 10 March 1950; DCER/1952 – Document 1008, Memorandum from Acting Secretary of State for External Affairs to Cabinet, 1 November 1952, Recognition of Vietnam, Laos and Cambodia; Deleuze, "Canada, les Canadiens."
26 Bothwell, *Alliance and Illusion*, 197. For a discussion of Indo-Canadian relations, see Touhey, "Dealing with the Peacock."
27 Milloy, *North Atlantic Treaty Organization*, chapter 2. See Latham, *Liberal Moment*, 61-64, for an exploration of the question of American power in North Atlantic relations.
28 Cogan, *Forced to Choose*, 106.
29 DEA/5872/50163-40/1.1 – Canadian Ambassador, Paris to SSEA, 28 October 1952; DEA/5872/50163-40/1.2 – Canadian Ambassador, Paris to SSEA, 25 April 1953.
30 Brogi, *Question of Self-Esteem*, 124; Hitchcock, *France Restored*, 135-168; Cogan, *Forced to Choose*, 91-116; Grosser, *Western Alliance*, 121-125.
31 DEA/3284/6956-40/1 – Canadian Ambassador, Paris to SSEA, 12 January 1954.
32 DEA/284/6956-40/1 – Pearson to Guérin, 30 December 1953.
33 The Western European Union was established through an amending of the 1948 Brussels Treaty. The new organization abandoned the EDC's supranational aspects, maintaining national armed forces. West Germany regained full sovereignty and entered NATO in return for allied control over German air and naval production and an effective ban on German bacteriological, chemical, and nuclear weapons.
34 Grosser, *Western Alliance*, 126; Hitchcock, *France Restored*, 197-202; DEA/6647/11562-39-40/1.3 – Léger to Holmes and Chapdelaine, 16 November 1954.
35 Jacques Portes, "Pierre Mendès-France au Canada," 786; DDF/1954(2) – Document 110, M. Hubert Guérin, Ambassadeur de France à Ottawa, à M. Mendès-France, Ministre des Affaires étrangères, 30 August 1954; DDF/1954(2) – Document 116, M. Mendès-France, Ministre des Affaires étrangères, à M. Hubert Guérin, Ambassadeur de France à Ottawa, 1 September 1954; DEA/3775/7839-40/1 – Roy and Ford, Departmental Memorandum, 26 November 1954.
36 DEA/6829/2727-AD-40/7.1 – Canadian Embassy, Paris to SSEA, 22 June 1955.
37 Winand, *Eisenhower, Kennedy*, 51; Wall, *United States*, 263-296; Rioux, *Fourth Republic*, 204-209.
38 Thomas, Moore, and Butler, *Crises of Empire*, 127-151, 209-251; Brogi, *Question of Self-Esteem*, 104; Betts, *France and Decolonisation*, 65-93; Marshall, *French Colonial Myth*, 302-315.
39 Gendron, *Towards a Francophone Community*, 218-232; MAE/95 – de Laboulaye to MAE, Amérique, 27 October 1952; DEA/5872/50163-40/1.1 – Canadian Ambassador, Paris to SSEA, 28 October 1952.
40 Gendron, *Towards a Francophone Community*, 23.
41 Betts, *France and Decolonisation*, 94-104; Thomas, *French North African Crisis*, 14-69.
42 Gendron, *Towards a Francophone Community*, 28-31, 38.
43 MAE/98 – Lacoste to Pineau, MAE, Amérique, 15 June 1956.
44 DEA/7043/6938-40/10 – Canadian Ambassador, Paris to SSEA, 7 March 1956; Gendron, *Towards a Francophone Community*, 33.
45 Thomas, *French North African Crisis*, 100-129; Rioux, *Fourth Republic*, 271-273; Coutau-Bégarie, "Comment on conduit une coalition," 101-104; Wall, *France, the United States*, 33-66; Vaïsse, "France and the Suez Crisis," 134-140.
46 English, *Worldly Years*, 116-118.

47 O'Reilly, "Following Ike?"; Kunz, *Economic Diplomacy;* Fry, "Canada, the North Atlantic Triangle," 288-313.
48 DEA/7068/7839-40/2 – Davis, Canadian Embassy, Paris to SSEA, 16 January 1957.
49 DEA/6461/5475-FA-17-40/1 – Robertson, Canadian High Commission, London to DEA, 13 December 1956.
50 DEA/7791/12515-40 – Visit of Premier Guy Mollet and Foreign Minister Pineau, Ottawa, 2-4 March 1957, Introduction to the Prime Minister's Brief.
51 Wall, *France, the United States,* 58-62; Vaïsse, "Post-Suez France," 143.
52 MAE/104 – Lacoste to MAE, Amérique, 3 December 1956.
53 DEA/5872/50163-40/1.2 – DEA to Canadian Embassy, Paris, 12 April 1958; Gendron, *Towards a Francophone Community,* 42.
54 Wall, *France, the United States,* 99-133; Thomas, *French North African Crisis,* 130-157.
55 MAE/103 – Lacoste to MAE, Amérique, 19 February 1958.
56 Connelly, *Diplomatic Revolution,* 142-170; Wall, *France, the United States,* 134-156.
57 DEA/7044/6938-40/11.2 – Davis, Canadian Embassy, Paris to SSEA, 18 April 1958.
58 DEA/7044/6938-40/12 – Davis, Canadian Embassy, Paris to SSEA, 4 June 1958.
59 MAE/98 – Lacoste to MAE, Amérique, 24 September 1959; Gendron, *Towards a Francophone Community,* 47-52; Lefèvre, *Charles de Gaulle,* 63.
60 DEA/4125/14003-F-5-1-40/1 – Canadian Embassy, Paris to USSEA, 13 July 1957; DEA/4125/14003-F-5-1-40/1 – Canadian High Commission, London to DEA, 16 December 1957.
61 DEA/4125/14003-F-5-1-40/1 – Canadian Embassy, Paris to DEA, 8 March 1958; Grosser, *Western Alliance,* 166-173; Granatstein, *Man of Influence,* 333.
62 DEA/6009/50271-L-40/1.2 – Canadian Embassy, Paris to DEA, 26 November 1959; DEA/7044/6956-40/4.1 – Holmes to the Minister, 3 November 1959.
63 DEA/7045/6956-A-40/1.1 – European Division to Davis, 21 April 1960.
64 DEA/7068/7839-40/2 – Davis, Canadian Embassy, Paris to SSEA, 12 April 1955; Brogi, *Question of Self-Esteem,* 90, 120-122, 148.
65 North Atlantic Treaty Organization, *The Committee of Three – Le comité des Trois Sages,* http://www.nato.int/archives/committee_of_three/CT.pdf. Accessed 7 June 2010.
66 Aglion, *Roosevelt and De Gaulle,* 181.
67 De Gaulle, *Memoirs of Hope,* 10. See also Berstein, *Histoire du gaullisme,* 293-306.
68 Berstein, *Histoire du gaullisme,* 294; Grosser, *Western Alliance,* 183-185; Morse, *Foreign Policy and Interdependence,* 117-118.
69 DEA/4881/50115-1-40/1 – Defence Liaison(1) Division to Under-Secretary, 29 May 1958; DEA/7068/7839-40/2.2 – Canadian Embassy, Paris to DEA, 30 July 1958.
70 Vaïsse, *La grandeur,* 116-123.
71 Milloy, *North Atlantic Treaty Organization,* 191-197.
72 Igartua, *The Other Quiet Revolution,* 115-129; Aronsen, "An Open Door to the North," 186.
73 English, *Worldly Years,* 180; Granatstein, *Yankee Go Home?* 112-120.
74 Whitaker, *Government Party,* 208-211; Robinson, *Diefenbaker's World,* 4-23.
75 DEA/4881/50115-1-40/1 – Robinson, SSEA to USSEA, 9 October 1958.
76 DEA/7068/7839-40/2.2 – Prime Minister's Brief, November 1958, General de Gaulle and NATO.
77 DEA/4881/50115-1-40/1 – Léger to the Minister, 16 October 1958.
78 DEA/7045/6956-A-40 – Canadian Embassy, Paris to DEA, 6 November 1958; DDF/1958(2) – Document 314, Compte Rendu de l'entretien du Général De Gaulle et de M. Diefenbaker, le 5 novembre 1958, à l'Hôtel Matignon.
79 DEA/3496/19-1-D-1958(1) – Prime Minister's Tour, October-December 1958.

80 DEA/7068/7839-40/2.2 – Memorandum for the Prime Minister, 22 October 1958.
81 DEA/4003/10117-AD-40/1.1 – Dupuy, Canadian Embassy, Paris to USSEA, 15 March 1960.
82 MAE/114 – Lacoste to Couve de Murville, MAE, Amérique, 4 February 1959.
83 DEA/7666/11562-126-40/1 – Davis, European Division to USSEA, 28 November 1959; DEA/7666/11562-126-40/1 – DEA to Canadian Embassy, Paris, 4 January 1960; MAE/100 – Lacoste to Couve de Murville, MAE, Amérique, 30 April 1960; DEA/7666/11562-126-40/1.2 – Keith, European Division to Acting USSEA, 5 May 1960.

Chapter 2: Stagnation amid Growth, Growth amid Stagnation

1 Portes, "'La Capricieuse' au Canada."
2 Kennedy, *Rise and Fall*, 357-358; Gaddis, *We Now Know*, 36-39; Latham, *Liberal Moment*, 33, 51.
3 Aronsen, "World War to Cold War," 189-194; Hart, *Trading Nation*, 127-133, 145-157; Canada, Minister of Reconstruction, *Employment and Income*; Cuff and Granatstein, *Canadian-American Relations*, 69-92; Muirhead, *Development of Postwar*, 16-46.
4 Aronsen, "Open Door to the North," 182-184; Rooth, "Australia, Canada."
5 Aronsen, "Open Door to the North," 173-184.
6 Rioux, *Fourth Republic*, 21
7 Grosser, *Western Alliance*, 75; Lynch, *France and the International Economy*, 40-59; Rioux, *Fourth Republic*, 133-134; Judt, *Postwar*, 220.
8 Hitchcock, *France Restored*, 39; Lynch, *France and the International Economy*, 72-102.
9 Miller, *French Atlantic Triangle*, 27.
10 Savard, *Le Consulat Général de France*, 65-70; Phillipe Prévost, *La France et le Canada*, 17-21.
11 Prévost, *La France et le Canada*, 22, 219-230, 269-280, 414-420.
12 ITC/296/T-10243 – Compte-rendu de l'entretien du vendredi, 5 avril 1946 de Monsieur Léon Blum avec des membres du Gouvernement canadien.
13 ITC/281/36619 – Copy of a Minute of a Meeting of the Committee of the Privy Council, 12 October 1945; Lescop, *Le pari québécois*, 14.
14 MAE/53 – de Hauteclocque to MAE, Amérique, 14 March 1945; ITC/281/36619 – Ilsey to Monnet, 16 August 1945; ITC/281/36619 – Credits for France, 19 November 1945.
15 DEA/5693/1-C(s) – Howe to Robertson, 3 May 1946; DEA/5693/1-C(s) – Mackenzie to Robertson, 3 May 1946; DEA/5693/1-C(s) – Robertson to King, 8 May 1946.
16 Aronsen, "World War to Cold War," 193.
17 Muirhead, *Development of Postwar*, 47-75, 109-111; Milloy, *North Atlantic Treaty Organization*, chapters 2 and 3.
18 DEA/3310/9245-40/1 – McDermot, Memorandum for the File, 6 July 1949; MAE/54 – Guérin to Schuman, MAE, Affaires Économiques et Financières, 15 December 1949.
19 DEA/6243/9245-G-40/1.1 – Plumptre to Heeney, 21 February 1950; MAE/54 – Heeney to Guérin, 28 December 1949; MAE/54 – Guérin to MAE, Amérique, 30 January 1950.
20 ITC/719/7-872/2 – Gauthier, Canadian Embassy, Paris, to Heasman, Trade Commissioner Service, 9 March 1950; DEA/6243/9245-G-40/1.1 – Heeney to Mackenzie, 3 February 1950; DEA/6243/9245-G-40/1.2 – Ritchie, Economic Division to European Division, 20 December 1952.
21 DEA/6243/9245-G-40/1.1 – SSEA to Canadian Ambassador, Paris, 8 March 1950.
22 DEA/6243/9245-G-40/1.1 – Canadian Ambassador, Paris to SSEA, 6 April 1950.
23 ITC/1948/20-2-2/1 – Vanier, Canadian Embassy, Paris, 12 October 1950.
24 Lynch, *France and the International Economy*, 36, 111, 130; Todd, *L'Identité économique*.

25 Lynch, *France and the International Economy*, 128-141.
26 Lynch, *France and the International Economy*, 104, 124-125, 143-144; Muirhead, *Postwar Canadian Trade Policy*, 109-114, 127-129.
27 MAE/141 – Guérin to Mendès-France, MAE, Affaires Économiques et Financières, 2 November 1954.
28 DEA/3495/19-1-B-1954(1) – Economic and International Trade Position of France, 18 January 1954; DEA/7157/9245-40/3.1 – Pearson to Guérin, 8 September 1955.
29 DEA/3493/18-1-D-FRA-1953/1 – Briefing for French Ministerial Visit, March 1953; DEA/6243/9245-G-40/1.2 – Meagher, Economic Division, to Ritchie and MacDonnell, 27 March 1953.
30 MAE/143 – Lacoste to MAE, Amérique, 25 March 1958; MAE/143 – Lacoste to MAE, Amérique, 25 June 1958; DEA/7158/9245-40/5 – Dupuy to Robertson, 24 November 1958; MAE/43 – Lacoste to MAE, Amérique, 31 January 1959.
31 DEA/6519/9245-40/2.2 – SSEA to Canadian Ambassador, Paris, 11 September 1954.
32 DEA/7157/9245-40/3.1 – Léger to Pearson, 8 September 1955.
33 DEA/6519/9245-40/2.2 – Plumptre to Harris, 23 August 1955.
34 MAE/142 – Lacoste to MAE, Amérique, 5 October 1956; MAE/142 – Relations Économiques Franco-Canadiennes, 28 February 1957.
35 MAE/142 – Lacoste to MAE, Amérique, 2 May 1957; DEA/7158/9245-40/4.1 – Record of Cabinet Decision, Meeting of May 9th, 1957; MAE/142 – Lacoste to MAE, Amérique, 13 November 1957.
36 Giauque, *Grand Designs*, 19-33; Lynch, *France and the International Economy*, 169-183.
37 Hart, *Trading Nation*, 155; Muirhead, *Postwar Canadian Trade Policy*, 164, 174; MAE/143 – Note, Direction des Affaires Économiques et Financières, 29 October 1958.
38 Muirhead, *Postwar Canadian Trade Policy*, 109, 177; Hart, *Trading Nation*, 148, 219.
39 Vaïsse, *La grandeur*, 170; Frieden, *Global Capitalism*, 296.
40 British and West German exports to Canada in 1958 were valued, respectively, at $526.6 million and $105.9 million. The value of French exports was $41 million, outpacing Belgian sales – $36 million – for the first time that decade. By comparison, American exports to Canada exceeded $3.57 billion. Canada, Minister of Trade and Commerce, Dominion Bureau of Statistics, *Canada Year Book 1960*, 1003-1004; Muirhead, *Postwar Canadian Trade Policy*, 132.
41 François-Richard, "La France et le Québec," 156; AHC/WB/3/5 – Bousquet to Couve de Murville, MAE, Affaires Économiques, 13 July 1962.
42 MAE/141 – Guérin to MAE, Affaires Économiques et Financières, 27 October 1953.
43 Pépin, "Les relations économiques franco-canadiennes," 485-486; Mehling, "Remarques sur le commerce franco-canadien," 614-617; ITC/1949/20-2-2/3 – T&C, Paris to T&C, Ottawa, 18 August 1965.
44 Latham, *Liberal Moment*, 40, 112.
45 Cooper, *Economics of Interdependence*, 151-152. Cooper acknowledges that the pre-1914 world was more integrated in the sense that government barriers to the movement of goods, capital, and labour were minimal; however, he counters that those imposed by nature were much greater, meaning that economic integration after 1945 was of a different order.
46 Lawrence, "Universal Claims," 231.
47 Osterhammel and Petersson, *Globalization: A Short History*, 122; Camps, *Management of Interdependence*, 8-13; Cooper, *Economics of Interdependence*, 61.
48 This remains a highly contested debate given that the ideal of state sovereignty is just that, since there never has existed a golden age when sovereignty was not challenged by forces

in both the domestic and international environments. In this regard, see Wallerstein, "States? Sovereignty?"; Krasner, "Globalization and sovereignty"; Rosenau, *Turbulence in World Politics*, 109.

49 Vinant, *De Jacques Cartier*, 109, 293, 305; Barjot, *Fougerolle*, 65-66.
50 MAE/143 – Lacoste to Couve de Murville, MAE, Affaires Économiques et Financières, 2 June 1959; Barjot, "Lafarge: l'ascension d'une multinationale," 56-59.
51 Vinant, *De Jacques Cartier*, 334.
52 DEA/6173/72-ALB-40/1.3 – Canadian Embassy, Paris to SSEA, 9 April 1951.
53 MAE/5 – French Consulate, Montreal, Chronique mensuelle, May 1951; MAE/95 – Guérin to Schuman, MAE, Amérique, 11 August 1952; MAE/95 – Guérin to Bidault, MAE, Affaires Économiques et Financières, 28 April 1953; Vinant, *De Jacques Cartier*, 103-104.
54 MAE/141 – MAE to Ministre des Affaires Économiques, Relations Économiques Extérieures, Service de l'Expansion Économique et des Foires, 12 March 1953; MAE/141 – Guérin to Bidault, MAE, Amérique, 13 February 1954; MAE/141 – Guérin to MAE, Amérique, 13 September 1954; MAE/141 – Guérin to MAE, Affaires Économiques et Financières, 2 November 1954.
55 DEA/8059/2727-AD-40/6.1 – Désy to DEA, 25 May 1955; DEA/6829/2727-AD-40/7.1 – Memorandum for the Acting Minister, 23 June 1955.
56 ANQ/E5/1960-01-027/196 – *L'Espoir* (Nice), 18 January 1958, "3000 Personnes ont inauguré hier l'exposition 'Visages du Canada'"; ANQ/E5/1960-01-027/196 – Présence du Québec à Paris par Armour Landry – Paris, 24 January 1958.
57 DEA/6243/9245-G-40/1.1 – Report, Canadian Embassy, Paris, 23 October 1950; MAE/141 – Échanges commerciaux entre la France et le Canada, 1 February 1954.
58 MAE/99/Séjour à Paris de M. St. Laurent – Visite de M. Saint Laurent, Chef du Gouvernement canadien, undated; Vinant, *De Jacques Cartier*, 113-114; *Informations canadiennes* January 1957, 2(12): 13.
59 DEA/6829/2727-AD-40/7.1 – Désy, Canadian Embassy, Paris to SSEA, 22 June 1955; Vinant, *De Jacques Cartier*, 128-134.
60 For a discussion of the French context, see Clarke, *France in the Age of Organization*.
61 Cullather, "Modernization Theory," 216-218.
62 One of the clearest statements of the alleged dynamic is Kerr, "Changing Social Structures."
63 Engerman, "To Moscow and Back," 54-58; Gilman, "Modernization Theory," 50-51; Cooper, *Colonialism in Question*, 118.
64 Barjot, "Americanisation," 41. See also Cooper, *Colonialism in Question*, 147.
65 Cullather, "Modernization Theory," 218. See also de Grazia, *Irresistible Empire*, 94-95; McKenzie, *Remaking France*, 13.
66 Rostow, *Stages of Economic Growth*, 17-18, 67.
67 Reynolds, "American Globalism," 253.
68 Christie and Gauvreau, "Introduction," 7.
69 Kuffert, "'Stabbing our spirits broad awake,'" 31.
70 Canada, Minister of Reconstruction, *Employment and Income*, 3-5, 18.
71 Francis, *The Technological Imperative*, 159-265. Francis recounts how numerous English-Canadian intellectuals wrestled with questions related to the links between technology and American power, and Canada's place in and response to technological civilization.
72 Massolin, *Canadian Intellectuals*, 134, 199.
73 Ibid., 214.
74 Quoted in Massolin, *Canadian Intellectuals*, 186. See also Cook, *The Maple Leaf Forever*, 60-61.
75 MAE/141 – Guérin to Bidault, MAE, Affaires Économiques et Financières, 27 October 1953; MAE/141 – Guérin to MAE, Amérique, 27 September 1955.

76 Azzi, *Walter Gordon*, 34-65; Aronsen, "Open Door to the North," 186-187; MAE/128 – Lacoste to MAE, Amérique, 9 July 1957.
77 Ryan, *Penser la nation*, 106-107.
78 Hamelin and Gagnon, *Histoire du catholicisme*, 359-451.
79 Gélinas, *La droite intellectuelle*, 4. Along with Gélinas's work, Ryan's *Penser la nation* and Foisy-Geoffroy's "Le Rapport de la Commission Tremblay" have nuanced the traditional nationalist antipathy for an activist state that has been depicted in the historiography.
80 Behiels, *Prelude*, 8-14.
81 Trudeau, "The Province of Quebec"; Foisy-Geoffroy, "Le Rapport de la Commission Tremblay," 261.
82 Behiels, *Prelude*, 38-40.
83 Behiels, *Prelude*, 102-103; Brunelle, *La désillusion tranquille*, 97-99.
84 Quoted in Jones, "French Canada," 343.
85 Coleman, *Independence Movement*, 94-95.
86 Behiels, *Prelude*, 97-115.
87 Léger, *Le Temps dissipé*, 141-142; Behiels, *Prelude*, 51.
88 Behiels, *Prelude*, 43-47; Gélinas, *La droite intellectuelle*, 64-65.
89 MAE/43 – Moeneclaey to de Hauteclocque, 20 March 1945; MAE/54 – de Vial to MAE, Affaires Économiques, 16 November 1951.
90 MAE/26 – Lorion to Bidault, MAE, Amérique, 13 May 1947; MAE/54 – Lorion to Bidault, MAE, Amérique, 22 October 1947; MAE/54 – Duranthon to Schuman, MAE, Amérique, 4 January 1950; MAE/176 – Guérin to Schuman, MAE, Amérique, 29 January 1952; MAE/44 – Guérin to Schuman, MAE, Amérique, 13 February 1951.
91 Kuisel, *Seducing the French*, 52-69; Wall, *The United States*, 121-126; MAE/12 – Guérin to Schuman, MAE, Affaires Économiques et Financières, 4 April 1950.
92 MAE/143 – Lacoste to Couve de Murville, MAE, Affaires Économiques et Financières, 15 October 1958.
93 Kuisel, *Seducing the French*, 3, 101-102.
94 Grosser, *Western Alliance*, 217.
95 Caron, *Histoire économique*, 153, 203, 232; Hecht, *Radiance of France*, 27; Kuisel, *Capitalism and the State*, 277-280. Jackie Clarke, in "France, America," provides an important corrective to the modernization discourse that informs much of the post-war (notably American) historiography of France.
96 Bloch-Lainé and Bouvier, *La France restaurée*, 38-40; Caron, *Histoire économique*, 205.
97 Kuisel, *Capitalism and the State*, 223-227; Kuisel, *Seducing the French*, 70; Taylor, "Izations of the World," 57.
98 Souillac, *Le mouvement Poujade*.
99 Judt, *Past Imperfect*, 200-201.
100 Quoted in Winock, "The Cold War," 74.
101 MAE/53 – Renseignement, Ministère de la Guerre, État-Major de l'armée, 5ème bureau, 29 May 1945; MAE/43 – L'intérêt que présente le développement des relations franco-canadiens, undated [circa 1946].
102 MAE/86 – Queuille to Mouton, French Embassy, Ottawa, 3 March 1952; MAE/142 – Lacoste to Pineau, MAE, Amérique, 22 March 1956.
103 MAE/53 – de Hauteclocque to MAE, Amérique, 28 August 1945; MAE/53 – de Hauteclocque to MAE, Amérique, 12 July 1945.
104 MAE/43 – L'intérêt que présente le développement des relations franco-canadiens, undated [circa 1946].
105 MAE/127 – Guérin to Mendès-France, MAE, Amérique, 16 October 1954; MAE/142 – Ribère to Lacoste, 13 May 1957.

106 MAE/41 – Del Perugia to MAE, Amérique, 21 May 1949; MAE/170 – Guérin to MAE, Relations Culturelles, 16 July 1952.
107 MAE/96 – Lacoste to Pineau MAE, Amérique, 29 January 1958; Behiels, *Prelude*, 100.
108 Vinant, *De Jacques Cartier*, 101.
109 MAE/141 – Guérin to Mendès-France, MAE, Affaires Économiques et Financières, 2 November 1954.
110 MAE/142 – Relations économiques franco-canadiennes, 28 February 1957; Black, *Duplessis*, 492.
111 MAE/129 – Lacoste to Couve de Murville, MAE, Amérique, 12 December 1959.
112 MAE/141 – Treuil to Secrétaire d'État aux Affaires Économiques, Service de l'Expansion Économique, 12 August 1952; Vinant, *De Jacques Cartier*, 142.
113 MAE/142 – Lacoste to Pineau, MAE, Affaires Économiques et Financières, 15 March 1956.
114 ANF/5AG1/404/Documentation sur le Canada – Documentation destinée au Général de Gaulle, à l'occasion de son voyage officiel au Canada, 18-22 avril 1960.
115 De Gaulle, *Memoirs of Hope*, 242.
116 ANF/5AG1/284 – Discours du Président de la République Française à l'issue du dîner d'État, au Château Frontenac; MAE/100 – Allocution Prononcée par le Général de Gaulle à la fin du Banquet offert par la Ville de Montréal à l'Hôtel Queen Elizabeth, le vendredi, 21 avril 1960.
117 DEA/807/593 – Skelton to King, 3 February 1940; MAE/63 – Lechartier to de Hauteclocque, 15 September 1945.
118 Thomson, *Vive*, 29; MAE/129 – Lacoste to MAE, Amérique, 2 March 1960.

Chapter 3: "More Necessary than Ever"

1 Roussel, "Relations culturelles," 193-194.
2 MAE/RCST/Enseignement/132/Collège "Marie de France" de Montréal – de Hauteclocque to MAE, Relations Culturelles, 4 April 1946. See attached Note de M. René de Messières, Conseiller Culturel.
3 "Le Québec signe sa 1ère entente internationale," *Le Devoir*, 27 February 1965, 1.
4 In addition to Roussel's "Relations culturelles," for discussions of links between France and Quebec prior to 1945, see Canada, Centre culturel canadien, *Les Relations*; Harvey, "Les relations culturelles"; Lamonde, *Allégeances et dépendances*, 137-165; Pomeyrols, *Les intellectuels québécois*; Savard, "Les Canadiens français."
5 MAE/33 – de Hauteclocque to MAE, 24 March 1945; MAE/33 – Dennery to French Embassy, Ottawa, 3 April 1945.
6 MAE/Schuman/105 – L'importance internationale du Canada, 10 September 1949; Savard, "L'Ambassade de Francisque Gay," 6-7.
7 MAE/170 – Guérin to Bidault, MAE, Amérique, 16 March 1953.
8 Behiels, *Prelude*.
9 Nardout, "Le Champ littéraire," 85-97.
10 Roussel, "Relations culturelles," 164-171.
11 Gauvreau, *Catholic Origins*, 25; Roy, "Le personnalisme."
12 Gauvreau, *Catholic Origins*, 43; Meunier and Warren, *Sortir de la "Grande noirceur"*; Behiels, *Prelude*, 20-36, 61-83; Hamelin, *Histoire du catholicisme québécois*, 86-87.
13 See especially Blain, "Sur la liberté de l'esprit"; Pelletier, "D'un prolétariat spirituel"; MAE/170 – de Vial to Schuman, MAE, Relations Culturelles, 24 October 1952.
14 Behiels, *Prelude*, 55-57.
15 Meunier and Warren, *Sortir de la "Grande noirceur,"* 15-16, 90.

16 MAE/171 – Rapport annuel du service culturel de l'Ambassade de la France au Canada, 31 July 1957.
17 Lapointe, *Maison des étudiants canadiens*, 76, 96-104, 114; Roussel, "Relations culturelles," 229.
18 MAE/66 – Gay to MAE, Relations Culturelles, 1 March 1949.
19 MAE/170 – de Laboulaye to Bidault, MAE, Relations Culturelles, 29 July 1953; MAE/99/ Séjour à Paris de M. St. Laurent – Visite de M. Saint Laurent, Chef du Gouvernement Canadien, undated.
20 Rudin, *Making History*, 142-145; MAE/172 – Lacoste to Couve de Murville, MAE, Affaires Culturelles, 8 August 1958.
21 MAE/64 – Note to Direction Générale des Relations Culturelles, 18 June 1946.
22 Cloutier, "Sartre à Montréal," 268-270.
23 MAE/89 – Triat to French Ambassador, Ottawa, Chronique Mensuelle, October 1952; MAE/171 – de Villelume to Pinay, MAE, Relations Culturelles, 10 November 1955; *Informations canadiennes* February 1956, 1(2): 7; *Informations canadiennes* May 1957, 2(16): 13.
24 Nardout, "Le Champ littéraire," 170-175.
25 Bouchard, *Entre l'Ancien*, 33-39; Lamonde, *Allégeances et dépendances*, 89-90. See also Nardout, "Le Champ littéraire," 190-227; Roussel, "Relations culturelles," 166-167.
26 MAE/RCST/EC/60/Livres – Note du Conseiller culturel concernant la réimpression de livres français au Canada, undated [circa March 1947]; MAE/RCST/EC/60/Livres – de Hauteclocque to MAE, Relations Culturelles, 4 June 1947.
27 Duc, "La langue française," 466-467.
28 Duc, "La langue française," 481; François-Richard, "La France et le Québec," 76-77.
29 Nardout, "Le Champ littéraire," 384-385.
30 Richard, "La politique culturelle," 155.
31 Gérols, *Le Roman québécois*, 89, 111, 132, 149-150; Nardout, "Le Champ littéraire," 244-245, 378-385.
32 MAE/43 – de Hauteclocque to Bidault, MAE, Revue de l'Année 1945; MAE/170 – Triat to French Ambassador, Ottawa, 17 December 1953; MAE/5 – Revue mensuelle, January 1952; Roussel, "Relations culturelles," 233-235.
33 MAE/70 – Henry, President, founder of Fédération Normandie-Canada, Société d'Amitié Franco-Canadienne, Lisieux, France, 9 March 1948.
34 DEA/3271/6420-40/1 – Vanier to Pearson, 8 February 1947; MAE/70 – Accueil Franco-Canadien to MAE, Amérique, December 1948.
35 MAE/70 – Form Letter, *Accueil Franco-Canadien*, 15 April 1951; MAE/175 – Note for Secrétaire d'État, MAE, Amérique, 28 March 1957; Roussel, "Relations culturelles," 244-245.
36 DEA/8059/2727-AD-40/6.1 – Désy to USSEA, 30 March 1954; DEA/6829/2727-AD-40/7.1 – Canadian Embassy, Paris to SSEA, 22 June 1955.
37 MAE/175 – Brochure, *L'Accueil franco-canadien fait appel à votre collaboration, Association d'amitié franco-canadienne, œuvre d'assistance à l'immigrant français*; MAE/175 – Kosczuisko-Morizet to de Boisanger, 4 September 1953; Léger, *Le Temps dissipé*, 200.
38 MAE/60 – Basdevant to MAE, Accords Techniques, 2 September 1949; DEA/6331/232-C-40/2 – Heeney to Pearson, 17 April 1950.
39 MAE/171 – Rapport annuel du service culturel de l'Ambassade de la France au Canada, 31 July 1957; Pépin, "Les relations économiques," 487.
40 MAE/43 – de Hauteclocque to MAE, Amérique, Bilan des activités françaises au Canada en 1946.

41 DEA/3592/2727-AD-40/3 – Bellemare to Anderson, 19 April 1947; Donneur, "Les relations Franco-Canadiennes," 182.
42 MAE/64 – Négrier to Bidault, MAE, 5 July 1946.
43 Roussel, "Relations culturelles," 194-195; Nardout, "Le Champ littéraire," 239-240.
44 Linteau et al., *Quebec Since 1930*, 285-286; MAE/172 – Lacoste to Couve de Murville, MAE, Affaires Culturelles et Techniques, 19 November 1958; MAE/89 – Triat to French Ambassador, Ottawa, Chronique Mensuelle, May 1953; Vineberg, "Filming in Poetry," 87-89; Leach, *Claude Jutra*, 53-58, 83-84.
45 Trofimenkoff, *Dream of Nation*, 282-285.
46 MAE/171 – Rapport du Service culturel de l'Ambassade de France à Ottawa, 1955-1956, 19 September 1956.
47 D'Allemagne, *Le colonialisme au Québec*, 116.
48 Léger, *Le Temps dissipé*, 253-257.
49 MAE/175 – Guérin to Pinay, MAE, Relations Culturelles, 3 May 1955; Léger, *Le Temps dissipé*, 367-372; Roussel, "Relations culturelles," 264-265.
50 MAE/173 – Lacoste to MAE, Amérique, 23 January 1966 [sic, 1961]; DEA/5057/2727-14-40/1 – Projet de Statuts, Préambule.
51 Bouchard, *La langue et le nombril*, 89, 93, 211.
52 Levine, *Reconquest of Montreal*, 7-38; MAE/171 – Lacoste to Pineau, MAE, Amérique, 17 July 1957.
53 Bouchard, *La langue et le nombril*, 213-214.
54 Desbiens, *Les insolences du Frère Untel*, 17.
55 Borduas et al., *Refus global*, 2-3.
56 Monière, *André Laurendeau*, 79-103.
57 Judt, *Postwar*, 209-210.
58 Meunier and Warren, *Sortir de la "Grande noirceur,"* 115.
59 Pelletier, *Les années d'impatience*, 37-38.
60 Léger, *Le Temps dissipé*, 139; see also 94-99, 112-144, 178, 362-376.
61 MAE/RCST/EC/59/Canada, Direction générale, 1945-1947 – Lorion to Bidault, MAE, Relations Culturelles, 12 November 1947.
62 Roussel, "Relations culturelles," 204-205; Aird, *André Patry*, 12-38.
63 Osterhammel and Petersson, *Globalization*, 7.
64 Iriye, *Cultural Internationalism*, 82-84, 157-160; Taylor, "Izations of the World," 53-54.
65 Iriye, *Cultural Internationalism*, 51-130. For an overview of early German cultural diplomacy, see Aguilar, *Cultural Diplomacy*, 25-28, and Michels, "Deutsch als Weltsprache?" The origins of the British Council are outlined in Donaldson, *The British Council*. American cultural diplomacy is explored in Ninkovich, *Diplomacy of Ideas*.
66 Lebovics, *Mona Lisa's Escort*, 24, 28; Poirrier, *Histoire des politiques culturelles*, 8-17.
67 Pendergast, "UNESCO"; Roche and Pigniau, *Histoire de diplomatie*, 8-89; François-Richard, "La France et le Québec," 47-48.
68 François-Richard, "La France et le Québec," 45.
69 MAE/2 – de Hauteclocque to MAE, 28 February 1945.
70 MAE/Schuman/105 – L'importance internationale du Canada, 10 September 1949.
71 MAE/RCST/Enseignement/131/Canada, Dir. Gal., 1947 [henceforth, Canada] – Lorion to MAE, Relations Culturelles, 5 June 1947; MAE/95 – Lapierre to MAE, Amérique, 17 August 1955.
72 MAE/63 – Relations culturelles franco-canadiennes, 5 October 1945; MAE/RCST/EC/181 – Guérin to MAE, Relations Culturelles, 15 November 1950; MAE/62 – Guérin to Schuman, MAE, Relations Culturelles, 15 August 1951.

73 Roche and Pigniau, *Histoire de diplomatie*, 80-82; Pendergast, "UNESCO," 459.
74 DEA/3796/8260-AD-40/1 – Vanier to SSEA, 30 March 1946; DEA/8274/9456-LN-40 – Canadian Consulate General, Boston to USSEA, 24 July 1952; Roussel, "Relations culturelles," 247-250.
75 Roussel, "Relations culturelles," 201-202, 233-235; MAE/63 – Relations culturelles franco-canadiennes, 5 October 1945.
76 DEA/3796/8260-AD-40/1 – Laugier to Vanier, 2 June 1945; MAE/171 – Communiqué, DEA, Ottawa, 16 November 1956.
77 Leeson and Vanderelst, *External Affairs*, 88. I discuss this court ruling and its implications in chapter 7.
78 MAE/RCST/Enseignement/132/Établ.ts d'Enseignement – de Hauteclocque to MAE, 25 March 1946. Also during this exchange, Robertson shocked de Hauteclocque by referring to Nazi propaganda efforts in discussing the complications that could arise from Paris appointing a cultural councillor, including the question of how Ottawa would be able to turn down a Soviet request given the French precedent.
79 Carr, "Non-State Actors"; Cooper, "Canadian Cultural Diplomacy," 11-12.
80 Hilliker, *Canada's Department of External Affairs*, 275; Hilliker and Barry, *Canada's Department of External Affairs*, 10-11.
81 DEA/3197/5175-40 – Pearson to Robertson, 2 June 1943; DEA/3197/5175-40 – Robertson to Pearson, 25 June 1943.
82 Roussel, "Relations culturelles," 229.
83 DEA/3592/2727-AD-40/2 – Beaulieu to the Ambassador, 27 May 1946.
84 DEA/3495/19-1-B-1954(1)/1– Relations between Canada and France, 18 January 1954.
85 Lapointe, *Maison des étudiants canadiens*, 87, 97; Roussel, "Relations culturelles," 230.
86 Royal Commission on National Development in the Arts, Letters and Sciences, *Report, 1949-1951*, 253-254.
87 Roussel, "Relations culturelles," 186-189; DEA/5261/8260-AD-40/2 – Berlis to Canadian Embassy, Paris, 18 February 1960.
88 Litt, *Muses*, 24, 28, 239-241.
89 MC/2/7/Cadieux to Heeney, 30 November 1949; Roussel, "Relations culturelles," 231-232.
90 DEA/4003/10117-AD-40/1 – Notes on the Information and Cultural Section, Paris Embassy, 13 September 1957.
91 The French figure is somewhat misleading as it includes monies earmarked for "technical cooperation" (foreign aid). Nevertheless, from 1945 to 1956, when the Direction générale des Relations culturelles absorbed the French government's technical cooperation programs, approximately 30 percent of France's foreign affairs budget was devoted to cultural relations. Conversely, in the fiscal year 1961-62, the DEA budget amounted to just under $93.8 million, which suggests that only approximately 0.008 percent of the departmental budget was earmarked *specifically* for cultural diplomacy. Even if one expands this amount by including monies allocated to the Information Division, funds granted by the Canada Council, and Ottawa's indirect cultural action through the CBC, Radio-Canada, the National Film Board, and the Royal Society of Canada, the 1963 Glassco Report on the federal civil service was correct to describe Ottawa's cultural diplomacy as pitiful.
92 Tovell, "Comparison," 74; Canada, Department of Finance, *Estimates*, 4; DEA/5056/2727-AD-40/9 – France-Canada Cultural Relations, 25 November 1963.
93 Handler, *Nationalism*, 82.
94 MAE/96 – Lacoste to Pineau, MAE, Amérique, 27 September 1956; Roussel, "Relations culturelles," 229.
95 Léger, *La Francophonie*, 83.

96 Roussel, "Relations culturelles," 174-183; Gérin-Lajoie, *Combats d'un révolutionnaire*, 162; Black, *Duplessis*, 320.
97 Roger, *American Enemy*, 122, 275-276.
98 Ibid., 272-273.
99 Ibid., 340-341.
100 Arnavon, *L'américanisme et nous*; Camus cited in McKenzie, *Remaking France*, 231.
101 Roger, *American Enemy*, 442-443.
102 MAE/66 – Gay to MAE, Relations Culturelles, 1 March 1949; MAE/62 – Basdevant to MAE, Relations Culturelles, 28 June 1950.
103 MAE/41 – del Perugia to MAE, Amérique, 21 May 1949, Influence des États-Unis dans la Province de Québec; MAE/171 – Rapport annuel du service culturel de l'Ambassade de la France au Canada, 31 July 1957.
104 MAE/175 – de Vial to MAE, Amérique, 24 September 1953.
105 Hertel, "Les évolutions," 50.
106 MAE/95 – de Vial to MAE, Amérique, 23 July 1955.
107 MAE/170 – Copie du Rapport annuel du Service Culturel de l'Ambassade, 26 July 1954.
108 Lamonde, "Regard sur les États-Unis," 69-73; Lamonde and Bouchard, *Québécois et Américains*, 70-84.
109 MAE/170 – Copie du Rapport annuel du Service Culturel de l'Ambassade, 26 July 1954.
110 Bouchard and Lamonde, *Québécois et Américains*, 76; Lamonde, *Allégeances et dépendances*, 91.
111 Gélinas, *La droite intellectuelle*, 338-339, 356-358; Foisy-Geoffroy, "Le rapport"; Roussel, "Relations culturelles," 225-227; Desbiens, *Les insolences du Frère Untel*, 29-30; ANQ/E4/1960-01-483/436/Conseil Culturel du Québec – Paul Gouin, Le Conseil Culturel du Québec (projet), 25 October 1952.
112 MAE/179 – de Laboulaye to Schuman, MAE, Conventions Administratives et Sociales, 30 September 1952.
113 ANQ/E4/1960-01-483/436/Conseil Culturel du Québec – Paul Gouin, Le Conseil Culturel du Québec (projet), 25 October 1952.
114 Lapalme, *Le vent*, 238-239.
115 Litt, *Muses*, 107; Thompson and Randall, *Canada and the United States*, 115-26.
116 Litt, *Muses*, 17, 22.
117 Rutherford, "The Persistence of Britain," 196; Kuffert, "'Stabbing our Spirits,'" 28-33, 44-45; Litt, *Muses*, 108.
118 Scott, "Canada et Canada français," 182.
119 Massey, *On Being Canadian*; Massolin, *Canadian Intellectuals*, 196-197.
120 Behiels, *Prelude*, 207-208.
121 Gélinas, *La droite intellectuelle*, 306, 316; Behiels, *Prelude*, 206-211.
122 Behiels, *Prelude*, 207.
123 DEA/7069/7839-40/3 – Canadian Ambassador, Lima to SSEA, 7 September 1959; Poirrier, *Histoire des politiques culturelles*, 35-50.
124 MAE/100 – Allocution Prononcée par le Général de Gaulle à la fin du Banquet offert par la Ville de Montréal à l'Hôtel Queen Elizabeth, le vendredi, 21 avril 1960.
125 Saint-Gilles, *Présence culturelle*, 243.

Chapter 4: A "French" Fact

1 DEA/5692/1-A(s)/4 – Stone to Robertson, 13 June 1944.
2 Bell, *Cult of the Nation*, 21.

3 Breton, "Ethnic to Civic Nationalism"; Igartua, *Other Quiet Revolution*; Silver, *The French-Canadian Idea*.
4 Martel, *French Canada*.
5 Aquin, "L'Existence politique," 69.
6 Igartua, *Other Quiet Revolution*, 98-101, 164-168; Breton, "Ethnic to Civic Nationalism," 92.
7 Grant, *Lament for a Nation*, 20-21.
8 Igartua, *Other Quiet Revolution*, 96, 177-222. For an alternative and provocative account of this period, see Champion, *The Strange Demise of British Canada*.
9 Igartua, *Other Quiet Revolution*, 168-169.
10 MAE/134 – Bousquet to MAE, Amérique, 19 August 1963.
11 Igartua, *Other Quiet Revolution*, 193-222.
12 ANQ/P688/S1/SS1/1986-03-007/17/150 – Discours, Université de Montréal, 3 May 1961.
13 MAE/146 – Lacoste to MAE, Amérique, 18 May 1961.
14 Thomson, *Vive*, 95; ANQ/P776/2001-01-006/1/Délégation, Inauguration, 1961-1967 – Lussier to Chapdelaine, 27 July 1981.
15 ANQ/P762/1999-10-011/29/Discours de Jean Lesage par Claude Morin [Discours] – Alliance française de Montréal, 11 March 1962; MAE/146/Agence Générale de la province du Québec à Paris – *Europe-Canada, Bulletin d'Information*, 14 October 1961.
16 Bouchard, *Entre l'Ancien et le Nouveau*, 37-38.
17 MAE/146/Agence Générale de la province de Québec à Paris – *Europe-Canada, Bulletin d'Information*, 14 October 1961; ANQ/P688/S1/SS1/18/18 – Dîner pour Ministre des Affaires culturelles de la France, André Malraux, 11 October 1963.
18 MAE/209/Discours prononcés – Allocution de M. Daniel Johnson, Dîner Offert par le Général de Gaulle, 25 July 1967.
19 "Conférence de Presse donnée à Paris le 11 octobre 1963 par André d'Allemagne, vice-président du Rassemblement pour l'indépendance Nationale," *Québec Libre* 1963, 1(1): 1-12.
20 MAE/277 – Charleboix to de Gaulle, 18 March 1966.
21 Léger, "Une responsabilité commune," 567-568.
22 Duc, "La langue française," 423.
23 Bouchard, *La langue et le nombril*, 226, 250-251.
24 Bouchard, *La langue et le nombril*, 229-262; Desbiens, *Les insolences du Frère Untel*, 26-27.
25 Bouchard, *La langue et le nombril*, 254-261.
26 ANQ/P688/S1/SS1/1986-03-007/17/174 – Réception à l'Hôtel de Ville de Paris, 6 October 1961.
27 MAE/209/Discours prononcés – Allocution de M. Daniel Johnson, Dîner Offert par le Général de Gaulle, 25 July 1967.
28 ANQ/P422/S2/1995-01-008/2/1 – Cholette, Document de Travail, 14 June 1968; ANQ/P599/2001-01-001/4/Causeries et conférences, 1952-1996 – *La Presse*, octobre 1969, "Jean-Marc Léger énumère six domaines de coopération entre les pays de la francophonie."
29 Léger, "Une responsabilité commune," 569.
30 MAE/206/Visite de Daniel Johnson – Leduc to MAE, Amérique, 9 May 1967.
31 DEA/5289/9245-30/6.1 – Martin to Pearson, 12 September 1963; DEA/10097/20-1-2-FR/1.1 – Canadian Embassy, Washington to DEA, 9 September 1963; DEA/10097/20-1-2-FR/1.1 – Enclosure, Canadian Embassy, Paris to DEA, 21 October 1963.
32 DDF/1964(1) – Document 29, Compte rendu de l'entretien entre le Général de Gaulle et M. Lester Pearson, Premier Ministre du Canada à Paris, le 15 janvier 1964; DDF/1964(1) – Document 31, Compte rendu de l'entretien entre M. Georges Pompidou et M. Lester Pearson, Premier Ministre du Canada, à l'Hôtel Matignon, le 16 janvier 1964.

33 Lebovics, *Mona Lisa's Escort*, 4.
34 Étiemble, *Parlez-vous franglais?*; Bourniquel and Domenach, "Le français, langue vivante," 562-563.
35 DEA/10684/26-2/1 – Canadian Embassy, Paris to DEA, 15 November 1966.
36 Julien, *L'Empire américain*, 299.
37 Roger, *American Enemy*, 405; Ross, *May '68*, 8-10.
38 Brubaker, *Citizenship and Nationhood*, 1-13; Weber, *Peasants into Frenchmen*.
39 Brubaker, *Citizenship and Nationhood*, 94-102.
40 Wilder, *French Imperial Nation-State*, 15-19.
41 Comeau and Fournier, *Le Lobby du Québec*, 44; Peyrefitte, *De Gaulle*, 37.
42 DEA/10098/20-1-2-FR/2.1 – Léger to DEA, 4 June 1964.
43 DEA/9568/18-1-D-FRA-1967(1) – Le Général de Gaulle en Visite au Canada, 12.
44 MAE/135 – Note sur la Province de Québec, MAE, Amérique, 9 October 1961.
45 Peyrefitte, *De Gaulle*, 30. Malraux's attitudes toward Quebec remain unclear, and his rhetorical flourishes contribute to this obscurity. He harboured a certain (but limited) interest in Quebec, and figures such as René Garneau, cultural councillor at Canada's embassy, and painter Alfred Pellan kept him informed. André Patry's impression, based on a conversation following de Gaulle's 1967 visit, was that Malraux felt that independence was a "debatable, even harmful" option. See Bastien, "Malraux et le Québec," 196-199.
46 Mills, *Empire Within*, 5.
47 MAE/146 – de Boyer de Ste-Suzanne to Roux, 23 August 1961.
48 DEA/5232/6956-40/5 – Halstead to USSEA, 31 May 1963; MAE/101 – Bosson and Thorailler, Rapport d'Information, 18 March 1963.
49 Domenach, "Le Canada Français," 321-322.
50 Domenach, "Urgence au Québec," 4.
51 Dumazedier quoted in DEA/10045/20-1-2-FR/9 – Pierre Godin, "L'indépendance économique de la France se joue dans la lutte du Québec pour la libération," *La Presse*, 5 September 1967.
52 Lists of members of the Quebec lobby exist elsewhere and so will not be repeated here; instead, members will be identified as such throughout the rest of this work. The most comprehensive discussions are found in Bosher, *Gaullist Attack on Canada*, 63-83, and Comeau and Fournier, *Le Lobby du Québec*.
53 Comeau and Fournier, *Le Lobby du Québec*, 28-29.
54 Wilder, *French Imperial Nation-State*, 4, 28-33.
55 Roger, *American Enemy*, 165, 175-176.
56 Comeau and Fournier, *Le Lobby du Québec*, 27.
57 Gagliardi and Rossillon, *Survivre à De Gaulle*, 7, 93-110.
58 Untitled editorial, *Patrie et progrès*, December 1961, (1): 2.
59 MAE/RCST/DG2/94/Haut comité pour la Défense de la langue française – MAE, Bureau des Échanges culturels et socio-culturels, Organisations internationales, Note sur le Haut comité de la langue française, 24 February 1970.
60 The most prominent statement of the two-nation thesis contemporaneous to the events studied is Johnson, *Égalité ou indépendance*.
61 Lebovics, *Mona Lisa*, 29; Fenet, "Difference Rights," 22.
62 Berstein, *Histoire du gaullisme*, 294.
63 Cerny, "De Gaulle," 254-278; Kolodziej, *French International Policy*, 22-29; Anderson, *Imagined Communities*, 83.
64 Berstein, *Histoire du gaullisme*, 294.

65 MAE/100 – Allocution Prononcée par le Général de Gaulle à la fin du Banquet offert par la Ville de Montréal à l'Hôtel Queen Elizabeth, le vendredi, 21 avril 1960; Jean-François Lisée, *Dans l'œil de l'aigle*, 75.
66 MAE/135 – Levasseur to Couve de Murville, MAE, Amérique, 14 June 1961; MAE/87 – Lacoste to MAE, Amérique, 15 April 1962, Annexe V.
67 Lescop, *Le pari québécois*, 30.
68 DDF/1964(1) – Document 29, Compte rendu de l'entretien entre le Général de Gaulle et M. Lester Pearson, Premier Ministre du Canada à Paris, le 15 janvier 1964.
69 Julien, *Le Canada*, 264-265.
70 MAE/101 – Bousquet to Couve de Murville, MAE, Amérique, 21 October 1963. See also Lebovics, *Mona Lisa*, 5; Saint-Gilles, *Présence culturelle*, 239.
71 MAE/198 – Bousquet to Couve de Murville, MAE, Amérique, 18 November 1964.
72 MAE/278 – Picard to Leduc, 14 October 1966.
73 MAE/146 – de Boyer de Ste-Suzanne to Roux, 23 August 1961; MAE/135 – Note sur la Province de Québec, MAE, Amérique, 9 October 1961.
74 De Gaulle, "Note pour Étienne Burin des Roziers, Secrétaire Général de la Présidence de la République, 4 September 1963," in *Lettres, notes et carnets, janvier 1961-décembre 1963*, 369.
75 DEA/10098/20-1-2-FR/2.1 – Canadian Embassy, Paris to DEA, 4 June 1964.
76 MAE/331 – Rossillon, Note sur le Bilinguisme au Canada, 22 October 1968.
77 Peyrefitte, *De Gaulle*, 83.
78 DEA/10098/20-1-2-FR/4.2 – Léger to Cadieux, 2 December 1966.
79 MAE/202 – Secrétaire Général, Présidence de la République, to Debré, 28 March 1969.
80 DEA/9809/21-F-11-1979/1/MF4153 – IAC Assessment 4/79, Canadian National Unity: Current French Attitudes and Policies.
81 Thomson, *Vive*, 199; English, *The Worldly Years*, 340; Bouthillier, "Les indépendantistes," 523.
82 Thomson, *Vive*, 14, 199; Rouanet and Rouanet, *Trois derniers chagrins*, 24-31; Bergeron, *Le Canada-Français*, 85; MAE/208/Antérieur au Voyage – Note, 4 March 1967.
83 Rouanet and Rouanet, *Trois derniers chagrins*, 27.
84 Knapp, *Le Gaullisme après de Gaulle*, 15.
85 ANQ/P776/2001-01-006/4/Ministère des Affaires intergouvernementales, 1969-1996 – Dorin to Masse, 25 March 1996; Comeau and Fournier, *Le Lobby du Québec*, 51; Thomson, *Vive*, 197; Rouanet and Rouanet, *Trois derniers chagrins*, 103-133; Hébert and Roy, "Amour scénarisé."
86 Lescop, *Le pari québécois*, 154-173.
87 ANF/5AG1/199/Québec-Entretiens – de Gaulle to Johnson, 8 September 1967.
88 MAE/210/Réactions – de Leusse, Telegram circulaire à tous postes diplomatiques, 28 July 1967.
89 DEA/10045/20-1-2-FR/9 – Léger to Cadieux, 20 September 1967; DEA/10045/20-1-2-FR/9 – Léger to Cadieux, 22 September 1967.
90 De Gaulle, "Conférence de presse tenue au Palais de l'Élysée," in *Discours et messages*, 239-240.
91 Bourgault, *Écrits polémiques*, 133-135. In this account, Bourgault categorically rejects the idea that the RIN harboured an exaggerated Francophilia.
92 Jasmin, *Rimbaud, mon beau salaud!* 41-43.
93 Aquin, "Nos cousins de France."
94 Angers, "Épilogue," 180. See also Angers, "'Le monde saura,'" 8-9.

95 Thomson, *Vive*, 214-16, 236.
96 ANQ/P776/2001-01-006/1/Réportage Politique, 1967-1974 – Chapdelaine to Morin, 5 December 1967.
97 De Gaulle, "Allocution radiodiffusée et télévisée prononcée au Palais de l'Élysée," in *Discours et messages*, 251; MAE/268 – du Boisberranger to French Embassy, Ottawa, 28 September 1968; ANQ/E42/1960-01-054/81/Correspondance "E" – "Drapeaux en berne aujourd'hui," *Courrier de l'Ouest*, 30 September 1968.
98 MAE/RCST/Enseignement/132/Établ.ts d'Enseignement – de Hauteclocque to MAE, 25 March 1946.
99 ANQ/P776/2001-01-006/3/Ministres du Québec en France, 1969-1972 – "Le toast du général," *Le Devoir*, 23 January 1969.

Chapter 5: *Vive le Québec libre?*

1 Thomson, *Vive*, 30, 173-175; Gros d'Aillon, *Daniel Johnson*, 151; Rouanet and Rouanet, *Trois derniers chagrins*, 61.
2 Behiels, *Prelude*, 185-186; Foisy-Geoffroy, "Le Rapport," 259.
3 Behiels, *Prelude*, 257-265.
4 MAE/95 – Guérin to Schuman, MAE, Amérique, 17 December 1952; MAE/127 – Guérin to Mendès-France, MAE, Amérique, 16 October 1954.
5 MAE/176 – Guérin to Schuman, MAE, Amérique, 29 January 1952.
6 MAE/44 – Guérin to Schuman, MAE, Amérique, 13 February 1951.
7 MAE/87 – Couve de Murville, MAE to Bousquet, 22 May 1962.
8 ANQ/E6/1976-00-066/26/Annuel, Délégation culturelle du Québec à Paris – Lussier to Lévesque, 11 December 1962; DEA/10492/55-3-1-FR-QUÉBEC/1 – Canadian Embassy, Paris to USSEA, 12 October 1964.
9 MAE/135 – Levasseur to Couve de Murville, MAE, Amérique, 18 October 1961.
10 MAE/136 – Le Consul Général de France à Montréal à Son Excellence Monsieur L'Ambassadeur de France au Canada, 6 September 1962.
11 MAE/135 – Lacoste to Couve de Murville, MAE, Amérique, 27 June 1961.
12 MAE/132 – Bousquet to Couve de Murville, MAE, Amérique, 23 January 1963.
13 MAE/Schuman/105 – L'importance internationale du Canada, 10 September 1949; MAE/126 – Guérin to Bidault, MAE, Amérique, 27 January 1954; MAE/127 – Guérin to Couve de Murville, MAE, Amérique, 16 October 1954; Jenkins and Copsey, "Nation, Nationalism," 101-102.
14 Legrand, "L'axe missionnaire catholique"; Beaudet, *Qui aide qui*, 40-42; Deleuze, *L'une et l'autre indépendance*.
15 Beaudet, *Qui aide qui*, 59.
16 Betts, *Decolonization*, 51-52.
17 Mills, *The Empire Within*. The work most widely associated with this trend was Vallières, *Nègres blancs d'Amérique*.
18 Brittain, "Unlikely Warriors."
19 Roger, *The American Enemy*, 129-130; 142-145, 321-335.
20 Shepard, *Invention of Decolonization*, 2-7, 75, 271-272.
21 Vaïsse, *La grandeur*, 452-460, 501-503.
22 Domenach, "Le Canada Français," 310; "Elizabeth II au Canada," *Le Monde*, 14 October 1964, 1; Berque, "Les révoltés du Québec," 10-11; Berque, "Préface," 7-16; Memmi, *Portrait du colonisé*, 137-146.
23 Bosher, *Gaullist Attack*, 76.

24 MAE/132 – Bousquet to Couve de Murville, MAE, Amérique, 23 January 1963; MAE/174 – Bousquet to Couve de Murville, MAE, Service d'Information et de Presse, 1 March, 1963; MAE/132 – Bousquet to MAE, Amérique, 28 March 1963.
25 Peyrefitte, *De Gaulle*, 17, 28-29.
26 Connelly, *Diplomatic Revolution*, 279.
27 Judt, *Past Imperfect*, 42.
28 Winock, *Parlez-moi de la France*, 63.
29 Létourneau, *History for the Future*, 128-132; Meren, "De Versailles à Niamey," 99-124.
30 MAE/135 – Lacoste to Couve de Murville, MAE, Amérique, 12 December 1960; MAE/135 – MAE, Amérique, Note sur la Province de Québec, 9 October 1961; MAE/87 – Couve de Murville, MAE, to Bousquet, 22 May 1962.
31 MAE/87 – Bousquet to Roché, 30 August 1962; MAE/132 – Bousquet to Couve de Murville, MAE, Amérique, 23 January 1963; MAE/136 – Bousquet to Couve de Murville, MAE, Amérique, 18 June 1963.
32 MAE/132 – Bousquet to Couve de Murville, MAE, Amérique, 3 January 1963.
33 MAE/133 – Bousquet to MAE, Amérique, 24 April 1963; English, *Worldly Years*, 267.
34 Peyrefitte, *De Gaulle*, 27.
35 MAE/259 – Bousquet to MAE, Amérique, 5 May 1964; MAE/275 – Bousquet to Couve de Murville, MAE, Amérique, 27 April 1964.
36 DDF/1964(1) – Document 31, Compte rendu de l'entretien entre M. Georges Pompidou et M. Lester Pearson, Premier Ministre du Canada, à l'Hôtel Matignon, le 16 janvier 1964; MAE/192 – Bousquet to Couve de Murville, MAE, Amérique, 28 April 1964; Couve de Murville, "Pearson et la France," 30.
37 MAE/275 – Bousquet to MAE, Amérique, 6 April 1964; MAE/262 – de Pampelonne to MAE, Amérique, 4 August 1965; English, *Worldly Years*, 280-283, 350-354.
38 MAE/318 – de Pampelonne to Couve de Murville, MAE, Amérique, 3 March 1965.
39 Despite Pearson's qualification, the MAE subsequently told American and West German diplomats that Paris foresaw an "Austro-Hungarian solution" for Canada. Leduc's original report is underlined and circled in different inks, suggesting that Pearson's words were subsequently used against him. MAE/198 – Leduc to MAE, Amérique, 1 April 1965; DEA/10046/20-1-2-FR/11 – Canadian Embassy, Paris to DEA, 5 January 1968.
40 DEA/10098/20-1-2-FR/4.1 – Léger, Canadian Embassy, Paris to DEA, 1 April 1966; MAE/276 – Leduc to Couve de Murville, MAE, Amérique, 9 June 1965; MAE/262 – Leduc to MAE, Amérique, 10 November 1965.
41 DEA/9809/21-F-11-1979/1/MF4153 – IAC Assessment 4/79, Canadian National Unity: Current French Attitudes and Policies; DDF/1964(1) – Document 30, Compte rendu de l'entretien entre le Président de la République et le Premier Ministre du Canada à l'Élysée, le 16 janvier 1964.
42 ANQ/P776/2001-01-006/1/Délégation du Québec en France, 1964-1966 – Chapdelaine to Lesage, 3 December 1965; de Gaulle, *De Gaulle*, 362.
43 MAE/205/Deuxième séjour à Paris de Monsieur Lesage, Premier Ministre du Québec – Partial Transcript, to Ministre de l'Information, 12 November 1964; Thomson, *Vive*, 137.
44 MAE/198 – Leduc to MAE, Amérique, 8 April 1965.
45 MAE/277 – Leduc to Couve de Murville, MAE, Amérique, 3 June 1966; MAE/277 – Leduc to MAE, Amérique, 6 June 1966; MAE/199 – Leduc to MAE, Amérique, 25 July 1966.
46 ANF/5AG1/199/Québec-Entretiens – de Gaulle to Johnson, 24 September 1966.
47 ANQ/P776/2001-01-006/2/Daniel Johnson, 1966-1969 [DJ] – Chapdelaine to Johnson, 14 February 1967 (3).
48 Rouanet and Rouanet, *Trois derniers chagrins*, 61.

49 Fontaine, "La France et le Québec," 395.
50 MAE/199 – Jurgensen to Couve de Murville, 2 May 1967; MAE/279 – Leduc to Couve de Murville, MAE, Amérique, 30 June 1967.
51 MAE/265 – Leduc to MAE, Amérique, 4 January 1967; MAE/278 – Leduc to MAE, Amérique, 11 May 1967.
52 MAE/199 – Jurgensen to de Saint-Légier, 13 July 1966.
53 ANQ/P422/S2/1995-01-008/3/9 – Deniau to Patry, 6 October 1966; MAE/208/Antérieur au Voyage – Note, 4 March 1967.
54 ANQ/P776/2001-01-006/4/Ministère des Affaires intergouvernementales, 1969-1996 [MAI] – Dorin to Masse, 25 March 1966.
55 DEA/8910/20-FR-1-3-USA/1 – Canadian Embassy, Washington to DEA, 21 July 1967.
56 MAE/199 – Jurgensen to Secrétaire-Général, MAE, 9 December 1966; AHC/CM/8/1966 – Secrétaire Général, Présidence de la République to Couve de Murville, 9 December 1966.
57 DEA/9568/18-1-D-FRA-1967(1) – Le Général de Gaulle en Visite au Canada, 54.
58 ANF/5AG1/144/Voyage au Canada du Général de Gaulle, Président de la République, Notes Politiques – MAE, Amérique, Note, Canada, Le Problème constitutionnel, Pouvoir fédéral et pouvoir provincial; ANF/5AG1/144/Voyage au Canada du Général de Gaulle, Président de la République, Notes Politiques (II)/Politique intérieure – Résumé de l'Histoire des Canadiens français.
59 DEA/5289/9245-40/6 – Joncas, Economic Division to Stoner, undated; JL/1/12 – Léger to Cadieux, 25 November 1964.
60 Black, *Direct Intervention*, 15; JL/1/12 – Cadieux to Léger, 23 November 1964.
61 Bothwell, "Marcel Cadieux," 210-212; MC/8/14/Journal – 17 February 1968.
62 JL/1/12 – Cadieux to Léger, 23 November 1964.
63 DEA/10078/20-FR-9/2.2 – Halstead to USSEA, 13 January 1967.
64 DEA/10045/20-1-2-FR/5 – Martin to Pearson, 24 January 1967.
65 English, *Worldly Years*, 84; DEA/10098/20-1-2-FR/3.1 – Léger to DEA, 8 September 1965.
66 DEA/10045/20-1-2-FR/5 – Martin to Pearson, 24 January 1967.
67 DEA/10045/20-1-2-FR/5 – Martin to Pearson, 24 February 1967.
68 DEA/10045/20-1-2-FR/5 – Cadieux to Léger, 23 March 1967.
69 JL/1/12 – Léger to Cadieux, 25 November 1964.
70 ANQ/E6/1976-00-066/29/Maison des étudiants canadiens à Paris – Chapdelaine to Morin, 27 June 1967. See also Bosher, *Gaullist Attack*, 122.
71 Vaïsse, *La grandeur*, 306, 309; Comeau and Fournier, *Le Lobby du Québec*, 72-73; JL/1/12 – Léger to Cadieux, 25 November 1964. Léger acknowledged that whereas on the whole the Quai followed Couve de Murville's more nuanced approach, some officials were less discreet, and "one or two younger members" had "advanced, even separatist ideas."
72 DEA/10078/20-FR-9/4 – Halstead to Cadieux, 7 July 1967; DEA/9568/18-1-D-FRA-1967(1) – Le Général de Gaulle en Visite au Canada, 65-68.
73 Bothwell, "Marcel Cadieux," 211-215.
74 MAE/209/Discours prononcés – Textes et Notes, Voyage du Général de Gaulle au Québec, Président de la République [Textes], À son arrivée à l'anse au Foulon, le 23 juillet 1967.
75 MAE/209/Discours prononcés – Textes, Au dîner offert par M. Daniel Johnson, Premier Ministre du Québec, à Québec, le 23 juillet 1967.
76 Thomson, *Vive*, 203; Lescop, *Le pari québécois*, 154-166.
77 ANQ/P776/2001-01-006/4/MAI – Dorin to Masse, 25 March 1996. See also Lescop, *Le pari québécois*, 171.
78 Létourneau, *History for the Future*, 67, 131.
79 Thomson, *Vive*, 232-236.
80 JL/1/11 – Cadieux to Pearson, 10 January 1968.

81 Thomson, *Vive*, 212, 234-236; Morin, *L'art de l'impossible*, 82; Godin, *Daniel Johnson*, 241; Lescop, *Le pari québécois*, 60.
82 Vaïsse, "Réactions françaises."
83 DEA/10045/20-1-2-FR/7 – "Le gauche gaulliste: De Gaulle a eu raison au Québec," *France Soir*, 8 August 1967.
84 Thomson, *Vive*, 230-231; DEA/10046/20-1-2-FR/11 – Canadian Embassy, Paris to DEA, 6 December 1967.
85 Quoted in Bozo, *Deux stratégies*, 167.
86 Alphand, *L'étonnement d'être*, 493; DEA/10045/20-1-2-FR/9 – Léger to Cadieux, 22 September 1967; DEA/10046/20-1-2-FR/9 – Léger to Cadieux, 17 October 1967. See also Thomson, *Vive*, 227. Thomson quotes Jurgensen's claim that "not one politician out of eight," even among Gaullists, supported de Gaulle's actions.
87 Lacouture, *De Gaulle*, 461. See also Peyrefitte, *De Gaulle*, 65.
88 ANQ/P776/2001-01-006/2/DJ – Chapdelaine to Johnson, 12 October 1967; DEA/10046/20-FR-1-2/13 – Fortier to USSEA, 27 March 1968; MAE/189 – Leduc to Debré, MAE, Amérique, 26 June 1968.
89 DEA/10046/20-1-2-FR/10 – Canadian Embassy, Paris to DEA, 27 November 1967.
90 DEA/10045/20-1-2-FR/7 – Memorandum for the Prime Minister, 24 July 1967; Martin, *Very Public Life*, 594.
91 Thomson, *Vive*, 209; DEA/10045/20-1-2-FR/6 – Christoff to Fortier, 28 July 1967; PM/225/10 – Hadwen, Memorandum to File, 14 August 1967; MC/8/15 – Journal, 25 July 1967.
92 PCO/6323/Cabinet Conclusion, 25 July 1967 – General de Gaulle; PCO/6323/Cabinet Conclusion, 25 July 1967a – General de Gaulle.
93 Lescop, *Le pari québécois*, 174-175; DEA/10045/20-1-2-FR/7 – Canadian Embassy, Paris to DEA, 11 August 1967.
94 ANF/5AG1/199/Québec-Entretiens – de Gaulle to Johnson, 8 September 1967.
95 Lescop, *Le pari québécois*, 185-189.
96 JL/1/11 – Léger to Cadieux, 14 December 1967; FCO/111 – Reilly, Record of Conversation with the Canadian Ambassador, 15 December 1967.
97 ANQ/P776/2001-01-006/2/DJ – Chapdelaine to Johnson, 12 October 1967; MAE/214/ Jean-Noël Tremblay, Ministre des Affaires culturelles du Québec – Jurgensen to Secrétaire-Général, 18 January 1968.
98 Peyrefitte, *De Gaulle*, 99-101.
99 MAE/279 – Leduc to MAE, Amérique, 5 October 1967; Thomson, *Vive*, 257-258; Gros d'Aillon, *Daniel Johnson*, 194-195.
100 ANQ/P776/2001-01-006/2/DJ – Chapdelaine to Johnson, 30 November 1967; ANQ/ P776/2001-01-006/1/Reportage Politique, 1967-74 [Reportage] – Chapdelaine to Morin, 12 June 1968.
101 ANQ/P776/2001-01-006/1/Reportage – Morin to Chapdelaine, 15 December 1967.
102 DEA/10046/20-1-2-FR/11 – Gotlieb, ANNEX – Federal action to deal with possible French support for separatism, 6 September 1967, attached to Memorandum from Martin to Pearson, 29 November 1967.
103 Cadieux even entertained extending asylum to various enemies of the Gaullist regime, notably Jacques Soustelle, who was living in exile to avoid French justice after breaking with de Gaulle over Algeria and joining the Organisation de l'armée secrète. MC/8/14/ Journal – 19 February 1968; MC/8/14/Journal – 12 March 1968.
104 DEA/10045/20-1-2-FR/7 – Draft Memorandum for the Prime Minister, 14 August 1967; DEA/10045/20-1-2-FR/9 – Léger to Cadieux, 20 September 1967.
105 DEA/10045, 20-1-2-FR/9 – Martin to DEA, 26 September 1967; DEA/10045/20-1-2-FR/9 – Canadian Embassy, Paris to DEA, 1 September 1967.

106 DEA/10046/20-1-2-FR/10 – Canadian Embassy, Paris to DEA, 28 November 1967; Black, *Direct Intervention*, 19-20.
107 DEA/10046/20-1-2-FR/10 – Cadieux to Martin, 27 November 1967; DEA/11632/30-10-FR/2 – Cadieux to Martin, 28 November 1967.
108 House of Commons, *Debates, Official Report (Hansard)*, 28 November 1967, 4774-4775.
109 DEA/10046/20-1-2-FR/11 – Martin to Pearson, 29 November 1967.
110 DEA/10047/20-1-2-FR/16.2 – DEA to Canadian Mission, UN, 4 October 1968.
111 Peyrefitte, *De Gaulle*, 106-110; Comeau and Fournier, *Le lobby du Québec*, 62-63; de Menthon, *Je témoigne*, 16-18.
112 MAE/212 – French Embassy, Ottawa to Jurgensen, 30 December 1968; MAE/215/Voyage en France du M. Bertrand, Premier Ministre du Québec, non-réalisé – Jurgensen to Debré, 23 December 1968.
113 Domenach, "Urgence au Québec."
114 MAE/202 – Siraud to MAE, 1 November 1968; MAE/281 – Siraud to MAE, Amérique, 16 October 1968; MAE/213 – Exposés faits par le Consul général de France à Québec sur "l'évolution politique au Québec (mai 1968-mai 1969)" et sur "la coopération franco-québécoise" lors de la réunion consulaire qui s'est tenue à Ottawa les 9 et 10 mai 1969.
115 MAE/193 – Siraud to Schumann, MAE, Amérique, 9 June 1970; DEA/8647/20-1-2-FR/27 – Canadian Embassy, Paris to DEA, 16 May 1970.
116 Duchesne, *Jacques Parizeau*, 599-605.
117 De Menthon, *Je témoigne*, 19.
118 ANF/5AG2/1021/Correspondance – Siraud to MAE, Amérique, 13 December 1969.
119 MAE/218 – Note pour Monsieur le Ministre, 3 October 1970.
120 MAE/463/Francophonie, Conférence de Paris – de Menthon to MAE, 29 March 1968. As the Liberal leadership race reached its end, Johnson told Jurgensen that he hoped that Paul Martin would win, given his more conciliatory attitude and willingness to grant "concessions substantielles."
121 MAE/218 – Note pour Monsieur le Ministre, 3 October 1970.

Chapter 6: Atlanticism in Conflict

1 Vaïsse, *La grandeur*, 387.
2 Ibid., 45, 119-139.
3 Giauque, *Grand Designs*, 98-125; Grosser, *Affaires extérieures*, 200.
4 Giauque, *Grand Designs*, 115-118; Cogan, *Oldest Allies*, 95.
5 Giauque, *Grand Designs*, 166-223; Vaïsse, *La grandeur*, 452-460; 501-503.
6 MAE/105 – Bousquet to MAE, Amérique, 13 July 1962.
7 Minifie, *Peacemaker*; Robinson, *Diefenbaker's World*, 47-51, 92.
8 Diefenbaker, *Years of Achievement*, 151, and *The Tumultuous Years*, 16. See also Stairs, "Present in Moderation."
9 MAE/115 – Note, Les États-Unis et le Canada, Fin de mai 1961; MAE/101/Voyage de la Commission des Affaires étrangères de l'Assemblée Nationale au Canada – Bosson and Thorailler, Rapport d'Information, 18 March 1963.
10 Robinson, *Diefenbaker's World*, 29, 86, 106.
11 DEA/7045/6956-A-40 – Report on Meeting held in Ottawa, 19 April 1960, between President de Gaulle and Members of the Canadian Cabinet; DEA/7045/6956-A-40 – Dupuy, Account of Conversation at Government House between Green and de Murville, 19 April 1960.
12 Nash, *Kennedy and Diefenbaker*, 283-311.

13 English, *Worldly Years*, 249-251; Granatstein, *Yankee Go Home?* 143.
14 English, *Worldly Years*, 89, 191.
15 English, "Problems in Middle Life"; Donaghy, *Tolerant Allies*, 92-122; Saul, "Regards officiels"; LBP/N6/9/NATO, Memoranda, Pearson and Paul Martin, Private Statements, Pearson, 1959-1967 [NATO] – Pearson to Martin, 20 April 1966.
16 DEA/10097/20-1-2-FR/1.1 – Robertson to Martin, 30 August 1963; DEA/10097/20-1-2-FR/1.1 – Canadian Embassy, Washington to DEA, 9 September 1963; DEA/5289/9245-40/6.1 – European Division to USSEA, 10 September 1963; DEA/10097/20-1-2-FR/1.1 – Canadian Embassy, Washington to DEA, 25 September 1963; DEA/10097/20-1-2-FR/1.1 – Canadian Mission, UN, to DEA, 3 October 1963.
17 DDF/1964(1) – Document 29, Compte rendu de l'Entretien entre le Général de Gaulle et M. Lester Pearson, Premier Ministre du Canada à Paris, le 15 janvier 1964.
18 DEA/3497/19-1-BA-FR-1964(3) – Halstead to DEA, 21 February 1964.
19 Locher, "A Crisis Foretold," 118.
20 Donaghy, *Tolerant Allies*, 105-106; Vaïsse, *La grandeur*, 372-377; DDF/1963(1) – Document 174, Compte Rendu, Entretien de M. Couve de Murville avec M. Paul Martin, 21 mai 1963.
21 DEA/10098/20-1-2-FR/3.1 – Cadieux to Martin, 10 November 1964.
22 DEA/10097/20-1-2-FR/1.1 – European Division to File, 10 October 1963; DEA/10097/20-1-2-FR/1.1 – Robertson to Martin, 18 September 1963.
23 MAE/137 – Bousquet to Couve de Murville, MAE, Amérique, 31 December 1963.
24 DEA/10098/20-1-2-FR/1.2 – George to USSEA, 31 March 1964.
25 DDF/1964(1) – Document 31, Compte rendu de l'entretien entre M. Georges Pompidou et M. Lester Pearson, Premier Ministre du Canada, à l'Hôtel Matignon, le 16 janvier 1964; DEA/3497/19-1-BA-FR-1964(3) – Halstead to DEA, 21 February 1964; Thomson, *Vive*, 124-125.
26 DEA/10295/27-4-NATO-3-1-FR/1 – Canadian Embassy, Paris to USSEA, 8 October 1965; DEA/10098/20-1-2-FR/3.1 – Léger to DEA, 8 September 1965; DEA/10097/20-1-2-FR/1 – Robertson to Martin, 18 September 1963. Paris was not alone in looking askance on Ottawa's linchpin efforts; the American ambassador told the DEA that Ottawa's bid to improve Franco-American relations was "*not* welcome" in Washington.
27 DEA/10098/20-1-2-FR/4.1 – Léger to Cadieux, 12 July 1966.
28 LBP/N6/9/NATO – Pearson to Martin, 20 April 1966.
29 FRUS, 1964-1968, v. XIII – Document 196, Memorandum of Conversation, Chamcock, New Brunswick, 21 August 1966.
30 LBP/N6/9/NATO – Pearson to Martin, 20 April 1966; LBP/N6/9/NATO – Martin to Pearson, 6 May 1966.
31 DEA/10045/20-1-2-FR/5 – Martin to Pearson, 24 January 1967; MC/8/15/Journal – 14 July 1967.
32 Filion, "De Gaulle," 317-318.
33 MAE/42 – Duranthon to MAE, Amérique, 4 July 1950; MAE/114 – Triat to Guérin, 17 March 1955; DDF/1964(1) – Document 29, Compte rendu de l'entretien entre le Général de Gaulle et M. Lester Pearson, Premier Ministre du Canada à Paris, le 15 janvier 1964; de Gaulle, *Memoirs of Hope*, 240.
34 MAE/101 – Bosson and Thorailler, Rapport d'Information, 18 March 1963; Julien, *Canada*, 12.
35 DEA/10077/20-FR-9/2.1 – Halstead, European Division to Wylie, 14 October 1966.
36 DEA/10045/20-1-2-FR/9 – Léger to Cadieux, 20 September 1967.
37 MAE/278 – Leduc to MAE, Amérique, 11 May 1967; MAE/189 – Leduc to MAE, Amérique, 26 June 1968.

38 Lacouture, *De Gaulle*, 452.
39 MAE/210/Réactions – de Leusse, Télégramme circulaire à tous postes diplomatiques, 28 July 1967.
40 DEA/10045/20-1-2-FR/7 – FBIS, French Minister's Article, Paris, AFP, 4 August 1967.
41 Foccart, *Tous les soirs*, 684-686.

Chapter 7: Parisian *pied-à-terre*

1 DEA/5753/54-C(s) – Cadieux to Wrong, 19 May 1943.
2 Leeson and Vanderelst, *External Affairs*, 61-63.
3 DEA/4305/11333-40 – Burbridge to Acting USSEA, 13 July 1951.
4 DEA/4286/10605-A-40 – Read, Provincial Government Representation Abroad, 11 May 1955.
5 Hilliker, *Canada's Department*, 17, 22-23, 72-74; Patry, *Québec dans le monde*, 47.
6 Dehousse, "Fédéralisme," 284-288.
7 DEA/4092/11336-14-40/1 – Heeney to Pearson, 6 February 1951. See also Hilliker and Barry, *Canada's Department*, 26, 217-218.
8 DEA/4092/11336-14-40/1 – Cadieux to Moran, 23 October 1950; MC/2/8 – Cadieux to Chapdelaine, 13 December 1950.
9 English, *Worldly Years*, 20; Hilliker, *Canada's Department*, 47, 120-122, 237, 259.
10 Hilliker and Barry, *Canada's Department*, 90.
11 JL/1/1 – Interview avec le Très Honorable Jules Léger par H.H. Carter, 24 September 1980; JL/2/8 – Watters to Léger, 28 November 1956.
12 MC/2/7 – Cadieux to Dumas, 25 November 1949; Bothwell, "Marcel Cadieux," 211-212.
13 Lalande, *Department of External Affairs*, 28, 43-45; Royal Commission on Bilingualism and Biculturalism, *Report, Book 3*, 145-146.
14 Patry, "Ce qu'on attend d'un diplomate canadien," *Le Nouveau Journal*, 28 April 1962, Section Arts et Spectacles, iv.
15 MAE/44 – Guérin to MAE, 25 December 1950, St. Laurent visit.
16 Auriol, *Journal du Septennat*, 175; Guillaume, "Montaigne et Shakespeare," 107.
17 Portes, "Pierre Mendès-France," 783-784.
18 MAE/102 – Guérin to Schuman, MAE, Amérique, 29 April 1952; MAE/95 – Guérin to Mendès-France, Cabinet du Ministre, 2 November 1954.
19 GV/21/35 – Vanier to Duplessis, 12 January 1952; MC/2/12 – Cadieux to USSEA, 6 March 1957.
20 MAE/95 – Guérin to MAE, 19 November 1953; MAE/91 – Derival to MAE, Amérique, 12 March 1954.
21 Black, *Duplessis*, 493-494.
22 DEA/7666/11562-126-40/1 – Translation, *Le Devoir* article of March 24 1960; Gendron, *Towards a Francophone Community*, 74.
23 Thomson, *Vive*, 90-93; Lapalme, *Le paradis du pouvoir*, 42-48.
24 ANQ/P776/2001-01-006/1/Délégation, Inauguration, 1961-1967 [Inauguration] – Lussier to Chapdelaine, 27 July 1981.
25 MAE/146 – Lacoste to MAE, Amérique, 23 January 1961.
26 DEA/7044/6956-40 – Beaulne, Memorandum to File, 2 May 1960; DEA/3197/5175-40 – European Division to the USSEA, 31 May 1960.
27 MAE/144 – Lacoste to MAE, Amérique, 2 December 1960; MAE/146 – Roché to French Embassy, Ottawa, 19 January 1961; MAE/146 – Roché to French Embassy, Ottawa, 24 January 1961; MAE/146 – Lacoste to MAE, Amérique, 25 January 1961; *Informations canadiennes* June-July 1961, 6(53): i-iv.

28 DEA/3197/5175-40 – Robertson to Green, 8 November 1961; MAE/146/Agence Générale de la province du Québec à Paris, Inauguration par M. Lesage – *Europe-Canada, Bulletin d'Information,* 14 October 1961; DEA/5232/6956-40/5 – Dupuy to DEA, 11 October 1961; Thomson, *Vive,* 100.
29 MAE/146 – Lacoste to MAE, Amérique, 23 January 1961.
30 MAE/146 – Jurisconsulte to Secrétaire Général, 3 February 1961; MAE/146 – Roché to French Embassy, Ottawa, 9 February 1961; DEA/3197/5175-40 – Cadieux to USSEA, 16 February 1961.
31 DEA/3197/5175-40 – Robertson to Green, 24 April 1961. See also DEA/3197/5175-40 – Lapalme to Robertson, 18 April 1961; DEA/3197/5175-40 – Cadieux to USSEA, 2 February 1961.
32 DEA/3197/5175-40 – Fournier/Cadieux to Canadian Embassy, Paris, 24 April 1961; ANQ/P776/2001-01-006/1/Inauguration – Adam to Lussier, 4 July 1962.
33 Thomson, *Vive,* 104.
34 Hilliker and Barry, *Canada's Department,* 348-349; MAE/133 – Bousquet to MAE, Amérique, 11 June 1963.
35 MAE/136 – Bousquet to MAE, Amérique, 29 July 1963.
36 DEA/10097/20-1-2-FR/1.1 – Robertson to Martin, 27 July 1963. See also Granatstein, *Man of Influence,* 362. Despite Martin's hesitation, Cadieux was appointed under-secretary, owing to the strong lobbying efforts of Norman Robertson, who felt that a francophone should succeed him.
37 DEA/10097/20-1-2-FR/1.1 – Robertson to Martin, 30 August 1963; DEA/3087/6 – Le Canada (Québec) et l'Europe Francophone, 1960-1966, Cahier II, 8.
38 MAE/204 – Bousquet to Roché, 16 October 1963; MAE/204 – Bousquet to Lucet, 22 November 1963.
39 DDF/1964(1) – Document 30, Compte rendu de l'entretien entre le Président de la République et le Premier Ministre du Canada à l'Élysée, le 16 janvier 1964; DEA/3497/19-1-BA-FR-1964(3) – Halstead to DEA, 21 February 1964; MAE/204 – Pampelonne to MAE, Amérique, 18 January 1964.
40 ANQ/P776/2001-01-006/1/Inauguration – Lussier to Arthur, 31 May 1963; ANQ/E42/1990-09-002/405/A – Blais to Lussier, 2 March 1964.
41 DEA/10098/20-1-2-FR/2.1 – Cadieux to Martin, 8 June 1964; DEA/10098/20-1-2-FR/2.1 – Cadieux, Mémoire pour le dossier, 25 June 1964; Thomson, *Vive,* 109-110, 122.
42 Lapalme, *Le paradis du pouvoir,* 251.
43 ANQ/P776/2001-01-006/1/Délégation du Québec en France, 1964-1966 – Martin, Memorandum for Cabinet, 2 October 1964; ANQ/E42/1990-09-002/405/A – DEA to Canadian Embassy, Paris, October 1964.
44 ANQ/P776/2001-01-006/1/Délégation du Québec en France, 1964-1966 – Martin, Memorandum for Cabinet, 2 October 1964; MAE/205/Deuxième séjour à Paris de Monsieur Lesage, Premier Ministre du Québec – Bousquet to MAE, Amérique, 19 October 1964; Thomson, *Vive,* 135-136; Morin, *L'art de l'impossible,* 23; Patry, *Le Québec dans le monde,* 60-61.
45 Balthazar, "Quebec's International Relations," 144-146; Painchaud, "The Epicenter," 93-94.
46 Thomson, *Vive,* 145-146.
47 RB/006/031 – Robertson; Morin, *L'art de l'impossible,* 9.
48 JL/56/5 – Chapdelaine to Léger, 15 June 1964; JL/56/5 – Cadieux to Léger, 28 September 1964; JL/56/5 – Léger to Cadieux, 2 October 1964; JL/56/5 – Cadieux to Léger, 16 October 1964.
49 Thomson, *Vive,* 150; Morin, *L'art de l'impossible,* 45-46; Patry, "Ce qu'on attend."

50 ANQ/P422/S2/1995-01-008/2/5 – Allocution du ministre de l'Éducation, Monsieur Paul Gérin-Lajoie, aux membres du Corps consulaire de Montréal, 12 April 1965; ANQ/P422/S2/1995-01-008/2/3 – Allocution du Vice-Président du Conseil et ministre de l'Éducation, Monsieur Paul Gérin-Lajoie, prononcée devant une délégation d'universitaires belges, français et suisses, au Parlement de Québec, 22 April 1965; Gérin-Lajoie, *Combats,* 325.
51 ANQ/P762/1999-10-011/60/Mémoires aux Premiers Ministres/Memos de M. Morin aux Premiers Ministres, 1962-1976 [Memos] – Morin to Lesage, 30 April 1965.
52 Thomson, *Vive,* 147-149; ANQ/E5/1986-03-007/94/1 – Mémoire des délibérations du Conseil Exécutif, Séance du 7 mai 1965; ANQ/E5/1986-03-007/94/1– Mémoire des délibérations du Conseil Exécutif, Séance du 25 août 1965; Patry, *Québec dans le monde,* 77.
53 DEA/10046/20-1-2-FR/1.1 – Canadian Embassy, Paris to DEA, 21 October 1963, Enclosure.
54 MAE/276 – Leduc to MAE, Amérique, 22 April 1965; Thomson, *Vive,* 148-149.
55 ANQ/P762/1999-10-011/60/Memos – Morin to Lesage, 30 April 1965.
56 LBP/N3/321/840-F815 – Martin to Pearson, 27 April 1965.
57 Thomson, *Vive,* 157; ANQ/E5/1986-03-007/94/1 – Mémoire des délibérations du Conseil Exécutif, Séance du 11 mai 1965; DEA/10141/30-12-QUE/3 – Cadieux to SSEA, 4 February 1966.
58 Larose, "Création de la délégation générale," 90.
59 MC/8/15 – Journal, 19 January 1968.
60 Thomson, *Vive,* 140; JL/2/3 – Léger to Chapdelaine, 20 October 1964.
61 ANQ/E6/1976-00-066/4 – Frégault to Laporte, 14 July 1965; ANQ/P422/S2/1995-01-008/2/6 – Patry to Johnson, 12 July 1966; ANQ/P422/S2/1995-01-008/3/9 – Extrait d'une lettre de monsieur Clément Saint-Germain, 29 September 1966; ANQ/P422/S2/1995-01-008/3/9 – Léger, Note sur la D.G. du Québec à Paris, undated.
62 Morin, *L'art de l'impossible,* 70.
63 ANQ/P776/2001-01-006/2/Daniel Johnson, 1966-1969 [DJ] – Chapdelaine to Johnson, 25 July 1966; ANF/5AG1/199/Québec-Entretiens – Johnson to de Gaulle, 13 September 1966; Gros d'Aillon, *Daniel Johnson,* 125-131; MAE/278 – Leduc to MAE, Amérique, 27 July 1966.
64 MAE/198 – Leduc to MAE, Amérique, 8 April 1965; MAE/204 – Bousquet to Roché, 16 October 1963.
65 MAE/199 – Leduc to MAE, Amérique, 3 March 1967; Rouanet and Rouanet, *Trois derniers chagrins,* 79.
66 MAE/328 – Note pour le Ministre, 4 June 1965. "Mains libres" should not be construed as meaning independence; this same report notes the Lesage government's determination to prevent a rupture with Ottawa. The way that the expression is employed suggests a reference to its Gaullist usage – freedom of action on the world stage.
67 MAE/276 – Message from Picard to Leduc, 31 August 1965; Aird, *André Patry,* 72.
68 Peyrefitte, *De Gaulle,* 38.
69 ANF/5AG1/199/Québec-Entretiens – de Gaulle to Johnson, 24 September 1966; Peyrefitte, *De Gaulle,* 55; Lacouture, *De Gaulle,* 450.
70 De Gaulle, "Lettre à Geoffroy de Courcel, Secrétaire Général de la Présidence de la République, 21 janvier 1961," in *Lettres, notes et carnets, janvier 1961-décembre 1963,* 26.
71 DEA/10098/20-1-2-FR/3.2 – Léger to Cadieux, 2 November 1965.
72 DEA/10098/20-1-2-FR/2.2 – Léger to Cadieux, 8 July 1964; DEA/10098/20-1-2-FR/3.1 – Léger to Cadieux, 6 October 1964; DEA/10098/20-1-2-FR/2.2 – Cadieux to Léger, 28 September 1964.
73 Quoted in Thomson, *Vive,* 139.
74 It was during this ceremony that de Gaulle referred to French Canadians as French in every respect except their sovereignty. DEA/10098/20-1-2-FR/2.1 – Léger to DEA, 4 June 1964; DEA/10098/20-1-2-FR/2.1 – Canadian Embassy, Paris to USSEA, 5 June 1964.

75 DEA/3497/19-1-BA-FRA-1964(3) – Martin to Léger, 25 November 1964; DEA/3497/19-1-BA-FRA-1964(3) – Cadieux to Martin, 10 December 1964; JL/1/12 – Léger to Cadieux, 25 November 1964; Thomson, *Vive*, 128-130.
76 DEA/11568/30-1-1-QUE/1 – Gotlieb to Cadieux, 28 February 1966; DEA/11568/30-1-1-QUE/1 – Cadieux to Robertson, 9 March 1966.
77 MAE/199 – Jurgensen to Couve de Murville, 26 September 1966; ANQ/E42/2004-01-002/70/Projet d'accord général Franco-Québécois – Cholette to Morin, 19 September 1966.
78 DEA/10077/20-FR-9/1.2 – Cadieux to Collins, 22 September 1966; DEA/10077/20-FR-9/1.2 – Cadieux to Halstead, 26 September 1966; Bosher, *Gaullist Attack*, 93.
79 DEA/10078/20-FR-9/2.2 – SSEA to Canadian Embassy, Paris, 1 November 1966; DEA/10077/20-FR-9/2.1 – Halstead to Martin, 3 October 1966; Peyrefitte, *De Gaulle*, 89.
80 MAE/278 – Leduc to MAE, Amérique, 2 March 1967; Hilliker and Barry, *Canada's Department*, 397.
81 DEA/10045/20-1-2-FR/5 – Martin to Pearson, 24 January 1967; DEA/10045/20-1-2-FR/5 – Martin to Pearson, 14 April 1967.
82 DEA/10098/20-1-2-FR/2.1 – Cadieux, Memorandum to File, 25 June 1964.
83 DEA/10492/55-3-1-FR-QUEBEC/2.2 – Martin to Pearson, 22 March 1965.
84 DEA/10098/20-1-2-FR/3.2 – Cadieux to Léger, 6 December 1965.
85 DEA/10098/20-1-2-FR/4.2 – Cadieux to Halstead, 19 December 1966.
86 DEA/10098/20-1-2-FR/3.2 – Cadieux to Léger, 6 December 1965.
87 DEA/10045/20-1-2-FR/5 – Martin to Pearson, 24 February 1967.
88 DEA/10098/20-1-2-FR/3.1 – Léger to DEA, 8 September 1965; DEA/10098/20-1-2-FR/4.2 – Canadian Embassy, Paris to DEA, 16 January 1967; DEA/10045/20-1-2-FR/5 – Martin to Pearson, 24 January 1967.
89 DEA/10045/20-1-2-FR/5 – Canadian Embassy, Paris to DEA, 15 February 1967.
90 DEA/10045/20-1-2-FR/5 – Martin to Pearson, 14 April 1967; Loiselle, *Daniel Johnson*, 132.

Chapter 8: Crisis

1 ANQ/P422/S2/1995-01-008/3/10 – Morin to Johnson, 11 May 1967.
2 DEA/10077/20-FR-9/1.1 – George to Canadian Embassy, Paris, 2 May 1966.
3 MAE/208/Antérieur au Voyage – Léger to de Gaulle, 6 September 1966; MAE/208/Antérieur au Voyage – Johnson to de Gaulle, 13 September 1966; MAE/208/Antérieur au Voyage – Curien, Cabinet du Ministre, to MAE, Amérique, 24 September 1966.
4 ANQ/P776/2001-01-006/2/Daniel Johnson, 1966-1969 [DJ] – Chapdelaine to Johnson, 14 February 1967 (2).
5 DEA/9568/18-1-D-FRA-1967(1) – Le Général de Gaulle en Visite au Canada, 15; DEA/10078/20-FR-9/2.2 – Cadieux to Hodgson, 4 January 1967.
6 MAE/208/Antérieur au Voyage – Note for Secrétaire Général, 22 March 1967; English, *Worldly Years*, 333.
7 DEA/10045/20-1-2-FR/5 – Eberts to USSEA, 14 March 1967; DEA/10045/20-1-2-FR/5 – Eberts to USSEA, 13 April 1967.
8 De Gaulle, "Lettre à Étienne Burin des Roziers, Secrétaire Général de la Présidence de la République, 13 janvier 1967," in *Lettres, notes et carnets, juillet 1966-avril 1969*, 62; DEA/9568/18-1-D-FRA-1967(1) – Le Général de Gaulle en Visite au Canada, 32-47.
9 DEA/10045/20-1-2-FR/5 – George to Halstead, 22 March 1967.
10 DEA/10045/20-1-2-FR/7 – Martin to DEA, 23 April 1967; DEA/10078/20-FR-9/3 – Martin to Pearson, 3 April 1967.
11 DEA/10078/20-FR-9/4 – Cadieux to Hodgson, 15 May 1967. See also DEA/10078/20-FR-9/3 – Robinson, Memorandum for File, 18 April 1967; André Patry, *Le Québec dans le monde*, 98.

12 ANQ/P422/S2/1995-01-008/3/10 – Morin to Johnson, 11 May 1967; MAE/208/Antérieur au Voyage – de Leusse to French Embassy, Ottawa, 26 May 1967; DEA/10078/20-FR-9/4 – Canadian Embassy, Paris to DEA, 18 May 1967.
13 DEA/10078/20-FR-9/4 – Lalonde to Cadieux, 30 May 1967; DEA/10045/20-1-2-FR/6 – Memorandum from Moncel, 14 June 1967; DEA/10045/20-1-2-FR/6 – Moncel, Note for File, 16 July 1967.
14 MC/8/15 – Journal, 12 July 1967.
15 DEA/10045/20-1-2-FR/6 – Williamson to USSEA, 22 June 1967; Thomson, *Vive*, 197-198.
16 DEA/9568/18-1-D-FRA-1967(1) – Le Général de Gaulle en Visite au Canada, 65-68.
17 DEA/10045/20-1-2-FR/7 – Memorandum to Pearson, 24 July 1967.
18 Lescop, *Le pari québécois*, 160-167.
19 ANQ/E42/2002-10-005/44/Voyages Europe, Claude Morin [Voyages] – Morin to Jurgensen, 14 August 1967; MAE/212 – Leduc to MAE, Amérique, 24 August 1967.
20 ANQ/E42/2002-10-005/44/Voyages – Jurgensen to Morin, 18 August 1967; MAE/200 – Conseil Restreint sur l'aide économique et culturelle au Québec, 5 September 1967; MAE/200 – Letter from Chapdelaine, 14 September 1967.
21 ANQ/P776/2001-01-006/4/Ministère des Affaires intergouvernementales, 1969-1996 [MAI] – Dorin to Masse, 25 March 1996; Peyrefitte, *De Gaulle*, 88-90.
22 ANQ/E6/1976-00-066/21/Coopération à l'extérieur, 1966-1971 – Procès-verbal des décisions arrêtées entre MM. Daniel Johnson, premier ministre, Jean-Jacques Bertrand, vice-président du Conseil, ministre de l'Éducation et de la Justice, Jean-Noël Tremblay, ministre des Affaires culturelles, Marcel Masse, ministre d'État à l'Éducation, d'une part, et M. Alain Peyrefitte, ministre de l'Éducation nationale, représentant le Gouvernement Français, d'autre part; MAE/212 – Leduc to MAE, Amérique, 18 September 1967.
23 ANQ/P776/2001-01-006/2/DJ – Chapdelaine to Johnson, 12 October 1967.
24 MAE/200 – Leduc to MAE, Amérique, 14 October 1967; ANQ/E42/1995-02-001/147/CME, Statut du Québec, Général [CME] – Morin to Johnson, 22 December 1967.
25 MAE/191 – Couve de Murville to Leduc, 14 March 1968; MAE/212 – Instructions à M. Pierre de Menthon (Projet); DEA/10046/20-FR-1-2/13 – European Division to USSEA, 26 February 1968; de Menthon, *Je témoigne*, 24-26.
26 DEA/10046/20-1-2-FR/13 – Canadian Embassy, Paris to DEA, 3 April 1968.
27 DEA/10045/20-1-2-FR/7 – Draft Memorandum for the Prime Minister, 14 August 1967.
28 DEA/10078/20-FR-9/8.1 – Martin to Canadian Embassy, Paris, 6 September 1967; DEA/11642/30-14-7-1/1 – Martin to Pearson, 22 September 1967; DEA/10045/20-1-2-FR/9 – Head to Trudeau, 2 October 1967.
29 ANQ/P776/2001-01-006/4/MAI – Dorin to Masse, 25 March 1996.
30 Black, *Direct Intervention*, 14; DEA/11642/30-14-7-1/1 – Martin to Pearson, 31 October 1967.
31 DEA/10098/20-1-2-FR/4.2 – Canadian Embassy, Paris to DEA, 16 January 1967; DEA/10045/20-1-2-FR/5 – Cadieux to Léger, 28 February 1967; DEA/10045/20-1-2-FR/5 – Léger, Relations Franco-Canadiennes – draft article; DEA/10045/20-1-2-FR/5 – Cadieux to Martin, 30 March 1967.
32 DEA/10045/20-1-2-FR/9 – Canadian Embassy, Paris to DEA, 15 September 1967; DEA/10078/20-FR-9/8.1 – Canadian Embassy, Paris to DEA, 12 September 1967.
33 DEA/10078/20-FR-9/8.1 – Canadian Embassy, Paris to DEA, 12 September 1967.
34 DEA/20-1-2-FR/9 – Canadian Embassy, Paris to USSEA, 13 October 1967; DEA/10046/20-1-2-FR/9 – Cadieux to Léger, 17 October 1967.
35 DEA/10046/20-1-2-FR/10 – Memorandum for the Minister, 11 November 1967.
36 JL/1/12 – Cadieux to Léger, 25 September 1967; JL/1/11 – Cadieux to Léger, 14 November 1967; JL/1/11 – Cadieux to Léger, 10 January 1968; JL/1/11 – Cadieux to Léger, 28 February 1968.

37 JL/1/12 – Léger to Cadieux, 25 November 1964.
38 ANQ/P776/2001-01-006/2/DJ – Chapdelaine to Johnson, 30 November 1967.
39 DEA/10045/20-1-2-FR/9 – Martin to Pearson, 29 September 1967; DEA/11642/30-14-7-1/1 – Martin to Pearson, 31 October 1967.
40 MC/8/15 – Journal, 12 July 1967; MC/8/15 – Journal, 25 July 1967; MC/8/15 – Journal, 26 July 1967. Martin told Cadieux that Pearson was "catastrophé, désespéré" to learn de Gaulle would not visit Ottawa, prompting Cadieux to allow Léger to make his *démarche*. However, according to Cadieux, Martin had lied; apparently, Pearson believed that the abbreviated itinerary was the best decision and nothing should be done to change de Gaulle's mind. Cadieux was so angered by the deception that he complained to Gordon Robertson, clerk of the Privy Council, and the two officials agreed that in the future Pearson would tell Robertson of his dealings with Martin, and Robertson would keep Cadieux informed.
41 DEA/10046/20-1-2-FR/11 – Cadieux to Martin, 8 December 1967; DEA/10046/20-1-2-FR/11 – Cadieux to Pearson, 26 December 1967.
42 Lefèvre, "Les États-Unis," 147-169, 201-204; Vaïsse, *La grandeur,* 452-500; Tétu, *La Francophonie,* 56-58; Peyrefitte, *De Gaulle,* 52.
43 DEA/11632/30-10-FRAN/1 – Visit of President Senghor, September 19-21, "La Francophonie," 13 September 1966; DEA/10685/26-2-CDA-QUE/1 – Gotlieb to European Division, 27 September 1966.
44 ANQ/P776/2001-01-006/1/Délégation du Québec en France, 1964-1966 – Chapdelaine to Lesage, 3 March 1965; Gérin-Lajoie, *Combats,* 319.
45 ANQ/P422/S2/1995-01-008/3/5 – Chapdelaine to Morin, 11 July 1966; ANQ/E42/1990-09-002/405/B – Morin to Chapdelaine, 26 July 1966; ANQ/E42/1995-02-001/147/CME – Mémoire du Ministre d'État à l'Éducation au Conseil des Ministres, 7 December 1966; MAE/322 – Basdevant to Secrétaire-Général, 21 September 1966; ANQ/E42/1995-02-001/147/CME – Léger to Morin, 13 January 1967.
46 MAE/199 – Entretien entre M. Couve de Murville et M. Paul Martin, 29 September 1966; Thomson, *Vive,* 186.
47 Gendron, *Towards a Francophone Community,* 122-123.
48 DEA/10045/20-1-2-FR/5 – Martin to Pearson, 24 February 1967; Department of External Affairs, "Canada and 'la Francophonie': Speech by the Secretary of State for External Affairs, the Honourable Paul Martin, Montreal, March 11, 1967"; DEA/10045/20-1-2-FR/5 – George to Halstead, 22 March 1967.
49 DEA/10045/20-1-2-FR/5 – DEA to Canadian Embassy, Paris, 1 March 1967.
50 DEA/10046/20-1-2-FR/11 – Gotlieb, ANNEX – Federal action to deal with possible French support for separatism, 6 September 1967, attached to Memorandum from Martin to Pearson, 29 November 1967.
51 MAE/460/Francophonie au Canada – Note, 7 July 1967.
52 DEA/11632/30-10-FRAN/1 – Beesley to Cadieux, 14 December 1967.
53 MAE/462/Francophonie – Conférence de Libreville et rupture des relations diplomatiques Canada-Gabon [Libreville] – Foccart to Raimond, 30 December 1967; ANQ/P776/2001-01-006/4/MAI – Dorin to Masse, 25 March 1996; Peyrefitte, *De Gaulle,* 85, 110.
54 MAE/462/Libreville – Peyrefitte to Couve de Murville, 30 November 1967; Claude Morin, *L'art de l'impossible,* 116; ANQ/E42/1995-02-001/147/CME – Morin to Johnson, 22 December 1967; MAE/462/Libreville – Leduc to MAE, Amérique, 22 December 1967.
55 ANQ/P776/2001-01-006/3/Ministère de l'Éducation, 1965-1969 – Chapdelaine to Morin, 11 January 1968.
56 DEA/10046/20-1-2-FR/11 – European Division to Francophonie Division, 8 December 1967; Gendron, *Towards a Francophone Community,* 130.

57 DEA/10046/20-1-2-FR/11 – Cadieux to Martin, 8 December 1967; JL/1/11 – Cadieux to Pearson, 10 January 1968; JL/1/11 – Cadieux to Léger, 10 January 1968; Morin, *L'Art de l'impossible*, 117.
58 MAE/462/Libreville – Note to file, undated; MAE/462/Libreville – Author unknown to Delauney, Ambassadeur de France, Libreville, 10 January 1968; MAE/462/Libreville – Projet de lettre de M. Malékou à M. Cardinal, 6 January 1968; MAE/462/Libreville – Delauney to MAE, Amérique, 12 January 1968. See also ANQ/P776/2001-01-006/4/Divers – Morin to Chapdelaine, 14 August 1998; Peyrefitte, *De Gaulle*, 112. There exists a story, likely apocryphal, that Gabon's Washington embassy sent the invitation to the DEA by mistake and a departmental official then mistakenly forwarded it to Quebec City. Claude Morin dismisses the idea, arguing that the time frame did not permit this. What appears closer to the truth is Alain Peyrefitte's claim that the Gabonese embassy almost sent the invitation to Ottawa, but that an alert official ensured that it was sent directly to Quebec City.
59 DEA/11652/30-16-QBC/1 – Martin to Pearson, 18 January 1968; MAE/462/Libreville – Leduc to MAE, Amérique, 18 January 1968; MC/8/15 – Journal, 18 January 1968; MC/8/14 – Journal, 27 February 1968.
60 Gendron, *Towards a Francophone Community*, 133; Morin, *L'art de l'impossible*, 125-133; Thomson, *Vive*, 270.
61 MAE/462/Libreville – Déclaration de M. Alain Peyrefitte, Ministre Français de l'Éducation nationale, undated, attached to letter from Delauney to Couve de Murville, MAE, Affaires africaines et malgaches, 10 February 1968.
62 Gendron, *Towards a Francophone Community*, 134.
63 MC/8/14 – Journal, 27 February 1968; MC/8/14 – Journal, 10 March 1968; MC/8/13 – Journal, 19 March 1968; MC/8/13 – Journal, 21 March 1968.
64 JL/1/11 – Léger to Cadieux, 23 February 1968; MC/8/14 – Memorandum for the Prime Minister, 27 February 1968; JL/1/11 – Cadieux to Léger, 28 February 1968; MC/8/14 – Cadieux to Tremblay, 29 February 1968; MC/8/14 – Journal, 27 February 1968.
65 MAE/462/Libreville – de Menthon to MAE, Amérique, 25 January 1968; MAE/462/Libreville – de Menthon to MAE, 27 January 1968; MAE/462/Libreville – de Menthon to MAE, Amérique, 5 March 1968; MAE/463/Francophonie, Conférence de Paris [Paris] – de Menthon to MAE, Amérique, 6 March 1968. Further evidence of the change of mood was an MAIQ official requesting that the Quebec delegation to Libreville be received with maximum discretion when it stopped in Paris en route; the aim was to avoid provoking Ottawa further.
66 MC/8/14 – Journal, 7 February 1968.
67 ANQ/E42/1995-02-001/147/CME – Pearson to Johnson, 5 April 1968.
68 ANQ/E42/1995-02-001/147/CME – Patry to Johnson, 9 April 1968; ANQ/E42/1995-02-001/147/CME – Patry to Johnson, 10 April; Morin, *L'art de l'impossible*, 134-137.
69 MAE/463/Paris – de Menthon to MAE, Amérique 6 March 1968; MAE/463/Paris – Leduc to MAE, 12 March 1968.
70 Black, *Direct Intervention*, 35; JL/1/11 – Cadieux to Léger, 28 February 1968; JL/1/11 – Cadieux to Léger, 26 March 1968; Canada, Secretary of State for External Affairs, Paul Martin, *Federalism and International Relations*; Canada, Secretary of State for External Affairs, Mitchell Sharp, *Federalism and International Conferences on Education*.
71 Godin, *Daniel Johnson*, 337-338.
72 MAE/463/Paris – de Menthon to MAE, 29 March 1968; MAE/461/Francophonie – Note for Secrétaire Général, 9 March 1968; MAE/463/Paris – Leduc to MAE, 18 April 1968; Schlegel, "Containing Quebec Abroad," 159; Peyrefitte, *De Gaulle*, 121.
73 MAE/201 – Canadian Embassy, Paris to MAE, 3 May 1968; Black, *Direct Intervention*, 38.

74 DEA/10046/20-1-2-FR/14 – Cadieux to European Division, 28 May 1968.
75 MC/8/13 – Journal, 22 March 1968.

Chapter 9: Missions Impossible?

1 Savard, *Le Consulat Général*, 40.
2 Huntington, "Transnational Organizations."
3 Original figures obtained from Lundestad, *The United States and Western Europe*, 77, and adjusted for inflation using the calculator provided by the American Bureau of Labor Statistics at http://www.bls.gov/data/inflation.calculator.htm, accessed 10 July 2010. See also de Grazia, *Irresistible Empire*, 367-369.
4 Lundestad, *"Empire" by Integration*, 52-54.
5 MAE/144 – Lacoste to MAE, Amérique, 8 October 1960; Comeau and Fournier, *Le Lobby du Québec*, 113-114.
6 Levine, *Reconquest of Montreal*, 22; Coleman, *Independence Movement*, 12-19.
7 MAE/146/Agence Générale de la province du Québec à Paris, Inauguration par M. Lesage – *Europe-Canada, Bulletin d'Information*, 14 October 1961; MAE/276 – Leduc to MAE, Amérique, 21 July 1965.
8 ANQ/E16/1960-01-035/56/Chambre de Commerce France-Canada – Speech by G.-D. Lévesque, 30 May 1963; Arbour, *Québec Inc.*, 20-24; McRoberts, *Quebec: Social Change*, 132-135.
9 Maul, "'Help Them Move,'" 393; Behiels, *Prelude*, 114; MAE/146 – Denizeau to Levasseur, 16 October 1961.
10 MAE/143 – MAE, Affaires Économiques et Financières, Note to File, 29 October 1958; MAE/145 – Bousquet to MAE, Affaires Économiques et Financières, 16 February 1963; MAE/205/Deuxième séjour à Paris de Monsieur Lesage, Premier Ministre du Québec – Partial Transcript, to Ministre de l'Information, 12 November 1964; MAE/293 – Leduc to MAE, Amérique, 26 November 1965.
11 ANQ/E16/1960-01-035/56/Chambre de Commerce France-Canada – Speech by G.-D. Lévesque, 30 May 1963.
12 ANQ/P776/2001-01-006/1/Délégation du Québec en France, 1964-1966 [DGQ] – Chapdelaine to Lesage, 27 July 1965.
13 ANF/5AG1/199/Québec-Entretiens – Lesage to de Gaulle, 8 October 1963.
14 ANQ/E16/1960-01-035/56/Chambre de Commerce France-Canada – Speech by G.-D. Lévesque, 30 May 1963; *Informations canadiennes* March 1965, 10(87): advertisement between 17-18; ANQ/P776/2001-01-006/1/DGQ – Chapdelaine to Lesage, 27 July 1965; McKenna and Pucell, *Drapeau*, 153.
15 Mouré, "French Economy," 372; Berstein, *La France de l'expansion*, 145.
16 Morse, *Foreign Policy*, 13-17; Caron, *Histoire économique*, 179; Berstein, *La France de l'expansion*, 151.
17 Grosser, *Affaires extérieures*, 219; Caron, *Histoire économique*, 181; Berstein, *La France de l'expansion*, 177.
18 Giauque, *Grand Designs*, 33-43; Vaïsse, *La grandeur*, 164-169, 545-549, 553-560; Grosser, *Affaires extérieures*, 219-220.
19 Vaïsse, *La grandeur*, 398-399; Kuisel, *Seducing the French*, 159-162.
20 Vaïsse, *La grandeur*, 400-407; Kolodziej, *French International Policy*, 184-191.
21 Grosser, *Western Alliance*, 224-225; Servan-Schreiber, *Le défi américain*.
22 MAE/135 – Lacoste to Couve de Murville, MAE, Amérique, 12 December 1960.
23 ANQ/E6/1976-00-066/26/Annuel, Délégation culturelle du Québec à Paris [Annuel] – Lussier to Lévesque, 11 December 1962.

24 MAE/146 – Bousquet to Couve de Murville, MAE, Affaires Économiques et Financières, 4 November 1963.
25 Cholette, *Coopération économique*, 237; MAE/226 – Note to File, March 1968.
26 MAE/136 – Note to File, 7 May 1963; MAE/278 – Leduc to Couve de Murville, MAE, Amérique, 17 March 1967; MAE/202 – Siraud to MAE, 1 November 1968; AHC/WB/5/1 – La Mission de M. Baumgartner et la situation au Canada et au Québec, 3 October 1962.
27 Couve de Murville, *Une politique étrangère*, 451-453.
28 Peyrefitte, *De Gaulle*, 21; MAE/209/Discours prononcés – Textes et Notes, Voyage du Général de Gaulle au Québec, Président de la République [Textes], Au dîner offert par M. Daniel Johnson, Premier Ministre du Québec, à Québec, le 23 juillet 1967.
29 Grosser, *Western Alliance*, 218.
30 François-Richard, "La France et le Québec," 187, 281-282; Saint-Gilles, *Présence culturelle*, 243.
31 DEA/11642/30-14-7-1 – "Plaidoyer d'un diplomate français en faveur d'une alliance plus étroite entre son pays et le Québec," *Le Devoir*, 7 April 1966, 1; MAE/136 – Bousquet to Couve de Murville, MAE, Amérique, 27 June 1962; MAE/145 – Bousquet to Couve de Murville, MAE, Affaires Économiques et Financières, 13 July 1963.
32 ANQ/P776/2001-01-006/1/Délégation du Québec en France, 1964-1966 – Chapdelaine to Lesage, 14 May 1965; MAE/200 – Leduc to MAE, 23 August 1967 (2).
33 McKenna and Pucell, *Drapeau*, 138-140. See also MAE/97 – Bousquet to Couve de Murville, MAE, Amérique, 26 May 1962.
34 Vinant, *De Jacques Cartier à Péchiney*, 355-356; MAE/199 – Jurgensen to de Saint-Légier, 13 July 1966.
35 ANQ/P776/2001-01-006/2/Général de Gaulle, 1967 – Allocution du Général de Gaulle à L'Hôtel de Ville de Montréal, le 24 juillet 1967 (sur la terrasse); MAE/209/Discours prononcés – Textes, Au déjeuner offert par le maire de Montréal à Montréal, le 26 juillet 1967.
36 Lescop, *Le pari québécois*, 169.
37 MAE/200 – Conseil Restreint sur l'aide économique et culturelle au Québec, 5 September 1967; Cholette, *Coopération économique*, 40-41; de Gaulle, "Toast adressé à M. J.G. Cardinal, Vice-Président du Conseil des ministres du Québec," in *Discours et messages*, 373-374.
38 ITC/1949/20-2-2/3 – Kniewasser to Halstead, 11 October 1963; DEA/7158/9245-40/5.2 – Crean to Ritchie, 22 September 1959; DEA/7666/11562-126-40/1.2 – Franco-Canadian Trade, 7 April 1960; MAE/144 – Lacoste to Couve de Murville, MAE, Affaires Économiques et Financières, 21 March 1961; Vaïsse, *La grandeur*, 168-170; DEA/5232/6956-40/5 – Programme de la visite de la mission économique et financière française au Canada.
39 Azzi, *Walter Gordon*, 64.
40 Hart, *A Trading Nation*, 197-198; Levitt, *Silent Surrender*; Muirhead, "Development," 693.
41 DEA/6519/9245-G-40 – Interdepartmental Committee on Canada-France Relations, 1 October 1963.
42 DDF/1964(1) – Document 30, Compte rendu de l'entretien entre le Président de la République et le Premier Ministre du Canada à l'Élysée, le 16 janvier 1964; DDF/1964(1) – Document 31, Compte Rendu de l'Entretien entre M. Georges Pompidou et M. Lester Pearson, Premier Ministre du Canada, à l'Hôtel Matignon, le 16 janvier 1964; MAE/198 – Telegram from Bousquet to MAE, Amérique, 27 February 1964.
43 DEA/6519/9245-G-40 – Interdepartmental Committee on Canada-France Relations, 1 October 1963; DDF/1964(1) – Document 29, Compte rendu de l'entretien entre le Général de Gaulle et M. Lester Pearson, Premier Ministre du Canada à Paris, le 15 janvier 1964.
44 MAE/97 – Bousquet to MAE, 23 August 1962; MAE/199 – Leduc to MAE, Amérique, 18 October 1966; DDF/1964(1) – Document 29, Compte rendu de l'entretien entre le Général

45 MAE/AE-CE/1474/Canada, 1961-1966 – Note, 12 October 1966; Muirhead, *Dancing Around the Elephant*, 226-239.
46 DEA/6830/2927-AD-40/8.2 – Notes on Some Trade and Economic Aspects of Canada-France Relations, undated [circa 1963].
47 DEA/4125/14003-F-5-3-40 – Stoner to Ritchie, 12 December 1962; MAE/258 – MAE, Service des Affaires atomiques, Note: Approvisionnement en uranium au Canada, 1 December 1964; English, *Worldly Years*, 321; MAE/258 – MAE, Service des Affaires atomiques, Note: Uranium canadien, 17 February 1965; DEA/10077/20-FR-9/1.1 – DEA to Canadian Embassy, Paris, 13 April 1965; MAE/258 – Martin, MAE, Service des Affaires atomiques to French Embassy, Ottawa, 24 May 1965.
48 ANQ/E42/1990-09-002/405/A – Chapdelaine to Morin, 17 February 1966; JL/4/10 – Léger to Martin, 3 February 1965; MAE/199 – Audience accordée par le Secrétaire Général à M. Cadieux, Secrétaire-Général du Ministère Canadien des Affaires Extérieures, 19 November 1966.
49 Hecht, *Radiance of France*, 2.
50 DEA/10098/20-1-2-FR/3.1 – Léger to DEA, 8 September 1965; DEA/10046/20-1-2-FR/9 – Yalden to Léger, 25 October 1967; Foccart, *Tous les soirs*, 425.
51 MAE/114 – Lacoste to Couve de Murville, MAE, Amérique, 4 February 1959; MAE/115 – Lacoste to MAE, Amérique, 7 March 1962; MAE/133 – Bousquet to MAE, Amérique, 17 April 1963.
52 English, *Worldly Years*, 276; Pearson, *Mike*, 107.
53 Donaghy, *Tolerant Allies*, 25-66.
54 Merchant and Heeney, *Canada and the United States*; MAE/243 – Leduc to MAE, Amérique, 15 July 1965; MAE/AE-CE/957/Canada, 1961-1965 – Note, 26 January 1965.
55 MAE/293 – Leduc to MAE, Amérique, 2 December 1965; MAE/265 – Leduc to MAE, Amérique, 4 January 1967; Julien, *Le Canada*, 53.
56 Vinant, *De Jacques Cartier*, 296-297, 320; Cholette, *Coopération économique*, 260; MAE/205/ Deuxième séjour à Paris de Monsieur Lesage, Premier Ministre du Québec – Partial Transcript, to the Ministre de l'Information, 12 November 1964.
57 ANQ/E6/1976-00-066/26/Annuel, Délégation culturelle du Québec à Paris – Lussier to Rousseau, 15 June 1962; ANQ/E42/2002-04-003/210/Agent Général de la P.Q. à Paris, Rapports activités 1961 [Rapports] – Lussier to Lévesque, 14 May 1964.
58 ANQ/E6/1976-00-066/26/Annuel – Lussier to Lapalme, 5 May 1961; ANQ/E42/2002-04-003/210/Rapports – Lussier to Lévesque, 14 May 1964.
59 Cholette, *Coopération économique*, 36-37; MAE/293 – Bousquet to Couve de Murville, MAE, Affaires Économiques et Financières, 27 November 1964; Thomson, *Vive*, 102.
60 ANQ/E42/2002-04-003/210/Rapports – Lussier to Lévesque, 27 May 1963.
61 DEA/10098/20-1-2-FR/2.1 – Canadian Embassy, Paris to DEA, 22 June 1964; DEA/10098/20-1-2-FR/3.1 – Léger to Cadieux, 6 January 1965.
62 ANQ/E42/2002-04-003/210/Rapports – Lussier to G.-D. Lévesque, 14 May 1964.
63 Comeau and Fournier, *Le Lobby du Québec*, 86.
64 MAE/293 – Leduc to MAE, Amérique, 26 November 1965; MAE/294 – Couve de Murville to Ministre de l'Économie et des Finances, 18 February 1966.
65 ITC/2785/810-F2-4/1 – Reny to Barrow, 9 March 1962; François-Richard, "La France et le Québec," 292; ANQ/E42/1995-02-001/7/France-Actim, Ententes and Accords – Treuil to Bousquet, 8 January 1963.
66 MAE/144 – Bousquet to MAE, Amérique, 5 July 1962; MAE/144 – Bousquet to MAE, Amérique, 17 January 1963; MAE/173 – Bousquet to MAE, Amérique, 2 April 1963.

67 Cholette, *Coopération économique*, 34.
68 The ensuing agreement with the University of Toronto remained a dead letter, owing to that institution's lack of initiative. DEA/5232/6956-40/5 – Robertson to Martin, 15 August 1963; MAE/145 – Bousquet to Couve de Murville, MAE, Affaires Économiques et Financières, 1 June 1963; DEA/10045/20-1-2-FR/6 – Procès-verbal d'une Réunion Inter-Ministérielle sur les Échanges de Jeunes avec la France, 27 April 1967.
69 Hecht, *Radiance of France*, 206.
70 MAE/145 – Bousquet to MAE, Amérique, 5 March 1963; MAE/145 – Bousquet to MAE, Amérique, 27 April 1963.
71 DEA/5289/9245-40/6.1 – Stone to Acting USSEA, 21 August 1963.
72 DEA/5289/9245-40/6.1 – European Division to USSEA, 10 September 1963.
73 DEA/5289/9245-30/6.1 – Martin to Pearson, 12 September 1963; DEA/5289/9245-40/6.1 – Dier to USSEA, 16 September 1963; MAE/204 – Bousquet to MAE, Amérique, 24 September 1963.
74 MAE/164 – Bousquet to MAE, Amérique, 11 June 1963; DEA/5289/9245-30/6.1 – Hooten to Economic Division, 25 October 1963; DEA/10098/20-1-2-FR/2.1 – Cadieux, Memorandum to File, 25 June 1964; MAE/145 – Bousquet to MAE, Amérique, 6 November 1963; MAE/164 – Bousquet to MAE, Amérique, 16 November 1963; ANQ/E5/1986-03-007/93/4 – Mémoire des délibérations du Conseil Exécutif, 6 November 1963.
75 The Gordon affair erupted when the head of Canadian National Railway, Donald Gordon, explained that the lack of French Canadians on the company's board of directors was due to what he claimed was an absence of competent candidates. For Quebec opinion, the remarks underscored French Canada's economic marginalization, and provoked a large demonstration that was held in front of the company's Montreal offices.
76 MAE/165 – Bousquet to MAE, Amérique, 12 December 1963; MAE/165 – Bousquet to MAE, Amérique, 13 December 1963; Pépin, "Les relations économiques," 503-504.
77 MAE/275 – Bousquet to Couve de Murville, MAE, Amérique, 27 April 1964; ANQ/E42/2002-04-003/210/Rapports – Lussier to Lévesque, 14 May 1964.
78 ANQ/E42/2004-01-002/70/Projet d'accord général Franco-Québécois – Aide-mémoire to Johnson, 30 September 1966.
79 MAE/294 – Jurgensen, Note, 28 October 1966; ANQ/E42/1990-09-002/405/B – Chapdelaine to Morin, 6 December 1966.
80 DEA/10141/30-12-QUE/4 – Cadieux to Martin, 1 December 1966; DEA/10141/30-12-QUE/4 – Langley to USSEA, 7 December 1966; DEA/10098/20-1-2-FR/4.2 – Léger to Cadieux, 5 January 1967.
81 MAE/199 – Leduc to Couve de Murville, MAE, Cabinet du Ministre, 18 January 1967; ANQ/P776/2001-01-006/2/Daniel Johnson, 1966-1969 – Chapdelaine to Johnson, 14 February 1967(3); ANQ/E42/2002-10-005/44/Voyages Europe, Morin – Jurgensen to Parizeau, 25 August 1967.
82 MAE/206/Visite de M. Daniel Johnson – Leduc to MAE, Amérique, 1 May 1967; MAE/199 – Compte-Rendu de la séance de travail franco-québécoise présidée par M. Hervé Alphand, 18 May 1967; MAE/228 – Note pour le Cabinet du Secrétaire d'État, à l'attention de M. Malaud.
83 MAE/281 – Transcript, Conférence de Presse de M. Daniel Johnson, 25 September 1968; MAE/214/Voyage en France de M. Daniel Johnson, Premier Ministre du Québec – Substance de la conversation chez le Ministre le 25 septembre 1968, concernant la visite de M. Daniel Johnson, 26 September 1968.
84 DEA/6519/9245-G-40 – Interdepartmental Committee on Canada-France Relations, 1 October 1963; MAE/204 – Bousquet to MAE, Amérique, 24 September 1963; MAE/204 – Lucet to French Embassy, Ottawa, 27 September 1963; DDF/1964(1) – Document 29,

Compte rendu de l'entretien entre le Général de Gaulle et M. Lester Pearson, Premier Ministre du Canada à Paris, le 15 janvier 1964; DDF/1964(1) – Document 28, Compte rendu de l'entretien entre M. Couve de Murville et M. Paul Martin, Ministre des Affaires étrangères du Canada, le 15 janvier 1964.

85 MAE/205/Deuxième séjour à Paris de M. Paul Martin – Entrevue de M. Paul Martin, Ministre des Affaires étrangères du Canada avec M. Couve de Murville, 13 December 1964.
86 DEA/10098/20-1-2-FR/3.1 – European Division to USSEA, 26 September 1965; MAE/293 – Leduc to Couve de Murville, MAE, Affaires Économiques et Financières, 3 December 1965.
87 MAE/143 – MAE, Affaires Économiques et Financières, Investissements Français à l'Étranger, Canada, March 1959; Dominion Bureau of Statistics, *Canada Year Book 1961*, 964-966.
88 DEA/10098/20-1-2-FR/2.1 – George to Léger, 19 May 1964.
89 MAE/293 – Bousquet to MAE, Amérique, 15 September 1964, pour la Direction Économique; DEA/10097/20-1-2-FR/5 – Smith to Warren, 28 February 1967; MAE/145 – Bousquet to MAE, Affaires Économiques et Financières, 11 July 1963.
90 ANQ/E42/1995-08-010/27/Mission Économique du Canada en France – Mission book; DEA/3163/32-A-1967(1) – Canada-France Economic Committee, Canadian Brief, October 1967; MAE/258 – MAE, Service des Affaires atomiques to Service de Presse, 10 October 1968.
91 ANF/5AG1/199/Canada I-II, Entretiens, Correspondances, 1958-1968 avec le Général de Gaulle [Canada] – Léger to de Gaulle, 31 March 1966; ANF/5AG1/199/Canada – de Gaulle to Pearson, 5 April 1966; DEA/10098/20-1-2-FR/4.1 – Canadian Embassy, Paris to DEA, 1 April 1966; Canada, Statistics Canada, *Canada Year Book 1972*, 1074-1081.
92 MAE/200 – Leduc to MAE, Amérique, 23 September 1967.
93 MC/8/14 – Journal, 13 February 1968; MC/8/14 – Journal, 19 February 1968.
94 DEA/8646/20-1-2-FR/19 – Canadian Embassy, Paris to DEA, 27 January 1969; MAE/227 – Rapport de la Commission Franco-Québécoise pour l'Étude des Investissements, January 1969.
95 Knapp, *Le Gaullisme*, 20; Berstein, *République gaullienne*, 148-153.
96 Ross, *Fast Cars*, 42.
97 Latham, *Liberal Moment*, 21.
98 Vinant, *De Jacques Cartier*, 51; ITC/2866/810-F2-1/5 – Warren to Pépin, 15 October 1970. The memorandum refers to French investments growing from $64 million to $250 million. These figures were adjusted for inflation using the Bank of Canada calculator available at http://www.bankofcanada.ca/en/rates/inflation_calc.html, accessed 10 July 2010.
99 ANQ/P776/2001-01-006/1/Délégation Organisation, 1967-1973 – Discours d'adieu de Monsieur Patrick Hyndman devant la Chambre de Commerce France-Canada, 14 January 1970; Taton, "Investissements," 42-44; Cholette, *Coopération économique*, 254.
100 Hence the Élysée's fury over Pierre Trudeau's parliamentary quip, "Vive le franc libre!"
101 Morse, *Foreign Policy*, 250-251; Grosser, *Western Alliance*, 256; DEA/10047/20-1-2-FR/18 – Black to Halstead, 28 November 1968; Vaïsse, *La grandeur*, 406-407; Kolodziej, *French International Policy*, 206-210; Black, *Direct Intervention*, 44; Berstein, *République gaullienne*, 334-336.
102 Vaïsse, *La grandeur*, 403-407; Kolodziej, *French International Policy*, 204-211.
103 ANQ/P776/2001-01-006/1/Reportage Politique, 1967-1974 – Chapdelaine to Morin, 5 December 1967; Thomson, *Vive*, 271.
104 MAE/233/Comité franco-québécois sur les investissements – Chauvet to MAE, 30 July 1969.
105 MAE/226 – de Courson to French Embassy, Ottawa, 22 September 1967; MAE/226 – de Menthon to MAE, Amérique, 18 April 1968.

106 MAE/278 – Leduc to MAE, Amérique, 10 February 1967; MAE/294 – Leduc to MAE, Amérique, 21 November 1966; ANF/5AG1/199 – Compte rendu avec le Général de Gaulle, 24 January 1969; ANF/5AG2/1021 – de Menthon to MAE, 17 December 1969; Bastien, *Relations particulières*, 83-84; Cholette, *Coopération économique*, 240.
107 MAE/278 – Leduc to MAE, Amérique, 11 May 1967; MAE/284 – de Menthon to MAE, Amérique, 20 October 1969; Bastien, *Relations particulières*, 75.
108 Jean-Marie Domenach, "Le Canada français," 322.

Chapter 10: Rivalry, Recrimination, and Renewal

1 DEA/10098/20-1-2-FR/3.2 – Cadieux to Léger, 6 December 1965.
2 Larose, "Création de la délégation générale," 43.
3 ANQ/E6/1976-00-066/26/Annuel, Délégation culturelle du Québec à Paris – Lussier to Rousseau, 15 June 1962; ANQ/E6/1976-00-066/26/Annuel – Lussier to Lévesque, 11 December 1962; ANQ/E42/2002-04-003/210/Agent Général de la P.Q. à Paris, Rapports activités 1961 – Lussier to Lévesque, 27 May 1963.
4 MAE/87 – Lacoste to MAE, Amérique, 23 January 1961; MAE/87 – Basdevant to Couve de Murville, 27 January 1961; MAE/87 – Basdevant to Lacoste, 6 February 1961; MAE/87 – Lacoste to MAE, Amérique, 20 March 1961; MAE/87 – MAE, Amérique to MAE, Affaires Culturelles et Techniques, 23 March 1961; MAE/87 – Lacoste to Couve de Murville, MAE, Affaires Culturelles et Techniques, 9 June 1961.
5 DEA/5232/6956-40/5 – Robertson to Green, 4 May 1961.
6 DEA/5232/6956-40/5 – Cadieux to Robertson, 9 May 1961; DEA/5232/6956-40/5 – Canadian Embassy, Paris to DEA, 3 June 1961.
7 DEA/5057/2727-14-40/1 – Cadieux to Robertson, 2 February 1961; DEA/5232/6956-40/5 – Cadieux to Information Division, 6 June 1961; Thomson, *Vive*, 151.
8 Gendron, *Towards a Francophone Community*, 73-75.
9 DEA/5057/2727-15-40/1 – Cadieux to Robertson, 23 April 1963; DEA/10097/20-1-2-FR/1.1 – Robertson to Martin, 30 August 1963; DEA/5057/2727-15-40/1 – Cadieux to Martin, 19 August 1963.
10 DEA/5057/2727-15-40/1 – Cadieux to Martin, 19 August 1963. The Belgians and Swiss also rejected the proposal, fearing complications with their francophone populations.
11 DEA/5056/2727-AD-40/9 – France-Canada Cultural Relations, 25 November 1963; Thomson, *Vive*, 117.
12 ANQ/P422/S2/1995-01-008/2/2 – J.-Y. Morin to Frégault, undated; ANQ/E42/1995-02-001/7/France-Actim, Ententes and Accords [France-Actim] – Note to R. Morin, 13 February 1964; Morin, *L'art de l'impossible*, 39.
13 ANQ/E6/1976-00-066/4 – Frégault to Morin, 7 January 1964; ANQ/E5/1986-03-007/93/5 – Mémoire des délibérations du Conseil Exécutif, Séance du 30 janvier 1964; Martin, *Very Public Life*, 578.
14 DEA/5057/2727-15-40/1 – Garneau to Robertson and Cadieux, 21 October 1963.
15 Garrigues, *La France de la Ve République*, 564; Poirrier, *Histoire des politiques*, 53.
16 ANQ/E6/1976-00-066/4 – French Embassy, Ottawa, Compte-Rendu de la réunion du 15 octobre 1963 à Montréal, 25 October 1963; Thomson, *Vive*, 108; Lapalme, *Le paradis du pouvoir*, 241-244.
17 MAE/101 – Bousquet to MAE, Amérique, 21 October 1963; MAE/204 – Bousquet to Rocher [sic, Roché], 16 October 1963.
18 MAE/173 – Accord sur les Relations Cinématographiques Franco-Canadiennes, 11 October 1963; DEA/5057/2727-15-40/1 – Garneau to Robertson and Cadieux, 21 October 1963; DEA/5056/2727-AD-40/9 – European Division to Cadieux, 21 October 1963.

19 DEA/5057/2727-15-40/1 – Garneau to Robertson and Cadieux, 21 October 1963.
20 ANQ/P776/2001-01-006/4/Ministère des Affaires intergouvernementales, 1969-1996 [MAI] – Dorin to Masse, 25 March 1996; ANQ/E42/1995-02-001/7/France-Actim – Note to R. Morin, 13 February 1964; DEA/10098/20-1-2-FR/2.1 – Cadieux, Memorandum to File, 25 June 1964; Comeau and Fournier, *Le Lobby du Québec*, 69.
21 Hobsbawm, *Age of Extremes*, 295-297; Jobs, *Riding the New Wave*, 84; Mesli, "La coopération franco-québécoise," 24 (citing Louis Dollot, *Les relations culturelles internationales* [Paris: PUF, 1964], 21).
22 Behiels, *Prelude*, 149-151, 160-163; Gauvreau, *Catholic Origins*, 249-251.
23 Mesli, "La coopération franco-québécoise," 40. See also Levine, *The Reconquest of Montreal*, 163.
24 Coleman, *Independence Movement*, 157.
25 Gérin-Lajoie, *Combats*, 322; MAE/327 – Bousquet to MAE, Affaires Culturelles et Techniques, 18 July 1964; DEA/10492/55-3-1-FR-QUÉBEC/1 – Dench to Cadieux, 25 June 1964; DEA/10492/55-3-1-FR-QUÉBEC/1 – European Division to USSEA, 30 June 1964; MAE/327 – Programme de Coopération et d'Échanges Universitaires entre la France et la Province du Québec, 2 November 1964, Annexe.
26 MAE/327 – Bousquet to Couve de Murville, MAE, Affaires Culturelles et Techniques, 18 July 1964; MAE/205/Deuxième séjour à Paris de Monsieur Lesage, Premier Ministre du Québec – Lesage to de Gaulle, 9 November 1964.
27 Peyrefitte, *De Gaulle*, 40-41.
28 MAE/320 – Bousquet to MAE, Amérique, 18 July 1964; MAE/327 – Bousquet to MAE, Affaires Culturelles et Techniques, Accords de coopération éducationnelle franco-québécois, Projet "large."
29 MAE/RSCT/DG1/70/Ententes franco-québécoises, 1963-1967 [Ententes] – de Saint-Légier, Note, 9 November 1964; Thomson, *Vive*, 136.
30 DEA/3497/19-1-BA-FRA-1964(3) – Léger to Martin, 13 November 1964; JL/1/12 – Cadieux to Léger, 19 November 1964; JL/1/12 – Léger to Cadieux, 25 November 1964; JL/1/12 – Cadieux to Léger, 3 December 1964.
31 DEA/3497/19-1-BA-FRA-1964(3) – Procès-verbal de la réunion tenue le 18 novembre 1964 à 9:30 à l'occasion de la visite de Monsieur Basdevant à Ottawa [Procès-verbal].
32 DEA/10492/55-3-1-FR-QUÉBEC/2 – Cadieux to Martin, 19 January 1965; DEA/10492/55-3-1-FR-QUÉBEC/2 – Cadieux to Martin, 21 January 1965.
33 MAE/327 – Pampelonne to MAE, Amérique, 27 February 1965; Thomson, *Vive*, 142.
34 MAE/327 – Note to File, 1 March 1965; DEA/10492/55-3-1-FR-QUÉBEC/2 – Halstead to Cadieux, 5 March 1965.
35 DEA/10492/55-3-1-FR-QUÉBEC/1 – European Division to USSEA, 30 June 1964.
36 DEA/3497/19-1-BA-FRA-1964(3) – Procès-verbal; MAE/328 – Canadian Counter-Proposal, Canadian Embassy, Paris, 10 September 1965; MAE/198 – Leduc to MAE, Amérique, 1 April 1965.
37 ANQ/P762/1999-10-011/60/Mémoires aux Premiers Ministres, Memos de M. Morin aux Premiers Ministres, 1962-1976 [Memos] – Morin to Lesage, 30 April 1965.
38 MAE/327 – Leduc to MAE, Amérique, 31 May 1965; MAE/327 – Note for the Minister, 31 May 1965; MAE/328 – Note to File, 2 June 1965.
39 DEA/10492/55-3-1-FR-QUEBEC/1 – Canadian Embassy, Paris to DEA, 25 November 1964; MAE/327 – Leduc to MAE, Amérique, 13 April 1965; MAE/328 – Jurgensen to MAE, Affaires Culturelles et Techniques, 11 June 1965.
40 MAE/328 – Leduc to MAE, Amérique, 13 September 1965.
41 ANQ/P422/S2/1995-01-008/2/5 – Chapdelaine to Morin, 20 September 1965.

42 MAE/RCST/DG1/57/Accord culturel franco-canadien – Note from MAE to Leduc, 18 November 1965.
43 ANQ/P422/S2/1995-01-008/2/5 – Chapdelaine to Morin, 20 September 1965; ANQ/P422/S2/1995-01-008/3/9 – Patry to Basdevant, 13 July 1965; ANQ/P422/S2/1995-01-008/3/9 – Patry to de Saint-Légier de la Saussaye, 11 September 1965; Thomson, *Vive*, 165.
44 MAE/327 – Basdevant to French Embassy, Ottawa, 21 May 1965; MAE/328 – Leduc to MAE, Amérique, 13 September 1965; ANQ/E5/1986-03-007/94/1 – Mémoire des délibérations du Conseil Exécutif, Séance du 11 mai 1965; Patry, *Le Québec dans le monde*, 64.
45 MAE/327 – Basdevant to French Embassy, Ottawa, 21 May 1965; MAE/327 – Leduc to MAE, Amérique, 31 May 1965; ANQ/P776/2001-01-006/1/Délégation du Québec en France, 1964-1966 – Chapdelaine to Lesage, 27 July 1965.
46 DEA/10492/55-3-1-FR-QUEBEC/2.2 – SSEA to Canadian Embassy, Paris, 19 May 1965; Thomson, *Vive*, 156, 160.
47 DEA/10492/55-3-1-FR-QUEBEC/2.2 – Cadieux to Martin, 1 September 1965; DEA/10492/55-3-1-FR-QUEBEC/2.2 – Canadian Embassy, Paris to DEA, 23 August 1965; DEA/11642/30-14-7-1/1 – Morin to Cadieux, 26 August 1965.
48 ANQ/P762/1999-10-011/60/Memos – Morin to Lesage, 15 September 1965; ANQ/E5/1986-03-007/94/1 – Mémoire des délibérations du Conseil Exécutif, Séance du 15 septembre 1965.
49 Thomson, *Vive*, 163-164; Roussel, "Relations culturelles," 308.
50 MAE/328 – Leduc to MAE, Amérique, 23 November 1965; ANQ/P762/1999-10-011/61/Rélations internationales du Québec/1 – Morin, Chronological Notes, undated; DEA/10492/55-3-1-FR-QUÉBEC/2.2 – Memorandum for the Prime Minister, 20 November 1965.
51 In addition to the stated excuse, Malraux's decision not to sign can also be attributed to the rivalry between the Quai d'Orsay and France's ministry of culture, along with his stated scepticism over the value of such agreements. MAE/RCST/DG1/57/Réunions culturelles franco-canadiennes, 29 septembre 1965 – Leduc to Basdevant, 23 September 1965; MAE/RCST/DG1/57/Accord culturel franco-canadien – de Menthon to French Embassy, Ottawa, 9 November 1965; DEA/5056/2727-AD-40/9 – Garneau to Robertson and Cadieux, 21 October 1963; ANQ/P422/S2/1995-01-008/3/9 – Chapdelaine to Morin, 20 September 1965.
52 MAE/RCST/DG1/57/Accord culturel franco-canadien – Leduc to MAE, 15 November 1965; MAE/RSCT/DG1/70/Ententes – Leduc to MAE, 25 November 1965.
53 DEA/10492/55-3-1-FR-QUÉBEC/2.2 – Memorandum to Martin, 17 November 1965; Thomson, *Vive*, 163; Roussel, "Relations culturelles," 309-310.
54 MAE/328 – Leduc to MAE, Amérique, 13 September 1965; MAE/328 – Note to Secrétaire-Général, 3 November 1965; Thomson, *Vive*, 163; Patry, *Québec dans le monde*, 65.
55 LBP/N3/321/840-F815 – Memorandum from Martin to Pearson, 27 April 1965.
56 MAE/327 – Note for the Minister, 31 May 1965; DEA/10935/56-1-2-FR/1.1 – Martin to Favreau et al., 12 January 1965; JL/1/12 – Léger to Cadieux, 12 July 1966; Canada (Ambassade du Canada [Paris]), *Centre Culturel Canadien, 25 ans d'activité, 1970-1995*, 22-23; Thomson, *Vive*, 151.
57 Quebec, Minister of Cultural Affairs, L'Allier, *Pour l'évolution de la politique culturelle, Document de travail*, 18.
58 ANQ/E6/1976-00-066/26/Délégation culturelle du Québec à Paris, Trimestriels – Rapport de la Section Culturelle pour les mois d'octobre, novembre et décembre 1965; ANQ/P422/S2/1995-01-008/3/9 – Léger, Note sur la D.G. du Québec à Paris, undated [circa autumn 1966].
59 ANQ/P776/2001-01-006/3/Personnel, Missions de France au Québec, 1966-1971 – Morin to Chapdelaine, 2 June 1966; ANQ/E42/1995-02-001/147/CME, Statut du Québec, Général – Chapdelaine to Morin, 1 December 1966.

60 ANQ/P776/2001-01-006/2/Daniel Johnson, 1966-1969 – Visite à Paris du Premier Ministre M. Daniel Johnson; MAE/206/Johnson Visit – Leduc to MAE, Amérique, 9 May 1967.
61 ANQ/E5/1986-03-007/94/1 – Mémoire des délibérations du Conseil Exécutif, Séance du 7 mai 1965; ANQ/P762/1999-10-011/62/Relations internationales du Canada, Documents Divers – Memorandum for the Prime Minister, 1 May 1967; Thomson, *Vive*, 193-194.
62 DEA/10045/20-1-2-FR/6 – Procès-verbal d'une Réunion Inter-Ministérielle sur les Échanges de Jeunes avec la France, 27 April 1967; MAE/199 – Leduc to Couve de Murville, MAE, Amérique, 3 March 1967; MAE/199 – Jurgensen to Couve de Murville, 2 May 1967.
63 DEA/10098/20-1-2-FR/1.2 – Halstead to Cadieux, 19 February 1964; MAE/198 – Bousquet to MAE, Amérique, 10 May 1964.
64 DEA/10098/20-1-2-FR/4.1 – George to USSEA, 27 June 1966.
65 ANQ/E6/1976-00-066/4 – Frégault to Laporte, 14 July 1965; Behiels, *Quebec and the Question*, 17-19.
66 MAE/199 – Leduc to Couve de Murville, MAE, Conventions Administratives et des Affaires Consulaires, Conventions, 27 October 1966; MAE/199 – Jurgensen to Couve de Murville, 2 May 1967; ANQ/P776/2001-01-006/1/Reportage Politique, 1967-1974 – Chapdelaine to Morin, 5 December 1967.
67 DEA/10098/20-1-2-FR/4.2 – Léger to Cadieux, 2 December 1966.
68 MAE/200 – Conseil Restreint sur l'aide économique et culturelle au Québec, 5 septembre 1967; ANQ/E6/1976-00-066/21/Coopération à l'extérieur, 1966-1971 [Coopération] – Procès-verbal des décisions arrêtées entre MM. Daniel Johnson, premier ministre, Jean-Jacques Bertrand, vice-président du Conseil, ministre de l'Éducation et de la Justice, Jean-Noël Tremblay, ministre des Affaires culturelles, Marcel Masse, ministre d'État à l'Éducation, d'une part, et M. Alain Peyrefitte, ministre de l'Éducation nationale, représentant le Gouvernement Français, d'autre part.
69 JL/1/11 – Cadieux to Pearson, 10 January 1968.
70 MAE/455/Acadiens, Coopération franco-acadienne, Dossier général [Acadiens] – Note pour le Secrétaire-Général, 2 April 1968.
71 ANQ/E42/1995-02-001/203/Parlementaires français – Note sur la coopération franco-québécois, 1 September 1970.
72 MAE/190 – Note pour la Direction du personnel et de l'Administration générale, 9 December 1967; ANQ/P422/S2/1995-01-008/2/8 – L'Allier to Héroux, 4 January 1968; de Menthon, *Je témoigne*, 14-18.
73 DEA/10046/20-1-2-FR/9 – Léger to Cadieux, 13 October 1967.
74 DEA/10047/20-1-2-FR/16.2 – Canadian Embassy, Paris to DEA, 17 September 1968; DEA/10047/20-1-2-FR/17 – Black to Stephens, 7 November 1968; Black, *Direct Intervention*, 67-70, 146.
75 Morin, *L'Art de l'impossible*, 24.
76 DEA/10046/20-1-2-FR/11 – Bilan des échanges entre la France et le Canada depuis la signature de l'Accord culturel [undated, circa May 1967]; DEA/10045/20-1-2-FR/6 – Halstead to USSEA, 31 May 1967.
77 MAE/RSCT/DG1/70/Ententes – Basdevant to French Embassy, Ottawa, 13 July 1965.
78 DEA/10140/30-6-QUE/1 – DEA to Léger, 1 May 1967; MAE/194 – MAE, Service Juridique, to MAE, Amérique, 17 February 1967.
79 MC/8/15 – Cadieux to Tremblay, 19 September 1967; MAE/200 – Leduc to MAE, Amérique, 23 September 1967; MAE/219 – Leduc to MAE, Amérique, 28 September 1967.
80 DEA/10046/20-1-2-FR/9 – Cadieux to Martin, 13 October 1967.
81 MAE/219 – Relations culturelles franco-québécoises, 10 November 1967.
82 DEA/10046/20-1-2-FR/10 – Léger to DEA, 23 November 1967.
83 MAE/237 – Leduc to Couve de Murville, MAE, Amérique, 1 November 1967.

84 MAE/237 – Leduc to MAE, Amérique, 6 February 1968; MAE/237 – de Bresson to Leduc, 8 February 1968.
85 DEA/10046/20-1-2-FR/12.2 – Roquet to Halstead, 8 February 1968; MAE/237 – Note to File, 9 February 1968; DEA/10046/20-1-2-FR/12.2 – Memorandum for USSEA, 15 February 1968.
86 Gélinas, *La droite intellectuelle*, 123, 358; Coleman, *Independence Movement*, 151-152.
87 MAE/RCST/DG1/71/Quebec: Commissions interministérielles – Compte rendu final de la séance du 5 décembre 1967 de la Commission interministérielle pour les questions de coopération entre la France et le Québec, 29 February 1968. See also Friesen, *Citizens and Nation*, 198; MAE/199 – Compte-Rendu de la séance de travail franco-québécoise présidée par M. Hervé Alphand, 18 May 1967.
88 DEA/10045/20-1-2-FR/6 – Canadian Embassy, Paris to DEA, 26 June 1967. See also DEA/10045/20-1-2-FR/6 – Canadian Embassy, Paris to Cadieux, 28 April 1967; DEA/10045/20-1-2-FR/9 – Canadian Embassy, Paris to DEA, 15 September 1967.
89 ANQ/E10/1983-05-000/157/Relations Fédérales-Provinciales, Satellites (1) – Rapport préliminaire sur les communications par satellites pour le Québec, 12 July 1967.
90 MAE/225/Voyage de M. Peyrefitte, ministre de l'Éducation nationale au Québec – Jurgensen to MAE, Relations Culturelles, 8 September 1967.
91 DEA/10046/20-1-2-FR/9 – Halstead to Cadieux, 17 October 1967. See also DEA/10046/20-1-2-FR/9 – Léger to Cadieux, 13 October 1967.
92 MAE/257 – Jurgensen to Debré, 14 October 1968; MAE/215/Voyage en France du M. Bertrand, Premier Ministre du Québec, non-réalisé – Compte Rendu des Entretiens Officiels entre la Délégation Française et la Délégation Québécoise au Département, le 22 janvier 1969.
93 DEA/11604/30-6-QUE/5 – Black to Halstead, 25 November 1968; DEA/10047/20-1-2-FR/18 – Canadian Embassy, Paris to DEA, 20 December 1968; DEA/11604/30-6-QUE/6 – Beaulieu to DEA, 17 January 1969; DEA/11604/30-6-QUE/6 – Sharp to Trudeau, 17 January 1969.
94 ANQ/E5/1985-05-002/1/De Gaulle 1967 – Debré to Cardinal, 24 January 1969.
95 DEA/8646/20-1-2-FR/19 – Canadian Embassy, Paris to DEA, 27 January 1969; DEA/8646/20-1-2-FR/19 – Legal Affairs Division to Legal Adviser, 29 January 1969; DEA/8646/20-1-2-FR/20 – Canadian Embassy, Paris to DEA, 6 February 1969.
96 ANQ/E10/1983-05-000/157/Relations Fédérales-Provinciales, Satellites (1) – Simon to L'Allier, 22 June 1970.
97 Hayday, *Bilingual Today*, 36-37, 42.
98 ANQ/P776/2001-01-006/4/MAI – Dorin to Masse, 25 March 1996; MAE/457/Acadiens, Séjour en France d'une délégation acadienne [Acadiens]/Protocole – Note pour la direction générale des relations culturelles from MAE, Amérique, 26 December 1967; MAE/455/Acadiens – Azan to French Ambassador, Ottawa, 19 September 1968; MAE/457/Acadiens/Séjour en France de la délégation acadienne – MAE to French Embassy, Ottawa, 23 January 1968; Peyrefitte, *De Gaulle*, 95-97, 105, 112-116.
99 DEA/10046/20-1-2-FR/12 – Martin to Pearson, 17 January 1968.
100 MC/8/15 – Journal, 8 January 1967. See also MC/8/15 – Journal, 15 January 1968; DEA/10046/20-1-2-FR/12 – Cadieux to Pearson, 19 January 1968.
101 MAE/455/Acadiens – Leduc to Couve de Murville, MAE, Amérique, 29 December 1967; MAE/457/Acadiens/Réunions de Travail – Compte rendu de la séance de travail tenue le 11 janvier avec les représentants de la Société nationale des acadiens sous la présidence de Monsieur André Bettencourt, Secrétaire d'État aux Affaires Extérieures.
102 MAE/455/Acadiens – Note for the Secrétaire-Général, 2 April 1968; MAE/455/Acadiens – Note, 11 April 1968.

103 MAE/455/Acadiens – Note pour le Secrétaire-Général, 17 April 1968; MAE/455/Acadiens – Note pour le Cabinet du Ministre, 30 December 1968; MAE/456/Acadiens – Note pour le ministre, 25 February 1969.
104 DEA/10046/20-FR-1-2/13 – DEA to Canadian Embassy, Paris, 3 April 1968.
105 MAE/455/Acadiens – Compte rendu de la réunion organisée par la Direction d'Amérique, le vendredi 15 décembre 1967 sur la coopération Franco-Acadienne; MAE/455/Acadiens – Leduc to MAE, Relations Culturelles, 22 May 1968.
106 Pichette, *L'Acadie par bonheur*, 140-141.
107 MAE/455/Acadiens – Leduc to MAE, Relations Culturelles, 22 May 1968.
108 MC/4/10/Journal – 27 August 1968; MAE/211/Voyage de M. Rossillon au Manitoba et incident entre la France et le Canada, septembre 1968 [Rossillon] – Bourdon to Siraud, 4 September 1968; DEA/10046/20-1-2-FR/16 – Cultural Affairs Division to Gotlieb, 6 September 1968.
109 DEA/10046/20-1-2-FR/16 – Cadieux to Sharp, Conversation with the French Ambassador, 11 September 1968.
110 *The Ottawa Citizen*, 17 September 1968, "Rossillon termed 'sympathetic' visitor," 11. See also DEA/10046/20-1-2-FR/16 – Cadieux to Sharp, 16 September 1968.
111 MC/4/10/Journal – 27 August 1968.
112 *The Globe and Mail*, 12 September 1968, "PM assails 'secret agents' of Paris," A1.
113 Trudeau denied referring to Rossillon as a "secret agent." In his account, Eldon Black echoes this position, suggesting that the press combined the prime minister's use of the word "agent" and his reference to "surreptitious." Black, *Direct Intervention*, 47-51. See also *The Globe and Mail*, 16 September 1968, "Was no secret over Rossillon, Trudeau says," A8.
114 Black, *Direct Intervention*, 51; MAE/211/Rossillon – Siraud to MAE, 11 September 1968; Thomson, *Vive*, 282.
115 DEA/10046/20-1-2-FR/16 – Léger to DEA, 17 September 1968; MC/4/9/Journal – 19 September 1968.
116 Bosher, *Gaullist Attack*, 24-25, 106-107. Bosher is critical of Trudeau's handling of the Rossillon affair, accusing him of going off "half-cocked" and consequently being forced to retreat.
117 RB/006/35 – Siraud; Bastien, *Relations particulières*, 104; MAE/RCST/DG2/94/Haut comité pour la défense de la langue française – MAE, Bureau des Échanges culturels et socio-culturels, Organisations internationales, Note sur le Haut comité de la langue française, 24 February 1970. See also Peyrefitte, *De Gaulle*, 79. Peyrefitte claims that Georges Pompidou described Rossillon as an "extremist" and a trouble-maker.
118 MAE/211/Rossillon – Jurgensen to Debré, 11 September 1968.
119 DEA/8647/20-1-2-FR/26 – Blanchette to GEU, 17 December 1969; DEA/8647/20-1-2-FR/27 – Sharp to Trudeau, 28 April 1970.
120 DEA/8647/20-1-2-FR/26 – Black to Halstead, 16 January 1970; Black, *Direct Intervention*, 52, 95; Donneur, "Les relations Franco-Canadiennes," 194.
121 DEA/8647/20-1-2-FR/26 – Black to Halstead, 16 January 1970. See also MAE/201 – Siraud to MAE, Amérique, 26 September 1968.
122 DEA/8647/20-1-2-FR/27 – Tremblay to Sharp, 11 May 1970; Black, *Direct Intervention*, 144-146.
123 MAE/216 – de Menthon to MAE, Amérique, 17 October 1969; DEA/8647/20-1-2-FR/27 – Canadian Embassy, Paris to DEA, 16 March 1970.
124 MAE/203 – Sharp to Siraud, 11 May 1970; Black, *Direct Intervention*, 151-152.
125 ANF/5AG2/1021 – Note, 5/6 février 1970; MAE/203 – Siraud to MAE, Amérique, 12 May 1970; MAE/203 – Morin to Chapdelaine, 19 May 1970.

126 ANF/5AG2/1021 – Siraud to MAE, 12 May 1970.
127 MAE/203 – French Embassy, Rome to MAE, Amérique, 27 May 1970; DEA/8647/20-1-2-FR/27 – Canadian Embassy, Rome, to DEA, 27 May 1970.

Chapter 11: Is Paris Turning?

1 Black, *Direct Intervention*, 98.
2 PCO/6323/Cabinet Conclusion, 28 November 1967, Reply of the Canadian Government to General de Gaulle. See also DEA/10097/20-1-2-FR/5 – George to Halstead, 17 January 1967; Hilliker and Barry, *Canada's Department*, 397; Thomson, *Vive*, 232.
3 Axworthy, "'To Stand Not So High,'" 23. See also Schlegel, "Containing Quebec Abroad," 160.
4 MC/8/14 – Journal, 27 February 1968; MC/8/13 – Cadieux to Tremblay, 16 May 1968.
5 FCO/113 – Account of Conversation between Reilly and Léger, 5 June 1968.
6 LBP/N7/1/De Gaulle 1967 – Note to File, undated; Black, *Direct Intervention*, 37.
7 MAE/RCST/DG1/58/Canada, Dossier ensemble 1961-1968/Visites personnalités – Leduc to MAE, 7 April 1968. See also MAE/201 – Leduc to MAE, Amérique, 8 April 1968; MAE/267 – Leduc to MAE, Amérique, 9 May 1968; MAE/463/Francophonie, Conférence de Paris [Paris] – Leduc to MAE, 10 April 1968.
8 DEA/9809/21-F-11-1979/1/MF4153 – IAC Assessment 4/79, Canadian National Unity: Current French Attitudes and Policies.
9 Black, *Direct Intervention*, 37.
10 House of Commons, *Debates, Official Report, (Hansard)*, 16 September 1968, 66-67; Black, *Direct Intervention*, 51; MAE/201 – Siraud to MAE, Amérique, 26 September 1968.
11 Peyrefitte, *De Gaulle*, 99-101; Lescop, *Le pari québécois*, 69.
12 MAE/214/Voyage en France de M. Daniel Johnson, Premier Ministre du Québec [Johnson] – de Menthon to MAE, Amérique, 4 March 1968; MC/8/14 – Cadieux to Tremblay, 11 March 1968; MAE/214/Johnson – de Menthon to MAE, Amérique, 25 July 1968.
13 MAE/215/Voyage en France du M. Bertrand, Premier Ministre du Québec, non-réalisé [Bertrand] – de Menthon to MAE, Amérique, 3 October 1968.
14 Morin, *L'art de l'impossible*, 89-95.
15 MAE/215/Bertrand – de Menthon to MAE, Amérique, 23 December 1968; MAE/213 – de Menthon to MAE, Amérique, 18 February 1969.
16 MAE/201 – de Menthon to MAE, Amérique, 7 June 1968; DEA/10046/20-1-2-FR/15 – Canadian Embassy, Paris to DEA, 15 July 1968; MC/8/13 – Cadieux to Tremblay, 27 June 1968.
17 ANQ/P776/2001-01-006/1/Reportage Politique, 1967-1974 [Reportage] – Chapdelaine to Morin, 2 August 1968; DEA/10046/20-1-2-FR/16 – Canadian Embassy, Paris to DEA, 17 September 1968.
18 MAE/467/Francophonie, Conférence de Niamey [Niamey] – de Lipkowski to Foccart, 2 February 1970; Gaillard, *Foccart Parle*, 266-267.
19 ANQ/E42/1995-02-001/147/Statut du Québec, CME Conférence générale, 1968 [CME] – Morin, Quelques Brèves Réflexions sur Kinshasa, 20 December 1968.
20 MC/8/13 – Journal, 25 March 1968.
21 Schlegel, *Deceptive Ash*, 261; DEA/3163/32-1968-1 – Chevrier Mission Report.
22 Gendron, *Towards a Francophone Community*, 134-135; MAE/462/Francophonie, Conférence de Libreville et rupture des relations diplomatiques Canada-Gabon [Libreville] – Delauney to Couve de Murville, MAE, Affaires africaines et malgaches, 30 March 1968.
23 MC/8/13 – Journal, 14 March 1968; MC/8/13 – Cadieux to Tremblay, 27 June 1968. See also Schlegel, *Deceptive Ash*, 271. Canadian aid to francophone Africa rose by 87 percent from 1967 to 1968.

24 DEA/10140/30-12-QUE/1 – Lesage to Pearson, 19 February 1965; ANQ/E42/1995-02-001/7/ France-Actim, Ententes and Accords – Note to R. Morin, 13 February 1964.
25 DEA/10140/30-12-QUE/1 – European Division to USSEA, 1 April 1965; LBP/N3/321/840-F815 – Martin to Pearson, 26 April 1965; DEA/10140/30-12-QUE/4 – Yalden to Economic Division, 28 August 1967; Gendron, *Towards a Francophone Community*, 107-114.
26 Gendron, *Towards a Francophone Community*, 87-88; JL/4/10 – Léger to Martin, 27 January 1966.
27 DEA/8647/20-1-2-FR/25 – Sharp to Trudeau, 20 October 1969; Schlegel, *Deceptive Ash*, 374.
28 MAE/249 – Leduc to MAE, Amérique, 27 January 1968; ANQ/E42/1988-08-021/16/Agence canadienne de développement international, A – Tremblay to Minister of Education, undated; MAE/249 – Note, 13 February 1968; MAE/RCST/DG1/71/Québec, Commissions interministérielles – Compte rendu final de la séance du 5 février 1968 de la Commission interministérielle pour les questions de coopération entre la France et le Québec, 22 April 1968; MAE/249 – MAE, Affaires Politiques, to French Embassy, Algiers, Tunis, Rabat, Dakar, Yaounde, Abidjan, Niamey, etc., 14 February 1968.
29 ANQ/P422/S2/1995-01-008/2/8 – Note de Service, 22 October 1968; ANQ/E42/1995-02-001/147/CME – Chapdelaine to Morin, 19 September 1968; ANQ/P762/1999-10-011/61/ Relations internationales du Québec, Conférence de Niamey au Niger, 1969-1970 [Niamey] – Chapdelaine to Morin, 28 November 1968. See also Baulin, *Conseiller du Président Diori*, 58.
30 MAE/462/Libreville – de Menthon to MAE, Amérique, 5 March 1968; MAE/463/Paris – Leduc to MAE, 26 April 1968; MAE/465 – de Menthon to MAE, 18 October 1968; MAE/465 – Jurgensen to de Lipkowski, 28 January 1969.
31 ANQ/P762/1999-10-011/61/Niamey – Chapdelaine to Morin, 28 November 1968.
32 Lefèvre, *Charles de Gaulle*, 179-180; Baulin, *Conseiller du Président*, 60.
33 Morin, *L'art de l'impossible*, 146-147.
34 MAE/461/Francophonie – Annexe, Historique des conférences des Ministres de l'Éducation des pays africains et malgache d'Expression française [Historique].
35 MAE/461/Francophonie – Historique; MAE/464/Francophonie, Conférence de Kinshasa [Kinshasa] – Souza to French Consulate, Quebec, 23 December 1968; ANQ/E42/1995-02-001/147/CME – Morin, Quelques Brèves Réflexions sur Kinshasa, 20 December 1968; ANQ/E42/1995-02-001/147/CME – Chapdelaine to Morin, 21 December 1968.
36 MAE/465 – Alphand to French Consulate, Québec, 30 November 1968; MAE/464/Kinshasa – de Menthon to MAE, Amérique, 23 December 1968; MAE/464/Kinshasa – de Menthon to MAE, 24 December 1968.
37 MAE/465 – de Menthon to MAE, 31 December 1968.
38 MAE/464/Kinshasa – MAE, Afrique-Levant to French Embassy, Kinshasa, 31 December 1968; MAE/464/Kinshasa – Courson to MAE, Amérique, 7 January 1969; MAE/464/Kinshasa – Chenet to MAE, pour Délégation Générale Québec, 7 January 1969.
39 MAE/213 – de Menthon to unknown, MAE, 8 January 1969.
40 MAE/331 – Siraud to MAE, Amérique, 13 January 1969; Granatstein and Bothwell, *Pirouette*, 139; Morin, *L'art de l'impossible*, 148-154; Foccart, *Le Général en mai*, 533.
41 MAE/464/Kinshasa – Bourges to MAE, 13 January 1969; DEA/10687/26-4-1969-NIAMEY/2 – Report of a Meeting February 5, 1969 in Quebec City concerning the Niamey Conference, 6 February 1969; DEA/8646/20-1-2-FR/20 – Canadian Embassy, Paris to DEA, 6 February 1969.
42 ANQ/P776/2001-01-006/3/Dossier Personnel – Morin to Chapdelaine, 8 January 1969; Morin, *L'art de l'impossible*, 198-199.
43 MAE/465 – Alphand to French Embassy, Niamey, 8 November 1968.

44 DEA/10687/26-4-1969-NIAMEY/1 – SSEA to Trudeau, 25 November 1968; Black, *Direct Intervention*, 89.
45 DEA/10687/26-4-1969-NIAMEY/1 – Canadian High Commission, Accra to DEA, 24 January 1968; MAE/465 – Debré to French Embassy, Niamey, 1 November 1968; MAE/465 – Alphand to French Embassy, Niamey, 8 November 1968; MAE/465 – Wintrebert to MAE, 14 November 1968; MAE/465 – MAE, Amérique to French Embassy, Niamey, 15 November 1968.
46 DEA/10687/26-4-1969-NIAMEY/1 – Diori to Trudeau, 18 November 1968; DEA/10687/26-4-1969-NIAMEY/1 – Malone to DEA, 20 November 1968; MAE/465 – de Menthon to MAE, Amérique, 21 November 1968.
47 MAE/465 – de Menthon to MAE, Amérique, 21 November 1968; MAE/465 – de Menthon to MAE, Amérique, 2 December 1968.
48 MAE/465 – Jurgensen to French Consulate, Quebec, 23 December 1968.
49 Decisions at the Niamey conference were reached by consensus, so that this condition, although significant in the abstract, remained without practical effect.
50 MAE/464/Kinshasa – de Menthon to MAE, 24 December 1968; ANQ/P776/2001-01-006/4/Niamey, 1969-1970 [Niamey] – Morin to Chapdelaine, 21 February 1969; Black, *Direct Intervention*, 90.
51 MAE/465 – de Menthon to MAE, 7 February 1969; MAE/465 – Siraud to MAE, 14 February 1969; Morin, *L'Art de l'impossible*, 154-155; Léger, *La Francophonie*, 105-106.
52 Black, *Direct Intervention*, 91; Léger, *Le Temps dissipé*, 400-403.
53 ANQ/P776/2001-01-006/3/Dossier Personnel – Morin to Chapdelaine, 8 January 1969; ANQ/P776/2001-01-006/3/Dossier Personnel – Chapdelaine to Héroux, 21 November 1969.
54 DEA/10046/20-1-2-FR/9 – Cadieux to Yalden, 25 October 1967; ANQ/E42/2002-04-003/210/Délégation du Québec à Paris – Morin to Loiselle, 12 February 1968.
55 ANQ/P776/2001-01-006/1/Reportage – Chapdelaine to Morin, 7 May 1969; ANQ/P762/1999-10-011/60/Mémoires aux Premiers Ministres, Memos de M. Morin aux Premiers Ministres, 1962-1976 [Memos] – Morin to Bertrand, 15 July 1969.
56 ANQ/P762/1999-10-011/60/Memos – Morin to Bertrand, 15 July 1969.
57 Ibid.
58 MC/12/11 – Cadieux to Tremblay, 5 May 1969.
59 DEA/8647/20-1-2-FR/21 – Canadian Embassy, Paris to DEA, 30 April 1969.
60 DEA/8647/20-1-2-FR/22 – Périard to Halstead, 5 June 1969.
61 DEA/8647/20-1-2-FR/22 – Beaulieu to DEA, 2 June 1969.
62 ANQ/P762/1999-10-011/60/Memos – Morin to Bertrand, 15 July 1969.
63 DEA/8647/20-1-2-FR/23 – Canadian Embassy, Paris to DEA, 30 June 1969; DEA/8647/20-1-2-FR/25 – Black to Halstead, 24 October 1969; Black, *Direct Intervention*, 101-103.
64 DEA/8647/20-1-2-FR/22 – Les élections présidentielles en France: L'avenir des relations France-Canada, undated; Black, *Direct intervention*, 103-105.
65 Comeau and Fournier, *Le Lobby du Québec*, 89; Black, *Direct Intervention*, 99.
66 Knapp, *Le Gaullisme*, 29-42; Berstein and Rioux, *La France de l'expansion*, 72; Garrigues, *La France de la Ve République*, 24, 330; Vallon, *L'Anti de Gaulle*.
67 Bastien, *Relations particulières*, 31-34; Black, *Direct Intervention*, 108.
68 ANQ/P762/1999-10-011/60/Memos – Morin to Bertrand, 15 July 1969; ANQ/P776/2001-01-006/1/Reportage – Chapdelaine to Morin, 27 May 1970.
69 ANQ/P776/2001-01-006/1/Reportage – Chapdelaine to Morin, 10 July 1969; DEA/8647/20-1-2-FR/24 – Robinson to Sharp, 17 July 1969.
70 DEA/8647/20-1-2-FR/24 – Beaulieu to DEA, 21 July 1969; DEA/8647/20-1-2-FR/24 – Les relations France-Canada, Perspectives à moyen terme, 13 August 1969.

71 DEA/10079/20-FR-9/11 – Black to DEA, 22 August 1969.
72 ANF/5AG2/1049/Annotations du Président – Canada 18/19 septembre 1969, tél no. 659/61 d'Ottawa, cl. Canada.
73 ANF/5AG2/1021/Correspondance – Note, tél no. 610/18 de Québec du 20/21 août 1969; Black, *Direct Intervention,* 109.
74 DEA/8647/20-1-2-FR/24 – Sharp to DEA and PMO (Lalonde), 24 September 1969.
75 DEA/8647/20-1-2-FR/25 – Black to Halstead, 10 October 1969.
76 ANF/5AG2/1021/correspondance – Note, 30 septembre/1 octobre 1969, tél no. 723/30 d'Ottawa, cl. Québec, visite Lipkowski et Canada. See also ANF/5AG2/1021 – Gaucher to Pompidou, 6 October 1969; Bastien, *Relations particulières,* 38-43.
77 MC/12/11 – Journal, 14 October 1969.
78 PCO/6340/Cabinet Conclusion, 15 October 1969, Question of the relations between France and Canada; Black, *Direct Intervention,* 113-116.
79 DEA/8647/20-1-2-FR/25 – Black to Halstead, 7 November 1969. See also ANF/5AG2/1021/ Correspondance – Note, 23 octobre 1969, tél no. 927/30 d'Ottawa, cl. Canada (et Notes du Président), rappel à Québec; ANF/5AG2/1021/Correspondance – Siraud to MAE, 24 October 1969; ANF/5AG2/115/Correspondances avec le Président Pompidou – Entretien entre M. de Lipkowski et l'Ambassadeur du Canada à Paris, 28 October 1969; Black, *Direct Intervention,* 118.
80 DEA/8647/20-1-2-FR/25 – Mathieu to Black, 18 November 1969.
81 DEA/8647/20-1-2-FR/26 – Beaulieu to DEA, 12 December 1969; DEA/8647/20-1-2-FR/26 – Cadieux to Canadian Embassy, Paris, 29 December 1969; Black, *Direct Intervention,* 125.
82 MC/12/11 – Cadieux to Tremblay, 5 May 1969; DEA/8647/20-1-2-FR/23 – Canadian Embassy, Paris to DEA, 19 June 1969.
83 ANQ/P762/1999-10-011/60/Memos – Morin to Bertrand, 15 July 1969; ANQ/P776/2001 -01-006/4/Ministère des Affaires intergouvernementales, 1969-1996 – Dorin to Masse, 25 March 1996; Peyrefitte, *De Gaulle,* 79.
84 MAE/466/Francophonie, Conférence de Paris [Paris] – Canadian Embassy, Paris, Aide Mémoire, 27 March 1969; MC/12/11 – Aide Mémoire, 23 September 1969.
85 MAE/466/Paris – Jurgensen to Secrétaire-Général, 3 April 1969; MAE/466/Paris – Alphand to French Consulate, Québec, 17 March 1969.
86 MAE/466/Paris – Chauvet to MAE, 23 July 1969; Morin, *L'art de l'impossible,* 159-161; MAE/466/Paris – De Sourza to French Consulate, Quebec, 11 September 1969; MAE/466/ Paris – De Sourza to French Embassy, Ottawa, 11 September 1969.
87 DEA/8647/20-1-2-FR/24 – Sharp to DEA and PMO (Lalonde), 24 September 1969; Black, *Direct Intervention,* 111.
88 MAE/466 – Siraud to MAE, 19 September 1969; MC/12/11 – Record of Conversation, 29 September 1969; MAE/466/Paris – Siraud to MAE, 28 September 1969.
89 Pompidou had declared that "it was necessary to not give in" to Ottawa. ANF/5AG2/1021/ Correspondance – Note, 24/25 septembre 1969, Entretien entre M. Sharp, Secrétaire aux Affaires Extérieures du Canada, et M. Maurice Schumann, tél no. 2889/99 de New-York, cl. Conférence des Ministres de l'Éducation – Annotation du Président de la République; Black, *Direct Intervention,* 124.
90 DEA/8647/20-1-2-FR/25 – Sharp to Trudeau, 20 October 1969; DEA/10688/26-4-1969 -NIAMEY/8 – Canadian Embassy, Paris to DEA, 23 October 1969; MAE/467/Francophonie, Conférence de Nouakchott, 23-27 février 1970 [Nouakchott] – Treca to French Embassy, Nouakchott, 28 January 1970.
91 MAE/467/Nouakchott – de Menthon to MAE, Amérique, 20 December 1969; MAE/467/ Nouakchott – de Menthon to MAE, Amérique, 29 January 1970; MAE/467/Nouakchott – Alphand to French Embassy, Nouakchott, 21 December 1969; MAE/467/Nouakchott

- Dufour to MAE, 9 February 1970; Patry, *Le Québec dans le monde,* 125; Black, *Direct Intervention,* 124.
92 MAE/474 – Suggestions pour une position française sur les principaux problèmes soulevés par la création de l'Agence de coopération culturelle et technique, undated [circa 13 November 1969]; MAE/461/ Francophonie – de Beaumarchais to French Embassy, Niamey, 11 December 1969.
93 Foccart, *Dans les bottes,* 208; MAE/474 – de Menthon to MAE, 5 November 1969; MAE/467/ Nouakchott – de Menthon to MAE, Amérique, 31 January 1970; MAE/467/Niamey – de Menthon to MAE, 6 February 1970; MAE/474 – Wintrebert to MAE, 1 December 1969; MAE/467/Niamey – Compte rendu de l'entretien de M. de Lipkowski et de M. Alliot, Conseiller de Président Diori, 23 January 1970 [compte rendu]; MAE/467/Niamey – Jurgensen to French Embassy, Niamey, 10 February 1970.
94 MAE/467/Niamey – Wibaux to MAE, 3 February 1970; MAE/467/Niamey – de Lipkowski to French Embassy, Dakar and Abidjan, 4 February 1970; MAE/467/Niamey – Raphael-Leygues, French Embassy, Abidjan, 14 February 1970; DEA/10688/26-4-1969-NIAMEY/11 – de Goumois to DEA, 15 February 1970.
95 MAE/474 – Wintrebert to MAE, 1 December 1969; MAE/467/Niamey – Wintrebert to MAE, 12 February 1970; Baulin, *Conseiller du Président,* 80-81.
96 MAE/467/Niamey – Chateauvieux to MAE, 18 February 1970; MAE/467/Niamey – Alphand to de Menthon, 18 February 1970; MAE/467/Niamey – de Menthon to MAE, 19 February 1970.
97 MAE/232 – Note for the Secrétaire d'État, 16 September 1969; MAE/474 – Note pour le Cabinet du Secrétaire d'État, 13 November 1969; MAE/474 –Alphand to French Embassy, Niamey, 29 November 1969; MAE 474 – Wintrebert to MAE, 1 December 1969; MAE/467/ Niamey – Compte rendu; MAE/474 – Alphand to French Embassy, Ottawa, 27 January 1970.
98 MAE/474 – Suggestions pour une position française sur les principaux problèmes soulevés par la création de l'Agence de coopération culturelle et technique, undated [circa 13 November 1969]; MAE/467/Niamey – Jurgensen, Circular Telegram 90, 7 March 1970.
99 DEA/10688/26-4-1969-NIAMEY/10 – Stansfield to SSEA (PDM), 6 February 1970.
100 DEA/8647/20-1-2-FR/26 – Canadian Embassy, Paris to DEA, 20 February 1970; DEA/10691/26-4-1970-NIAMEY/2 – de Goumois to Bissonnette, 12 March 1970; Foccart, *Dans les bottes,* 233-234.
101 MAE/467/Niamey – Compte rendu.
102 DEA/10688/26-4-1969-NIAMEY/11 – de Goumois to DEA, 15 February 1970; MAE/467/ Niamey – Chateauvieux to MAE, 18 February 1970. See also Baulin, *Conseiller du Président,* 66, 80-81; Schlegel, *Deceptive Ash,* 299.
103 DEA/10691/26-4-1970-NIAMEY/1 – Tremblay, Discuté avec l'Ambassadeur de France, 27 February 1970.
104 Bastien, *Relations particulières,* 57; DEA/8647/20-1-2-FR/26 – Canadian Embassy, Paris to DEA, 6 March 1970.
105 ANF/5AG2/1039 – Raimond to Jobert, 6 March 1970.
106 MAE/467/Niamey – de Menthon to MAE, 19 February 1970; MAE/467/Niamey – Alphand to de Menthon, 20 February 1970.
107 Foccart, *Dans les bottes,* 241.
108 Ibid., 208, 237.
109 MAE/467/Niamey – Alphand to de Menthon, 9 March 1970.
110 DEA/10691/26-4-1970-NIAMEY/1 – Trudeau to Bertrand, 6 March 1970.

111 ANQ/P776/2001-01-006/4/Niamey – Morin to Chapdelaine, 9 March 1970; ANQ/P762/1999-10-011/62/Relations Internationales du Québec/Documents portant sur la participation du Québec à l'ACCT, 1970-1971 – Bertrand to Trudeau, 10 March 1970.
112 ANQ/P776/2001-01-006/4/Niamey – Morin to Chapdelaine, 13 April 1970; Morin, *L'art de l'impossible*, 217-218.
113 DEA/10691/26-4-1970-NIAMEY/2 – Memorandum to Trudeau, 17 March 1970; Foccart, *Dans les bottes*, 253-254; DEA/10691/26-4-1970-NIAMEY/2 – Pelletier to DEA, 16 March 1970.
114 The federal counter-proposal was that the French provision would not apply to federal states that were themselves signatories to the ACCT charter, thereby ruling it a dead letter in terms of Quebec.
115 DEA/10691/26-4-1970-NIAMEY/2 – Pelletier to DEA, 18 March 1970; Bastien, *Relations particulières*, 66-68; Granatstein and Bothwell, *Pirouette*, 149-152.
116 ANQ/P776/2001-01-006/4/Niamey – Chapdelaine, Conférence de Niamey II, 16-20 mars 1970, 31 March 1970; ANQ/P776/2001-01-006/4/Niamey 1969-1970 – Morin to Chapdelaine, 13 April 1970.
117 MAE/474 – MAE, Affaires Politiques, Le Directeur Adjoint, Note sur la conférence de Niamey, 24 March 1970.
118 Léger, *La Francophonie*, 119.
119 DEA/10691/26-4-1970-NIAMEY/2 – Bissonnette to GRF, 26 March 1970; DEA/10691/26-4-1970-NIAMEY/2 – Black to DEA, 23 March 1970.
120 PT/8/7 – GEU to PDM (Roquet), 4 August 1970.
121 Black, *Direct Intervention*, 144-148; ANF/5AG2/1021/Correspondance – Siraud to MAE, 12 December 1969; ANF/5AG2/1049/Annotations du Président, 8/9 janvier 1970, tél no. 8/15 d'Ottawa, cl. Canada; ANF/5AG2/1021/Correspondance – Note, 5/6 février 1970, tél no. 113/115 d'Ottawa, cl. Canada, "Visites" rappel à Québec – "Notes du Président."
122 MAE/475 – Chauvet to MAE, Amérique, 18 January 1971; Léger, *La Francophonie*, 131-132.

Conclusions

1 Steger, *Globalization*, 14-15; Cooper, *Colonialism in Question*, 96.
2 Charles A. Cerami, "The U.S. Eyes Greater Europe," *The Spectator*, 5 October 1962, 495; Robert, *Le Nouveau Petit Robert*, 1624.
3 Reynolds, "American Globalism," 258.
4 Taylor, "Izations of the World," 53.
5 Betts, *Decolonization*, 38; Latham, *Liberal Moment*, 49.
6 Latham, *Liberal Moment*, 33, 124-126.

Bibliography

Archival Sources

Library and Archives Canada

MG 26, N3, N6, N7 – Fonds Lester B. Pearson (LBP)
MG 31-E1 – Fonds Marcel Cadieux (MC)
MG 32-B12 – Fonds Paul Martin (PM)
MG 32-A2 – Fonds Georges Vanier (GV)
MG 32-A3 – Fonds Jules Léger (JL)
R285 – Fonds Paul Tremblay (PT)
RG 2 – Privy Council Office (PCO)
   Series A-5-a
RG 20 – Industry, Trade and Commerce (ITC)
   Series A-3, A-4
RG 25 – Department of External Affairs (DEA)
   Series A-3-b, A-3-c, A-4, D-1, G-2

Bibliothèque et Archives nationales du Québec (ANQ)

E4 – Fonds Secrétariat de la Province
E5 – Fonds Conseil Exécutif
E6 – Fonds Ministère de la Culture et des Communications
E10 – Fonds Ministère des Communications
E16 – Fonds Ministère de l'Industrie et Commerce
E42 – Fonds Ministère des Relations internationales
P422 – Fonds André Patry
P599 – Fonds Jean-Marc Léger
P688 – Fonds Jean Lesage
P762 – Fonds Claude Morin
P776 – Fonds Jean Chapdelaine

Archives d'histoire contemporaine (AHC)

4BA – Fonds Wilfrid Baumgartner (WB)
CM – Fonds Maurice Couve de Murville (CM)

Archives du Ministère des Affaires étrangères, France (MAE)

Séries B, Amérique
   Sous-séries Canada, 1944-1952, 1952-1963, 1964-1970, 1971-1975
Séries Cabinet du Ministre, Schuman, 1948-1953 (Schuman)
Service de Coopération économique, 1945-1966
   Série Affaires Économiques et Financières
   Sous-série Coopération économique, 1945-1966 (AE-CE)
Direction générale des Relations culturelles, scientifiques et techniques (RCST)
Cabinet du Directeur Général, 1946-1968 (DG1)
Cabinet du Directeur Général, 1969-1972, Pierre Laurent (DG2)
Œuvres diverses – échanges culturels, 1945-1959 (EC)
Enseignement, 1945-1961 (Enseignement)

Archives nationales, France (ANF)

3AG1 – Fonds De Gaulle
5AG1 – Fonds De Gaulle (Fifth Republic)
5AG2 – Fonds Pompidou

National Archives, United Kingdom

FCO 23 – Commonwealth Office: Atlantic Department (FCO)

University of Toronto Archives

Fonds Robert Bothwell (RB)
   B-88-007
   B-89-0044B-90-0034-006

Government Collections (various dates)

Canada. Parliament. House of Commons, *Debates, Official Report (Hansard)*. Ottawa: Queen's Printer and Controller of Stationery.
Documents on Canadian External Relations (DCER).
Documents diplomatiques français (DDF).
Foreign Relations of the United States (FRUS).

Newspapers and Periodicals (various dates)

Le Devoir
The Globe and Mail
Informations canadiennes
Le Monde
Le Nouveau Journal
The Ottawa Citizen
Patrie et progrès
Québec Libre
The Spectator

Other Sources

Aglion, Raoul. *Roosevelt and De Gaulle, Allies in Conflict: A Personal Memoir.* New York: The Free Press, 1988.

Aguilar, Manuela. *Cultural Diplomacy and Foreign Policy: German-American Relations, 1955-1968.* New York: Peter Lang, 1996.

Aird, Robert. *André Patry et la présence du Québec dans le monde.* Montreal: VLB éditeur, 2005.

Alphand, Hervé. *L'étonnement d'être, Journal 1939-1973.* Paris: Fayard, 1977.

Amyot, Éric. *Le Québec entre Pétain et de Gaulle: Vichy, la France libre et les Canadiens français, 1940-1945.* Saint-Laurent, QC: Fides, 1999.

Anderson, Benedict. *Imagined Communities: Reflections on the Origin and Spread of Nationalism.* Revised edition. New York: Verso, 1991.

Angers, François-Albert. "L'épilogue de la visite du Général de Gaulle." *L'Action nationale* 57, 2 (1967): 175-180.

–. "'Le monde saura que nous existons, et nous ne sommes plus seuls.'" *L'Action nationale* 57, 1 (1967): 1-10.

Aquin, Hubert. "L'Existence politique." *Liberté* 21 (1962): 67-76.

–. "Nos cousins de France." In *Point de Fuite,* 67-70. Montreal: Cercle du Livre de France, 1971.

Arbour, Pierre. *Québec Inc., and the Temptation of State Capitalism.* Translated by Madeleine Hébert. Montreal: Robert Davies Publishing, 1993.

Arnavon, Cyrille. *L'américanisme et nous.* Paris: Del Duca, 1958.

Aronsen, Lawrence. "From World War to Cold War: Cooperation and Competition in the North Atlantic Triangle, 1945-1949." In *The North Atlantic Triangle in a Changing World: Anglo-American-Canadian Relations, 1902-1956,* edited by B.J.C. McKercher and Lawrence Aronsen, 184-219. Toronto: University of Toronto Press, 1996.

–. "An Open Door to the North: The Liberal Government and the Expansion of American Foreign Investment, 1945-1953." *American Review of Canadian Studies* 22, 2 (1992): 167-197.

Auriol, Vincent. *Journal du Septennat, 1947-1954, tome 5, 1951,* edited by Laurent Theis. Paris: Librairie Armand Colin, 1975.

Axworthy, Thomas S. "'To Stand Not So High Perhaps but Always Alone': The Foreign Policy of Pierre Elliott Trudeau." In *Towards a Just Society: The Trudeau Years,* edited by Thomas S. Axworthy and Pierre Elliott Trudeau, 12-48. Markham: Viking, 1990.

Azzi, Stephen. *Walter Gordon and the Rise of Canadian Nationalism.* Montreal and Kingston: McGill-Queen's University Press, 1999.

Balthazar, Louis. "Quebec's International Relations: A Response to Needs and Necessities." In *Foreign Relations and Federal States,* edited by Brian Hocking, 140-152. London: Leicester University Press, 1993.

Barjot, Dominique. "Americanisation: Cultural Transfers in the Economic Sphere in the Twentieth Century." *Entreprises et Histoire* 32 (2003): 41-58.

–. *Fougerolle, Deux siècles de savoir-faire.* Caen: Éditions du Lys, 1992.

–. "Lafarge: l'ascension d'une multinationale à la française (1833-2005)." *Relations internationales* 124 (2005): 51-67.

Bastien, Frédéric. *Relations particulières: La France face au Québec après de Gaulle.* Montreal: Boréal, 1999.

Bastien, Hervé. "Malraux et le Québec au service du Général." In *André Malraux et le rayonnement culturel de la France,* edited by Charles-Louis Foulon, 191-200. Brussels: Éditions Complexe, 2004.

Baulin, Jacques. *Conseiller du Président Diori*. Paris: Eurafor Press, 1986.
Beaudet, Pierre. *Qui aide qui? Une brève histoire de la solidarité internationale au Québec*. Montreal: Boréal, 2009.
Behiels, Michael D. *Prelude to Québec's Quiet Revolution: Liberalism versus Neo-Nationalism, 1945-1960*. Montreal and Kingston: McGill-Queen's University Press, 1985.
–. *Quebec and the Question of Immigration: From Ethnocentrism to Ethnic Pluralism, 1900-1985*. Ottawa: Canadian Historical Association, 1991.
Bell, David A. *The Cult of the Nation in France: Inventing Nationalism, 1680-1800*. Cambridge: Harvard University Press, 2001.
Bergeron, Gérard. *Le Canada-Français après deux siècles de patience*. Paris: Éditions du Seuil, 1967.
Berque, Jacques. "Préface." In *Parti pris, Les québécois*, 7-16. Paris/Montreal: Librairie François Maspero/Éditions Parti pris, 1967.
–. "Les révoltés du Québec." *France-Observateur* 1, 2 (1963): 10-11.
Berstein, Serge. *La France de l'expansion, tome 1, La République gaullienne, 1958-1969*. Paris: Éditions du Seuil, 1989.
–. *Histoire du gaullisme*. Paris: Perrin, 2001.
Berstein, Serge, and Jean-Pierre Rioux. *La France de l'expansion, tome 2, L'apogée Pompidou, 1969-1974*. Paris: Éditions du Seuil, 1995.
Betts, Raymond F. *Decolonization*. Routledge, 1998.
–. *France and Decolonization, 1900-1960*. New York: St. Martin's Press, 1991.
Black, Conrad. *Duplessis*. Toronto: McClelland and Stewart, 1977.
Black, Eldon. *Direct Intervention: Canada-France Relations, 1967-1974*. Ottawa: Carleton University Press, 1997.
Blain, Maurice. "Sur la liberté de l'esprit." *Esprit* 20, 193-194 (1952): 201-213.
Bloch-Lainé, François, and Jean Bouvier. *La France restaurée, 1944-1954. Dialogue sur les choix d'une modernisation*, prologue de Jean-Pierre Rioux. Paris: Fayard, 1986.
Borduas, Paul-Émile, et al. *Refus global, En regard du surréalisme actuel*. Montreal: Mithra-Mythe éditeur, 1948.
Bosher, J.F. *The Gaullist Attack on Canada, 1967-1997*. Montreal and Kingston: McGill-Queen's University Press, 1999.
Bothwell, Robert. *Alliance and Illusion, Canada and the World, 1945-1984*. Vancouver: UBC Press, 2007.
–. "Marcel Cadieux: The Ultimate Professional." In *Architects and Innovators: Building the Department of Foreign Affairs and International Trade, 1909-2009*, edited by Greg Donaghy and Kim Richard Nossal, 207-222. Montreal and Kingston: School of Policy Studies, Queen's University and McGill-Queen's University Press, 2009.
Bouchard, Chantal. *La langue et le nombril: Histoire d'une obsession québécoise*. Montreal: Fides, 1998.
Bouchard, Gérard. *Entre l'Ancien et le Nouveau Monde: Le Québec comme population neuve et culture fondatrice*. Ottawa: Les Presses de l'Université d'Ottawa, 1996.
Bourgault, Pierre. *Écrits polémiques 1960-1981, tome 1, Le politique*. Montreal: VLB éditeur, 1983.
Bourniquel, Camille, and J.-M. Domenach. "Le français, langue vivante." *Esprit* 30, 311 (1962): 561-563.
Bouthillier, Guy. "Les indépendantistes québécois et le général de Gaulle." In Institut Charles de Gaulle, *De Gaulle en son siècle, tome 6, Liberté et dignité des peuples*, 1417-1435. Paris: La Documentation Française-Plon, 1992.
Bozo, Frédéric. *Deux stratégies pour l'Europe, De Gaulle, les États-Unis et l'Alliance atlantique*. Paris: Plon/Fondation Charles de Gaulle, 1996.

Breton, Raymond. "From Ethnic to Civic Nationalism: English Canada and Quebec." *Ethnic and Racial Studies* 11, 1 (1988): 85-102.
Brittain, Donald. "Unlikely Warriors." *The Champions*, part 1. Montreal: National Film Board of Canada, 1978.
Brogi, Alessandro. *A Question of Self-Esteem: The United States and the Cold War Choices in France and Italy, 1944-1958*. Westport, CT: Praeger, 2002.
Brubaker, Rogers. *Citizenship and Nationhood in France and Germany*. Cambridge: Harvard University Press, 1992.
Brunelle, Dorval. *La désillusion tranquille*. Montreal: Hurtubise HMH, 1978.
Camps, Miriam. *The Management of Interdependence: A Preliminary View*. New York: Council of Foreign Relations, 1974.
Canada. Ambassade du Canada (Paris). *Centre culturel canadien/Canadian Cultural Centre, 25 ans d'activité, 1970-1995*. Paris: Ambassade du Canada, 1997.
Canada. Centre culturel canadien. *Les Relations entre la France et le Canada au XIXe siècle, Colloque, 26 avril 1974, organisé par le Centre culturel canadien*. Paris: Centre culturel canadien, 1974.
Canada. Department of External Affairs. "Canada and 'la Francophonie': Speech by the Secretary of State for External Affairs, the Honourable Paul Martin, Montreal, March 11, 1967." *Statements and Speeches 1967-1968*. Government of Canada, 1968.
Canada. Department of Finance. *Estimates for the Fiscal Year ending March 31, 1963*. Ottawa: Queen's Printer, 1962.
Canada. Minister of Reconstruction. *Employment and Income, with Special Reference to the Initial Period of Reconstruction*. Ottawa: King's Printer, 1945.
Canada. Minister of Trade and Commerce. Dominion Bureau of Statistics. *Canada Year Book 1960*. Ottawa: Queen's Printer, 1960.
–. *Canada Year Book 1961*. Ottawa: Queen's Printer, 1961.
Canada. Secretary of State for External Affairs. Martin, Paul. *Federalism and International Relations*. Ottawa: Queen's Printer, 1968.
–. Sharp, Mitchell. *Federalism and International Conferences on Education*. Ottawa: Queen's Printer, 1968.
Canada. Statistics Canada. *Canada Year Book 1972*. Ottawa: Information Canada, 1972.
Caron, François. *Histoire économique de la France, XIXe-XXe siècles*. 2nd edition. Paris: Armand Colin, 1995.
Carr, Graham. "Non-State Actors, Border Security, and Cultural Diplomacy in Canada's Cold War." Paper presented at the Annual Meeting of the Canadian Historical Association, University of British Columbia, 2008.
Cerny, P.G. "De Gaulle, the Nation-State and Foreign Policy." *The Review of Politics* 33, 2 (1971): 254-278.
Champion, C.P. "Mike Pearson at Oxford: War, Varsity, and Canadianism." *Canadian Historical Review* 88, 2 (2007): 263-290.
–. *The Strange Demise of British Canada: The Liberals and Canadian Nationalism, 1964-68*. Montreal and Kingston: McGill-Queen's University Press, 2010.
Chapnick, Adam. *The Middle Power Project: Canada and the Founding of the United Nations*. Vancouver: UBC Press, 2005.
Cholette, Gaston. *La coopération économique franco-québécoise, de 1961 à 1997*. Sainte-Foy: Les Presses de l'Université Laval, 1998.
Christie, Nancy, and Michael Gauvreau. "Introduction: Recasting Canada's Post-war Decade." In *Cultures of Citizenship in Post-war Canada, 1940-1955*, edited by Nancy Christie and Michael Gauvreau, 3-26. Montreal and Kingston: McGill-Queen's University Press, 2003.

Clarke, Jackie. "France, America and the Metanarrative of Modernization: From Postwar Social Science to the New Culturalism." *Contemporary French and Francophone Studies* 8, 4 (2004): 365-377.

–. *France in the Age of Organization: Factory, Home and Nation from the 1920s to Vichy.* New York: Berghahn Books, 2011.

Cloutier, Yvan. "Sartre à Montréal en 1946: une censure en crise." *Voix et images* 32, 2 (1998): 266-280.

Cogan, Charles G. *Forced to Choose: France, the Atlantic Alliance, and NATO – Then and Now.* Westport, CT: Praeger, 1997.

–. *Oldest Allies, Guarded Friends: The United States and France since 1940.* Westport, CT: Praeger, 1994.

Coleman, William D. *The Independence Movement in Quebec, 1945-1980.* Toronto: University of Toronto Press, 1984.

Comeau, Paul-André, and Jean-Pierre Fournier. *Le Lobby du Québec à Paris: Les précurseurs du général de Gaulle.* Montreal: Québec-Amérique, 2002.

Connelly, Matthew. *A Diplomatic Revolution: Algeria's Fight for Independence and the Origins of the Post-Cold War Era.* New York: Oxford University Press, 2002.

Cook, Ramsay. *The Maple Leaf Forever: Essays on Nationalism and Politics in Canada.* Toronto: Macmillan of Canada, 1977.

Cooper, Andrew Fenton. "Canadian Cultural Diplomacy: An Introduction." In *Canadian Culture: International Dimensions,* edited by Andrew Fenton Cooper, 3-26. Waterloo: Centre on Foreign Policy and Federalism, University of Waterloo/Wilfrid Laurier University and Canadian Institute of International Affairs, 1985.

Cooper, Frederick. *Colonialism in Question: Theory, Knowledge, History.* Berkeley and Los Angeles: University of California Press, 2005.

Cooper, Richard N. *The Economics of Interdependence: Economic Policy in the Atlantic Community.* New York: McGraw-Hill, 1968.

Coutau-Bégarie, Hervé. "Comment on conduit une coalition: La France et la Grande Bretagne dans l'affaire de Suez." *Histoire, Économie et Société* 13, 1 (1994): 101-109.

Couture, Paul M. "The Politics of Diplomacy: The Crisis of Canada-France Relations, 1940-1942." PhD thesis, York University, 1981.

Couve de Murville, Maurice. "Pearson et la France." *International Journal* 29, 1 (1973/1974): 24-32.

–. *Une politique étrangère, 1958-1969.* Paris: Plon, 1971.

Cuff, R.D., and J.L. Granatstein. *Canadian-American Relations in Wartime: From the Great War to the Cold War.* Toronto: Hakkert, 1975.

Cullather, Nick. "Modernization Theory." In *Explaining the History of American Foreign Relations,* edited by Michael J. Hogan, 212-220. Cambridge: Cambridge University Press, 2004.

d'Allemagne, André. *Le colonialisme au Québec.* Montreal: Les éditions R-B, 1966.

de Gaulle, Charles. *Discours et messages, Vers le terme, janvier 1966-avril 1969.* Paris: Plon, 1970.

–. *Lettres, notes et carnets, janvier 1961-décembre 1963.* Paris: Plon, 1987.

–. *Lettres, notes et carnets, juillet 1966-avril 1969.* Paris: Plon, 1987.

–. *Memoirs of Hope.* Translated by Terence Kilmartin. New York: Simon and Schuster, 1971.

de Gaulle, Philippe. *De Gaulle, mon père: Entretiens avec Michel Tauriac, tome 2.* Paris: Plon, 2004.

de Grazia, Victoria. *Irresistible Empire: America's Advance through Twentieth-Century Europe.* Cambridge: The Belknap Press of Harvard University Press, 2005.

de Menthon, Pierre. *Je témoigne: Québec 1967, Chile 1973*. Paris: Les Éditions du Cerf, 1979.

Dehousse, Renaud. "Fédéralisme, asymétrie et interdépendance: aux origines de l'action internationale des composantes de l'État fédéral." *Études internationales* 20, 2 (1989): 283-309.

Deleuze, Magali. "Le Canada, les Canadiens et la guerre d'Indochine: quelques intérêts communs?" *Guerres mondiales et conflits contemporains* 54, 223 (2006): 17-29.

–. *L'une et l'autre indépendance, 1954-1964: Les médias au Québec et la guerre d'Algérie*. Outremont, QC: Éditions Point de fuite, 2001.

Desbiens, Jean-Paul. *Les insolences du Frère Untel*. Montreal: Éditions de l'Homme, 1960.

Diefenbaker, John G. *One Canada, Memoirs of the Right Honourable John G. Diefenbaker, volume 2, Years of Achievement, 1957-1962*. Toronto: Macmillan, 1976.

–. *One Canada, Memoirs of the Right Honourable John G. Diefenbaker, volume 3, The Tumultuous Years, 1962-1967*. Toronto: Macmillan, 1977.

Domenach, Jean-Marie. "Le Canada Français, Controverse sur un nationalisme." *Esprit* 33, 335 (1965): 290-328.

–. "Urgence au Québec." *Esprit* 37, 383 (1969): 3-6.

Donaghy, Greg. *Tolerant Allies: Canada and the United States, 1963-1968*. Montreal and Kingston: McGill-Queen's University Press, 2002.

Donaldson, Frances. *The British Council: The First Fifty Years*. London: Jonathan Cape, 1984.

Donneur, André. "Les relations Franco-Canadiennes: Bilan et Perspectives." *Politique Étrangère* 38, 2 (1973): 179-199.

Duc, Édouard. "La langue française dans les relations entre le Québec et la France (1902-1977): de la 'survivance' à l'unilinguisme français au Québec." PhD thesis, Université Paris IV, 2007.

Duchesne, Pierre. *Jacques Parizeau, tome 1, Le Croisé, 1930-1970*. Montreal: Québec-Amérique, 2001.

Engerman, David C. "To Moscow and Back: American Social Scientists and the Concept of Convergence." In *American Capitalism, Social Thought and Political Economy in the Twentieth Century*, edited by Nelson Lichtenstein, 47-68. Philadelphia: University of Pennsylvania Press, 2006.

English, John. "Problems in Middle Life." In *Canada and NATO, Uneasy Past, Uncertain Future*, edited by Margaret O. MacMillan and David S. Sorensen, 47-66. Waterloo: University of Waterloo Press, 1990.

–. *The Worldly Years: The Life of Lester Pearson, 1949-1972*. Toronto: Alfred A. Knopf Canada, 1992.

Étiemble, René. *Parlez-vous franglais?* Paris: Gallimard, 1964.

Fenet, Alain. "Difference Rights and Language in France." In *Language, Nation, and State: Identity Politics in a Multilingual Age*, edited by Tony Judt and Denis Lacorne, 19-61. New York: Palgrave Macmillan, 2004.

Filion, Jacques. "De Gaulle, la France et le Québec." *Revue de l'Université d'Ottawa* 45, 3 (1975): 295-319.

Foccart, Jacques. *Dans les bottes du Général, Journal de l'Élysée, volume 3, 1969-1971*. Paris: Fayard/Jeune Afrique, 1999.

–. *Le Général en mai, Journal de l'Élysée, volume 2, 1968-1969*. Paris: Fayard/Jeune Afrique, 1998.

–. *Tous les soirs avec de Gaulle, Journal de l'Élysée, volume 1, 1965-1967*. Paris: Fayard/Jeune Afrique, 1997.

Foisy-Geoffroy, Dominique. "Le Rapport de la Commission Tremblay (1953-1956), testament politique de la pensée canadienne-française." *Revue d'histoire de l'Amérique française* 60, 3 (2007): 257-294.

Fontaine, André. "La France et le Québec." *Études Internationales* 8, 2 (1977): 303-402.

Francis, R. Douglas. *The Technological Imperative in Canada: An Intellectual History.* Vancouver: UBC Press, 2009.

François-Richard, Nathalie. "La France et le Québec, 1945-1967 dans les archives du MAE." PhD thesis, Université Paris VIII, 1998.

Frieden, Jeffry A. *Global Capitalism: Its Fall and Rise in the Twentieth Century.* New York: W.W. Norton, 2006.

Friesen, Gerald. *Citizens and Nation: An Essay on History, Communication, and Canada.* Toronto: University of Toronto Press, 2000.

Fry, Michael. "Canada, the North Atlantic Triangle, and the United Nations." In *Suez 1956: The Crisis and its Consequences,* edited by W. Roger Louis and Roger Owen, 285-316. Oxford: Clarendon Press, 1989.

Gaddis, John Lewis. *We Now Know: Rethinking Cold War History.* Oxford: Clarendon Press, 1997.

Gagliardi, Jacques, and Philippe Rossillon. *Survivre à De Gaulle.* Paris: Plon, 1959.

Gaillard, Philippe. *Foccart Parle: Entretiens avec Philippe Gaillard, tome 1.* Paris: Fayard/Jeune Afrique, 1995.

Garrigues, Jean, ed. *La France de la Ve République, 1958-2008.* Paris: Armand Colin, 2008.

Gauvreau, Michael. *The Catholic Origins of Quebec's Quiet Revolution, 1931-1970.* Montreal and Kingston: McGill-Queen's University Press, 2005.

Gélinas, Xavier. *La droite intellectuelle québécoise et la Révolution tranquille.* Quebec City: Les Presses de l'Université Laval, 2007.

Gendron, Robin. *Towards a Francophone Community: Canada's Relations with France and French Africa, 1945-1968.* Montreal and Kingston: McGill-Queen's University Press, 2006.

Gérin-Lajoie, Paul. *Combats d'un révolutionnaire tranquille: Propos et confidences.* Montreal: Centre Éducatif et Culturel, 1989.

Gérols, Jacqueline. *Le Roman québécois en France.* Lasalle: Hurtubise HMH, 1984.

Giauque, Jeffrey Glen. *Grand Designs and Visions of Unity: The Atlantic Powers and the Reorganization of Europe, 1955-1963.* Chapel Hill: University of North Carolina Press, 2002.

Gilman, Nils. "Modernization Theory, the Highest Stage of American Intellectual History." In *Staging Growth, Modernization, Development and the Global Cold War,* edited by David C. Engerman, Nils Gilman, Mark H. Haefele, Michael E. Latham, 47-80. Amherst: University of Massachusetts Press, 2003.

Godin, Pierre. *Daniel Johnson, 1964-1968: La difficile recherche de l'égalité.* Montreal: Éditions de l'Homme, 1980.

Granatstein, J.L. *A Man of Influence: Norman A. Robertson and Canadian Statecraft, 1929-1968.* Ottawa: Deneau Publishers, 1981.

–. *Yankee Go Home? Canadians and Anti-Americanism.* Toronto: Harper Collins, 1996.

Granatstein, J.L., and Robert Bothwell. *Pirouette: Pierre Trudeau and Canadian Foreign Policy.* Toronto: University of Toronto Press, 1990.

Grant, George. *Lament for a Nation.* Toronto: McClelland and Stewart, 1965.

Gros d'Aillon, Paul. *Daniel Johnson: L'égalité avant l'indépendance.* Montreal: Stanké, 1979.

Grosser, Alfred. *Affaires extérieures: La politique de la France, 1944-1984.* Paris: Flammarion, 1984.

–. *The Western Alliance: European-American Relations since 1945*. Translated by Michael Shaw. New York: Continuum, 1980.

Guillaume, Pierre. "Montaigne et Shakespeare, Réflexions sur le voyage du Président Vincent Auriol au Canada, en avril 1951." *Études canadiennes/Canadian Studies* 4 (1978): 97-119.

Hamelin, Jean. *Histoire du catholicisme québécois: Le XXe siècle, tome 2, De 1940 à nos jours*. Saint-Laurent, QC: Boréal Express, 1984.

Hamelin, Jean, and Nicole Gagnon. *Histoire du catholicisme québécois: Le XXe siècle, tome 1, 1898-1940*. Saint-Laurent, QC: Boréal Express, 1984.

Handler, Richard. *Nationalism and the Politics of Culture in Québec*. Madison: University of Wisconsin Press, 1988.

Harrison, Michael M. *The Reluctant Ally: France and Atlantic Security*. Baltimore: Johns Hopkins University Press, 1981.

Hart, Michael. *A Trading Nation: Canadian Trade Policy from Colonialism to Globalization*. Vancouver: UBC Press, 2002.

Harvey, Fernand. "Les relations culturelles entre la France et le Canada (1760-1960)." In *France-Canada-Québec: 400 ans de relations d'exception*, edited by Serge Joyal and Paul-André Linteau, 95-126. Montreal: Les Presses de l'Université de Montréal, 2008.

Hayday, Matthew. *Bilingual Today, United Tomorrow: Official Languages in Education and Canadian Federalism*. Montreal and Kingston: McGill-Queen's University Press, 2005.

Hébert, Michel, and Lyse Roy. "Amour scénarisé, amour vécu: l'entrée solennelle de Charles de Gaulle au Québec en juillet 1967." *Bulletin d'histoire politique* 14, 1 (2005): 147-159.

Hecht, Gabrielle. *The Radiance of France: Nuclear Power and National Identity after World War II*. Cambridge: MIT Press, 1998.

Hertel, François. "Les évolutions de la mentalité au Canada français." *Cité libre* 10 (1954): 40-52.

Hilliker, John. *Canada's Department of External Affairs, volume 1, The Early Years, 1909-1946*. Montreal and Kingston: McGill-Queen's University Press, 1990.

–. "The Canadian Government and the Free French: Perceptions and Constraints 1940-44." *International History Review* 2, 1 (1980): 87-108.

Hilliker, John, and Donald Barry. *Canada's Department of External Affairs, volume 2, Coming of Age, 1946-1968*. Montreal and Kingston: McGill-Queen's University Press, 1995.

Hitchcock, William I. *France Restored: Cold War Diplomacy and the Quest for Leadership in Europe, 1944-1954*. Chapel Hill: University of North Carolina Press, 1998.

Hobsbawm, E.J. *The Age of Extremes: A History of the World, 1914-1991*. New York: Vintage, 1994.

Huntington, Samuel P. "Transnational Organizations in World Politics." *World Politics* 25, 3 (1973): 333-368.

Igartua, José. *The Other Quiet Revolution: National Identities in English Canada, 1945-1971*. Vancouver: UBC Press, 2006.

Iriye, Akira. *Cultural Internationalism and World Order*. Baltimore: Johns Hopkins University Press, 1997.

Jasmin, Claude. *Rimbaud, mon beau salaud!* Montreal: Éditions du Jour, 1969.

Jenkins, Brian, and Nigel Copsey. "Nation, Nationalism and National Identity in France." In *Nation and Identity in Contemporary Europe*, edited by Brian Jenkins and Spyros A. Sofos, 101-124. London: Routledge, 1996.

Jobs, Richard Ivan. *Riding the New Wave: Youth and the Rejuvenation of France after the Second World War*. Stanford: Stanford University Press, 2007.

Johnson, Daniel. *Égalité ou indépendance*. Montreal: Éditions Renaissance, 1965.

Jones, Richard A. "French Canada and the American Peril in the Twentieth Century." *The American Review of Canadian Studies* 14, 3 (1984): 333-350.
Judt, Tony. *Past Imperfect: French Intellectuals, 1944-1956.* Berkeley and Los Angeles: University of California Press, 1992.
–. *Postwar: A History of Europe since 1945.* New York: Penguin, 2005.
Julien, Claude. *Le Canada, dernière chance de l'Europe.* Paris: Bernard Grasset, 1965.
–. *L'Empire américain.* Paris: Bernard Grasset, 1968.
Kennedy, Paul. *The Rise and Fall of the Great Powers: Economic Change and Military Conflict from 1500 to 2000.* New York: Random House, 1987.
Kerr, Clark. "Changing Social Structures." In *Labor Commitment and Social Change in Developing Areas,* edited by Wilbert E. Moore and Arnold S. Feldman, 348-359. New York: Social Science Research Council, 1960.
Kitchen, Martin. "From the Korean War to Suez: Anglo-American-Canadian Relations, 1950-1956." In *The North Atlantic Triangle in a Changing World: Anglo-American-Canadian Relations, 1902-1956,* edited by B.J.C. McKercher and Lawrence Aronsen, 220-255. Toronto: University of Toronto Press, 1996.
Knapp, Andrew. *Le Gaullisme après de Gaulle.* Paris: Éditions du Seuil, 1996.
Kolodziej, Edward A. *French International Policy under De Gaulle and Pompidou: The Politics of Grandeur.* Ithaca: Cornell University Press, 1974.
Krasner, Stephen D. "Globalization and sovereignty." In *States and Sovereignty in the Global Economy,* edited by David A. Smith, Dorothy J. Solinger, and Steven C. Topik, 34-52. London: Routledge, 1999.
Kuffert, Leonard. "'Stabbing our Spirits Broad Awake': Reconstructing Canadian Culture, 1940-1948." In *Cultures of Citizenship in Post-war Canada, 1940-1955,* edited by Nancy Christie and Michael Gauvreau, 27-62. Montreal and Kingston: McGill-Queen's University Press, 2003.
Kuisel, Richard F. *Capitalism and the State in Modern France: Renovation and Economic Management in the Twentieth Century.* Cambridge: Cambridge University Press, 1981.
–. *Seducing the French: The Dilemma of Americanization.* Berkeley and Los Angeles: University of California Press, 1993.
Kunz, Diane B. *The Economic Diplomacy of the Suez Crisis.* Chapel Hill: University of North Carolina Press, 1991.
Labreque, Jean-Claude. *La visite du Général de Gaulle au Québec.* Quebec: L'Office d'information et de Publicité du Québec, 1967.
Lacouture, Jean. *De Gaulle: The Ruler, 1945-1970.* Translated by Alan Sheridan. New York: W.W. Norton, 1992.
Lalande, Gilles. *The Department of External Affairs and Biculturalism, Diplomatic Personnel (1945-1965) and Language Use (1964-1965).* Ottawa: Queen's Printer, 1969.
Lamonde, Yvan. *Allégeances et dépendances: L'histoire d'une ambivalence identitaire.* Quebec: Éditions Nota bene, 2001.
–. "Le regard sur les États-Unis: Le révélateur d'un clivage social dans la culture nationale québécoise." *Journal of Canadian Studies* 30, 1 (1995): 69-74.
Lamonde, Yvan, and Gérard Bouchard. *Québécois et Américains: La culture québécoise aux XIXe et XXe siècles.* Saint-Laurent, QC: Fides, 1995.
Langer, William L. *Our Vichy Gamble.* New York: A. Knopf, 1947.
Lapalme, Georges-Émile. *Le paradis du pouvoir, mémoires, tome 3.* Montreal: Leméac, 1973.
–. *Le vent de l'oubli, mémoires, tome 2.* Montreal: Leméac, 1970.
Lapointe, Linda. *Maison des étudiants canadiens: Cité internationale universitaire de Paris, 75 ans d'histoire, 1926-2001.* Saint-Lambert: Éditions Stromboli, 2001.

Larose, Sylvain. "La création de la délégation générale du Québec à Paris (1958-1964)." MA thesis, Université du Québec à Montréal, 2000.

Latham, Robert. *The Liberal Moment: Modernity, Security and the Making of Postwar International Order.* New York: Columbia University Press, 1997.

Lawrence, Mark Atwood. "Universal Claims, Local Uses: Reconceptualizing the Vietnam Conflict, 1945-1960." In *Global History: Interactions between the Universal and the Local,* edited by A.G. Hopkins, 229-256. New York: Palgrave Macmillan, 2006.

Leach, Jim. *Claude Jutra, Filmmaker.* Montreal and Kingston: McGill-Queen's University Press, 1999.

Lebovics, Herman. *Mona Lisa's Escort: André Malraux and the Reinvention of French Culture.* Ithaca: Cornell University Press, 1999.

Leeson, Howard A., and Wilfrid V. Vanderelst. *External Affairs and Canadian Federalism: The History of a Dilemma.* Toronto: Holt, Rinehart and Winston of Canada, 1973.

Lefèvre, Marine. *Charles de Gaulle: Du Canada français au Québec.* Ottawa: Leméac, 2007.

–. "Les États-Unis face à la Francophonie: Les stratégies américaines en Afrique francophone, 1960-1970." PhD thesis, Université de Montréal and Université Paris IV, 2005.

Léger, Jean-Marc. *La Francophonie: Grand dessein, grande ambiguité.* Lasalle: Hurtubise HMH, 1987.

–. *Le Temps dissipé: Souvenirs.* Montreal: Hurtubise HMH, 1999.

–. "Une responsabilité commune." *Esprit* 30, 311 (1962): 564-571.

Legrand, Catherine. "L'axe missionnaire catholique entre le Québec et l'Amérique latine. Une exploration préliminaire." *Globe, Revue internationale d'études québécoises* 12, 1 (2009): 43-66.

Lescop, Renée. *Le pari québécois du général de Gaulle.* Montreal: Boréal Express, 1981.

Létourneau, Jocelyn. *A History for the Future: Rewriting Memory and Identity in Quebec.* Translated by Phyllis Aronoff and Howard Scott. Montreal and Kingston: McGill-Queen's University Press, 2004.

Levine, Marc V. *The Reconquest of Montreal: Language Policy and Social Change in a Bilingual City.* Philadelphia: Temple University Press, 1990.

Levitt, Kari. *Silent Surrender: The Multinational Corporation in Canada.* Toronto: Macmillan, 1970.

Linteau, Paul-André, René Durocher, Jean-Claude Robert, and François Ricard. *Quebec since 1930,* translated by Robert Chados and Ellen Garmaise. Toronto: James Lorimer, 1991.

Lisée, Jean-François. *Dans l'œil de l'aigle: Washington face au Québec.* Montreal: Boréal, 1990.

Litt, Paul. *The Muses, the Masses, and the Massey Commission.* Toronto: University of Toronto Press, 1992.

Locher, Anna. "A Crisis Foretold: NATO and France 1963-66." In *Transforming NATO in the Cold War: Challenges beyond Deterrence in the 1960s,* edited by Andreas Wenger, Christian Nuenlist, and Anna Locher, 107-127. New York: Routledge, 2007.

Loiselle, Jean. *Daniel Johnson: Le Québec d'abord.* Montreal: VLB éditeur, 1999.

Lundestad, Geir. *"Empire" by Integration: The United States and European Integration, 1945-1957.* Oxford: Oxford University Press, 1998.

–. *The United States and Western Europe since 1945: From "Empire" by Invitation to Transatlantic Drift.* Oxford: Oxford University Press, 2003.

Lynch, Frances M.B. *France and the International Economy: From Vichy to the Treaty of Rome.* New York: Routledge, 1997.

Mann Trofimenkoff, Susan. *The Dream of Nation: A Social and Intellectual History of Quebec.* Toronto: Gage, 1983.

Marshall, D. Bruce. *The French Colonial Myth and Constitution-Making in the Fourth Republic*. New Haven: Yale University Press, 1973.
Martel, Marcel. *French Canada: An Account of its Creation and Break-up, 1850-1967*. Ottawa: Canadian Historical Association, 1998.
Martin, Paul. *A Very Public Life, volume 2, So Many Worlds*. Toronto: Deneau, 1985.
Massey, Vincent. *On Being Canadian*. Toronto: J.M. Dent and Sons, 1948.
Massolin, Philip. *Canadian Intellectuals, the Tory Tradition, and the Challenge of Modernity, 1939-1970*. Toronto: University of Toronto Press, 2001.
Maul, Daniel. "'Help Them Move the ILO Way': The International Labour Organization and the Modernization Discourse in the Era of Decolonization and the Cold War." *Diplomatic History* 33, 3 (2009): 387-404.
Mazlish, Bruce. "Comparing Global History to World History." *Journal of Interdisciplinary History* 28, 3 (1998): 385-395.
Mazlish, Bruce, and Akira Iriye. "Introduction." In *The Global History Reader*, edited by Bruce Mazlish and Akira Iriye, 1-13. New York: Routledge, 2005.
McKenna, Brian, and Sarah Pucell. *Drapeau*. Toronto: Clarke, Irwin, 1980.
McKenzie, Brian Angus. *Remaking France: Americanization, Public Diplomacy, and the Marshall Plan*. New York: Berghahn Books, 2005.
McLuhan, Marshall. *The Gutenberg Galaxy: The Making of Typographic Man*. Toronto: University of Toronto Press, 1962.
McRoberts, Kenneth. *Quebec: Social Change and Political Crisis*. 3rd edition. Toronto: McClelland and Stewart, 1988.
Mehling, Jean. "Remarques sur le commerce franco-canadien et les importations canadiennes." *L'Actualité économique* 34, 4 (1958-1959): 581-617.
Memmi, Albert. *Portrait du colonisé, précédé du Portrait du colonisateur et d'une préface de Jean-Paul Sartre, suivi de Les Canadiens français sont-ils des colonisés?* Montreal: L'Étincelle, 1972.
Merchant, Livingston T., and A.D.P. Heeney. *Canada and the United States: Principles for Partnership*. Ottawa: Queen's Printer, 1965.
Meren, David. "De Versailles à Niamey: Le patrimoine constitutionnel canado-brittanique du Québec et sa participation au sein de la Francophonie." *Globe, Revue internationale d'études québécoises* 13, 1 (2010): 99-124.
–. "Strange Allies: Canada-Quebec-France Triangular Relations, 1944-1970." PhD thesis, McGill University, 2007.
Mesli, Samy. "La coopération franco-québécoise dans le domaine de l'éducation de 1965 à nos jours." PhD thesis, Université du Québec à Montréal and Université Paris VIII, 2006.
Meunier, E.-Martin, and Jean-Philippe Warren. *Sortir de la "Grande noirceur": L'horizon "personnaliste" de la Révolution tranquille*, preface by Éric Bédard. Sillery: Septentrion, 2002.
Michels, Eckhard. "Deutsch als Weltsprache? Franz Thierfelder, the Deutsche Akademie in Munich and the Promotion of the German Language Abroad, 1923-1945." *German History* 22, 2 (2004): 206-228.
Miller, Christopher L. *The French Atlantic Triangle: Literature and Culture of the Slave Trade*. Durham: Duke University Press, 2008.
Milloy, John. *The North Atlantic Treaty Organization 1948-1957: Community or Alliance?* Montreal and Kingston: McGill-Queen's University Press, 2006.
Mills, Sean. *The Empire Within: Postcolonial Thought and Political Activism in Sixties Montreal*. Montreal and Kingston: McGill-Queen's University Press, 2010.
Minifie, James M. *Peacemaker or Powder-Monkey: Canada's Role in a Revolutionary World*. Toronto: McClelland and Stewart, 1960.

Monière, Denis. *André Laurendeau et le destin d'un peuple*. Montreal: Québec-Amérique, 1983.

Morin, Claude. *L'art de l'impossible: La diplomatie québécoise depuis 1960*. Montreal: Boréal, 1987.

Morse, Edward L. *Foreign Policy and Interdependence in Gaullist France*. Princeton: Princeton University Press, 1973.

Mouré, Kenneth. "The French Economy since 1930." In *French History since Napoleon*, edited by Martin S. Alexander, 364-390. London: Arnold, 1999.

Muirhead, Bruce. *Dancing Around the Elephant: Creating a Prosperous Canada in an Era of American Dominance, 1957-1973*. Toronto: University of Toronto Press, 2007.

–. "The Development of Canada's Foreign Economic Policy in the 1960s: The Case of the European Union." *Canadian Historical Review* 82, 4 (2001): 690-718.

–. *The Development of Postwar Canadian Trade Policy: The Failure of the Anglo-European Option*. Montreal and Kingston: McGill-Queen's University Press, 1992.

Nardout, Élisabeth. "Le Champ littéraire québécois et la France 1940-50." PhD thesis, McGill University, 1987.

Nash, Knowlton. *Kennedy and Diefenbaker: Fear and Loathing across the Undefended Border*. Toronto: McClelland and Stewart, 1990.

Ninkovich, Frank A. *The Diplomacy of Ideas: U.S. Foreign Policy and Cultural Relations, 1938-1950*. Cambridge: Cambridge University Press, 1981.

O'Reilly, Marc J. "Following Ike? Explaining Canadian-United States Cooperation during the 1956 Suez Crisis." *Journal of Commonwealth and Comparative Politics* 35, 3 (1997): 75-107.

Osterhammel, Jürgen, and Niels P. Petersson. *Globalization: A Short History*, translated by Dona Geyer. Princeton: Princeton University Press, 2003.

Painchaud, Paul. "The Epicenter of Quebec's International Relations." In *Perforated Sovereignties and International Relations: Trans-Sovereign Contacts of Subnational Governments*, edited by Ivo D. Duchacek, Daniel Latouche, and Garth Stevenson, 91-97. New York: Greenwood Press, 1988.

Patry, André. *Le Québec dans le monde*. Montreal: Leméac, 1980.

Pearson, Lester B. *Mike: The Memoirs of the Rt. Hon. Lester B. Pearson, volume 2, 1948-1957*, edited by John A. Munro and Alex I. Inglis. Toronto: University of Toronto Press, 1973.

–. *Mike: The Memoirs of the Rt. Hon. Lester B. Pearson, volume 3, 1957-1968*, edited by John A. Munro and Alex I. Inglis. Toronto: University of Toronto Press, 1975.

Pelletier, Gérard. *Les années d'impatience, 1950-1960*. Montreal: Stanké, 1983.

–. "D'un prolétariat spirituel." *Esprit* 20, 193-194 (1952): 190-200.

Pendergast, William R. "UNESCO and French Cultural Relations, 1945-1970." *International Organization* 30, 3 (1976): 453-483.

Penisson, Bernard. "Le Commissariat canadien à Paris (1882-1928)." *Revue d'histoire de l'Amérique française* 34, 1 (1980): 357-376.

Pépin, Pierre-Yves. "Les relations économiques franco-canadiennes: données récentes et perspectives." *L'Actualité Économique* 40, 3 (1964): 482-504.

Peyrefitte, Alain. *De Gaulle et le Québec*. Montreal: Stanké, 2000.

Pichette, Robert. *L'Acadie par bonheur retrouvée: De Gaulle et l'Acadie*. Moncton, NB: Éditions d'Acadie, 1994.

Poirrier, Philippe. *Histoire des politiques culturelles de la France contemporaine*. 2nd edition. Dijon: Bibliest, 1998.

Pomeyrols, Catherine. *Les intellectuels québécois: formation et engagements, 1919-1939*. Paris: L'Harmattan, 1996.

Portes, Jacques. "'La Capricieuse' au Canada." *Revue d'histoire de l'Amérique française* 31, 3 (1977): 351-370.

–. "Pierre Mendès-France au Canada (15-17 novembre 1954)." *Études Internationales* 14, 4 (1983): 781-787.

Prévost, Philippe. *La France et le Canada: D'une après-guerre à l'autre, 1918-1944*. Saint-Boniface, MB: Les Éditions du Blé, 1994.

Quebec. Minister of Cultural Affairs. L'Allier, Jean-Paul. *Pour l'évolution de la politique culturelle, Document de travail*. Quebec: Government of Québec, Ministère des Affaires culturelles, 1976.

Reid, Escott. "The Birth of the North Atlantic Alliance." *International Journal* 22, 3 (1967): 426-440.

–. *Time of Fear and Hope: The Making of the North Atlantic Treaty, 1947-1949*. Toronto: McClelland and Stewart, 1977.

Reynolds, David. "American Globalism: Mass, Motion and the Multiplier Effect." In *Globalization in World History*, edited by A.G. Hopkins, 243-260. London: Pimlico, 2002.

Richard, Nathalie. "La politique culturelle de la France vis-à-vis du Québec, 1945-1967." In *Français et Québécois: Le Regard de l'autre*, Paris, 7-9 October 1999, edited by Jean-Pierre Bardet and René Durocher, 151-163. Paris: Centre de coopération interuniversitaire franco-québécoise, 1999.

Rioux, Jean-Pierre. *The Fourth Republic, 1946-1958*, translated by Godfrey Rogers. Cambridge/Paris: Cambridge University Press/Éditions de la Maison des Sciences de l'Homme, 1987.

Robert, Paul. *Le Nouveau Petit Robert, Dictionnaire alphabétique et analogique de la langue française,* edited by Josette Rey-Debove and Alain Rey. Paris: Dictonnaires Le Robert, 2008.

Robinson, H. Basil. *Diefenbaker's World: A Populist in Foreign Affairs*. Toronto: University of Toronto Press, 1989.

Roche, François, and Bernard Pigniau. *Histoire de diplomatie culturelle des origines à 1995*. Paris: ADPF, 1995.

Roger, Philippe. *The American Enemy: A Story of French Anti-Americanism*, translated by Sharon Bowman. Chicago: University of Chicago Press, 2005.

Rooth, Tim. "Australia, Canada, and the International Economy in the Era of Postwar Reconstruction, 1945-50." *Australian Economic History Review* 40, 2, (2000): 127-152.

Rosenau, James N. *Turbulence in World Politics: A Theory of Change and Continuity*. Princeton: Princeton University Press, 1990.

Ross, Kristin. *Fast Cars, Clean Bodies: Decolonization and the Reordering of French Culture*. Cambridge: MIT Press, 1995.

–. *May '68 and its Afterlives*. Chicago: University of Chicago Press, 2002.

Rostow, W.W. *The Stages of Economic Growth: A Non-Communist Manifesto*. Cambridge: Cambridge University Press, 1960.

Rouanet, Anne, and Pierre Rouanet. *Les trois derniers chagrins du Général de Gaulle*. Paris: Bernard Grasset, 1980.

Roussel, Luc. "Les Relations culturelles du Québec avec la France, 1920-1965." PhD thesis, Université Laval, 1983.

Roy, Christian. "Le personnalisme de *L'Ordre Nouveau* et le Québec (1930-1947): Son rôle dans la formation de Guy Frégault." *Revue d'histoire de l'Amérique française* 46, 3 (1993): 463-484.

Roy, Gabrielle. "The Theme Unfolded by Gabrielle Roy." In *Terre des hommes/Man and his World,* Jean-Marie Farber, 21-34. Ottawa: Canadian Corporation for the 1967 World Exhibition, 1967.

Royal Commission on Bilingualism and Biculturalism. *Report, Book 3, The Work World.* Ottawa: Queen's Printer, 1969.

Royal Commission on National Development in the Arts, Letters and Sciences. *Report, 1949-1951.* Ottawa: King's Printer, 1951.

Rudin, Ronald. *Making History in Twentieth-Century Quebec.* Toronto: University of Toronto Press, 1997.

Rutherford, Paul. "The Persistence of Britain: The Culture Project in Postwar Canada." In *Canada and the End of Empire*, edited by Phillip Buckner, 195-205. Vancouver: UBC Press, 2005.

Ryan, Pascale. *Penser la nation: La Ligue d'action nationale 1917-1960.* Montreal: Leméac, 2006.

Saint-Exupéry, Antoine de. *Terre des hommes.* Paris: Gallimard, 1939.

Saint-Gilles, Laurence. *La présence culturelle de la France aux États-Unis pendant la guerre froide, 1944-1963.* Paris: L'Harmattan, 2007.

Saul, Samir. "Regards officiels canadiens sur la politique étrangère de la France gaullienne, 1963-1969." *Guerres mondiales et conflits contemporains* 54, 223 (2006): 69-91.

Savard, Pierre. "L'Ambassade de Francisque Gay au Canada en 1948-49." *Revue de l'Université d'Ottawa* 44, 1 (1974): 5-31.

–. "Les Canadiens français et la France de la 'cession' à la 'Révolution tranquille.'" In *Le Canada et le Québec sur la scène internationale*, edited by Paul Painchaud, 471-495. Quebec: Centre québécois de relations internationales, 1977.

–. *Le Consulat Général de France à Québec et à Montréal, de 1859 à 1914.* Quebec: Les Presses de l'Université Laval, 1970.

Schlegel, John P. "Containing Quebec Abroad: The Gabon Incident, 1968." In *Canadian Foreign Policy, Selected Cases*, edited by John Kirton and Don Munton, 156-173. Scarborough, ON: Prentice-Hall, 1992.

–. *The Deceptive Ash: Bilingualism and Canadian Policy in Africa: 1957-1971.* Washington, DC: University Press of America, 1978.

Scott, Frank R. "Canada et Canada français." *Esprit* 20, 193-194 (1952): 178-189.

Servan-Schreiber, Jean-Jacques. *Le défi américain.* Paris: Denoël, 1967.

Shepard, Todd. *The Invention of Decolonization: The Algerian War and the Remaking of France.* Ithaca: Cornell University Press, 2006.

Silver, A.I. *The French-Canadian Idea of Confederation, 1864-1900.* 2nd edition. Toronto: University of Toronto Press, 1997.

Simpson, Erica. "The Principles of Liberal Internationalism According to Lester Pearson." *Journal of Canadian Studies/Revue d'études canadiennes* 34, 1 (1999): 75-92.

Souillac, Romain. *Le mouvement Poujade: De la défense professionnelle au populisme nationaliste (1953-1962).* Paris: Les Presses de Sciences Po, 2007.

Soutou, Georges-Henri. "La Sécurité de la France dans l'Après-guerre." In *La France et l'OTAN, 1949-1996*, edited by Maurice Vaïsse, Pierre Mélandri, and Frédéric Bozo, 21-52. Brussels: Éditions Complexe, 1996.

Stairs, Denis. *The Diplomacy of Constraint: Canada, the Korean War, and the United States.* Toronto: University of Toronto Press, 1974.

–. "Present in Moderation: Lester Pearson and the Craft of Diplomacy." *International Journal* 29, 1 (1973-1974): 143-153.

Steger, Manfred B. *Globalization: A Very Short Introduction.* New York: Oxford University Press, 2009.

Stueck, William. *The Korean War: An International History.* Princeton: Princeton University Press, 1995.

Taton, Robert. "Investissements, participations et réalisations françaises au Québec." *Le Québec, Un An Après, Europe-France-Outremer* 464 (1968): 42-44.
Taylor, Peter J. "Izations of the World: Americanization, Modernization and Globalization." In *Demystifying Globalization,* edited by Colin Hay and David Marsh, 49-70. New York: St. Martin's Press, 2000.
Tétu, Michael. *La Francophonie: Histoire, problématique et perspectives.* Montreal: Guérin Universitaire, 1992.
Thomas, Martin. *The French North African Crisis: Colonial Breakdown and Anglo-French Relations, 1945-1962.* New York: St. Martin's Press, 2000.
Thomas, Martin, Bob Moore, and L.J. Butler. *Crises of Empire: Decolonization and Europe's Imperial States*, 1918-1975. London: Hodder Education, 2008.
Thompson, John Herd, and Stephen J. Randall. *Canada and the United States: Ambivalent Allies.* 3rd edition. Montreal and Kingston: McGill-Queen's University Press, 2002.
Thomson, Dale. *Vive le Québec libre.* Toronto: Deneau, 1988.
Todd, David. *L'Identité économique de la France: Libre-échange et protectionnisme, 1814-1851.* Paris: Bernard Grasset, 2008.
Touhey, Ryan. "Dealing with the Peacock: India in Canadian Foreign Policy, 1941-1976." PhD thesis, University of Waterloo, 2006.
Tovell, Freeman M. "A Comparison of Canadian, French, British and German International Cultural Policies." In *Canadian Culture: International Dimensions,* edited by Andrew Fenton Cooper, 69-82. Waterloo: Centre on Foreign Policy and Federalism, University of Waterloo/Wilfrid Laurier University and Canadian Institute of International Affairs, 1985.
Trudeau, Pierre Elliott. "The Province of Quebec at the Time of the Strike." In *The Asbestos Strike,* edited by Pierre Elliott Trudeau, translated by James Boake, 1-81. Toronto: James Lewis and Samuel, 1974.
Vaïsse, Maurice. "France and the Suez Crisis." In *Suez 1956: The Crisis and its Consequences,* edited by Wm. Roger Louis and Roger Owen, 131-143. Oxford: Clarendon Press, 1989.
–. *La grandeur: Politique étrangère du général de Gaulle, 1958-1969.* Paris: Fayard, 1998.
–. "Post-Suez France." In *Suez 1956: The Crisis and its Consequences,* edited by Wm. Roger Louis and Roger Owen, 335-340. Oxford: Clarendon Press, 1989.
–. "Les réactions françaises à la visite de De Gaulle au Québec." In *Histoire des relations internationales du Québec,* edited by Stéphane Paquin with assistance from Louise Beaudoin, 56-61. Montreal: VLB éditeur, 2006.
Vallières, Pierre. *Nègres blancs d'Amérique: Autobiographie précoce d'un "terroriste" québécois.* Montreal: Éditions Parti pris, 1968.
Vallon, Louis. *L'Anti de Gaulle.* Paris: Éditions du Seuil, 1969.
Vinant, Jean. *De Jacques Cartier à Péchiney: Histoire de la coopération économique franco-canadienne.* Paris: Chotard, 1985.
Vineberg, Steve. "Filming in Poetry." *The Walrus* 3, 9 (2006): 86-89.
Wall, Irwin M. *France, the United States and the Algerian War.* Berkeley and Los Angeles: University of California Press, 2001.
–. *The United States and the Making of Post-War France, 1945-1954.* Cambridge: Cambridge University Press, 1991.
Wallerstein, Immanuel. "States? Sovereignty? The Dilemmas of Capitalists in an Age of Transition." In *States and Sovereignty in the Global Economy,* edited by David A. Smith, Dorothy J. Solinger, and Steven C. Topik, 20-33. London: Routledge, 1999.
Weber, Eugèn. *Peasants into Frenchmen: The Modernization of Rural France, 1870-1914.* Stanford: Stanford University Press, 1976.

Whitaker, Reginald. *The Government Party: Organizing and Financing the Liberal Party of Canada, 1930-1958*. Toronto: University of Toronto Press, 1977.
Wilder, Gary. *The French Imperial Nation-State: Negritude and Colonial Humanism between the Two World Wars*. Chicago: University of Chicago Press, 2005.
Winand, Pascaline. *Eisenhower, Kennedy and the United States of Europe*. New York: St. Martin's Press, 1993.
Winock, Michel. "The Cold War." In *The Rise and Fall of Anti-Americanism: A Century of French Perception*, edited by Denis Lacorne, Jacques Rupnik, and Marie France Toinet, 67-76. Translated by Gerry Turner. New York: St. Martin's Press, 1990.
–. *Parlez-moi de la France*. Paris: Éditions du Seuil, 1997.

Index

Notes: "ACCT" stands for Agence de coopération culturelle et technique; "ASTEF," for Association pour l'organisation des stages en France; "AUPELF," for Association des universités partiellement ou entièrement de la langue française; "DEA," for Department of External Affairs; "ENA," for École nationale d'administration; "MAE," for Ministère des Affaires étrangères; "MAIQ," for Ministère des Affaires intergouvernementales du Québec; "NATO," for North Atlantic Treaty Organization; and "SIDBEC," for Sidérurgie du Québec

Abadie affair, 58, 71, 72
Acadians, 208; federal government, 230, 231, 232; French cultural action, 70, 229-231; Quebec, 231. *See also* Société nationale des Acadiens
accord cadre (France-Canada Cultural Agreement), 237; Belgium, 223; cultural entente, 220; federal aims, 216-217; francophone minority communities, 217, 229, 231, 232; negotiation, 217-218, 221; Quebec concerns about, 217, 219; renewal, 233-234, 235-236; tensions surrounding operation, 225, 226, 231
Accueil Franco-Canadien (Canada), 65, 68
Accueil Franco-Canadien (France), 64
Les Affaires, 194
Agence de coopération culturelle et technique (ACCT), 262, federal objectives, 246, 255-256, 258, 259; French objectives, 257, 258, 259; Quebec participation in, 246, 248, 259, 260, 261; statutes, 256, 257, 260, 319n114. *See also* Francophonie; Niamey conference; Niamey II conference
Agence France-Presse, 65
Air France, 45
Air Liquide, 45

Alban Janin et Compagnie, 45
Alberta, 56
Alcan, 44
Algeria, 22, 28, 131, 268; Canada, 17, 23-24, 26-27, 293n103; Gouvernement provisoire de la République algérienne, 27; North Atlantic treaty, 17, 23; Quebec as colony analogy, 110-111, 119, 122, 187; Sakiet affair, 26; Suez Crisis, 24, 25, 26; war for independence, 23
Alliance française, 64, 68, 70, 71
Alliance laurentienne, 109
Alphand, Hervé, 198, 233, 258
L'américanisme et nous (Arnavon), 75
américanité, 63, 77, 90; Canada, 104
Americanization, 68, 69, 267; "American way of life," 35, 52, 75, 95, 266; Canada, 7, 48-49, 75, 80, 86, 280n71; and Canadian nationalist interest in Europe, 75, 78-79; *Le défi américain*, 186; education entente, 214; and events of May 1968, 93; France, 36, 52-54, 74, 75, 80, 94, 182; French Canada as a shield against, 92, 98; and French concern about Quebec, 55, 59, 76, 80, 101; modernization, 35, 47-48, 188-189, 266; Quebec, 76, 77, 90, 91, 266; Quebec neo-nationalism, 49, 59, 266. *See also* anti-Americanism

Angers, François-Albert, 102
anti-Americanism, 69, 87; Canada, 30, 31, 33, 78-79, 134, 266; Charles de Gaulle, 97, 138; France, 20, 27, 52-53, 59, 93, 96; French writings, 74-75; Quebec, 77, 95. *See also* Americanization
Aquin, Hubert, 87, 102
Arnavon, Cyrille: *L'américanisme et nous*, 75
Aron, Raymond, 16
Association canadienne-française pour l'avancement des sciences, 74
Association culturelle de la Vallée de la Rivière Rouge, 231
Association d'éducation des Canadiens Français du Manitoba, 232
Association de solidarité francophone, 175
Association des universités africaines, 176
Association des universités partiellement ou entièrement de langue française (AUPELF), 67, 68, 175, 210, 213
Association internationale des journalistes de langue française (AIJLF), 66, 68
Association pour l'organisation des stages en France (ASTEF), 195. *See also* ASTEF agreement
ASTEF agreement, 195, 214
Atlanticism, 132, 133; "Atlantic community," 17, 131, 134, 135, 136; Canadian, 16-17, 19, 24-25, 31, 39, 40, 43, 129, 133, 136, 265; and Canadian foreign policy establishment, 134;and Canadian linchpin efforts, 12, 20, 21, 30, 129, 130, 134, 136-138, 139, 140-141, 269; French, 16, 19; French reaction against, 12, 19-20, 22, 27; Gaullist challenge to, 27, 29, 129, 131, 132, 142; Jules Léger, 137-138; origins of, 15, 16; Lester Pearson, 134, 135, 142, 191; as response to preponderant American power, 15, 19, 30, 31; shapes Canadian reactions to decolonization, 23; as source of Franco-Canadian cooperation, 11, 15, 17, 265; as source of Franco-Canadian discord, 11, 12, 17, 19, 22, 26, 28, 31-32, 33, 129, 138-142, 265, 269; "Three Wise Men" committee, 24
Auriol, Vincent, 20, 65; visits Canada, 18, 149
Aventure, 76

Balcer, Léon, 196
Balfour Declaration (1926), 12
Banque Beaubien, 45
Banque canadienne nationale, 44
Barrettè, Antonio, 57
Basdevant, Jean, 175, 224, 230; *accord cadre*, 218; and cultural entente, 219; and education entente, 215; French cultural attachés episode, 209
Baumgartner, Wilfrid: economic mission to Canada, 186-187, 189, 200
Beaudry, Jean-Paul, 241
Beaulieu, Paul (diplomat), 68; ambassador to Paris, 250, 253, 254; Canadian cultural diplomacy, 72-73
Beaulieu, Paul (Quebec cabinet minister), 51, 56
Bedel, Maurice, 64
Belgium: *accord cadre*, 223; economic presence in Canada, 43-44, 279n40; francophone population, 115, 116, 308n10; Francophonie, 242, 245; *Tintin*, 66
Bergeron, Gérard: *Le Canada-Français après deux siècles de patience*, 114
Bernard, Louis, 154
Berque, Jacques, 110
Bertrand, Jean-Jacques, and government, 238; French scepticism regarding, 125, 241, 245-246, 247; Kinshasa conference, 245-246; more conciliatory approach, 240-241, 242, 248; Niamey conference, 247, 248; Niamey II conference, 257, 259; Paris follow-up meeting (1969), 255; unrealized visit to Paris, 125, 240, 241
Bettencourt, André, 121-122, 204
biculturalism, 80, 172, 215; and a distinctive Canadian identity, 79, 86, 88, 223, 268, 271; francophone minority communities, 229; French-Canadian nationalism, 87, 154; Claude Julien, 98; Lester Pearson, 88; Pearson government, 86, 93, 208, 217, 223, 224, 230, 243, 269. *See also* Royal Commission on Bilingualism and Biculturalism
Bidault, Georges, 21
bilingualism, 86, 236; in DEA, 148, 149-150, 152; and a distinctive Canadian identity, 268, 271; francophone minority

communities, 229; French scepticism regarding, 99; Claude Julien, 98. *See also* Royal Commission on Bilingualism and Biculturalism

Billecocq, Pierre, 261

Black, Eldon, 234, 261, 313n113

Blais, Jean-Éthier, 98

Bongo, Omar, 177, 178

Borduas, Paul-Émile: *Refus global*, 67

Bourassa, Henri, 87

Bourassa, Robert, and government: *accord cadre*, 235-236; criticizes Union nationale, 205; "cultural sovereignty," 236; election, 126, 229, 234, 273; relations with France, 234-235, 262; relations with Ottawa, 127

Bourgault, Pierre, 101, 119, 289n91

Bousquet, Raymond, 98, 116; Association de solidarité francophone, 175; ASTEF agreement, 195; Canada and "Grand Designs," 132; Caravelle affair, 196, 197; Diefenbaker government, 111-112; education entente, 214; ENA agreement, 213; French economic presence in Quebec, 187; NATO, 135, 136; Lester Pearson and government, 152, 153, 161, 190, 192, 212; proposed French loan to Quebec, 197; Quebec as colony analogy, 110, 112; Quebec's political future, 108, 112

Bretton Woods conference, 36

Britain, 12, 33, 40, 53, 55; Brussels treaty (1948), 15; Canada's international sovereignty, 145, 146, 161; Canada's "Vichy gamble," 13; Canadian Atlanticism, 17, 24-25, 30, 134, 137, 139; Canadian cultural life, 72, 76, 79; Canadian identity, 86, 87, 88; Diefenbaker government, 31, 49, 205; Directorate proposal, 30, 130; dismantles mercantile system, 34; Maurice Duplessis, 52; English Canada, 106, 149; European Common Market, 132, 183, 186, 189, 190-191; European Defence Community, 20; French search for parity with, 16, 18, 29, 54, 130; French views of Canadian relations with, 14, 18, 32, 142; Gaullist France, 29, 115, 131, 132, 136; and NATO, 16; post-war economic difficulties, 37; provincial representation in, 57, 147, 151, 152, 154; Quebec office, 57; Suez Crisis, 24-25, 26, 29. *See also* Commonwealth

British Council, 70, 72, 284n65

British North America, 12, 34, 38, 147, 182

British North America Act (1867): and culture, 78; foreign affairs, 146; French assessments of, 108, 115; residual powers, 80, 146. *See also* Constitution

Brossard, Jacques, 154

Broussine, Georges, 232

Bruchési, Jean, 74

Brunet, Michel, 51, 62

Brussels Treaty (1948), 15; and Western European Union, 21, 276n33

Cadieux, Marcel, 149; *accord cadre*, 217, 225; background, 115-116; Jean Chapdelaine, 117, 154-155; Maurice Couve de Murville, 117, 160; cultural diplomacy, 209, 210, 211; cultural entente, 219-220, 221; Charles de Gaulle, 117, 124, 241, 250; de Gaulle visit (1967), 121, 165, 167-168, 301n40; de Lipkowski affair, 253, 254; *Le Diplomate canadien*, 148; Maurice Duplessis, 159; education entente, 215-216; francophone minority communities, 230, 231; francophone presence in DEA, 147-148, 297n36; Francophonie, 175, 242, 243, 255; Gabon affair, 177, 178-179; Gérin-Lajoie doctrine, 145, 156-157, 163; Daniel Johnson, 174, 224, 240; Jules Léger, 159, 171-173, 179, 215; Charles Lussier, 157; mistrusts French, 115-116, 161-162; Paul Martin, 118, 173, 178-179, 301n40; Lester Pearson, 239; Peyrefitte visit, 226; proposed French loan to Quebec, 198; Quebec's place in triangular dynamic, 124, 174; retaliatory measures, 123, 201, 207, 293n103; Rossillon affair, 232, 233; satellite cooperation, 228

Caisse des Dépôts et Consignations, 187

Camus, Albert, 75

Canada (Attorney-General) v. Ontario (Attorney-General), 146, 155

Canada Council for the Arts, Letters, Humanities and Social Sciences, 73, 80, 210, 285n91

Le Canada-Français après deux siècles de patience (Bergeron), 114

Canada-France commercial agreement (1933), 38, 201
Canada-France Economic Committee, 46, 49; creation, 40; federal efforts to revive, 199-200
Canadair, 196
Canadian Cultural Centre, Paris, 222, 225, 234. *See also* Canadian embassy, Paris
Canadian embassy, Paris, 46, 56, 147-148; antecedents, 12-13; cultural diplomacy, 72-74, 78, 210, 222, 225; and DEA, 116, 250; and delegation-general of Quebec in Paris, 150, 151; economic officers, 200; impact of Léger's departure, 249-250; marginalization of, 159, 162, 171. *See also* Canadian Cultural Centre, Paris
Canadian Government Overseas Awards, 73
Canadian International Trade Fair, 56
Canadian University Service Overseas, 109
La Capricieuse, 34, 38, 54, 100; centenary of visit, 46, 76
Caravelle affair, 195-197
Cardinal, Jean-Guy, 247; exchange of letters with Debré, 201, 229; Gabon affair, 177-178; visits Paris, 125, 228, 241
Carnegie Foundation, 69
Carrefour, 65
Catholicism, 70; France, 60, 68; personalism, 61, 74-75; Quebec, 50, 55, 59-60, 213
Cazavan, Marcel, 197
CBC, 65, 78, 285n91. *See also* Radio-Canada
Centre du livre français, 63
Centre nationale d'études spatiales, 228
Centre nationale de la cinématographie française, 212
Césaire, Aimé: *Discours sur le colonialisme*, 109
Chambre de Commerce de la Province du Québec, 52
Chambre de Commerce française de Montréal, 46
Chambre de Commerce France-Canada, 46. *See also* Institut France-Canada
Chapdelaine, Jean, 114, 157, 160, 162, 185, 241; *accord cadre*, 218; concern about de Gaulle's actions, 102, 122; criticisms of, 157; cultural entente, 219, 220; de Gaulle visit (1967), 165; de Gaulle's resignation, 249; economic dimension of independence debate, 204; federal cultural diplomacy, 222; federal difficulties, 173; foreign aid, 244; French as workplace language, 169; Gabon affair, 177; Kinshasa conference, 244, 245; leaves DEA, 117, 154-155; Niamey II conference, 260; proposed French loan to Quebec, 198; uranium, 191
Chapleau, Adolphe, 12
Chaput, Marcel: *Pourquoi je suis séparatiste*, 108
Charbonneau, Robert, 68; Charbonneau affair, 63, 64
Charlebois, Robert, 215
Chevrier mission, 242-243, 244
Chevrier, Lionel, 165, 242. *See also* Chevrier mission
China, People's Republic of, 18, 132; Sino-Soviet split, 131
Cholette, Gaston, 92, 214
Chouinard, Julien, 260
Chrétien, Jean, 121
Churchill, Winston, 14
Les Ciments Lafarge, 45
Citélibre, 76; and *Citélibristes*, 61
Cité universitaire, 61
Coca-Cola, 52
Colbert, 100
Cold War, 11, 19, 20, 30, 133; Canada's participation in, 12, 22; encourages Franco-Canadian cooperation, 15, 139, 142, 264; international order, 29, 33, 45, 139; links between modernization and Americanization, 47
Collège Marie-de-France, 71. *See also* Abadie affair
Collège Stanislas, 71. *See also* Abadie affair
Comédie française, 63
Comité franc-dollar, 46
Comité France-Amérique, 57, 70
Comité France-technique, 46, 195
Comité franco-québécois sur les investissements, 198, 201
Comité national d'écrivains, 63
Comité permanent de la survivance française, 60, 71

Commission mixte franco-canadienne, 225, 234
Commission permanente de coopération franco-québécoise, 216, 221, 223, 226, 250
Commonwealth, 12, 14, 25, 86, 105; Canada as "middle power," 19; Canadian aid to African members, 150, 210, 244; Diefenbaker government, 27, 31, 132, 189. *See also* Britain
Communauté radiophonique des programmes de langue française, 65
Compagnie Générale d'Électricité, 193
Confederation, 12, 147, 182; centennial of, 1, 115, 129, 165, 192; "two nation" theory, 97
Confederation Development Corporation, 45
Conference of Independent African States, 27
Conquest, 12, 62, 90, 92; and cultural contact, 59; de Gaulle visit (1967), 100; and economic links, 38; Quebec's historical development, 51, 95; and Quebec's post-war challenges, 50. *See also* New France
Conseil de la Vie française, 76, 149-150
Conseil international de la langue française, 91, 176. *See also* Francophonie; French (language)
Conseil National de la Résistance, 53
constitution (Canadian), 7, 106, 162, 220; Marcel Cadieux, 172, 174, 210, 220; "colony to nation," 79, 145; communications, 227, 228; Confederation for Tomorrow Conference, 122; culture, 71-72, 73, 80, 208, 266, 267; Charles de Gaulle, 114, 118, 120, 121; de Lipkowski affair, 253; delegation-general of Quebec in Paris, 150, 151; foreign affairs, 8, 146-147, 153, 154, 156, 166, 167, 168, 218, 236, 268, 271, 272-273; French historical experience, 105, 111, 118; French views of, 105, 108, 111, 115, 126-127, 170, 181, 267; Fulton-Favreau formula, 113; Johnson government, 114, 122, 178, 179, 227, 240, 246; René Lévesque, 112; negotiations on reform of, 113, 115, 122, 124, 179, 227, 247, 255, 262; "two nations" thesis, 85, 89, 97. See also *British North America Act*; Gérin-Lajoie doctrine

Côté, Omer, 46
Couve de Murville, Maurice, 137, 159, 169; *accord cadre*, 218, 221; Canada-France economic committee, 199; de Gaulle visit (1967), 120, 166; Francophonie, 174-175; Gabon affair, 177; Paul Martin, 117, 118, 123-124, 171; meets with Trudeau, 125; named prime minister, 241; proposed French loan to Quebec, 198; Quebec as colony analogy, 187; Quebec policy, 117, 158, 292n71; SIDBEC, 194-195; visits Canada, 160-161
Creighton, Donald, 49
cri du balcon, xii, 2-3, 118, 127, 263; Marcel Cadieux, 173; Maurice Couve de Murville, 124; and "de Gaulle-centric" analysis, 5; Michel Debré, 141; federal response, 3, 121; Georges Pompidou, 251; Quebec reactions, 101, 102, 106, 119, 272; reactions in France, 119-120
Cuban missile crisis, 131, 133
cultural entente *(Entente sur la coopération culturelle entre le gouvernement de la République française et le gouvernement du Québec),* 208, 222, 226; monies spent on, 224-225; negotiation, 219-220, 221; renewal, 235, 236-237

Daddah, Moktar Ould, 256
d'Allemagne, André, 66, 90
Les damnés de la terre (Fanon), 109
David, Athanase, 74
Davis, Henry, 27
de Beauvoir, Simone, 54
de Belvèze, Henri (Captain), 34, 36
de Boyer de Sainte-Suzanne, Raymond, 107-108
de Broglie, Jean, 93, 175
de Gaulle, Charles, 91, 174-175, 203; Acadians, 230; Algeria, 27, 131, 293n103; announces withdrawal from NATO's integrated command, 138; Atlanticism, 28, 29, 131, 138; Marcel Cadieux, 117, 124, 174, 207, 230, 241, 250; on Canadian political order, 113, 114, 115, 123, 130, 140, 141, 232; capitalism, 201; centrality to federal analyses, 116, 123, 140, 161-162, 170, 238, 251, 252, 254, 261; criticized in

France, 119-120, 141, 293n86; criticizes Bertrand government, 246; cultural entente, 219; cultural relations with French Canada, 150, 209; Pierre de Menthon, 225; DEA reaction to return to power, 27, 30; delegation-general of Quebec in Paris, 153; John Diefenbaker, 28, 31-32, 132; directorate proposal, 30, 31, 130, 138; disappointed expectations regarding Quebec independence, 106, 126, 272; education entente, 214, 215, 216; European Common Market, 132, 186, 191; European Defence Community, 20; events of May 1968, 241; favours "two-nation" approach, 97-98, 99, 159; Franco-Canadian economic relations, 201; on francophones active at federal level, 99; Free French leader, 11, 13; French Canada as cultural entity, 81, 98; Gabon affair, 176; Grand Design, 131-132; Groupe de 29, 119; Daniel Johnson, 114, 119, 125, 157, 158-159, 169, 170; Claude Julien, 98, 140; François Leduc, 120, 158; Jules Léger, 116, 137-138, 159; Jean Lesage, 89, 98, 107, 151, 161-162, 179, 193, 195; Paul Martin, 117, 120, 173, 178; and modernization, 53, 188-189; November 1967 press conference, 101, 121, 122, 124, 125; nuclear weapons, 28, 132, 133; Paris follow-up meeting (1968), 181; Lester Pearson, 98, 121, 124, 137, 139, 190, 199, 200-201; Alain Peyrefitte, 169; Georges Pompidou, 251; prominence in historiography, 5; proposed French loan to Quebec, 198; Quebec as colony analogy, 110, 187; Quebec's economic development, 56, 187, 188-189, 204; Rassemblement du people français, 20; resignation (1946), 15; resignation (1969), 8, 234, 238, 249; return to power, 12, 27, 142; scepticism regarding bilingualism, 99; sense of history, 100; Société de montage automobile, 185, 194; supports Quebec independence, 113, 114, 118-119, 121, 122, 124, 127, 170; sympathy for Quebec neo-nationalism, 85; Pierre Trudeau, 99, 232, 239; and United States, 29, 130-131, 132, 135, 251; uranium, 192; Georges and Pauline Vanier, 105, 165-166; views Quebec as branch of French nation, 94, 100-103, 298n74; Vimy Ridge anniversary, 166; visits Canada (1944), 14, 39; visits Canada (1945), 39; visits Canada (1960), 28, 33, 56, 80-81, 133; visits Canada (1967), 2, 8, 90, 99-101, 102, 115, 118-119, 120, 121, 122, 141, 164, 168, 173, 187, 188, 198, 269, 301n40; visits Canada (1967) (preparations), 100, 114-115, 146, 164-165, 166-168. See also *cri du balcon*

de Gaulle, Philippe, 113

de Hauteclocque, Jean, 54, 70, 72, 103, 285n78

de la Fournière, Martial, 249

de La Noë, François, 64

de Lipkowski, Jean: de Lipkowski affair, 252-254, 255; and Niamey II conference, 257-258

de Menthon, Pierre, 180, 240, 241; appointed consul general, 169-170; French cultural action, 225; Kinshasa conference, 244, 245, 246; Niamey conference, 247; Niamey II conference, 259; Quebec's political future, 126

de Saint-Légier de la Saussaye, René, 166, 204, 224

de Vial, François, 76

Debré, Michel: conversation with Vaniers, 116; on *cri du balcon,* 141; exchanges letters with Cardinal, 201, 229; foreign minister, 99, 199; Laurent affair, 250-251; Niamey conference, 247; pro-Quebec sympathies, 228, 241

decolonization, 267-268; Canada as neo-colonial state, 232; Canadian policy, 22, 23, 26; France, 7, 12, 26, 109-110, 212; North Africa, 22, 23, 27; Quebec as colony analogy, 108-111, 112, 119, 121-122, 182, 187, 194. See also self-determination

Deferre, Gaston, 119

Le défi américain (Servan-Schreiber), 186

Delegation-General of Quebec in Paris, 157, 162, 169; antecedents, 12, 56, 147; calls for, 55, 56-57, 78; concern about eclipse, 222; cultural rationale, 208-209; economic rationale, 184; expansion, 225; federal response, 150, 151-152, 209-210; MAE response, 151; opening, 89, 150, 151; status of, 151-152, 153-154, 157, 159. See also Heeney, A.D.P.

Deniau, Xavier, 115; criticizes Jean Chapdelaine, 157; education entente, 214

Department of External Affairs (DEA): Acadians, 230-231; *accord cadre*, 216, 233-234; Algeria, 26, 27; Anglocentrism of, 138, 147-148, 242; ASTEF agreement, 195; Atlanticism, 25, 30, 31, 92, 130, 137; bilingualism and biculturalism, 152; "business as usual" approach, 123, 171, 252; Marcel Cadieux, 115, 118, 148, 172, 210, 297n36; Canada as "middle power," 13; Canada-France economic committee, 40, 199; on competence for foreign affairs, 146; concern about Franco-Canadian relationship, 32, 161; Couve de Murville visit, 160; cultural diplomacy, 72-73, 74, 157, 210-211, 222, 285n91; cultural entente, 219, 220; de Gaulle visit (1960), 33; de Gaulle visit (1967), 118, 123, 165, 168; de Gaulle-centric analysis, 123, 124, 170, 250-251; de Lipkowski affair, 253, 254; delegation-general of Quebec in Paris, 150, 151-152, 153; education entente, 214, 215, 216, 226; External Aid Office, 242, 243; Franco-Canadian economic relations, 191, 200; francophone presence in, 116, 147-150, 154, 155, 297n36; Francophonie, 174, 176, 177, 180, 247; Gabon affair, 302n58; growing unease about France-Quebec relations, 161, 209; Johnson-Peyrefitte agreement, 201; Laurent affair, 250-251; Malraux visit, 212; Martin visit to Paris, 168; Ministère des Affaires intergouvernementales du Québec, 161; Niamey II conference, 261; Office franco-québécois de la jeunesse, 227; opens consulates in France, 223; Pearson visit to Paris, 153; Prime Minister's Office, 239-240; and provinces, 145, 146, 147, 173, 174, 216; "quiet diplomacy," 117, 121, 164; task force on Quebec international action, 161; task force on relations with France, 134, 152

Department of Trade and Commerce, 39, 200

Desbiens, Jean-Paul, 78, 91; *Les insolences du Frère Untel*, 67

Deschamps, Jean, 194

Désy, Jean, 22, 46, 148; cultural diplomacy, 73; Institut France-Canada, 46, 65; lobbies to be Quebec representative in France, 149

Deutsche Akademie, 70

Le Devoir, 51, 98, 150; Jean-Marc Léger, 152; Quebec's cultural links with France, 58, 78

Diefenbaker, John, and government: Algeria, 27; Bomarc crisis, 133-134; and Britain, 132, 189, 190, 205; Caravelle affair, 196; criticizes Paul Martin, 156; cultural diplomacy, 210; Charles de Gaulle, 28, 31-32, 132; Directorate proposal, 31; election, 31, 49, 132; French Canada, 88; French perceptions of, 32-33, 111-112, 132-133, 192; and United States, 31, 132

Diori, Hamani: Niamey conference, 244, 247, 248; Niamey II conference, 256, 257, 258, 259

Le Diplomate canadien (Cadieux), 148

dirigisme: doubts about efficacy, 205; France, 40, 41, 53, 54; Gordon budget, 192; Quebec, 51, 184

Discours sur le colonialisme (Césaire), 109

Domenach, Jean-Marie, 205; on Americanization, 95; endorses Quebec independence, 125; on Quebec as colony analogy, 110

Dorin, Bernard, 96, 171, 213, 229; de Gaulle visit (1967), 114-115; Gabon affair, 176; and Niamey conference, 247; Alain Peyrefitte, 169

Drapeau, Jean: constitutional views, 112; de Gaulle visit (1967), 102, 118; Métro system, 188, 198

Drouin, Oscar, 72

Drury, Charles, 200

Duhamel, Georges, 64, 68

Dulles, John Foster, 21

Dumazedier, Joffre, 95-96

Duplessis, Maurice, and government, 56; abolishes Quebec's overseas offices, 147; attitudes toward France, 76, 52, 149; critiques of, 51, 61, 106; cultural affairs and diplomacy, 74, 80; economic interest in France, 46, 51-52; economic policy, 50; French views of, 55, 107, 108; Quebec office in Paris, 55, 57, 78, 150;

and St. Laurent government, 73, 106; Tremblay Commission, 107; Ungava deal, 184
Dupuy, Pierre, 28, 32, 42, 148, 209; and delegation-general of Quebec in Paris, 150, 151, 152

École nationale d'administration, 97-98; 213
Eden, Anthony, 25
Éditions de l'Arbre, 63
education: Canadian constitution, 78, 80, 211, 222, 242; communications, 227; ENA agreement, 213; as epicentre of triangular dynamic, 207, 213-214; exchanges, 61-62, 74, 209; French cultural diplomacy, 71, 72; Gabon affair, 176, 177-178; system in Quebec, 58, 67, 213-214. *See also* education entente
education entente *(Entente entre le Québec et la France sur un programme d'échanges et de coopération dans le domaine de l'éducation)*, 58, 222, 224-226, 235, 236; *accord cadre*, 214, 216, 217, 218; cultural entente, 219, 220; negotiation, 214-216; Office franco-québécois de la jeunesse, 227
Égalité ou indépendance (Johnson), 113, 288n60
Egypt, 24, 25, 109
Eisenhower, Dwight, and administration, 26, 27, 131
Elizabeth II, 105, 112
Ellul, Jacques, 49
Élysée Palace: battle of Vimy Ridge anniversary, 166; de Gaulle visit (1967), 165; ENA agreement, 213; Francophonie, 175, 258; and MAE, 99, 117, 146, 158-159, 169; proposed French loan to Quebec, 198; Quebec policy, 146, 162, 163, 168-169, 268. *See also* de Gaulle, Charles; Ministère des Affaires étrangères (MAE)
Les Enfants du paradis, 66
Entreprise de recherches et d'activités pétrolières, 199
Esprit, 93, 95, 125; issue on French Canada, 61, 68
Étiemble, René: *Parlez-vous franglais?* 93
European Coal and Steel Community, 41, 42

European Common Market: British membership, 132, 183, 189; Canada, 43, 190, 191, 199; France, 42-43, 44, 193, 201, 203; and Gaullist policy, 132, 186
European Defence Community (EDC), 20-21, 22, 131; Canadian policy, 20-21, 23, 24, 25-26; Pleven Plan, 20; Western European Union, 21, 276n33
European Free Trade Association, 186
European Payments Union (EPU), 41, 43
European Recovery Program. *See* Marshall Plan
L'Évangéline, 230
Expo '67, 1, 185; Charles de Gaulle, 2, 115, 164-165; and modernization, 188; official visits, 165, 167
External Aid Office. *See under* Department of External Affairs (DEA)

Fanon, Frantz: *Les damnés de la terre*, 109
Faure, Edgar, 101, 120
federalism: and Canada, 262, 266; cooperative federalism, 112, 210; Charles de Gaulle, 121, 159, 232; foreign affairs rivalry, 145-147, 154, 211, 268, 271; French attitudes, 105, 108, 126, 127, 267; French political culture, 97; "new federalism," 106; Pierre Trudeau, 239
Fédération des Sociétés Saint-Jean-Baptiste du Québec, 66, 78. *See also* Société Saint-Jean Baptiste de Montréal
Fédération Normandie-Canada, 64
Féquant, Albert, 235
Filion, Gérard, 51
film, 65-66, 212
First World War, 12, 13, 38, 69, 74; anniversary of battle of Vimy Ridge, 166
Foccart, Jacques, 233, 254, 259; Hamani Diori, 256; and Gabon affair, 177-178
foreign aid, 210, 242, 256, 258, 285n91; intergovernmental rivalry, 243, 244-245
Fortier, d'Iberville, 68
Fouchet, Christian, 216
Fougerolle, 45
Fournier, Sarto, 56
francité: cultural cooperation, 224, 226; education entente, 214; of Quebec, 95, 97, 101, 213

francophone minority communities, 55, 79, 176, 208, 234, 271; *accord cadre,* 217, 229; Francophonie, 180; Rossillon affair, 232, 233. *See also* Acadians

Francophonie: Marcel Cadieux, 174, 175; federal concern about, 174, 176, 260; federal initiatives, 175, 177; federal participation, 246, 248, 249; foreign aid rivalry, 244; and France, 174, 261; French support for Quebec participation in, 176, 241, 245, 252, 257-259, 269; Gabon affair, 178; Paul Gérin-Lajoie, 174-175; idea of, 174; institutionalization, 8, 93, 238, 245, 246, 251; Jean-Marc Léger, 92, 248-249; Jules Léger, 171; Paris follow-up meeting (1969), 255; Pompidou government, 254; Prime Minister's Office, 239-240; Quebec participation in, 8, 160-161, 164, 176, 238, 259, 260, 262, 271; Pierre Trudeau, 261; Union culturelle française, 66-67. *See also* Agence de coopération culturelle et technique

Frégault, Guy: and Jean Chapdelaine, 157; cultural entente, 219; federal cultural diplomacy, 211; historian, 51

French consulate general, Quebec City, 34, 38; reorganization, 169-170, 225

French embassy, Ottawa, 123; appointing of cultural councillor, 70; reorganization, 169-170, 225

French language, 67, 93, 94; Biennale de la langue française, 91; concern about in Quebec, 55, 67, 91, 95, 99, 107; Congrès de la langue française, 71; Conseil international de la langue française, 91-92; cultural entente, 219; economic cooperation, 185; French cultural diplomacy, 70, 71; *joual,* 91, 214; Georges Pompidou, 251; satellite cooperation, 227-228; as transnational bond, 66-67. *See also* Haut comité pour la défense et l'expansion de la langue française; Office de la langue française

French Revolution (1789), 94, 97, 110, 111

Front de libération du Québec, 194

Gabon affair, 176-179, 227, 244, 302n65; federal response, 177, 178-179, 242; French role in, 176, 177-178, 245; Libreville conference, 180-181; Quebec invitation, 176-178, 302n58; suspension of Canada-Gabon relations, 178, 179. *See also* Paris follow-up meeting (1968)

Gaillard, Félix, and government, 27

Garneau, René, 73, 212, 288n45

Gaullism, 100, 268; after de Gaulle, 249, 251, 262, 272; "Anglo-Saxons," 95; and Atlanticism, 29, 31, 33, 129, 130, 131-132, 134, 138-139; and Canada in geopolitical calculations, 134, 137, 138, 139, 141, 142, 269; capitalism, 184, 201-202; challenges American economic leadership, 182, 203, 205-206, 269, 270; cultural rivalry with United States, 208, 224; decolonization, 110, 119; economic cooperation with Quebec, 182, 193, 205, 270; economic policy, 185-186, 187, 201-202; European integration, 186, 190; francophone economic success, 56; nuclear policy, 28, 135-136, 191, 192; Quebec nationalism, 86, 101, 102, 103-104, 106, 119, 126, 127, 264, 271, 272; "two nation" approach, 97, 99, 103, 139-140, 159-160, 231, 241, 267; worldview, 7, 29, 85, 97, 105, 185, 267, 298n66. *See also* de Gaulle, Charles

Gay, Francisque, 14, 15, 60, 66

Gélinas, Gratien, 66

General Agreement on Tariffs and Trade (GATT), 39, 42, 189, 199; Dillon Round, 183; Kennedy Round, 183-184, 191, 192, 193

Gérin-Lajoie, Paul, 113, 207, 209, 221; *accord cadre,* 217; ASTEF agreement, 195; education entente, 58, 214, 215, 216, 219; Francophonie, 174-175; speech to Montreal consular corps, 155, 156, 160. *See also* Gérin-Lajoie doctrine

Gérin-Lajoie doctrine, 158, 207, 217, 253, 262; *accord cadre,* 218, 221; cultural entente, 220, 221; education entente, 216; federal opposition to, 156-157, 222, 268; Gabon affair, 176, 177-178; Kinshasa conference, 242; Jean Lesage, 155-156; Niamey conference, 242, 247; Niamey II conference, 260; Office franco-québécois de la jeunesse, 226; Paris follow-up meeting (1968), 180,

181; pronouncement, 255. *See also* Gérin-Lajoie, Paul
Germany, Federal Republic of, 15, 136; economic presence in Canada, 44, 56, 279n40; Élysée treaty (1963), 132; European Common Market, 42-43, 96, 203; rapprochement with France, 29, 132; rearmament, 16, 20, 21, 276n33
Giscard d'Estaing, Valéry, 120
Glassco Report, 285n91
globalization, 263-264, 268, 270, 272; United States, 264, 265
Godard, Jean-Luc, 66
Godbout, Adélard, and government, 72; and overseas offices, 56, 147
Godbout, Jacques, 91
Gordon, Donald, 306n75
Gordon, Walter, 49; 1963 federal budget, 192
Gordon affair, 197, 306n75
Gordon Commission (Royal Commission on Canada's Economic Prospects), 49; report, 30-31, 189
Gorse, Georges, 101, 141
Gotlieb, Allan, 123, 161
Gouin, Paul, 78
Gouvernement provisoire de la République française, 13, 85
Les Grands Travaux de Marseille, 45
Grant, George: anti-Americanism, 49, 189-190; Canadian nationalism, 79, 88, 190; French Canada, 88; on Gaullism, 270
Great Depression, 38, 47, 49, 53, 106
Green, Howard, 133, 210
Grégoire, Gilles, 119
Groulx, Lionel, 76, 77
Groupe de 29, 119
Groupe Schneider, 45
Guadeloupe, 38, 123
Guérin, Hubert, 21, 42, 44; American economic presence in Canada, 49; Canada's federal system, 108; Canadian Cold War policy, 18-19; criticizes Maurice Duplessis, 107; English Canada, 55, 60, 71; French Trade Exposition (1954), 41, 45-46, 55; Quebec attitudes regarding France, 60, 149; Quebec's development, 55, 107

Halstead, John, 160, 166

Hammarskjöld, Dag, 25
Hamon, Léo, 261
Haut Comité pour la défense et l'expansion de la langue française, 96, 99, 233. *See also* French (language)
Heeney, A.D.P., 147. *See also* Merchant-Heeney report
Hertel, François, 76
Hettier de la Boislambert, Claude, 166
Houde, Camillien, 149
Houphouet-Boigny, Félix, 256
Howe, C.D., 46, 73
Huntington, Samuel P., 183
Hydro-Québec, 109, 204; James Bay hydroelectric project, 193
Hyndman, Patrick, 202

immigration, 78, 223-224
In re Regulation and Control of Radio Communication in Canada, 146
independence movement (Quebec). *See* Separatism (Quebec)
India, 19
Indochina, Associated States of, 19; and France, 23, 41; International Commission on Supervision and Control, 19, 115-116
Innis, Harold, 49
Les insolences du Frère Untel (Desbiens), 67
Institut France-Canada, 46, 65
Institut international de Droit d'Expression et Inspiration française, 175
International Bank for Reconstruction and Development, 36
International Committee on Intellectual Cooperation, 69
International Monetary Fund, 36
International Trade Organization, 36, 37, 39
Iron Ore Company of Canada, 18
Israel, 24, 25

Jasmin, Claude, 101
Jeune Chambre de Commerce de Montréal, 150
Jobert, Michel, 254, 258
Johnson, Daniel, and government, 168, 223, 272; Couve de Murville visit, 160-161; Charles de Gaulle, 101, 114, 118,

121, 125, 157; de Gaulle visit (1967), 2, 3, 99, 118; 100, 101, 118, 119, 120, 165, 167, 274n5; death, 102-103, 125, 238, 240; *Égalité ou indépendance*, 106, 113, 288n60; election, 164, 197; federal Liberal leadership, 294n120; federal views of, 124, 174, 179; Francophonie, 175; on French assistance, 114, 224; French investment in Quebec, 198, 199; French reaction to election, 113; Gabon affair, 176, 177, 178, 179; Ministère des affaires intergouvernementales, 158; misgivings and hesitation, 122, 169, 240; Paris follow-up meeting (1968), 180; Alain Peyrefitte, 169, 170; proposed French loan, 197-198; Quebec international action, 157, 161, 240, 243; Quebec's distinctiveness, 90; Quebec's historic vocation, 92; satellite cooperation, 227, 228; unrealized second visit to Paris, 199, 240; visits Paris, 92, 105, 114, 158-159, 162, 198, 222-223, 227. *See also* Johnson-Peyrefitte agreement

Johnson, Lyndon B., and administration, 48, 132, 139

Johnson-Peyrefitte agreement, 169, 201, 240; federal response, 170, 171

Joxe, Louis, 181, 188

Judicial Committee of the Privy Council, 146

Julien, Claude, 93, 98, 140, 193

Julien, Pauline, 248

Jurgensen, Jean-Daniel, 122, 294n120; Acadians, 230; *accord cadre*, 217, 218; aid offer to PQ, 126; de Gaulle visit (1967), 113, 293n86; Gabon affair, 177; immigration, 224; Niamey conference, 244, 248; Niamey II conference, 260, 261; Quebec's political future, 114; Rossillon affair, 233; satellite cooperation, 227-228; Maurice Schumann, 250

Jutra, Claude, 66

Kennedy, John F., and administration: "Declaration of Interdependence" speech, 131, 132; John Diefenbaker, 132; Grand Design, 131, 183-184

Key Construction Company, 45

Keynesian liberalism, 35, 44, 264

King, Mackenzie, and government, 13, 14, 37

Kinshasa conference: federal-Quebec compromise, 246, 248, 254, 255; foreign aid rivalry, 244, 245; French intervention, 245; Quebec participation, 242, 244, 245, 246; tension between Paris and Quebec City, 246. *See also* Paris follow-up meeting (1969)

Korean War, 17-18, 20, 41

Labour Conventions case. See *Canada (Attorney-General) v. Ontario (Attorney-General)*

Lacoste, Francis, 23, 27; Canada-US relations, 32-33, 192; delegation-general of Quebec in Paris, 151; Maurice Duplessis, 55; French cultural attachés episode, 209; modernization, 54; nuclear testing, 28; on Quebec attitudes regarding France, 62, 67; Quebec's economic potential, 56, 186; separatist movement, 108; Louis St. Laurent, 26

Lamontagne, Maurice, 153

Lapalme, Georges-Émile: delegation-general of Quebec in Paris, 78, 150, 151, 153; federal annoyance with, 212; Lesage visit to Paris (1961), 89; Charles Lussier, 150, 157, 209

Laporte, Pierre, 113, 207; and cultural entente, 219, 221

Laurendeau, André, 51; American influences in Quebec, 77; opposes federal cultural action, 80; time in France, 67-68, 75

Laurent, Pierre: Laurent affair, 250-251

Laurier, Wilfrid, 12, 99

Leduc, François, 166, 171; Acadians, 231; *accord cadre*, 217, 218, 225; Canada's economic satellization, 192; Couve de Murville visit, 160; cultural entente, 219, 220, 221; de Gaulle visit (1967), 164, 167; dissent, 120, 141, 169, 239; economic cooperation, 188, 199-200, 201, 204-205; Francophonie, 175; Gabon affair, 176; immigration, 224; Johnson government, 92, 113, 157; Johnson-Peyrefitte agreement, 169, Jean Lesage, 113; named ambassador, 158; Paris follow-up meeting (1968), 180, 181; Lester Pearson, 113, 181,

291n39; Peyrefitte visit, 172, 226; Quebec's political future, 114; SIDBEC, 194; Pierre Trudeau, 239; youth exchanges, 223, 226

Léger, Jean-Marc, 51, 74, 91, 96; ACCT, 248-249, 257, 258; delegation-general of Quebec in Paris, 153, 222; *Le Devoir* articles, 152; francophilia of, 68; Francophonie, 91, 92, 175, 176; Niamey II conference, 261

Léger, Jules, 99, 101, 113, 141, 161, 170, 200; Algeria, 26, 27; appointed undersecretary of state for external affairs, 148; Marcel Cadieux, 117, 148, 171-173, 179, 215; Jean Chapdelaine, 154-155, 157; Maurice Couve de Murville, 117, 292n71; cultural diplomacy, 222, 225, 226; Charles de Gaulle, 116, 159, 162; de Gaulle visit (1967), 115, 121, 123, 164, 165, 167, 173, 301n40; end of posting, 181, 250; favours a more conciliatory approach, 116-117, 121, 123, 162, 172-173, 179, 215; francophones in DEA, 148; immigration, 223, 224; letters of credence ceremony, 94, 159-160; ostracization in Paris, 159-160, 162, 166, 207, 215; Paris follow-up meeting (1968), 181; Lester Pearson, 116; proposed French loan to Quebec, 198; questions Canadian Atlanticism, 137-138; Rossillon affair, 233; satellite co-operation, 227-228; separatism, 193; Pierre Trudeau, 239; uranium, 191

Léger, Paul-Émile (Cardinal), 46

Lesage, Jean, and government, 98, 200, 272; *accord cadre*, 217, 218, 221, 225; Caravalle affair, 196, 197; correspondence with de Gaulle, 161, 162; cultural activism, 109; cultural entente, 219, 220, 221; de Gaulle visit (1967), 119; defeat, 98; delegation-general of Quebec in Paris, 57, 89, 150, 151-152, 153, 184, 208-209; education, 213-214; education entente, 214, 215; election, 107; foreign aid, 243; French Canada's distinctiveness, 90, 92; French views of, 107, 113, 158, 298n66; Gérin-Lajoie doctrine, 155-156; immigration, 223; interministerial committee on Quebec's international action, 156, 158, 160; internal tensions, 156, 219; Malraux visit, 212; Société de montage automobile, 185, 194; Société générale de financement, 187; SIDBEC, 184; visits New York, 194; visits Paris (1961), 89-90, 95, 98, 150, 151, 184; visits Paris (1963), 113, 152, 195; visits Paris (1964), 153, 159, 193, 215

Lévesque, Georges-Henri, 79, 80, 176

Lévesque, Gérard-D., 185, 235

Lévesque, René, 112, 126; de Gaulle visit (1967), 100; Quebec as colony analogy, 109

Liberal Party (Quebec), 106-107, 119

Libreville conference. *See* Gabon affair

Ligue d'Action nationale, 227

Louis XIV, 70, 90

Louis XV, 100

Lucet, Charles, 28

Lussier, Charles, 150, 151, 152; criticism of, 157; French investment, 193, 194; Maison des étudiants canadiens, 209; proposed French loan to Quebec, 197

Lussier, Irénée (Monsignor), 213

MacArthur, Douglas (General), 18

MacGregor, Gordon, 197

Maison des étudiants canadiens (MEC), 61-62, 68, 71; federal cultural diplomacy, 73; Charles Lussier, 209; and Quebec government, 74

Maison du Québec. *See* Delegation-General of Quebec in Paris

Malraux, André, 80, 158, 209; attitude toward Quebec, 288n45; cultural entente, 219, 221, 310n51; delegation-general of Quebec in Paris, 89, 150, 153; on pro-autonomy sentiment in Quebec, 112; Quebec as colony analogy, 110; Quebec's "American" dimension, 95; visits Canada, 90, 95, 98, 110, 211-212, 213

Marchand, Jean, 99, 204, 223, 224, 241

Marshall Plan, 37-38, 47-48, 53; and Canada, 37, 39

Martin, Paul, 93, 116, 159, 200, 211, 217; ASTEF agreement, 195; bicultural foreign policy, 152; Marcel Cadieux, 118, 173, 178-179, 297n36, 301n40; Caravelle affair, 196; Jean Chapdelaine, 117, 154; Maurice Couve de Murville, 117, 123-124,

171; Couve de Murville visit, 160; Charles de Gaulle, 117, 162; de Gaulle visit (1967), 3, 120, 121, 166, 301n40; education entente, 214, 216; favours "business as usual" approach, 124; francophone minority communities, 230; Francophonie, 175, 210; Gabon affair, 178-179; Gérin-Lajoie doctrine, 156; Johnson-Peyrefitte agreement, 170; leadership ambitions, 117, 124, 294n120; linchpin efforts, 134-135, 137, 139, 140, 196, 295n26; Pearson visit to Paris, 153; Quebec's place in triangular dynamic, 161, 162, 173; tours Africa, 242; visits Paris, 117-118, 168

Martinique, 38, 123

Masse, Marcel, 99, 157, 175, 242; Niamey conference, 248

Massey Commission (Royal Commission on National Development in the Arts, Letters and Sciences), 73, 79, 227; report, 71, 73, 78, 80, 229

Massey-Ferguson, 44

Mauriac, François, 54

May 1968, events of, 241, 249, 251; anti-Americanism, 93; economic impact, 203, 243, 270

Mayer, René, 42

Memmi, Albert: *Portrait du colonisé*, 109, 110

Mendès-France, Pierre, and government, 21, 149

Merchant-Heeney Report (Canada and the United States: Principles for Partnership), 192

Mercier, Honoré, 12

Métro system (Montreal), 188, 198

Michaud, Yves, 96

Michelin, 204, 205

Michelin, François, 204

Minifie, James: *Peacemaker or Powder-Monkey?* 132

Ministère des Affaires étrangères (MAE): *accord cadre*, 217, 218; ACCT, 256; "Austro-Hungarian" solution, 291n39; Canada and United States, 18, 133, 149; Canada-France economic committee, 199; Canadian federalism, 108, 115; Chevrier mission, 244; cultural diplomacy, 70, 71, 81, 209, 225, 234, 310n51; and Charles de Gaulle, 146, 159, 169; de Gaulle visit (1967), 100, 141; delegation-general of Quebec in Paris, 151, 153; economic interest in Quebec, 54, 56; education entente, 225-226; federal estimations of, 250, 261; Francophonie, 175; Gabon affair, 177, 178; Daniel Johnson, 122; Kinshasa conference, 245; Malraux visit, 212; Montreal trade expositions, 45-46; more cautious approach, 122, 127, 128, 158, 162, 163, 268-269; Niamey II conference, 257; Paris follow-up meeting (1968), 180-181; Paris follow-up meeting (1969), 255; Pearson government, 112; postwar assessment of Canada, 14; proposed French loan to Quebec, 198; Quebec religious life, 60; Quebec's "American" dimension, 95; Quebec's political future, 127; support for Quebec in, 117, 125, 158, 163, 268-269, 292n71

Ministère des Affaires intergouvernementales du Québec, 158, 302n65; parallels to DEA, 161

Missoffe, François, 226

Mitterrand, François, 119-120, 249

Mobutu, Joseph-Désiré, 245, 246

modernization, 6, 35, 57, 266; Americanization, 47-48, 183; ASTEF agreement, 195; education, 213, 214; English Canada, 48-49; France, 36, 53-54, 192, 281n95; Gaullism, 188, 189, 201; modernization theory, 47-48, 184; Quebec, 49-50, 107, 184, 188, 189

Mollet, Guy, and government, 24; criticizes de Gaulle, 120; Suez Crisis, 25; visits Canada, 56, 149

Le Monde, 110

Le Monde français, 65

Monnet, Jean, 16, 53. *See also* Monnet Plan

Monnet Plan, 38, 53

Morin, Claude, 122, 169, 228; *accord cadre*, 217, 221, 225, 235; Jean-Jacques Bertrand, 240, 241; Marcel Cadieux, 155, 156, 160, 179; cultural entente, 219, 220, 221; de Gaulle visit (1967), 164, 167; on de Gaulle's resignation, 249-250; de Lipkowski affair, 252; education entente, 215-216; federal cultural diplomacy,

211, 222; foreign aid rivalry, 244; Gabon affair, 176, 177, 302n58; Gérin-Lajoie doctrine, 154, 155; Daniel Johnson, 157, 168; Kinshasa conference, 242, 245; Niamey conference, 244, 246-247, 249; Niamey II conference, 257, 258, 259, 260; Nouakchott conference, 256; Paris follow-up meeting (1968), 180; Paris follow-up meeting (1969), 255; Pompidou government, 250, 252, 254

Morin, Jacques-Yvan, 96, 154, 211
Morin, Jean-Marie, 246, 255
Morocco, 22, 23, 24
Mounier, Emmanuel, 61
Mouvement Souveraineté-Association, 125

Napoleon III, 34
Nasser, Gamal Abdel, 24, 25, 30
National Assembly (France), 21; foreign affairs committee, 95, 115, 140
National Film Board of Canada, 212, 285n91
nationalism, 7, 264; anti-colonial, 22, 23, 105; Canadian, 88-89, 104, 106, 264, 268; Canadian economic, 189-190, 192, 205; and Canadian internationalism, 17; class dimension of in Quebec, 77, 204-205, 215; economic, 38, 57, 205, 270; English Canada, 86, 87-88, 103, 211; English-Canadian cultural, 7, 59, 78-78; French, 16, 86, 94, 96, 111; French cultural, 74, 75; French economic, 35, 41, 42, 43, 186, 189, 201, 203, 265; Quebec, 6, 59, 103, 106, 215; traditional French-Canadian, 50, 51, 77, 87, 89, 266, 281n79. *See also* Gaullism; Quebec neo-nationalism
NATO (North Atlantic Treaty Organization), 33; article 2, 17, 39, 40; Canadian linchpin efforts, 20, 21, 30, 92, 134-135, 137-138, 139, 295n26; creation, 15, 16, 17; Directorate proposal, 30, 31-32, 138, European Defence Community, 20-21, 22, 276n33; "flexible response," 131; French frustration regarding, 12, 16, 18, 25, 27, 29; Gaullist challenge to, 30, 31, 129, 130, 138-139, 142; Multilateral Force (MLF), 131, 135-136; Mutual Aid program, 23; North Africa, 17, 22, 23, 24, 26; North Atlantic Council, 20-21, 24; North Atlantic treaty, 16, 17, 23, 39; nuclear weapons, 28, 131, 133; "Three Wise Men" committee, 24, 29; "two pillar" approach, 129, 139; United States predominance, 15, 136. *See also* Atlanticism

New Brunswick, 180, 230-231
New France, 2, 90, 100, 202. *See also* Conquest
New York, 60; Quebec office, 145, 147, 194
Niamey conference, 246, 248-249; federal-Quebec compromise, 248, 254; foreign aid rivalry, 244-245; Quebec participation, 242, 244, 247; tension between Paris and Quebec City, 247, 248
Niamey II conference, 255, 260, 261, 262; Quebec participation, 256, 257-259; tension between Paris and Quebec City, 258-259
Niger, 177, 242, 256; Canadian aid to, 244-245, 258. *See also* Niamey conference; Niamey II conference
NORAD (North American Air Defence Agreement), 31, 33
Norman, Herbert: Norman affair, 31
Notre Temps, 78
Nouakchott conference, 256
nuclear energy, 28, 192; plutonium, 200; uranium, 28, 191-192
nuclear weapons: Bomarc crisis, 133-134; command and control, 131, 133; disarmament movement, 133; *force de frappe*, 131, 192; French testing, 28, 29, 33; Nassau agreement (1962), 131, 132; non-proliferation, 28, 136, 191, 276n33. *See also* NATO

Office de la langue française, 98. *See also* French (language)
Office franco-québécois pour la jeunesse (OFQJ), 226-227, 228; origins, 223, 226
Official Languages Act (1969), 271
Ontario, 46, 56, 180, 195
Organisation commune africaine et malgache, 176
Organisation for Economic Co-operation and Development, 183
Organisation for European Economic Co-operation (OEEC), 41, 183

Paris: significance as place, 67-68, 75
Paris follow-up meeting (1968), 179-181, 239, 242, 245. *See also* Gabon affair
Paris follow-up meeting (1969), 254-255, 256. *See also* Kinshasa conference
Parizeau, Jacques, 197-198
Parlez-vous franglais? (Étiemble), 93
Parti pris movement, 91; *Parti pris,* 77
Parti Québécois, 126, 127, 154, 273; founding, 125
Patry, André, 68-69; *accord cadre,* 218; Marcel Cadieux, 148, 155; de Gaulle visit (1967), 167; Gérin-Lajoie doctrine, 180; interministerial committee, 156; André Malraux, 158, 288n45
Peacemaker or Powder-Monkey? (Minifie), 132
Pearson, Lester B., and government, 117, 127, 129, 140, 170; Atlanticism, 17, 23, 130, 134-135, 138, 139, 141, 142; and "Austro-Hungarian solution," 113, 291n39; bilingualism and biculturalism, 88, 93, 152, 208, 217, 223, 224, 230, 243, 269; Marcel Cadieux, 156, 160, 167-168, 239, 242; Canada-France economic committee, 40, 199; Canada-US economic relations, 192; Caravelle affair, 196; cooperation with Belgium and Switzerland, 116; creation of MAIQ, 161; cultural agreements, 217, 219, 226; cultural diplomacy, 72, 210, 212; de Gaulle's November 1967 news conference, 124; de Gaulle's visit (1967), 3, 121, 166, 167-168, 173, 301n40; delegation-general of Quebec in Paris, 153-154; economic relations with France, 42, 190, 200, 205; election, 112; ENA agreement, 213; European Common Market, 190-191; European Defence Community, 20-21; fails to win majority, 113; foreign aid rivalry, 243; francophones in DEA, 148; French hopes for, 112; French withdrawal from NATO integrated command, 138; Hubert Guérin, 18; Gérin-Lajoie doctrine, 156; Indochina, 19; interdepartmental committee on Franco-Canadian relations, 134, 152, 190; Daniel Johnson, 124, 177, 179-180; Korean war, 18; François Leduc, 181; Jules Léger, 116, 148, 162; Jean Marchand, 99; Paul Martin, 124, 178; Pierre Mendès-France, 21; Norman affair, 31; nuclear weapons, 134; "Pearsonian" diplomacy, 132, 138, 240; potential suspension of relations with France, 179; Quebec caucus, 112, 196, 197; retirement, 178, 179-180, 181; Suez Crisis, 24-25; surveillance of French embassy, 123; "Three Wise Men" committee, 24, 29; uranium, 191; visits Paris, 93, 98, 112, 113, 135, 137, 153, 190, 191, 211, 213, 243
Péchiney, 204
Pellan, Alfred, 288n45
Pelletier, Gérard, 99; significance of Paris, 68; Niamey conferences, 248, 249, 260
Perroux, François, 51
personalism. *See under* Catholicism
Pétain, Philippe, 13
Peugeot, 185, 194, 200, 204
Peyrefitte, Alain, 110, 214; Acadians, 229-230; de Gaulle visit (1967), 120; federal response to visit, 171-172, 226; Gabon affair, 178, 302n58; Philippe Rossillon, 313n117; uranium, 191; visits Quebec, 122, 169, 170, 224, 240
Picard, Robert, 98-99
Pinay, Antoine, and government, 22-23
Pineau, Christian, 25, 56, 149
Pleven, René, 18, 252. *See also* European Defence Community, Pleven Plan
Poher, Alain, 250
Polymer, 44
Pompidou, Georges, and government, 203, 272; on *cri du balcon,* 251; cultural agreements, 235, 236; de Lipkowski Affair, 252, 253-254, 255, 317n89; elected president, 249, 250; federal views of, 234, 254, 258, 261; maintains Quebec policy, 127, 251-252, 261; Niamey II conference, 256, 258-259, 260, 261; prime minister, 93, 137, 153, 188; Philippe Rossillon, 313n117
Portrait du colonisé (Memmi), 109, 110
Poujadiste movement, 53-54
Pouliot, Adrien, 60
Pourquoi je suis séparatiste (Chaput), 108
Prime Minister's Office (PMO), 148, 161, 165, 239-240

Prince Albert of Liège, 223
Prince Phillip, 166
Privy Council Office, 161
Prix France-Canada, 65

Quai d'Orsay. *See* Ministère des Affaires étrangères (MAE)
Quebec lobby, 96, 120, 163, 241, 267; Acadians, 229-230; criticism of Chapdelaine, 157; de Gaulle visit (1967), 168; ENA agreement, 213; Francophonie, 175, 176, 247, 248; members of, 96, 114-115, 214, 249, 288n52; Georges Pompidou, 251, 272; Quebec as colony analogy, 110; Maurice Schumann, 250
Quebec ministry of education, 215, 219; Service de la coopération avec l'extérieur, 214, 243
Quebec neo-nationalism, 7, 106, 107, 264; critique of post-war conditions, 51; decolonization, 109; education, 207, 213-214; foreign affairs, 145, 154, 155, 163, 207-208, 262, 268, 272; France in Quebec cultural life, 6, 59, 77-78, 89, 90, 102; francophone economic empowerment, 35-36, 52, 182, 184-185, 197, 266, 269, 270; French Canada's "break-up," 87, 154; Gaullism, 85, 86, 103-104, 106, 119, 126, 270, 271, 272; "Montreal School," 62, 109; origins, 49-50, 51, 61; Quebec's cultural vocation, 211, 266, 269; Quebec's historical mission, 92; "two nation" constitutional thesis, 97, 267
Quiet Revolution, 1, 6, 36, 89, 90, 103, 145; affects French policy, 107, 267; Canada, 88, 104; *cri du balcon,* 118; economic dimension, 182, 204; education, 207, 213-214; education entente, 214; federal concern about, 93, 152, 153, 190; French cultural influences on, 60, 266; French economic interest in, 36, 186, 194; Daniel Johnson, 114; Malraux visit, 98; Lester Pearson, 112; Quebec as colony analogy, 109

Radio Reference. *See In re Regulation and Control of Radio Communication in Canada*
Radio-Canada, 65, 66, 285n91. *See also* CBC

Radiodiffusion Française, 65
Raimond, Jean-Bernard, 249, 258
Rassemblement de l'Indépendance nationale (RIN), 90-91, 109, 289n91
Rassemblement du peuple français, 20
RCMP (Royal Canadian Mounted Police), 116, 171, 232
Refus global (Borduas), 67
La Relève, 68
Renaud, Jacques, 91
Renault, 185, 194, 200, 204
Rhône-Poulenc, 45
Richard, Léon, 230
Richer, Léopold, 78
Ritchie, A.E., 115
Rivard, Antoine, 51, 76
Robertson, Gordon, 140-141; de Gaulle visit (1967), 121, 301n40
Robertson, Norman, 133, 156; on Atlanticism, 16; and cultural diplomacy, 72, 103, 209, 210, 285n78; delegation-general of Quebec in Paris, 152; lobbies to have Marcel Cadieux succeed him, 297n36; review of Franco-Canadian relations, 136-137, 152-153, 190
Robichaud, Louis, 230-231, 246
Roosevelt, Franklin Delano, 14
Rossillon, Philippe, 96, 213, 233, 313n116; accused of being a spy, 232, 233, 313n113; on federal bilingualism efforts, 99; and francophone minority communities, 229-230, 231-232; Francophonie conferences, 176, 247, 260. *See also* Rossillon affair
Rossillon affair, 231-232, 233, 234, 240; Trudeau news conference, 232, 313n113, 313n116. *See also* Rossillon, Philippe
Rostow, Walt W.: *The Stages of Economic Growth: A Non-Communist Manifesto,* 48
Rouch, Jean, 66
Routière Colas, 193
Royal Bank of Canada, 44
Royal Commission of Inquiry on Constitutional Problems. *See* Tremblay Commission
Royal Commission on Bilingualism and Biculturalism, 88; report, 112-113, 229. *See also* bilingualism; biculturalism

Royal Commission on Canada's Economic Prospects. *See* Gordon Commission
Royal Commission on National Development in the Arts, Letters and Sciences. *See* Massey Commission
Royal Society of Canada, 73, 285n91
Rumilly, Robert, 61
Rusk, Dean, 115, 135

Saint-Exupéry, Antoine de: *Terre des hommes*, 1
Sartre, Jean-Paul, 62, 64
satellite cooperation, 227-229; and *Memini*, 229
Sauvé, Maurice, 217
Schuman, Robert, 16, 18, 40, 107, 149
Schumann, Maurice, 251, 255; cultural agreements, 235, 236; de Lipkowski affair, 252, 253, 254; federal views of, 261; Quebec government views of, 250; Quebec policy, 126-127
Scott, Frank, 79
Second World War, 106; cultural diplomacy, 70; decolonization, 268; France, 53, 93; Franco-Canadian relations during, 11, 13, 38, 85; Quebec, 13, 50, 60; Saint-Pierre-et-Miquelon affair, 13. *See also* Vichy France
Séguin, Maurice, 51
self-determination, 111, 268; Algeria, 23, 27; Bandung Declaration, 23; de Gaulle visit (1967), 105, 114, 118, 119, 120, 121, 141; and Gaullism, 97, 110; Quebec, 105, 113, 170. *See also* decolonization
Senghor, Léopold Sédar, 67
separatism (Quebec): 2, 97, 129; Algeria, 111, 122; Raymond Bousquet, 108, 112; Maurice Couve de Murville, 120, 125; André d'Allemagne, 90; Charles de Gaulle, 106, 113, 122, 124, 127, 269, 272; de Gaulle visit (1967), 101, 102, 106, 114, 119, 127; de Gaulle's November 1967 press conference, 101, 121, 124, 125; de Lipkowski affair, 253; Pierre de Menthon, 125; Xavier Deniau, 115; Jean-Marie Domenach, 125; Jean Drapeau, 112; foreign affairs as means to realize, 145, 156, 161, 163, 169, 174; Francophonie, 247, 249; French expectations of, 125, 127; and Gaullist geopolitical calculations, 130, 140, 141; Gaullist policy, 7, 164, 125-126, 203-204, 267; Daniel Johnson, 122; François Lacoste, 108; François Leduc, 120; Jean Lesage, 113; René Lévesque, 112; Claude Morin, 154; private sector concern about, 122, 194, 203, 270. *See also* self-determination
Servan-Schreiber, Jean-Jacques: *Le défi américain*, 186
Service de la coopération avec l'extérieur. *See* Quebec ministry of education
Sharp, Mitchell, 228, 240; *accord cadre*, 235, 236; de Lipkowski affair, 253; on importance of foreign aid, 244; Paris follow-up meetings, 181, 255; visits Paris, 234, 261
SIDBEC, 184, 194-195, 200; and proposed French loan to Quebec, 197
Siegfried, André, 64
Siraud, Pierre, 234, 235, 255; Quebec's political future, 126; Philippe Rossillon, 233; Rossillon affair, 232, 240
Société de montage automobile (SOMA), 194, 200, 204
Société générale de financement (SGF), 187, 194, 200
Société nationale des Acadiens (SNA), 229-230. *See also* Acadians
Société nationale des pétroles d'Aquitaine, 199
Société Saint-Jean-Baptiste de Montréal, 50-51. *See also* Fédération des Sociétés Saint-Jean-Baptiste
Sorel, Jean-Albert, 64
Soustelle, Jacques, 293n103
Soviet Union: and Gaullism, 15, 29, 131-132; modernization theory, 47-48; NATO, 16, 17, 129, 133; Suez Crisis, 25, 28
Sputnik, 133
St. Laurent, Louis, and government, 46, 65, 31; cultural diplomacy, 73; Charles de Gaulle, 99; French views of, 108; Gordon Commission, 49, Gray Lecture, 13-14; Jules Léger, 148; Pierre Mendès-France, 21; North Atlantic treaty negotiations, 17; Suez Crisis, 25, 26, 30; visits Paris, 18, 149

The Stages of Economic Growth: A Non-Communist Manifesto (Rostow), 48
Statute of Westminster (1931), 146
Stone, Thomas (Tommy), 85, 86
Sud-Aviation, 195, 196, 197
Suez Crisis, 24-25, 27, 131; Canada, 24-25, 30; France, 24, 26, 43; Gaullism, 29
Switzerland, 116, 242, 308n10

television, 66, 228
Terre des hommes (de Saint-Exupéry), 1
Théâtre du Nouveau Monde, 62-63
tourism, 65
Trade Expansion Act (1932) (United States), 184
Trans-Canada Airlines, 45, 195, 196, 197
Treaty of Paris (1763), 38
Treaty of Rome (1957), 43
Tremblay, Jean-Noël, 122, 157, 231
Tremblay, Michel, 214
Tremblay Commission (Royal Commission of Inquiry on Constitutional Problems), 106-107; report, 50, 78, 106-107
Trottier, Pierre, 137, 222
Trudeau, Pierre, and government, 88, 262, 270; *accord cadre*, 234; African tour, 175; Asbestos strike, 50; criticizes Pearson government, 239; de Gaulle visit (1967), 121; de Gaulle's antipathy for, 99, 239; de Lipkowski affair, 253, 254; francophone minority communities, 230; French views of, 126, 235, 242; Johnson-Peyrefitte agreement, 170; François Leduc, 239; meets with Couve de Murville, 124-125; Niamey II conference, 258, 259, 260, 261; Paris follow-up meeting (1968), 180; Paris follow-up meeting (1969), 255; rise to power, 124, 127, 179, 181, 238, 239; Rossillon affair, 232, 233, 240, 313n113, 313n116
Truffaut, François, 66
Tunisia, 22-23, 24; and Quebec, 243; Sakiet affair, 26

UNESCO (United Nations Educational, Scientific and Cultural Organization), 70
Union culturelle française (UCF), 66-67, 68, 74

Union Nationale, 98, 126, 205; Duplessis era, 52, 74; internal division, 125
United Nations, 18; and Canada as "middle power," 14, 17; French nuclear testing, 28, 33; North African decolonization, 22-23, 26, 27; San Francisco conference, 14-15; Suez Crisis, 24-25
United States: Algeria, 26-27; and Atlanticism, 11, 16, 265; Vincent Auriol criticizes, 20; Blum-Byrnes agreement, 37; Canada's economic relations with, 34, 35, 37, 43, 199-200, 205, 265, 266; Canada's relations with, 13, 14, 18, 149, 262; and Canadian Atlanticism, 12, 17, 19, 20, 30, 39, 129, 135, 136, 137, 139; and Canadian economic nationalism, 49, 183, 189-190, 206; cultural influence in Canada, 59, 75, 78, 80, 228; cultural influence in France, 74, 75, 93, 96, 266; cultural influence in Quebec, 55, 59, 76, 77, 95, 227, 266; cultural strength, 7, 69, 95, 266, 267; and Diefenbaker government, 31, 32-33, 132-133; economic presence in Quebec, 52, 55, 184, 187, 194-195, 198, 204; economic strength, 6, 34-35, 36, 44, 48, 57, 265; English Canada, 7, 78-79, 266; European Defence Community, 20-22; *"fait français"* as a shield against, 86, 88, 92, 104, 106, 268; France's economic relations with, 35, 41, 52, 186, 188; France's relations with, 14, 26, 27, 136-137, 251; and French Atlanticism, 16, 19; French cultural rivalry with, 59, 74, 81, 85, 100, 208, 224, 271; French nuclear activities, 131, 192; and Gaullism, 29, 262; and Gaullist challenge to Atlanticism, 29, 30, 31, 129, 130-132, 135, 137, 139; and Gaullist economic challenge, 182, 186, 191, 201-202, 203, 205-206, 269, 270; as imperial power, 109-110, 111; Claude Julien, 140, 193; Korean War, 18; André Malraux, 98; Marshall Plan, 37-38; Pierre Mendès-France, 21; and modernization, 35, 47-49, 52-53, 54; Monroe Doctrine, 123; NATO, 15, 16, 18, 20, 136; nuclear weapons, 131, 133-134; opposes Canadian linchpin efforts, 295n26; Péchiney, 204; Pinay affair, 22-23; preponderant power of, 4, 19, 33, 87, 142,

263, 264; Quebec economic dependence on, 197, 270; and Quebec in Gaullist geopolitical calculus, 140, 141, 142; in Quebec nationalist thought, 50, 51, 76, 77, 95; Antoine Rivard, 76; Suez Crisis, 24, 25, 28, 43; and Vichy France, 13; Vietnam war, 134. *See also* Americanization; anti-Americanism

Université de Montréal, 62, 95, 110, 188; and AUPELF, 67, 213; "Montreal School," 109

Université Laval, 184; and Annales school, 62; centennial of, 107

University of Toronto, 195, 306n68

Valéry, Paul, 101

Vanier, Georges, 40, 116, 148; Atlanticism, 17, 20; Charles de Gaulle, 30, 105; funeral, 166; retirement as ambassador, 149; unrealized state visit to France, 105

Vanier, Pauline, 105, 116, 166

Variétés, 63

Vaugeois, Denis, 96

Vercors, 64

Vichy France, 54, 59, 60, 94; Canada's relations with, 13

West Canadian Oil and Gas, 45

Wrong, Hume, 17